an artist's guide to drawing clothed characters

Learn to draw clothing and drapery with **tomfoxdraws**

3dtotal Publishing

Correspondence: publishing@3dtotal.com
Website: store.3dtotal.com

First published in the United Kingdom, 2025, by 3dtotal Publishing.

Address: 3dtotal.com Ltd,
6 Sansome Street, Worcester,
WR1 1UH, United Kingdom.

Soft cover ISBN: 978-1-915992-23-9
Printed and bound in Shanghai,
China by KS Printing.

Visit **store.3dtotal.com** for a complete list of available book titles.

Editor: Marisa Lewis
Designer: Matthew Lewis
Lead Editor: Samantha Rigby
Lead Designer: Joseph Cartwright
Studio Manager: Simon Morse
Managing Director: Tom Greenway

Cover images © Tom Fox

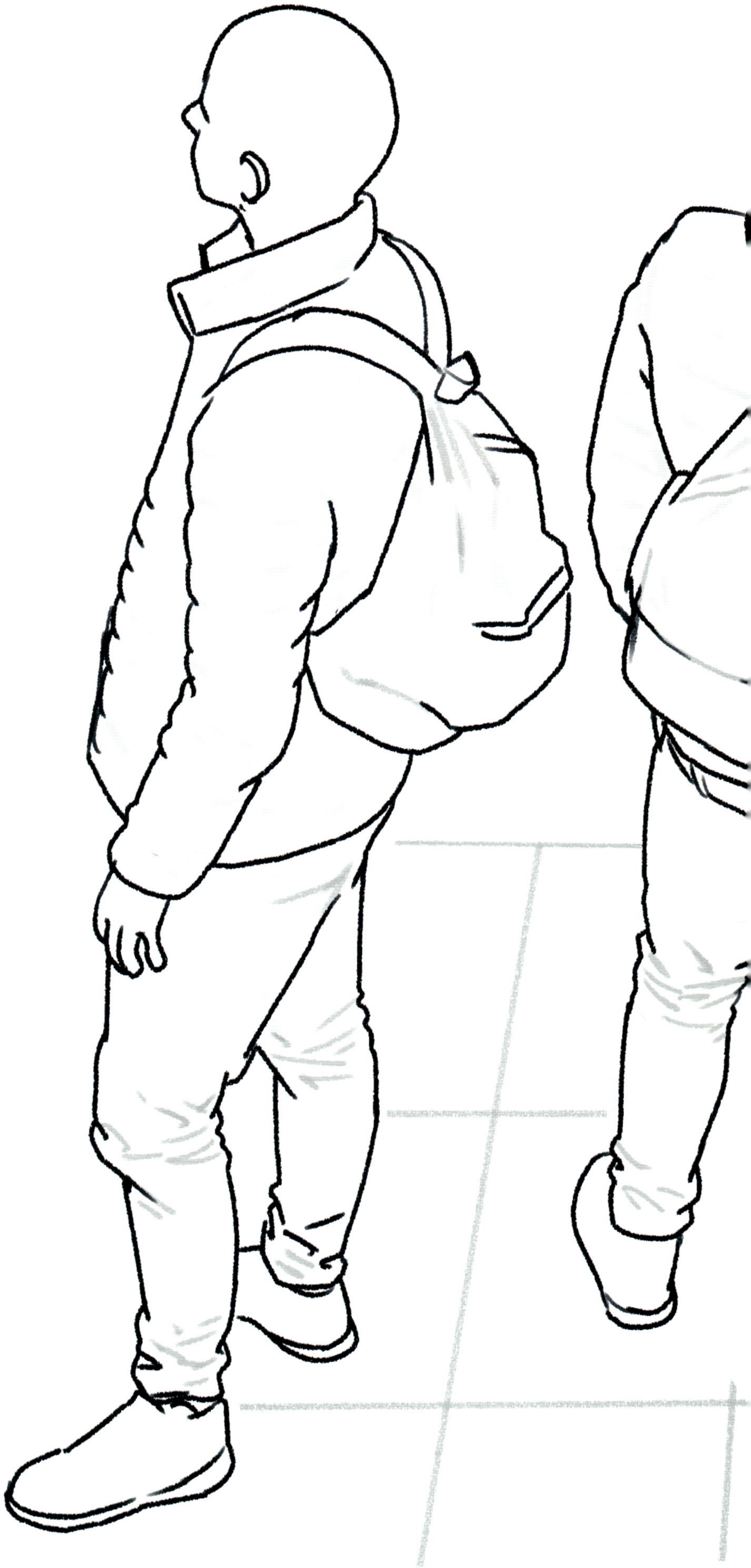

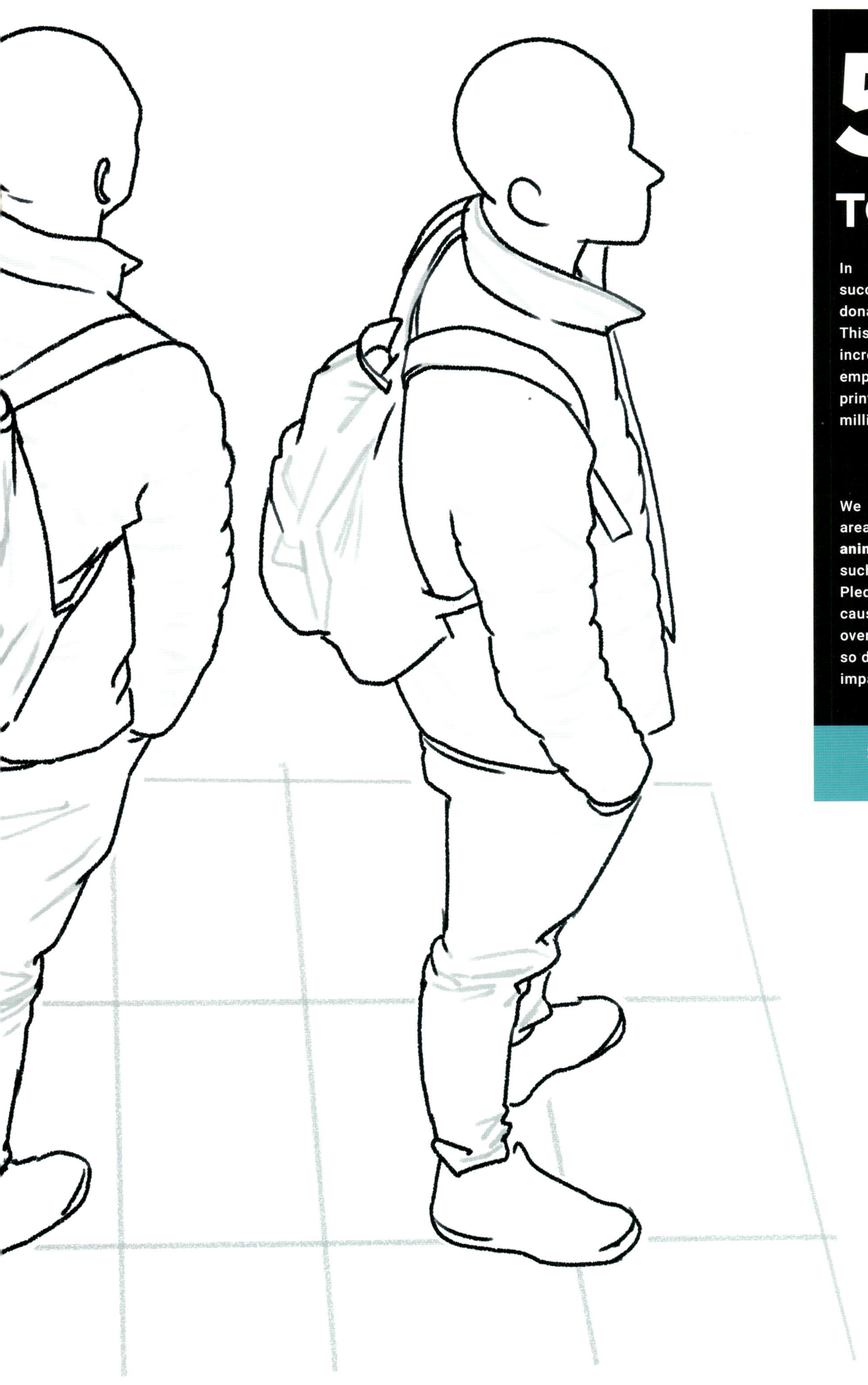

contents

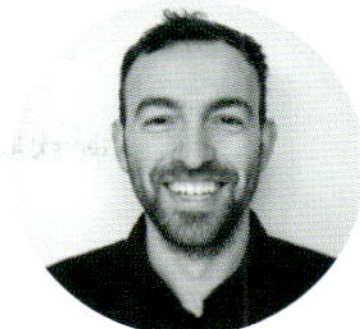

hello, i'm tom

Over the years, I've often found myself wondering: why doesn't anyone teach how to clothe characters? I've seen plenty of resources on 'tips for drawing folds' or 'the seven types of fold'. But let's be honest – the only reason we care about folds is because we want to draw people wearing clothes. So why not teach the thing we actually want to learn? That's how the idea for this book came about.

If you've already read *Anatomy for Artists: Drawing Form & Pose*, you'll know how helpful fixed structures can be. Clothing doesn't offer that luxury. Fabric responds to movement, gravity, friction, resistance, and the size and shape of the mannequin. That makes drawing drapery less like recalling a form and more like making an educated guess. Learning to clothe characters isn't about memorizing folds. It's about simulation, not memorization.

And because we're simulating, not memorizing, we need a different method. This book doesn't follow the same structure as the previous one. We can't move through folding 'regions' step by step, building complexity as we go. Drapery doesn't work like that. There's no fixed skeleton or underlying structure – everything is always shifting. So instead, we'll take a different approach.

Rather than learning about forms and saving them for later, we'll start by drawing – whatever your current skill level – and use that drawing, along with a set of prompts, to learn through adjustment. You'll try something, tweak it, see what's changed, and try again. These adjustments aren't rules or checkboxes – they're questions you can ask of your work. Small shifts in how you look, helping you revise with more clarity. It's more like building instincts than following steps. It's like an apprenticeship, with this book as an older colleague quietly guiding you.

There's also a companion workbook, *A Workbook for Drawing Clothed Characters*. It's not a sequel, and it doesn't add new information, but it gives you a place to apply what you've seen here. If this book is about observing and understanding, the workbook is about trying things out, making mistakes, and learning through doing. You'll draw directly onto examples, test your instincts, and return to the adjustments in this book as needed. The books work best as a pair, but this one can more than stand on its own.

You don't need to wait until you feel ready. Just begin. The sooner you start, the sooner you'll have something real to work with – and something to learn from. Start with what you already know how to do, and adjust from there.

Best of luck with your drawing,

tom fox

throughout this book, images are labelled with letters to help you follow them alongside the text

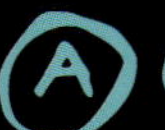
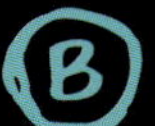
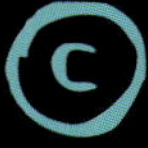

---

important sequences of smaller details are highlighted with numbers!

1 2 3

---

this book will always try to simplify and refer to forms rather than technical names where possible. if you're not sure, you can always check the glossary!

simulation, not memorization

If you picked up my previous book, *Anatomy for Artists: Drawing Form & Pose*, you'll remember we had the luxury of memorizing many anatomical forms. It's an approach that works well for learning anatomy. However, memorization isn't as effective for clothing characters because fabric doesn't have a fixed form to memorize.

Fabric is highly responsive. It changes shape according to what's going on around it and influencing it. The same piece of fabric can take on multiple forms **(A)**, displaying different 'drapery'. Drapery is what we see when fabric is formed into different positions by various forces.

As we can't memorize such a flexible subject, we must learn to **simulate** what it might do in different situations. The variables for simulation include: the mannequin, its position, the outfit, the forces generated, and the motion. These all affect the final drapery we see. Change even one variable and the resulting drapery will be different.

Finally, just as in the anatomy book, 'believable' is our goal. We aren't aiming to learn to simulate perfectly. Far from it. The simulation doesn't have to be one hundred per cent realistic - just good enough to look like it might happen!

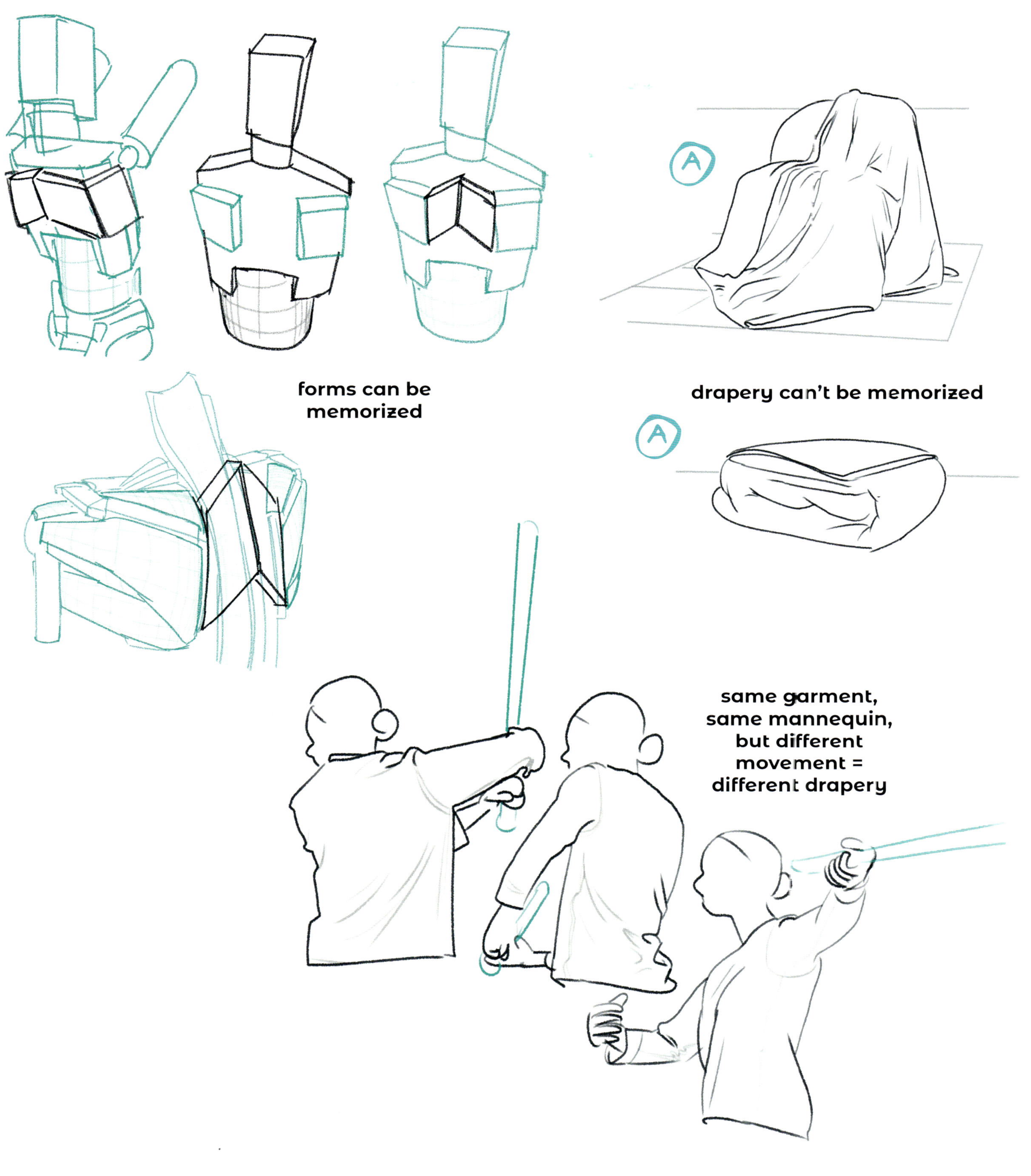
A
forms can be memorized
drapery can't be memorized
A
same garment,
same mannequin,
but different
movement =
different drapery

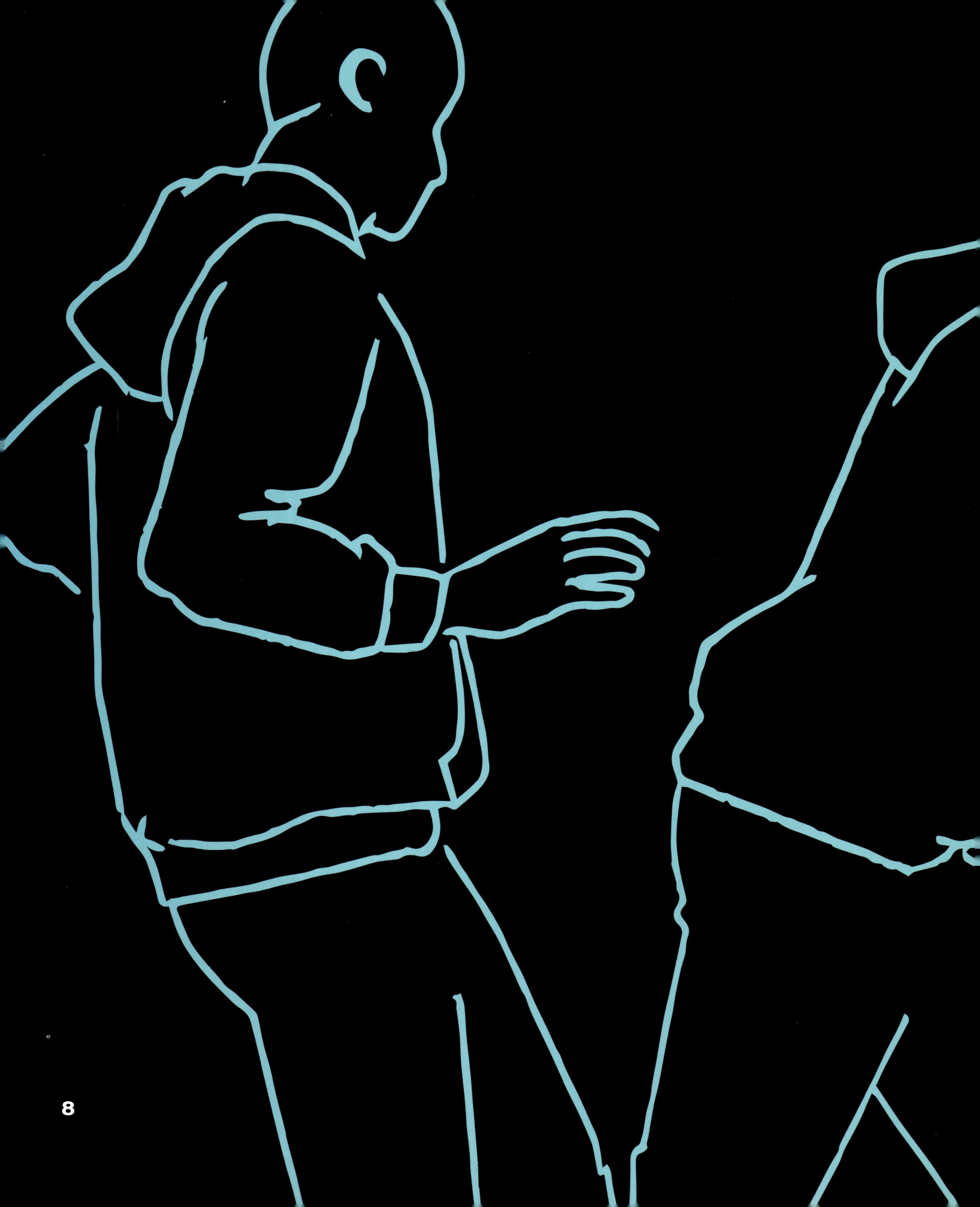

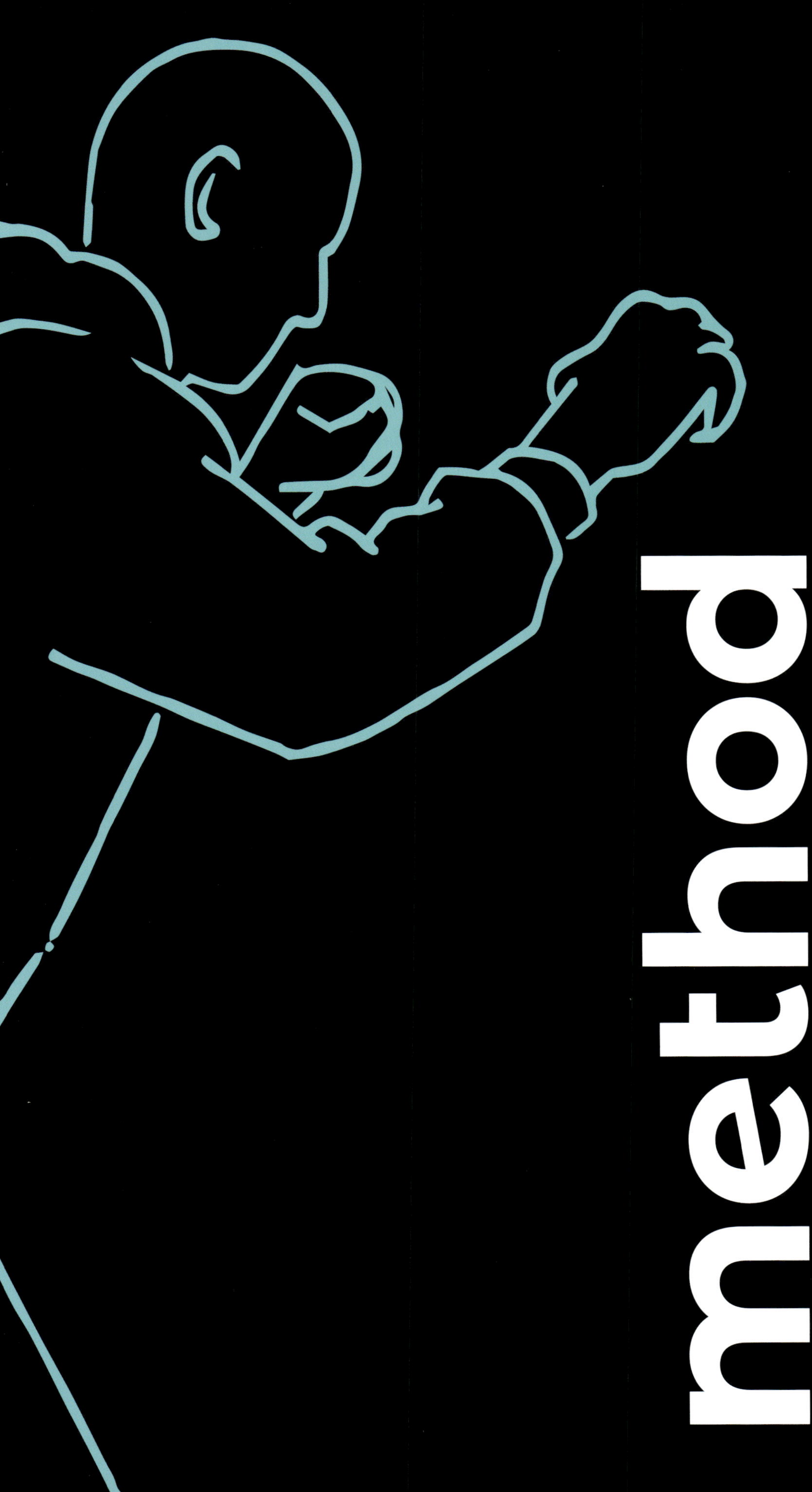

method

the usual method

Before we get into this book's learning method, here's the usual approach to learning a complex skill such as clothing characters. First, you visualize it as a whole skill made of smaller pieces, or components. Second, you identify the components – for example, anatomy, gesture, and drapery – and then study them separately. You believe that by studying the components, you'll eventually know how to perform the larger skill – in our case, of drawing clothed characters. We can use a brick wall as a metaphor (A). The wall is the whole skill. The bricks are the components.

After weeks of studying separate components, students begin to feel confident and knowledgeable about them. However, when they try to draw clothed characters, the results are disappointing. Here's why:

Distraction. The focus on learning about the individual components distracts us from actually trying to draw clothed characters. Unfortunately, the distraction leads to an...

Illusion of progress. It's easier to learn about the separate components than to try the whole skill. Because it's easier, you get a sense of rapid improvement. You feel encouraged to keep studying the components, which causes you to...

Postpone feedback. By studying components, you delay trying to draw clothed characters. This delays the valuable feedback you would be gaining if you actually tried the whole skill. In the end, rather than protecting you from negative feedback, postponing feedback makes you feel...

Anxiety. The longer you prepare to try something, rather than simply trying to do it, the greater the pressure you feel to be 'good' at it. That's a shame, because it's often more relaxing to *know* you're not proficient at something than to be unsure about your skill level. It's the uncertainty that's scary. Anxiety causes you to postpone drawing clothed characters in scenes, and the cycle continues.

In summary, this method is a nice idea, but it's not a great way to learn (B). At least, not as your *main* way to learn. Let's now consider a better method.

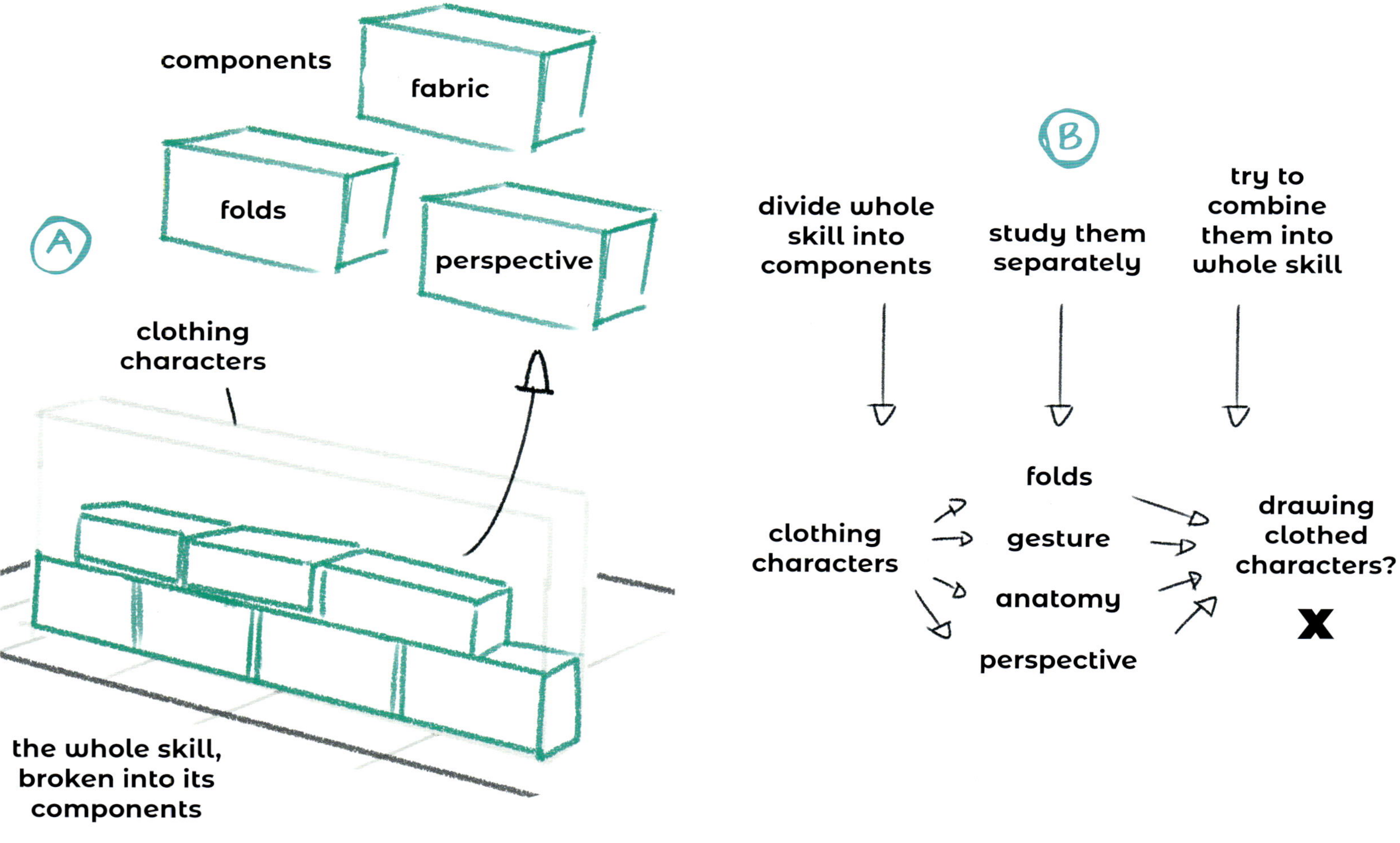

our approach

Instead, in this book, we'll work holistically. 'Holistic' simply describes a focus on the 'whole' rather than the components. To work this way, you must recognize that the components aren't separate, but influence each other. Abandon the brick wall metaphor (A). Instead, the skill of clothing characters is more like a web (B). Adjusting one component will affect the others. For example, adjusting the pose will affect the drapery, silhouette, tension, compression, and more.

It's not always effective to divide things into components to study. In fact, the best learning strategy is often to work 'directly' and simply try to do the thing you want to learn *without trying to break it into pieces*. In our case, this means trying to draw clothed characters. In doing so, you create something that can generate feedback. You can only see what works and what doesn't if you have something to compare against. Only with a drawing in front of you can you begin to explore ways to improve that drawing.

forget the 'component parts' approach

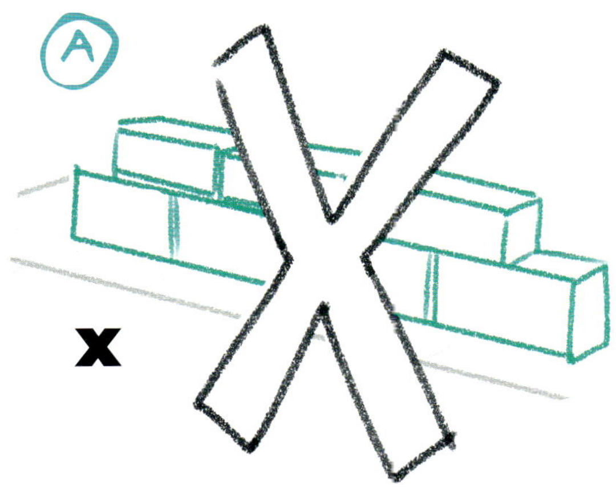

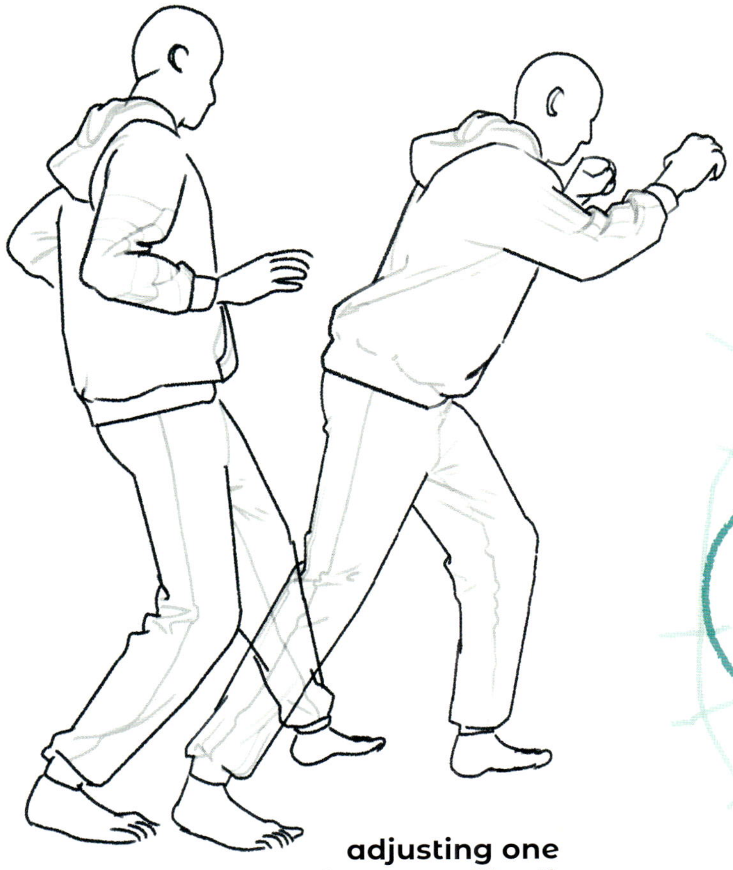

adjusting one element will adjust everything!

B

imagine a web of interconnected elements

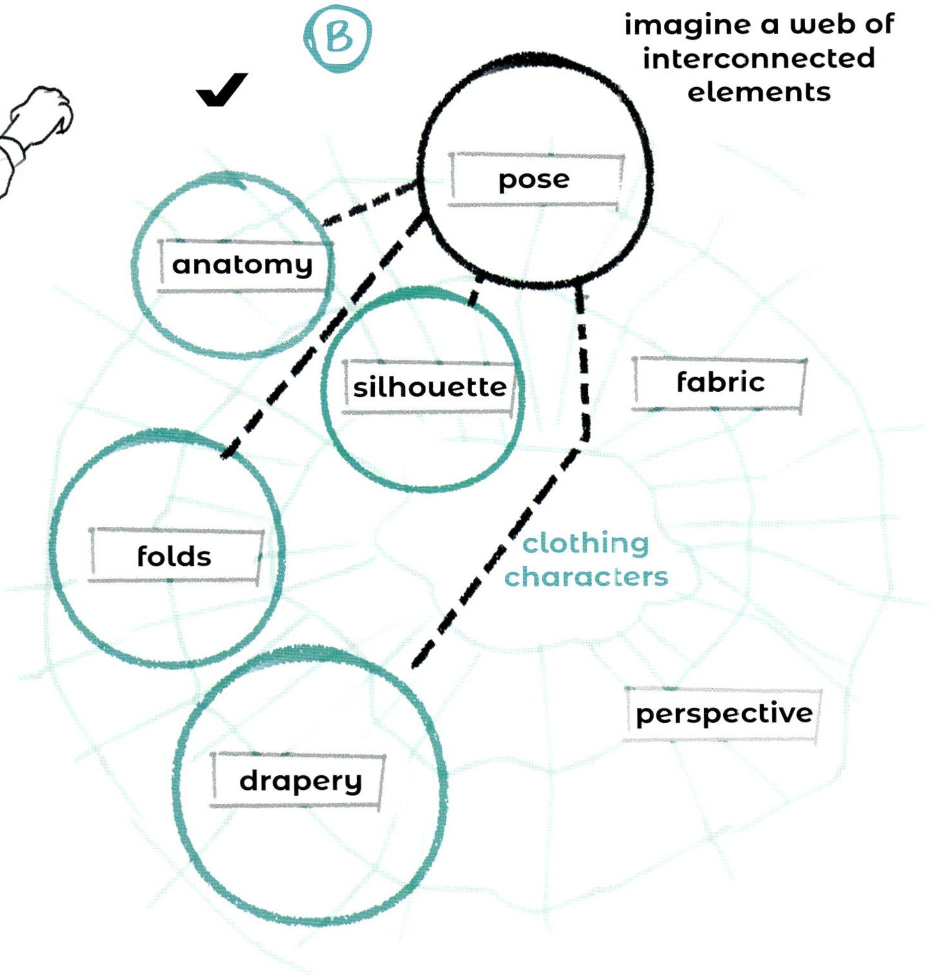

pose
anatomy
silhouette
fabric
folds
clothing characters
perspective
drapery

apprenticeship

This is essentially an 'apprenticeship' model of learning. You try, then you adjust. Apprenticeships have created some of the best draughtspeople from history. Here's why:

Holistic focus. Apprentices immediately tried the whole task. This reduced anxiety about negative feedback and discouraged avoidance. There was no 'illusion of progress'. You tried it and you knew exactly how capable you were (or weren't). You drew something and then you received...

Specific feedback and adjustments. You received immediate, direct, and targeted feedback. Senior artists suggested *specific* changes: 'Make this larger, move it here, add overlap, and improve the flow of this line.' Often these specific adjustments came in the form of...

Draw-overs. Within a few days, or even hours, you watched people draw over your work. You saw the before and after, which helped illustrate how seemingly minor changes could dramatically affect the whole drawing. This also reinforced the idea of the drawing as a whole, where seemingly minor adjustments have large effects.

To summarize: As an apprentice, you try to draw something; then, shortly after, someone else identifies something specific to change, and the image is redrawn. There are no long periods of 'learning' before being 'tested'. You're tested straight away and then you adjust what you did. That's how we'll do things in this book. The only difference is that we must learn to suggest our own adjustments and redraw our own drawings, in the absence of colleagues to give us feedback.

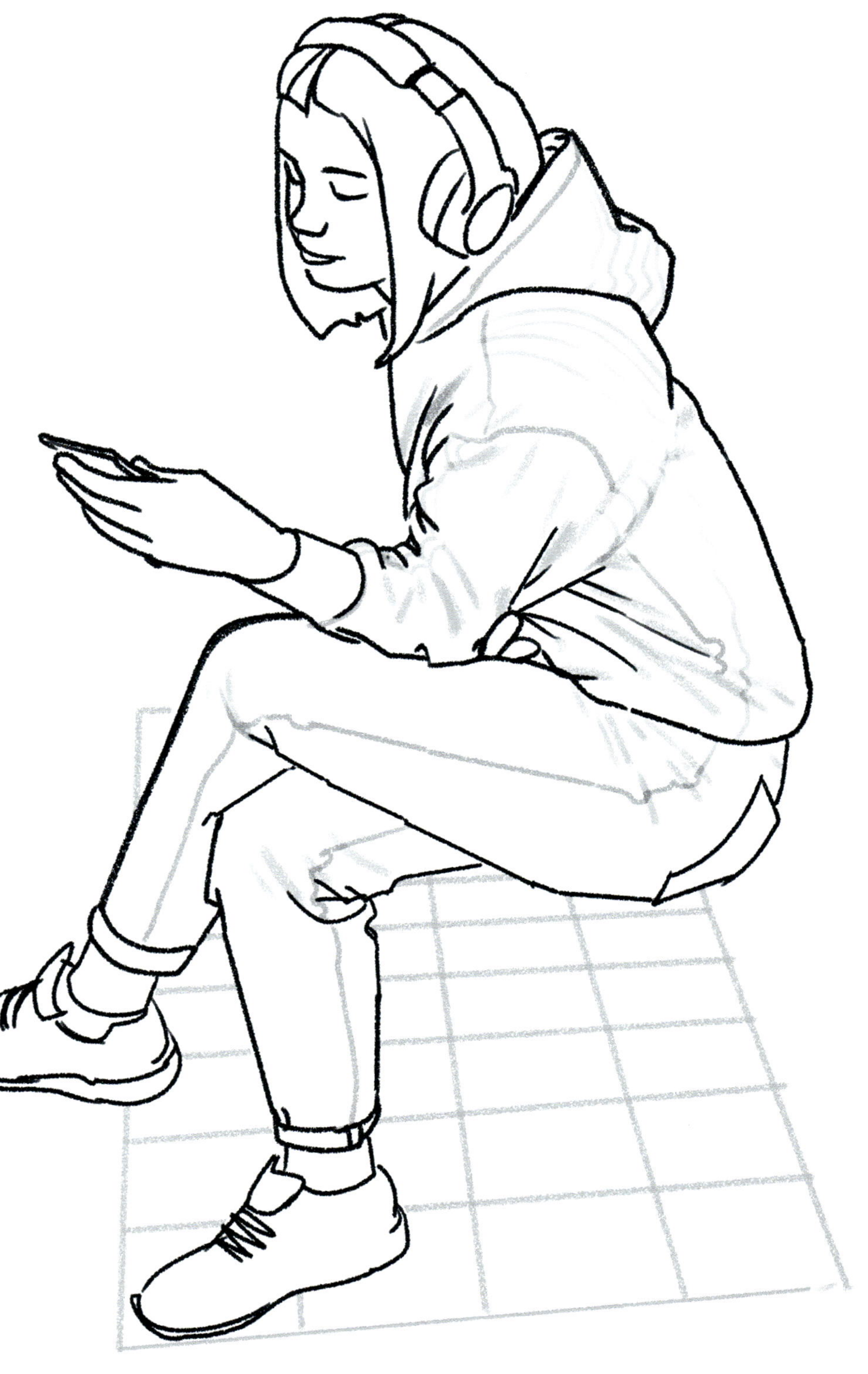

method example

attempt ...

Here's how we'll do it. Draw a clothed character (A). You need something to generate feedback and to redraw. Include the hands, head, and any objects the character is interacting with. Don't wait until you 'feel ready' or 'know enough'. If you're feeling anxious about this, let me reassure you: you are ready. There are no consequences – it's only lines on paper. You can throw it away afterwards! Keep your initial drawing time fairly short to ease any pressure. Perhaps set a ten-minute timer to remind yourself to work fast. For my own example below, I've drawn a man bending to fill a mug at a water cooler.

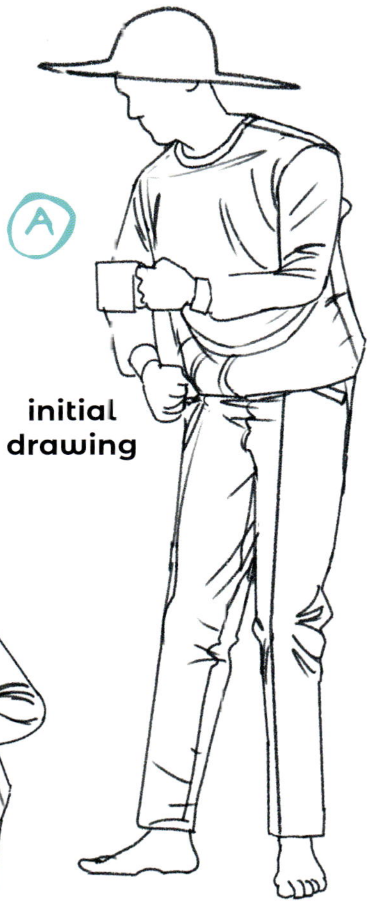

A
initial drawing

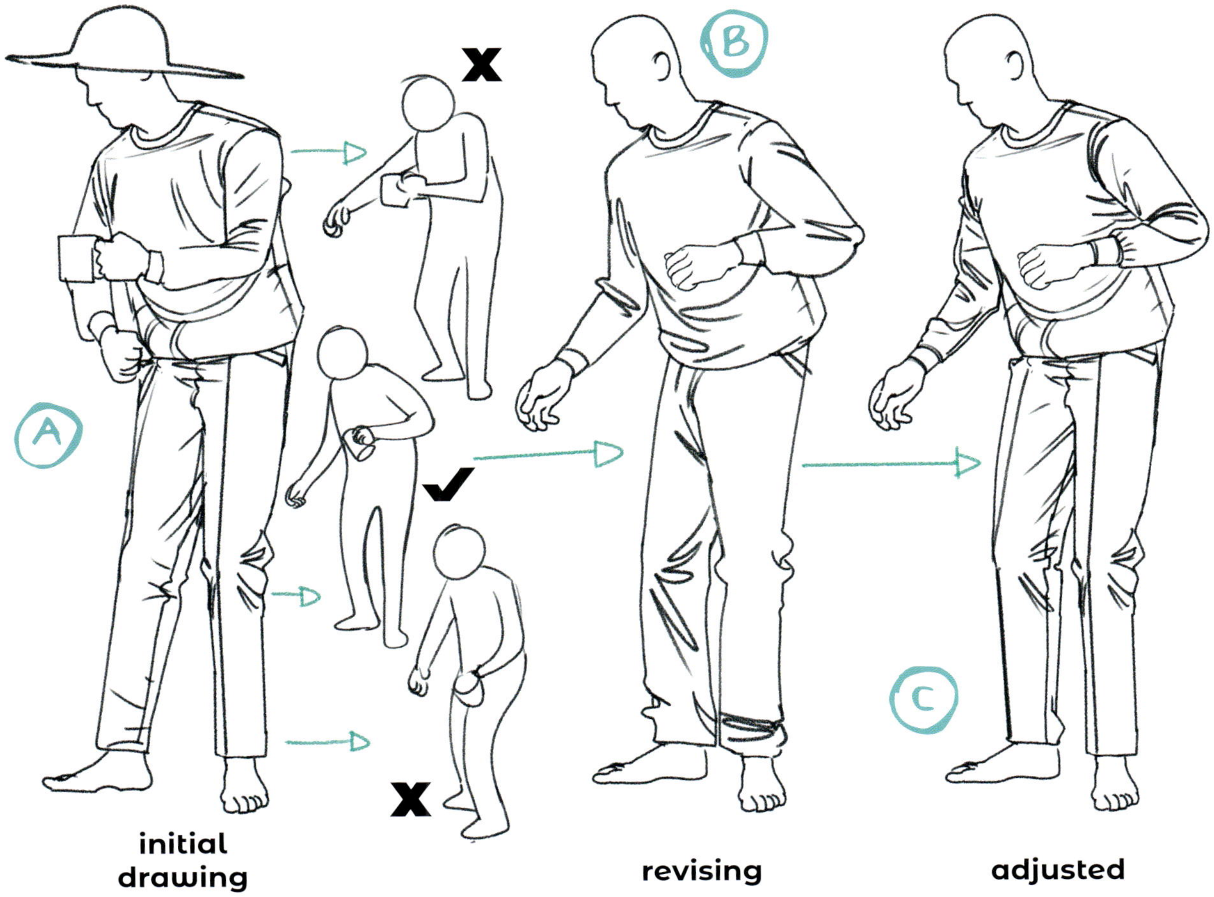

A
initial drawing

B
revising

C
adjusted

... and adjust

Use the Adjustments section (pages 18–93) to improve your initial drawing. These adjustments encourage you to look at your drawing in a different way – generating feedback – and usually to redraw some aspect of it. Work through them one at a time. Do as many as you like; you can even repeat the same adjustment at a later stage for different results. Pay attention to how each adjustment affects other parts of the drawing, because this reveals the relationships between components. For example, has altering the pose changed your impression of the perspective? Has adjusting overlapping lines changed the sense of volume? Learning happens not only by changing things, but by noticing what effect the change has had on the rest of the drawing. In my example, I notice that changing the pose makes me feel like I'm viewing the figure from a slightly higher angle (B).

The highest-priority adjustment to any clothed character is usually the pose itself. Above, I began by drawing thumbnails (as suggested by the 'priority pyramid' adjustment on page 24), then chose my favourite one. I continued revising this until I ended up with the adjusted drawing on the right (C).

continue adjusting

There are *forty-two* adjustments in the Adjustments section. For a clearer example of how they can be applied, I've combined a few of them here. In the first step, I use two adjustments (A): 'internals & noise' and 'line pressure'. The result is already a big improvement on the initial drawing, but it's good to keep adjusting if you still feel motivated! Next I apply another three adjustments (B). You may notice that after each adjustment, the number of lines is reduced rather than increased. This will be a recurring theme throughout this book: to improve most drawings, you need to remove or adjust existing lines, not add more.

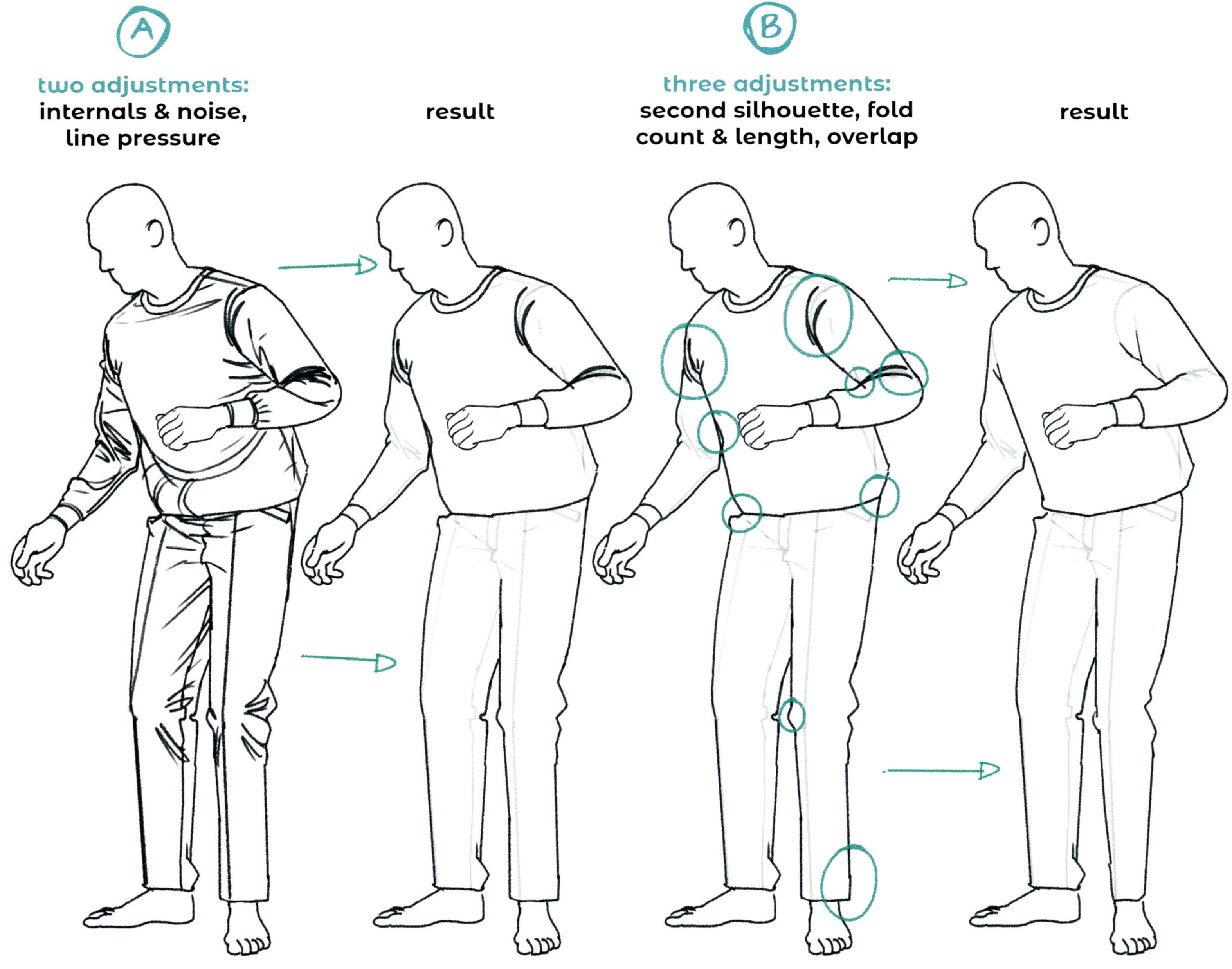

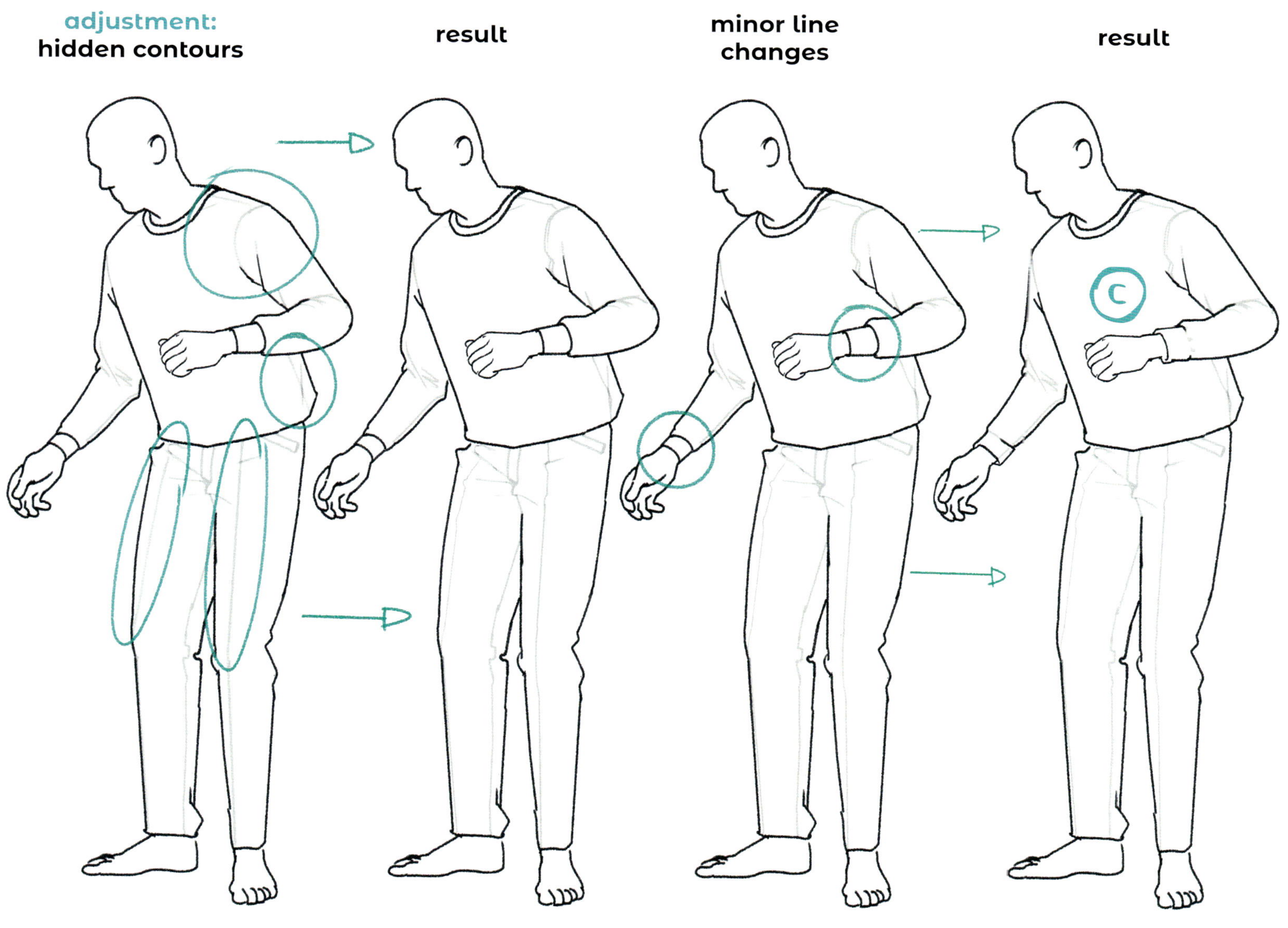

Let's continue revising. I apply two more adjustments here and it's starting to look like a different drawing! Notice that with some adjustments the improvement is only small. For example, here, we've just slightly changed the cuffs (C). That's all. Try to have a mindset of many small changes. They add up. The whole is greater than the sum of its parts, so these 'small' changes have a big impact on the overall result.

finally, reference

The last step, after you've done your own thinking and adjusting, is to look for reference images that are similar to your subject. This book includes a References section (page 94). You don't need to find an exact match for your pose and viewing angle. It's unlikely that you will, anyway. However, a similar reference will do nicely. Once you find one, observe it closely and compare it with your drawing. What differences stand out? In what ways does your simulation differ from what you see in the reference? Now draw over your work, incorporating these differences. Repeat this process as many times as needed.

In my example, I made the following changes: the neckline was dropping slightly too far down at the back (A). The pockets weren't angled enough (B). The fly of the trousers wasn't wrapping the form enough, which lowered the believability of the compressed folds in that area (C). The knees had no lines suggesting compression (D). And, finally, the bottoms of the trousers needed a contour around the hem (E).

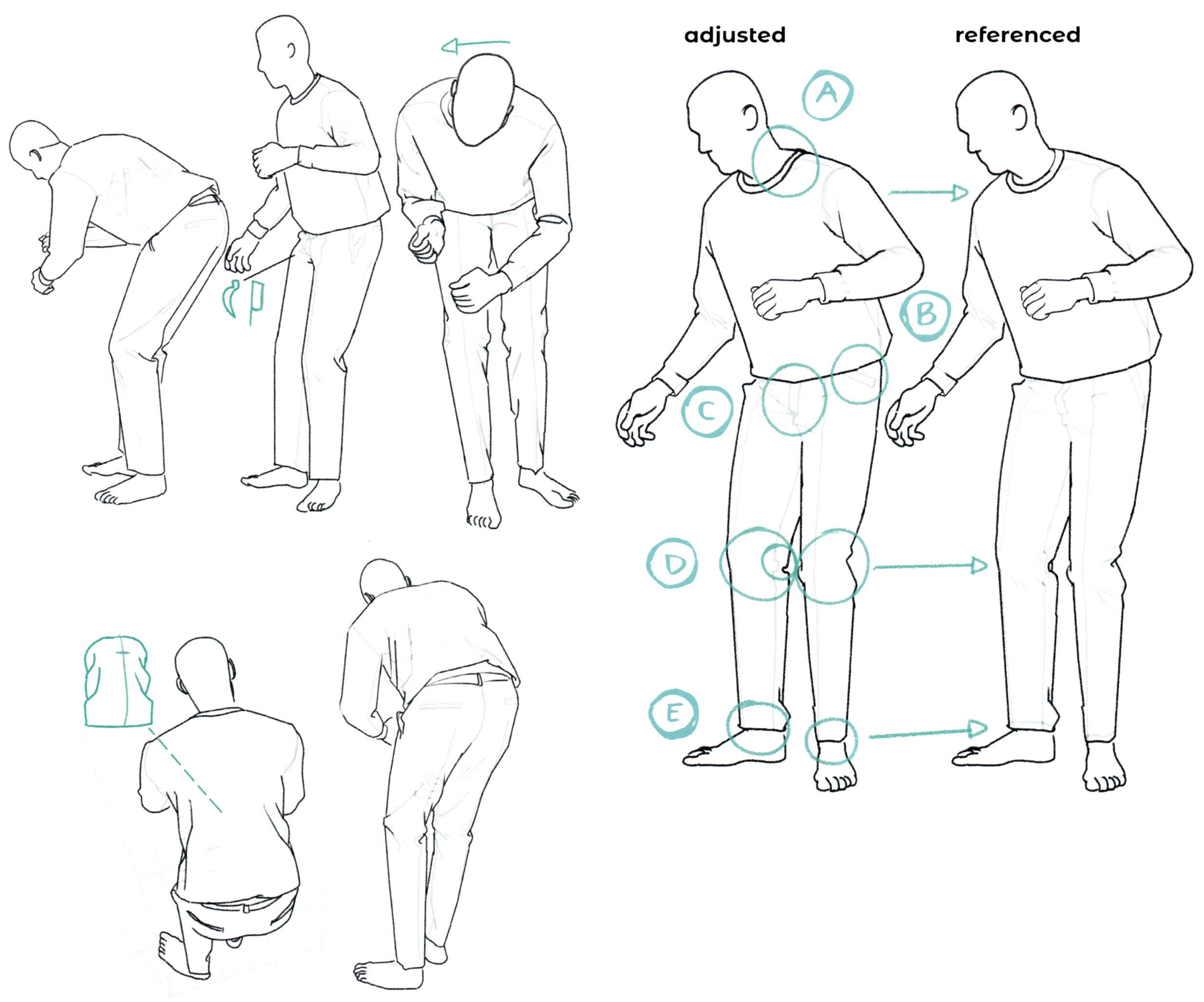

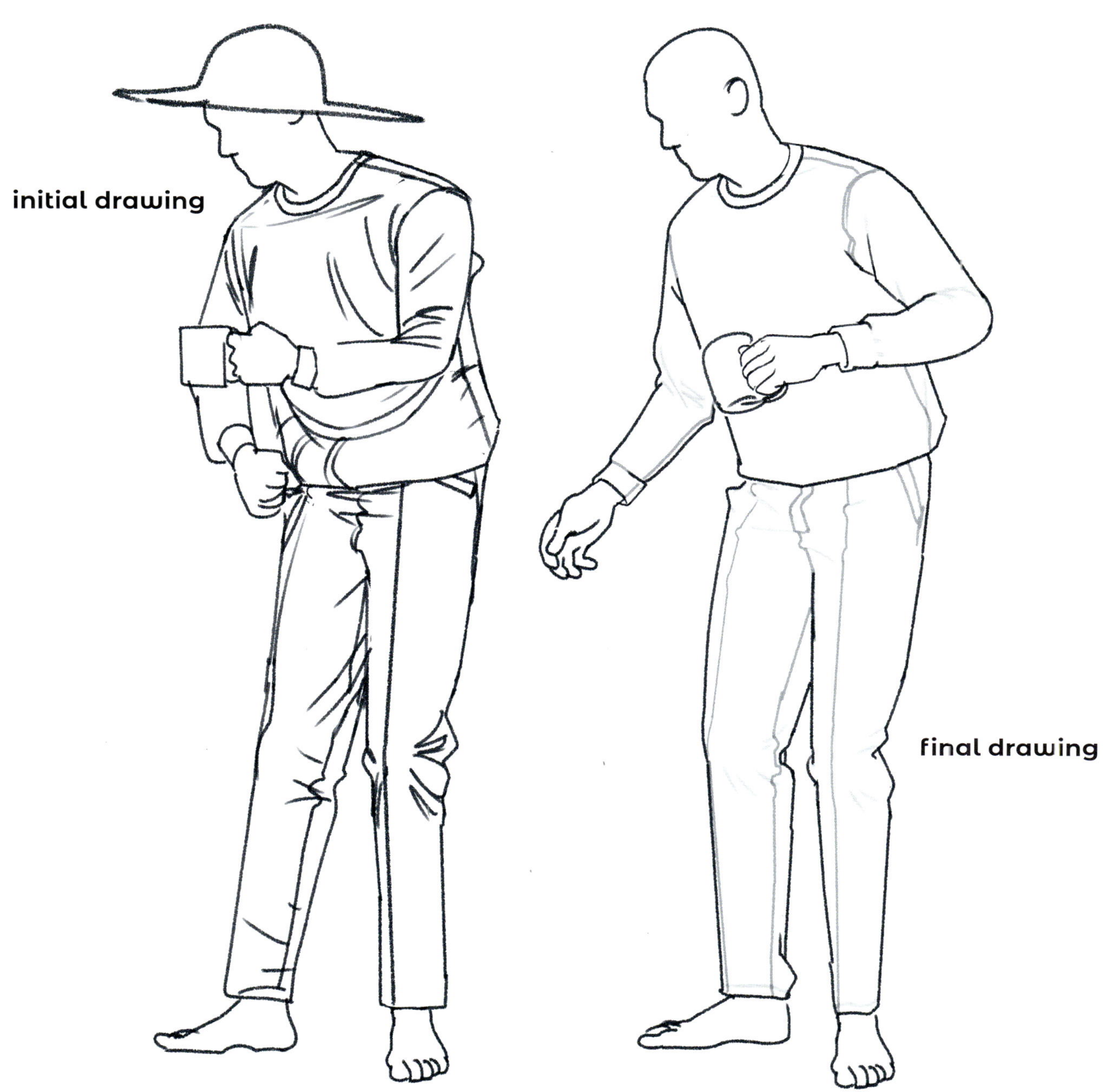

This is the difference all those small adjustments made, combined with a little referencing at the end. The character is in a much more natural pose and the forms feel 3D, without needing lighting or lots of additional marks. Notice, too, that the overall line count is greatly reduced. Less is more.

adjustments

adjustment web

This is a web of adjustments to consider when clothing characters. You can refer back to this once you're familiar with most of the adjustments as a quick reminder of potential issues in your work. This is by no means a complete list, and you may want to add to it over time, but it's a great place to start. There are 42 adjustments below, but add and remove ideas as you see fit.

No one adjustment is more important than the others. Remember: it all interacts. I recommend reading through the adjustments in the order they're presented the first time you go through this book. Ideas will build on each other, and may require some understanding of adjustments that have come before.

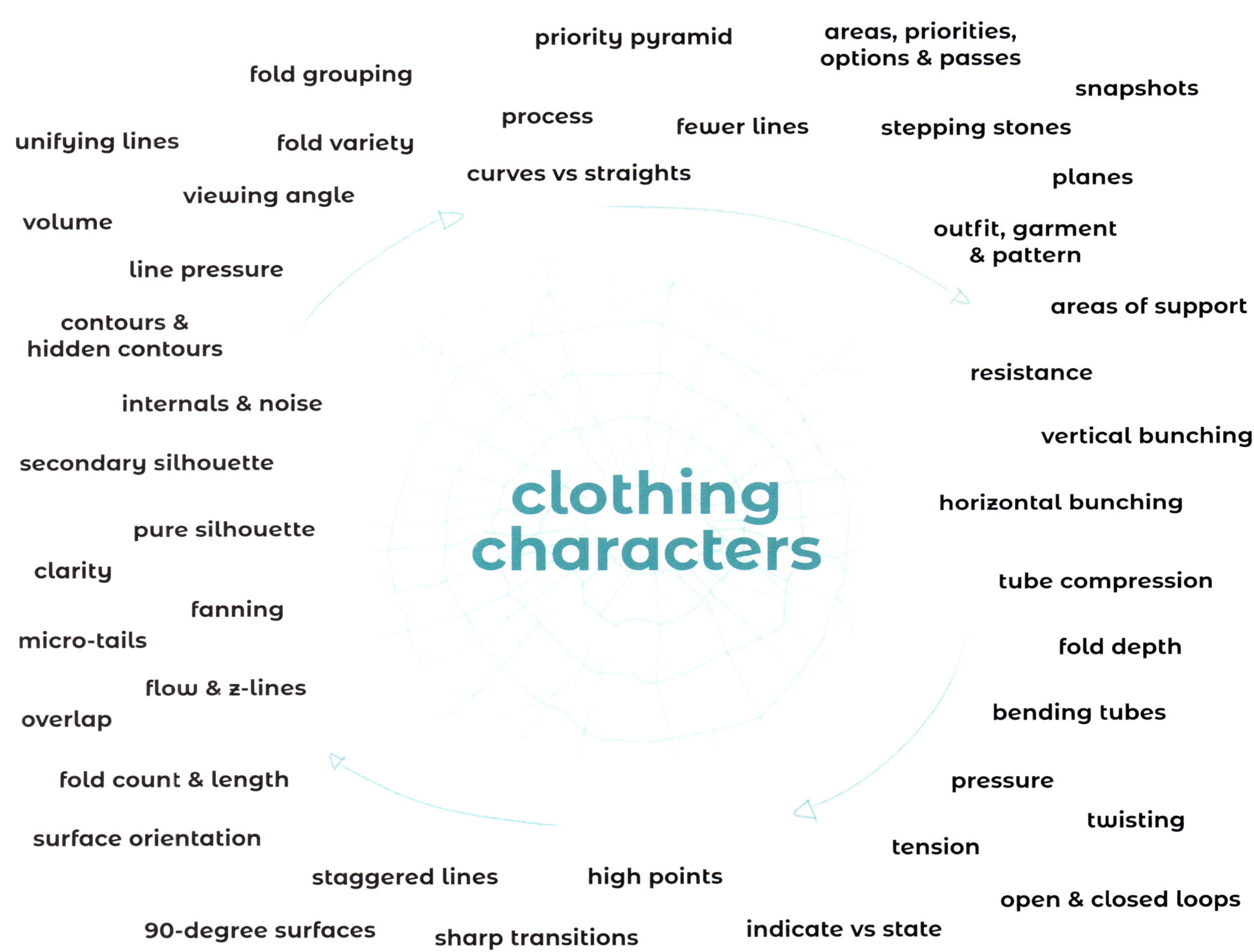

fewer lines

The first adjustment is simple but not easy: use fewer lines. Form can be conveyed with surprisingly few lines. The important thing is that the lines are in the right place, not that there are more of them. Add lots of details if you want, but don't expect more detail to equal more believability or clarity. If you find yourself thoughtlessly adding more lines, it's probably because you've lost focus. If so, you may be doing more harm than good to your drawing.

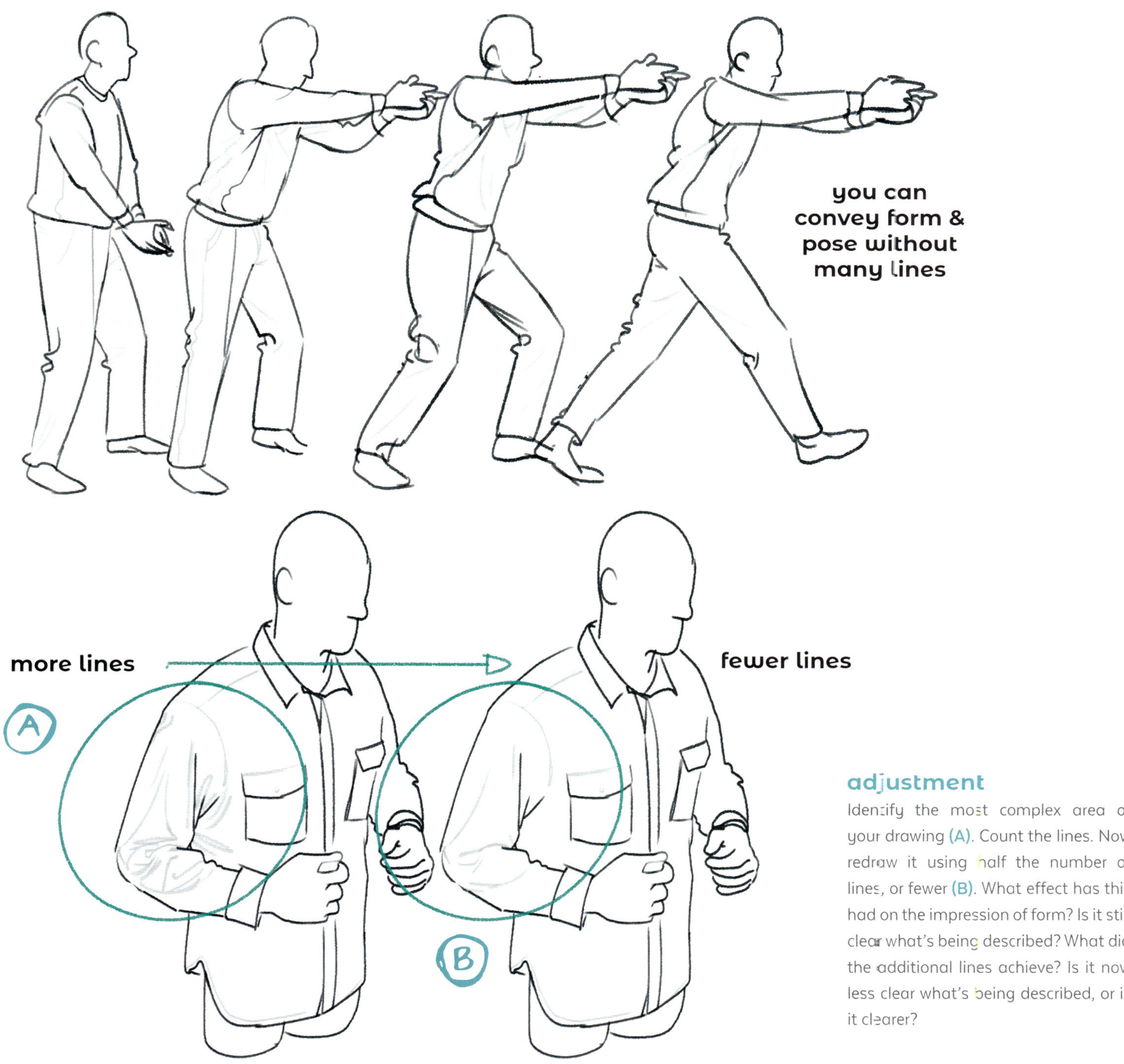

adjustment

Identify the most complex area of your drawing (A). Count the lines. Now redraw it using half the number of lines, or fewer (B). What effect has this had on the impression of form? Is it still clear what's being described? What did the additional lines achieve? Is it now less clear what's being described, or is it clearer?

areas, priorities, options & passes

Your process should include options. The most essential information is captured at the thumbnail stage, so always try to draw two or three thumbnails before investing time in a final drawing. The first thumbnail you draw (A) is rarely the best one (B).

However much time you have to draw a character, spend about a quarter of that time on thumbnails. If you have 20 minutes to draw, spend the first five minutes thumbnailing.

Your process should include **multiple passes** targeting the current priority. Most creative projects follow this pattern: try, adjust, try, adjust, and repeat. This is a craftsperson's mindset.

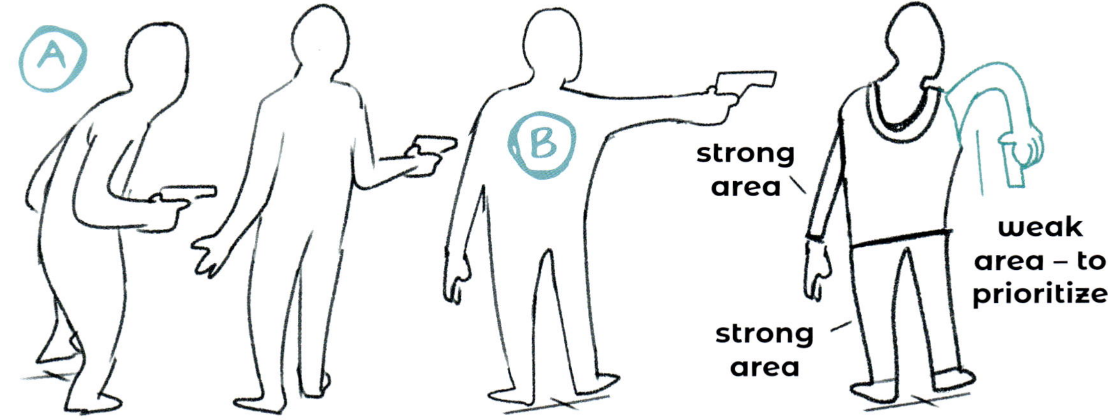

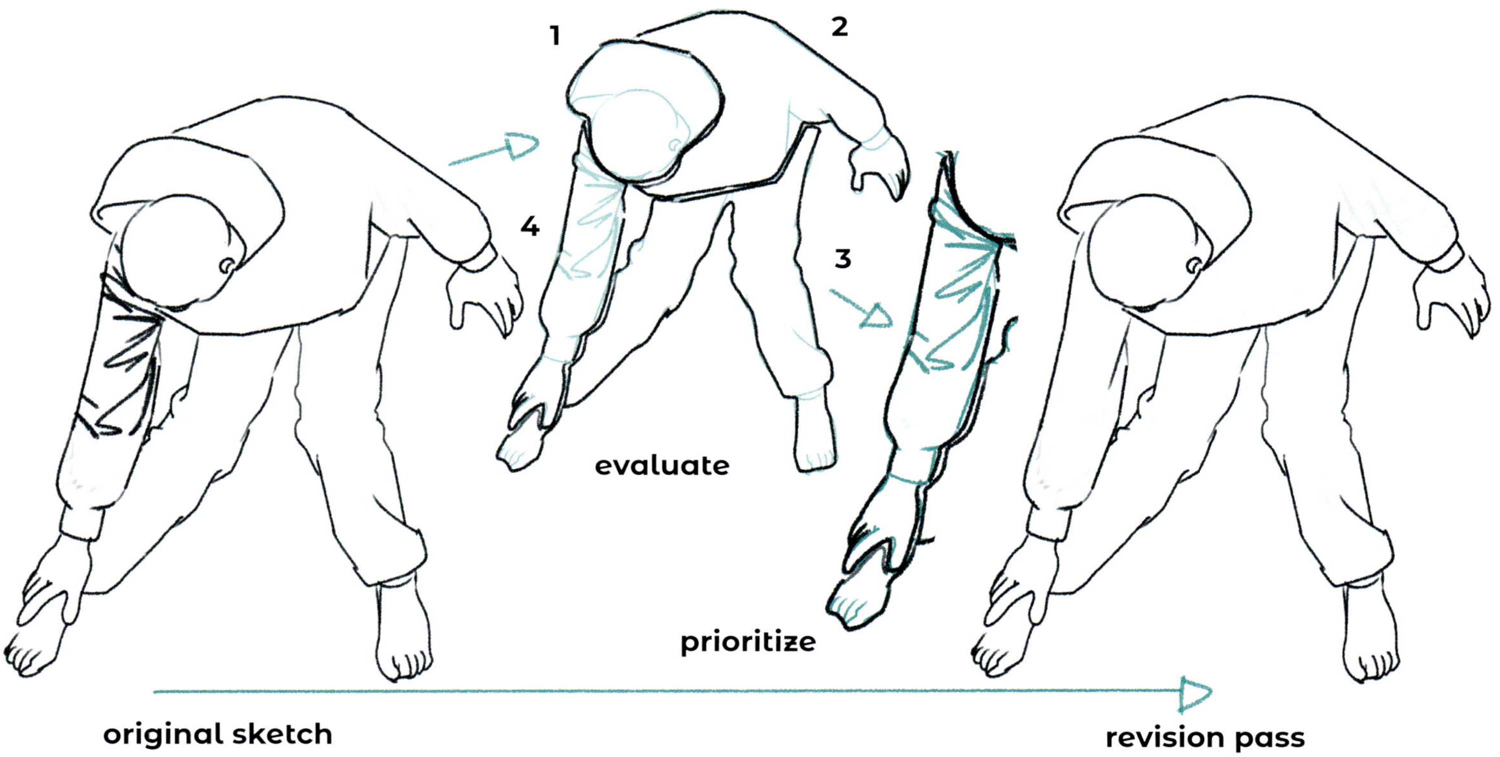

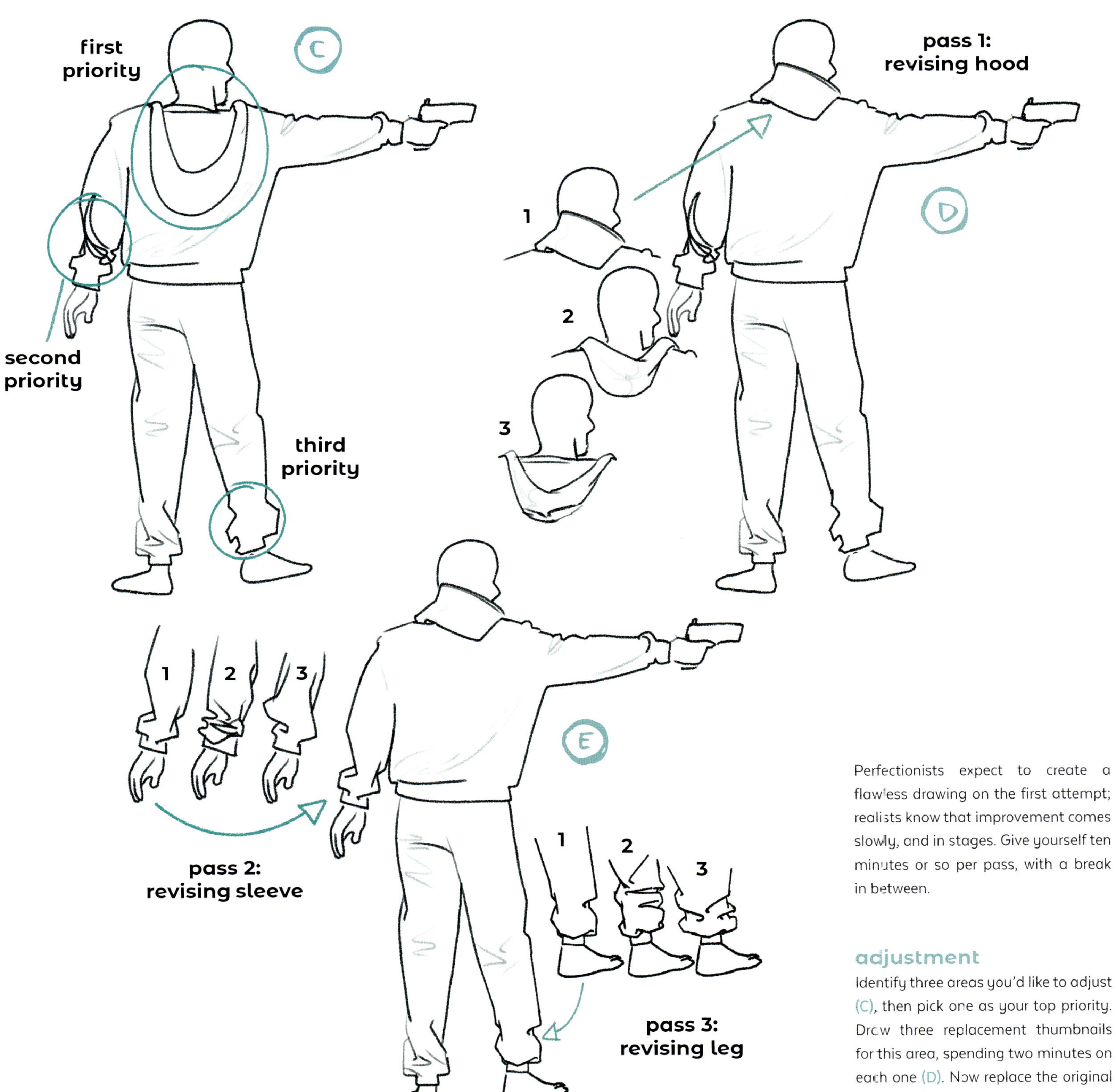

Perfectionists expect to create a flawless drawing on the first attempt; realists know that improvement comes slowly, and in stages. Give yourself ten minutes or so per pass, with a break in between.

adjustment

Identify three areas you'd like to adjust (C), then pick one as your top priority. Draw three replacement thumbnails for this area, spending two minutes on each one (D). Now replace the original with your favourite. Have a quick break, then repeat the process for the second and third priority areas you chose (E).

priority pyramid

For some reason, there's a natural tendency to focus most of our effort on drawing the 'folds', less effort on choosing the garments, and finally the least effort on the pose. This forms a sort of triangle of priorities, with pose at the narrow end and folds as the foundation (A).

However, we should rearrange this triangle. Ideally, we prioritize the pose, which forms the foundation of the drawing. Next, we build a solid garment choice on top of that. Finally, the folds and drapery are the icing on the cake, forming the top – and least important – layer (B).

You can draw great drapery, but if the pose is unnatural, the drawing will always look odd (C). Likewise, a strange outfit choice will also look odd, even if the folding is believable. Only after thumbnailing and finding a believable pose can we proceed onto the higher layers.

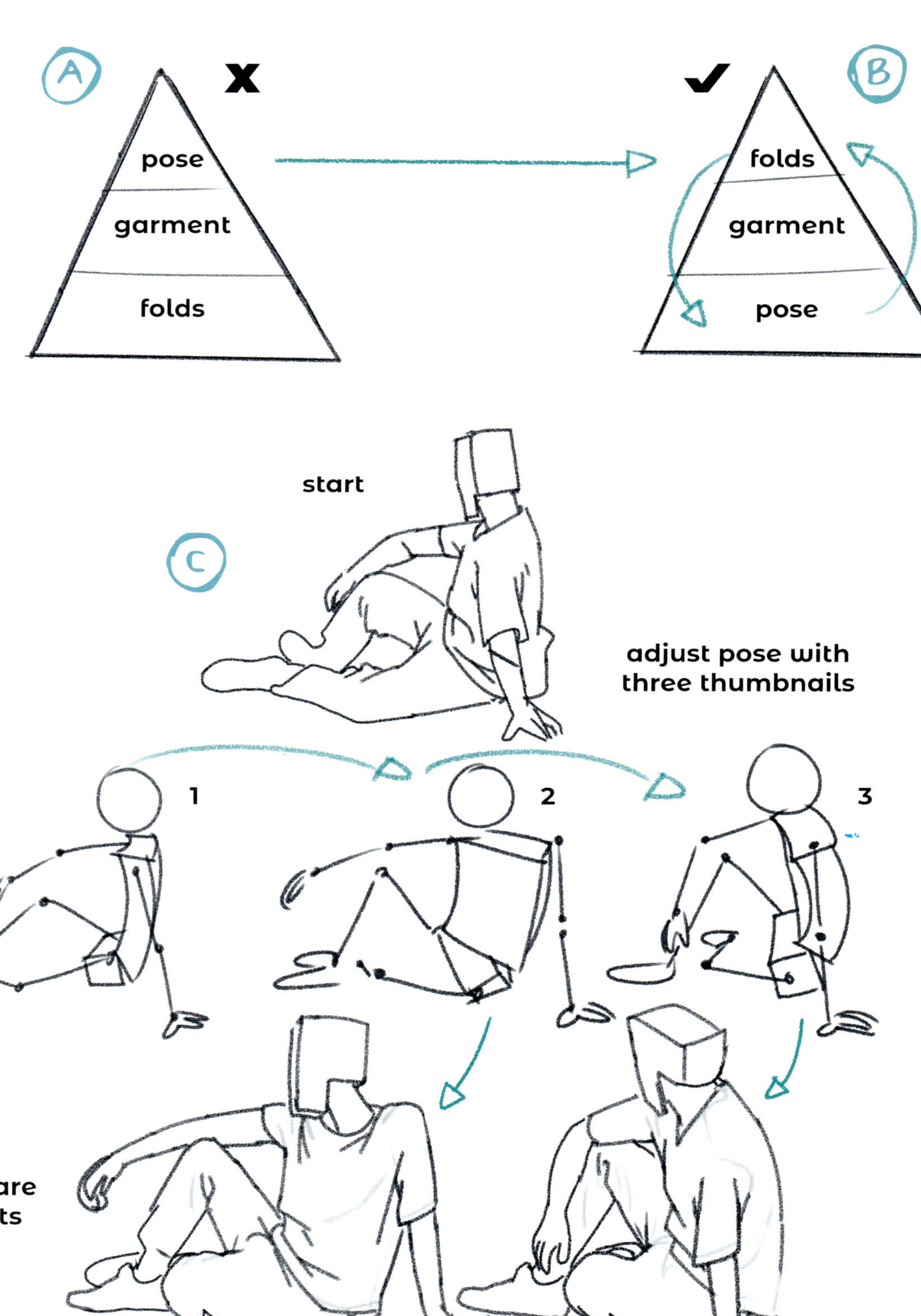

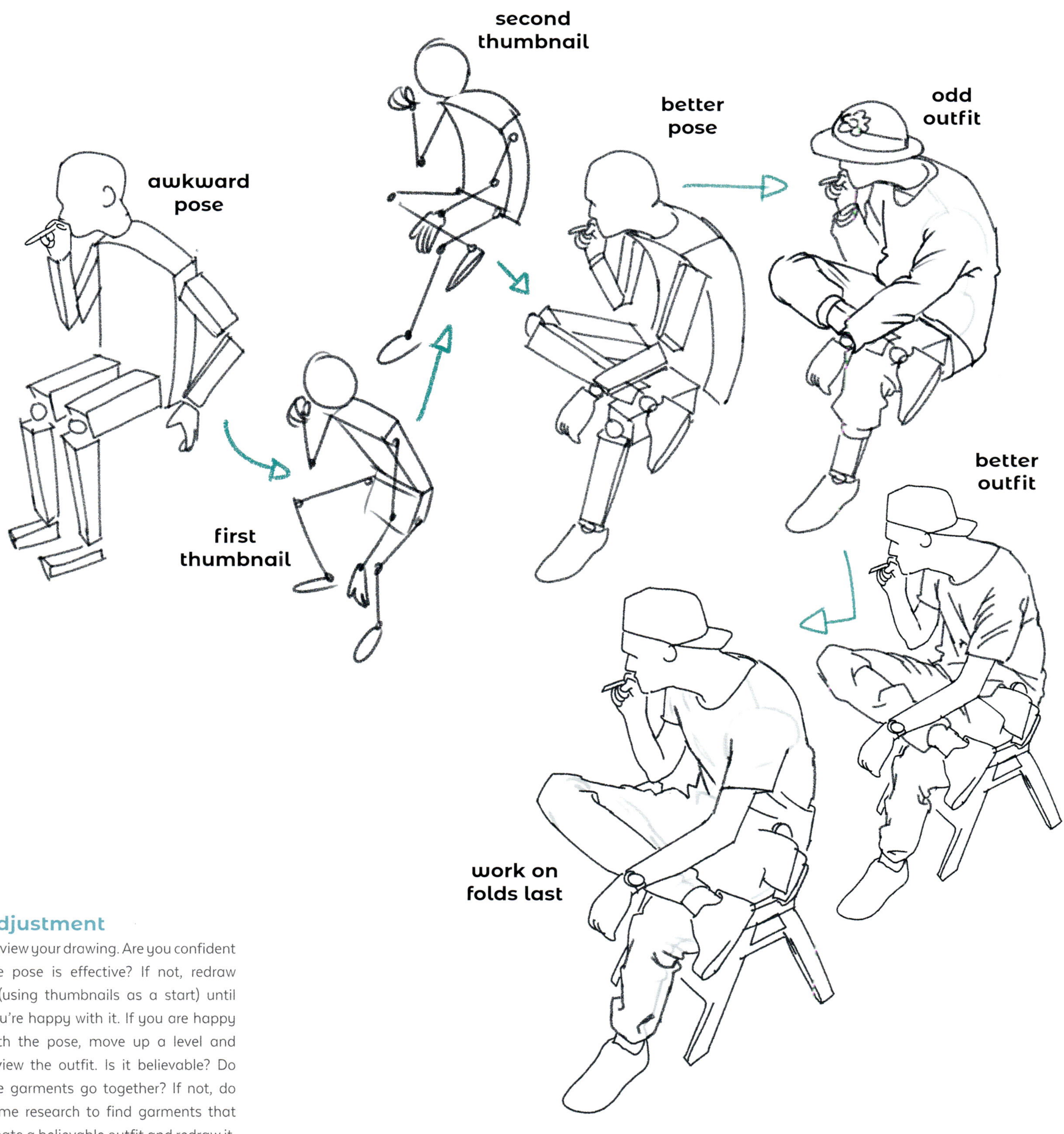

adjustment

Review your drawing. Are you confident the pose is effective? If not, redraw it (using thumbnails as a start) until you're happy with it. If you are happy with the pose, move up a level and review the outfit. Is it believable? Do the garments go together? If not, do some research to find garments that create a believable outfit and redraw it.

stepping stones

Most people draw linearly. This means that the drawing appears in a neat sequence on the page. Here's an example: the artist draws the head (A), then the next thing connected to it (B), then the arm (C), then the back (D), then the other arm (E), then one leg (F), and so on. This feels like a natural, logical way to draw for many people. The benefit of working this way is that the existing forms serve as cues for what to draw next. For example, it's easier to draw the arm when you've already drawn the head and hood (C), because the lines on the page help you visualize the perspective. There's nothing wrong with drawing linearly, but there are a couple of downsides.

The first downside is a tendency to 'zoom in' on whatever area you're drawing at the time (G). You may focus so much on one detail that you lose sight of the whole drawing (H). One sign of being mentally 'zoomed in' is trying to show as much as possible of whatever area you're currently drawing. For example, if you're focused on making these limbs look good (I), you'll naturally want to show as much of them as possible. Unfortunately, this focus discourages you from placing them behind another area. That's a shame, because the most natural poses have parts of the drawing that are tucked behind other parts (J). Only by working 'zoomed out' will you dare to tuck an arm behind the torso, or a leg behind another leg.

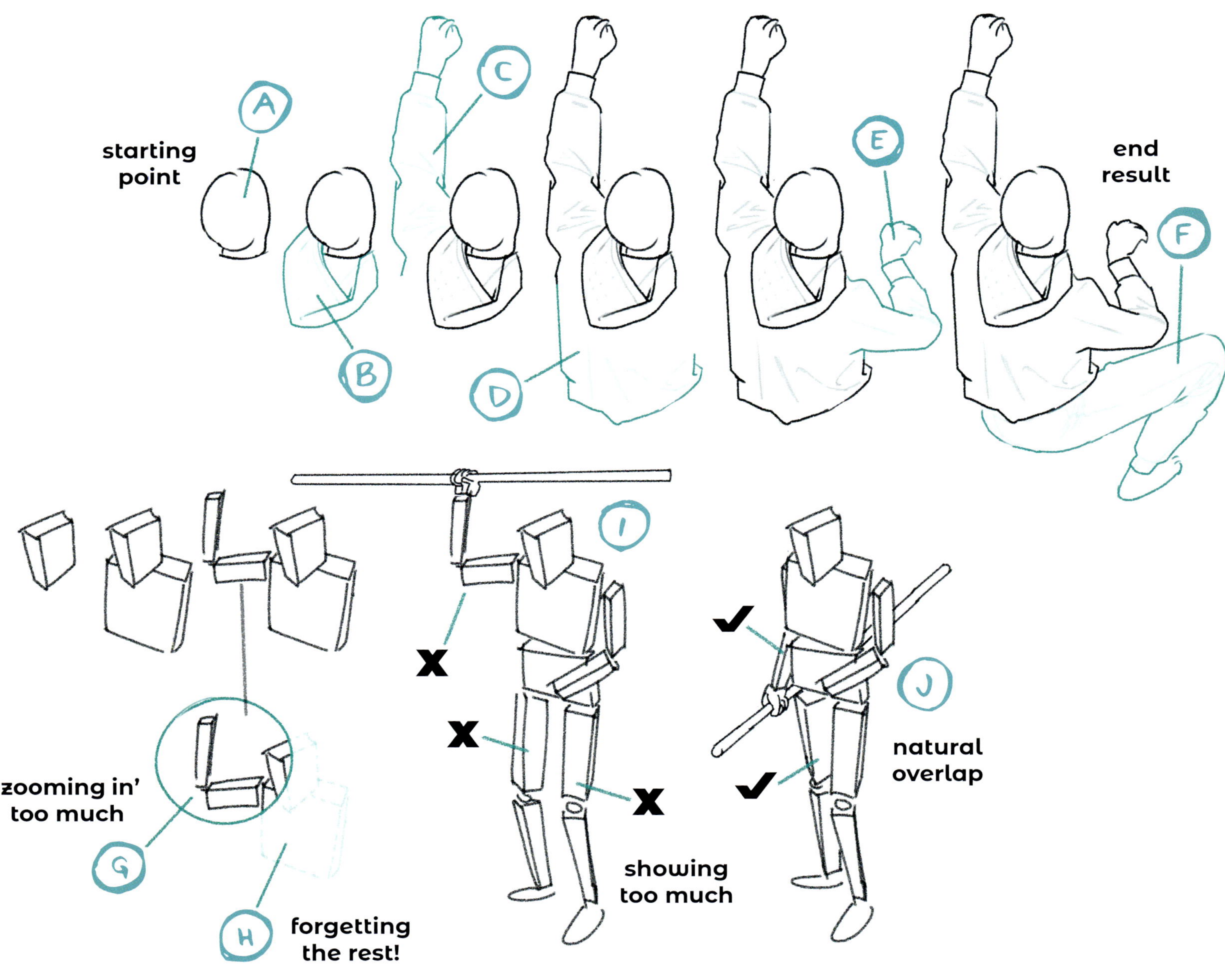

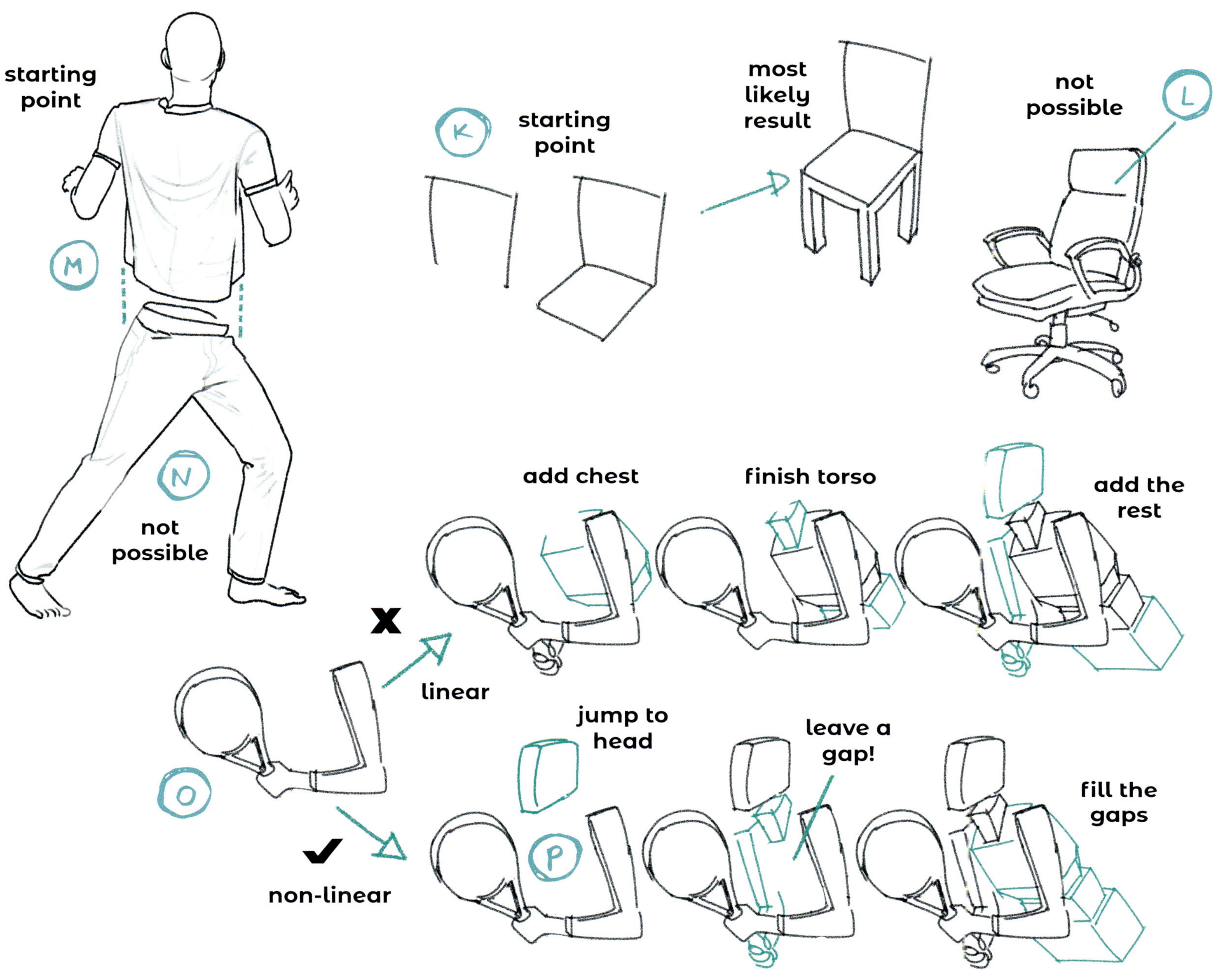

The existing lines on the page can help you to visualize the next part of a subject to draw, which leads us to the second downside: these lines can also limit your options. Every form you draw removes your options for a different final subject. For example, if you've drawn these lines (K), then the option of drawing this chair (L) has already been eliminated because the viewing angle is different and the chair has a different design. Another example: if you draw this character's torso (M), then you can't believably add these legs (N), because they're facing different directions and are viewed from a different angle. We should think carefully before we draw so that we don't eliminate too many options too early.

The alternative to linear drawing is to use 'stepping stones'. For example, you start with this arm holding a tennis racquet (O). You could draw linearly and keep adding the next connecting forms: chest, neck, head, and so on. However, if you draw non-linearly, you can 'jump' and draw a form that isn't directly connected. This means that there'll be a gap between them. You've made a mental 'leap'. In this case, it's jumping from the arm to the head (P). Next, you can fill in the neck and the far arm, skipping the torso, which leaves another gap.

It sounds more difficult to draw this way and, at the start of the drawing, it is. However, by the end of the drawing you'll have a lot of forms on the page that you simply need to connect; it's easier to add more to the drawing because you're just filling in the gaps. If you draw this way, it's a little harder at the start, but you generally end up with a more interesting drawing.

The main advantage of using some stepping stones in your process is that it forces you to try harder to visualize the final drawing. People often say 'I can't visualize at all', but that's almost never true. You often just need to give it a bit more time and focus. Visualization is one component of memory, and almost everyone has an amazing visual memory, even if they don't realize it!

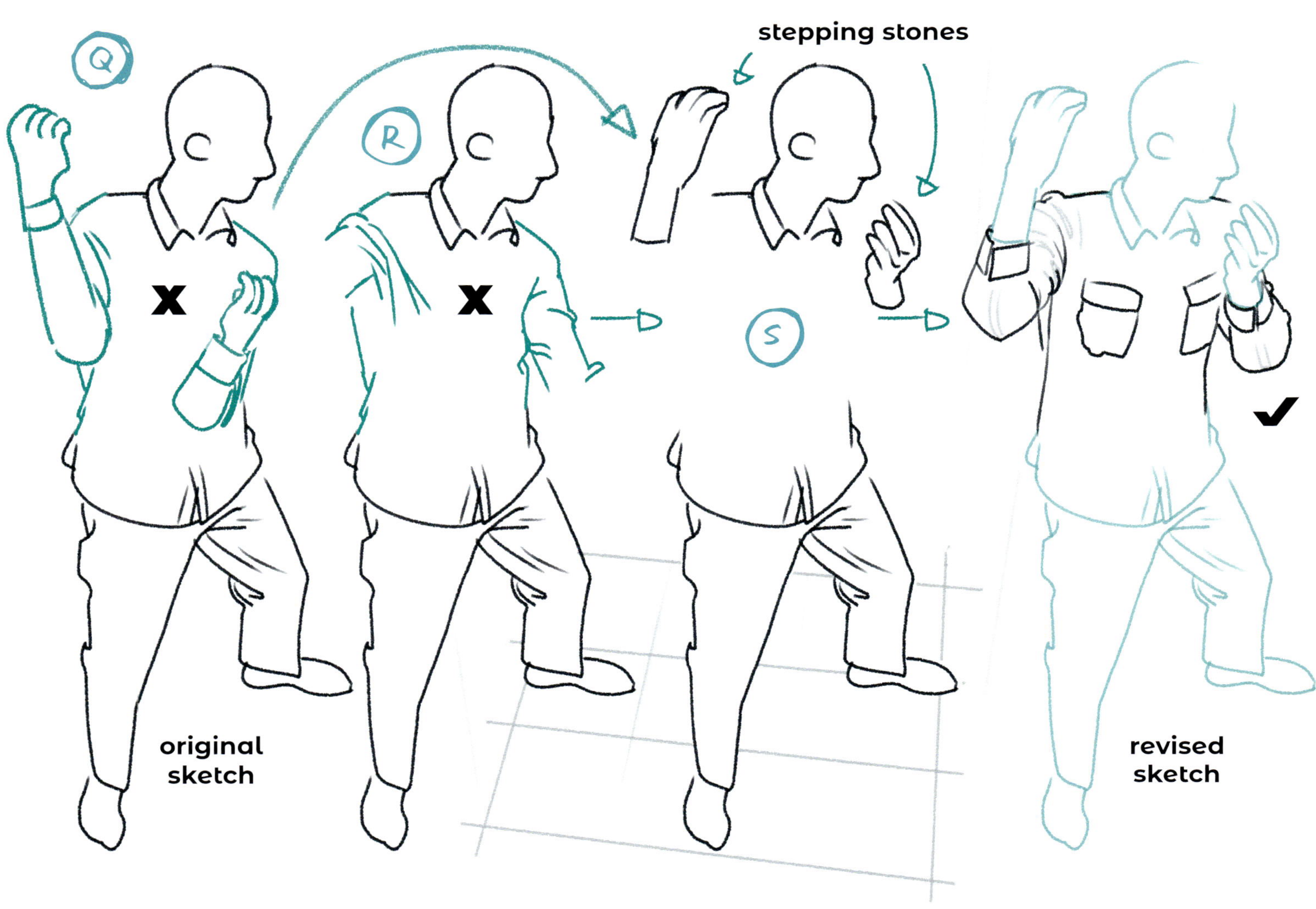

adjustment

Identify one or two priority areas in your drawing that could be improved (Q). Rather than erasing them and redrawing them linearly (R), spend a little longer than you normally would trying to visualize the pose and 'step across' (S). Give yourself some gaps to fill in. Trust that you will be able to fill the gap when you leave one. How does working this way affect your work and the way you feel about it?

snapshots

Characters are in constant motion. Avoid thinking in terms of 'stationary' and 'moving' poses. Even in 'stationary poses', such as sitting down, we constantly adjust ourselves to get more comfortable or respond to changes in emotion. Our goal is to capture a snapshot of a movement, rather than trying to draw static poses. Your drawing should communicate: 'this is a snapshot of a wider motion'.

If you're really getting advanced, the motion can show not just *what* they're doing, but *how they feel* about doing it. Try to demonstrate their mood through body language. Understanding the full motion greatly improves your ability to understand the forces generated by the mannequin on the outfit.

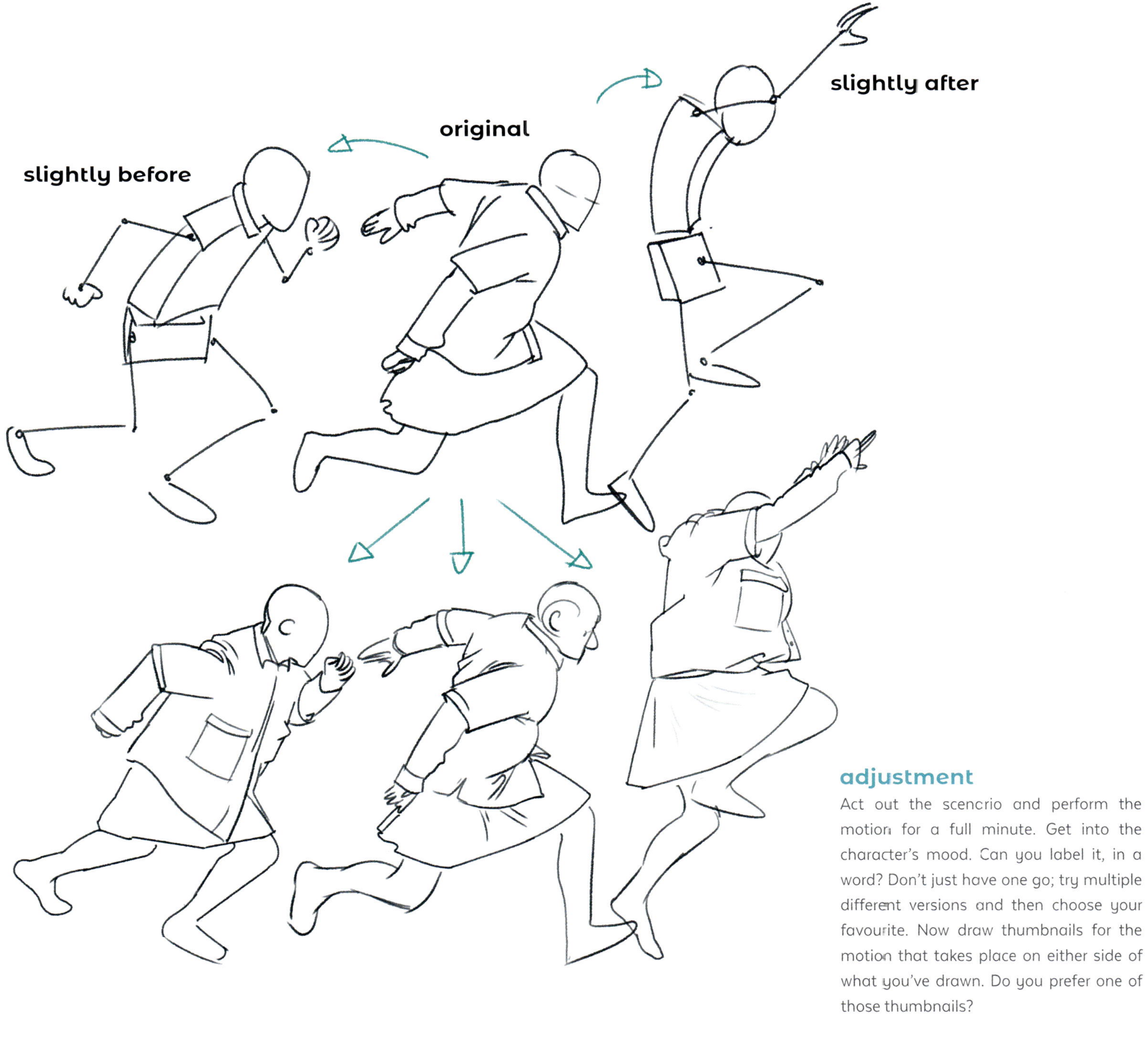

adjustment

Act out the scenario and perform the motion for a full minute. Get into the character's mood. Can you label it, in a word? Don't just have one go; try multiple different versions and then choose your favourite. Now draw thumbnails for the motion that takes place on either side of what you've drawn. Do you prefer one of those thumbnails?

outfit, garment & pattern

Let's get some terminology straight before we continue. The **mannequin** wears the **outfit**. The outfit is composed of several pieces of clothing called **garments**. A **pattern** is a blueprint for the garment which specifies the size and shape of the pieces of fabric. When the mannequin moves, the **drapery** changes, but the pattern always remains the same. Improve your 3D simulations by drawing the 2D pattern on the page next to the 3D version. This is a way of 'holding' some information on the page, so you don't have to remember it all. The more information you can 'hold' on the page, the easier the simulation will be. Try colour-coding your simulation and your pattern sometime – it's a great exercise to improve your simulation skills.

When two pieces of fabric are sewn together, a **seam** is created. A trouser leg is usually sewn from two pieces, for example; the front and back pieces are joined by two seams running down the sides of the leg (A). Sleeves are usually a single piece of fabric, rolled over to create a single seam on the underside of the arm (B). The seam runs the length of the arm, from the wrist to the armpit. Usually the seam side is turned over, so that the 'neat' side is on the outside of the garment, and appears as a single line (C).

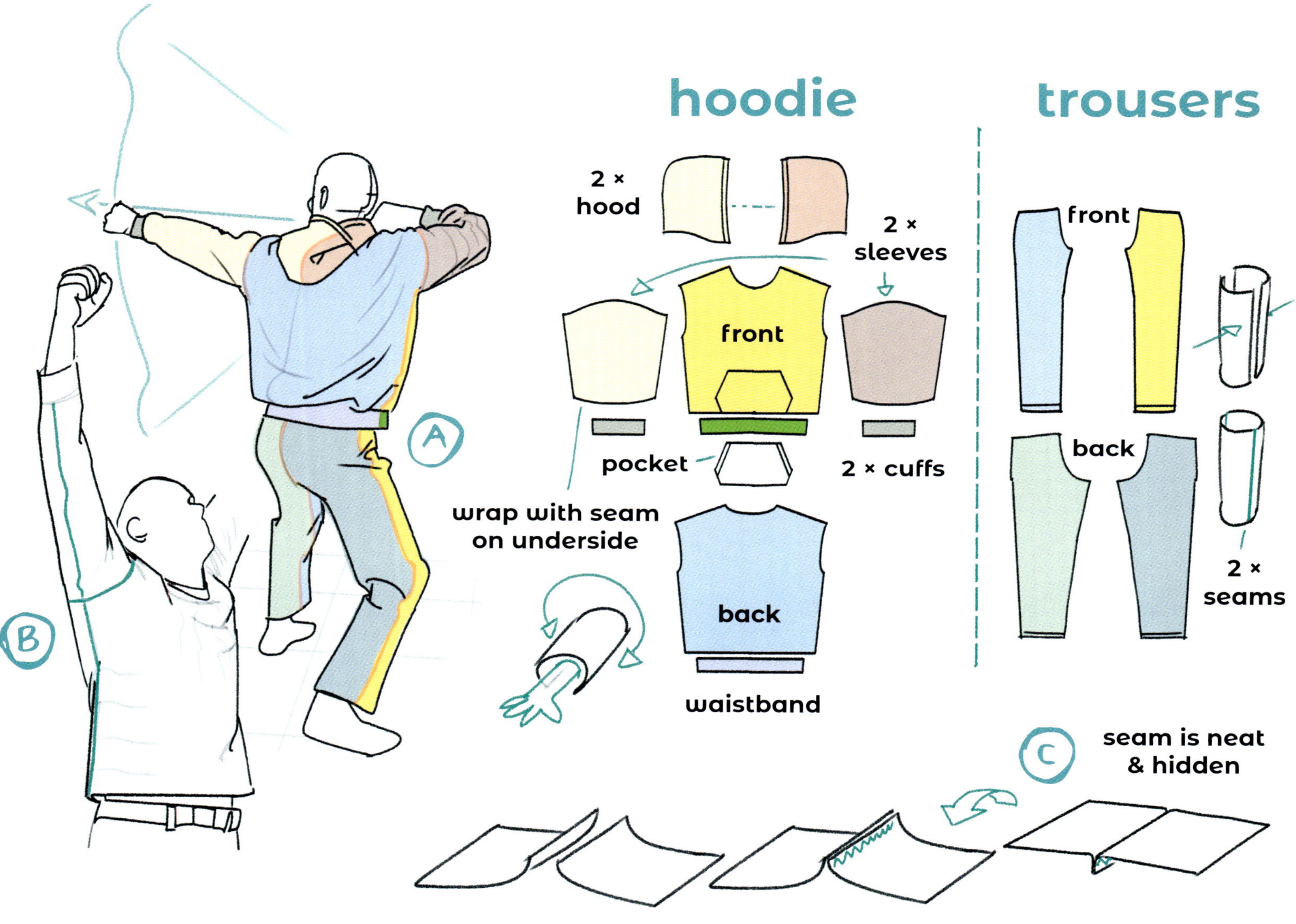

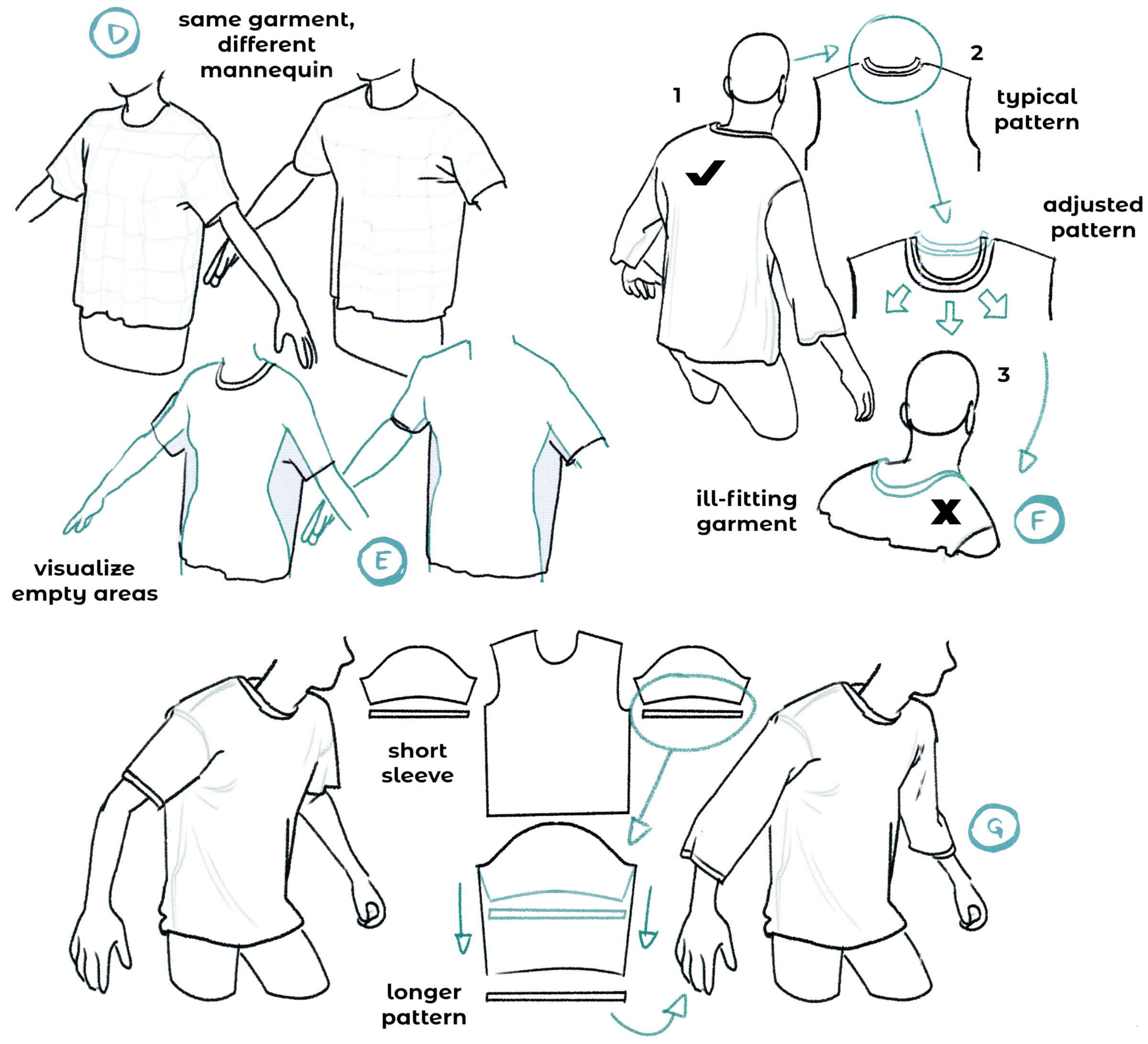

Larger garments have larger patterns. The same garment on a differently sized mannequin will create different drapery (D). Try to visualize the empty volume between the mannequin and the garment (E).

Adjusting the pattern changes the simulation. For example, most T-shirts have a round 'crew' neck which is higher at the back than the front. If you adjust the pattern and lower the back of the neck (F), the result is a poor fit in the simulation. Likewise, if you extend the sleeves of a T-shirt, the fit is changed (G). It's worth learning some basic garment patterns. Thankfully, although patterns can be complex, most everyday garments are just slight variations of a standard, classic design. You can find some of these in the Common Patterns section (page 278).

Here we have a pattern (H) and a mannequin in motion (I). But how do we know how large the pattern is, relative to the mannequin? How can we choose its overall scale? For example, how do we decide how low we want the bottom of this sweatshirt to fall (J)? This is important because we know the same pattern, but fifty per cent larger, would fit the mannequin very differently. To help figure this out, we can draw the major pieces of the pattern above the mannequin from a front view (K). This front-view mannequin should have the same proportions as the posed mannequin (I). When you draw a garment directly over the mannequin, it becomes much easier to choose the garment's size. For example, if we shrink the sweatshirt overall but keep the same pattern proportions (L), the waistband won't drop as low as J. Instead, it will have a slimmer fit overall. Overlaying the pattern is an important part of helping yourself visualize the drapery.

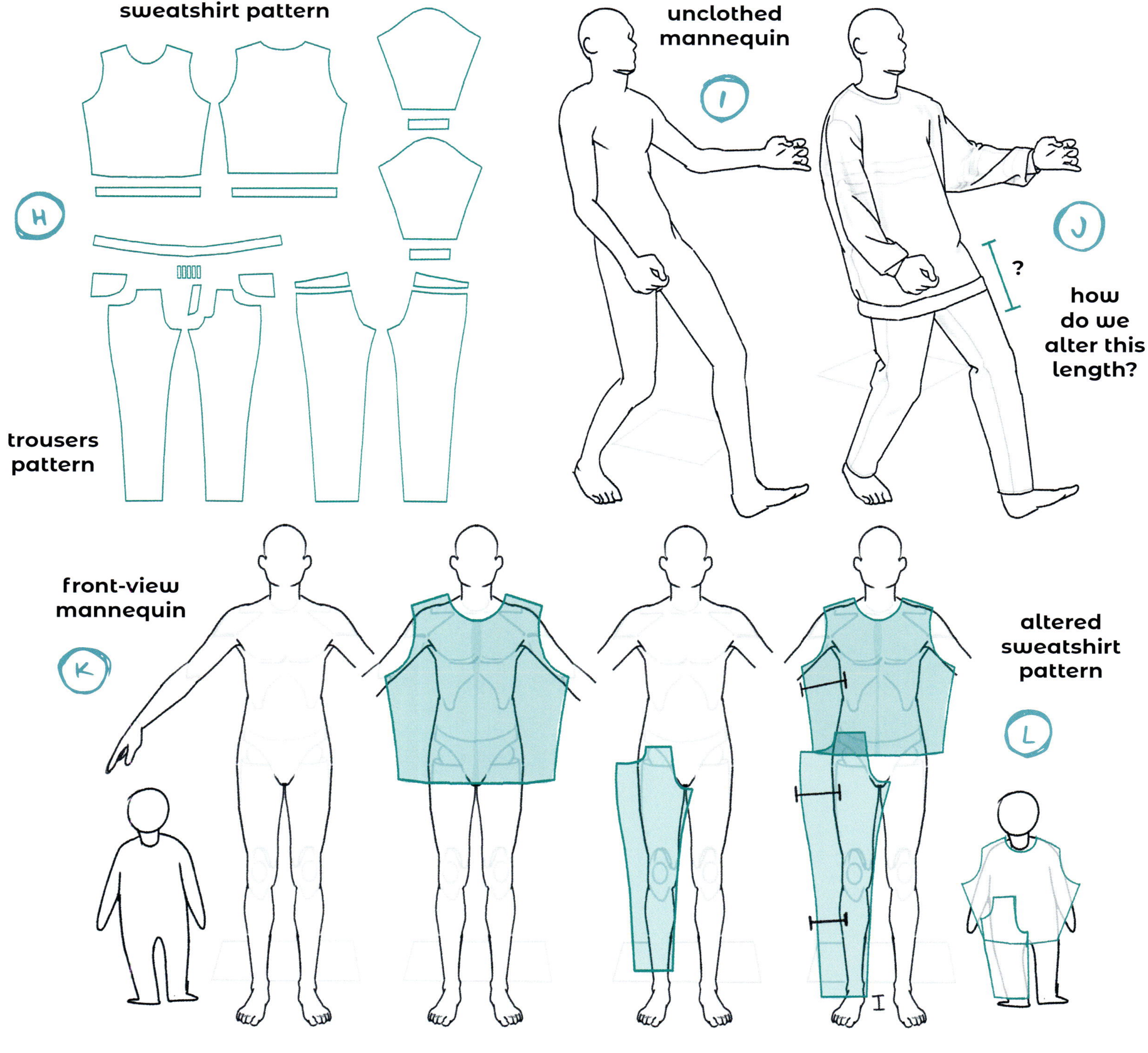

Don't forget to add any cuffs and waistbands to your pattern. Often, the reason a garment looks 'off' is simply that we've forgotten to add them (M). Cuffs are often slightly elasticated. Because of this, you can pull up a sleeve and it'll grip the arm without sliding down (N). When drawing a cuff 'holding' on to the arm, ensure that it's tight against the silhouette of the arm. If it's even slightly loose, it won't look elasticated.

Check that you've drawn the 'start' and 'end' points of the seams on both your pattern and the simulation (O). This is particularly helpful when drawing **twist** in your drapery.

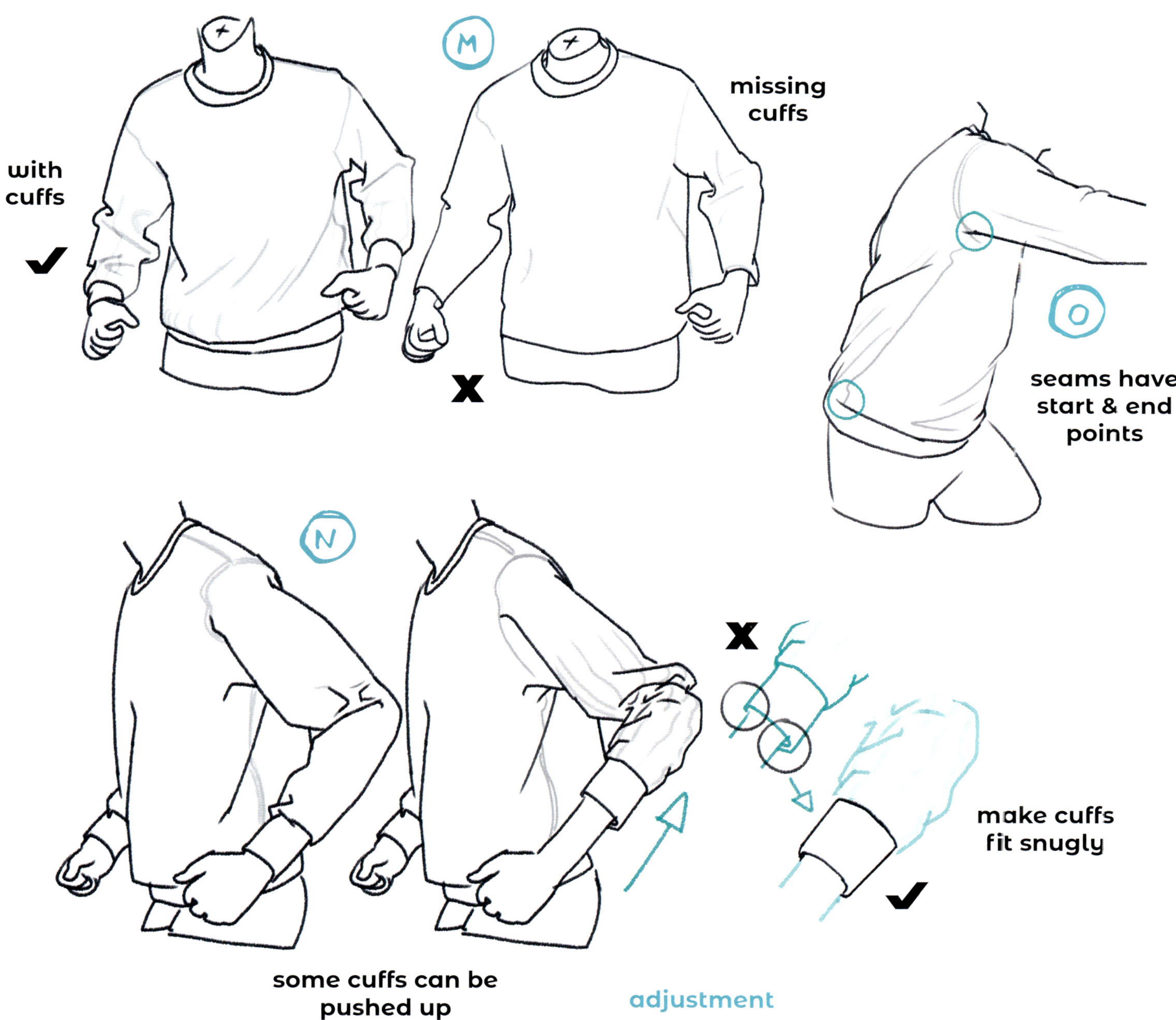

adjustment

Draw out the patterns for your whole outfit next to your simulation. Once you've drawn the pattern, try colour-coding it or numbering it. Make a note of which parts you're least confident about so you can review them later. Check that you've added elasticated regions. Draw in any seams that will help clarify the form. Try drawing a front view and drawing the major shapes over the top – use this to check the scale and distances between mannequin and seams.

areas of support

Areas of support (AoS) are regions where the garment is supported and therefore prevented from falling. Let's see an example. If we raise a central AoS in a circle of fabric, the garment attempts to hang directly below it (A). Because the fabric has to fit into a smaller area, it must fold. By pulling fabric below areas of support, gravity is also usually pulling fabric inwards (B).

Practice locating and labelling the AoS on both your pattern and the simulation. For example, there's one on this character's back (C). However, there are also more subtle ones on the tops of his thighs. In practice, areas of support are rarely horizontal. That would be too easy! Instead, they're often angled. Elasticated regions, such as cuffs, are also AoS. Without them, the fabric would hang loosely (D).

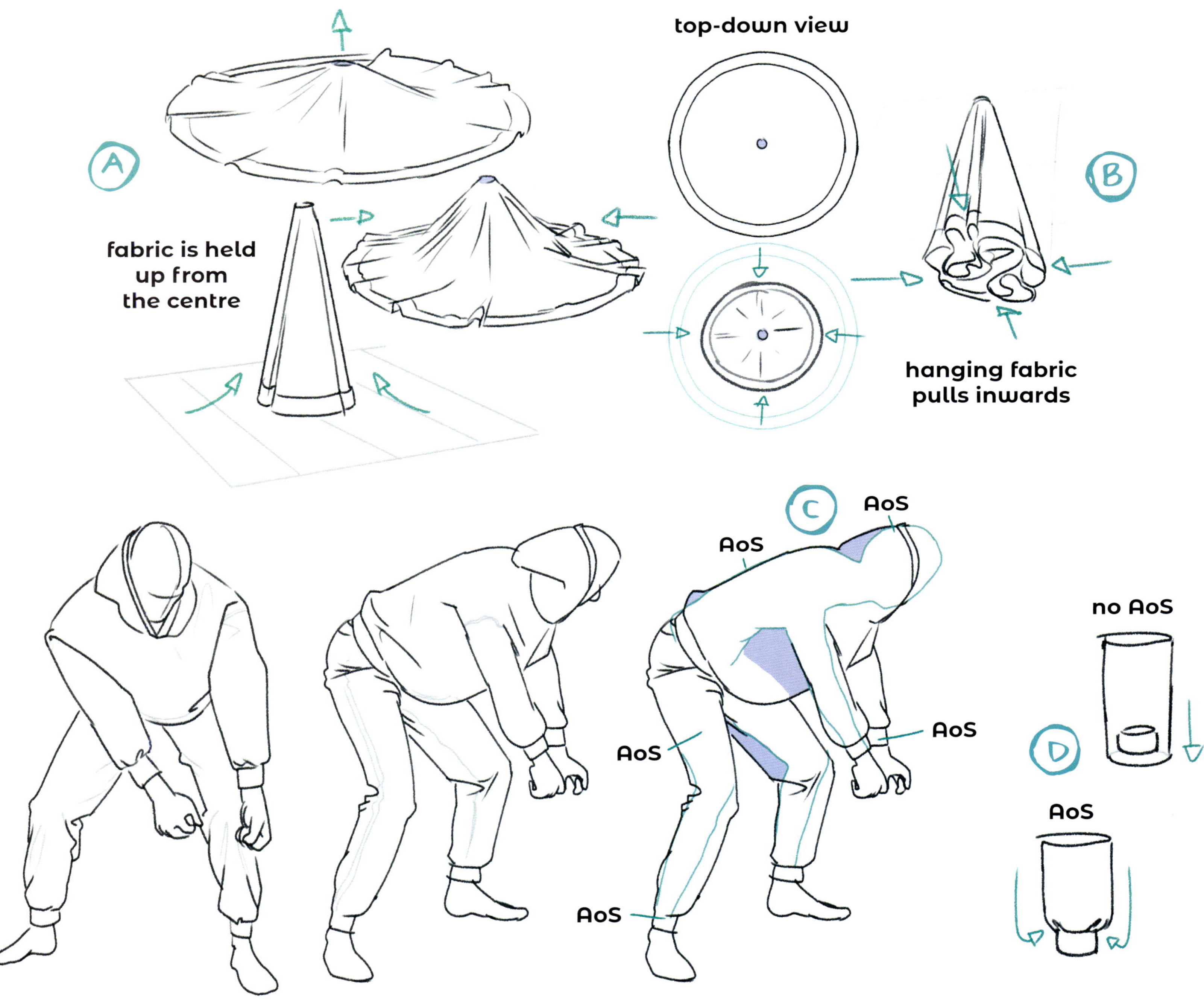

The greater the distance between the edge of the fabric and the AoS, the further the edge will fall. Here, the fabric at the side (E) is further from the AoS than the fabric at the ends (F). So it will hang further down – closer to the ground – than the fabric at the ends. If you know where the AoS are on the pattern, you can use that knowledge to predict the drapery. In the example at the bottom of the page, we'll lower a square of fabric onto a cuboid (G). We know that there's an AoS right in the middle (H), so we can make some measurements. We can predict that the corners will fall closest to the ground because they are furthest from the AoS. We can also predict that the corners will fold more, because they must fit under a smaller section of the AoS (I).

Finally, we know that the fabric along the sides of the cuboid will fall relatively flat, as it has an AoS the same length as the fabric.

In the resulting simulation (J), we see that our prediction was correct. The corners are the lowest points, and most of the folding is occurring near the small AoS of the corners.

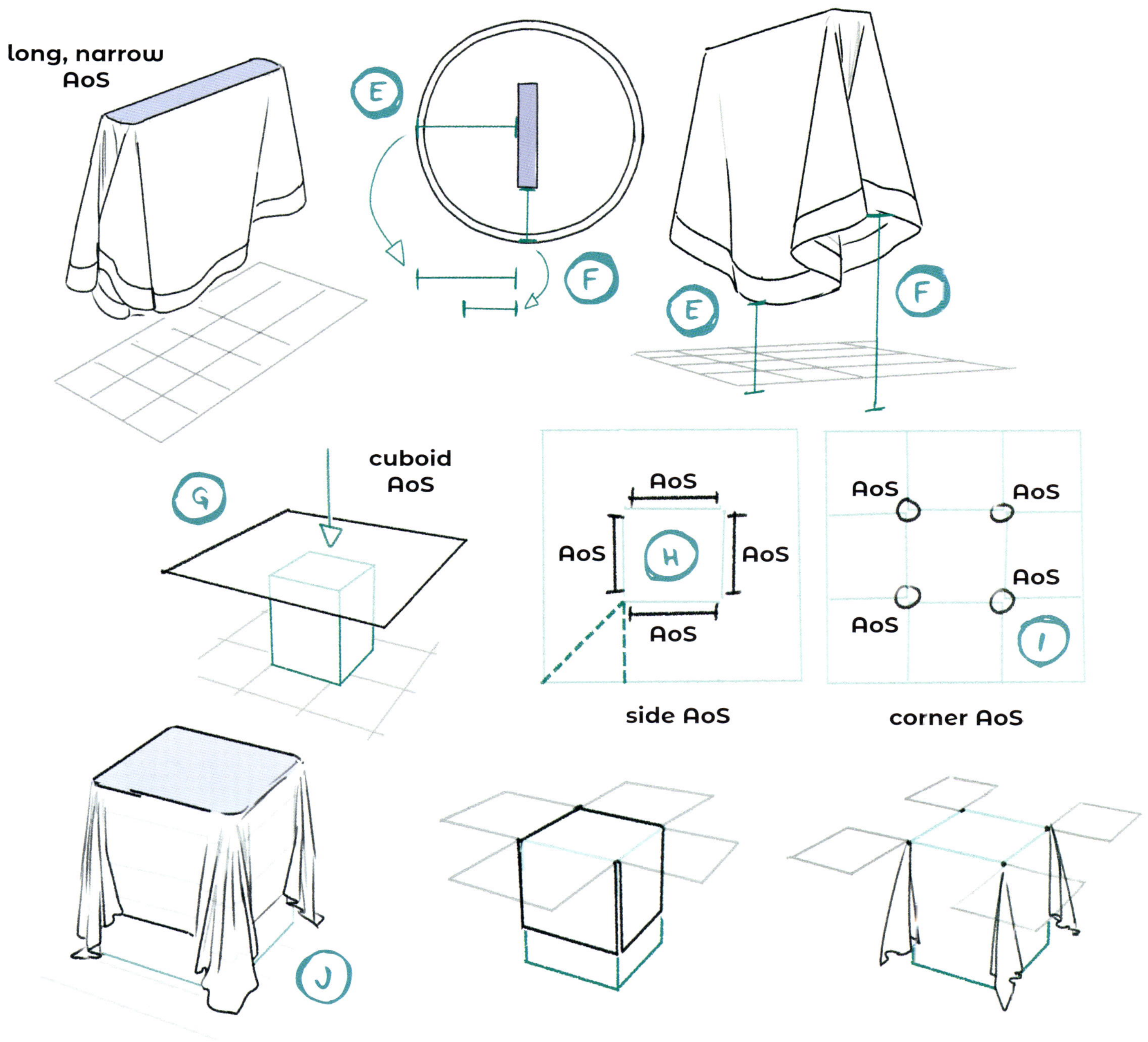

Now let's draw a shirt pattern on a mannequin (K). We want to know if the bottom of the shirt will be higher at the front or back. The first thing we notice is that the back of the pattern is longer than the front (L). Therefore, we might expect the back of the shirt to hang lower (M).

However, we know that the top of the shoulders is usually covered by the back yoke of the shirt, so we mark the AoS on the pattern and mannequin in red (N). This gives us something to measure.

Now, when we measure the distances from the AoS to the bottom of the shirt (red lines), we find that they're the same length. Therefore, we know the front and back of the shirt will be level.

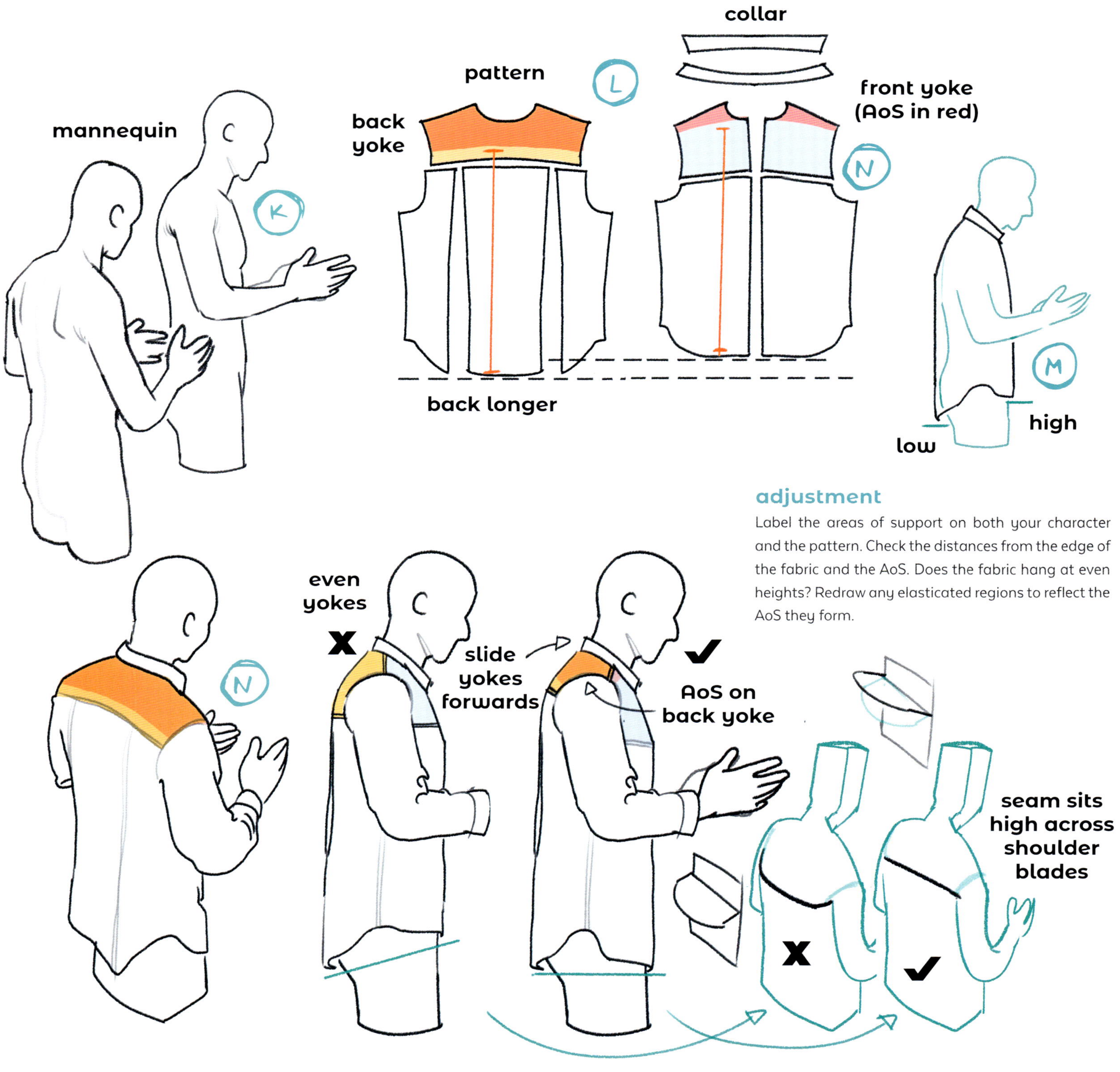

adjustment

Label the areas of support on both your character and the pattern. Check the distances from the edge of the fabric and the AoS. Does the fabric hang at even heights? Redraw any elasticated regions to reflect the AoS they form.

resistance

Resistance is a property of fabric – essentially whether it likes to be folded or not. High-resistance materials, like leather, don't like to bend or fold. Low-resistance materials, like silk, don't mind it. The level of resistance greatly affects the drapery.

Low-resistance fabric displays two behaviours. Firstly, the fold width is narrow, as opposed to broad. The individual folds are small in diameter (A). This shows that the fabric only weakly resists being deformed. By contrast, high-resistance materials form broad folds (B).

Secondly, the fabric shouldn't support its own weight very well. By contrast, high-resistance fabrics partially support their own weight (C).

The two jackets below are made from high-resistance fabrics. Notice that the interior folds are angular (D). The fabric doesn't want to bend. It can support its own weight further out from the mannequin. Not only are the interior folds more angular, but the silhouette is, too (E). This is a powerful tip – if you want to make your simulation appear high-resistance, make the silhouette angular.

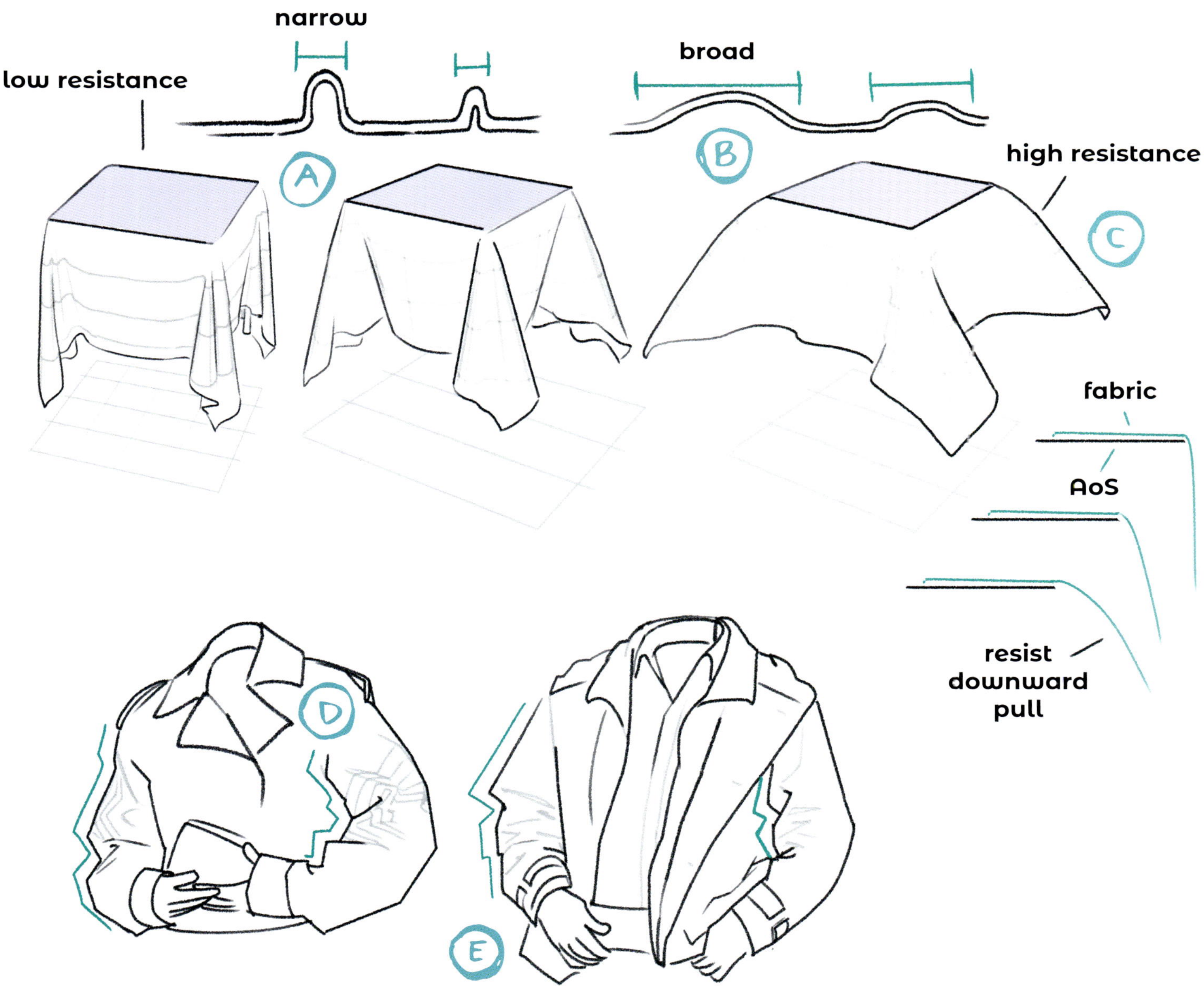

By contrast, low-resistance fabric hangs close to the mannequin's form, and the silhouette and interior folds are more 'flowing' and less angular. The opposite applies from what we said on the last page: if you want to draw low-resistance fabric (F), give the silhouette a lot of soft curves and don't make the interior folds too angular. The drapery should roll – think 'rolling hills' – rather than change orientation abruptly (G).

Don't assume that a thicker fabric will always be more resistant. Thicker fabrics generally have broader folds, but thicker material is also heavier, and heavier materials struggle to support their own weight. Resistance is determined by how a material is made, and what it's made from, rather than its thickness. Don't worry too much about what the fabric is. Instead, focus on choosing a level of resistance.

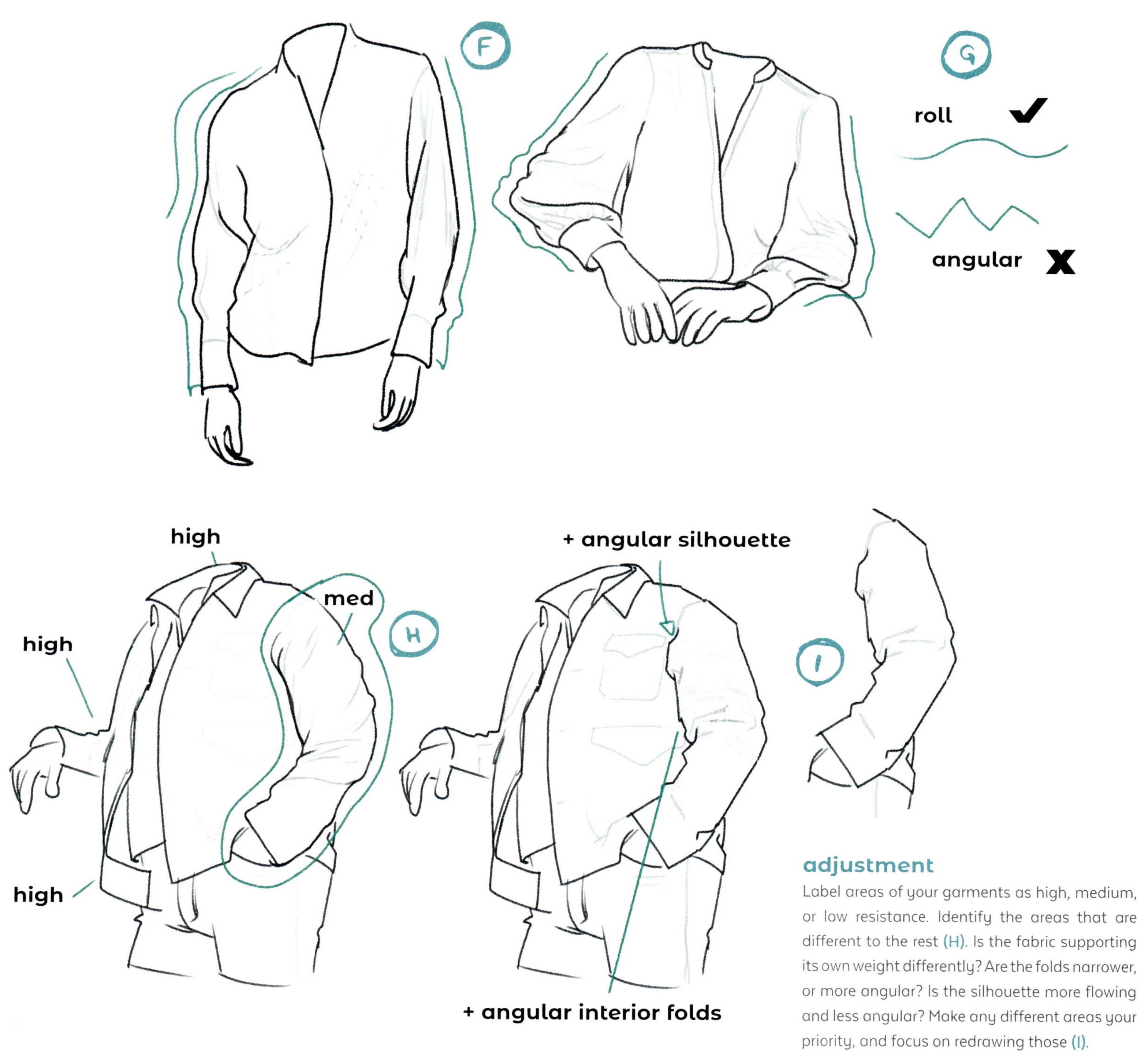

adjustment

Label areas of your garments as high, medium, or low resistance. Identify the areas that are different to the rest (H). Is the fabric supporting its own weight differently? Are the folds narrower, or more angular? Is the silhouette more flowing and less angular? Make any different areas your priority, and focus on redrawing those (I).

vertical bunching

If you lower an area of support closer to the ground, fabric will bunch vertically. The same length of fabric must now fit into the new reduced height, so it bulges out at the sides. However, the bunching isn't distributed evenly. Most of the folding happens near the ground, because fabric usually can't support much of its own weight (A). The higher the resistance of the fabric, the more of its own weight it can support, and the more evenly the folds will distribute between the ground and the area of support (B). The blue line indicates a region where the fabric must strongly resist folding (C).

Following this logic, many people draw complex bunching near the bottom of trousers (D). However, this is usually a mistake. Most trousers are carefully fitted so that they don't bunch around the tops of the feet/shoes. You see this sort of folding less often than you'd expect.

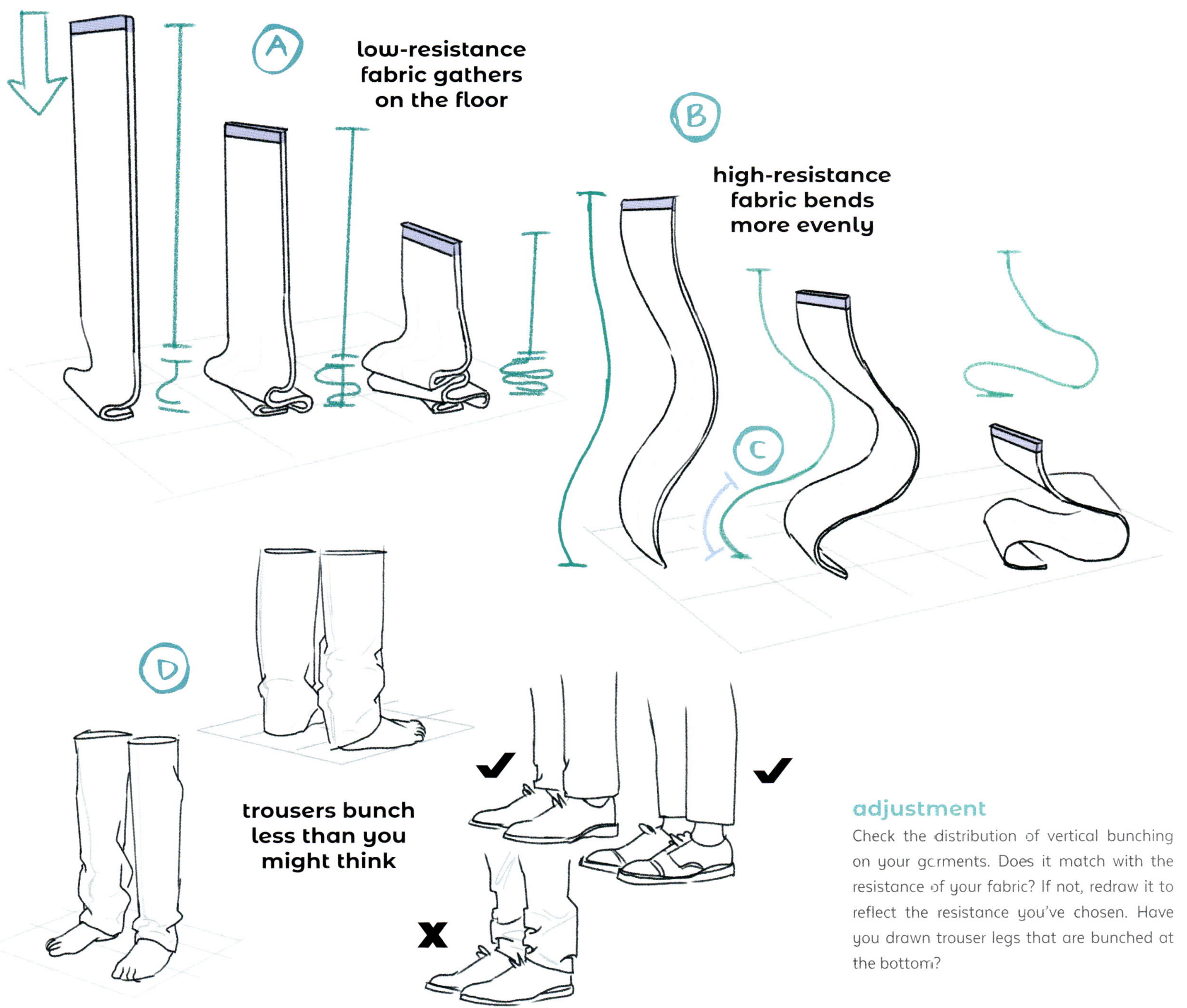

adjustment

Check the distribution of vertical bunching on your garments. Does it match with the resistance of your fabric? If not, redraw it to reflect the resistance you've chosen. Have you drawn trouser legs that are bunched at the bottom?

horizontal bunching

When compression occurs from the sides, we see horizontal bunching (A). This direction of folding is often overlooked, but it occurs more often than you'd imagine. The usual example of horizontal folding is seen in curtains, where it's often called a 'pipe fold'. In this direction gravity has less of an impact on the distribution of folds, so the folds are more evenly spaced rather than bunching towards one end. These curtains show more extreme horizontal compression at the top than the bottom (B). This 'fanning out' suggests that the material is resisting being horizontally bunched.

When the arms are held at the sides, there will usually be some horizontal bunching near the shoulders (C). In many types of shirt, it's also common to see some horizontal bunching built into the design at the centre. This is called a 'box pleat'.

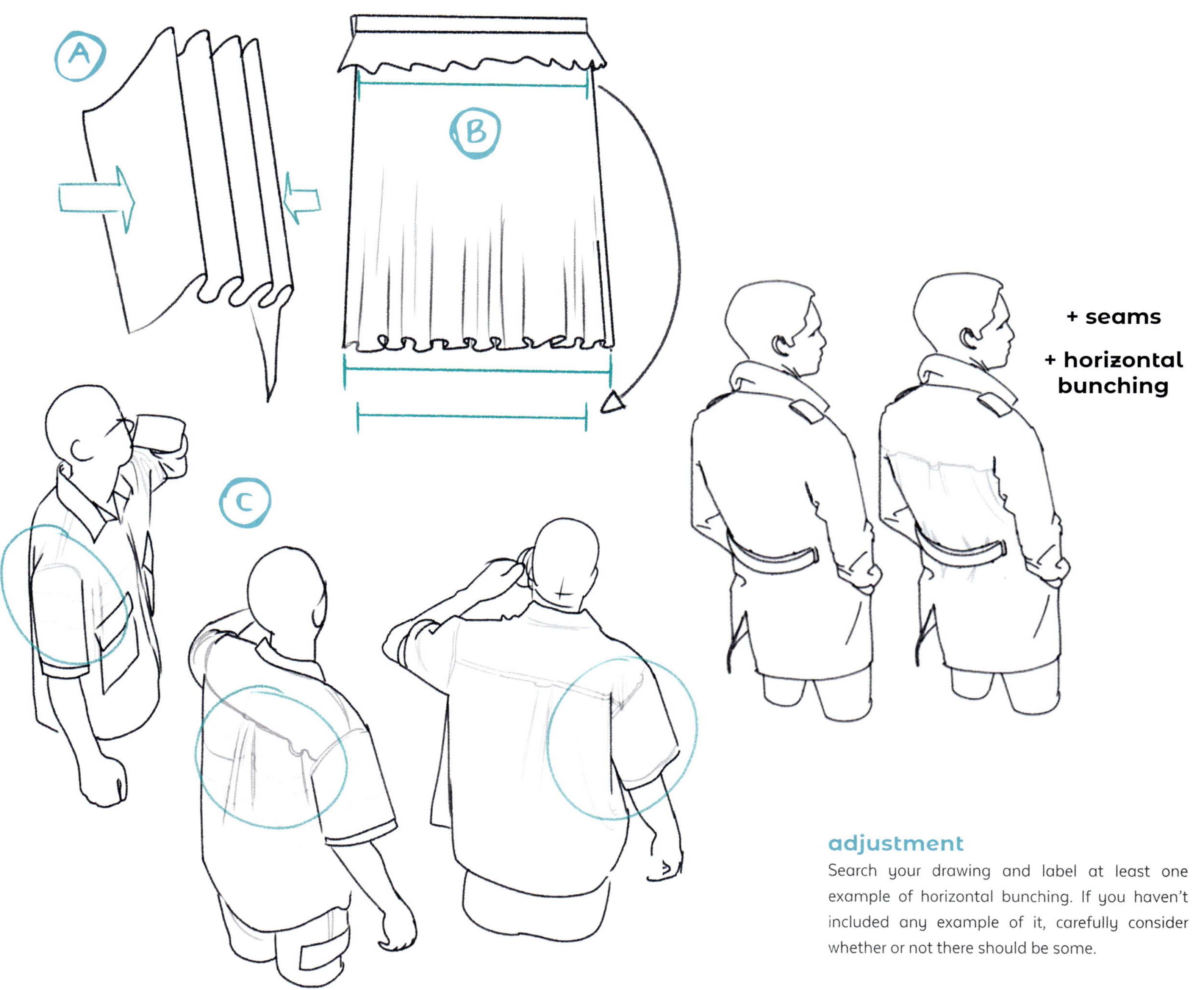

adjustment

Search your drawing and label at least one example of horizontal bunching. If you haven't included any example of it, carefully consider whether or not there should be some.

tube compression

Most clothing is some variation of a tube. We can learn a lot about drapery by looking at the behaviour of tubes of fabric under force. Let's start with a silk tube as an example (A). When lowered, it bunches near the ground. Some parts fold inwards and others fold outwards, but whichever direction they go in, they stay close to the area directly below the AoS. A more resistant fabric can support some of its own weight, so some folding occurs higher up (B). The greater the resistance, the more 'even' the vertical distribution of folds.

Let's see how this relates to drawing sleeves. When a sleeve is pushed up, the drapery will differ depending on the resistance. Low-resistance fabrics will show more condensed compression near the cuff (C). Higher-resistance fabrics will have more evenly distributed folds, and they will be more angular (D).

A tube will never form folds that taper outwards like this (E) when viewed from every angle. That would require the circumference of the tube to widen, and the pattern to change to something that isn't a tube.

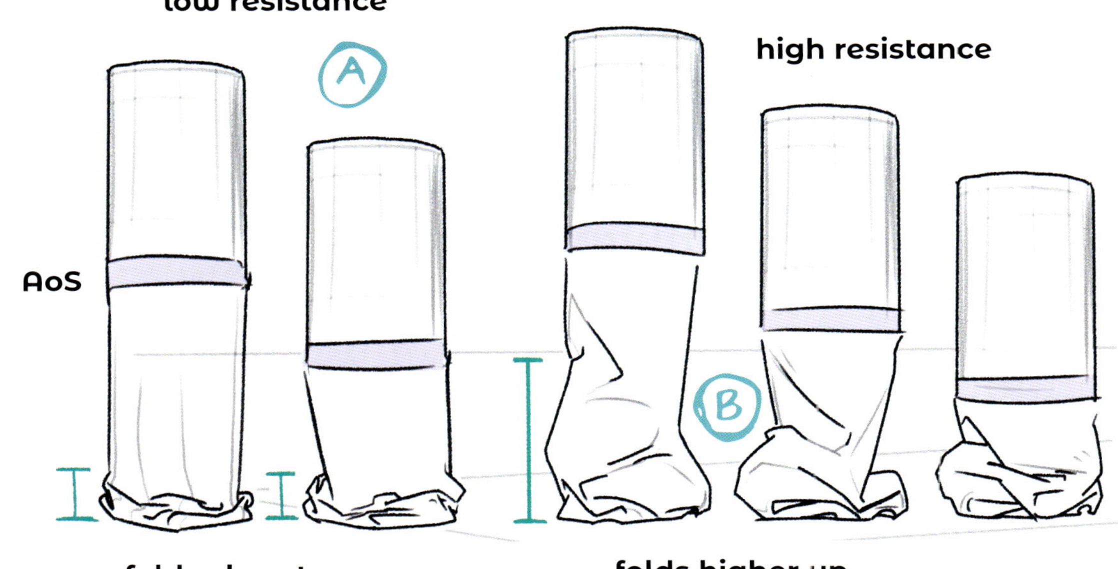

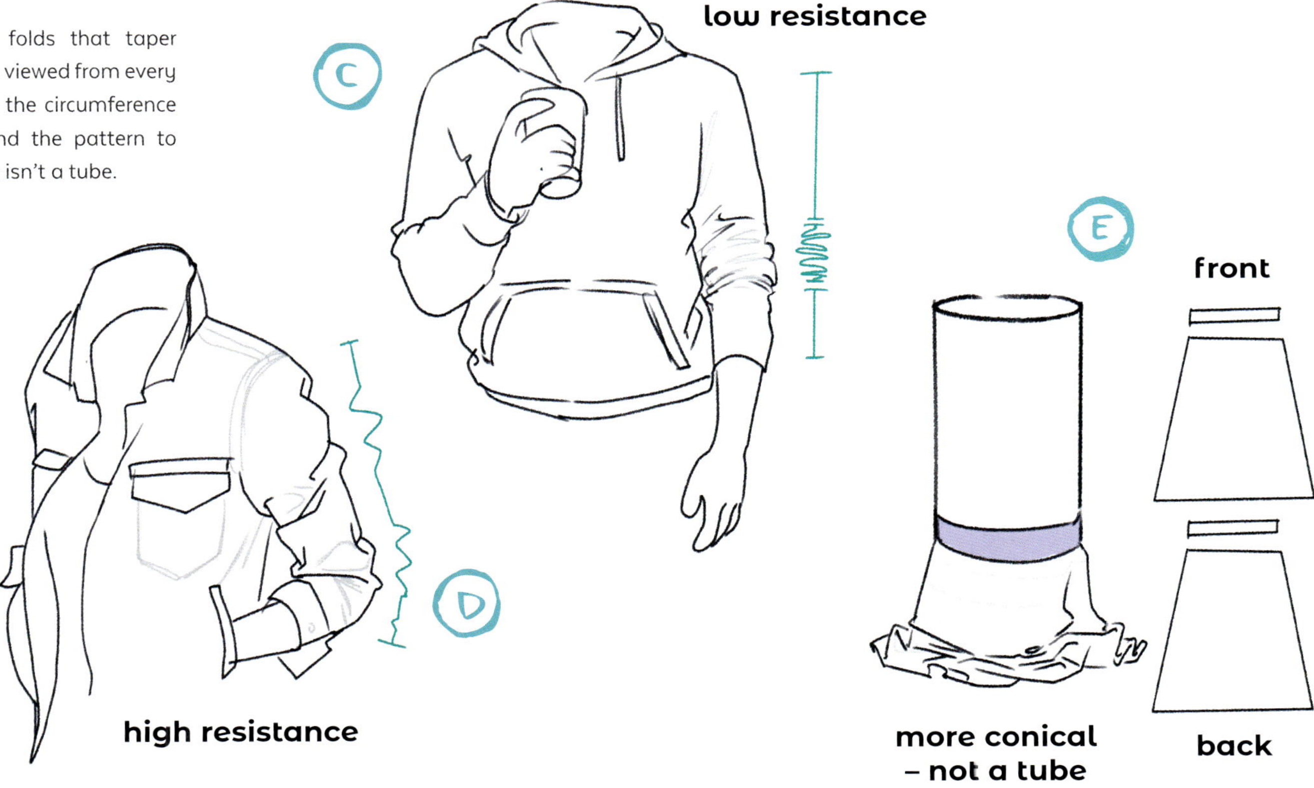

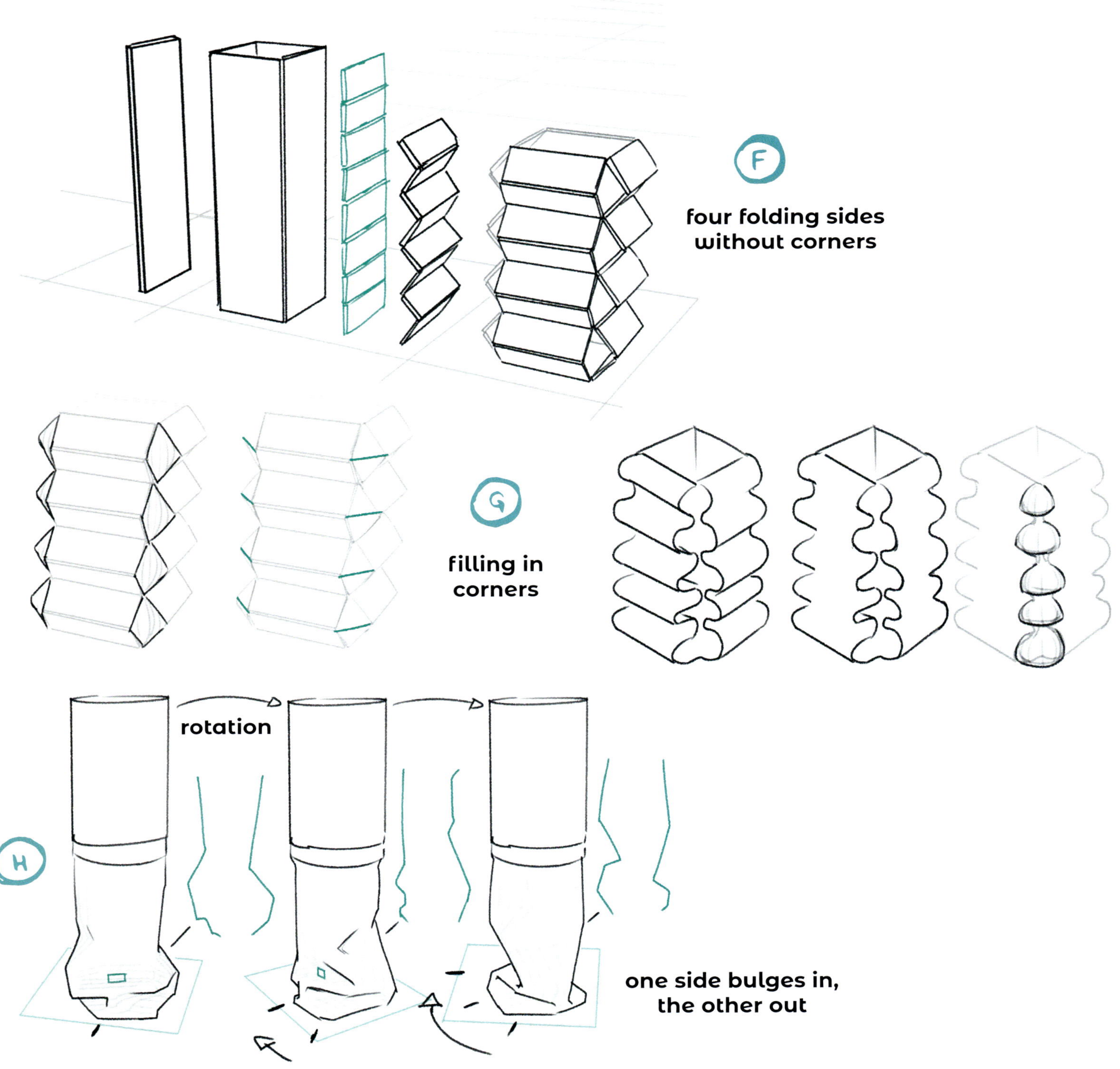

Let's consider how tubes compress. Start with a strip of fabric and multiply it to create four sides. Divide each side into sections. When each section is tilted the full length fits into a smaller height. Repeat on each side, and you get this (F). However, a tube cannot fold like this. Why? Because there are missing corners (G)! To fold like this, additional fabric would have to be added to fill these gaps. Instead, a tube must fold inwards and outwards unevenly. Each fold is influenced by folding happening on the other side of the tube. The circumference of the tube must remain constant. Therefore, if one side bulges out, the other side must bulge inwards to allow it to do so (H).

This doesn't mean that the silhouette has to be symmetrical. Often, a tube is wide in one axis, and another axis becomes narrow to accommodate that width. As the tube is rotated, so you can see the width from one angle and narrowness from another. It's wide near the base in one dimension, but narrow near the base from another angle.

What this means for us is that when drawing compressed tubes, like trousers or sleeves, we have a lot of freedom to draw the shapes we want. Silhouettes may be narrower or wider on paper than the diameter (width) of the tube, and it can still be believable. But remember: don't draw folds that move 'through' the inner form of the mannequin, or your character will have confusing anatomy (I).

We can visualize these compressed folds as being X- and Y-shaped (J). Rather than drawing these letter-forms separately, connect the arms of each one directly into each other (K). There should be a flow between the shapes so that they don't look like they exist in isolation. They should also wrap around the form and not sit flat on the surface (L).

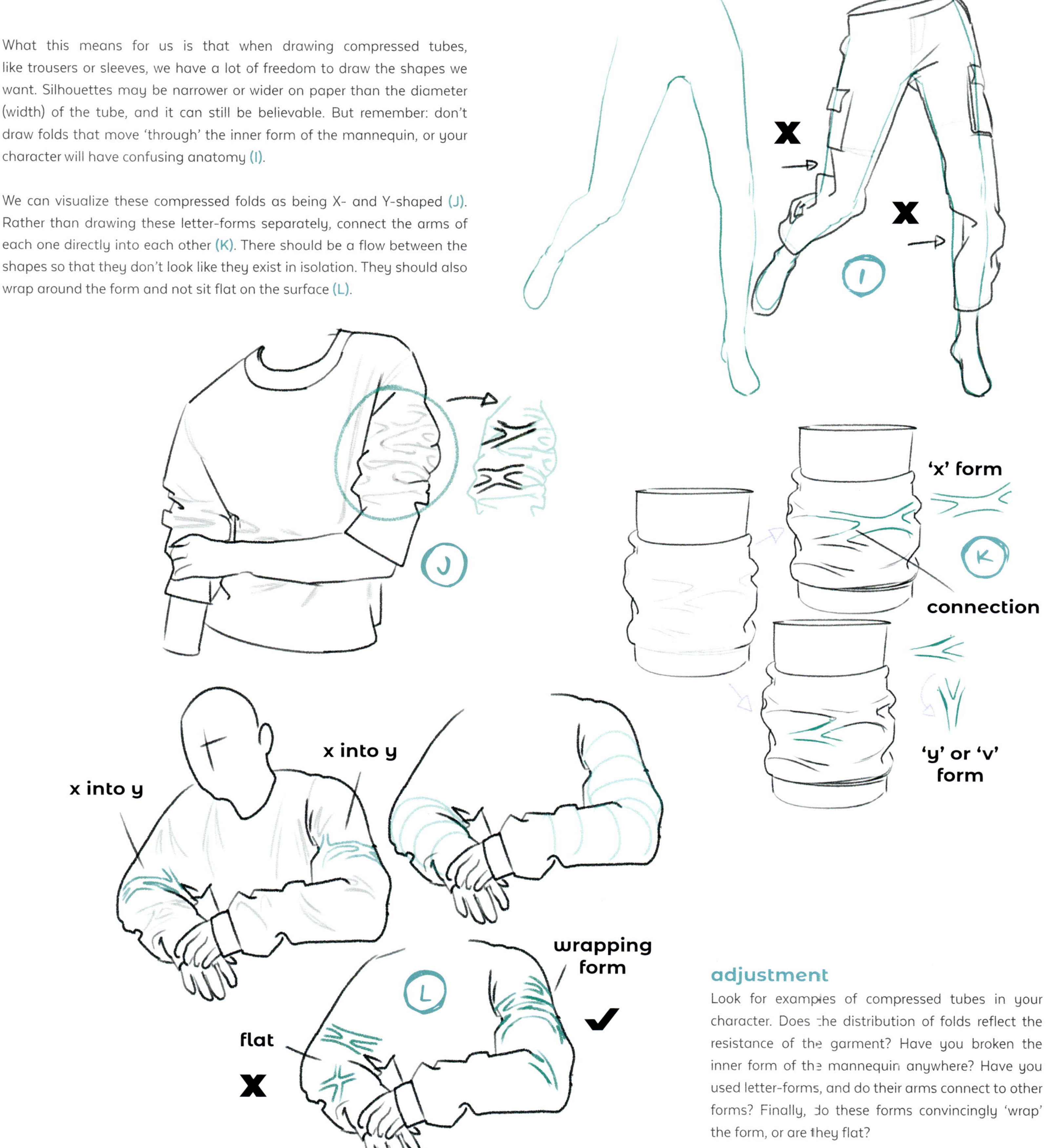

adjustment

Look for examples of compressed tubes in your character. Does the distribution of folds reflect the resistance of the garment? Have you broken the inner form of the mannequin anywhere? Have you used letter-forms, and do their arms connect to other forms? Finally, do these forms convincingly 'wrap' the form, or are they flat?

fold depth

Here, we have a flat piece of fabric (A). Next to it, we see some variations in fold depth: shallow folding and deep folding. The 'depth' is the distance of the highest point of the fold from the mannequin. Don't confuse this with fold width, which we've already covered – that describes how narrow or broad a fold is.

A common mistake is to draw most of your folds too narrow and too deep (B). Remember: most of the time garments aren't compressed enough to need to fold deeply or narrowly. These contours illustrate this (C). However, we don't want to cover our drawing in obvious contours, so we must be inventive in how we describe these shallow folds. We'll discuss how to do this later. For now, just know that most folds are shallow and broad rather than narrow and deep – and we should be careful not to draw folds too deep and narrow.

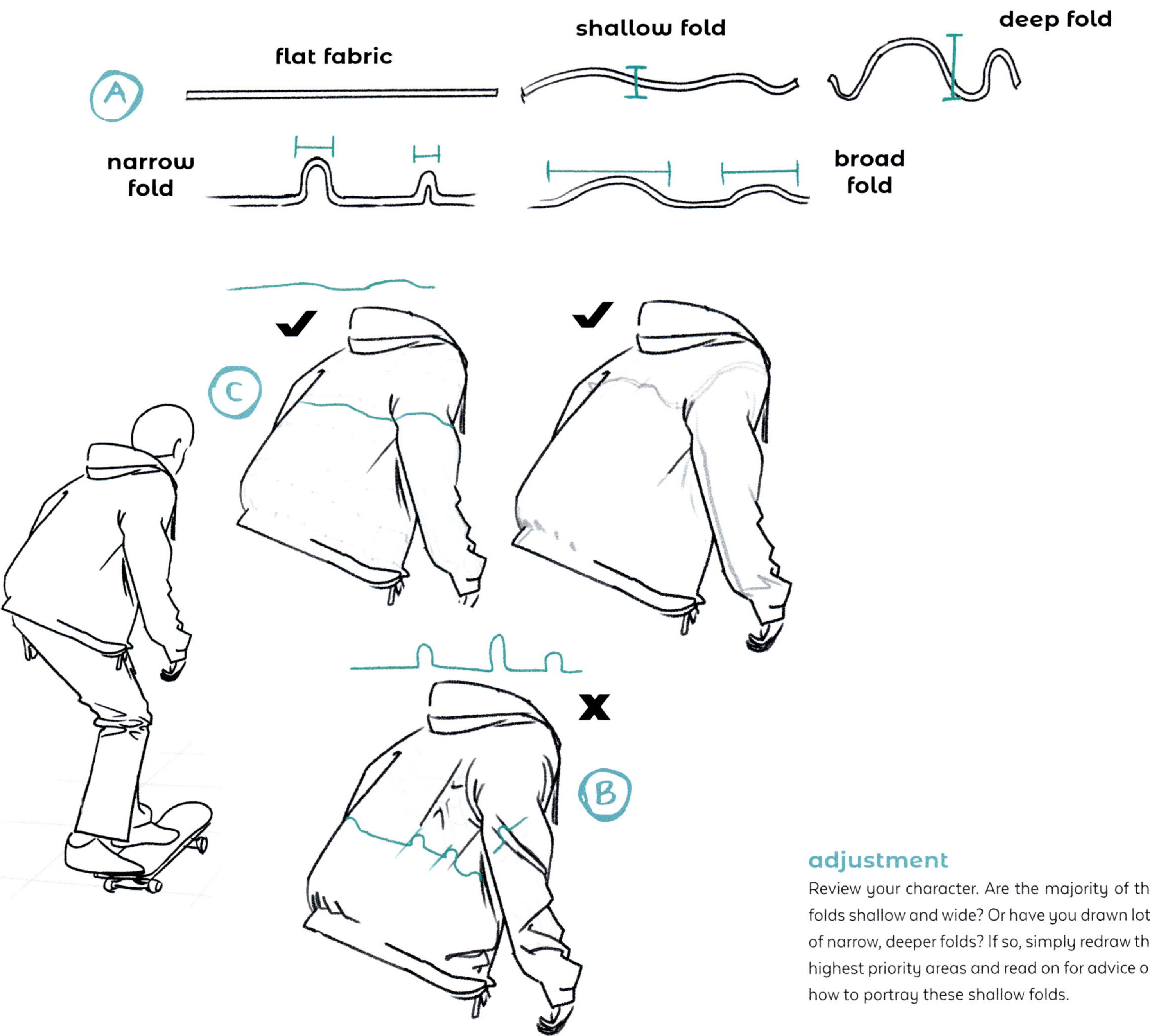

adjustment

Review your character. Are the majority of the folds shallow and wide? Or have you drawn lots of narrow, deeper folds? If so, simply redraw the highest priority areas and read on for advice on how to portray these shallow folds.

bending tubes

When a tube of fabric containing an anatomical form is bent, obviously the inner side is compressed. Less obviously, the outer side is also put under slight tension. This happens as a result of the underlying anatomy of elbows and knees; the outer length of the garment becomes slightly elongated.

To draw a bending tube, begin by drawing the outer side with fewer, straighter lines, then make the inner side more wavy and complex (A). Next, draw some lines that radiate out from the point of the knee or elbow (B). These lines indicate compression. Avoid drawing them all the way to the point of the elbow or knee.

It's helpful to add a slight curve to the lines, to indicate the compression (C). Try to visualize the 3D form of these folds. From some angles, these folds appear very different, and it requires a bit of focus to visualize them clearly.

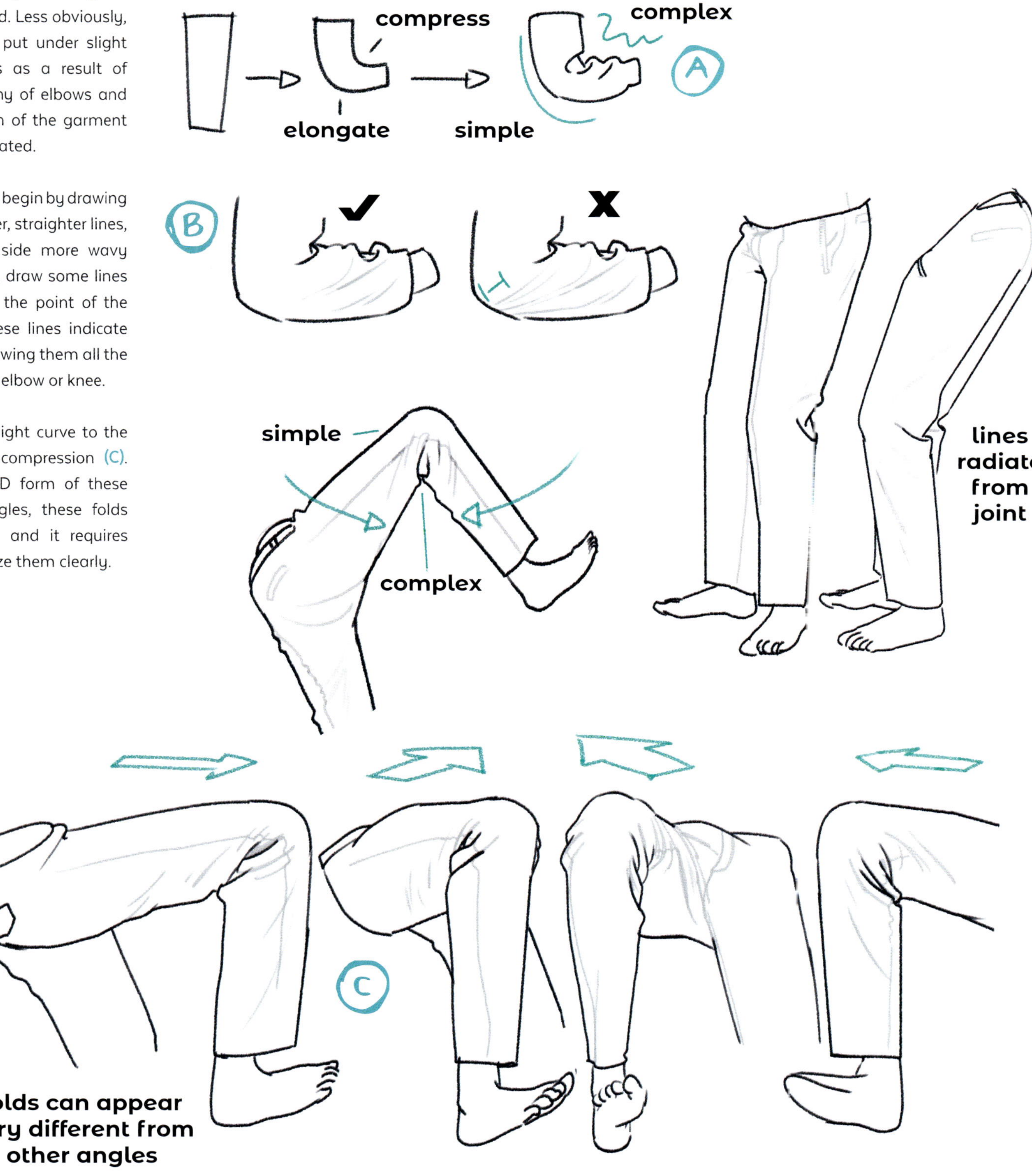

When seen from some angles, and when the garment is loose enough, the compression on the inside of the tube forces the fabric out to the sides, creating two bulges on either side of the bend (D).

When these side bulges are very pronounced, and are on looser garments, they create a near-vertical fold like this (E). Adding this line can add more believability to the compression (F). It helps indicate to the viewer that there's a form inside the tube. Don't let it connect right down to the elbow/knee (G). You'll only see this vertical line when the compression is really strong, so reserve it for when the arm is bent at 90 degrees or less. The bulging is also prominent from above and adds a lot of believability.

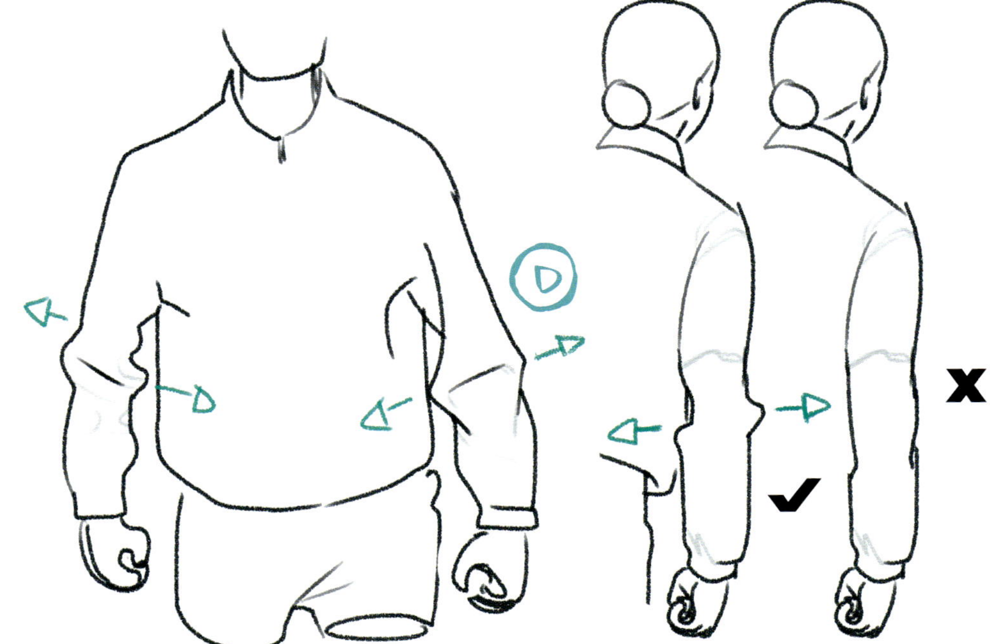

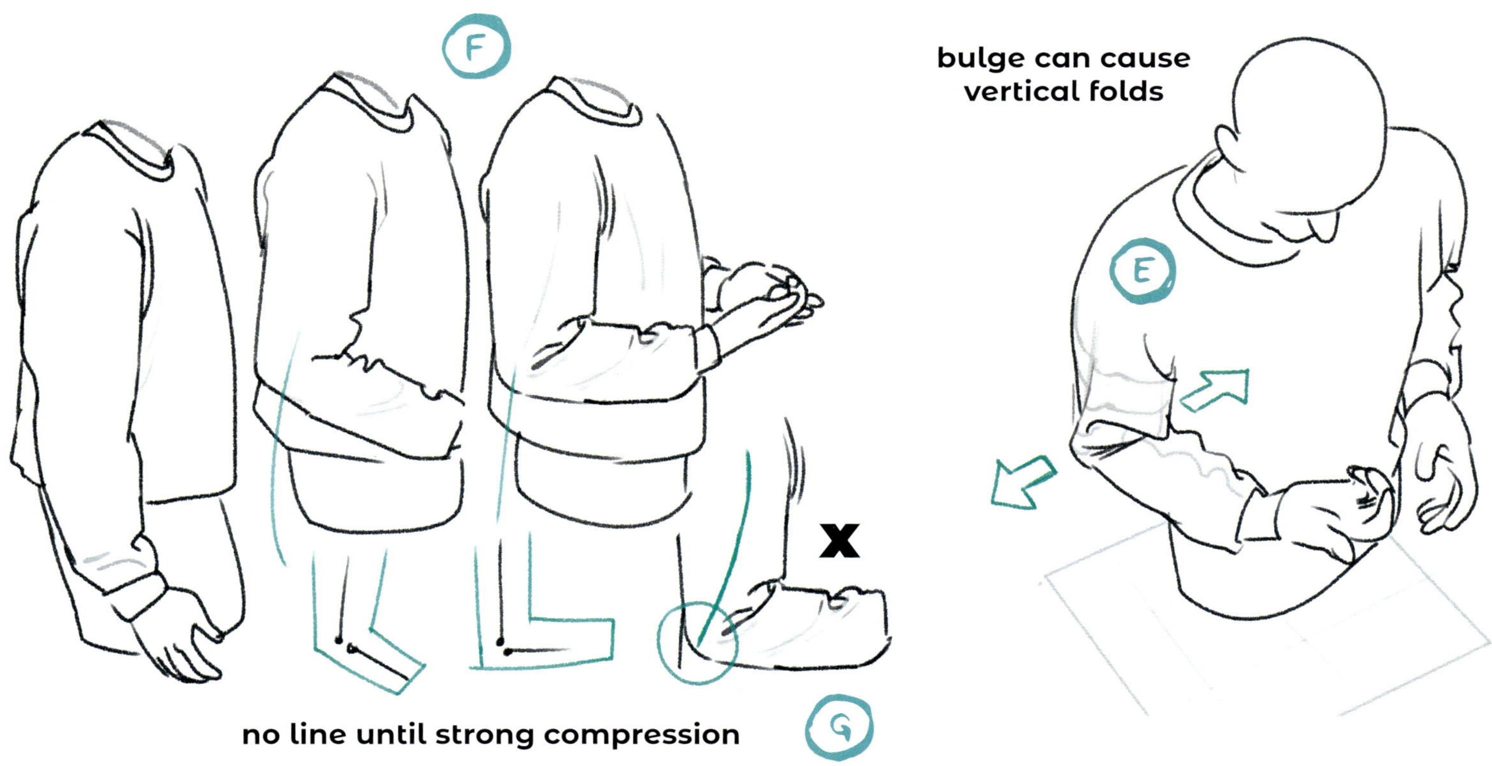

Be careful not to overdo this bulging at the sides. When the bend is gentler and there's less compression, there'll be only shallow folding (H). The folding often won't be deep enough to cause the side bulges. Often, all you need to indicate a slight bulging is a single, small mark (I). If your silhouette suggests compression, then the viewer is probably already 'looking for it' without knowing.

However, don't get carried away and assume that all folds need a small mark on the end. These bulges will usually only appear on a compressed tube. If you draw them in situations where there is no tube compression, they don't make sense. Why would there be bulging so near to a pulling area (J)?

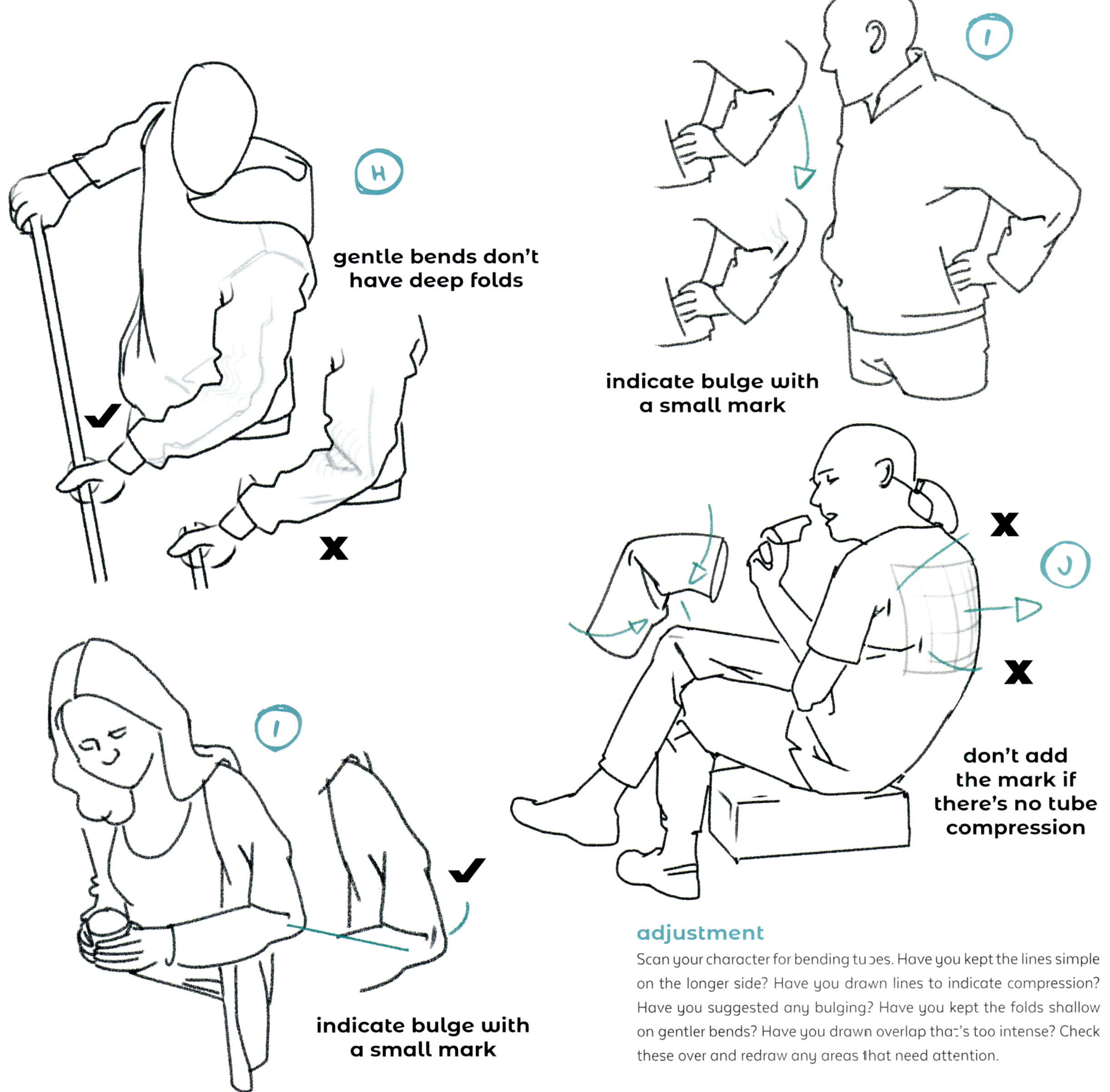

adjustment

Scan your character for bending tubes. Have you kept the lines simple on the longer side? Have you drawn lines to indicate compression? Have you suggested any bulging? Have you kept the folds shallow on gentler bends? Have you drawn overlap that's too intense? Check these over and redraw any areas that need attention.

pressure

When limbs are bent, or a limb is held against the body, two pieces of anatomy are forced against each other (A). As a result, two regions of fabric are often pressed together, too (B). When this happens, both sides of the fabric may deform in response to the pressure from the other. Here are a couple of ways to draw this so that the viewer can feel the pressure.

For the first way, find a location where you'd expect to see pressure between two regions of fabric. Erase any single lines, and redraw them with three 'sections' **(1, 2, 3)**. The **2** section is a sort of buffer between the two main pieces. Note that you don't always need to redraw a single line. From certain angles, and in some situations, a single line can be believable (C). However, for now, we want to practise 1-2-3s, so let's redraw our single lines like so (D). The important thing is to use these triple lines selectively – don't draw every fold this way. Sometimes there will be more than three sections. There might be four **(1, 2, 3, 4)** (E) or even five sections. The important thing is that there are more than just two.

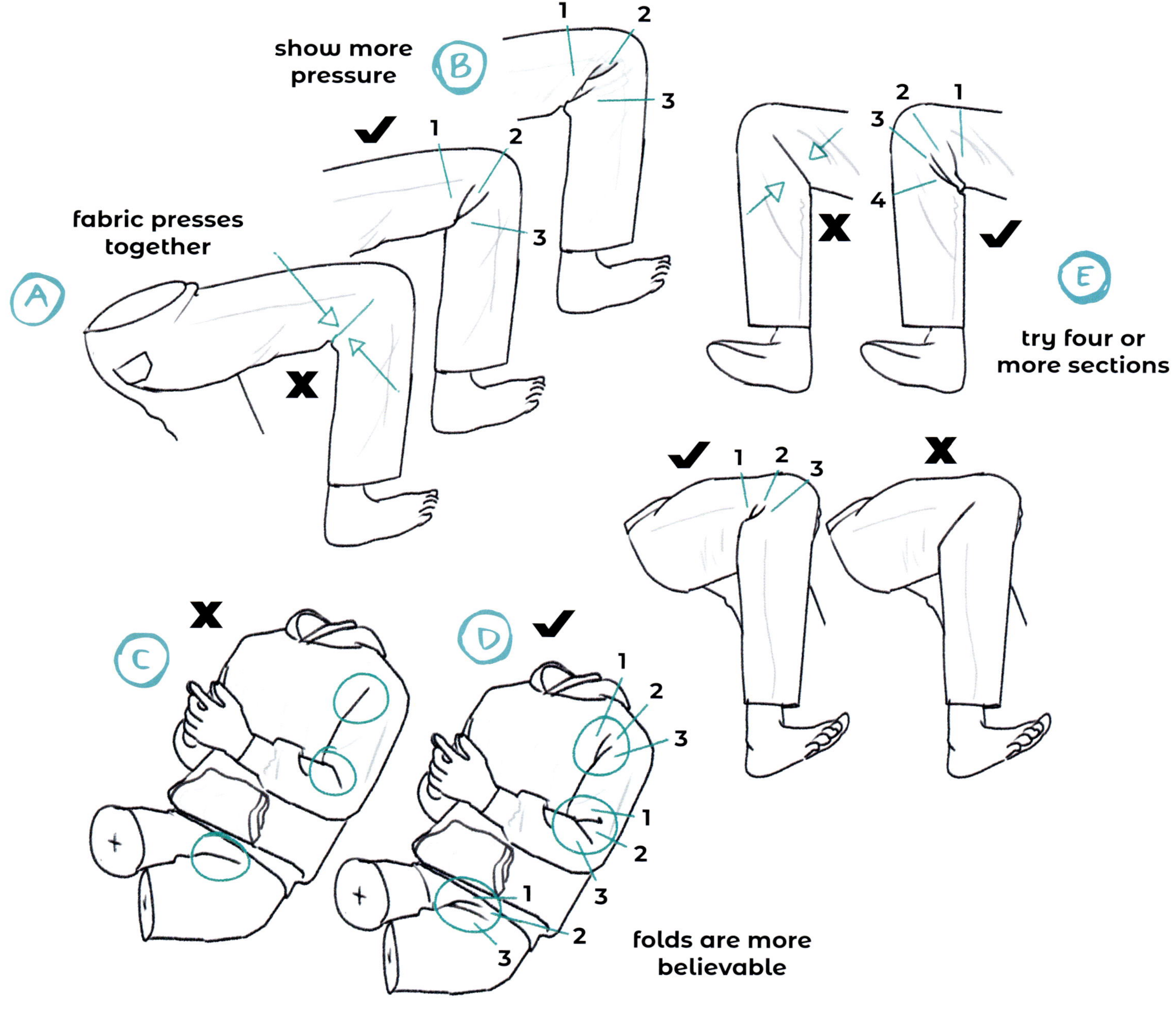

The second way to show pressure between two regions of fabric is to suggest bunching on either side of the fold. This can be done by using contours, by indicating a plane, or with a combination of the two. Let's see an example (F). To me, the fabric on this sleeve doesn't look like it's under much pressure. One solution is adding a '1-2-3' fold (G). Alternatively, we could add some 'planes' on either side of the fold (H) (see page 91), which would help to indicate that the surface of the fabric is bulging outwards as a result of the pressure. Another option is adding some contours to suggest the same bulging (I). Finally, we could combine the planes and the contours (J). Using some combination of planes and contours, rather than a simple 1-2-3, can add a bit more subtlety to your drapery – particularly if you can use a 'hidden contour', such as a seam.

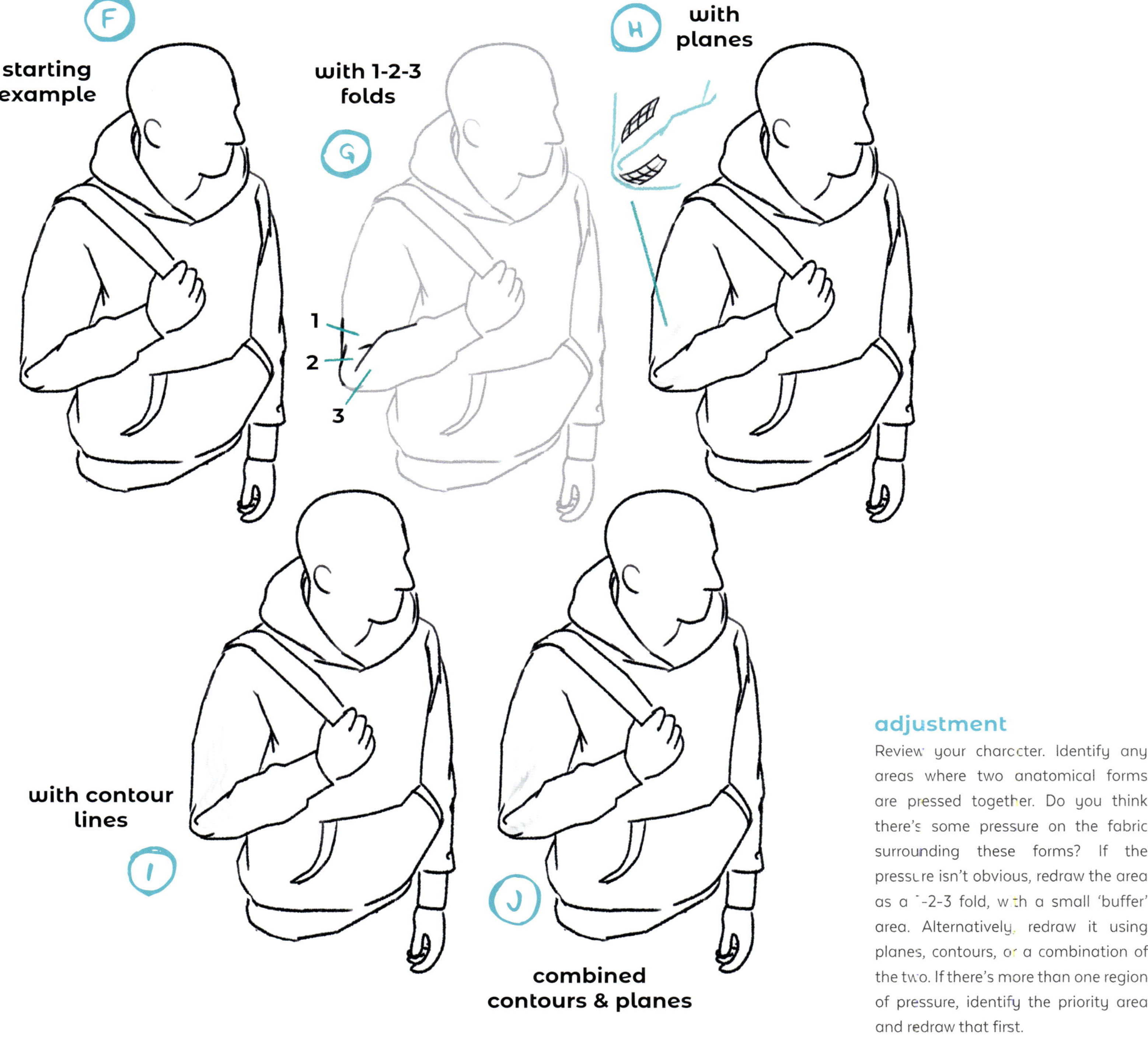

adjustment

Review your character. Identify any areas where two anatomical forms are pressed together. Do you think there's some pressure on the fabric surrounding these forms? If the pressure isn't obvious, redraw the area as a 1-2-3 fold, with a small 'buffer' area. Alternatively, redraw it using planes, contours, or a combination of the two. If there's more than one region of pressure, identify the priority area and redraw that first.

twisting

Let's discuss how to draw a twisting model more easily. Rather than starting at one end and working along (A), which can be difficult to visualize, you start with both 'ends' of the twist and a gap in between. Add a marker to these forms to help you remember which way they're facing (B), then fill in the gap with another simple form (C). Since you already have the two ends with markers, it's easier to visualize the middle section. Once you've done this, you have a twisting mannequin that'll help you draw the drapery (D).

The most common way to attempt to draw twist is by adding diagonal lines to shapes (E). Sometimes this is effective, but not always. Let's consider why. When you compress a tube evenly, horizontal folding occurs (F). When you then twist the compressed tube, these lines become diagonals (G) as the folds spiral. So, these lines represent compression *and* twist. Therefore, you should only draw these spiralling lines where fabric is twisting and also compressing.

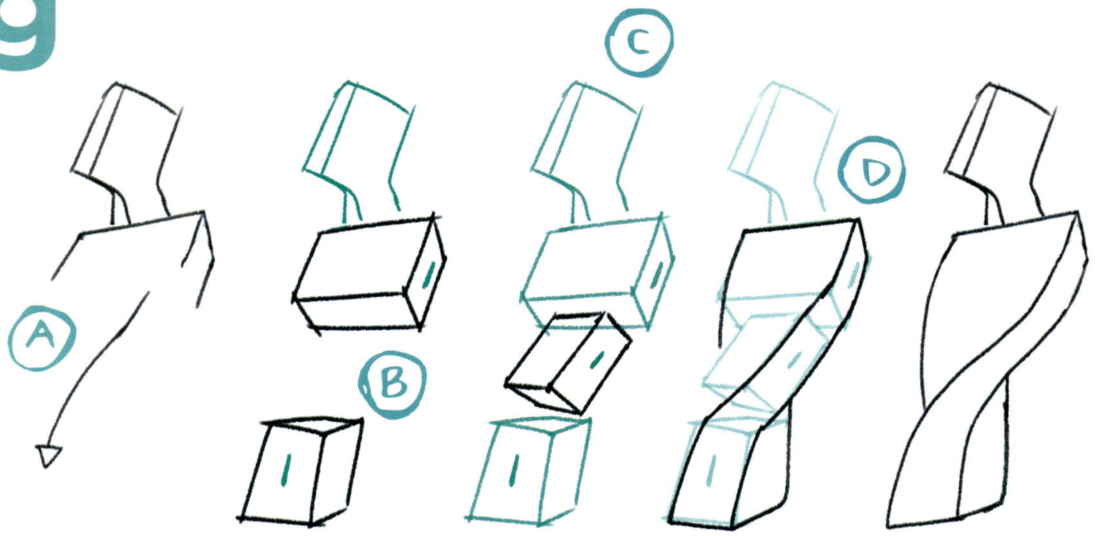

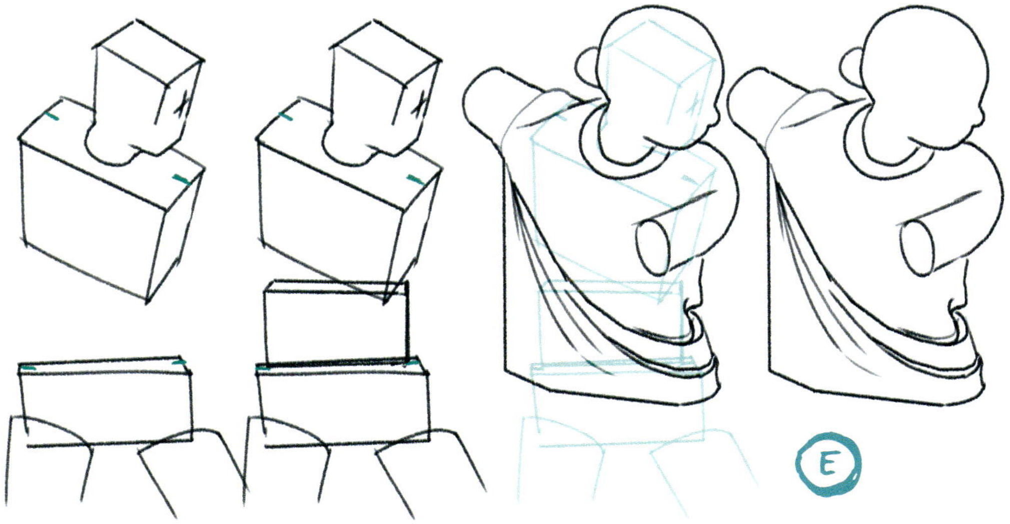

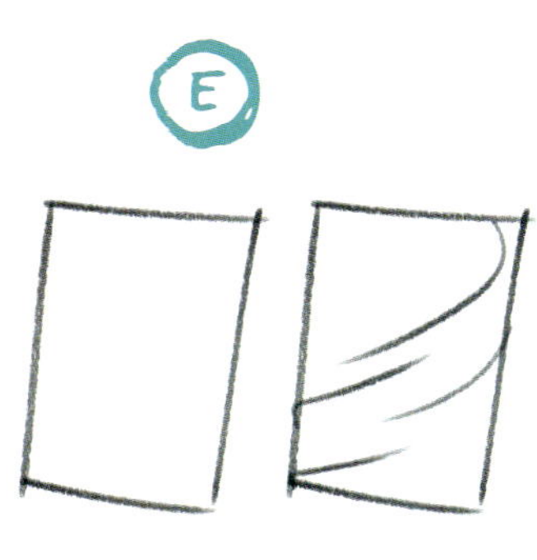

adding diagonal lines for twist

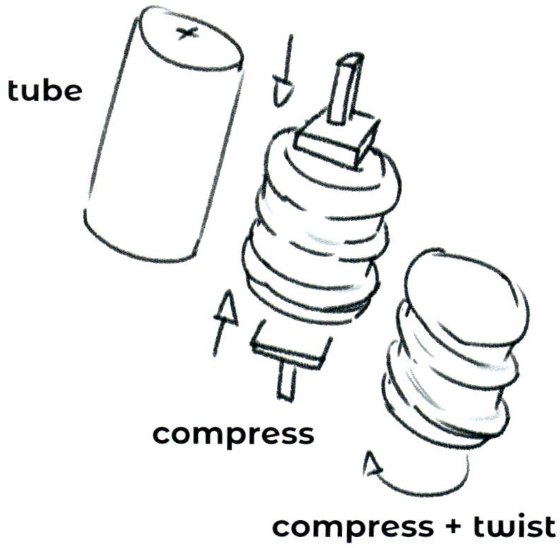

tube

compress

compress + twist

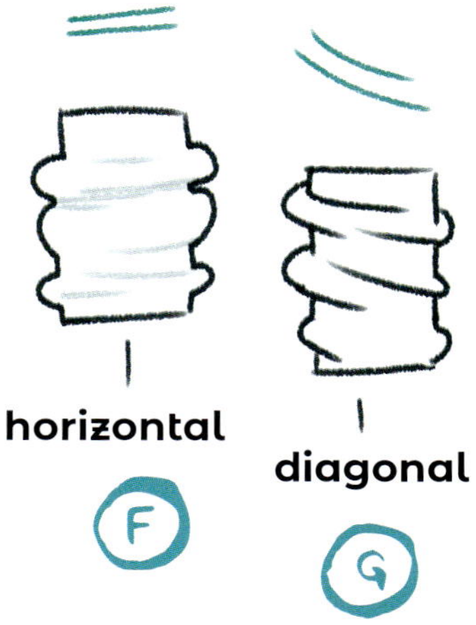

horizontal

diagonal

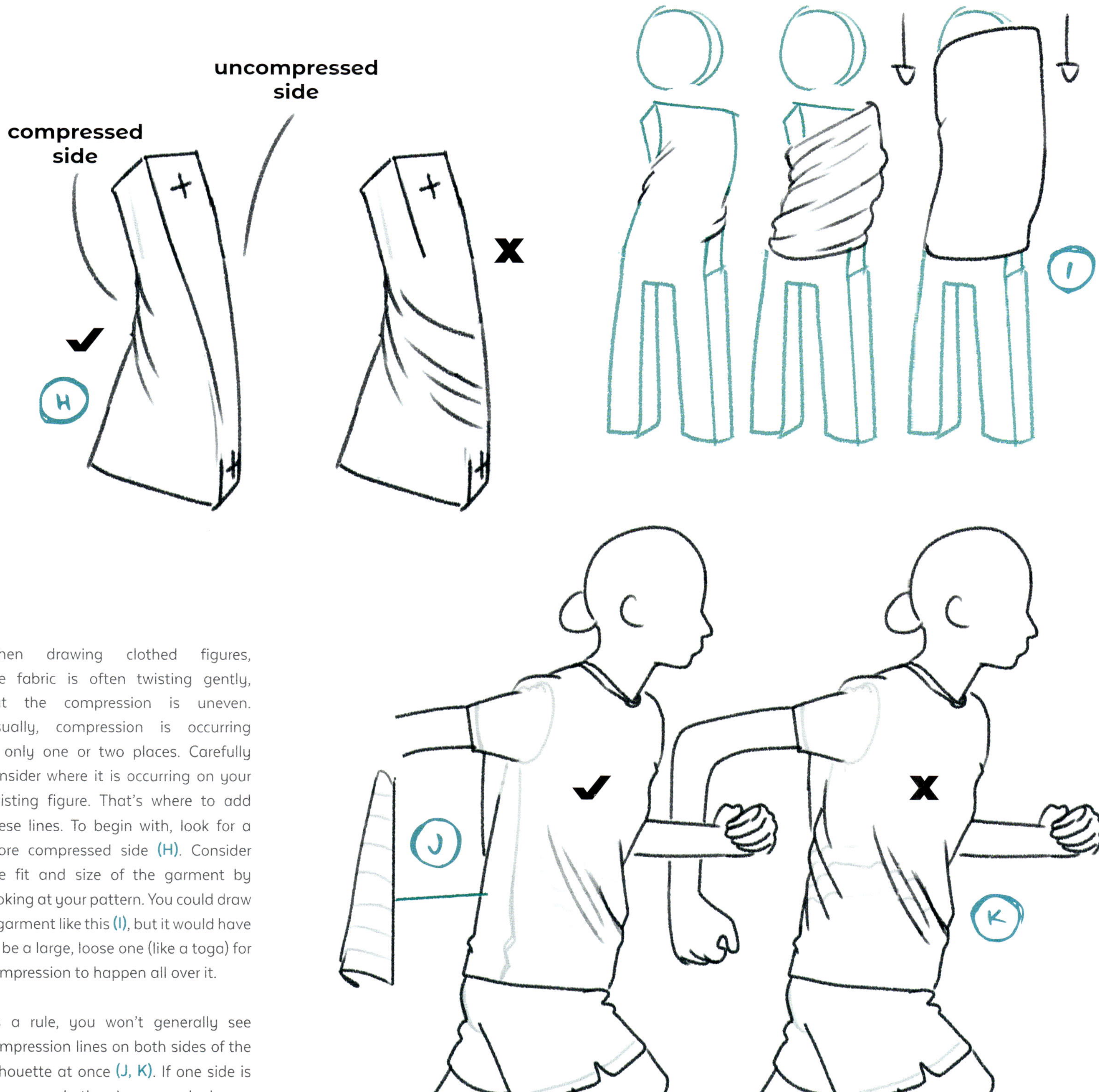

When drawing clothed figures, the fabric is often twisting gently, but the compression is uneven. Usually, compression is occurring in only one or two places. Carefully consider where it is occurring on your twisting figure. That's where to add these lines. To begin with, look for a more compressed side (H). Consider the fit and size of the garment by looking at your pattern. You could draw a garment like this (I), but it would have to be a large, loose one (like a toga) for compression to happen all over it.

As a rule, you won't generally see compression lines on both sides of the silhouette at once (J, K). If one side is compressed, there's a good chance that – at the same height – the other side will be hanging more loosely.

One way to describe twist is to emphasize relative markers. These are any two points on your garment that the viewer knows have a clear relationship to each other. The front of the collar and the belt buckle are a good example of this (L). The viewer recognizes the twist by looking at the relative positions of these markers. As the viewer knows that these face the same direction when the figure is untwisted, any difference must suggest a twist.

To help visualize the folding, draw the mannequin first, then the silhouette or secondary silhouette of the garments (M). (You can learn more about silhouettes and secondary silhouettes on pages 75 and 76.) Next, add two markers to clarify where the start and end points of a common seam should be. Once you've drawn these, draw the seam connecting them. This will help visualize the forms by clarifying the surface.

Consider the elasticated regions, like cuffs and waistbands. Because they grip the mannequin tightly, even slight twists in the mannequin's limbs will be clear in the drapery (N).

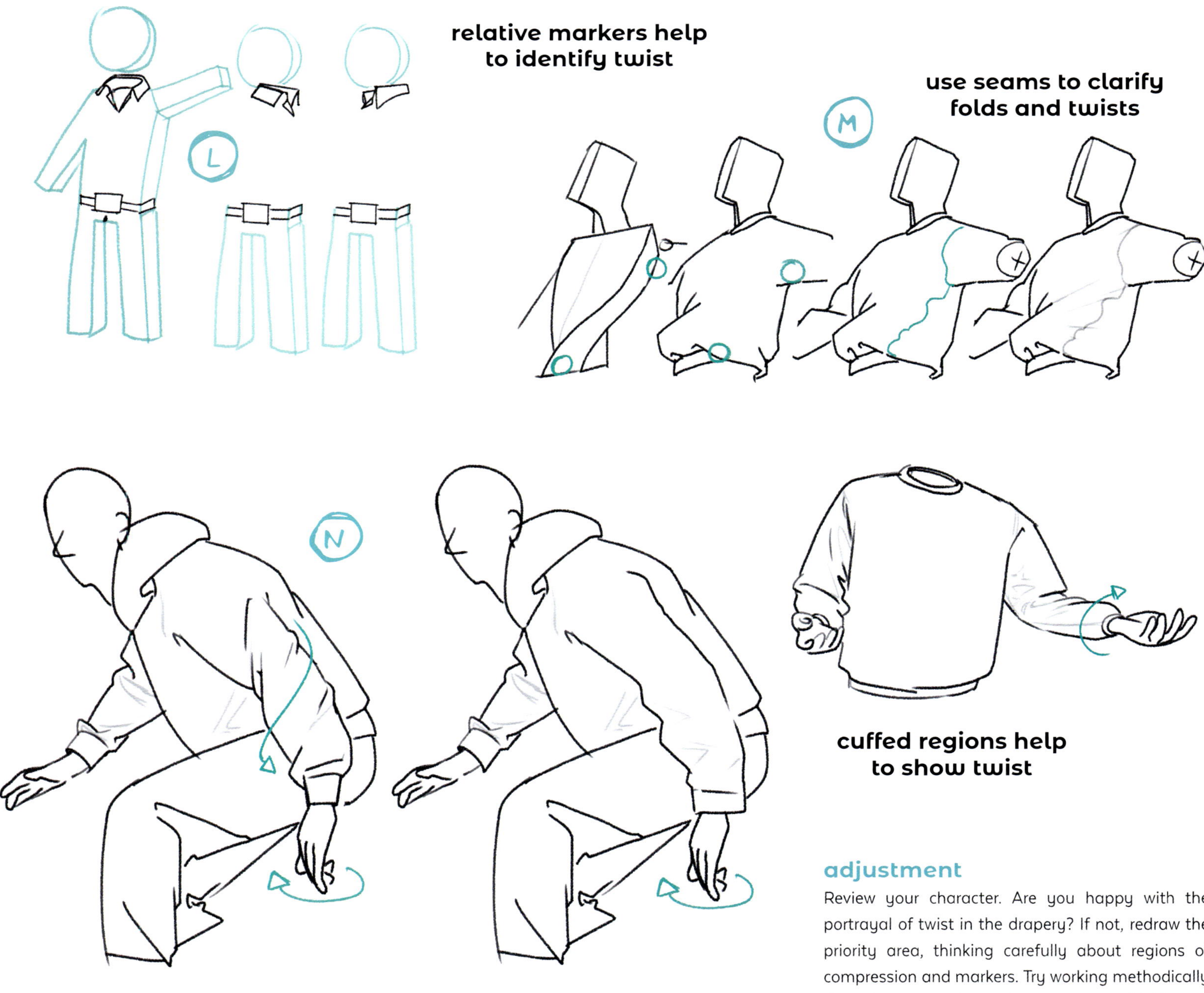

adjustment

Review your character. Are you happy with the portrayal of twist in the drapery? If not, redraw the priority area, thinking carefully about regions of compression and markers. Try working methodically through mannequin, markers, seams, and folds.

tension

Fabric may be relaxed or tense. Many people confuse tension with 'stretch'. When something stretches, its dimensions change: it becomes longer or wider. Under tension, fabric will assume its full length. If the tension increases, and the fabric isn't able to resist, it will begin to stretch (A). Although it's possible for fabric to be under tension without stretching, usually some level of stretching happens. The maximum amount of 'stretch' most garments can withstand, without breaking, is plus or minus twenty per cent of their length. Fortunately, with certain exceptions (like leggings), most garments aren't very stretchy. So we can focus on tension.

When a garment is placed over two forms which are moving apart, it is pulled in two directions, creating tension (B). The friction alone will generate some level of tension. The first step in simulating tension is to identify pairs of **opposing forms** (C). These are any forms moving apart that cause the garment to be pulled in two directions. The amount of tension is partly determined by the force of these opposing forms moving away from each other.

Obviously, human anatomy doesn't allow for two forms to remain parallel while moving apart. Therefore, most of the opposing forms you'll identify will have some degree of angle to them (D). There may still be a high level of tension between these forms, because of the level of friction between mannequin and garment. We'll cover this further on page 55.

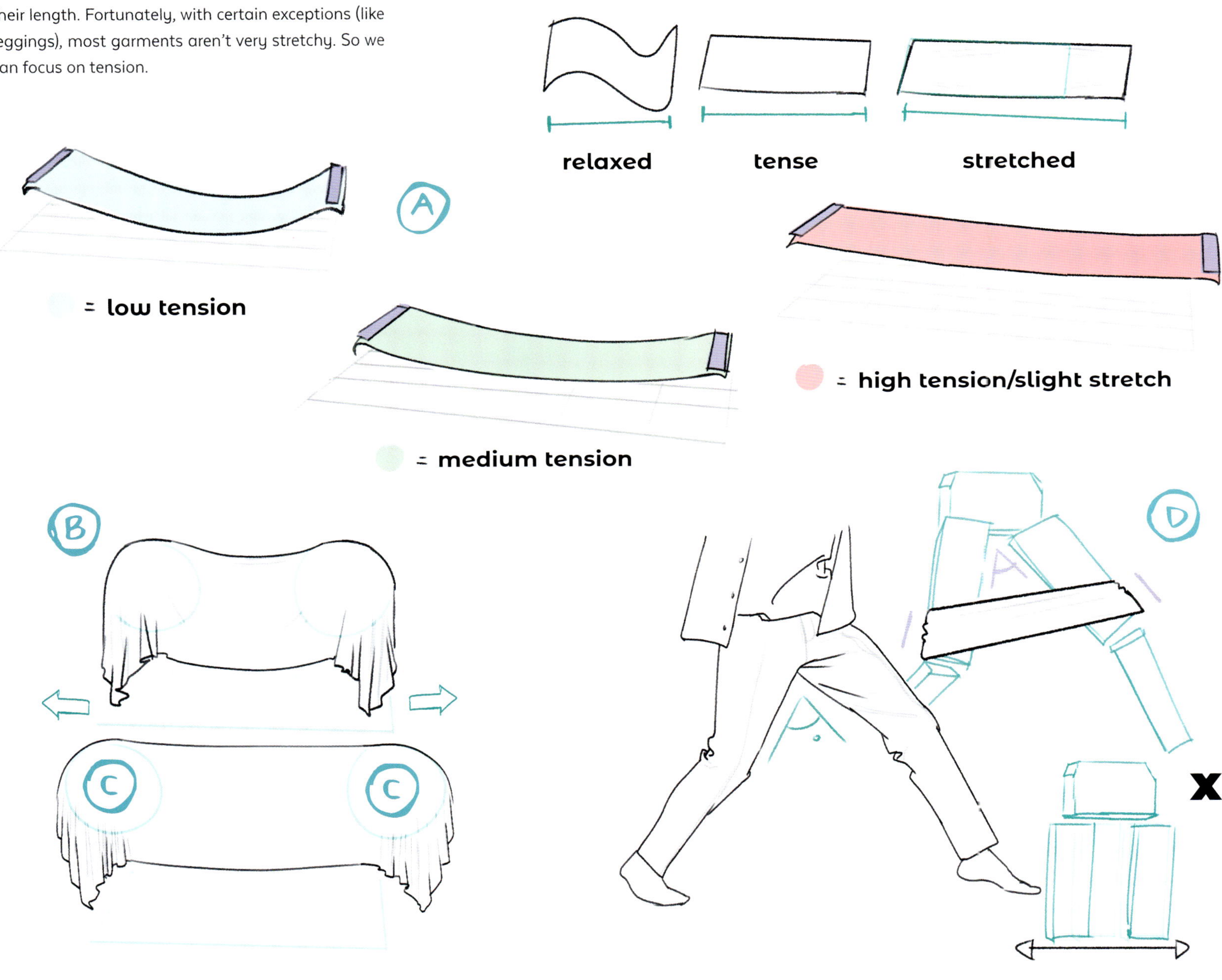

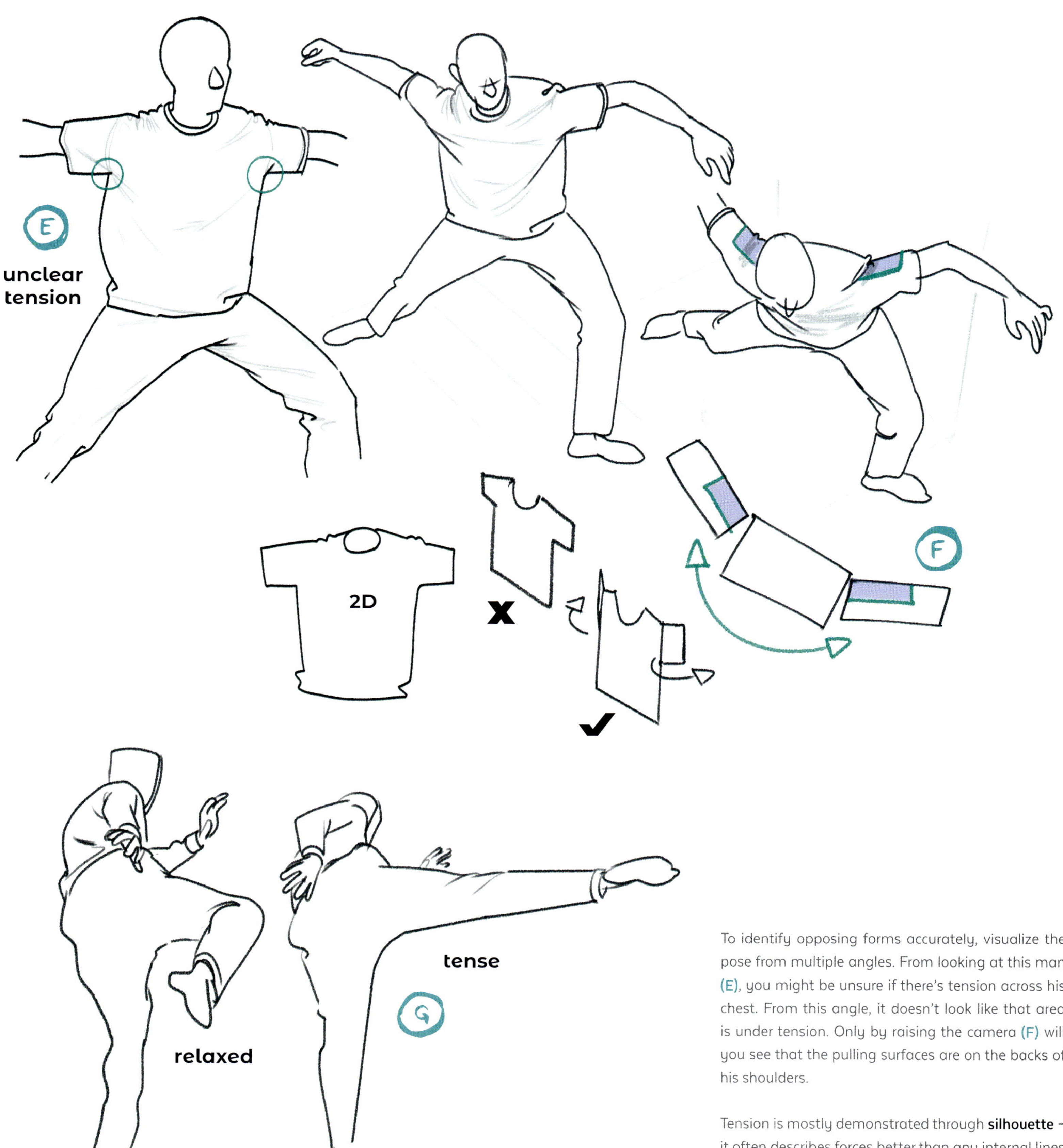

To identify opposing forms accurately, visualize the pose from multiple angles. From looking at this man (E), you might be unsure if there's tension across his chest. From this angle, it doesn't look like that area is under tension. Only by raising the camera (F) will you see that the pulling surfaces are on the backs of his shoulders.

Tension is mostly demonstrated through **silhouette** – it often describes forces better than any internal lines can (G). If you're not sure if you've achieved tension in your drawing, try hiding the internal lines to check.

Once you've identified the opposing forms, label the main 'pulling surfaces' of those forms. This is anywhere the opposing form is directly touching the fabric (H). Not where it's hanging between, or hanging 'off' the form. This is where most of the friction is.

The larger the surface area, the more evenly the force is distributed. However, a larger pulling surface doesn't indicate greater force. Here (I), the same amount of force as in H is distributed over a larger surface.

To create the illusion of tension, avoid drawing lines on the pulling surfaces. Lines to represent folding should sit mostly *between* the pulling surfaces (J).

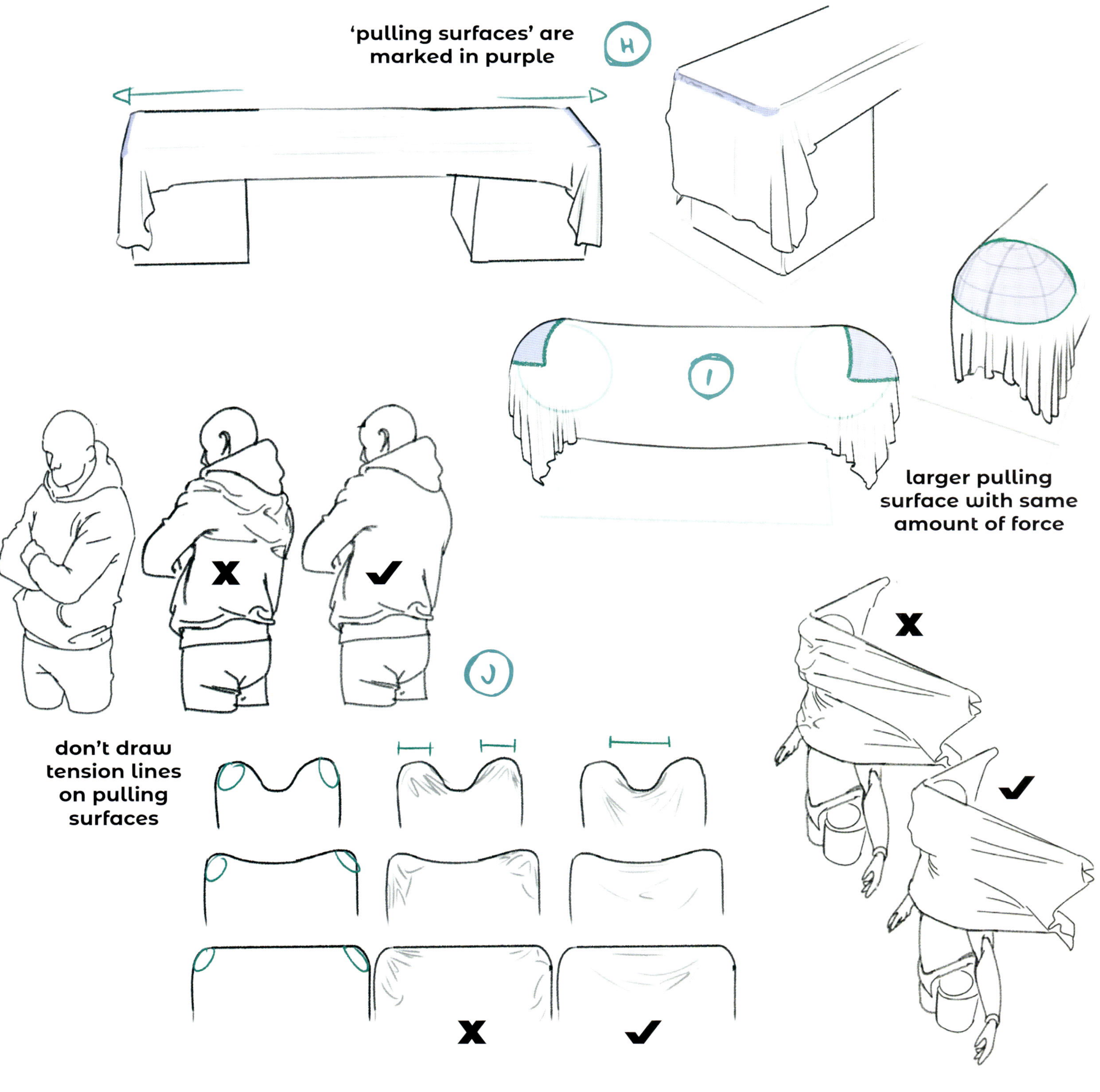

People often try to suggest tension by drawing lines between two pulling surfaces. Let's call them 'tension lines' (K). This choice is understandable because we often do see lines of folding where fabric is under tension. However, these lines represent **compression, not tension**. When seen from another angle, it's clear that the lines are the result of compression on another axis (L).

In another example, these two cylinders may be strongly pulling away from each other, but the lines don't convey that the fabric is compressed (M). If it were compressed, its width would also bunch up, and then these lines would be appropriate (N). The line across this character's torso represents compression caused by the arm swinging up, rather than tension, as you might assume (O).

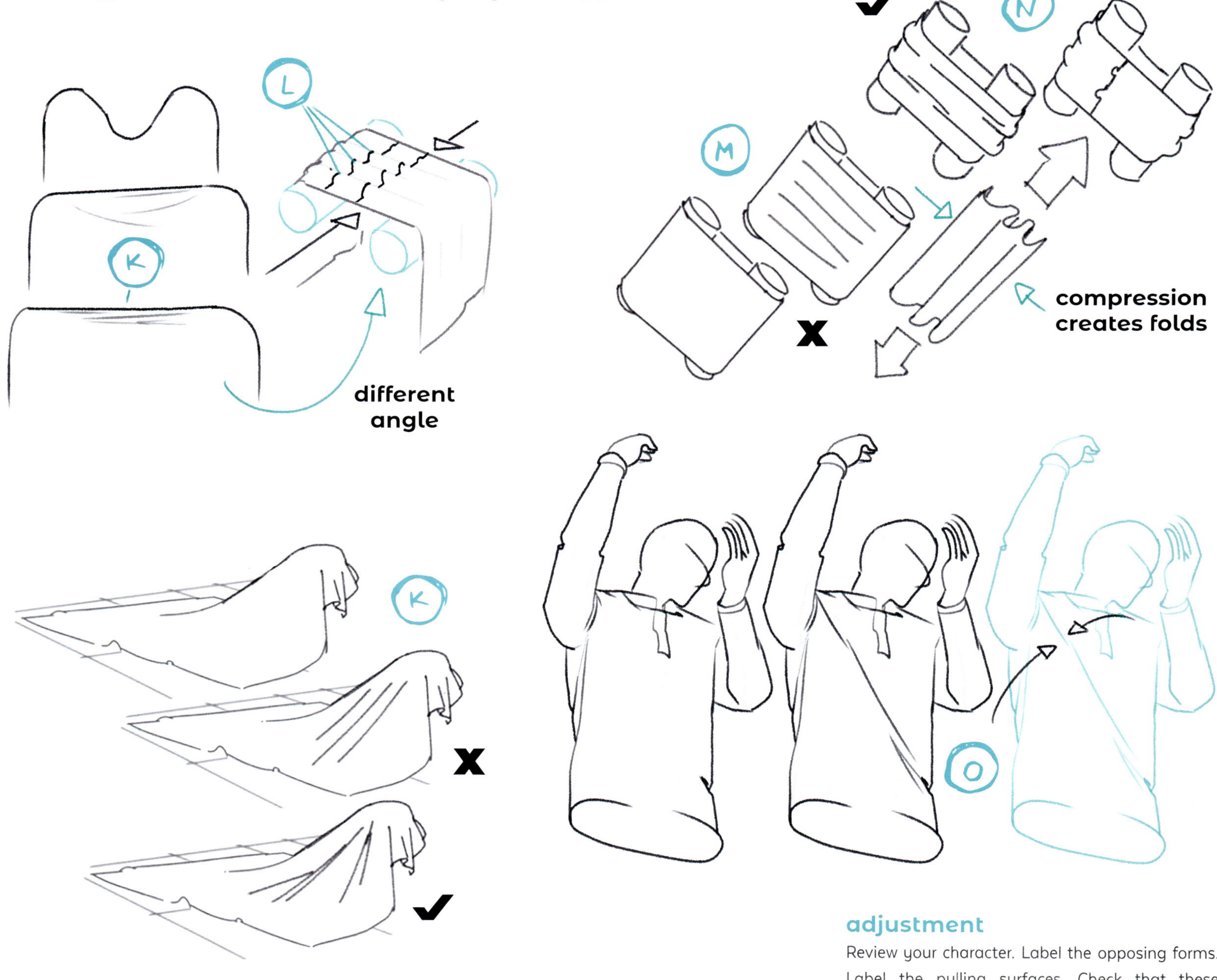

adjustment

Review your character. Label the opposing forms. Label the pulling surfaces. Check that these pulling surfaces are relatively free of internal lines. Do most of the lines in your drawing sit between the opposing forms? Check that you haven't drawn any 'tension lines' where there is no compression.

open & closed loops

When a garment is draped over the mannequin, but doesn't fully enclose it, we have an 'open loop' (A). Here, the cylinder mannequins aren't fully wrapped by the garment. As a result, when the cylinders move apart, the garment freely slides over the top of the cylinders (B). The freedom of the fabric allows it to continually move and thereby ease the tension.

When the ends of the garment are sewn together, we create a 'closed loop' that contains the mannequin(s). As the opposing forms move apart, the fabric cannot simply slide over it, because the bottom is attached (C). Tension between the forms rises until the fabric begins to stretch, before ultimately snapping.

As previously mentioned, a character's limbs rarely remain parallel while moving apart. Instead, we see tapering. The fabric at the widest part of the taper is under more tension – represented in red (D). In response, it will attempt to slide towards the closer ends of the forms (E).

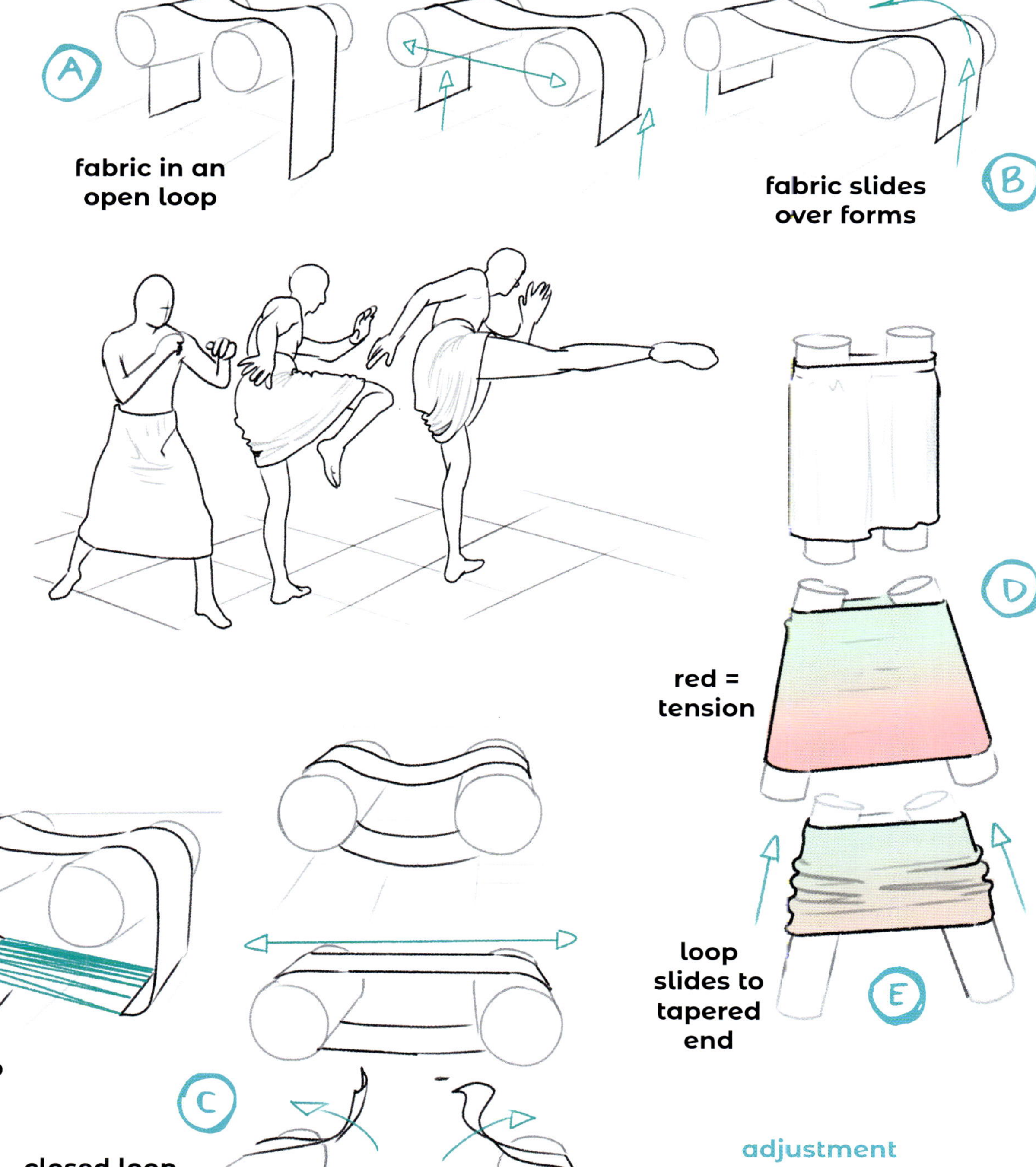

adjustment

Check your character for closed and open loops. If necessary, adjust any fabric that sits above tapered opposing forms.

indicate vs state

Using lines in a consistent way increases the believability of your drawing. Broadly speaking, you can draw folds in one of two ways. The first is to draw lines that simply **indicate** folding within the context. For example, if a viewer is looking at a drawing like this (A), then their brain is already expecting to see some internal folds. They have memories of seeing people in similar positions before, and they've been 'primed' to *expect* to see folding. Because of this, you can add lines that say to the viewer 'there's a fold going on here', and they won't look too closely. If we add some simple indicated folds to this drawing, they look quite believable (B). Indication relies on the fact that the viewer expects to see folds in certain places. They will partially 'fill in' the details that you leave out. As long as the lines you draw occur in a vaguely similar way to those that would occur in reality, the viewer will believe them.

The main benefit of 'indicating' folds is that it's fast, which means you can do more drawings in the same amount of time. Of course, indication only works when you have the context of the larger drawing. For example, if you've already drawn this (C), then a lot of the work of priming the viewer has already been done, and you can afford to indicate the folds loosely (D).

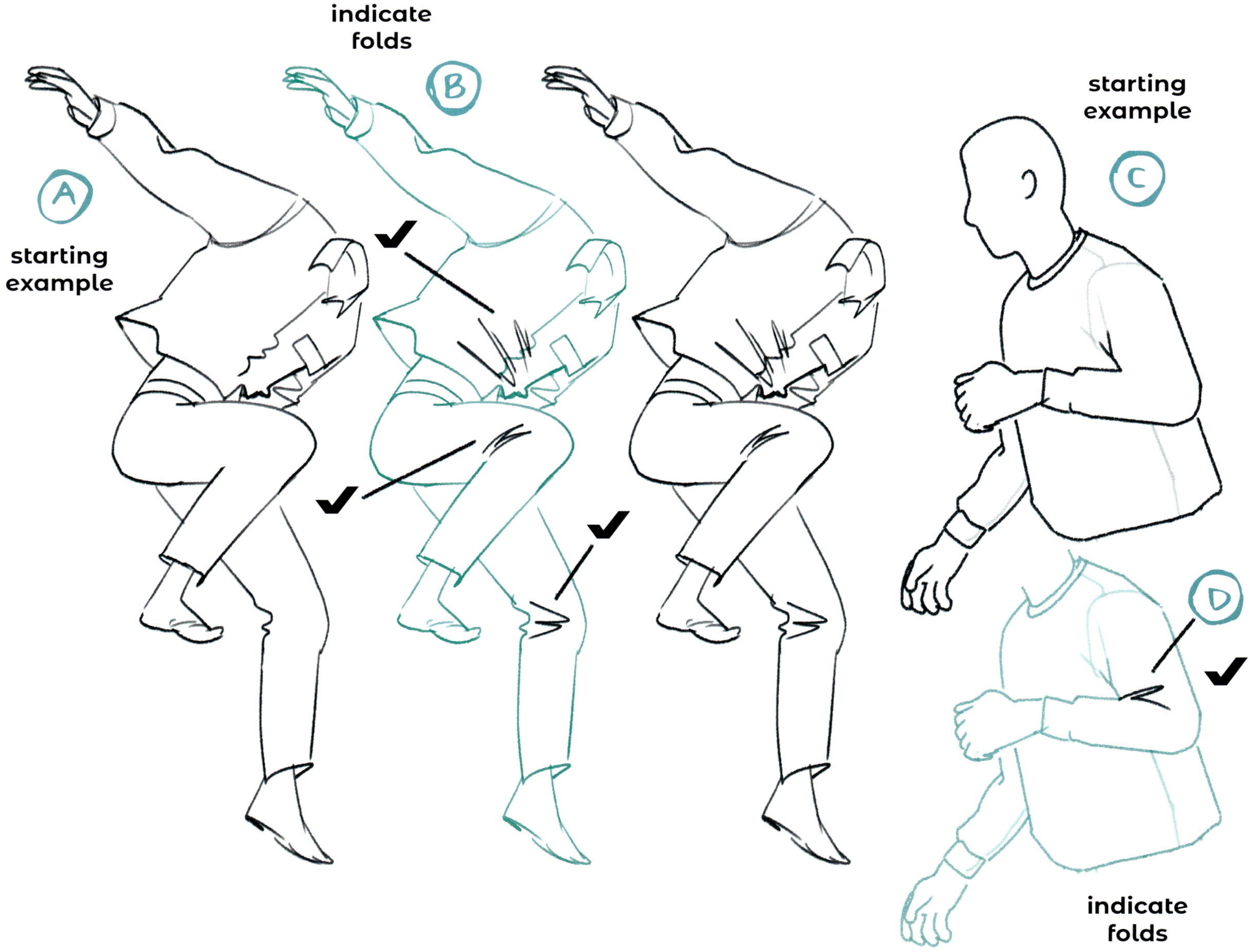

The second way to use lines is to **state** the forms of the folds exactly. You're saying to the viewer, 'this is the exact form of the fold that exists here'. Even if they look closely, the lines will still explain the form in detail. Stating folds is useful when you want to be really clear or accurate about the drapery and show the volumes. Let's compare the two: indicate (E) versus state (F). When viewed in isolation, you might think, 'Why wouldn't you always state? Indicating isn't as clear!' The answer is that stating drapery is much more time-consuming, and sometimes the reward isn't worth the effort. If you imagine example E is a background character in a storyboard, and has been drawn much smaller, then you can see why it wouldn't be worth spending your time stating the folds.

An effective compromise is to use a combination of the two, depending on the situation. You can even use both in the same character. For example, you could state the foreground elements and indicate the background elements (G), or you could indicate the top half and state the bottom half (H). Where you state or indicate affects the focal point. Experiment with this on your character. However, when learning, I suggest mostly stating the forms, rather than indicating. In doing so, you'll gain a better understanding. By always indicating folds, you delay your own learning process.

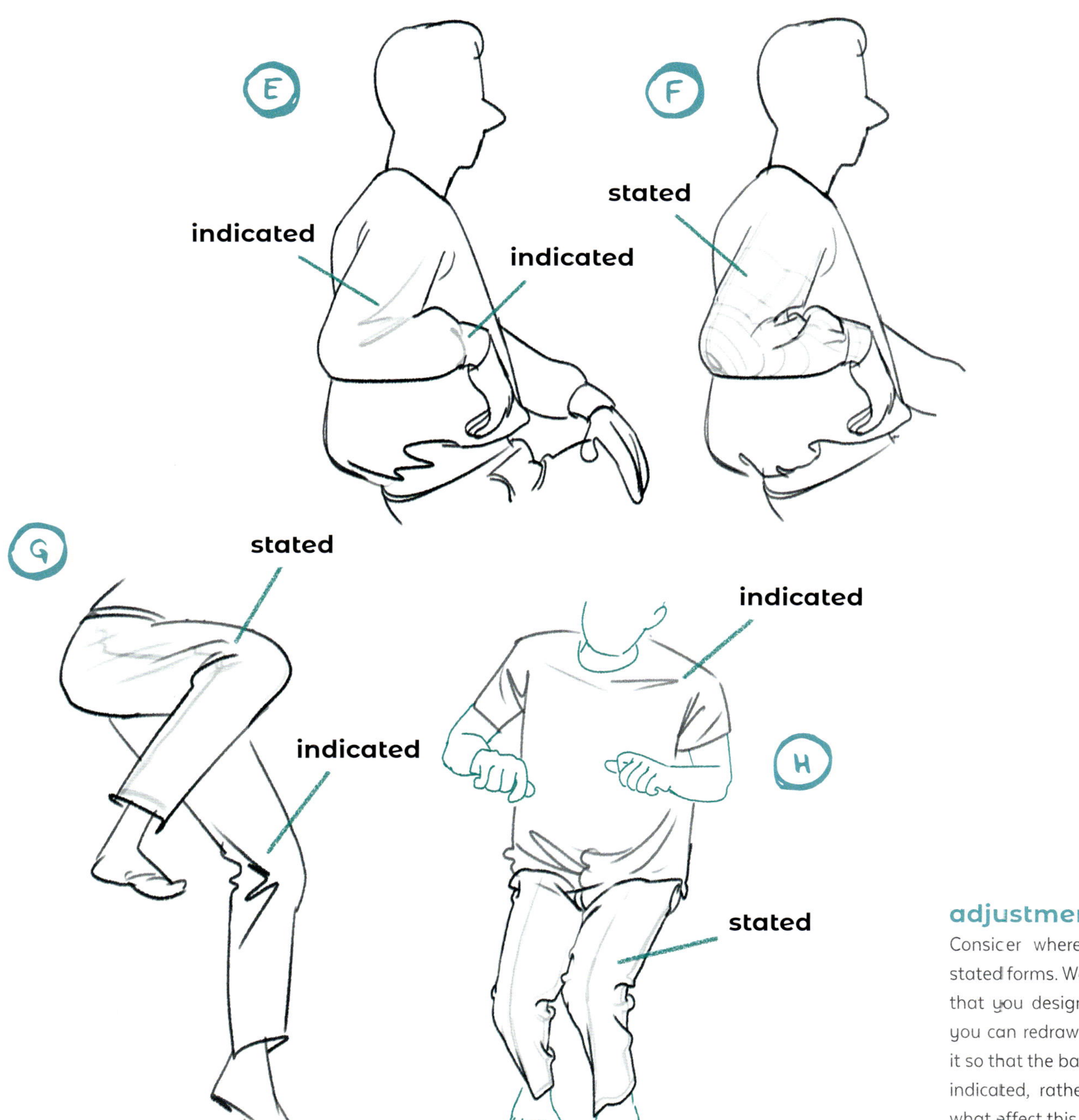

adjustment

Consider where you've indicated or stated forms. Was it a conscious choice that you designed or is it something you can redraw and improve? Redraw it so that the background elements are indicated, rather than stated, to see what effect this has.

high points

The simplest – and sometimes most effective – way to indicate a fold is to identify its 'high points', then use a single line to draw the fold. Here, we see a fold stated (A) and indicated (B). The shape of the fold has been identified with a line along the ridge of its high point (C). This can be incredibly powerful, but it does have its downsides. The problem with this method is that this doesn't work well to indicate folds that are broader (see Resistance on page 37). For drawing fabric that is high-resistance, this technique doesn't work as well because the drapery is more planar. It's hard to indicate high points on something like a thick leather jacket, for example.

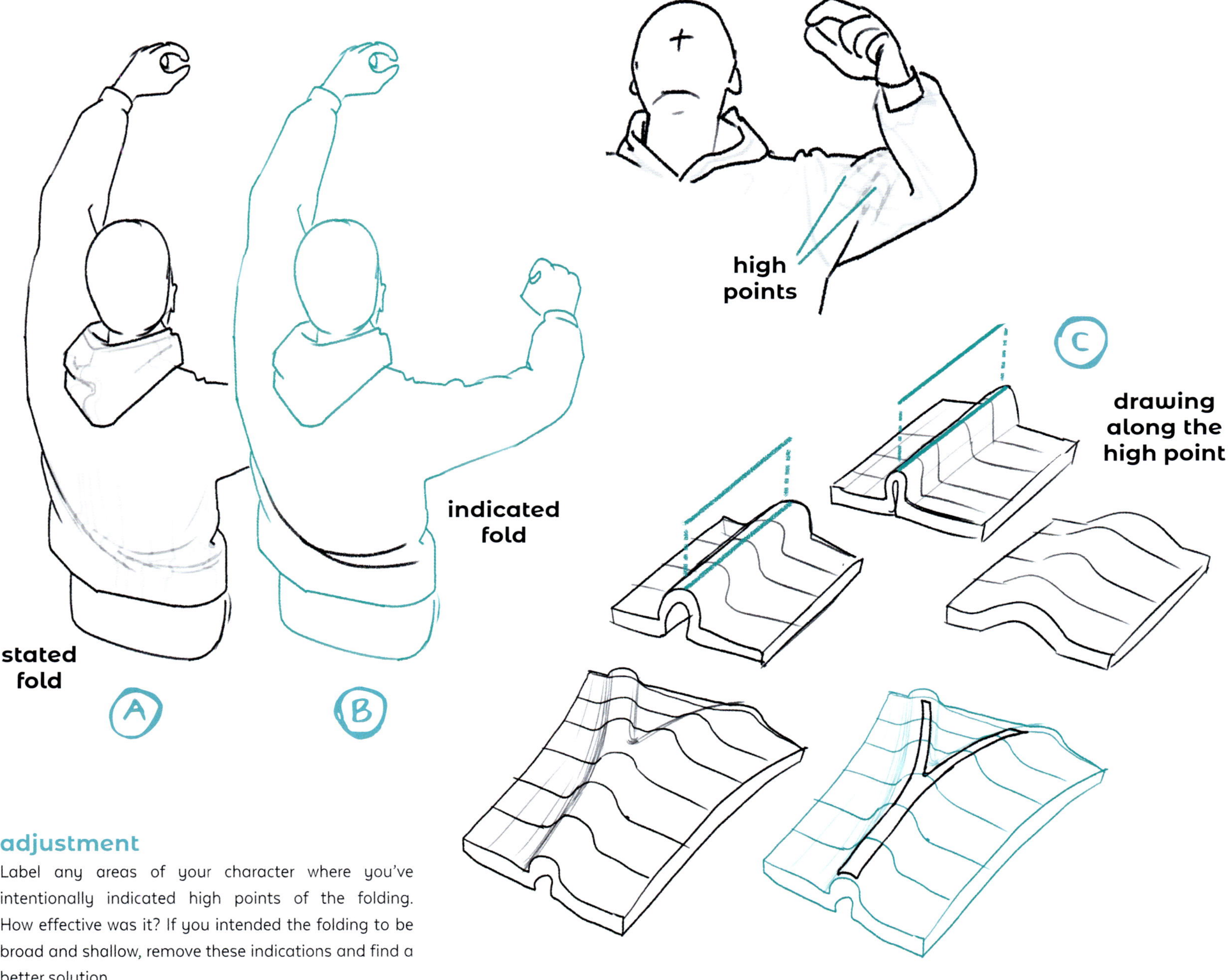

adjustment

Label any areas of your character where you've intentionally indicated high points of the folding. How effective was it? If you intended the folding to be broad and shallow, remove these indications and find a better solution.

sharp transitions

When we perceive objects, lighting provides a lot of information. Our brains use this information to guess what we're looking at. For example, the lighting information provided by this cube (A) helps us guess that there are three separate visible planes. When we remove the lighting, we lose this information (B). We can't leave this silhouette as it is - the interior form is too unclear. We need to add more information to help the viewer interpret the form. To do this, we can use lines to indicate sharp edges where one plane transitions into another (C). Because there are so few sharp transitions when drawing clothing, this is quite an uncommon line use, but it's still worth checking for.

If we zoomed in (D), we'd see that these edges aren't sharp at this scale. However, we're not drawing at this scale. From 'zoomed out', the transition does appear sharp. You can reverse-engineer this to improve your drawing. Look for parts of your drawing where you've drawn a line, and consider what this implies (E). If you've drawn **1**, it could communicate **2**, but it can't communicate **3**. Compare **1** and **4**; **1** indicates a much sharper transition, which could confuse the viewer if it's not what you meant to communicate.

On this clothed figure, we see a line across the chest, and lines down the arm (F). What are these lines communicating? If that's a sharp transition on the chest, then the orientation of the surface is unclear. That's the danger of using a single isolated line: you are indicating that something is happening, but it's not clear what. This can lead to confusion.

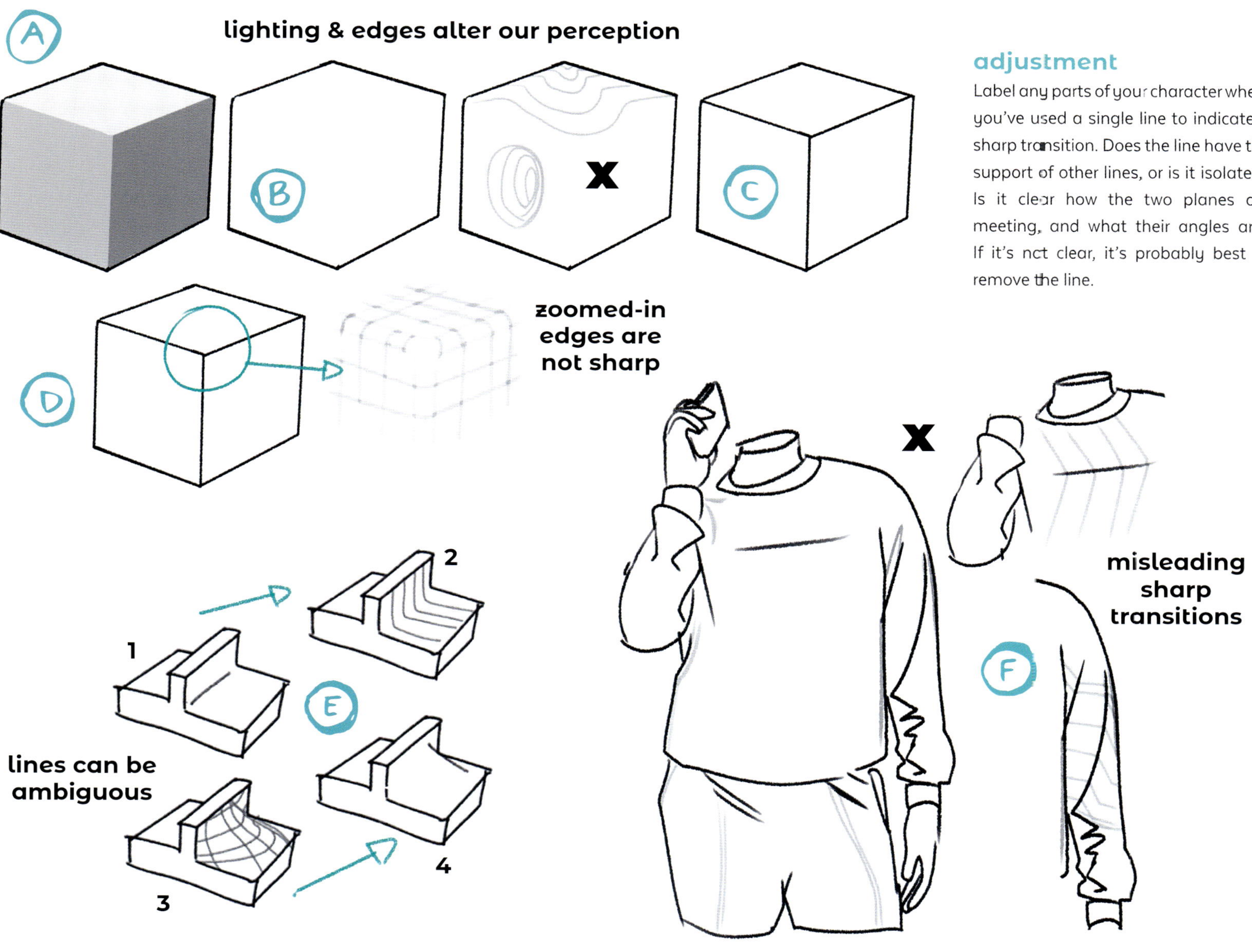

adjustment

Label any parts of your character where you've used a single line to indicate a sharp transition. Does the line have the support of other lines, or is it isolated? Is it clear how the two planes are meeting, and what their angles are? If it's not clear, it's probably best to remove the line.

staggered lines

When you want to indicate a sharp transition but don't want to use a single line, try using two lines instead of one. However, don't draw them parallel (A). You rarely see parallel lines in nature, and that's particularly true for drapery. Instead, stagger them slightly (A). Alternate the sides of the sharp transition, jumping back and forth. There should only be short sections where the lines both run parallel. This works well for describing continuous surfaces that fold multiple times. To improve these staggered lines, angle them slightly relative to each other, rather than having them running at the exact same angle.

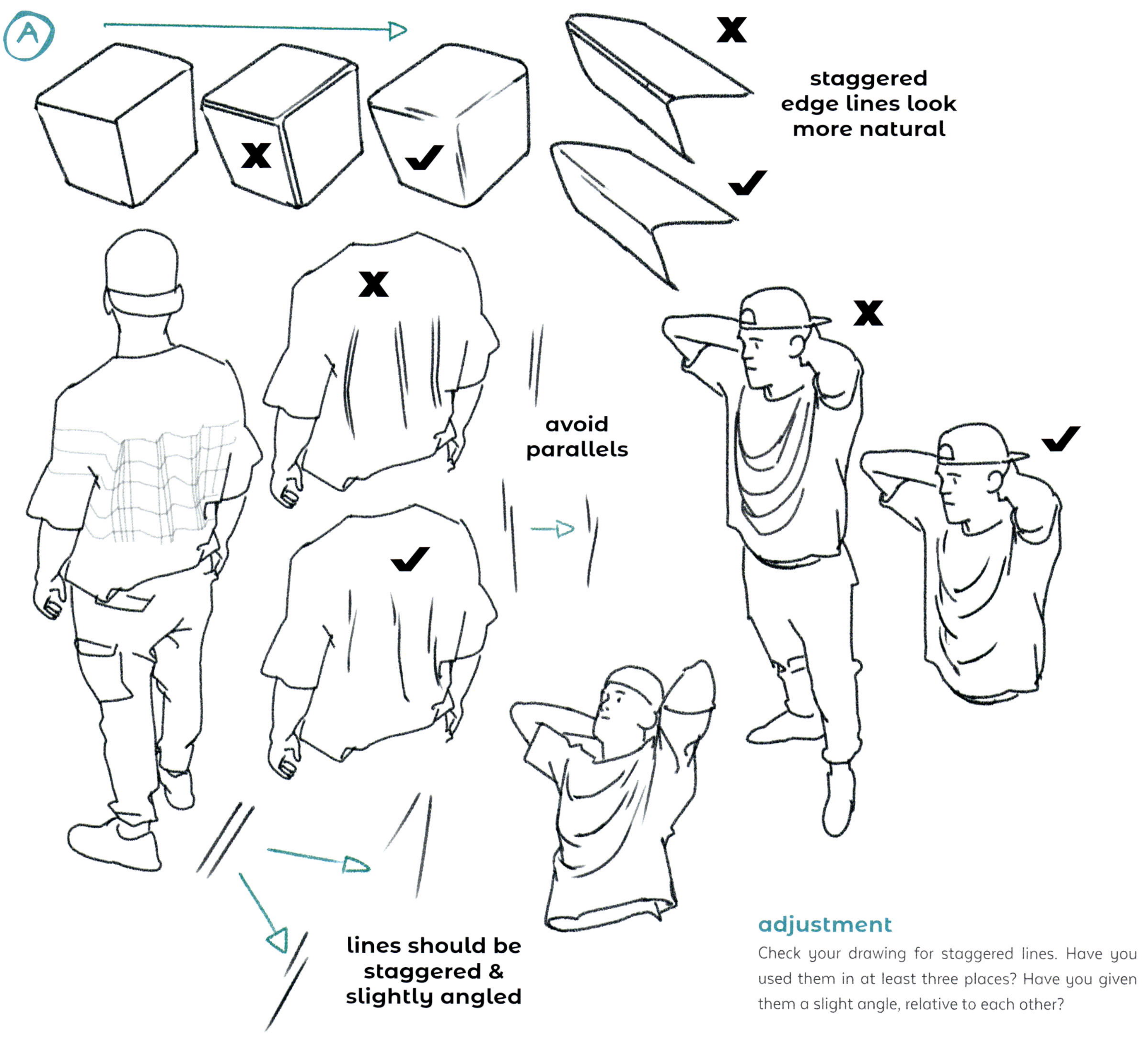

adjustment

Check your drawing for staggered lines. Have you used them in at least three places? Have you given them a slight angle, relative to each other?

90-degree surfaces

When the viewer looks at a form, all its surfaces are orientated at an angle relative to their eye. When the viewer moves from position **1** to position **2**, the relative angle of those surfaces changes, too (A). Parts that were not previously visible now become visible (B). This is important, because unless they're contours, we usually don't use lines to represent surfaces. For this reason, a flat rectangle or a curved surface will look almost identical from a distance, unless there are markings on the surface to differentiate them (C). However, wherever a surface faces 90 degrees or more from the viewer, they'll see what appears to be an 'edge', which we represent with a line. In reality, this is not a real 'edge' on the form – it's just as far around the surface *as the viewer can see*.

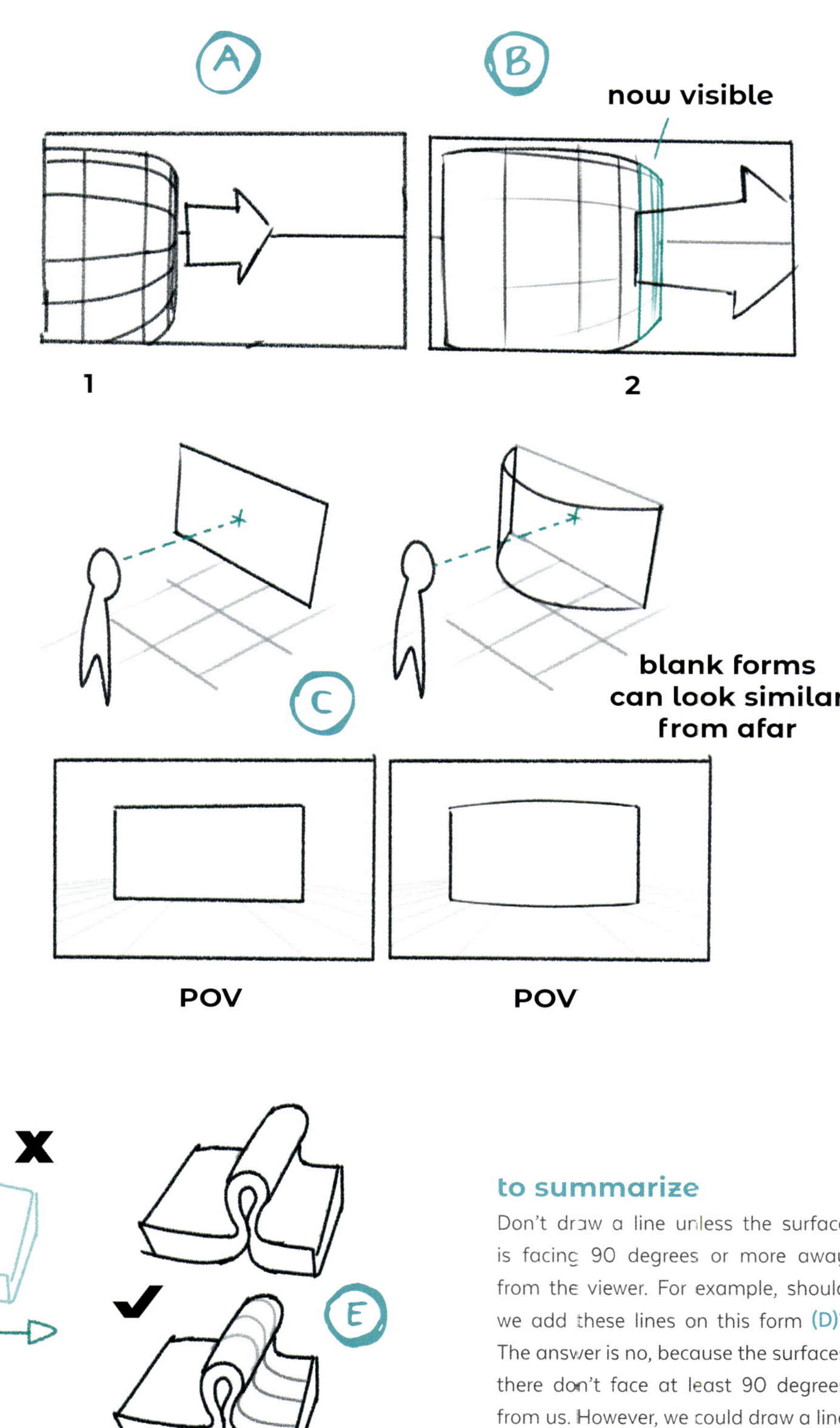

to summarize

Don't draw a line unless the surface is facing 90 degrees or more away from the viewer. For example, should we add these lines on this form (D)? The answer is no, because the surfaces don't face at least 90 degrees from us. However, we could draw a line here (E), because this surface does, and a line would clarify that.

When you change your viewing angle, you also change all the surfaces' relative orientation to you. Whether you see an 'edge' – and whether a line is drawn or not – depends on the angle from which you're viewing the subject. On this coat, we see this line (F). We can check if it should be there or not by drawing in the contours. With contours, we see that the surface is more or less facing the viewer, so, if we want to purely state forms, we should remove that line.

Below right, we see two angles of the same subject (G). On the right, there's a coloured line drawn where there shouldn't be one. However, when viewed from another angle, this part of the surface is now facing 90-plus degrees from the viewer, and we can use a line when drawing from that angle.

Most of the lines you use in a drawing should describe these surfaces angled at 90-plus degrees from you. This is the foundation of your drawing. Lines added for other reasons should be the icing on the cake, to bring your drawing to life. As we've seen, alternative uses of line include indicating graphics, sharp transitions, or contours.

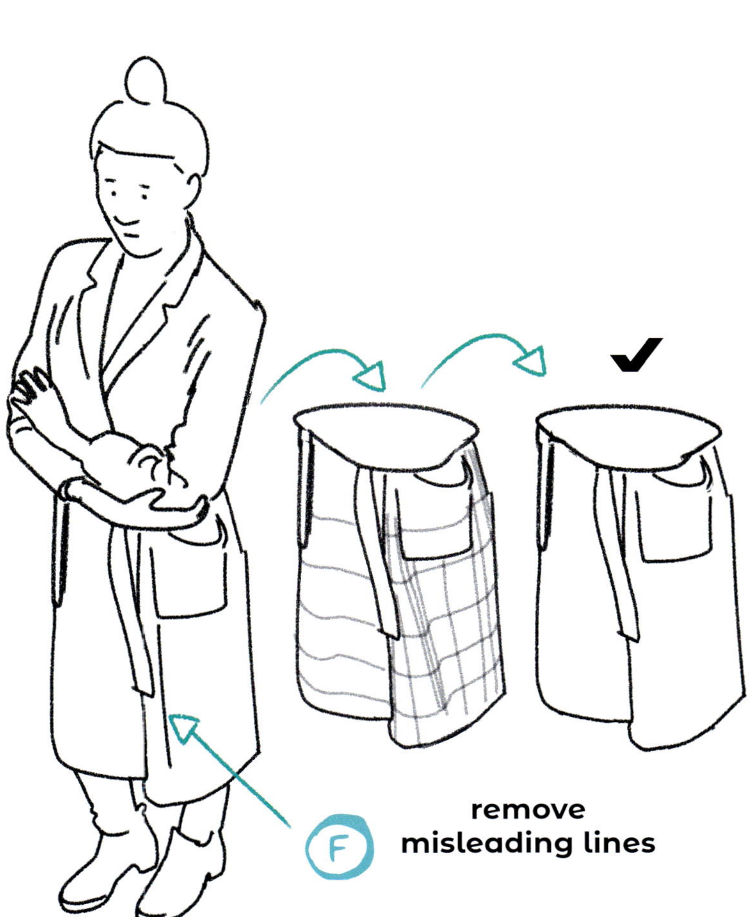

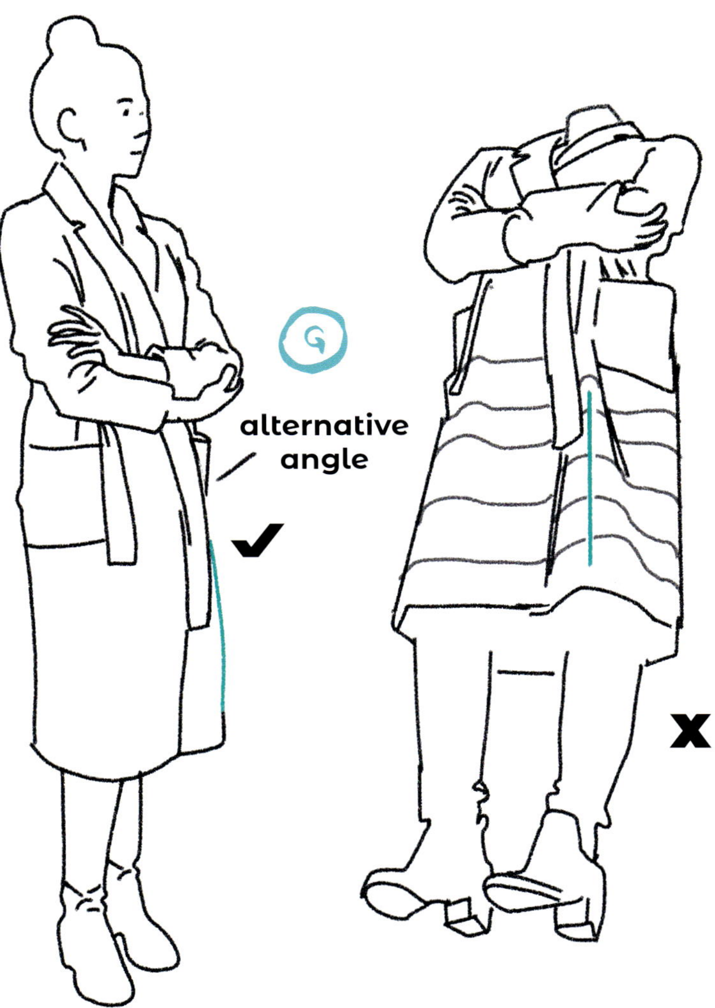

adjustment

Check your drawing for lines drawn on surfaces that aren't 90 (or more) degrees from the viewer. Why are they there? Do they fulfil some other role (like graphics, contours, or transitions) or should they be removed? Remove any lines that are unnecessary. Likewise, visualize these 90-plus-degree surfaces and add lines where necessary.

surface orientation

When viewing rounded subjects – including clothed people – surfaces facing 90-plus degrees from the viewer are more likely to be found at the sides of the subject, near the silhouette (A). On rounded objects, the surfaces in the middle of the subject mostly face the viewer. Therefore, the majority of lines we draw will be near the silhouette, and the middle of the subject will contain fewer lines (B).

On this cylinder, the folding happens all the way round, but we wouldn't use a line to describe the central folds because they're facing mostly towards us (C).

At its most basic, you can simply add lines near the sides of the form to make it appear more rounded (D).

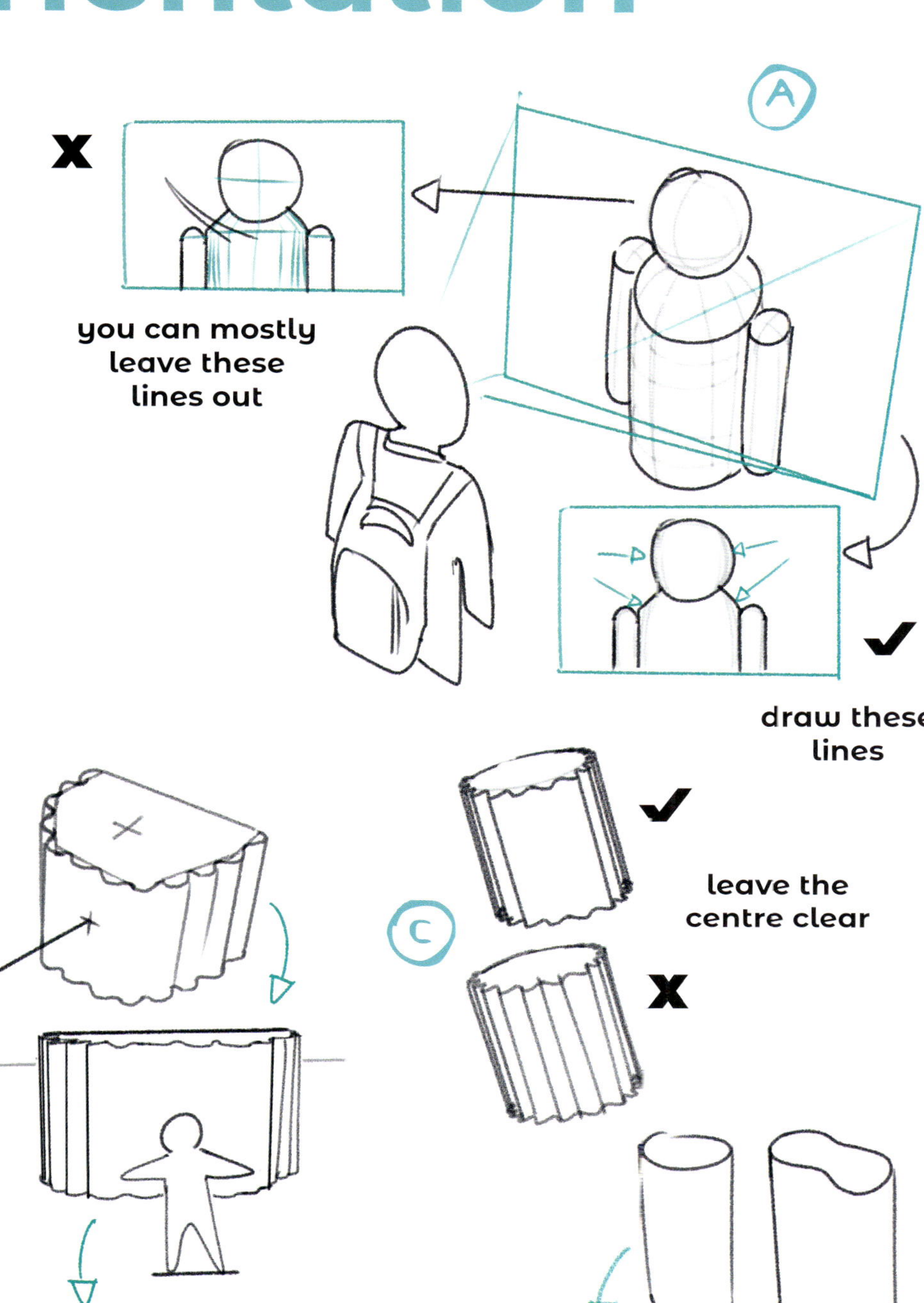

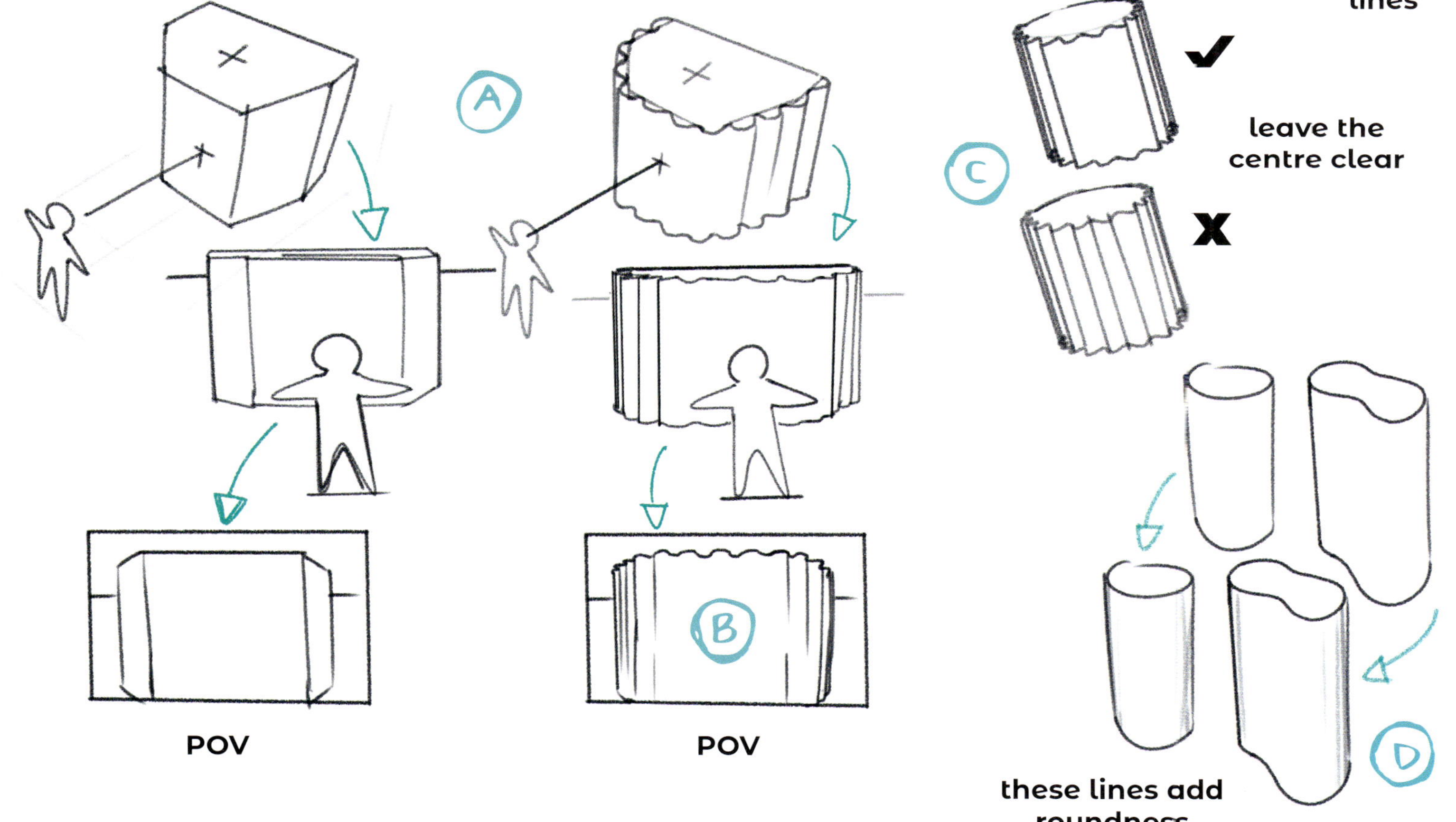

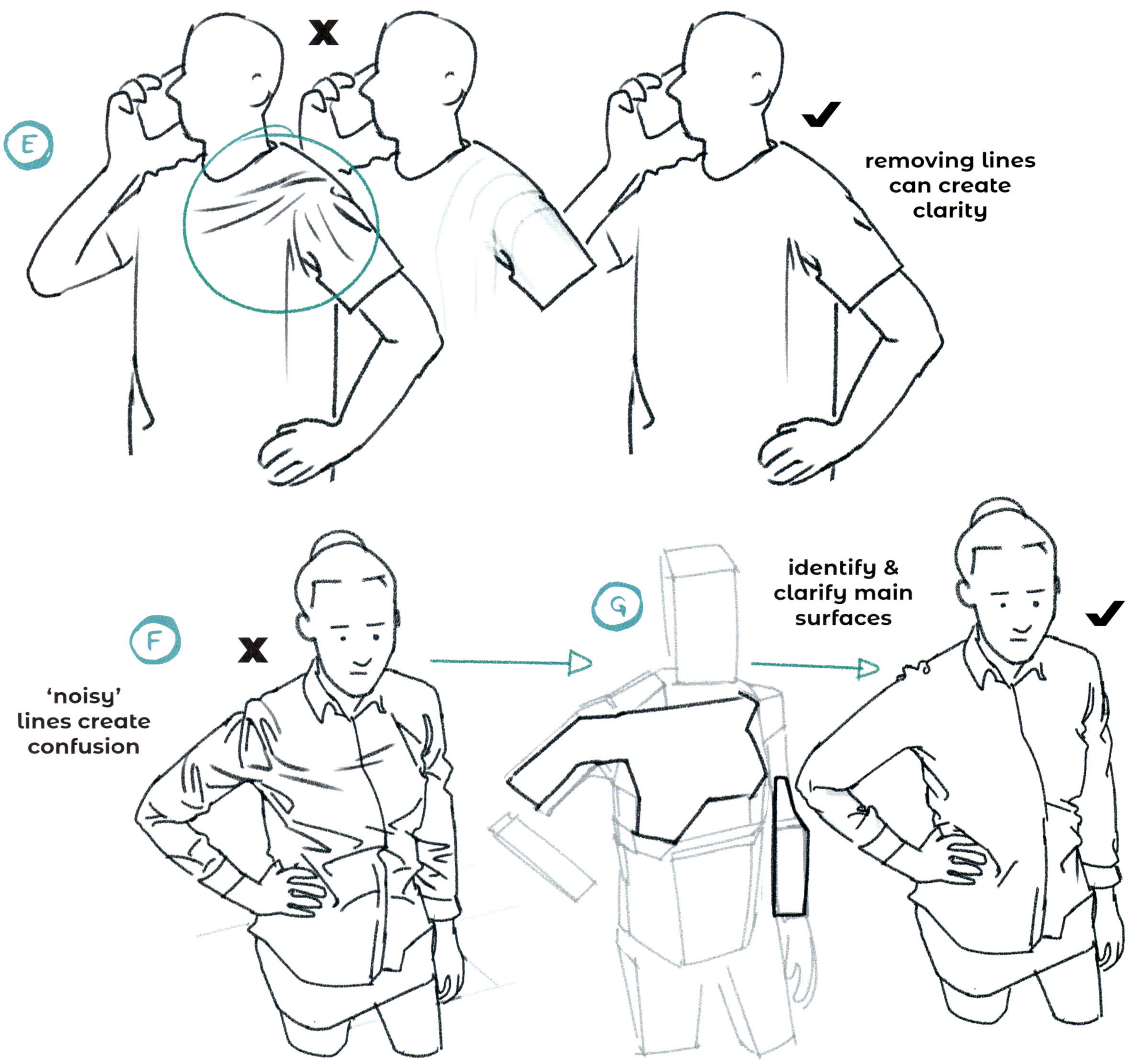

Again, you can reverse-engineer this. By removing lines from the middle of areas or subjects you'd like to be seen as rounded – as shown here in the shoulder (E) – you suggest to the viewer, 'This region is facing you.' If you want something to look like it's facing (or nearly facing) the viewer, you must often remove lines, not add them.

Here is a 'noisy' drawing (see Internals & noise on page 77) (F). There's a bit too much going on and the major surfaces are unclear. To improve it, we just need to identify the main surfaces facing towards us and remove most of the lines on those surfaces (G).

When a subject rotates towards you, the number of lines describing the folding will decrease (H). This is a little counter-intuitive – you'd think that the number of lines increases because you can see them more clearly! However, while you can see the surfaces more clearly, they are less likely to face 90-plus degrees from you. Folds are present, but you're not viewing them from an angle where they can be best described by lines. It takes confidence to portray this effect.

As this woman rotates, we see fewer and fewer lines across her upper back, even though the number of folds present remains the same (I).

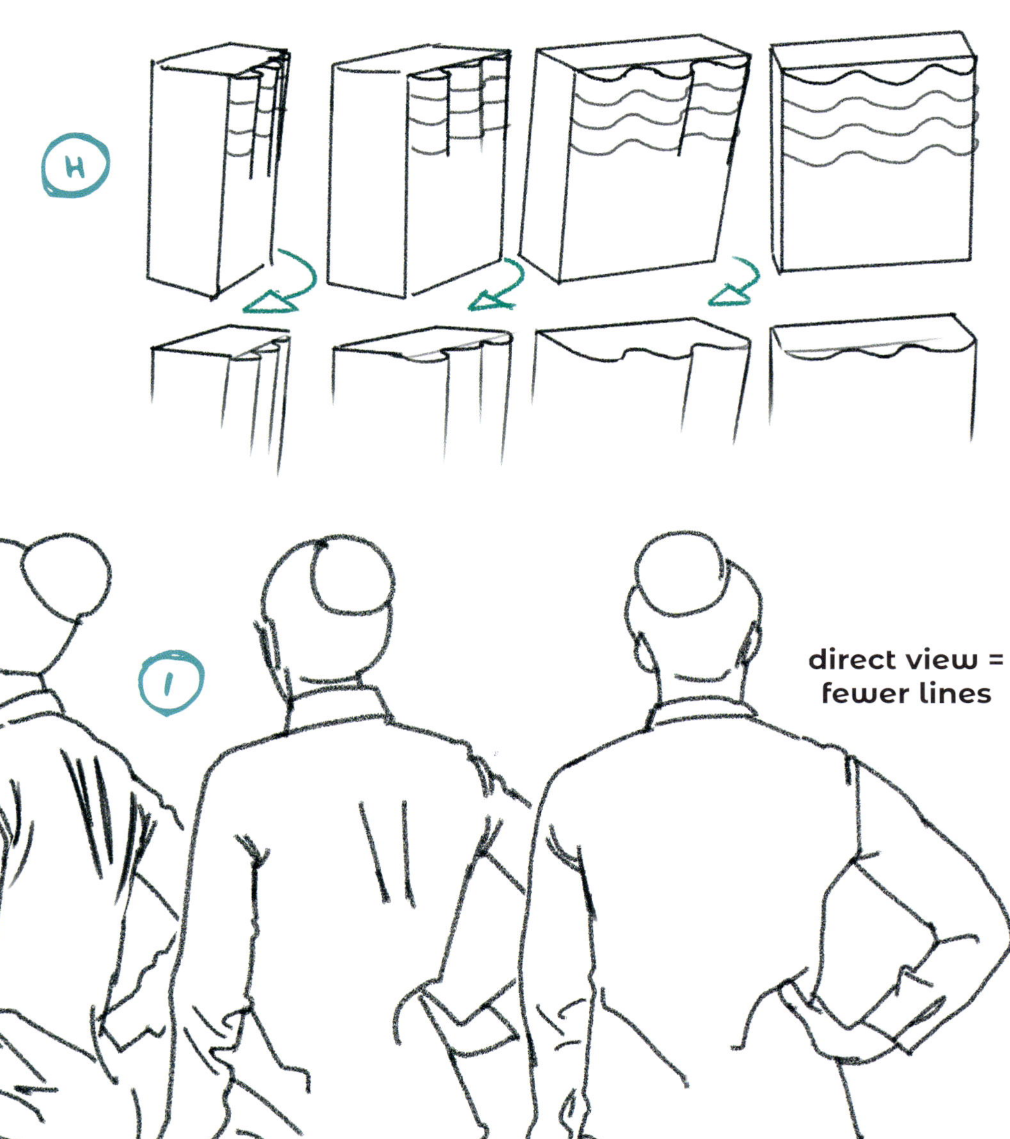

adjustment

Check that the distribution of folds is uneven. Are most of your lines located near the silhouette, at the sides of the forms? Label the two biggest surfaces facing you, and remove any lines in that area that don't fulfil some other role (e.g. they aren't contour, graphic, or sharp transition lines).

fold count & length

The fold 'count' is the number of lines used to describe a region of folding. The fold 'length' describes the distance these lines travel towards the interior, away from the silhouette. There's a tendency to draw both too many lines, and lines that are too long (A). Unfortunately, the urge to 'keep adding lines until it looks good' can override the fact that the drawing is becoming noisier and lower in clarity. (See Clarity on page 74 and Internals & noise on page 77 for more details.)

If you're going to add multiple interior lines and 'hidden contours' (page 79), it's best to keep your fold count low and the fold length short (B).

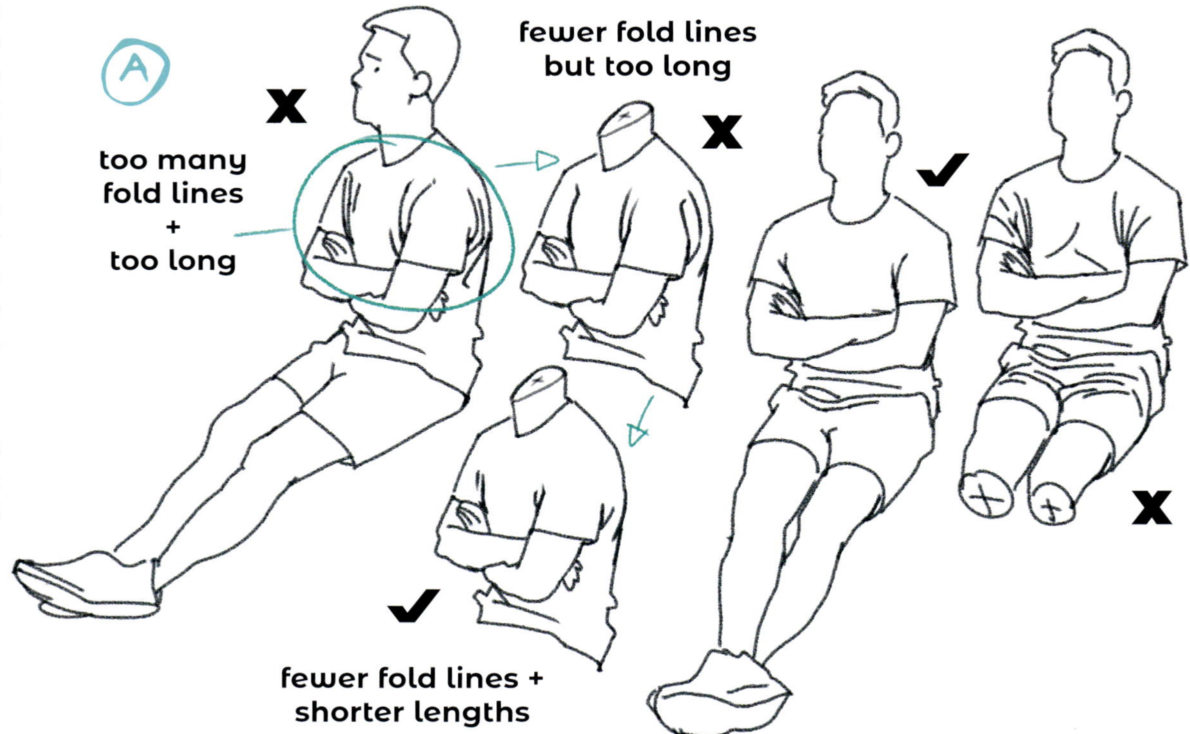

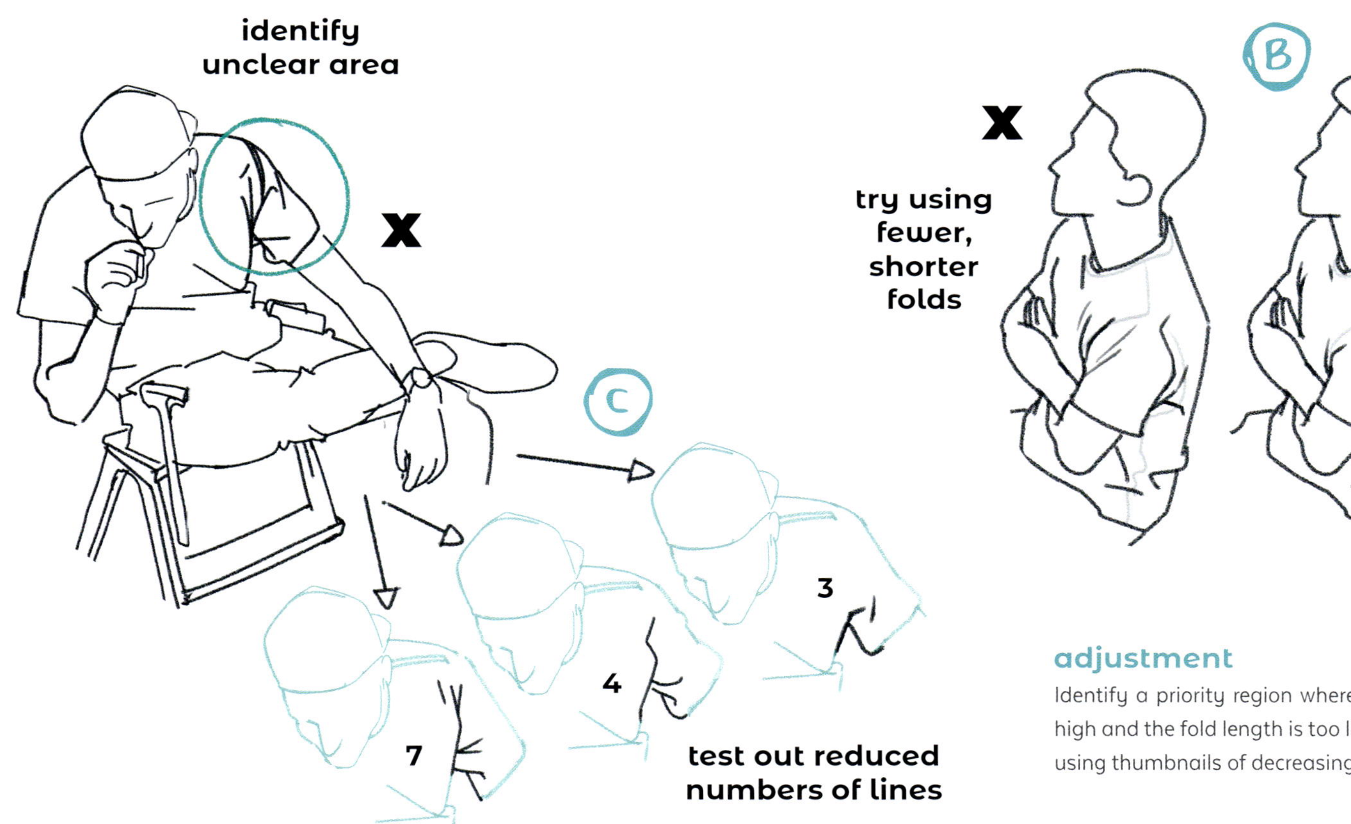

adjustment

Identify a priority region where the fold count is too high and the fold length is too long. Redraw that area using thumbnails of decreasing line count (C).

overlap

Overlaps occur when one thing is in front of another, relative to the viewer's position. Without overlap, the viewer can't be certain which subjects are closer or further from them. For example, if we draw four equally sized shapes, they appear to be the same distance away from us (A). If we draw some shapes larger and others smaller, we suggest depth, because viewers naturally assume that some are further away (B). However, the depth is only 'suggested' because we assume all the subjects are the same size. It's possible that they're the same distance away and happen to be different sizes. The only way for the viewer to be sure is to check for overlaps. These come in two main types:

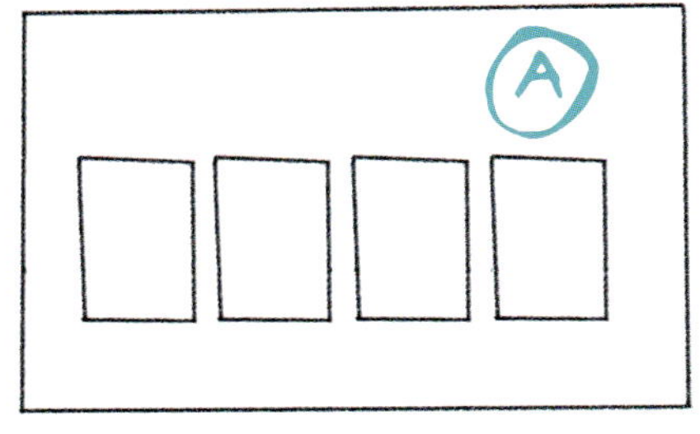

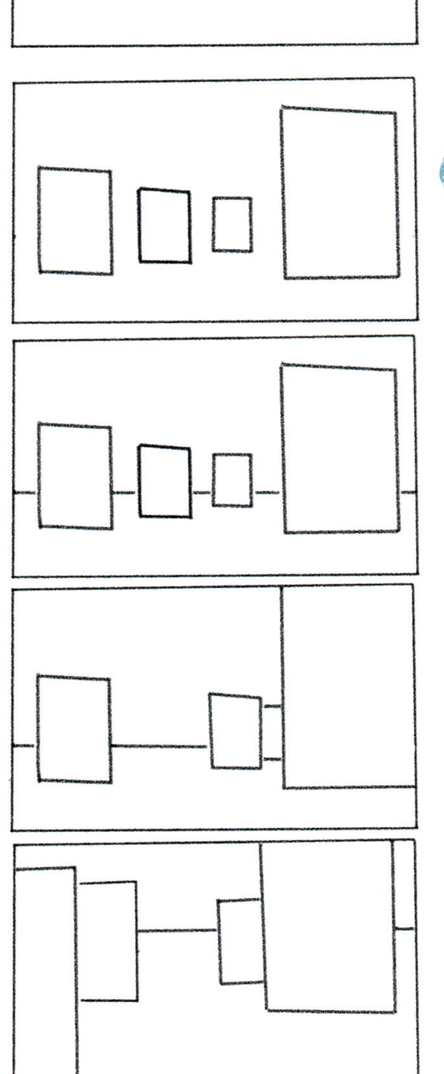

direct overlap

This is when one subject is in front of another, obscuring a section of the rear subject (C). This establishes a relationship between the locations of three things: both of the subjects and also the viewer. Direct overlap clarifies that one subject is between the viewer and the furthest subject.

contextual overlap

Here (D), subjects **1** and **3** have no obvious direct overlap, but subject **2** creates a sequence of overlaps that connects them. We know by instinct that if **1** is in front of **2**, and **2** is in front of **3**, then **3** must be behind **1**. Our brains are incredible at monitoring these contextual relationships. They do it without us even noticing.

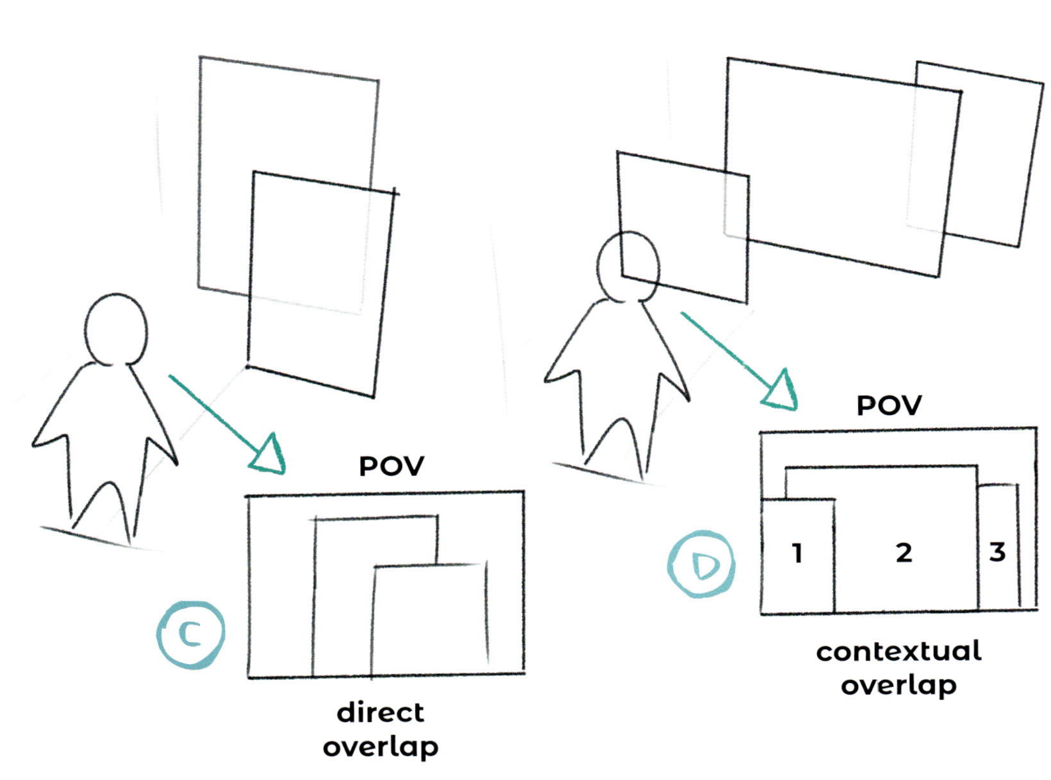

Even just one or two unclear overlaps can destroy a drawing's believability (E). We must carefully check what is in front of what. To do this, simply redraw what you've done as four or five simplified forms (F). This helps you check the overlaps.

To clarify your overlaps, **avoid tangents**. Tangents are situations when two or three lines meet, and it's not obvious which form is above or below (G). To prevent this from happening, avoid drawing overlaps close to a corner, and include a small gap between the form on top and the one below (H). This subtly emphasizes the top form, but be careful – if the gap is too large, it'll only make the overlap more confusing (I). Keep it subtle.

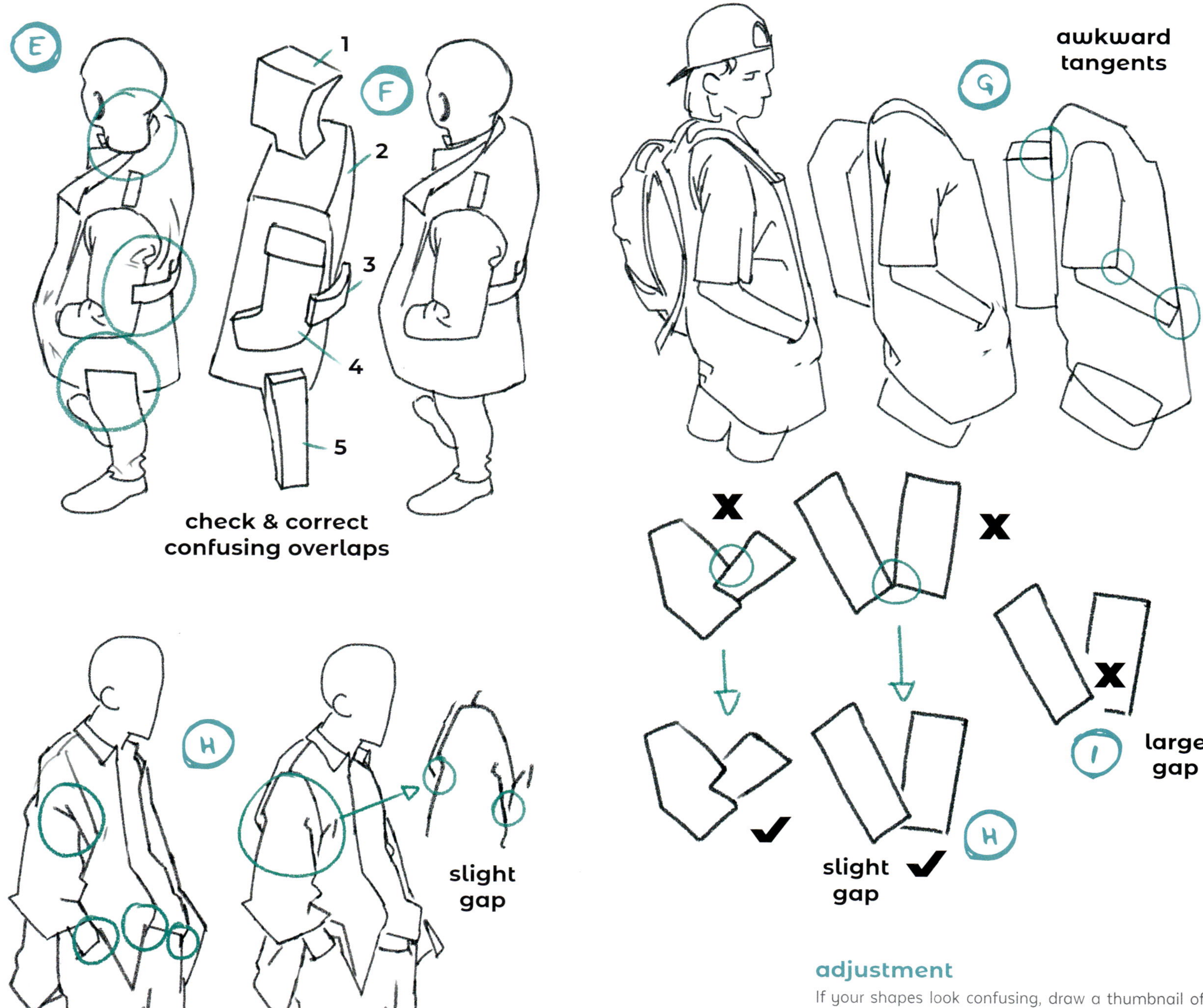

adjustment

If your shapes look confusing, draw a thumbnail of the figure with simplified forms. Use it to identify the three most important overlaps in the drawing. Now make the clarity of those overlaps your priority and make the changes to the original drawing.

flow & z-lines

Flow describes how smoothly the viewer's eyes move around the drawing without becoming 'trapped' in an area. For example, (A) has limited flow, with noisy lines creating dead ends that interrupt the viewer. Meanwhile, (B) has lots of flow. It's a common mistake to draw most folds as lines that run against the general flow of the main shape (C). This is something to avoid – we don't want to limit flow. We want to focus on the silhouette and the secondary silhouette (see pages 75 and 76), which doesn't block flow.

These are **Z-lines** (D). Using them is one way to increase flow. Use them as part of the secondary silhouette, rather than as internal lines. Follow three simple rules: the Z-line must have three sections, the end sections must turn in different directions, and it can't begin at the end of a previous Z-line. Z-lines are a great way to connect two sections of a drawing (E). Draw one, then begin the next by attaching it. Changing the orientation of your Z-lines can create the impression of looking up or down at the subject (F).

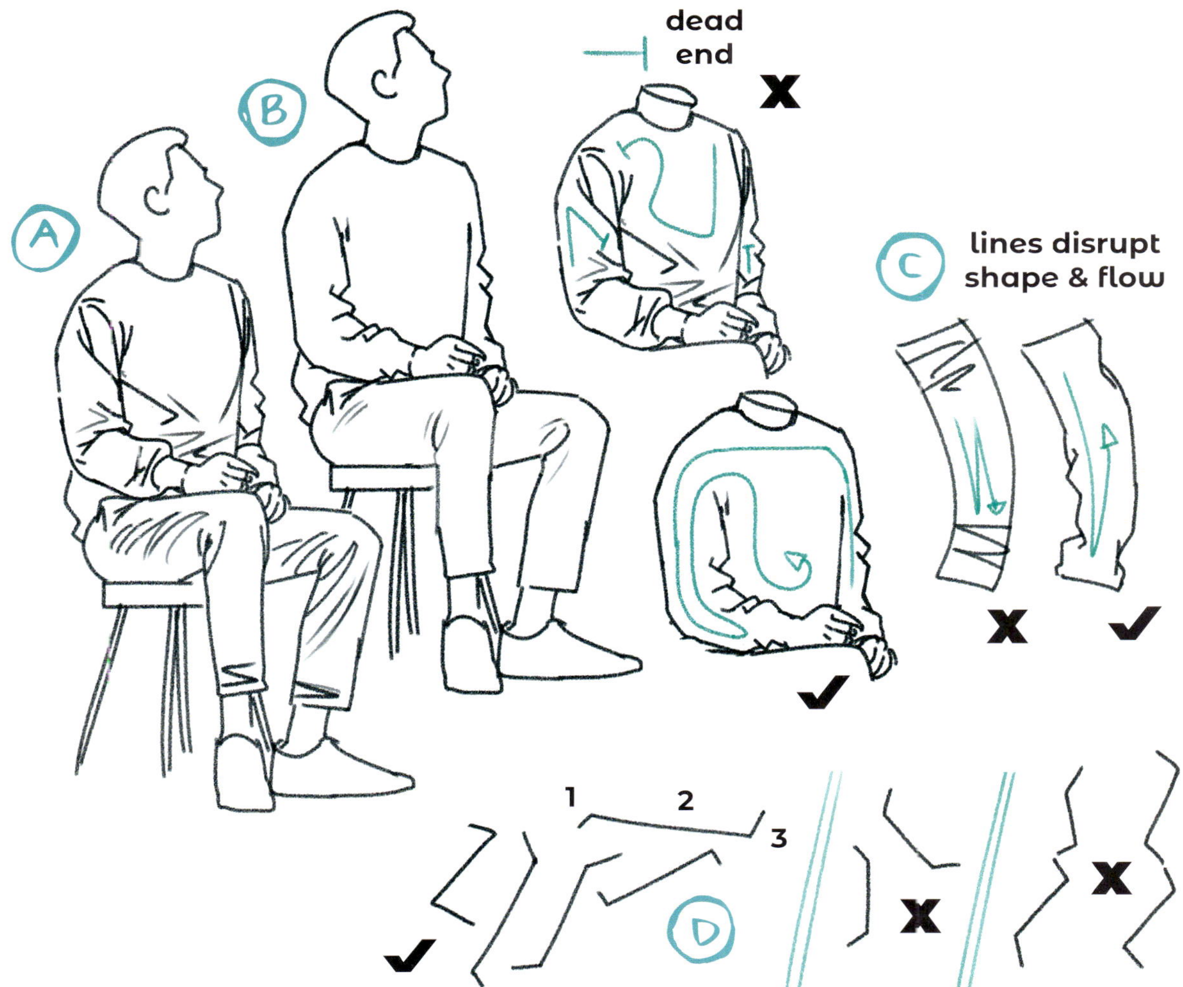

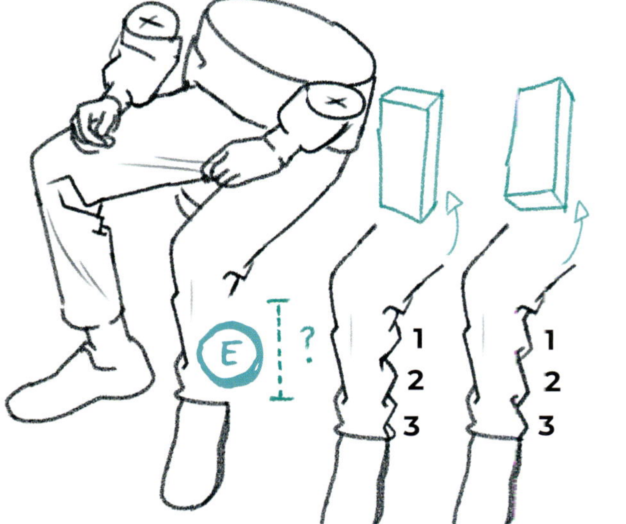

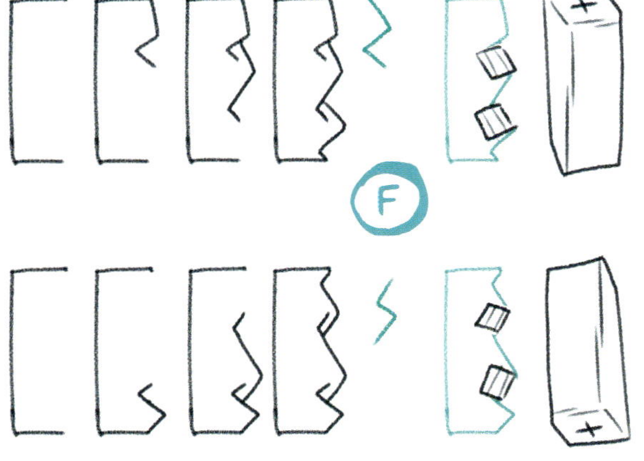

adjustment

With your finger, try to move through the drawing you've done, labelling areas where your finger hits a dead end and gets stuck. Erase the internal lines and redraw the silhouette using Z-lines.

micro-tails

Very often, the end of one form will run into another form, running at an angle to it (A). When this happens, it's not very effective to use straight lines to describe this meeting (B). They don't quite describe what's happening there. Instead of a simple, straight line, add a slight 'tail' at the end of the line (C). Let's call it a **micro-tail**. It helps the viewer understand that two forms are merging. If you draw this tail too long, it won't be as effective, so keep it short.

To take this a step further, add a slight 'shadow' to deepen the tail (D). This isn't lighting, but an indication that the form is turning sharply. It helps to round out the form. Don't add a shadow to the end of every micro-tail. Save shadows for a few select places in your drawing. If you draw them all over, it will look odd.

You can compress the angle at which the lines meet (E). Combining Z-lines with these little tails is so effective at suggesting 3D form that you can draw an almost random silhouette, incorporating Z-lines around these lines, and it'll look like a believable 3D form (F).

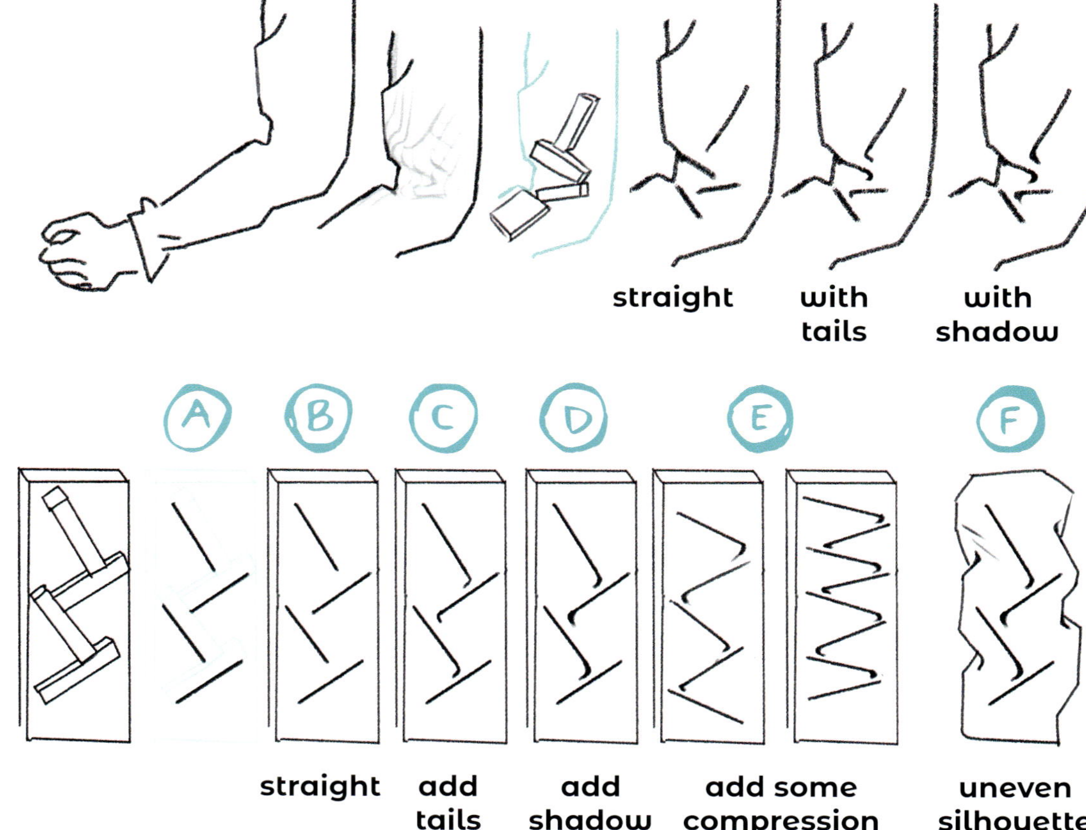

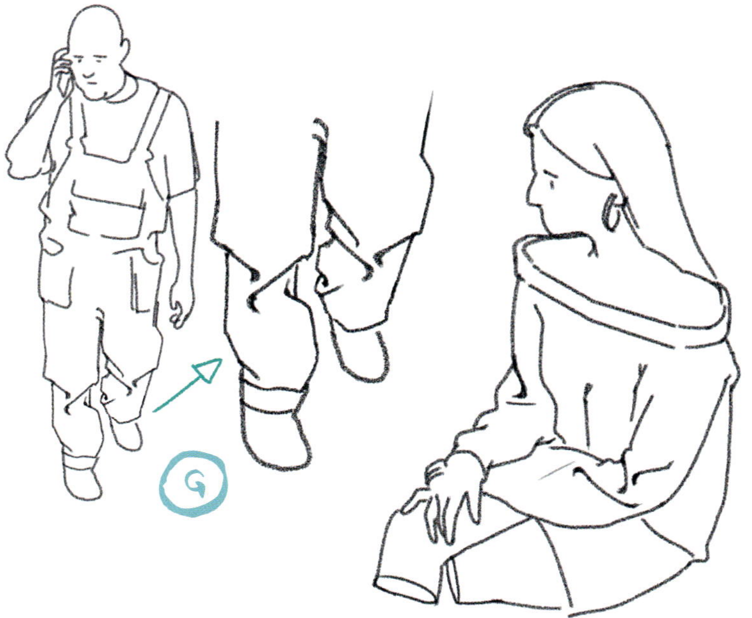

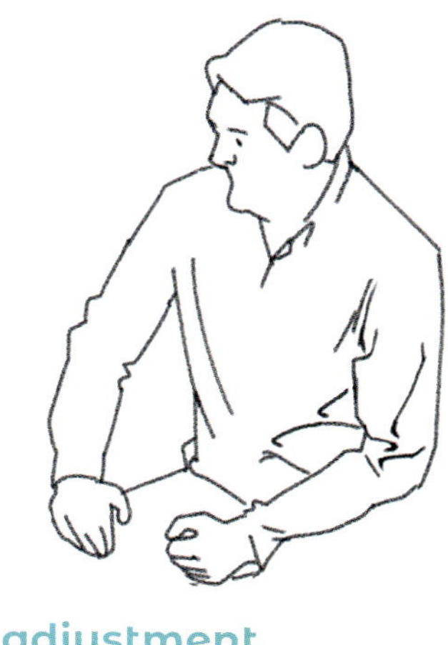

adjustment

Try redrawing the priority area of your drawing using Z-lines with micro-tails. Use them sparingly – don't draw too many across the whole drawing (G).

fanning

Fanning occurs when you try to draw a pinched area of overlap, and end up drawing a sort of 'mega-tangent': a single point where multiple lines radiate outwards, as if from the centre of a hand fan (A). These radiating lines don't make it clear what is overlapping what, and this confuses the viewer.

A

B

identify fanning tangents

revise clearer overlap

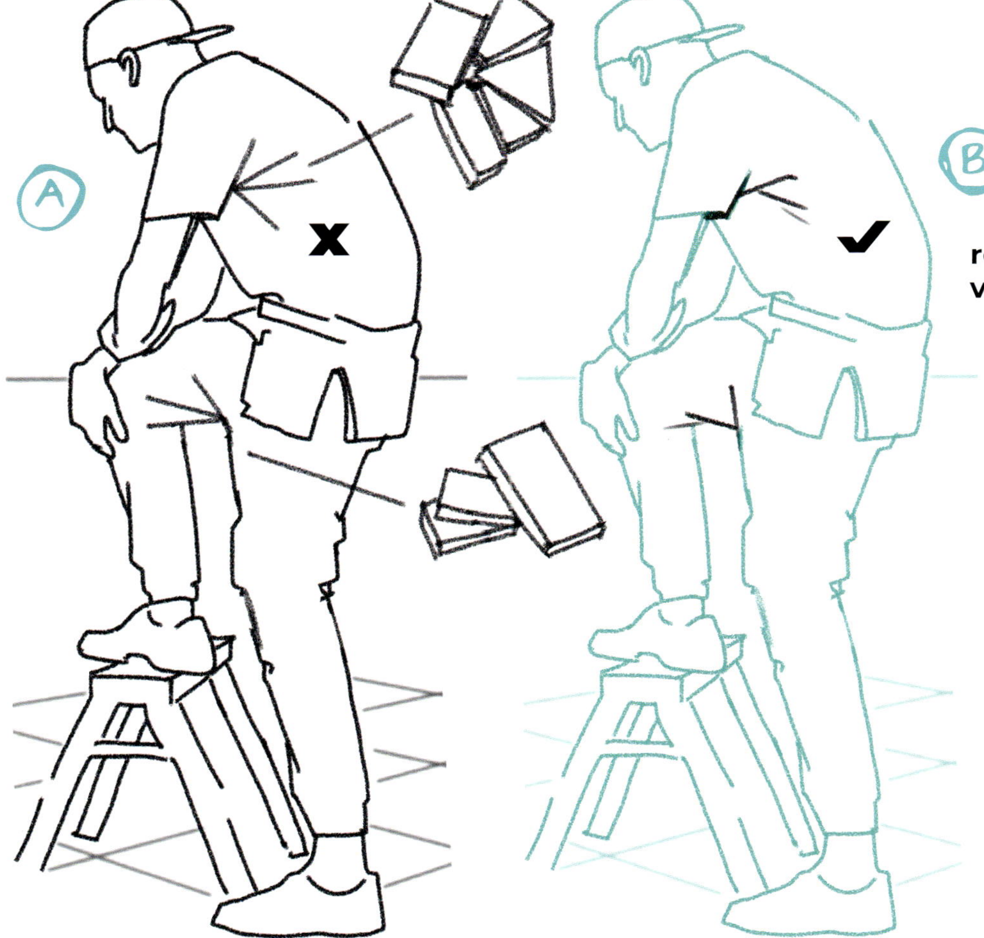

adjustment

Scan your drawing, looking for any fanning. If you're not sure about an area, redraw it with some simple forms to help focus on their sequence (B). Once you've done this, simply redraw the problem area with clearer overlaps.

clarity

Clarity is what gives us an instant 'read' of a drawing. It's the immediate understanding of what's being depicted. When clarity is low, the viewer can't easily grasp the forms and shapes (A). When clarity is high, they can quickly make sense of the drawing (B). Our goal as artists is to figure out which areas have the lowest clarity and then adjust those areas to raise it. Squinting at your drawing is a good test of clarity.

Alternatively, you can stand back or zoom out from your drawing enough that you've effectively 'shrunk' it (C). Do the major shapes still hold up? Is it clear what's in front of what, and where forms meet, or do they blur into each other?

adjustment

Label the two lowest clarity areas in your drawing and write down why you think they're low clarity. Putting it into words helps you to identify the cause. Are the overlaps unclear? Are there too many internals? If you're not sure, keep looking through other adjustments until you recognize what is reducing the clarity.

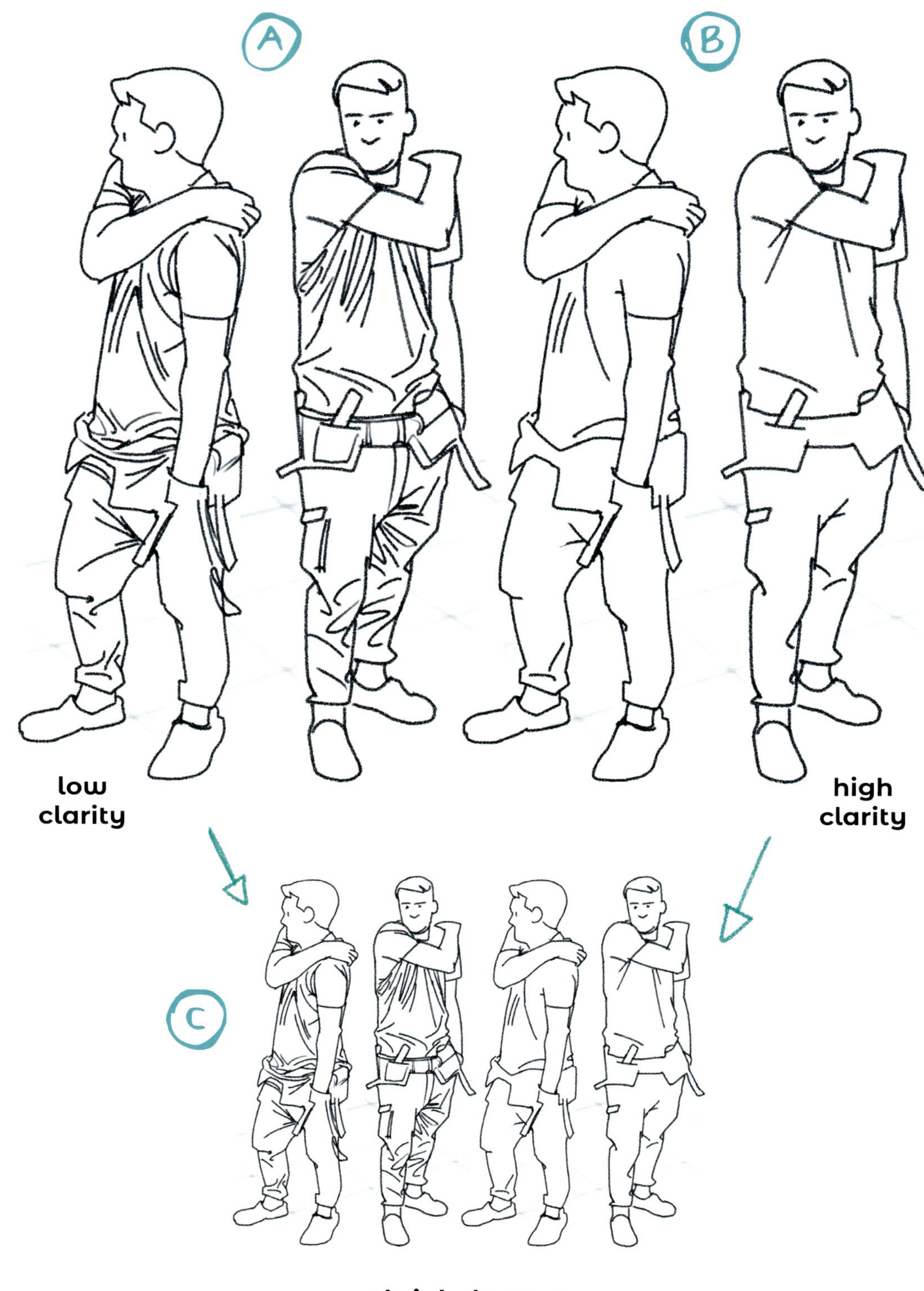

pure silhouette

Silhouettes come in two types. The first is 'pure silhouette'. This is the continuous line that outlines and unifies the drawing. When people say that a clear silhouette 'reads', they mean you can instantly tell both *what a subject is* and *what it's doing*. In short, it does a lot of the work in your drawing. Nothing improves the overall clarity of your drawing more than silhouette, so it's worth improving (A)!

The pure silhouette summarizes the relative proportions and angles of the subject: heights, widths, depths, relative angle of limbs, and so on. A clear silhouette also sometimes communicates mood, or *how something feels* (B). When the viewer looks at the drawing, their brain compares these relative proportions and angles to their memories, enabling them to guess what they're seeing. For a silhouette to be recognizable, it must match something in the viewer's memory. The more familiar the viewer is with a subject, the closer the match must be, because the more you see something, the more accurate your memory of it.

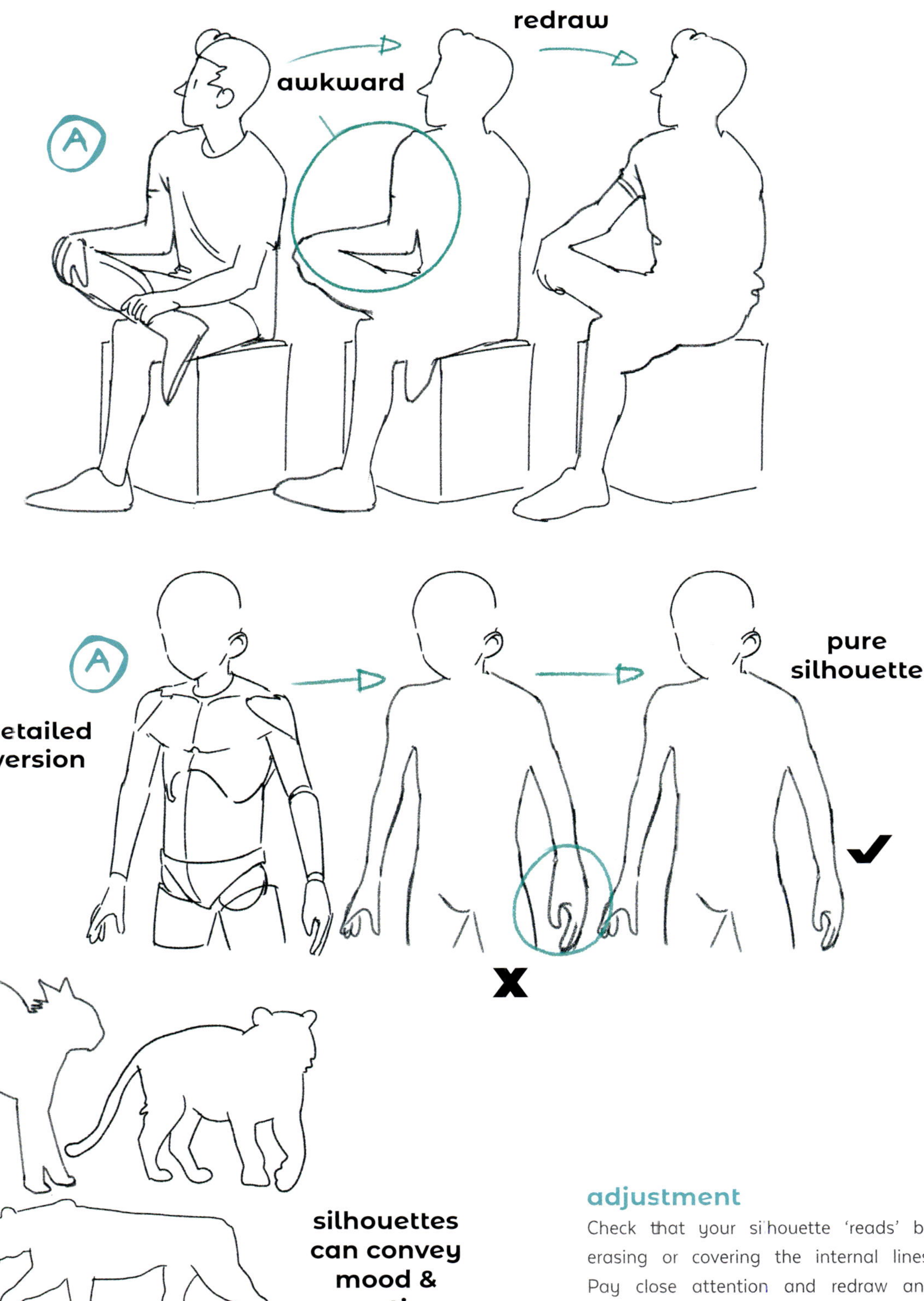

adjustment

Check that your silhouette 'reads' by erasing or covering the internal lines. Pay close attention and redraw any awkward areas where the silhouette isn't communicating what you'd like it to.

secondary silhouette

The other type of silhouette is the 'secondary silhouette'. This is the silhouette *plus any additional lines that touch it directly*. Any additional lines touching the pure silhouette – and heading towards the subject's interior – are called 'branches' (A). If it's not directly touching the silhouette, it's not a branch (B)! Branches help clarify overlap between different parts of the subject. As we saw in Fold count & length (page 68), they don't need to be very long to effectively communicate an overlap. Short branches do it clearly, too. Adjusting just a couple of short branches can instantly reduce the clarity of a drawing.

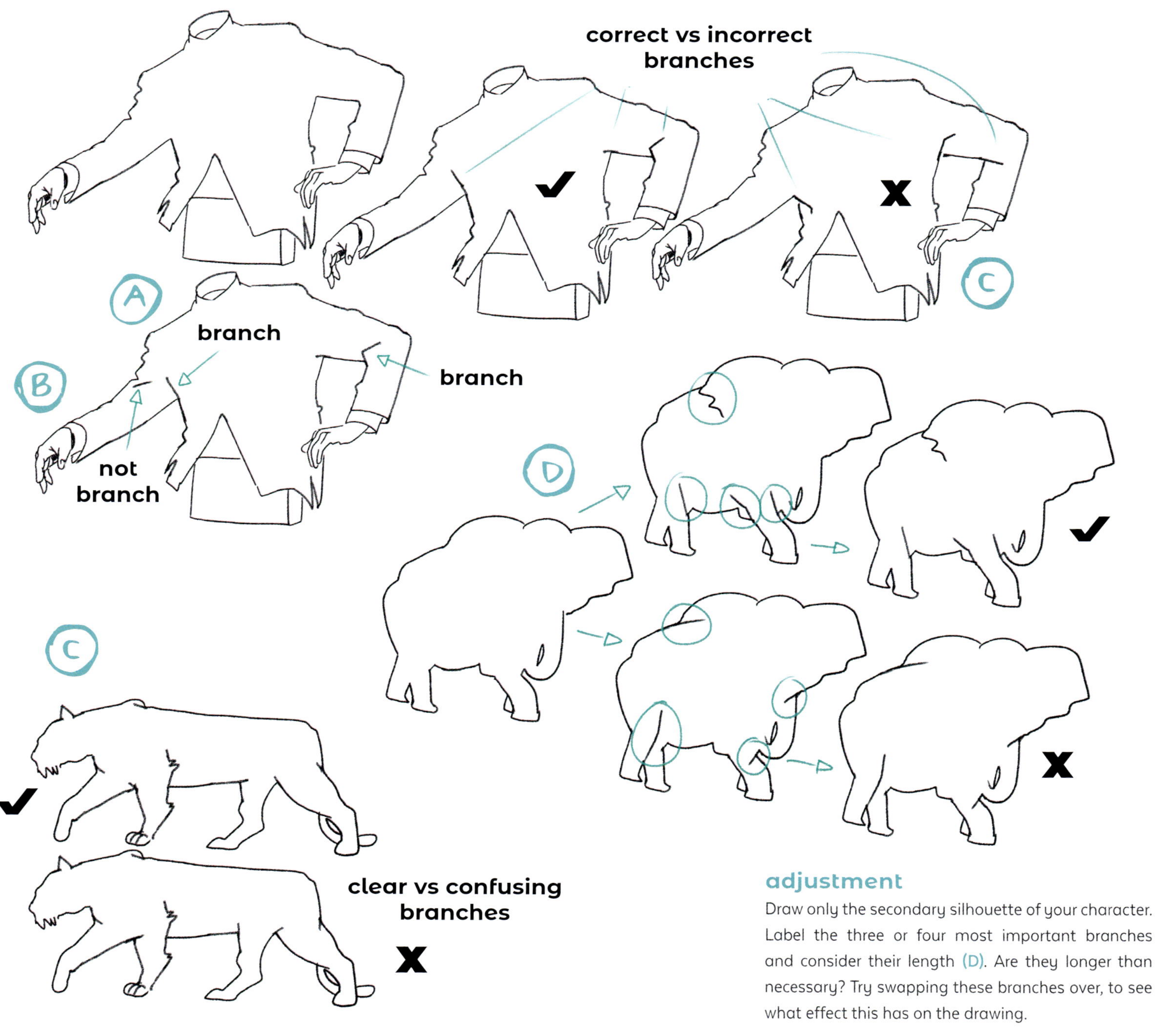

adjustment

Draw only the secondary silhouette of your character. Label the three or four most important branches and consider their length (D). Are they longer than necessary? Try swapping these branches over, to see what effect this has on the drawing.

internals & noise

'Internals' are lines completely separate from the silhouette or secondary silhouette (A). They can help to describe the surfaces and add clarity, but only if you don't overdo them. This is a graph of clarity versus internals (B): the **silhouette** and **secondary silhouette** do most of the heavy lifting – they get you to about eighty per cent clarity and understanding of the subject – and then the internals provide that last bit. They should be the spice, not the bulk of the meal. As the graph shows, adding too many internals damages your drawing. By adding too many, you create 'noise' and confuse the viewer (C). Having too many internals breaks up the main shapes and hides the key overlaps, making it difficult for the viewer to visualize the forms. A drawing is 'noisy' when too many internals have been added (D).

internals

A

100%

2

1

clarity

B

3

noise

number of internals

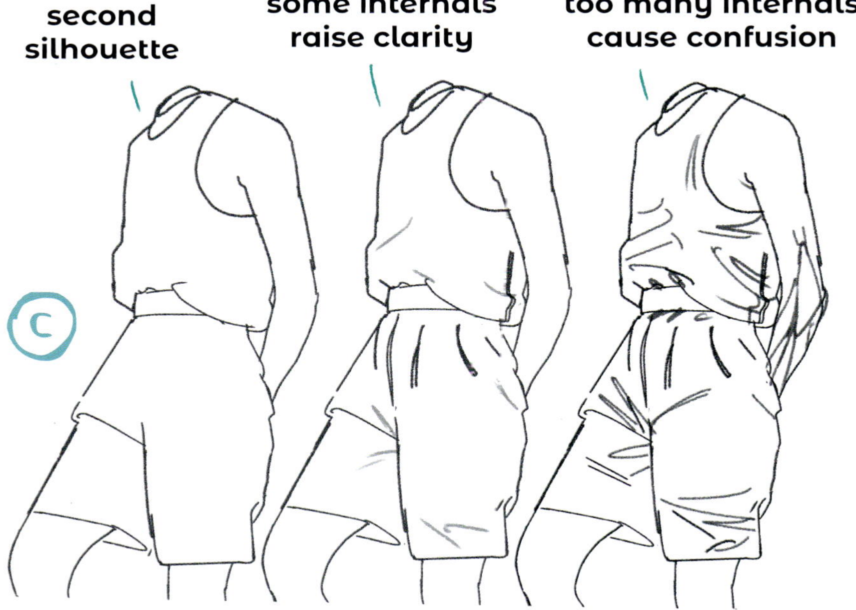

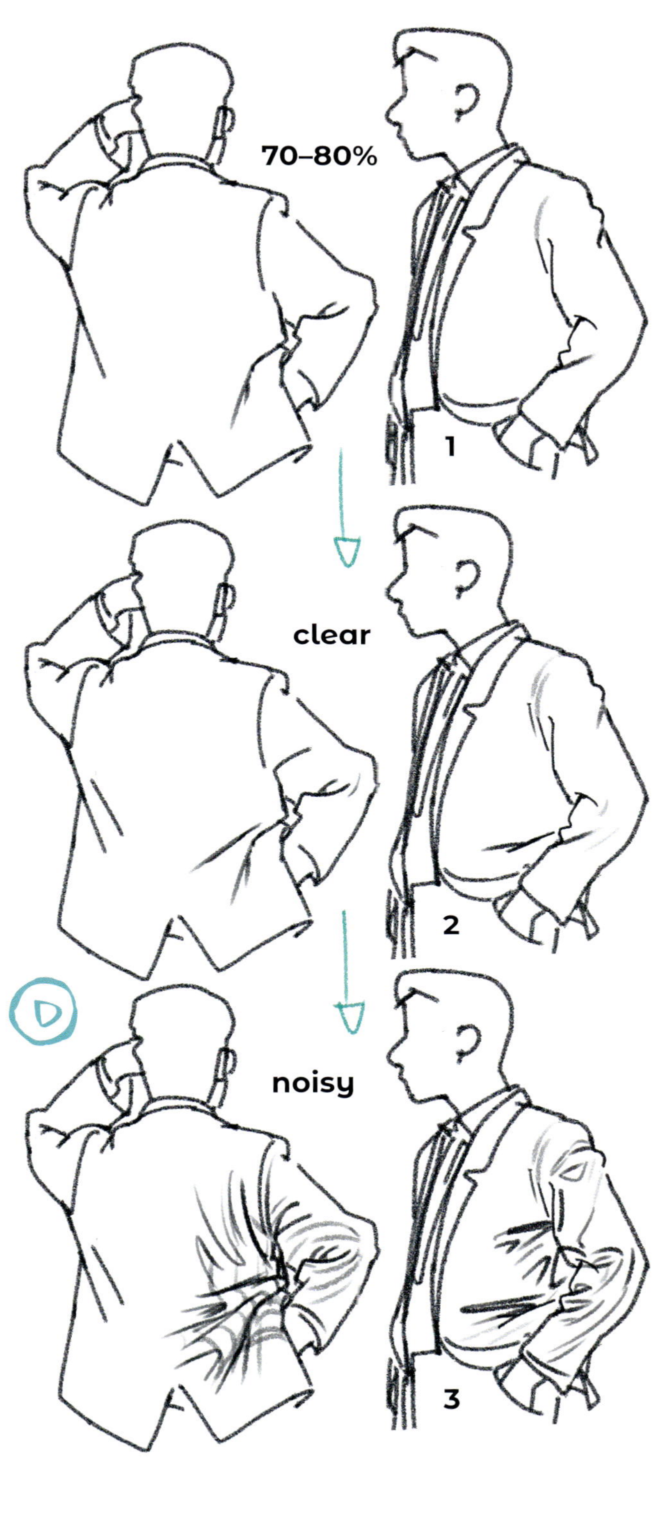

Let's briefly mention how internals relate to fold width and depth. When you draw parallel internals close together, you suggest to the viewer that narrow and fairly deep folds have formed on the garment (E). This is fine to do, but remember that – as we saw in Fold depth (page 44) – most of the folding on a garment will be broad and shallow. Therefore, you don't want to draw too many parallel internals close together. Instead, give them a bit of space to suggest broader folding (F).

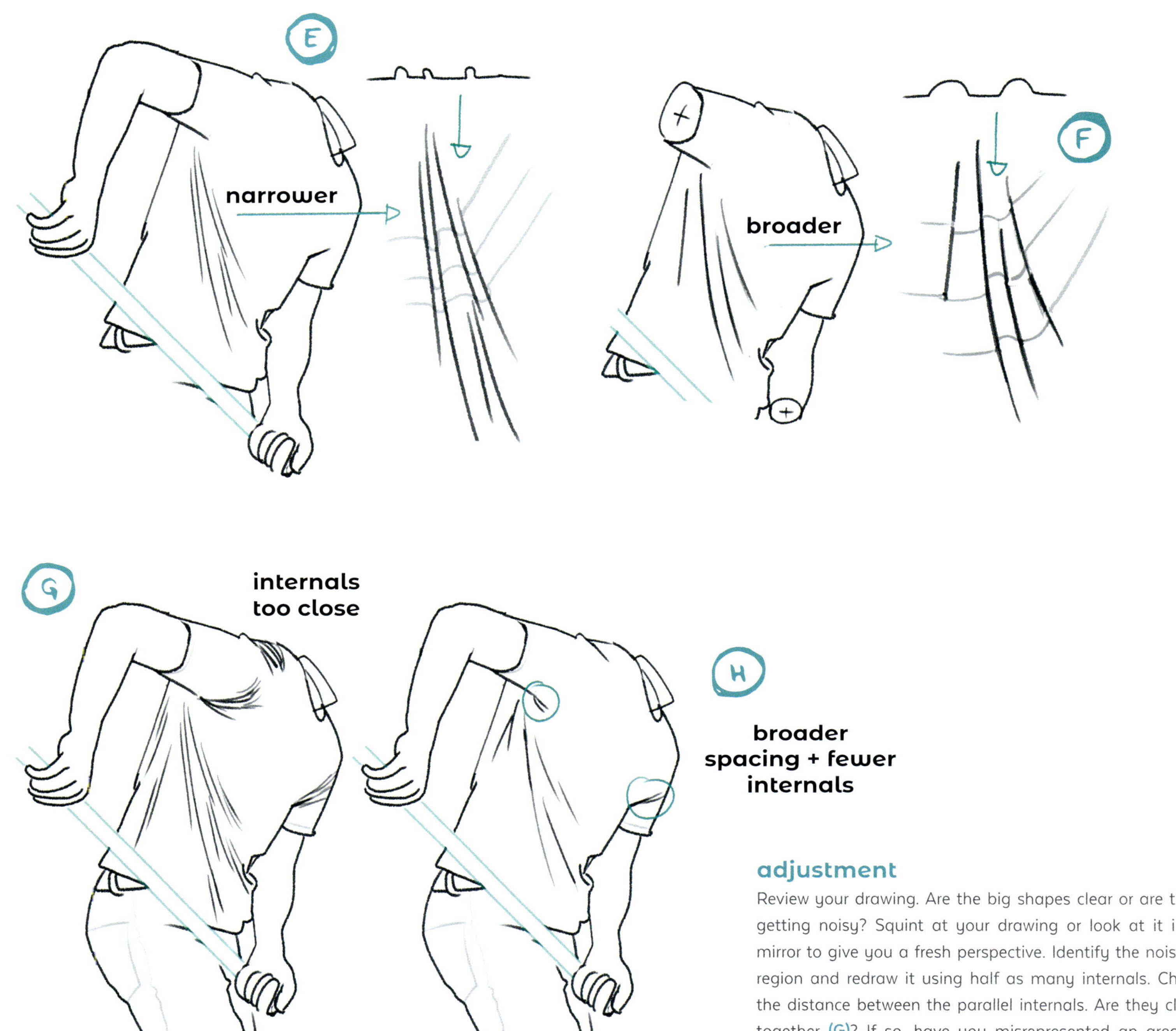

adjustment

Review your drawing. Are the big shapes clear or are they getting noisy? Squint at your drawing or look at it in a mirror to give you a fresh perspective. Identify the noisiest region and redraw it using half as many internals. Check the distance between the parallel internals. Are they close together (G)? If so, have you misrepresented an area of shallow and broad folds? Have you reserved only a few regions for this close folding, or do you need to remove a few (H)?

contours & hidden contours

Contour lines wrap the subject and help indicate the orientation of the surfaces (A). They can greatly improve clarity and help to explain volume, if they're not overused (B). We normally don't want to make our drawings look like 3D meshes, except for explanatory purposes, like some of the examples in this book (C)! Therefore, when we draw contours, we must do it sneakily. Where possible, disguise them as natural, everyday clothing elements – anything that already wraps the surface of the garment. Think waistbands, cuffs, zips, seams, and graphics. These are **hidden contours**. They describe the surfaces of the form, but don't look like they've been drawn exclusively to do that.

Graphics can be particularly helpful because they are usually found in places where seams aren't located. They're also often symmetrical, which makes it easier to draw them in perspective (D).

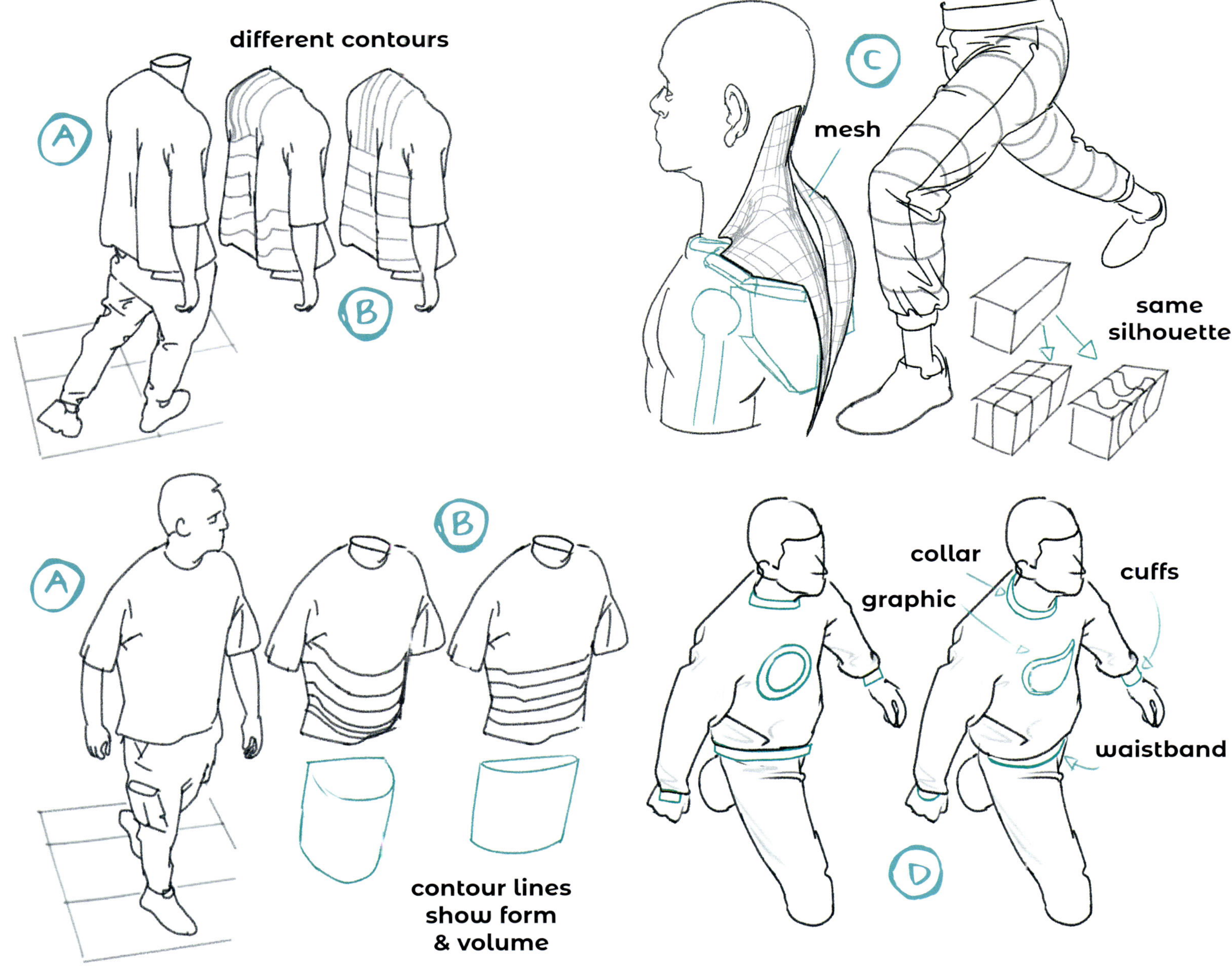

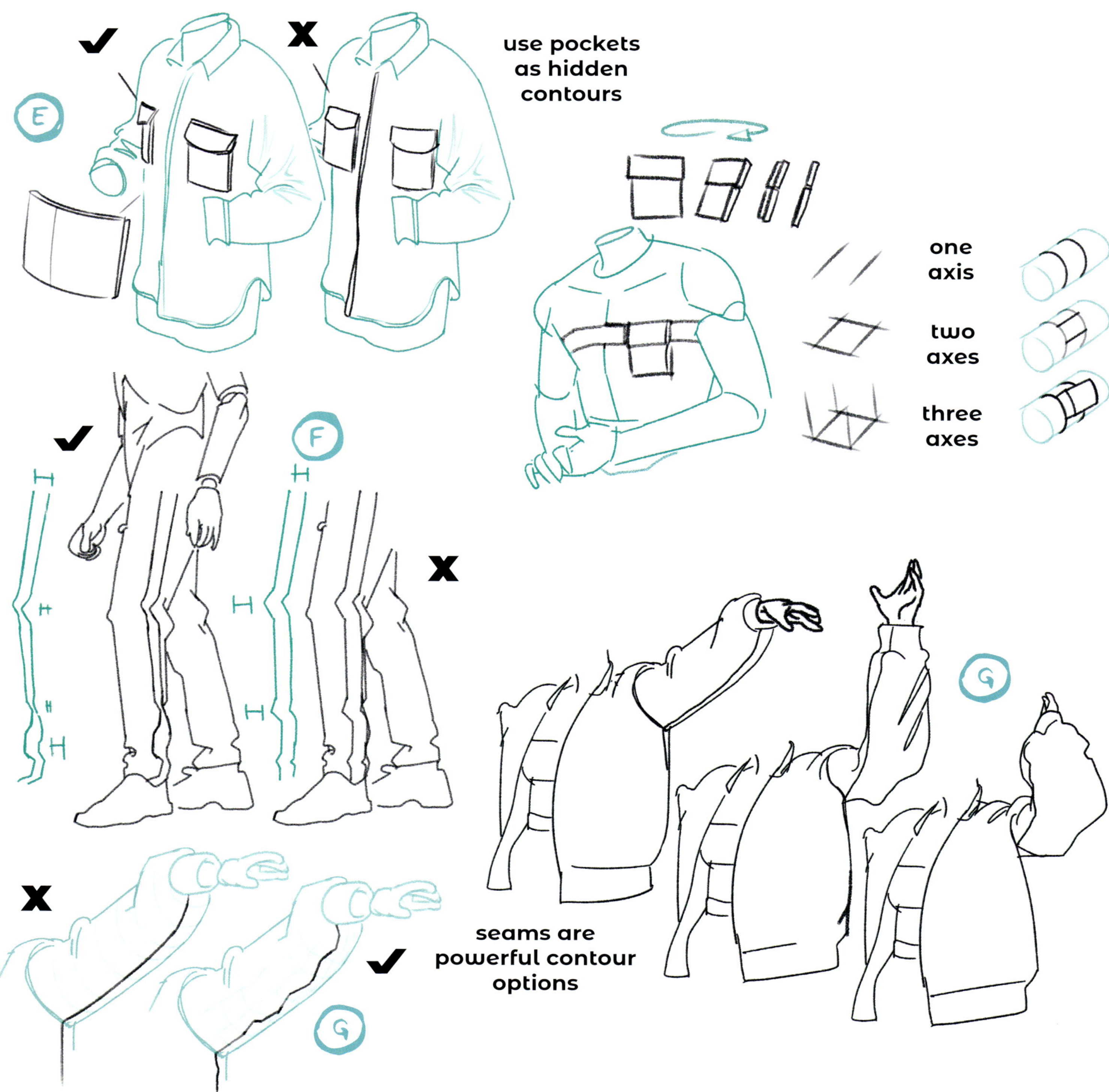

Pockets are also useful as hidden contours (E). Due to their size, shape, and the fact that they have two or three axes' worth of information, they can demonstrate surface orientation clearly.

Pay careful attention to any parallel lines on graphics. They might be parallel when laid flat on the pattern but, when seen in perspective, as the orientation of the surface changes, they will constantly move closer and further apart (F).

Seams are powerful hidden contours, but don't draw every seam or you'll create too much noise. Instead, focus on adding just one to three well-chosen seams.

Also, don't rush them! It's a common mistake to draw a fast, confident line where a seams sits (G), which implies that the seam is on a smooth, consistent surface. However, as we've seen, the surface of a garment is more commonly covered in shallow, broad folds. A smooth line wouldn't describe this surface well.

Most of the time, the contours on the surface of your drapery will be long, continuous lines (H) – particularly when the folds are broad and shallow, as most folds are. In this case, the planes are turning, but only on quite gentle angles relative to each other (I). However, this isn't *always* the case. Sometimes fabric will fold more sharply and deeply, and will wrap around under itself (J). When this happens, you'll have to resist the urge to draw a continuous line (K), and instead draw the same line 'offset' from itself (L). The line will break, then reappear again somewhere else. You probably won't need to draw this many times on a single clothed character, but if you can confidently offset your contours you'll add a lot of believability to those deeper folds.

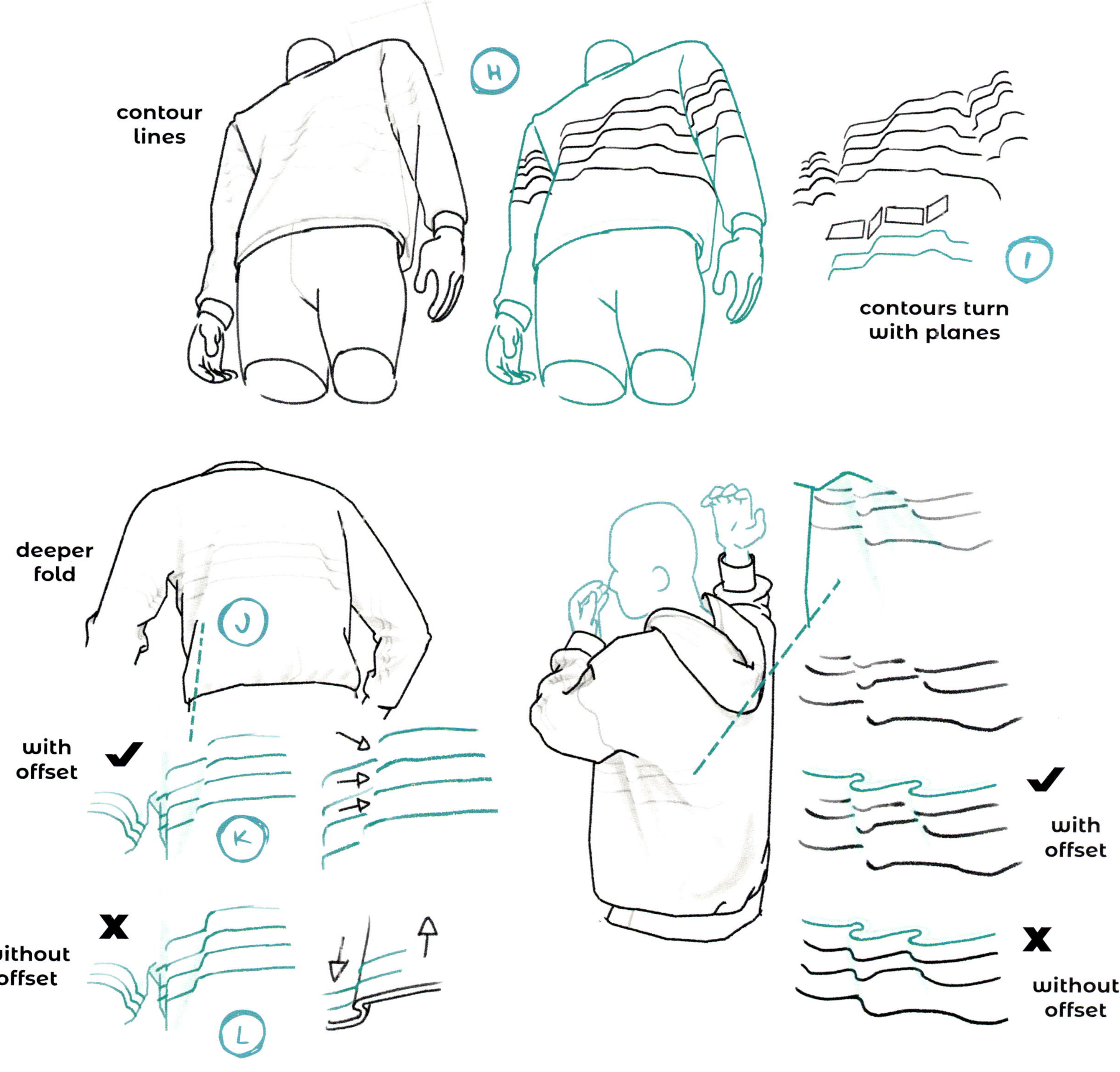

Seams are effective hidden contours because they describe both the surface and the twist. Practise 'pinning' your seams to the mannequin's wrists. In reality, cuffs can rotate slightly around the wrist, but for the sake of simplicity, imagine they're attached to the inner wrist by a pin (M). To draw a twisting arm, draw the silhouette (N), then the seam connecting the armpit to the inside of the wrist (O). This should help you visualize the drapery. Next, add the folds (P).

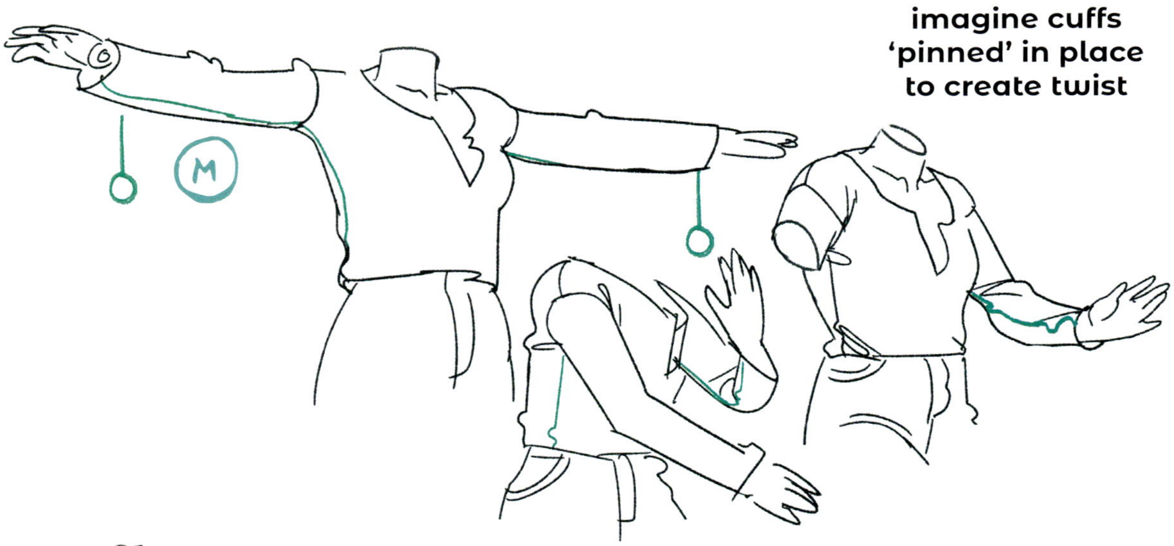

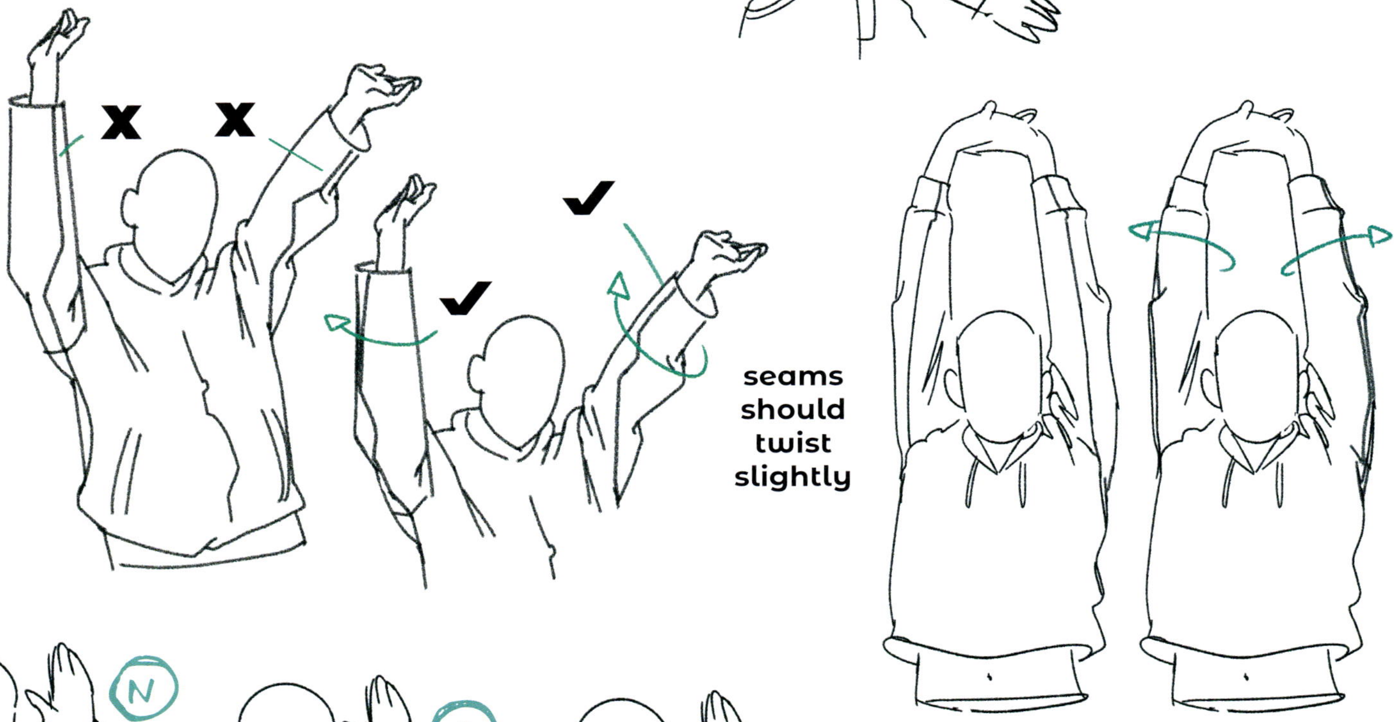

M

imagine cuffs 'pinned' in place to create twist

seams should twist slightly

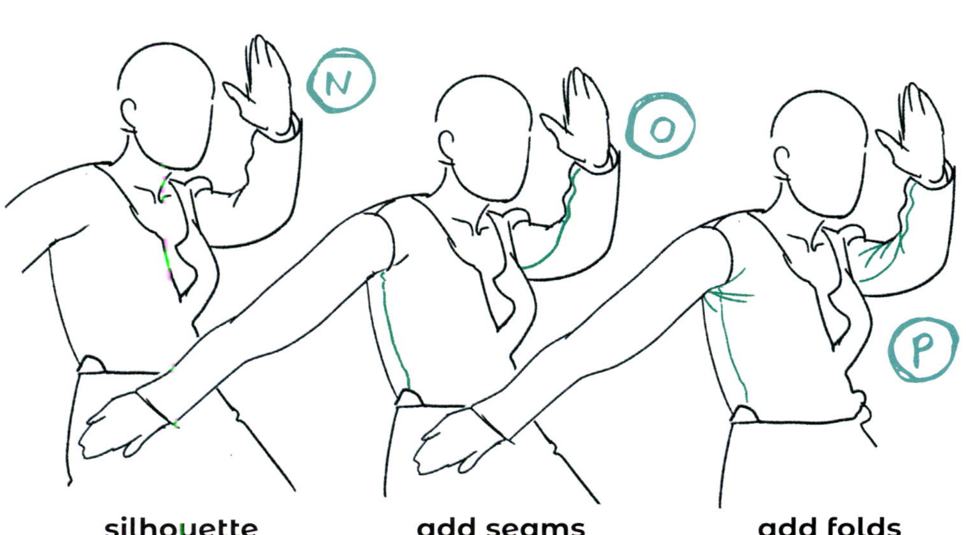

adjustment

Review your drawing. Have you included any hidden contours? Are there too many or too few? Are they making your drawing noisy? Have you pinned the seams to the wrist? Have you drawn contours too quickly and confidently – do you need to go back and add some variety into how you've drawn them? Check your drawing over for any examples of offset contours. If you don't have any, try to find at least one place where the fabric folds back upon itself, and add them in.

line pressure & curves vs straights

Perceptive readers will notice a pattern to the drawing examples in this book: with some exceptions, solid black lines are reserved for the silhouette and the major shapes. Lighter lines are used for the hidden contours and internals. This preserves the silhouette and helps to stop the internals from making the drawing noisy (A). This allows you to add more lines, which is sometimes necessary to explain a concept. If you squint, the drawing should still read. Give it a try.

Include a mix of curved and straight lines in your drawing – it's another way to add variety. I also find it helpful to keep the silhouette slightly more angular, and the internals and hidden contours slightly curved. The more angular lines encourage you to commit to your decisions and to focus on the bigger shapes. By contrast, the curving internals describe the roundedness of the form more clearly (B). As the majority of surfaces on a clothed figure are gently folding, curves are more suited to the interior.

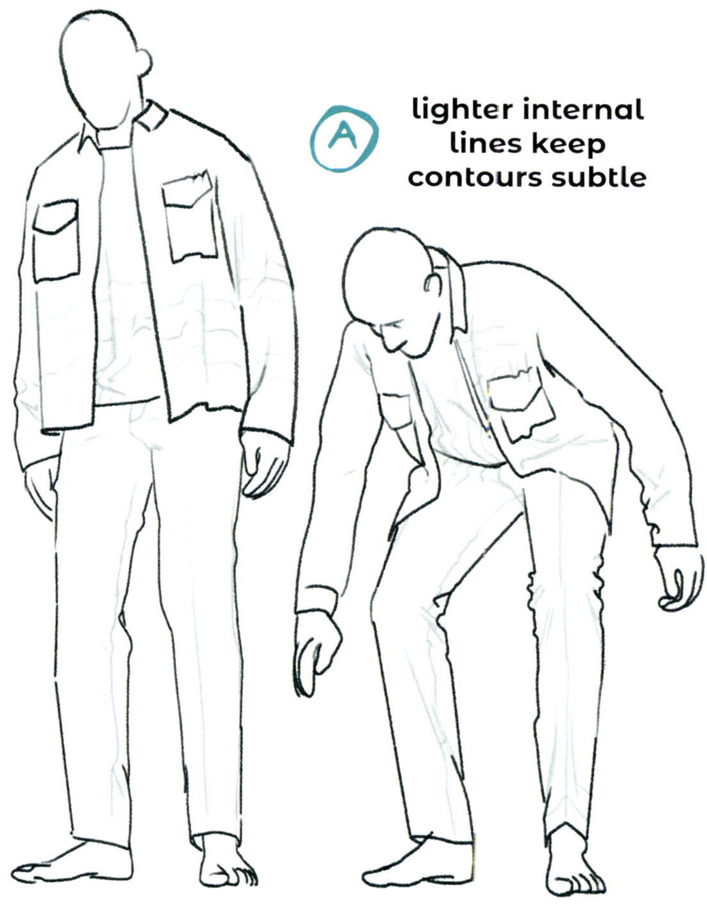

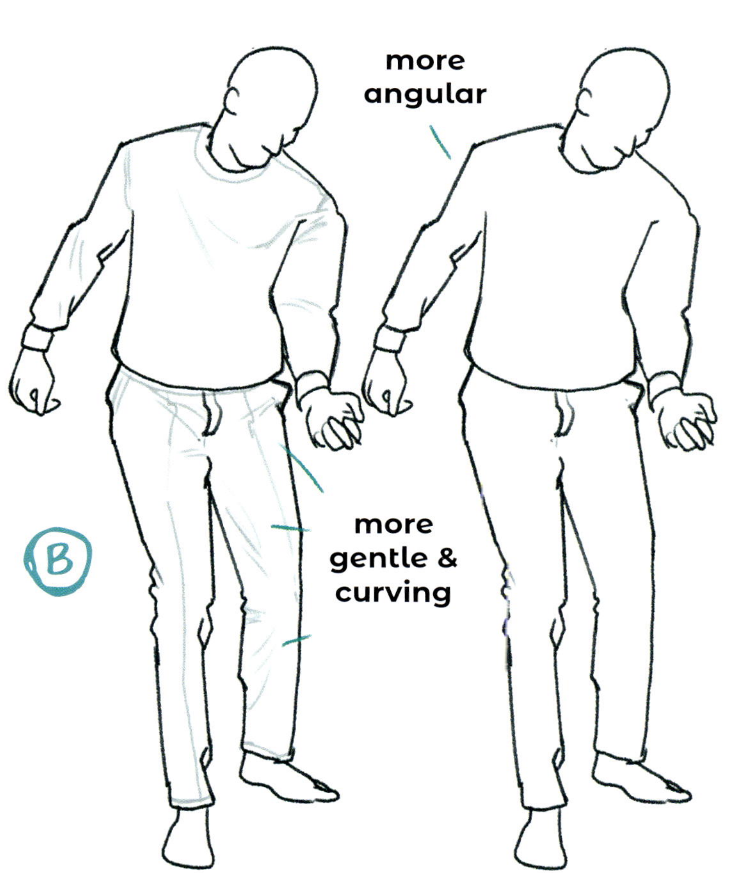

adjustment

Check your drawing for line pressure. Have you reserved the darkest lines for the silhouette and secondary silhouette? Have you kept the internals lighter, to preserve the big shapes? Have you used slightly more angular lines for the outer lines, and slightly curved lines for the internals and hidden contours? Redraw your priority region doing just this.

volume

Every shape within a drawing has a level of 'volume', which is how 3D it appears. Some shapes appear flat (low volume) (A) and some appear very 3D (high volume) (B). Don't assume that 'more volume = better'. It's often effective to keep some shapes low-volume to emphasize the higher-volume shapes (C). This provides a focal point and saves you time in situations where it's impractical to draw everything at a high level of volume.

To add volume, first taper a flat shape towards one or two vanishing points (labelled 'VP' on the right). When you've done this, the drawing will already look less flat. To clarify the taper, establish some common 'reference points' on either side of the figure (D). Next, add overlaps to your secondary silhouette that reinforce the taper. Z-lines help with this. Keep internals to a minimum (E).

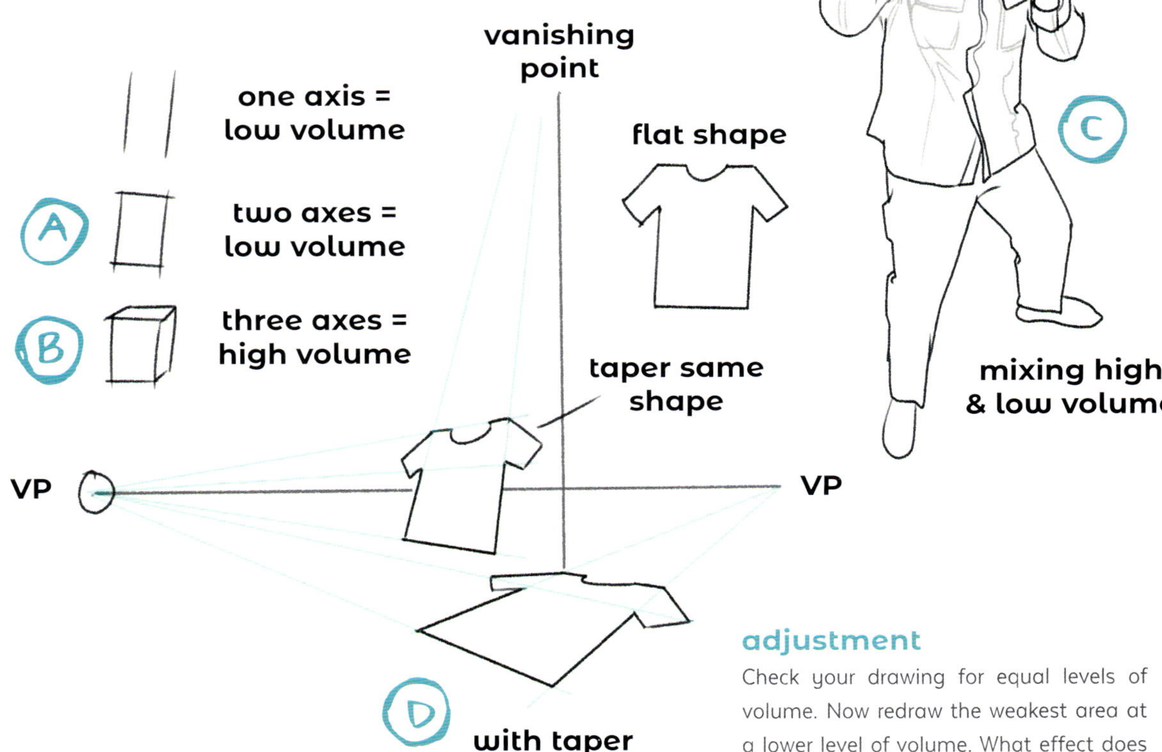

adjustment

Check your drawing for equal levels of volume. Now redraw the weakest area at a lower level of volume. What effect does this have? Has it made it easier to see the errors? Has it forced you to focus on the silhouette and the taper?

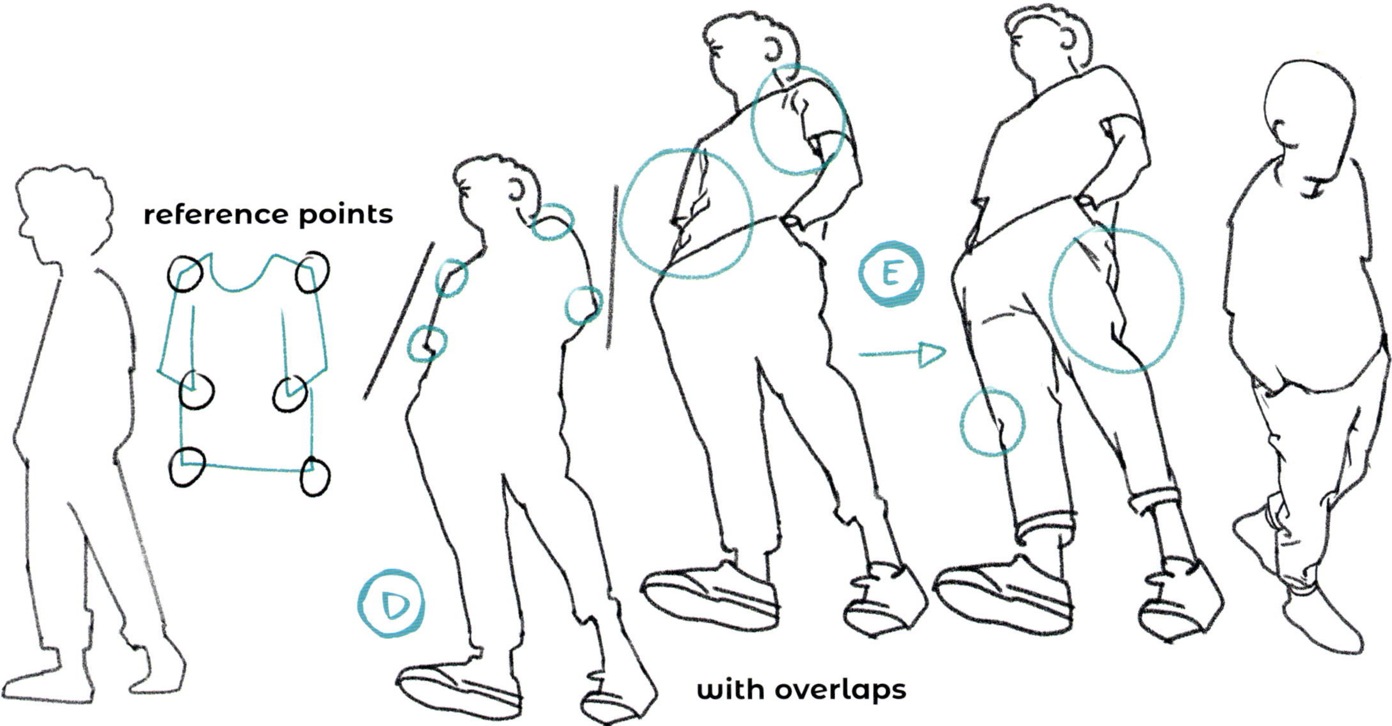

viewing angle

Your whole drawing, and each area within it, sends a message to the viewer. Something like, 'You're looking down at this,' or 'You're looking up at this.' Each area should communicate the same message and agree with the other areas. If one area says you're looking down, but the others say you're looking up, viewers will be confused (A). We must make these messages agree. Artists often try using a perspective grid to do this. However, this doesn't actually get these areas to agree; the grid just powerfully broadcasts the single message, 'You're looking up at this!' This might help to hide some of the disagreements in the drawing, but it doesn't resolve them (B). Ideally, the drawing shouldn't need a perspective grid – the viewing angle should be clear without it.

The first (and most underused) way to clarify viewing angle is to use **size difference**. Here, areas of this drawing have been resized (C). That's all, but it has changed our perception of the viewing angle. The second way to clarify viewing angle is to add an element of taper towards one or two vanishing points. Here, I've combined taper with subtle size differences (D). Again, nothing has been redrawn, and yet our perception of the viewing angle has changed. Taper and size adjustment do most of the work.

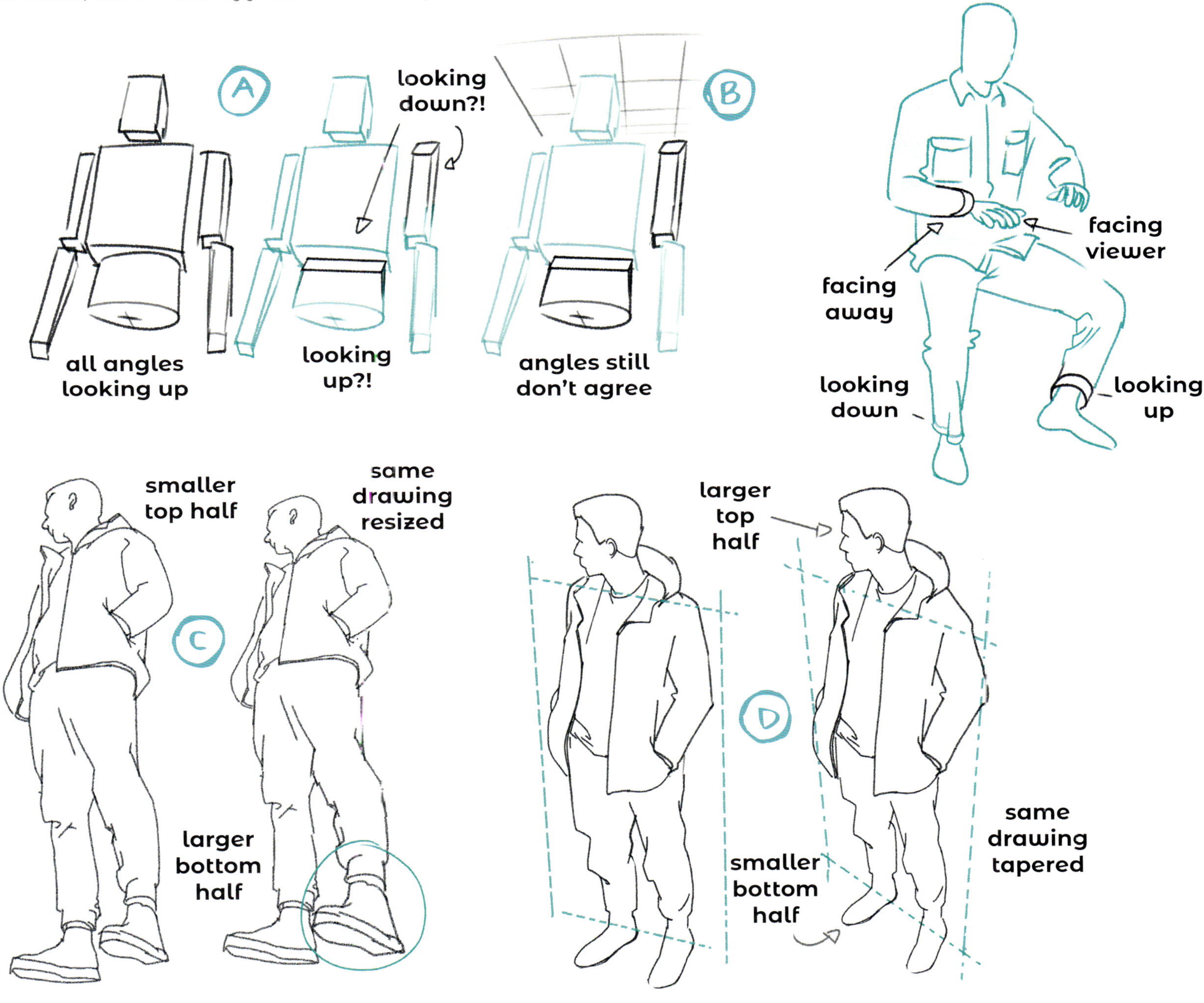

The third way to clarify viewing angle is to emphasize or add clothing elements with clearly orientated surfaces. These are any elements with clear planes, such as pockets, the tops of shoes, elasticated regions, and lapels (E). We can even add some bunching if it helps indicate the viewing angle.

The fourth and final way to clarify the viewing angle is to ensure that the secondary silhouette's overlaps – particularly the Z-lines – agree with the overall perspective (F).

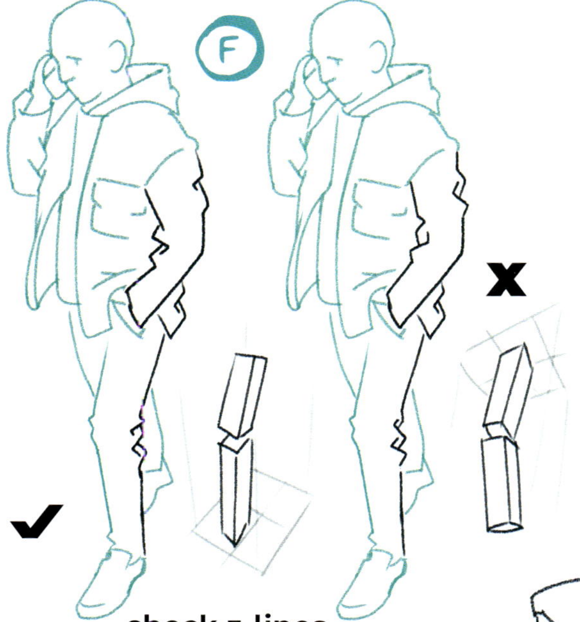

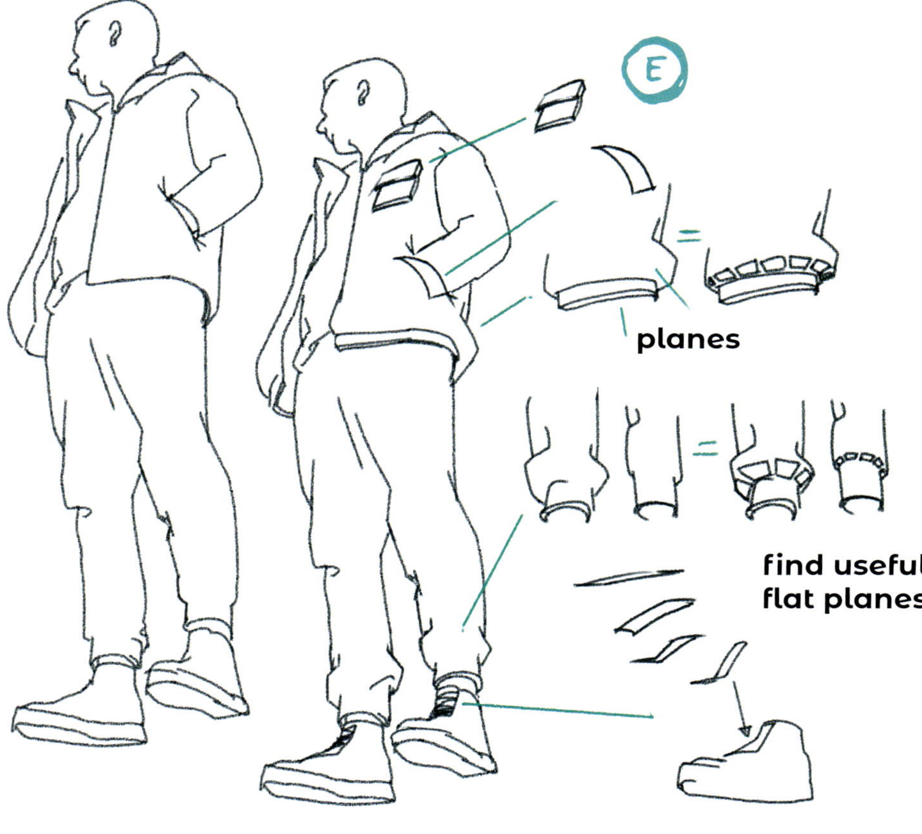

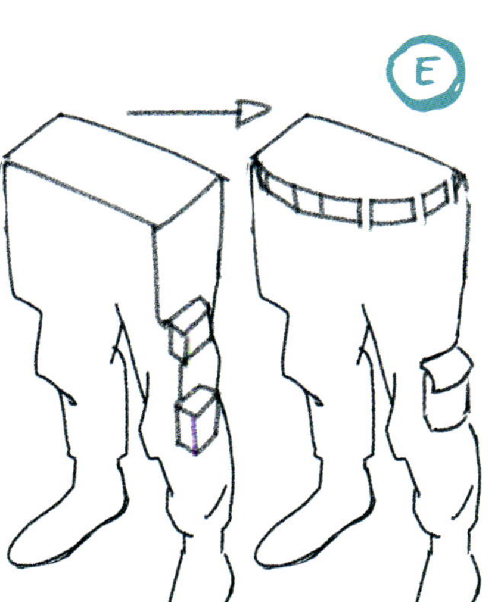

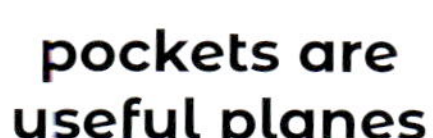

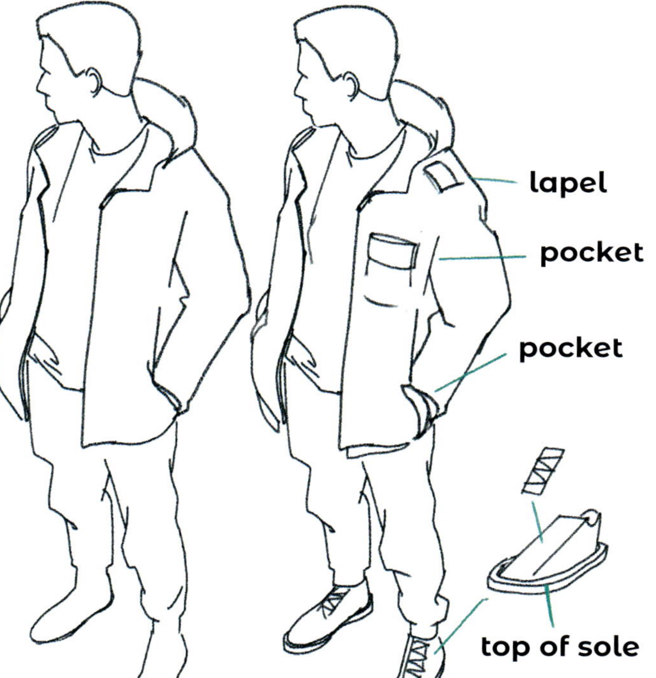

adjustment

Look for areas of your drawing that don't broadcast the same message about the viewing angle. Why do you think this is? Is the size difference correct? Does the character taper towards any vanishing points and, if so, do the areas agree? Can you clarify the viewing angle by clarifying the orientation of surfaces? Finally, can you redraw any disagreeing areas so that the Z-lines suggest the correct viewing angle?

unifying lines

Try drawing unified lines to replace collections of shorter, more 'feathery' lines. With these unifying lines, you make the key overlaps your priority. This adjustment is particularly effective when you're dissatisfied with the silhouette or secondary silhouette (A). It also helps you in another way: because the unified lines are continuous, they indicate confidence in your drawing abilities, which the viewer will find appealing.

Select a limb of your character that you'd like to adjust. Now draw the whole length of the limb using only two lines: **1** and **2** (B). Don't worry too much about getting them perfect. Now adjust the secondary silhouette of each line to include a maximum of two overlaps (C). This helps you prioritize only the most important information.

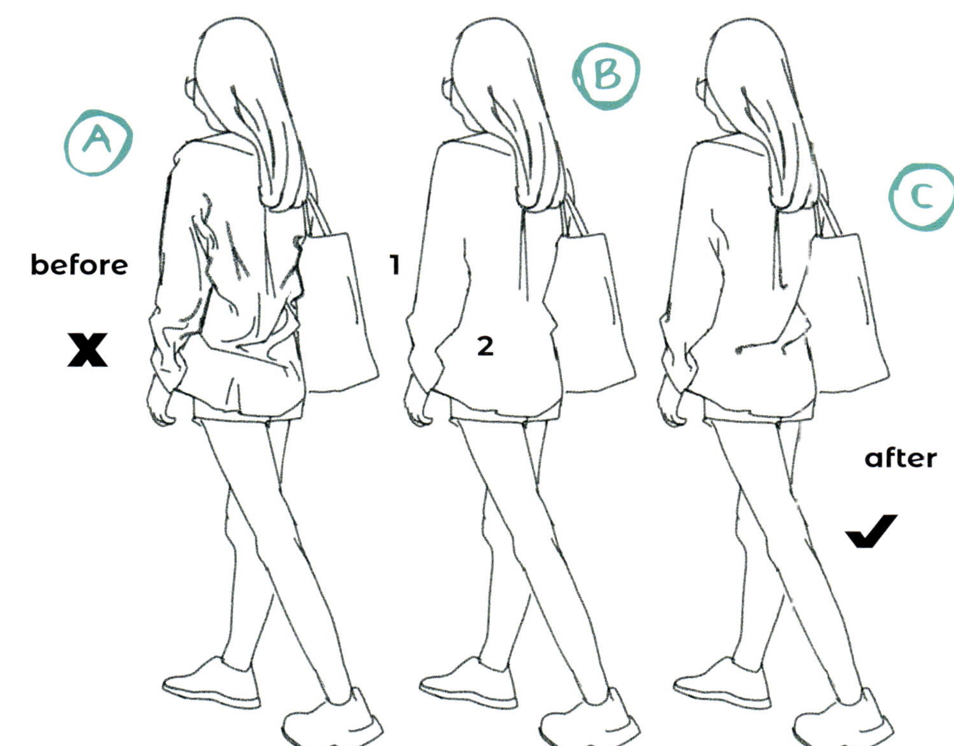

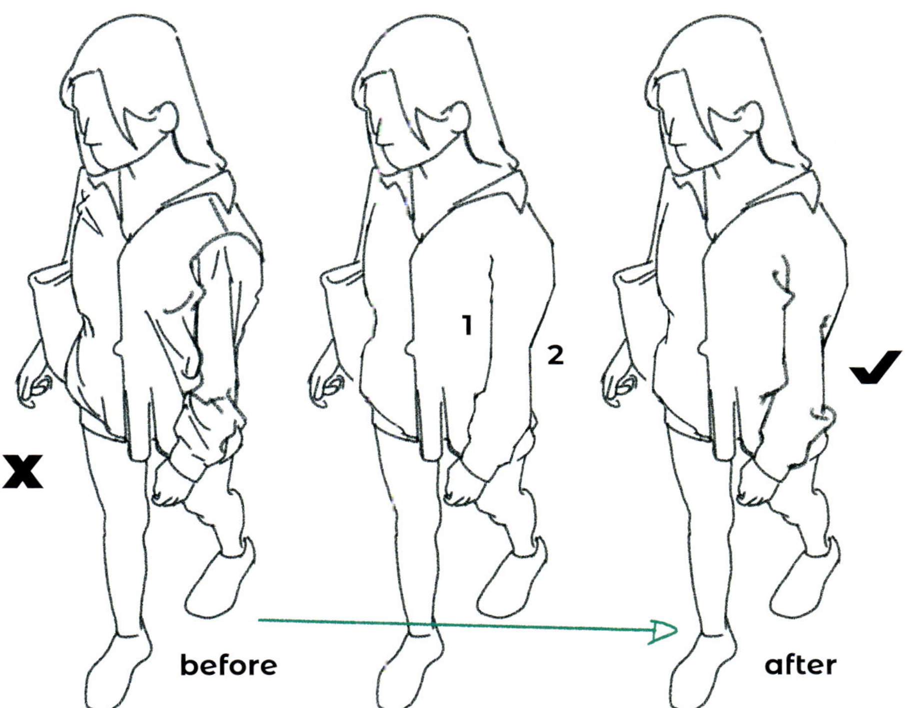

adjustment

Review your drawing, looking for opportunities to use a unifying line. Look for anywhere with 'feathery' lines, confused overlaps, or too much noise. Redraw the priority area with a single pair of lines, followed by a maximum of two overlaps in the secondary silhouette.

fold variety

Drapery that has believable 3D form is important, but making the drawing appealing is also important. A drawing can be 'realistic' but not visually satisfying. The world is full of visual variety, so we should aim to include variety in the composition of our drapery. To do this, we look for common mistakes that appear in the form of patterns, and then we replace them. These mistakes include: folds of equal horizontal or vertical length (A), parallel lines (B), tangents, repetitive lengths between overlaps and repetitive angles of those overlaps (C), and symmetry on either side of the centre line (either in the number of lines or in the distribution of folds) (D).

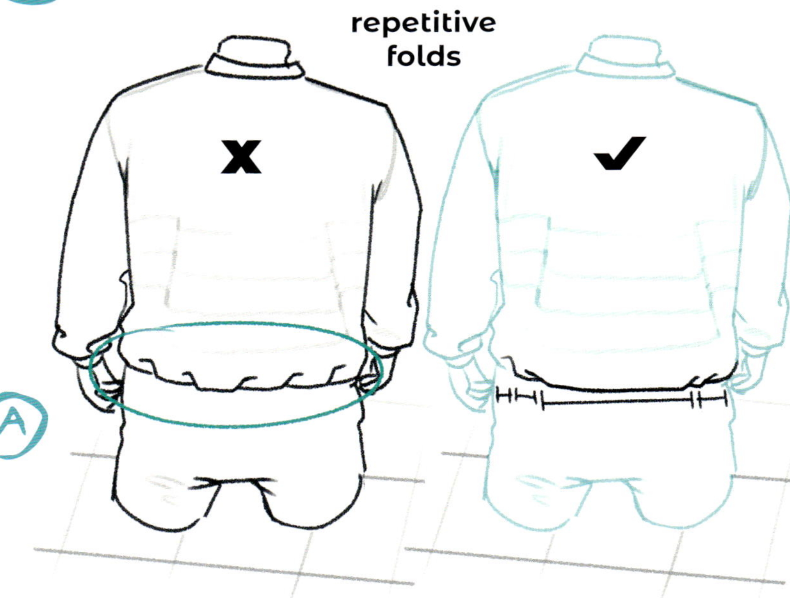

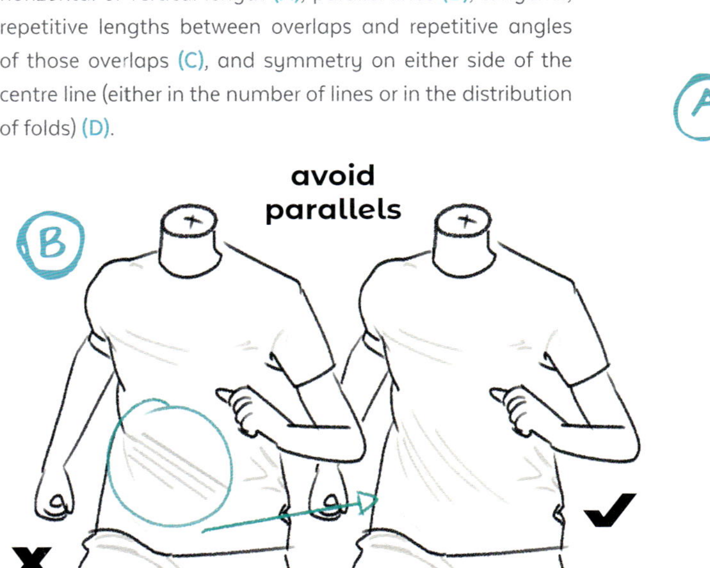

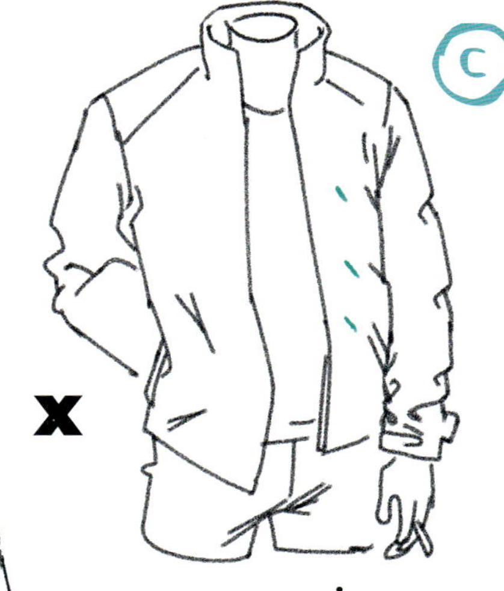
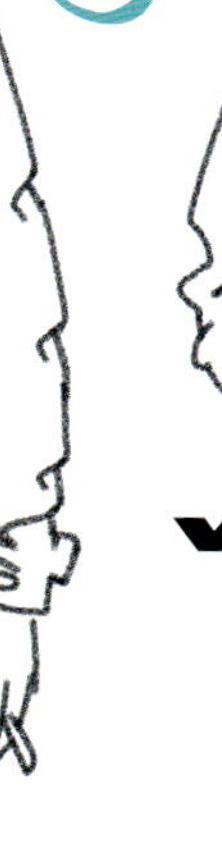

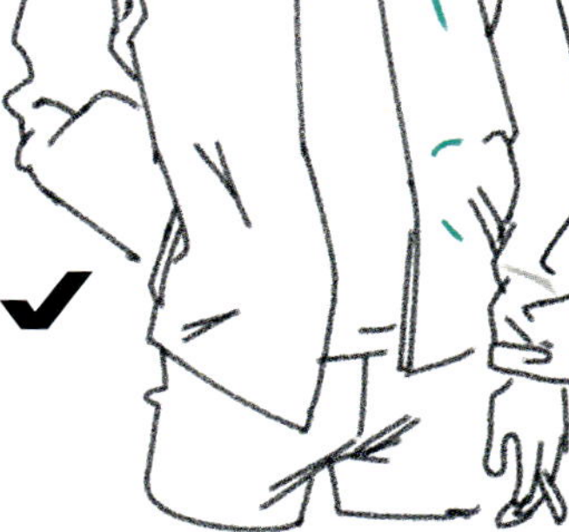

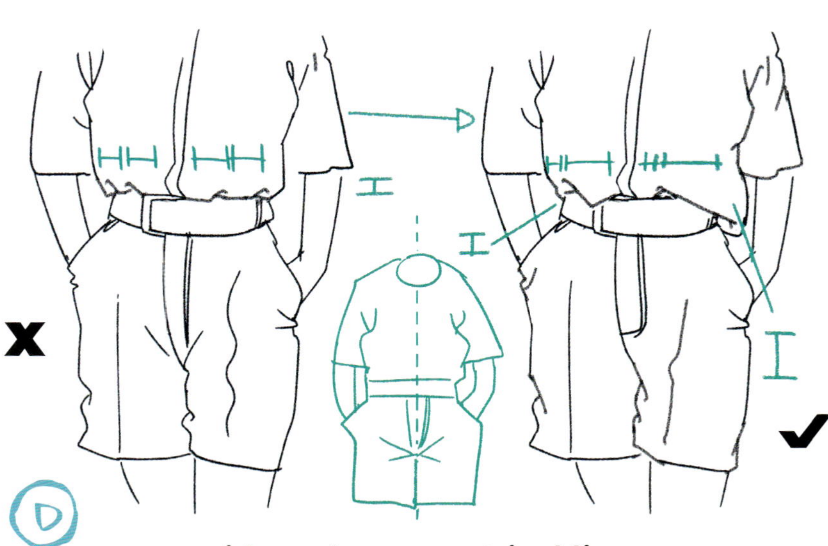

adjustment

Review your drawing, looking for the priority areas with any of these commonly seen patterns that reduce variety. If any are found, redraw those areas.

fold grouping

Grouping folds is one way to add some design to your work. Try experimenting with different groupings and observe the effect it has on your drapery. Here are some things to try: having a 'complex' and a 'simple' side of the silhouette (A); separating shapes into thirds, with folds condensed into one or two regions (B); and grouping folds into a left/right split or a foreground/background split (C).

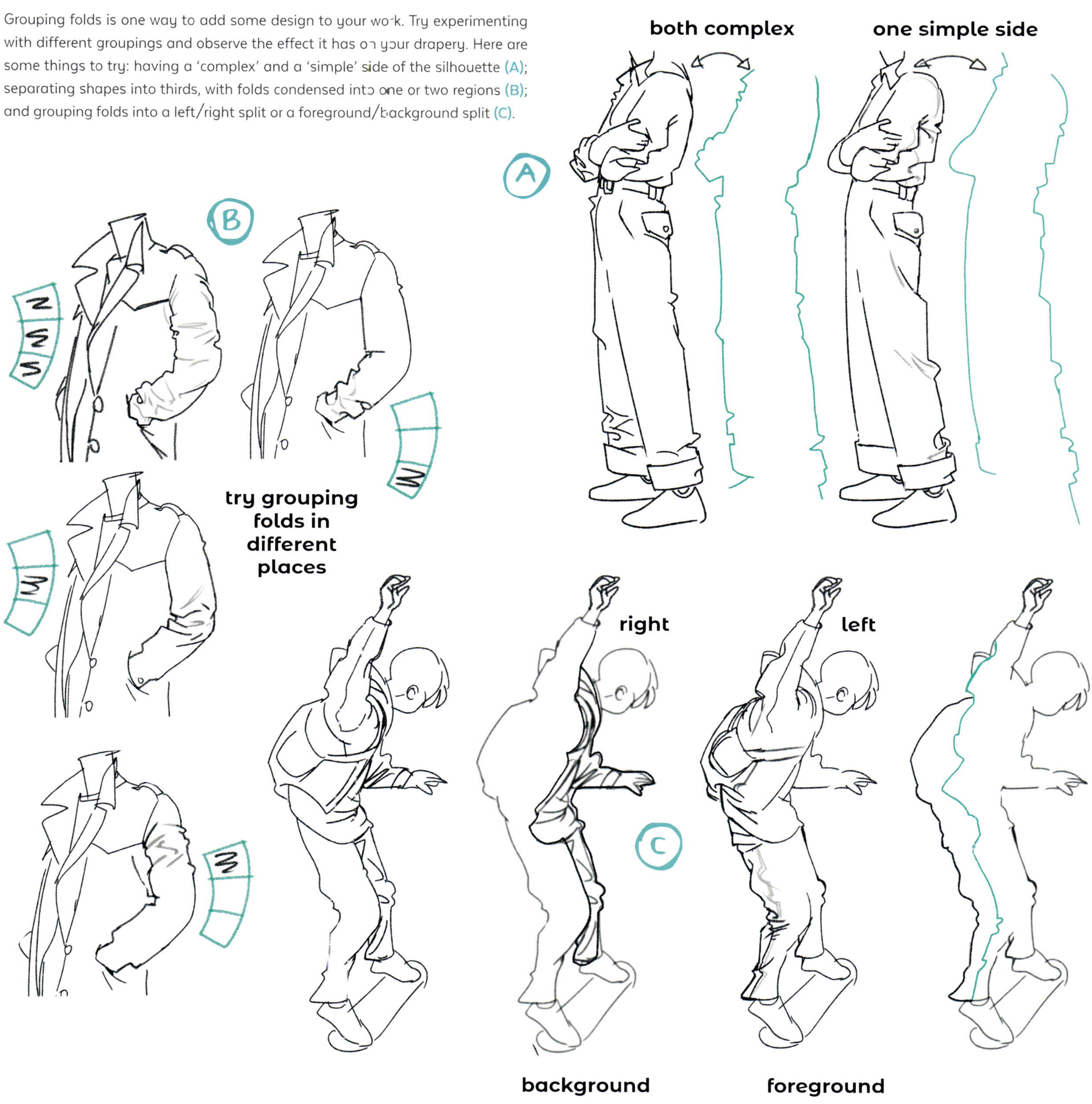

Try grouping folds to emphasize movement and momentum. First, create some quick thumbnails of your silhouette (D). On these, draw an arrow for the prevailing 'direction' in which the fabric is moving. Next, draw some indicated folds to plan where your main regions of folding will be. You can also use this method to analyse an existing drawing. Perhaps you have indicated drapery that has two directions. In this case, it might be worth consolidating the folds into a single direction.

The truth is, it's not really that important if the drawing is 'realistic'. It just needs to be believable. When grouping folds, the important thing is that the directions roughly agree – that they're consistent in their message (E). If they are, the viewer will probably assume the drapery is accurate.

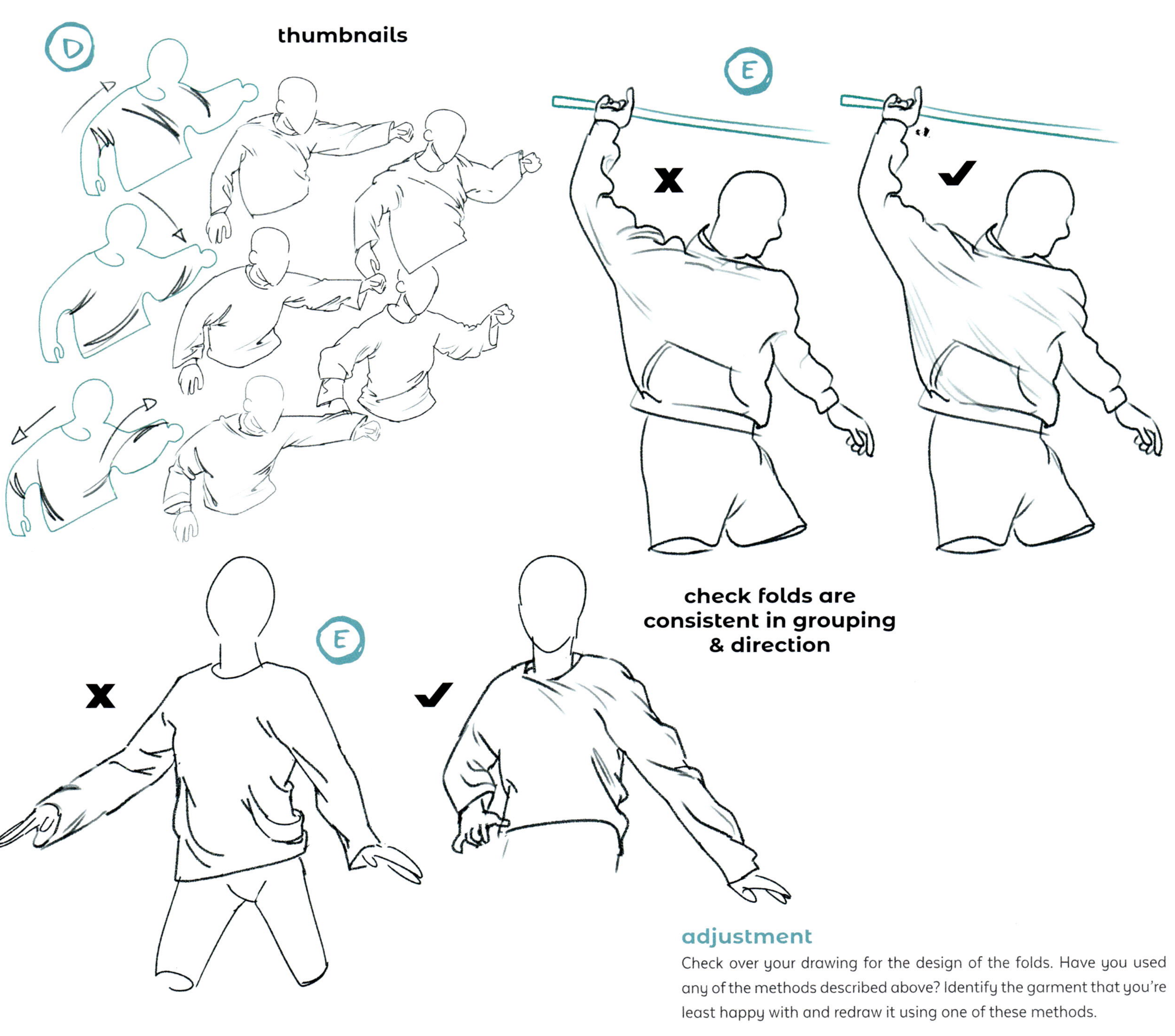

adjustment

Check over your drawing for the design of the folds. Have you used any of the methods described above? Identify the garment that you're least happy with and redraw it using one of these methods.

planes

Adding 'planes' is a very effective adjustment to help clarify your forms. This isn't adding 'lighting' in the normal sense, because that suggests relatively consistent lighting across the whole subject (A). We want something simpler. Instead, we can highlight just a few specific surfaces ('planes') by adding tone (B). You can also highlight these plane changes with contours (C), but combining the two is often the most efficient way to describe a plane (D). This is particularly effective when drawing a compressed fabric, where the planes alternate in the direction they face: **1**, **2**, **1**, **2**, and so on.

adjustment

To add planes, simply pick a direction and add tone to only those planes facing that direction (E). After a while, you'll notice that the shape of some planes often forms a 'sling' (F). Here are some baggy trousers where a lot of form is suggested by first adding triangles of tone, then adding just a couple of contours on top. To do this believably, you should always pay attention to what the contours are doing. If you put the triangles in the wrong places, it'll be much less effective.

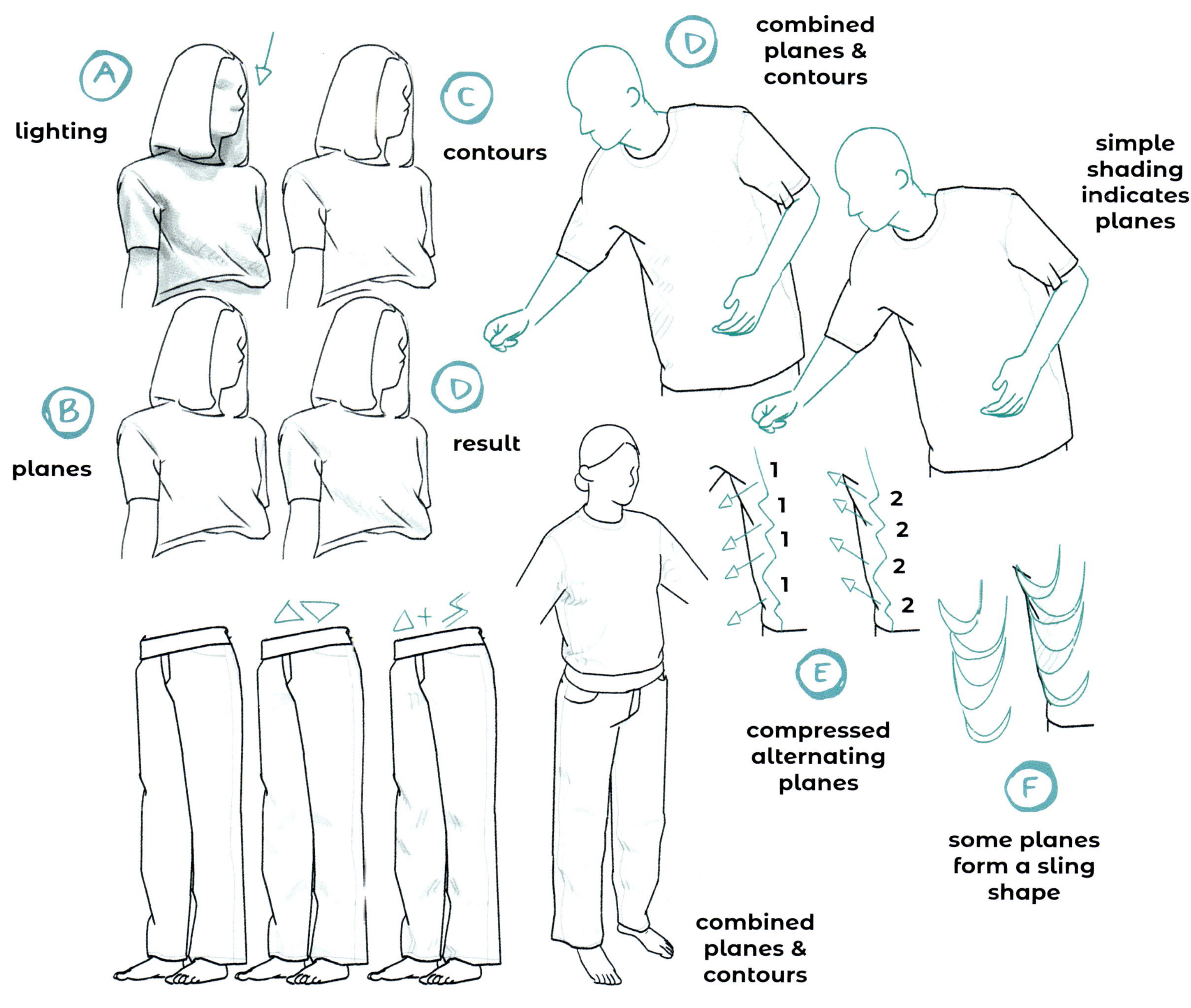

process

Now that we've covered all the adjustments, let's tie them together. I recommend using these as broad 'steps' in your clothing process. Obviously, it's very difficult to keep everything in mind at the same time – hence, a book of reminders – but it's worth giving it a go. Begin the drawing with the big decisions: thumbnails as options, then silhouette, then secondary silhouette, then hidden contours, and finally internals. In short, start 'zoomed out' and work from the outside inwards. We've covered many other adjustments so far, but this is the main process to remember. On top of this, insert the other adjustments where appropriate.

In practice, you won't work in such clear steps. You'll always jump around a bit, but try to generally work in this way. For example, it's fine to add the occasional internal line or hidden contour while working on the silhouette, but don't lose sight of the bigger process.

You might be working on one section of the secondary silhouette, then feel the urge to add in some seams as hidden contours. That's fine to do – just don't lose sight of the fact that you're focusing on the secondary silhouette right now.

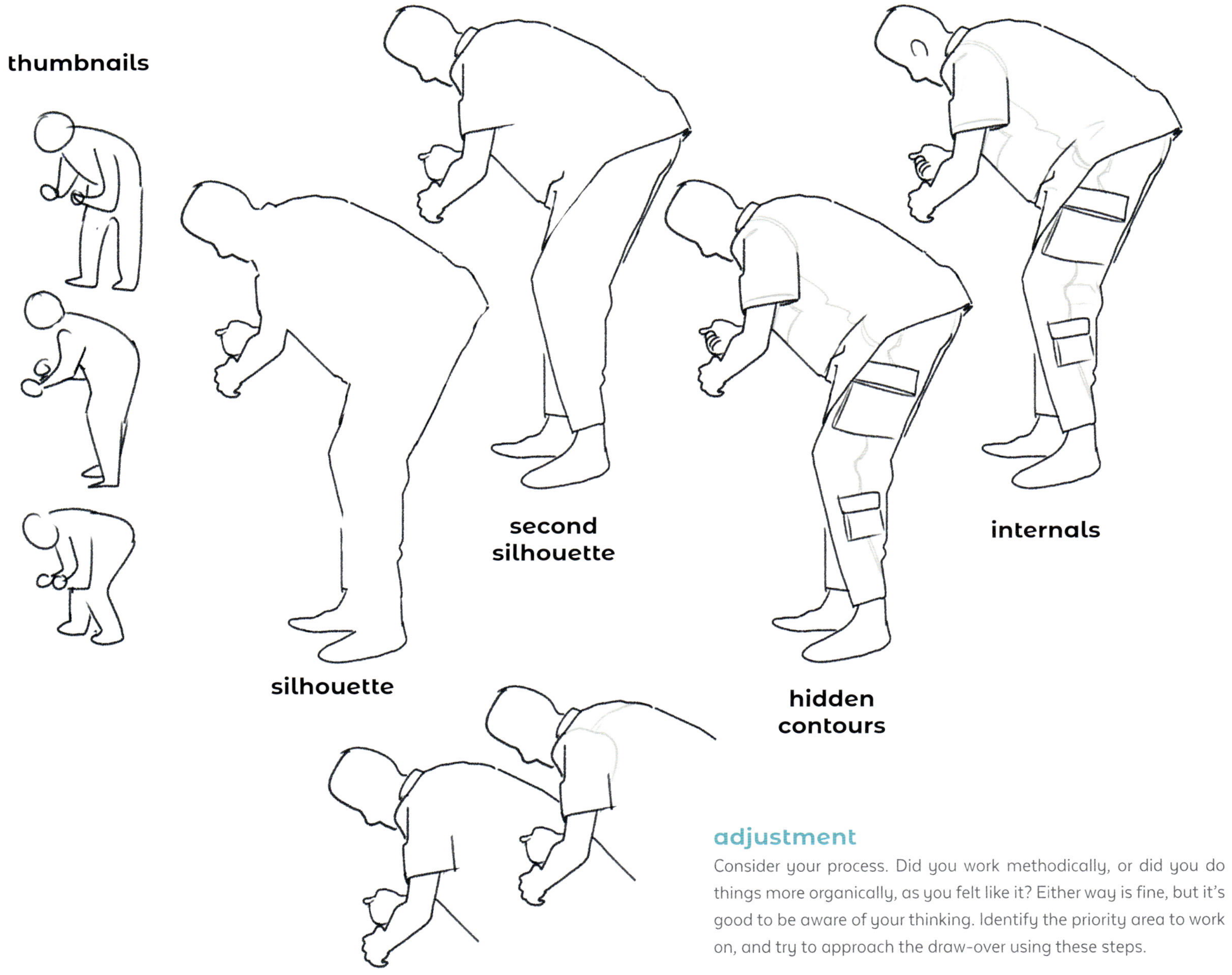

adjustment

Consider your process. Did you work methodically, or did you do things more organically, as you felt like it? Either way is fine, but it's good to be aware of your thinking. Identify the priority area to work on, and try to approach the draw-over using these steps.

clothing characters

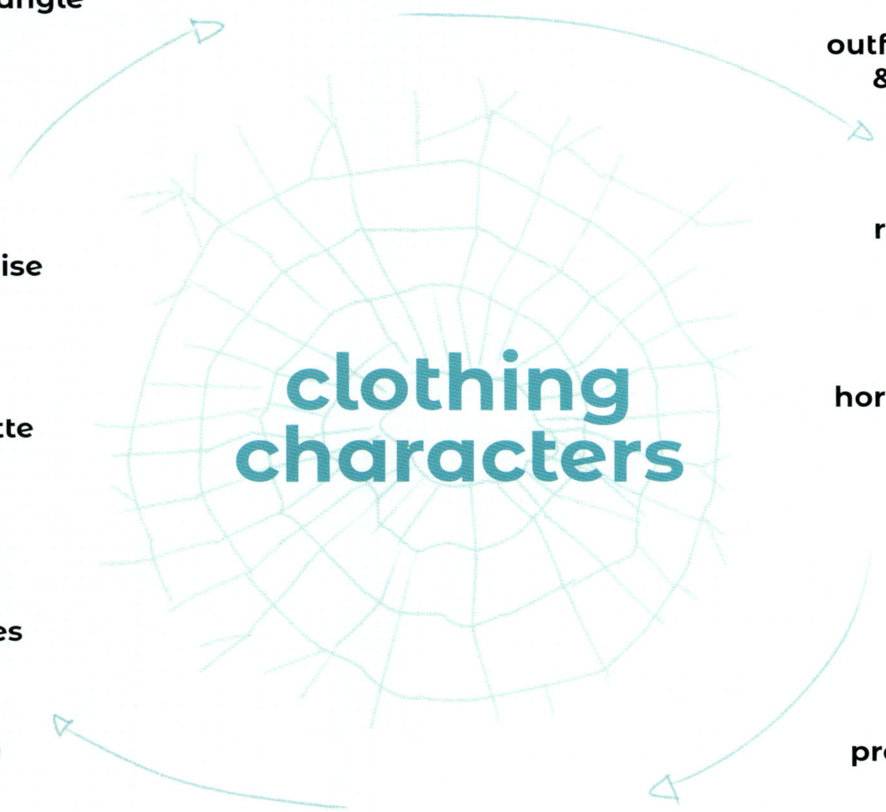

priority pyramid

areas, priorities, options & passes

fold grouping

snapshots

process

fewer lines

unifying lines

fold variety

stepping stones

curves vs straights

planes

viewing angle

volume

outfit, garment & pattern

line pressure

areas of support

contours & hidden contours

resistance

internals & noise

vertical bunching

secondary silhouette

horizontal bunching

pure silhouette

clarity

tube compression

fanning

micro-tails

fold depth

flow & z-lines

overlap

bending tubes

fold count & length

pressure

twisting

surface orientation

tension

staggered lines

high points

open & closed loops

90-degree surfaces

sharp transitions

indicate vs state

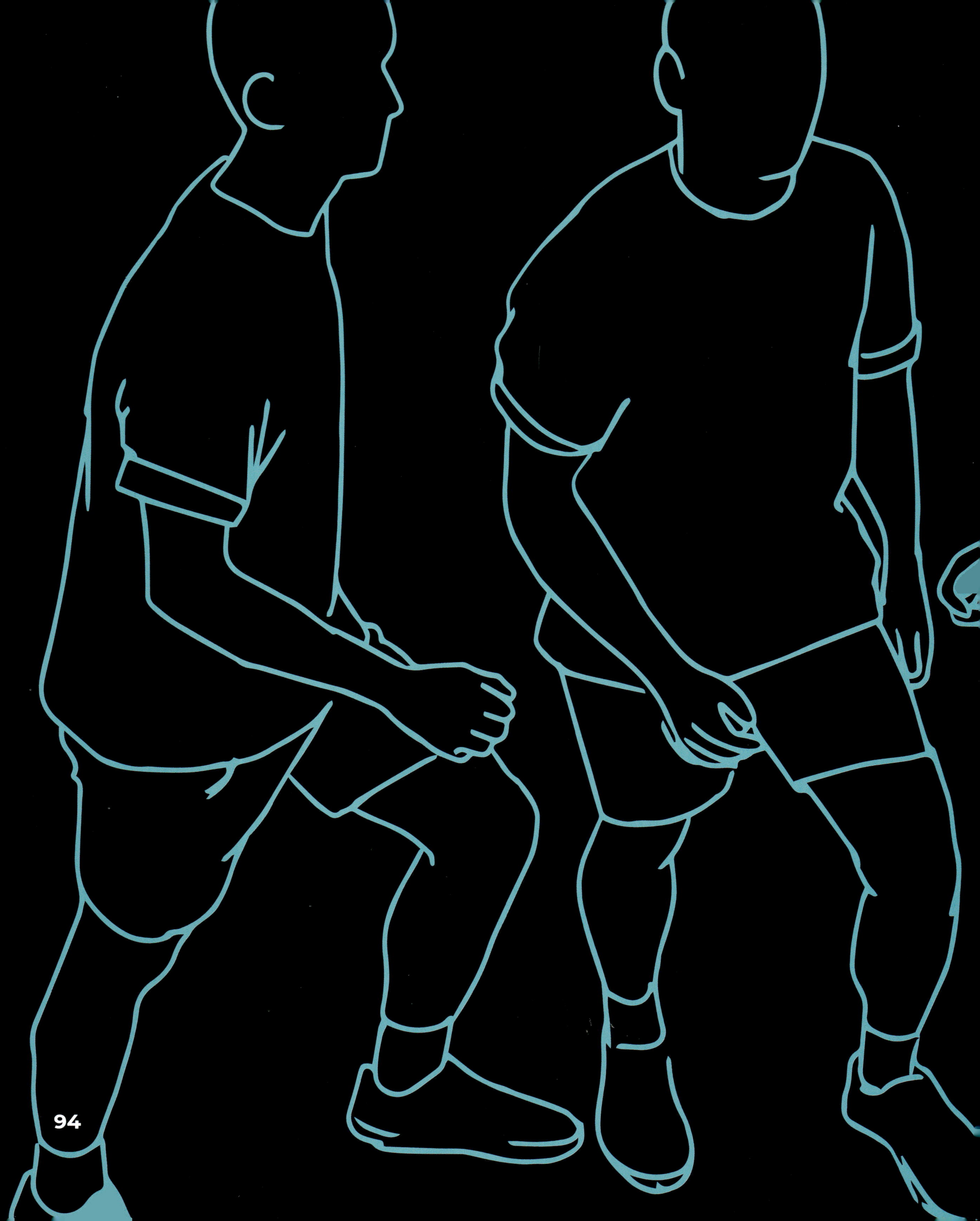

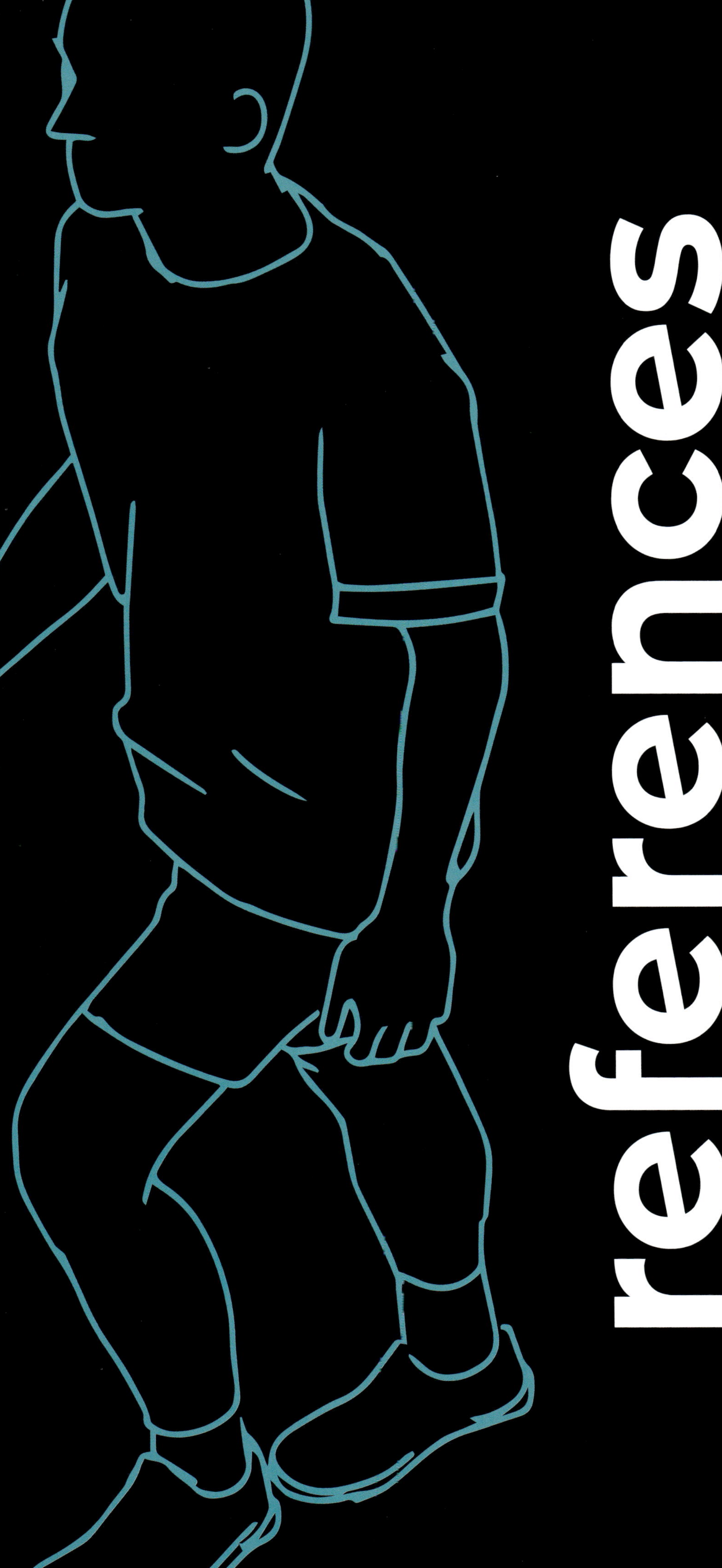

references

component parts 96

motions:

component parts

When using the reference drawings in this book, keep the idea of 'component parts' in mind. Each full-figure reference is a collection of smaller 'parts' (A). These parts themselves can often be separated into smaller parts (B). How does this help us? Well, rather than searching for the exact pose and outfit that you're drawing, look for components that resemble it, or that contain smaller specific components. Once you find these component parts, you can recombine them with other components to create a new figure. Mix and match, basically. There are over a thousand drawings in this book, so there are thousands of combinations available to you. Let's see some examples.

The simplest way to use components is to combine the upper and lower body of two references. In this case, the top and bottom halves of two different references have been combined (C). It's a very simple straight swap. The tiny green line, where one hand previously concealed the information, is the only 'welding' that was necessary to join these two parts (D).

Further below, the top and bottom halves of two different figures have been combined in another straight swap (E).

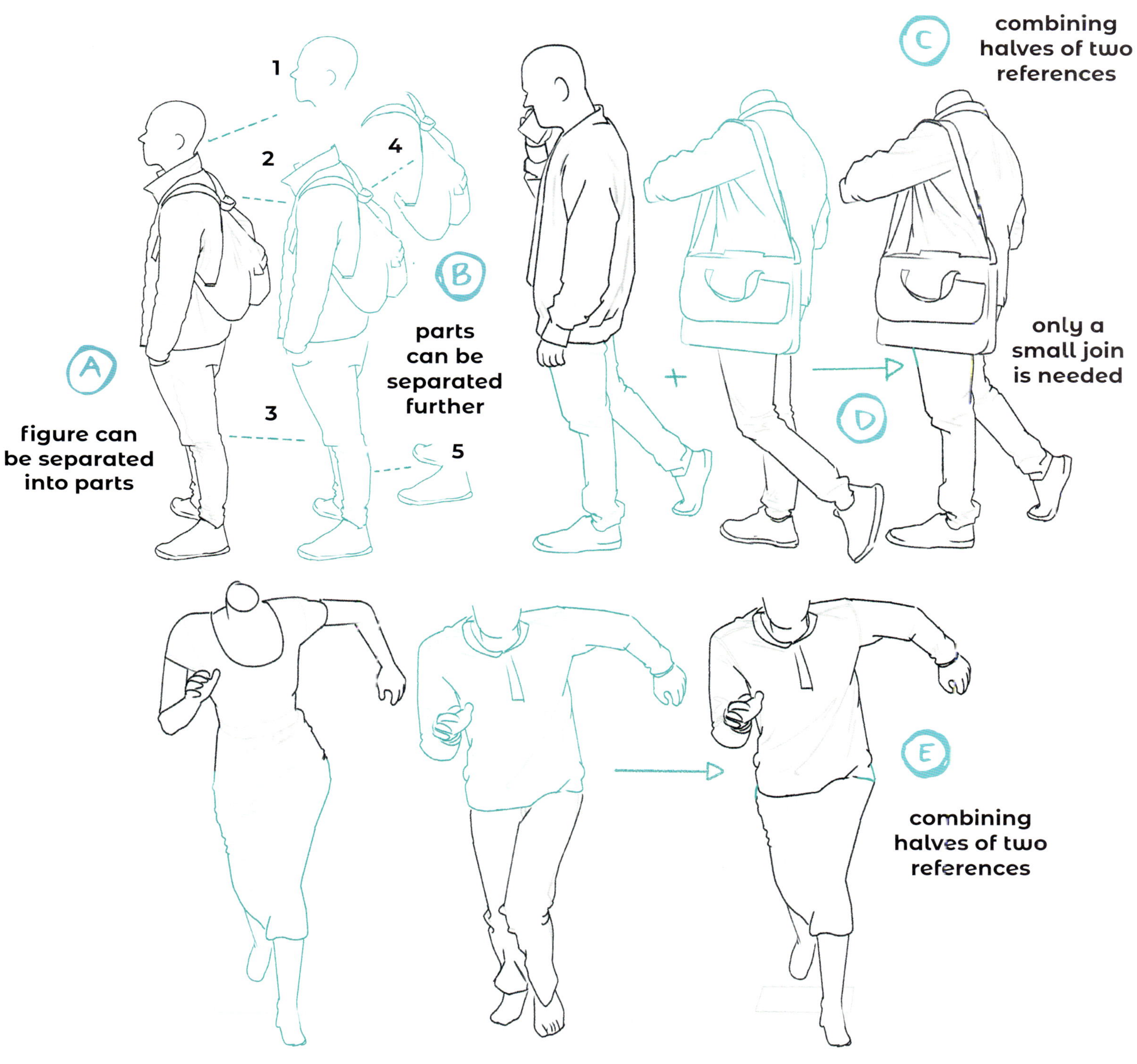

Once you can confidently combine two different halves, try combining smaller components, such as individual limbs. In this case, the 'welding' that joins the limb to the figure will be slightly trickier, and you'll probably have to adjust the pose slightly. However, most of the work is already done for you by using references. Here's an example. First, I wanted to swap this arm (A) for this one (B). To do so, I dropped the shoulder slightly to give a more natural pose (C). Next, I adjusted the legs and feet, as I thought they were a bit too grounded. I found a reference of a character wearing a tracksuit, with slightly raised feet. Although the tracksuit bottoms had a different fit to the chinos, there was enough information to help me redraw my character with chinos and raised heels (D). The final clothed character looks much more natural – a great example of using multiple components to assemble a clothed character.

It's important to remember: you often don't fully know what you want to draw until you see a partial reference for it. The references help you decide and inform the final drawing. When I began with character A, I didn't know I would end up with character E. I just knew that I wanted the figure to look more natural. This is the benefit of having a book of references nearby – to suggest ideas that you might like to incorporate into your drawing. The drawing evolves as you look through them.

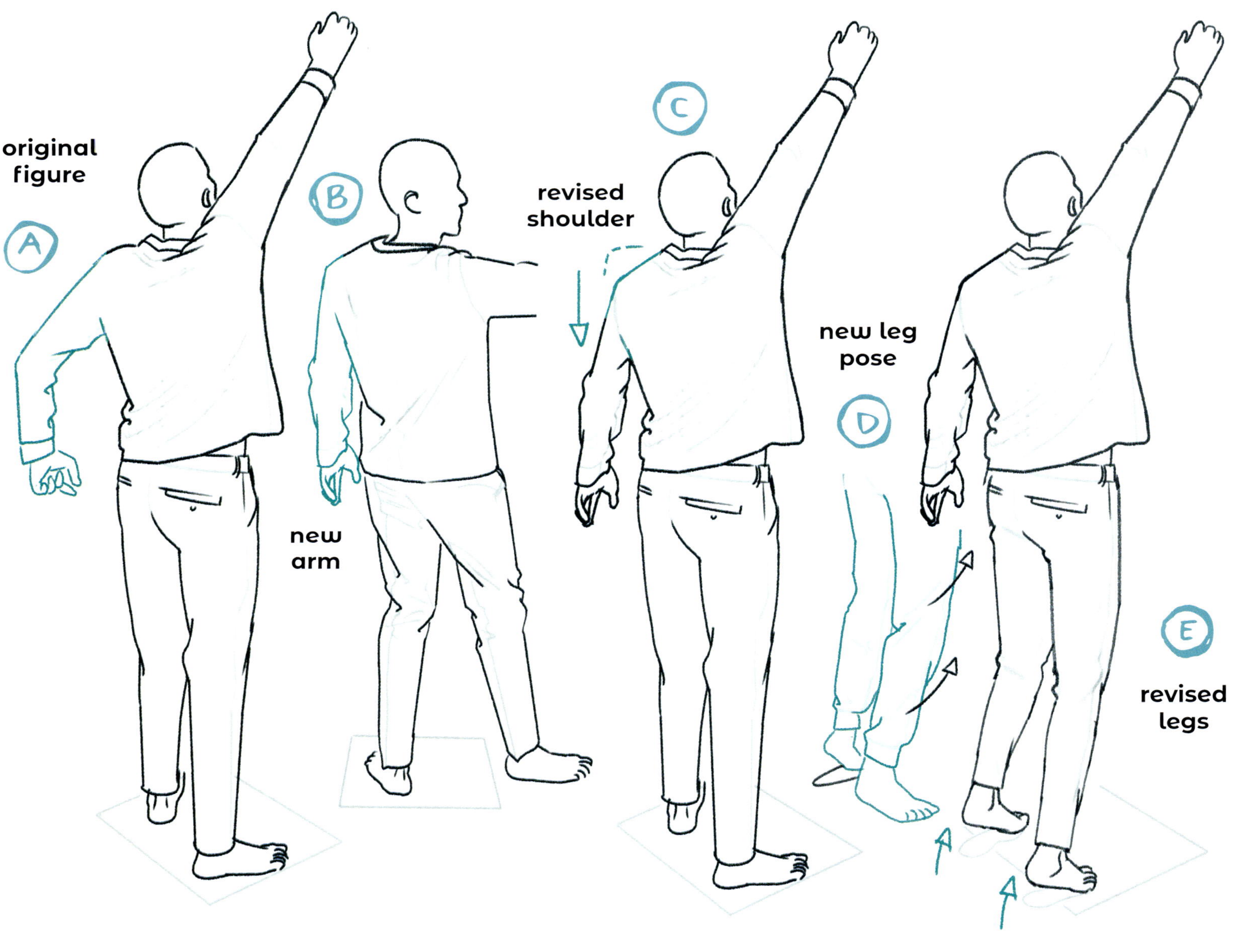

If you're comfortable swapping both halves of the body and individual limbs, you can start to swap garments. In this example, I want to draw a character in this position, but I'd like the sleeves to be looser (A). I skim through the reference pages until I find a sleeve in a fairly similar position. It doesn't have to be exact, but it should show some compression in similar places: for example, between the upper chest and the upper arm, and at the bends of the elbows. A helpful reference should also ideally show the level of resistance of the fabric I want to draw. This will help provide a reference for how angular the folds will be, and how deep the branches of the secondary silhouette might travel. Something like this (B). Now I can use both references to redraw the sleeves (C).

In the example below (D), I want to redraw the bottoms of the trousers to be tighter, to untuck and shorten the shirt, and to make the shirt fit more closely to the front of the torso. I use a reference of a character that has these component parts (E). It doesn't matter that this character isn't wearing the same shirt, or that he's wearing cargo trousers. What's important is the fit and the drapery that can be used. Here's the result (F).

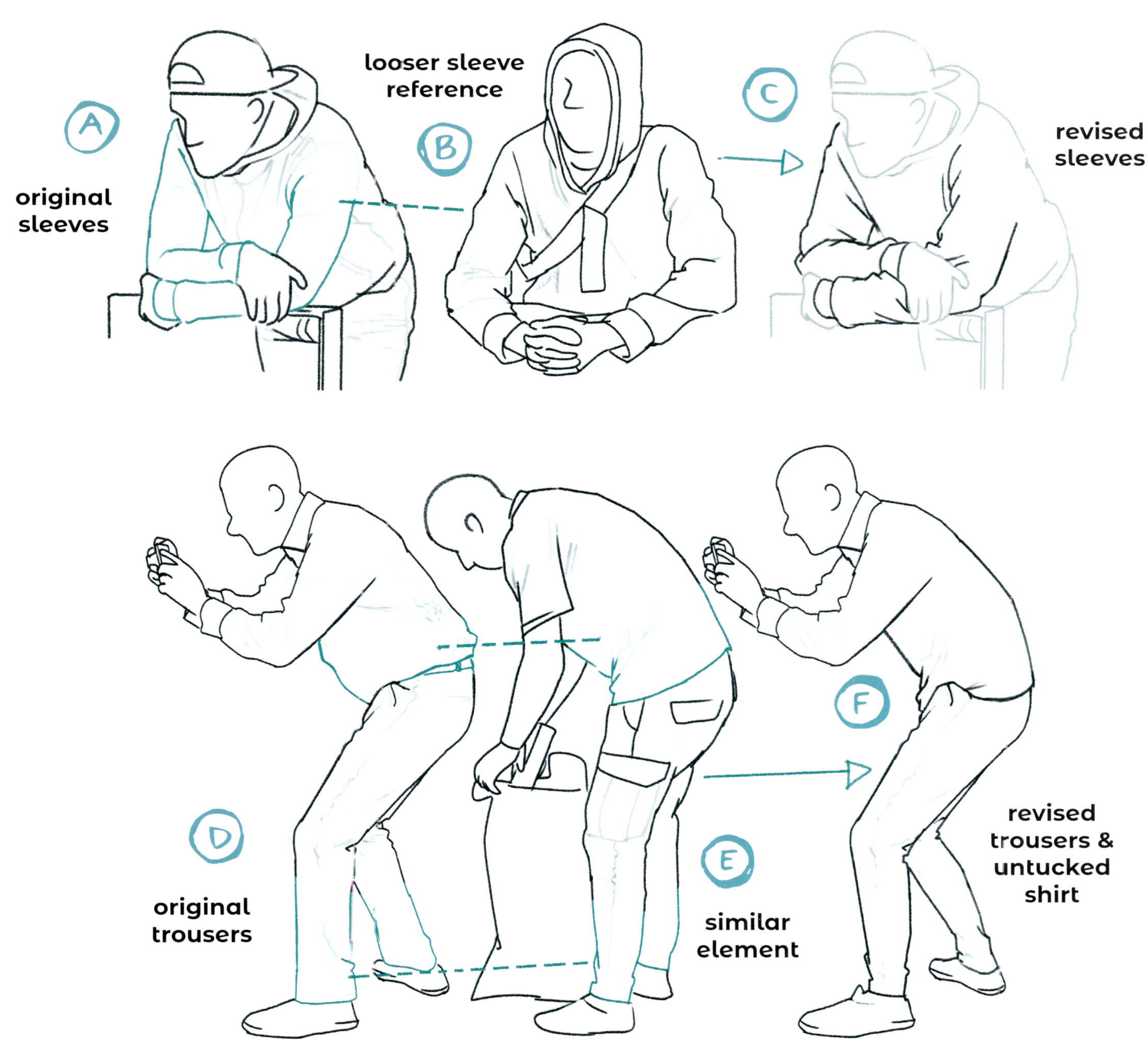

motions:

moving around

walking

When a leg is striding forwards, you often see compression at the top of the front of the thigh (A). Avoid drawing the fly too long – it shouldn't extend all the way down to the inseam (B). This compression is visible from both angles (C). The forwards leg will often cause the pocket to bend outwards (D). As the leg draws back, the fabric below the glutes should compress, and it also pulls the pocket a little flatter (E). When drawing someone walking from the front, don't draw the feet perfectly parallel (F). Instead, most people's feet angle out slightly. The bottom half of the shirt is often lifted slightly by the forward leg (G). Like the feet, the legs themselves aren't parallel, and the hip rarely sits perfectly horizontal. Instead, angle the legs inwards (H).

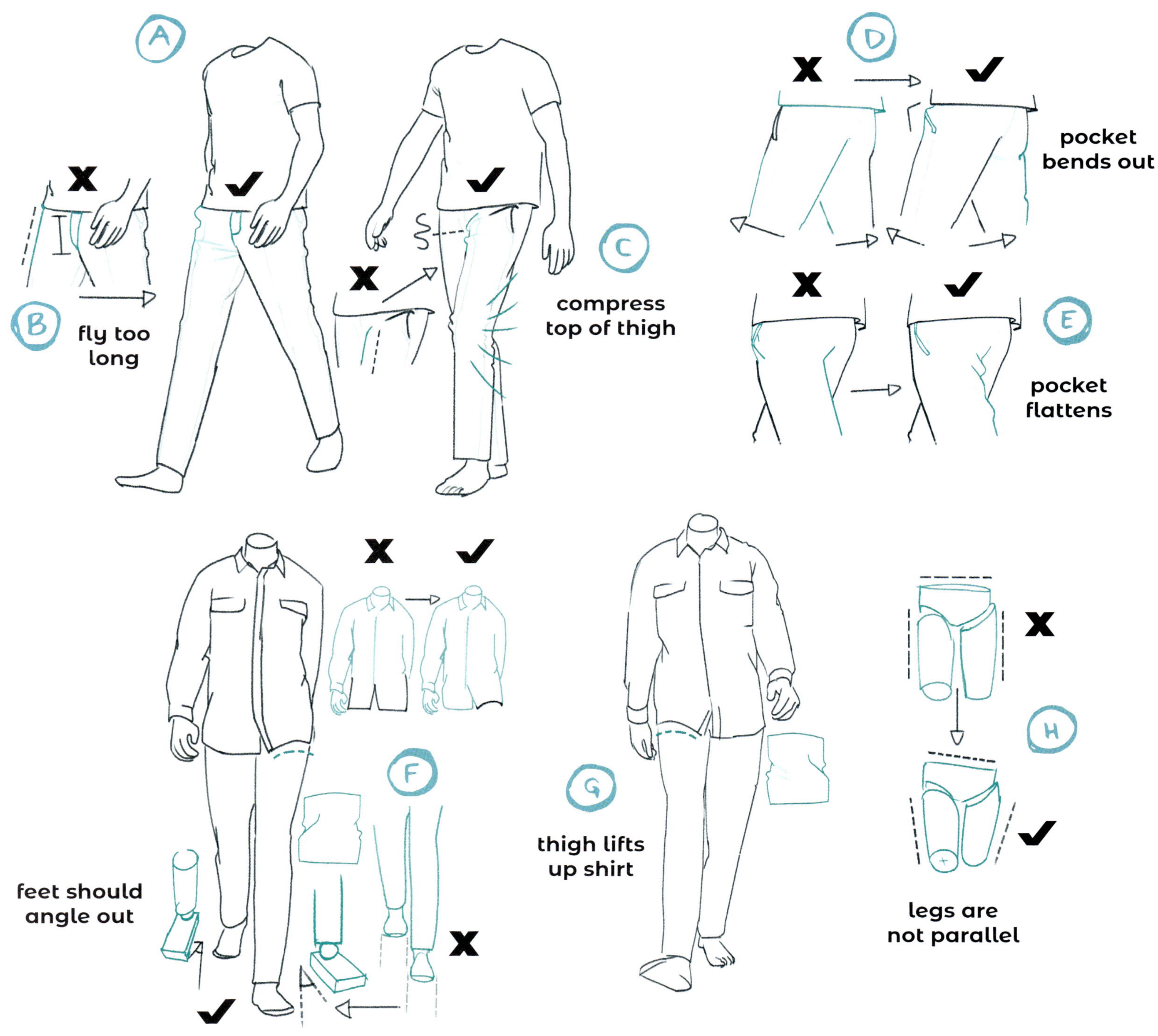

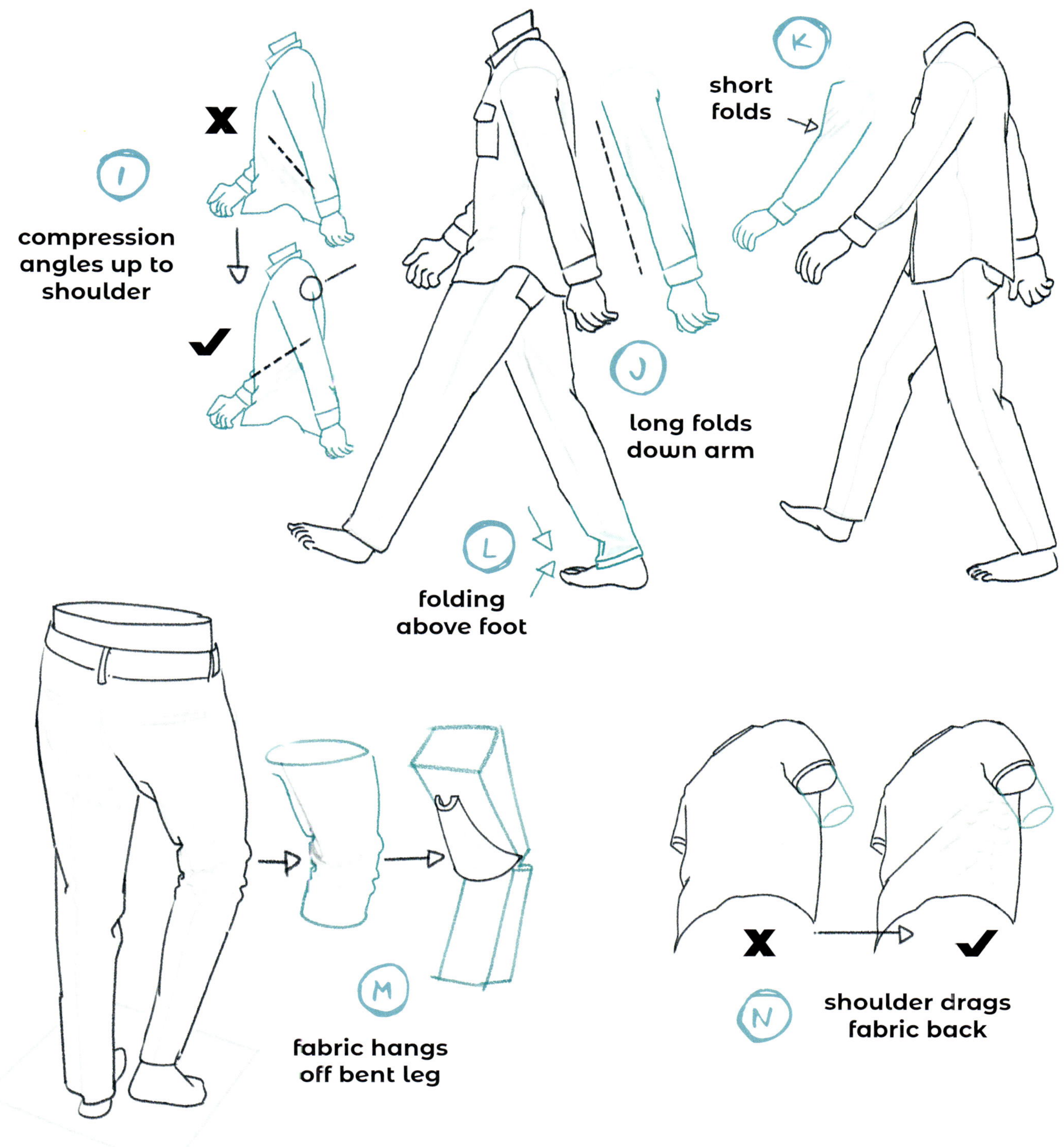

As the shoulder swings back, compression occurs on the same side and angles up towards it (I). When the arm swings back, it wil be almost completely straight, so you'll rarely see any folding across the arm. Instead, folds may appear down its length (J). When the arm swings forwards, it bends gently, and you'll often see compression occurring here (K). When the leg is fully extended back, some compression occurs between the shin and the top of the foot, causing folding to appear here (L). When the leg is bent, this form appears on the inside of the compression (M). It hangs off the bottom of the glutes, and merges into the folding at the back of the knee. When the shoulder swings back, it drags material with it, causing this pattern where fabric bunches behind the shoulder (N).

Looking closely at the collar of a T-shirt, you'll notice that the front section is angled backwards, and doesn't sit upright (O). The shoulders swing forwards and backwards, but also up and down. The folds converge on the highest shoulder (P). Most of the obvious folding occurs in the 'small' of the back, here (Q), because the upper back forms slight overhang. Usually there's a gap between the fly and the inseam. In this position, however, the line of the inseam often meets the bottom of the fly (R). Most of the time pockets are also more angled than you'd expect. When the leg is being raised, folds radiate outwards from the knee, as compression occurs on either side; this creates a star pattern when seen from the front (S).

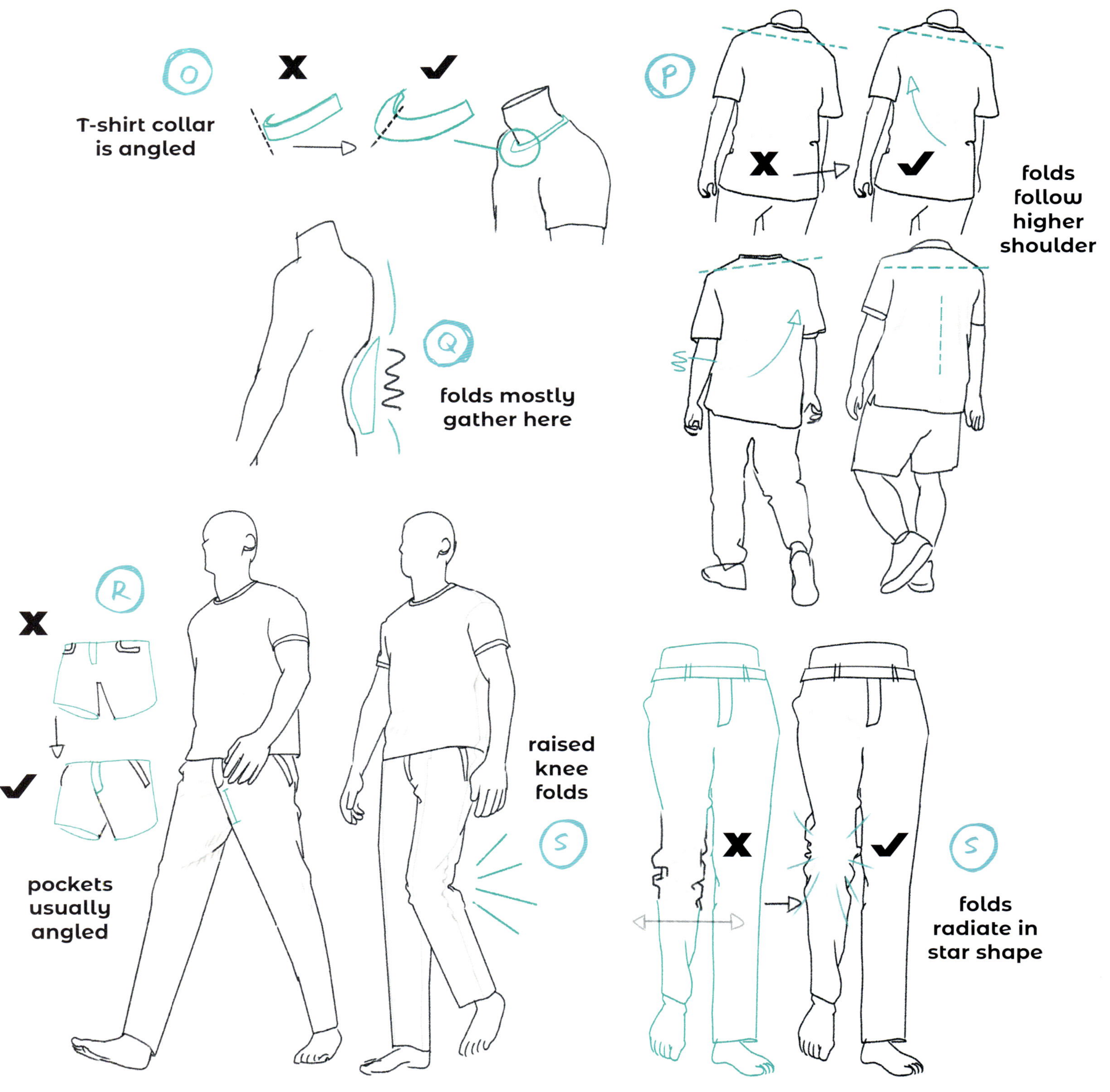

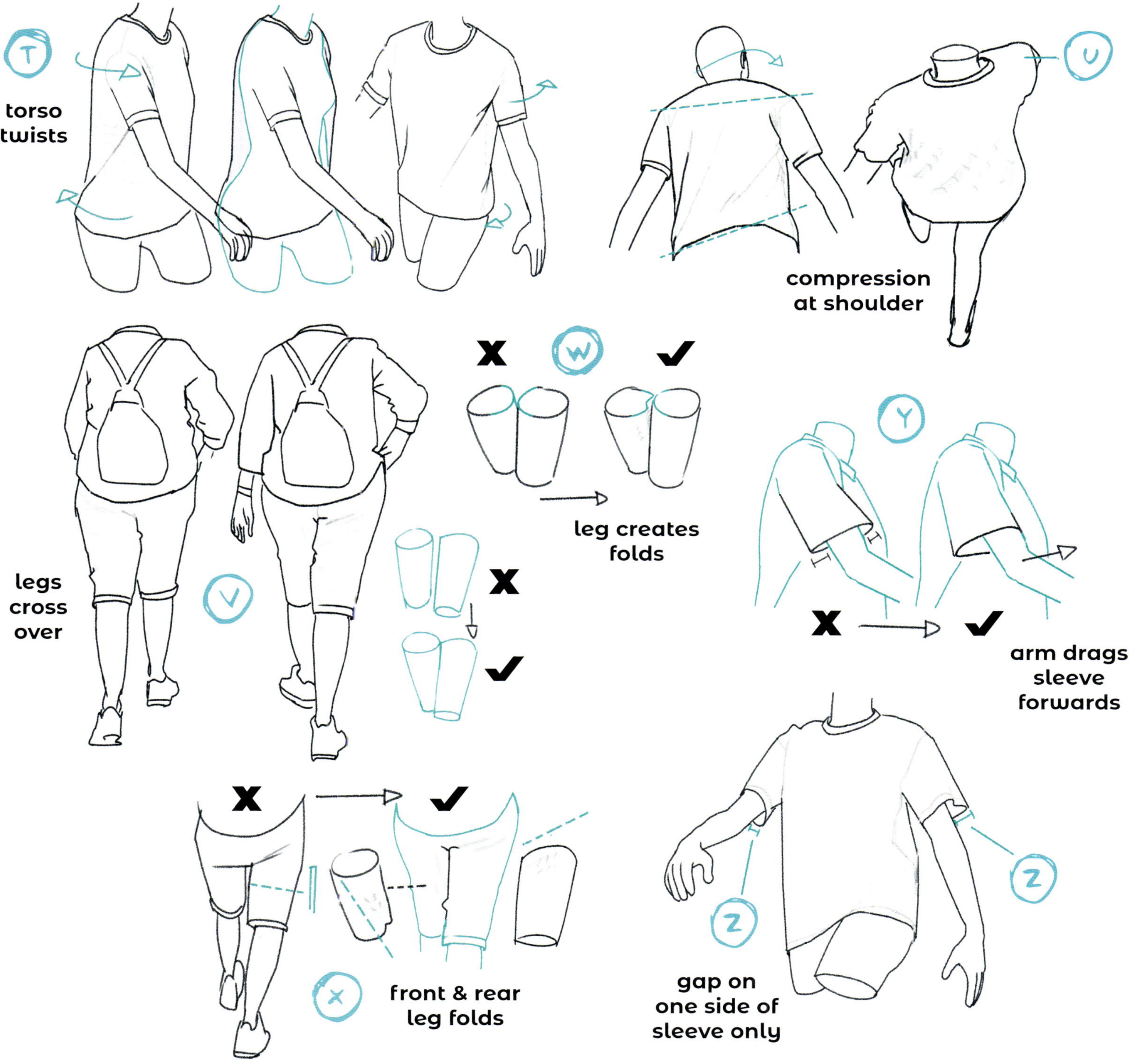

As the shoulder and hips rotate in opposite directions, the overall effect is a twisting pattern (T). When the arm swings forwards, it often causes gentle compression on top of the shoulder on the same side (U). From most viewing angles, the legs should cross over each other, rather than having a gap between them (V). They should also affect each other. They aren't completely solid, but subtly change shape (W). As they move forwards and backwards, the legs may display folds at these angles (X). As the arm swings forwards or back, think of it as 'dragging' the fabric with it. You'll rarely see a gap between the fabric and arm on both sides (Y). If one side is further from the arm, then check that you've drawn the other side close (Z).

When the leg swings back, compression occurs below the glutes and on the backs of the thighs (A). Make sure there are clear overlaps between the fabric of the chest, upper arm, and waist. This is a confused overlap (B), whereas this clearly shows the sequence of these forms (1, 2, 3) (C). Don't forget that the forward arm will show compression – particularly on the inside edge – and the rear arm will have longer folds along its length (D). When the arm is at the side, there will be some pressure on the fabric of the inner arm – often there'll be some vertical folding that demonstrates this (4, 5, 6) (E). When the arm swings back, you may see these folds on the back of the shoulder (F).

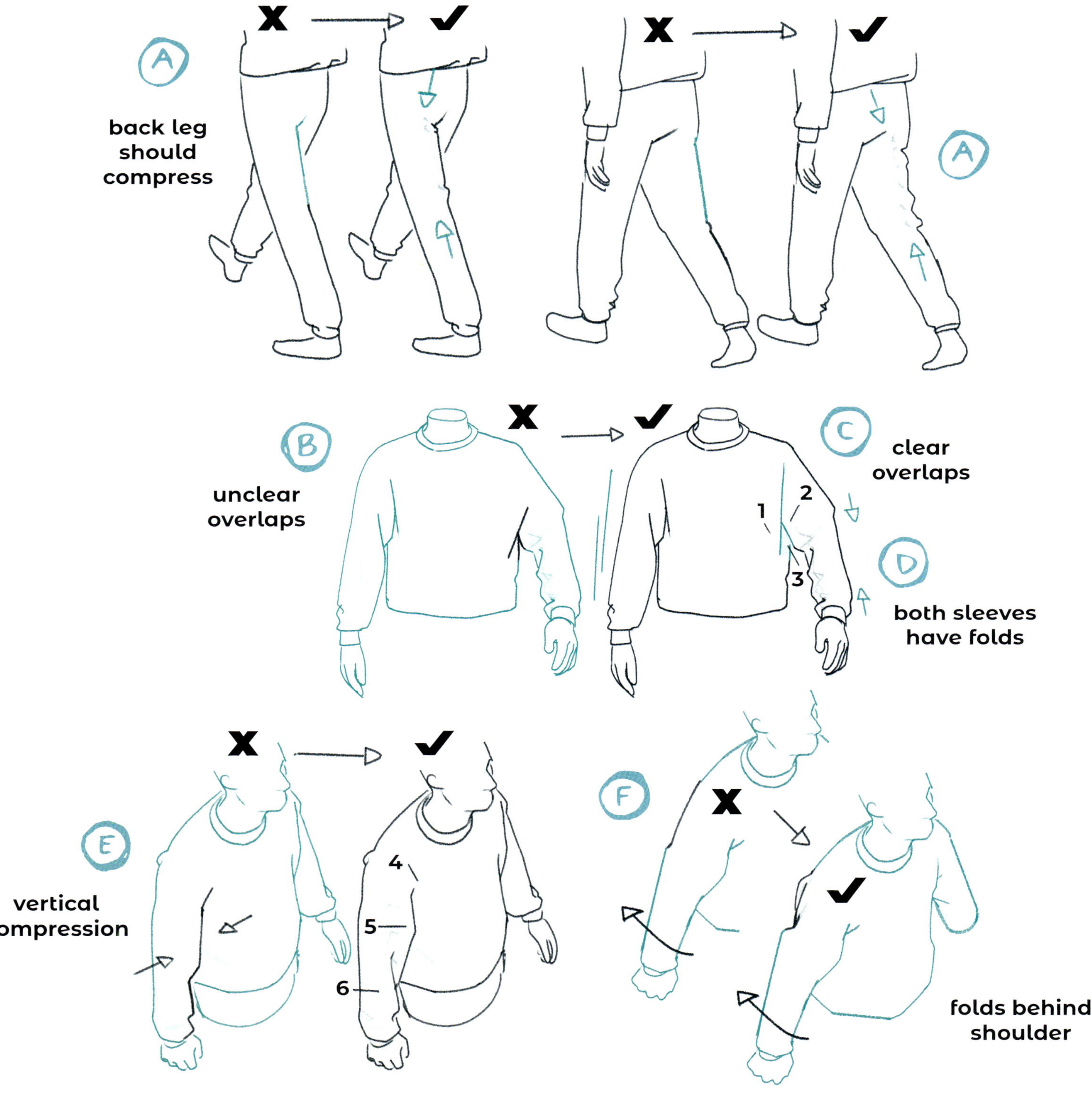

walking with a bag

Bags carried over the shoulder almost always sit at some sort of angle, rather than flat (A). The upper strap is usually twisted slightly as a result of the pressure from the hand (B). Sometimes when a hand is in the pocket, you'll see compression above the hand, between the hand and belt (C). The bottom section of the front leg often shows compression from two directions (D): fabric is dropping from above and is being pushed up by contact with the shoe or foot. The belt is usually higher at the back and angled forwards, rather than sitting flat (E). From behind, these angles are usually steeper than you'd expect (F). More often than not, the back of the shirt partially folds over the back of the belt (G). Finally, when the arm swings back, causing compression behind the arm, the drawing won't be fully believable until you include these diagonal folds that wrap around and up (H).

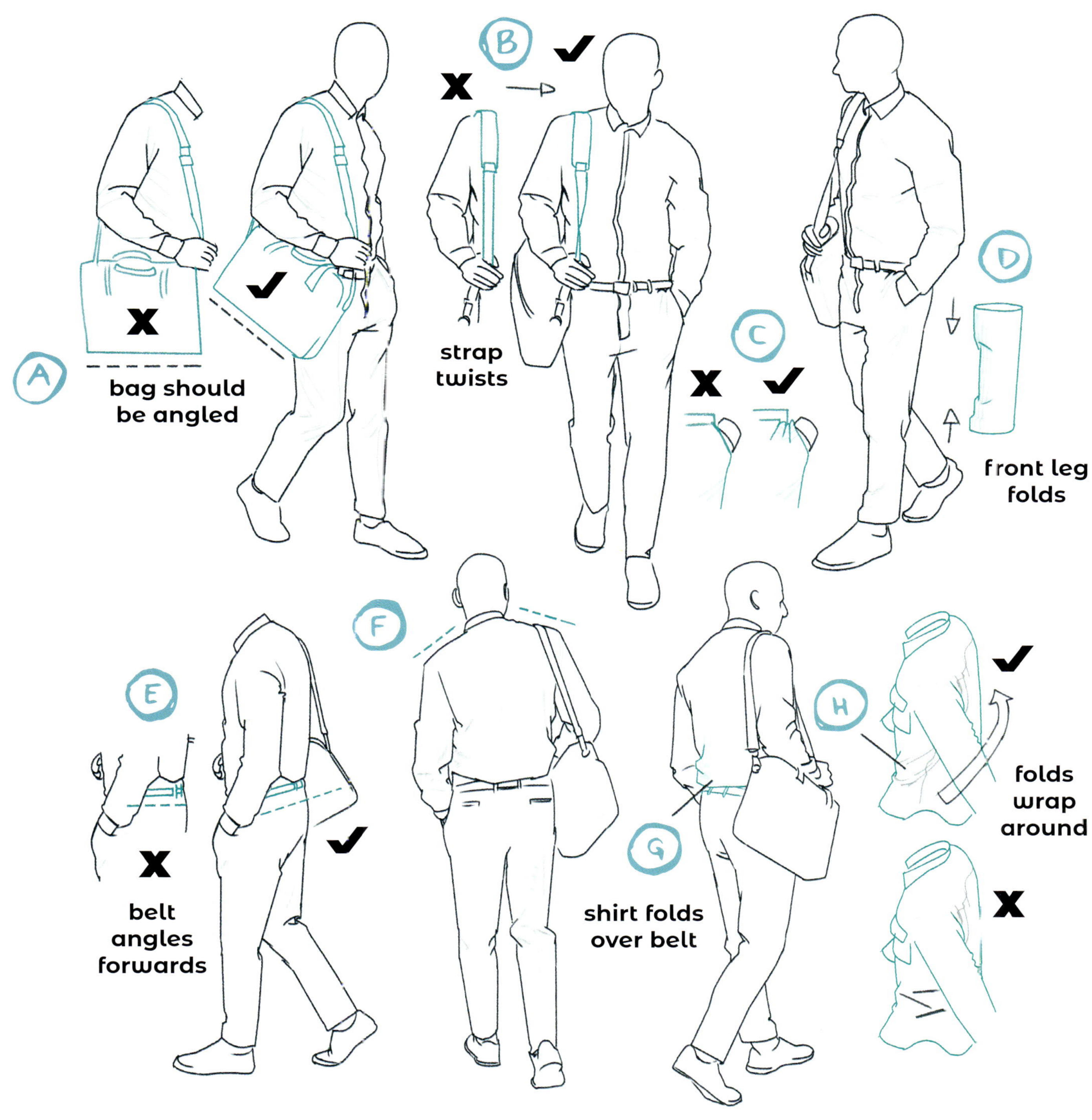

When looking down on the area around the fly, avoid drawing a 'V' shape. Instead, draw an almost horizontal line (I). The forward arm is slightly more bent, and shows more compression (J), whereas the rear arm is straighter and rotated slightly, so the folding will occur along its length (K). Leave a small gap between these lengthwise folds and the shoulder (L).

Remember to include the volume of the hand within the pocket, and to add these compression folds behind the pocket (M). A hand in the pocket causes the arm to be held back, which causes these folds to occur across the back of the shirt (N). They'll generally point towards the higher shoulder.

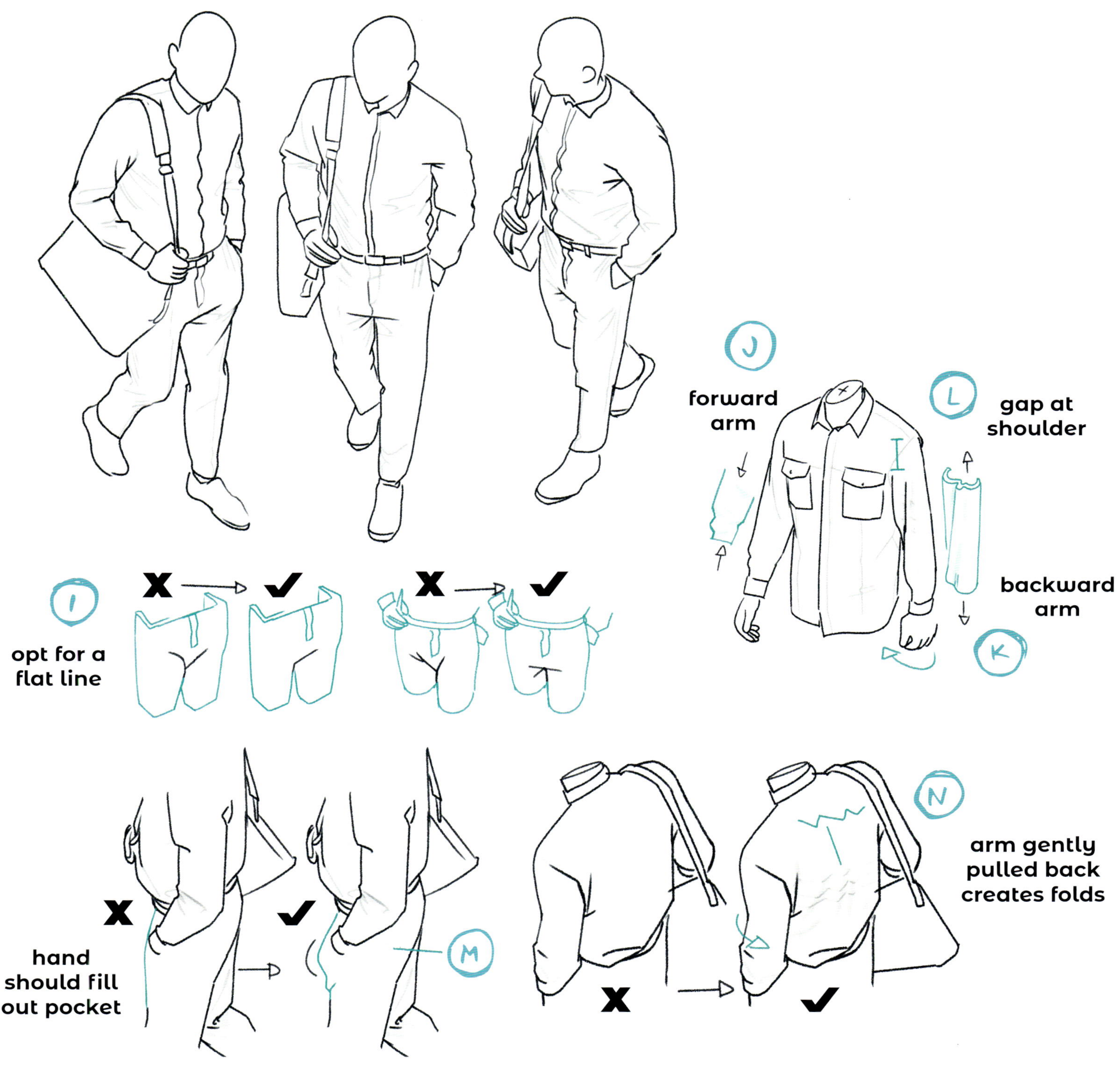

walking in a dress

The pattern of a dress is usually wider at the bottom than near the waist (A), because, when walking, the legs are further apart near the feet than at the thighs. If the pattern was closer to a rectangle, it would be impossible to walk – you'd have to shuffle (B). There's usually a small empty space at the crotch area, with shallow folds forming there (C). As the leg raises slightly, this folding is the first thing to appear (D). As the leg is raised higher, you'll start to see overlaps affecting the silhouette (E). Note the two main pulling areas: the front of the thigh and the back of the calf (F). The compression you see usually occurs between these two areas. When walking in a dress, there's rarely any folding on the front of the forward leg (G).

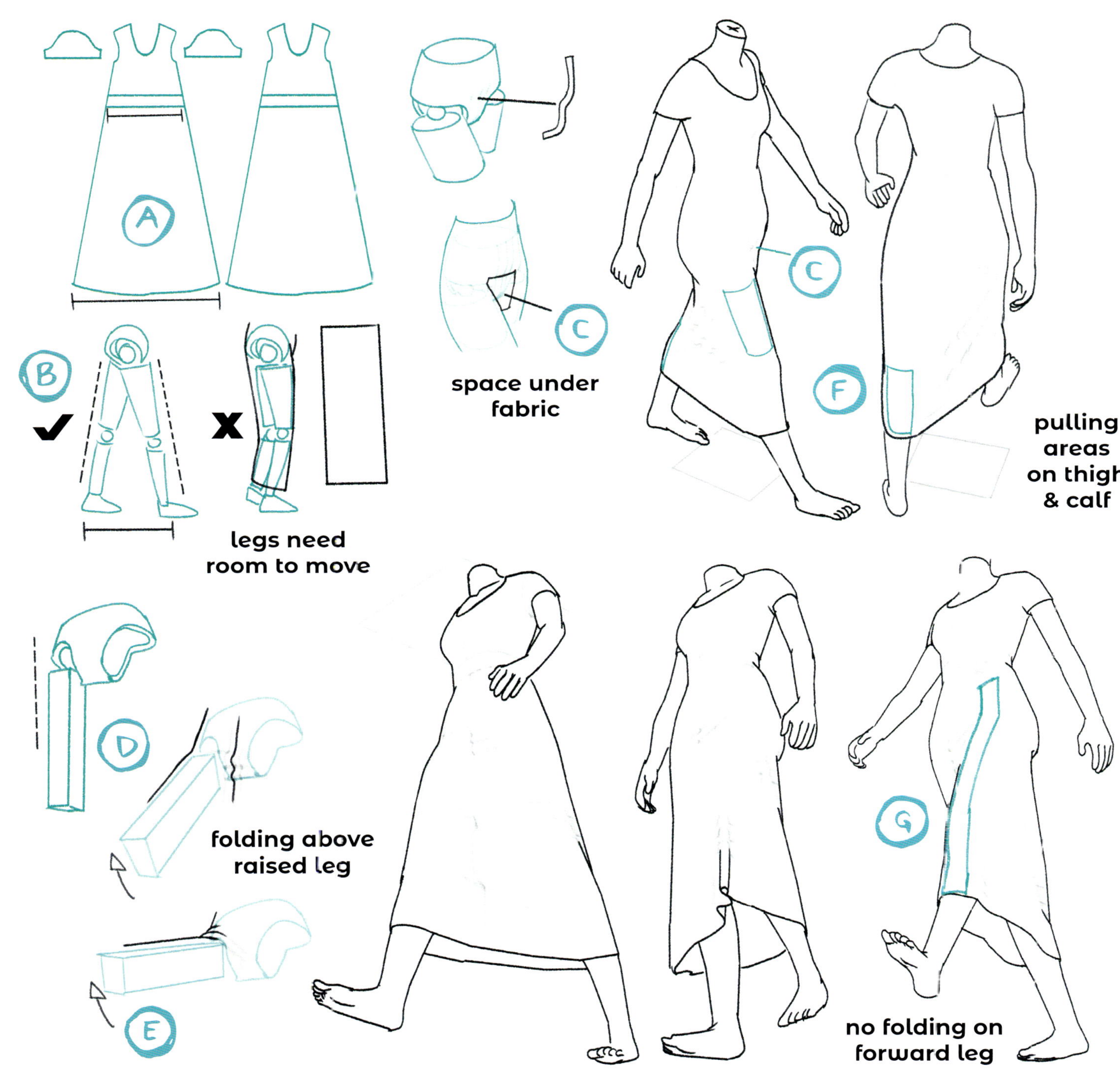

This dress is wider at the bottom than the dress on the previous page (H). As a result, there's more fabric at the bottom near the ankles. When striding, the forward and rear leg 'pull out' two partial cone shapes, and the vast majority of the bunching happens between them, sticking out to the sides (I). Seen from the side, try to keep the bunching in the middle, rather than across the whole width (J). As one thigh swings forwards, it gently pushes the fabric to the side (K). Folds won't drop straight down like this (L).

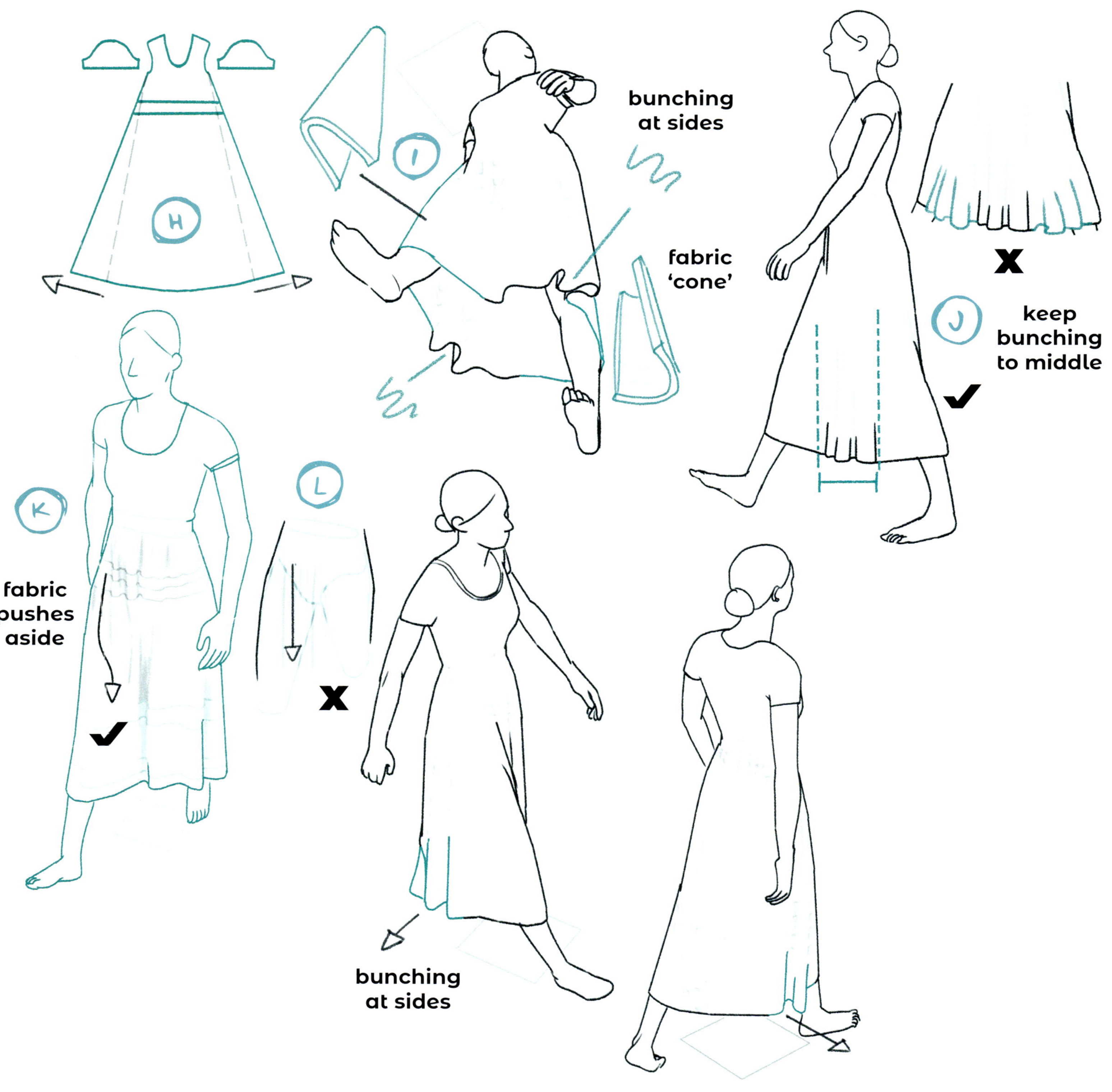

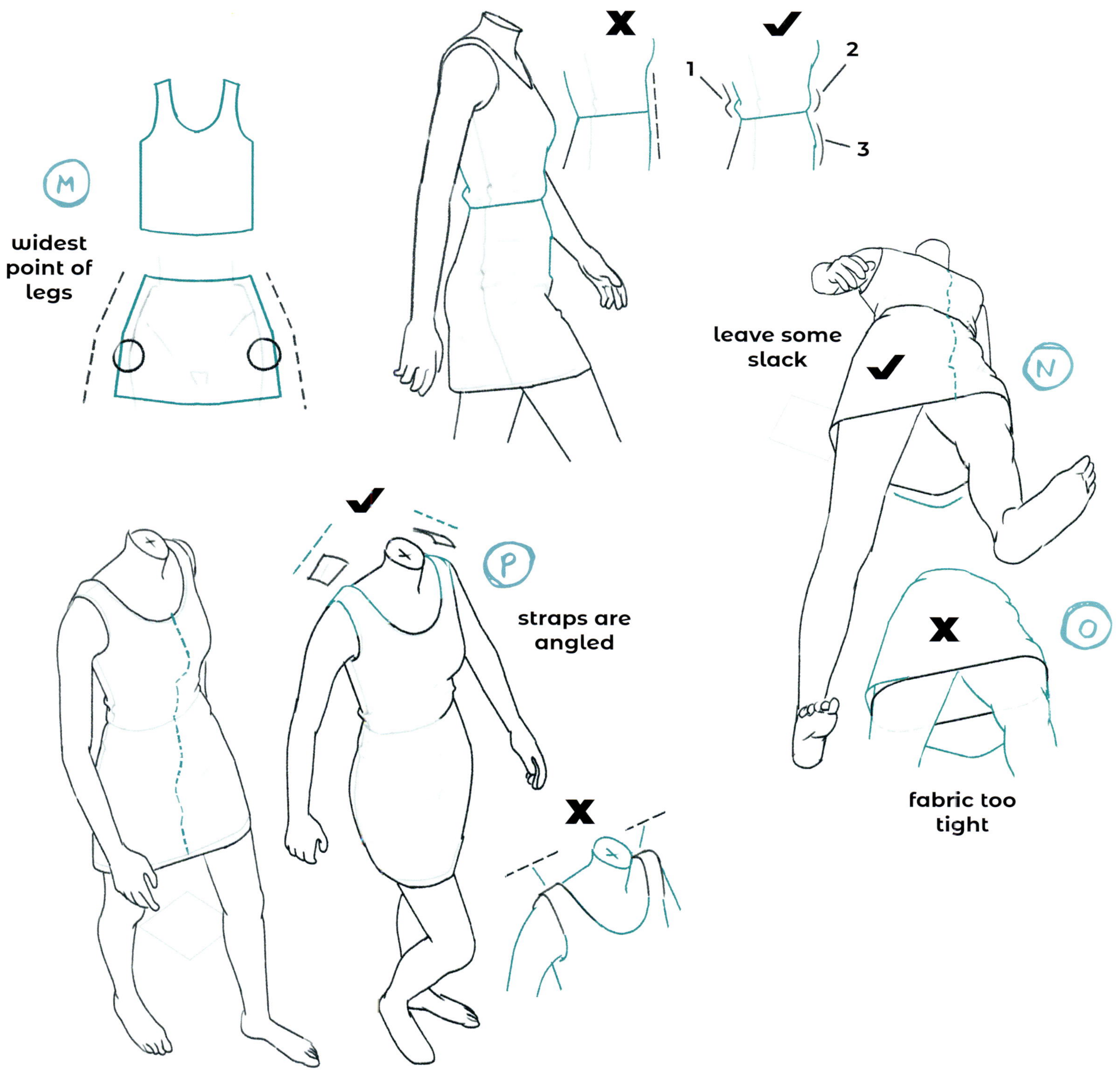

The widest point of our legs is usually near these circles (M). Therefore, the skirt should taper outwards towards the bottom. When drawing this high-waisted section, there will almost always be some bulging here **(1, 2, 3)**, which reflects the bunching of fabric at the back and anatomy at the front. When one leg is forwards, draw the skirt with a little slack (N), rather than this taut shape (O). Without that extra fabric, it would be extremely difficult to walk in the skirt. The shoulder straps of the vest aren't flat across the top, but angled (P).

tip: shirt collars

Shirt collars are formed of two parts, which we'll call the 'inner' and the 'outer' (A). The inner is not as tall as the outer, and it's slightly longer. The ends of the inner are often curved, rather than perfectly squared (B). The outer sits on top of the inner, but it doesn't run all the way to the end (C). When a collar is buttoned, the ends of the outer don't meet – there's a gap between them (D). When a collar is unbuttoned, it twists outwards, rather than staying flat (E). Behind the neck, our anatomy often creates a little 'ledge' just below the collar (F). The sides of the collar angle inwards, rather than being vertical (G). Men's shirts traditionally have the left side of the inner folded on top, and women's have the opposite (H).

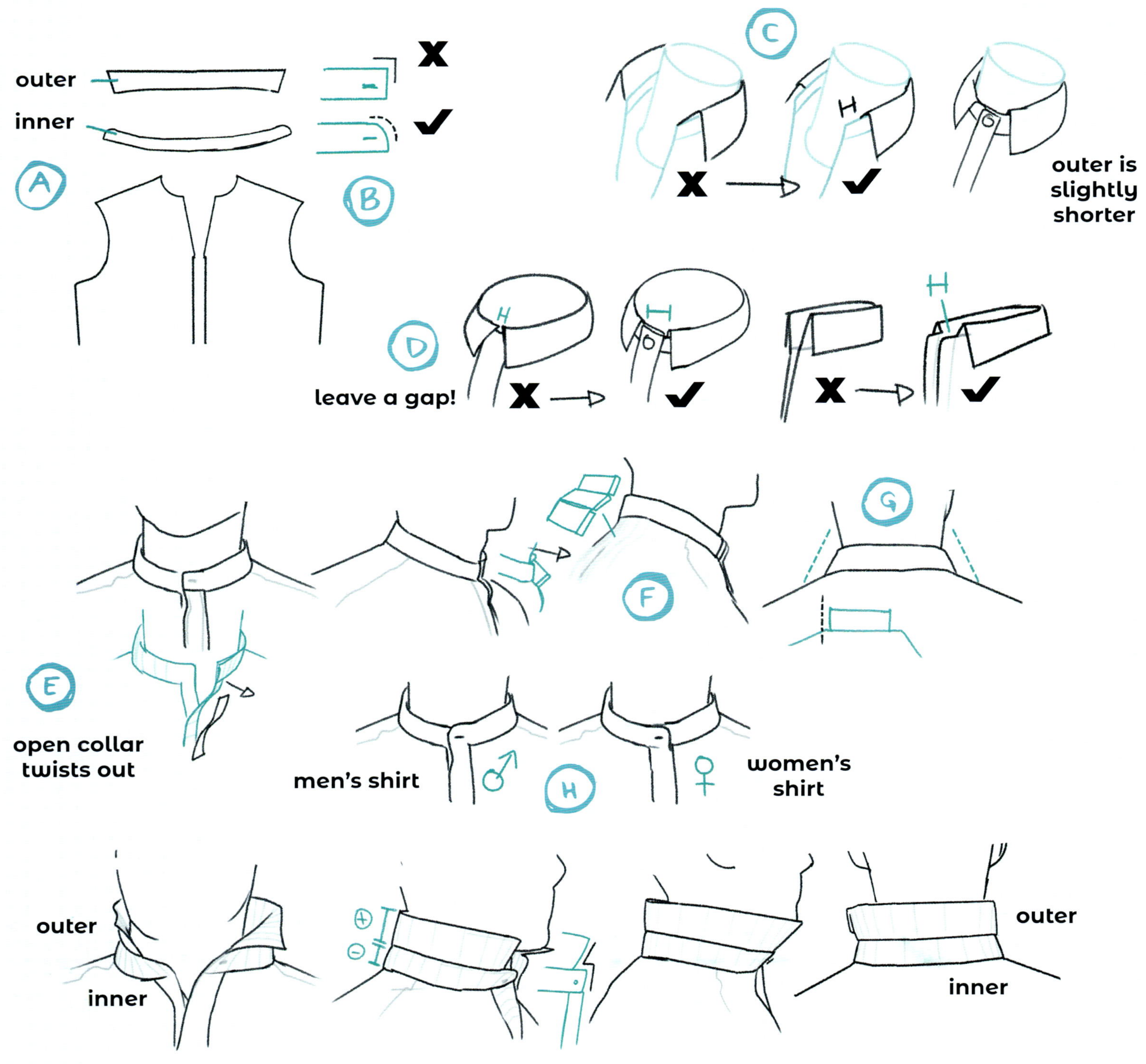

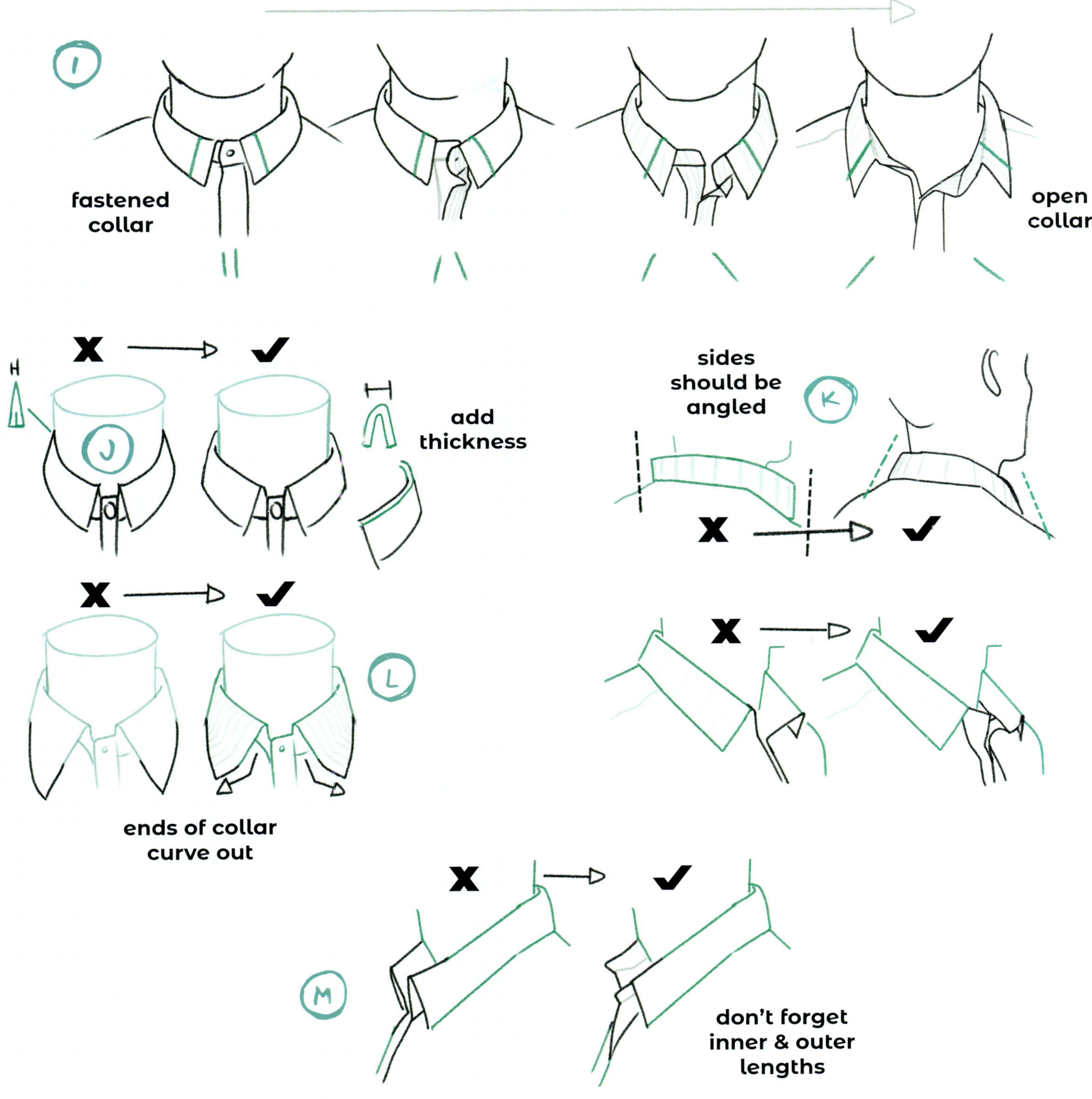

Notice the behaviour of these coloured lines when the collar is unbuttoned (I). As the collar falls open, the lines flatten out. The outside of the 'outer' faces upwards. Be mindful of the thickness of your collar (J). Some collars are very thin and will seem to form a sharp point at the neck. More often, however, the thickness can be drawn. From behind, the collar's angles shouldn't be vertical, but should taper in towards the top (K). When drawing larger collars, the bottoms will often curve outwards slightly (L). Drawing an open collar from the side can be tricky – don't forget to show the 'inner' extending further than the 'outer' (M).

phone call

When the arm is raised for a phone call, the shoulder and arm drag the material forwards and right around the back. The folding wraps around and affects the drapery all the way down to here (A). We tend to make the same mistake when drawing the front, too – we focus our efforts on the section right next to the arm, forgetting that raising this point (B) causes diagonal compression, indicated by the arrows. From behind, the fabric should be visibly pulled in towards the lower back (C).

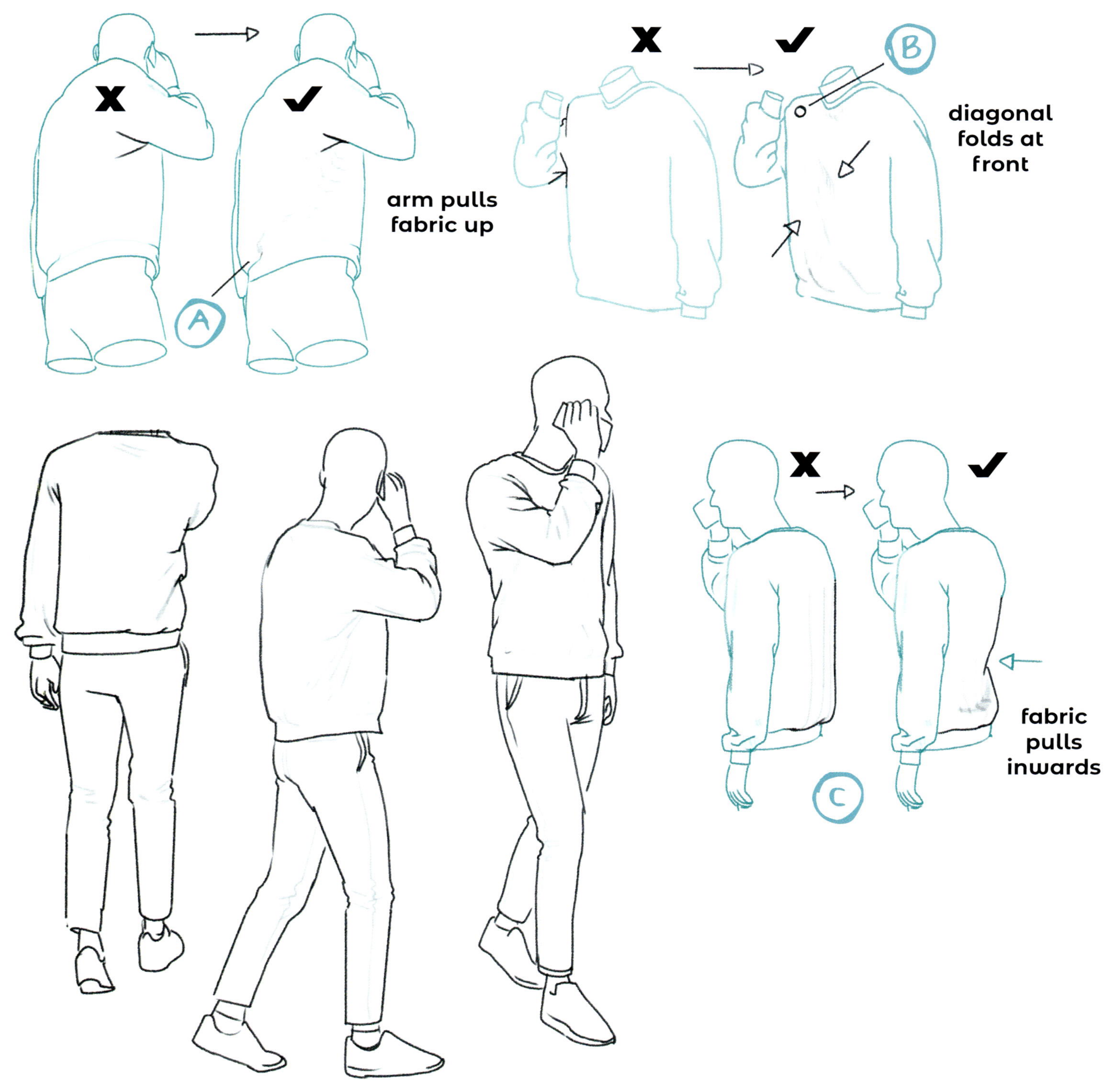

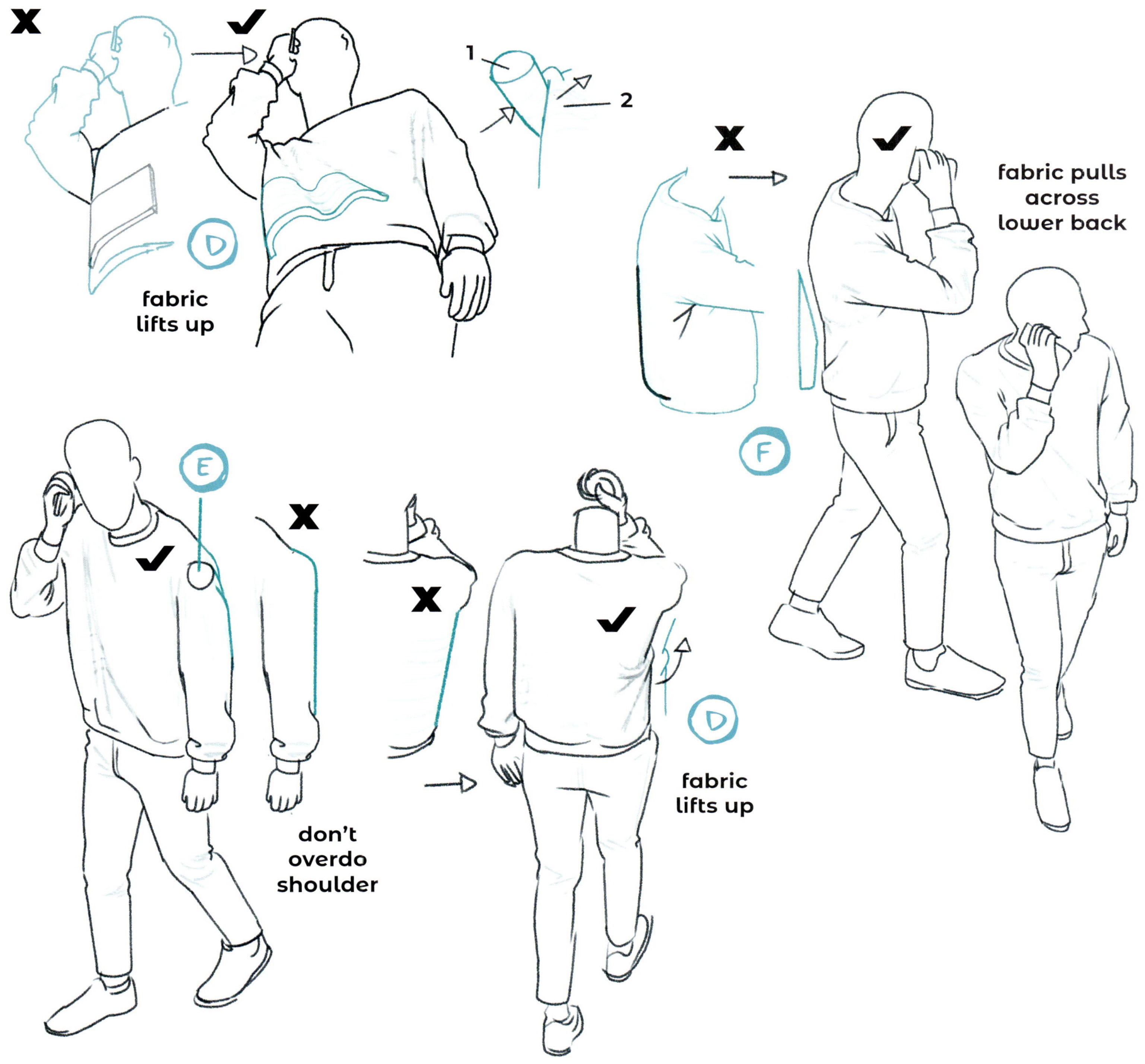

When viewed from below, the raised arm lifts up the fabric on the same side of the torso (D). The form of the arm **(1)** pushes against the form of the torso and deforms it **(2)**. It's a common habit to draw the 'bump' of the shoulder protruding from the silhouette, but it should sit within the silhouette instead (E). As we saw on the previous page, the raised arm pulls fabric more tightly across the lower back (F).

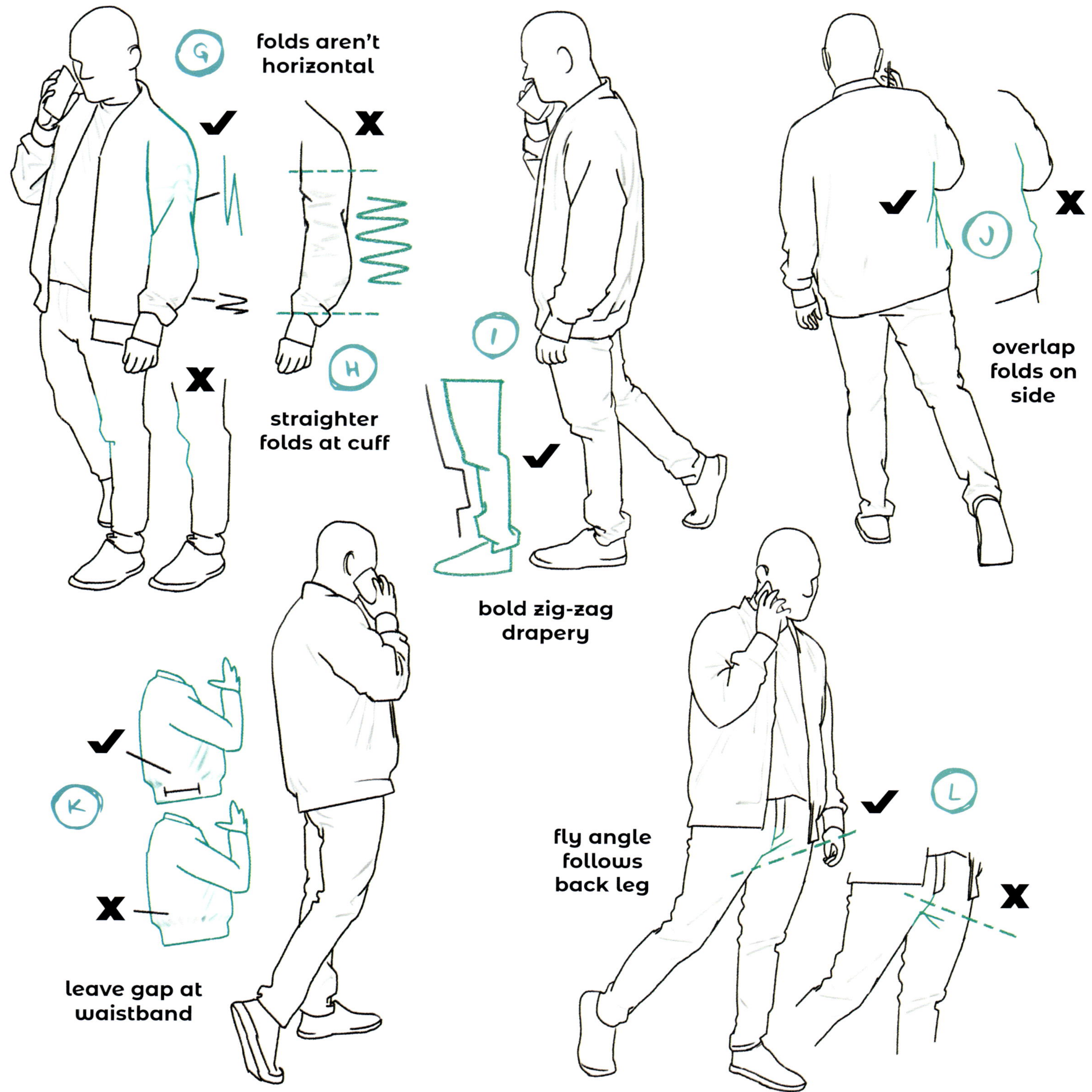

Rather than drawing horizontal folds across the whole arm, it's often better to keep the folds flowing vertically on the top part of the arm (G), and keep the horizontals for just above the cuff (H). Be bold with your drapery on a straight leg viewed from the side – it will often zig-zag (I). To show that one arm is raised and pulled forwards, these overlaps are essential (J). Small, shallow folds can make a big difference to your drawing. It's better to leave a gap here at the waistband (K), to help show that the material is being pulled upwards. With a leg held back, the folds near the fly often conform to this angle (L), rather than facing down.

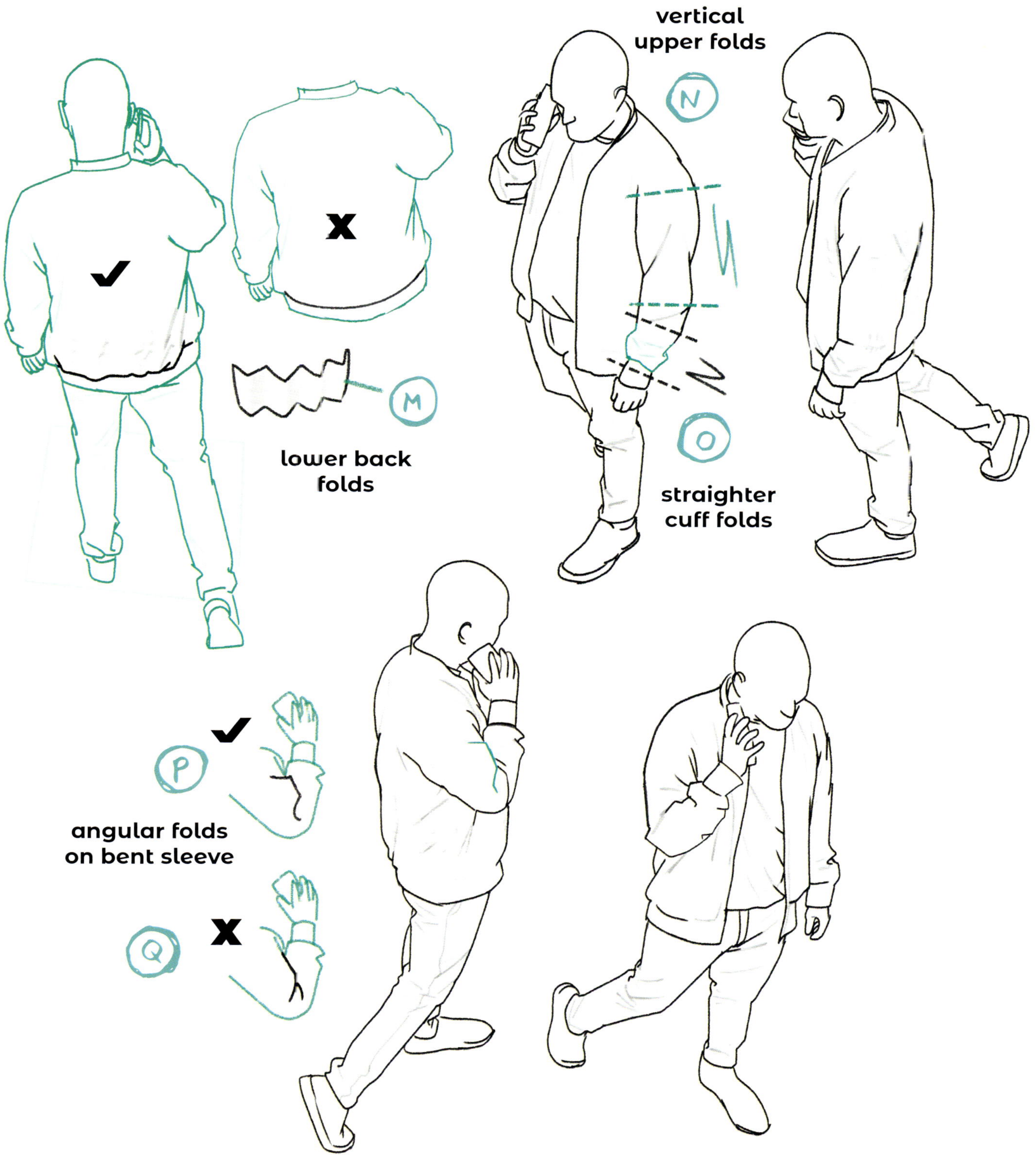

When one arm is raised, and the other is at the side, you'll often find this pattern across the lower back (M). This should be included in both the silhouette above the waistband and in the internal folds. As we saw on the previous page, you'll mostly want to use vertical folds for the upper arm (N) and reserve obvious vertical compression for the region just above the cuff (O). I find that I naturally want to draw a bent sleeve with a fold like this (P), despite the fact that I know this pattern (Q) is more accurate and often seen. Watch out for that shape.

checking a watch

When drawing rolled sleeves, it's often clearer to make them a little angular in cross-section rather than round (A). When the arm is raised, rolled sleeves often sit at an angle rather than perpendicular to the arm (B). Most rolls are also subtly tapered and get wider as you move higher up the arm. Similar to what we saw on the previous page, this is a helpful shape for drawing an arm bent at 90 degrees (C). When drawing a bag like this, it'll be more believable if you include some twist in the carry handles and straps (D).

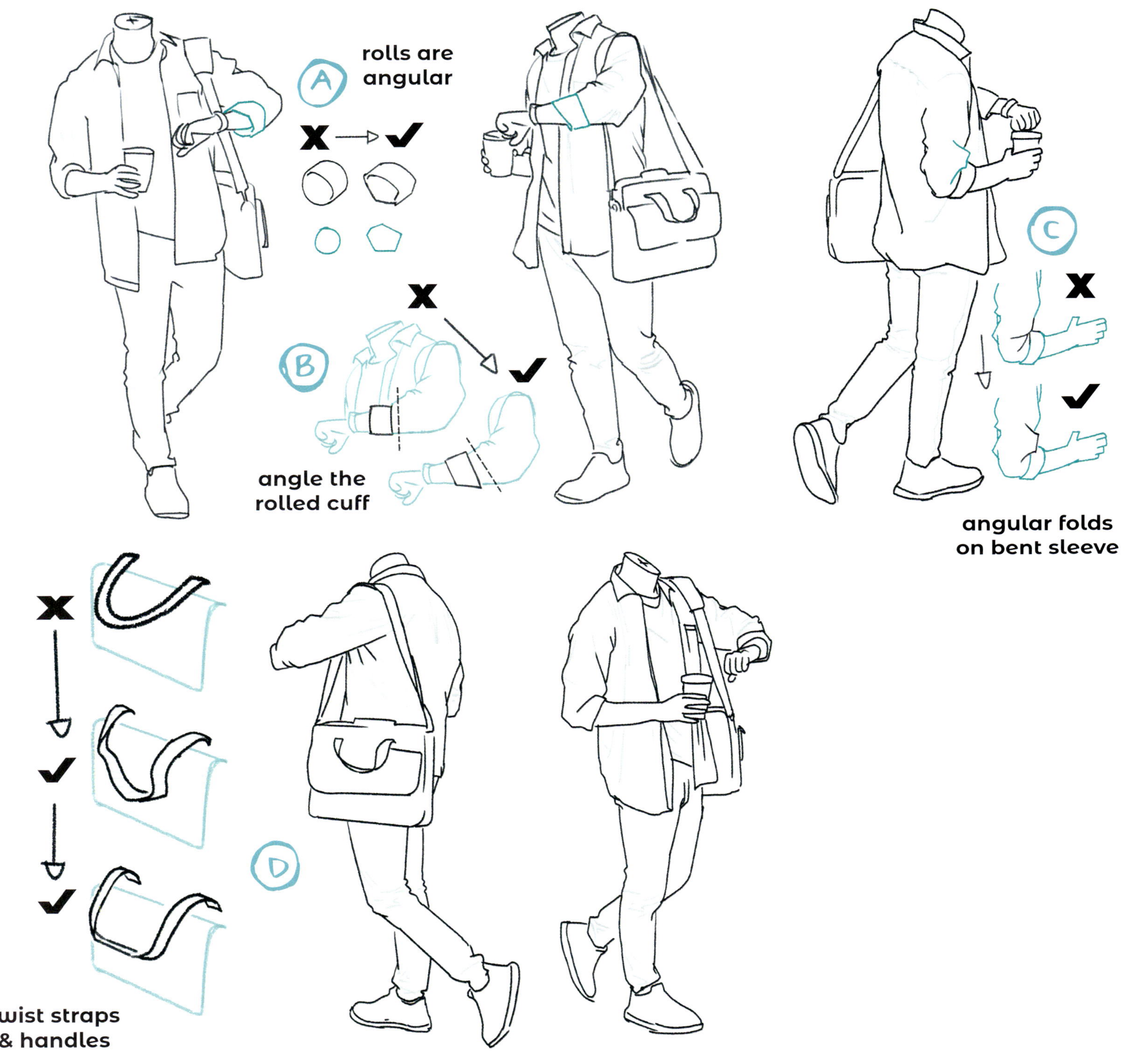

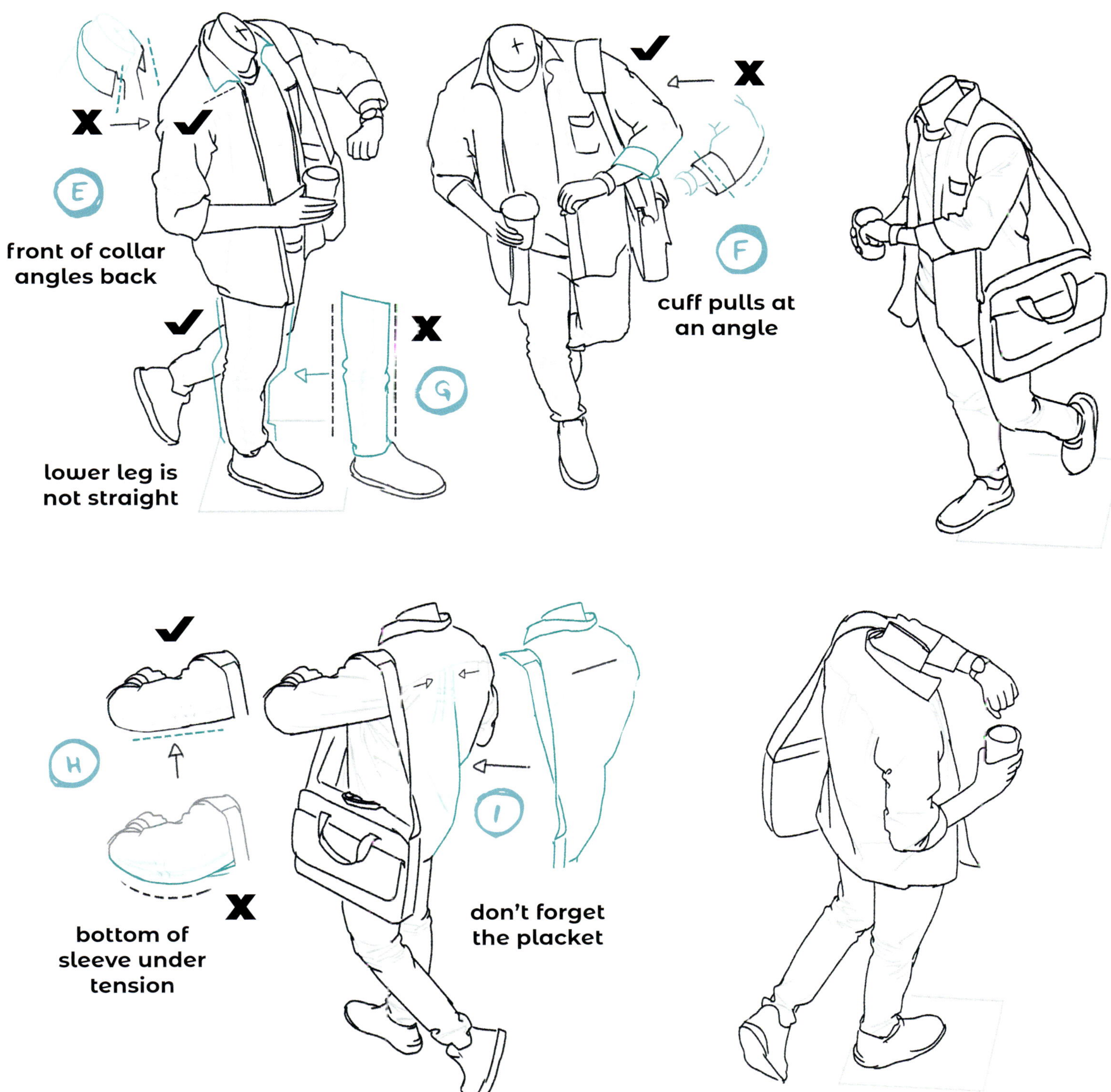

When a shirt is fully open, the front of the collar shouldn't be drawn too vertical. Instead, it should flare out to the sides (E). The partially rolled cuff will be pulled at an angle when the arm is raised and bent like this (F). When drawing a straight leg, remember the anatomy: the lower leg will be set back a little – it won't be straight (G). The sleeve is the same length on either side. When you bend the arm, the outer edge is lengthened, which pulls it tight and creates a straight line (H). Many shirts have a bunching of material in the centre of the back (I).

tip: open collar

When a shirt is fully unbuttoned, with both sides hanging loose, the collar may open out and backwards, losing some of its arch (A). The front of the outer part will be less vertical than you'd expect, and lean forwards. Here are a few examples (B). Learning to draw believable collars is essential to drawing clothed characters because the collar sits so close to the face, and it's so easy to draw it in a way that doesn't look believable.

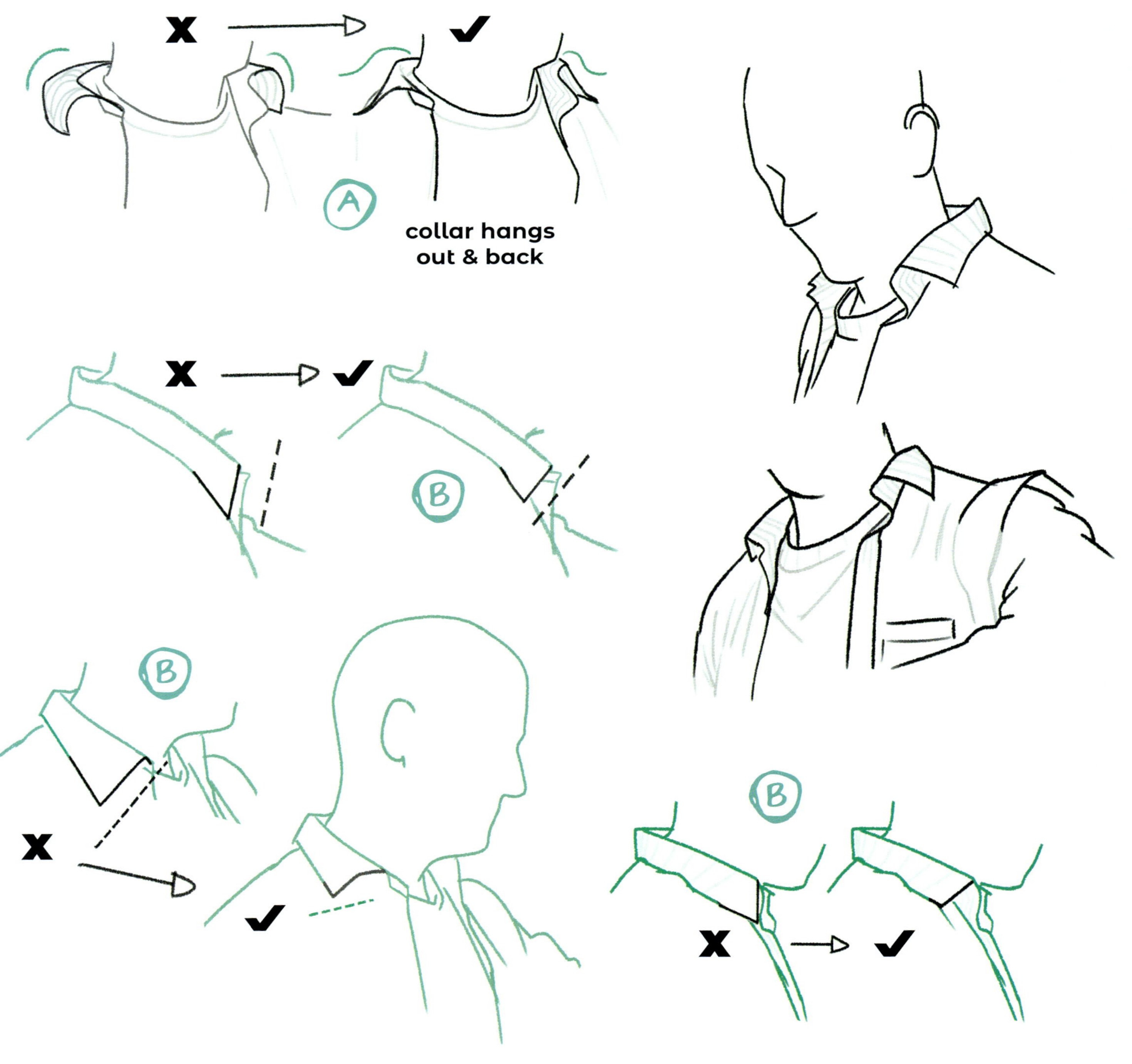

going up stairs

The collar usually curves down, rather than being straight and holding itself above the chest (A). The bottom of the sleeve is sometimes horizontal, but more often it's angled slightly (B). When one leg is raised, the fly may be partially hidden, and it may be pulled to one side (C). A raised leg may lift the fabric of the T-shirt on the same side, which causes compression above the thigh (D). This compression sometimes causes a large 'cone' of material to appear, which hangs from the centre of the chest (D). In turn, the folding above the thigh may also cause this form to hang off the centre of the chest (E).

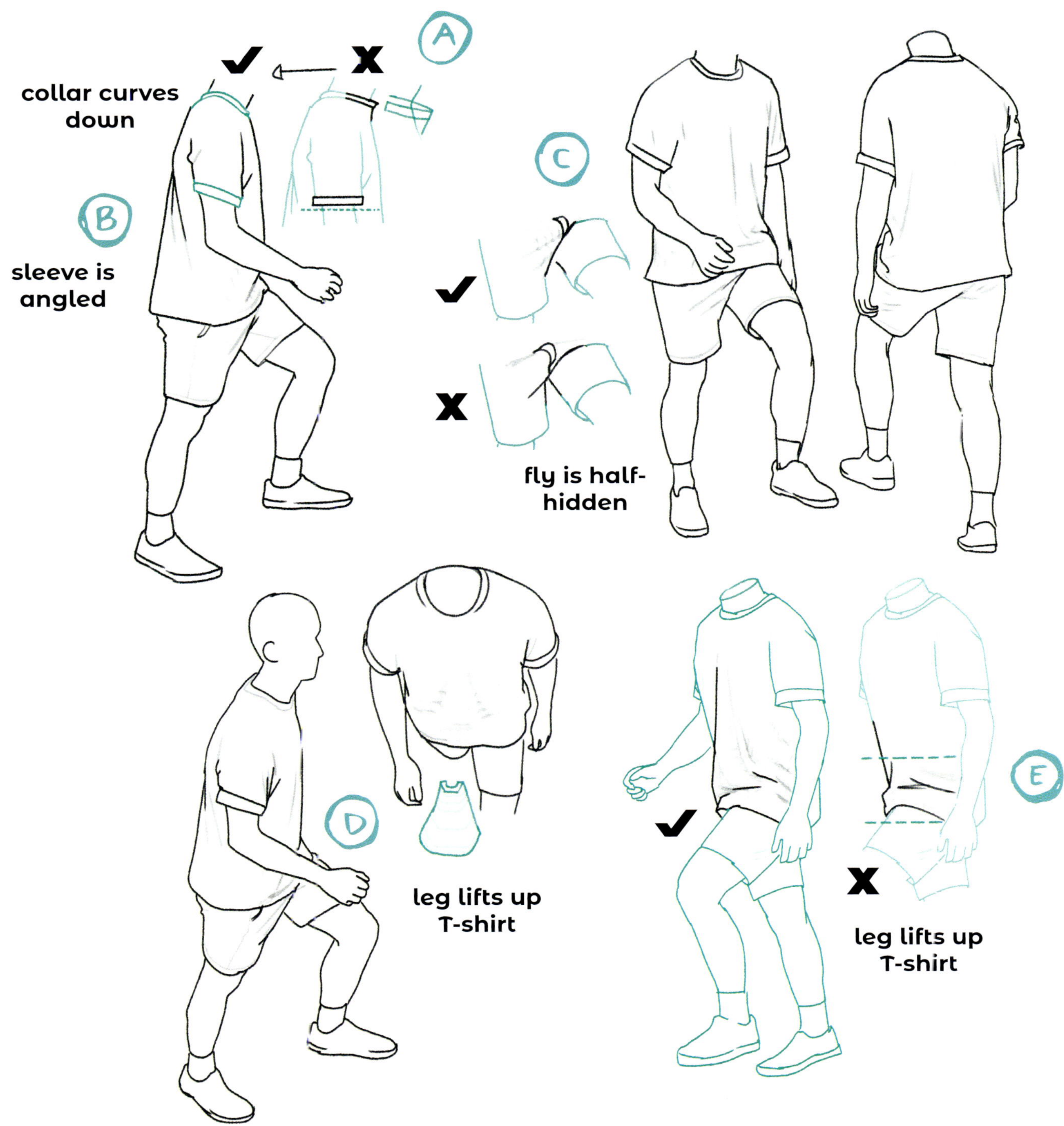

The seam on the inside of the thigh rarely runs into the underside of the crotch. Instead, it often connects into this fold and disappears (F). Most of the time, folding doesn't drop down below the glutes of the rear leg (G). Instead, it crosses over the glutes and the angle continues the line of the raised leg (H).

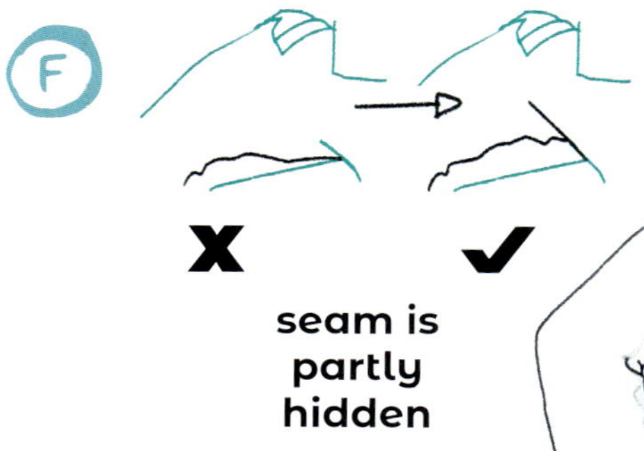

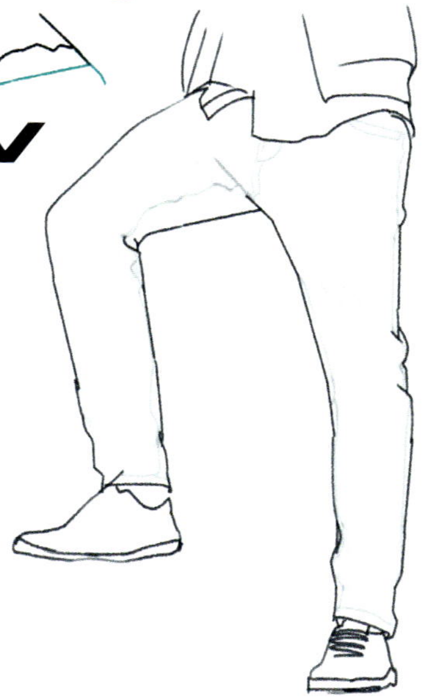

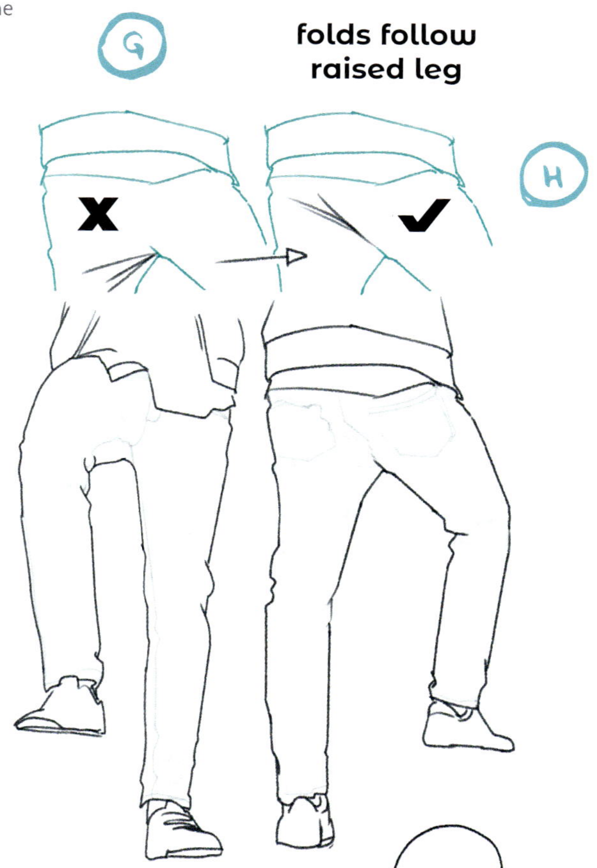

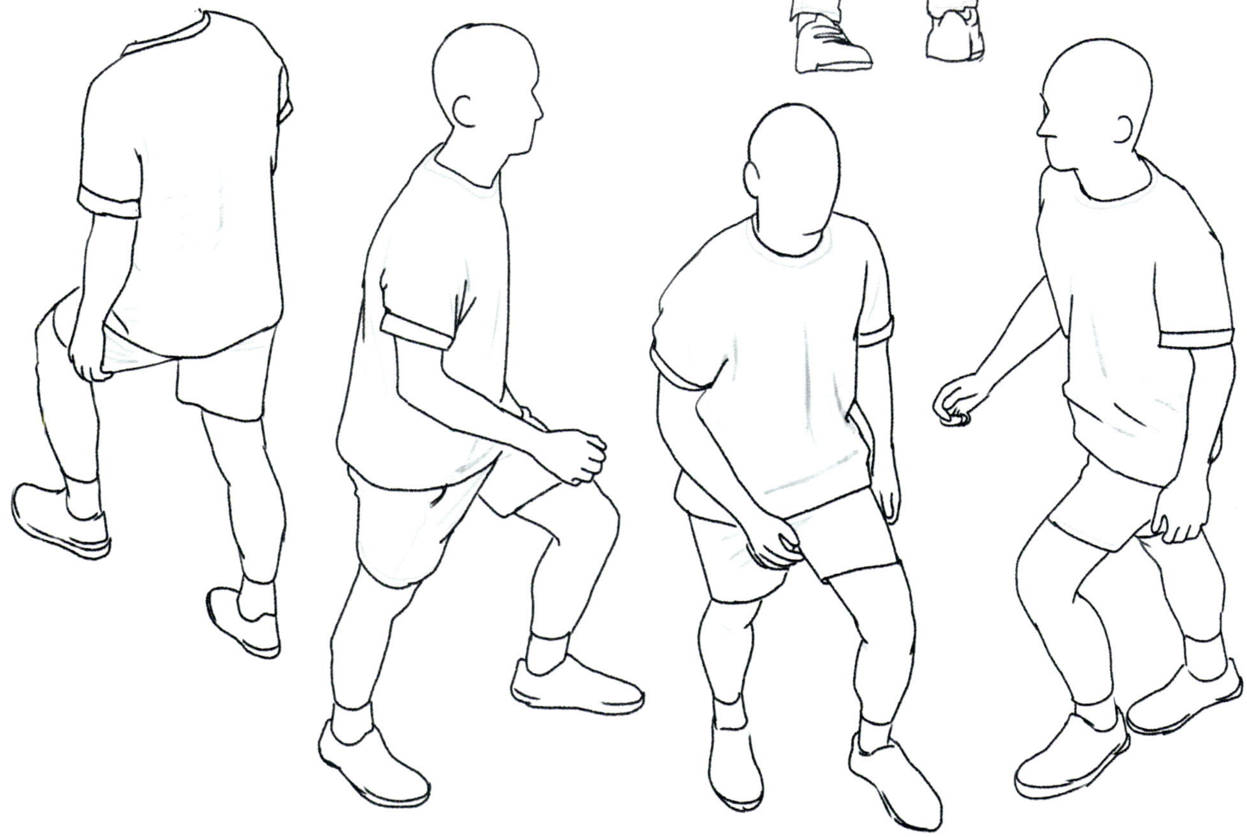

The outside edge of the trousers is rarely straight or vertical. Instead, the outer thigh bulges out before turning in (I). On most people, this is where the legs are widest. When the leg is bent, the bottom of the trousers won't form a circle. Instead, it will form a sort of 'V' that tapers up towards the knee (J). It's widest near the foot and narrower near the knee (K). When the leg is raised, it's tempting to draw the folds wrapping up and over the thigh (L). It's more accurate to draw folding heading up towards this circled point (M), to reflect the anatomy beneath. In most cases, the fly also deforms, and you'll see considerable bunching at the top, just below the belt or waistband.

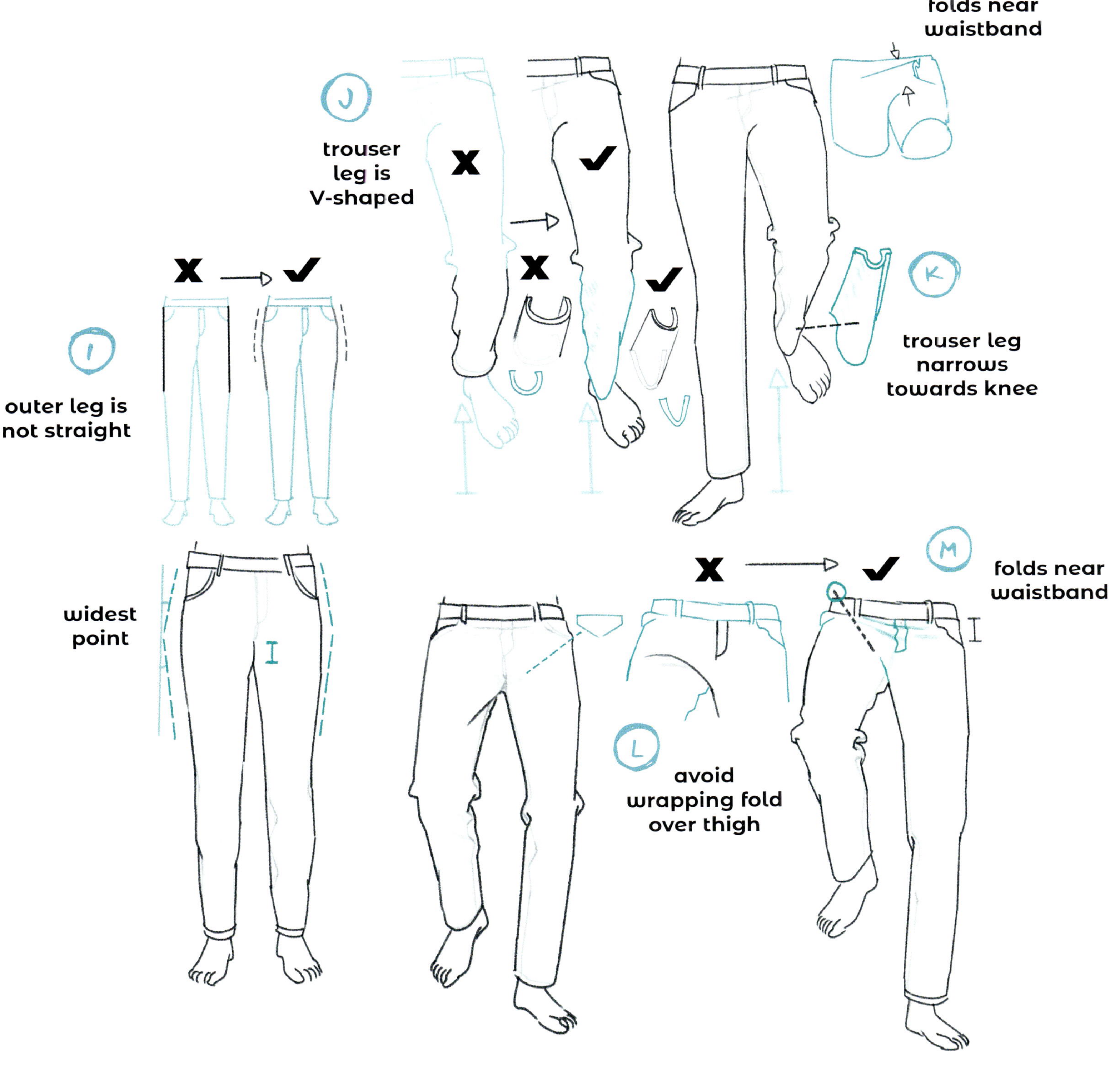

tip: flies & waistbands

Don't extend the fly too far down (A). From this angle, the back and kidneys often bulge out and hang over the belt, even on slimmer individuals (B). There's often an inwards tapering of this region (C). The belt and waistband should curve down towards the front-centre of the belt, rather than sitting flat (D). The section of waistband across the lower back is often straighter than you'd expect (E) – avoid drawing it curved, like you would draw the stomach. Avoid drawing the fly and lines of the inner legs too long – they shouldn't meet in the middle (F). The waistband usually drops in the middle to form a gentle 'V' (G).

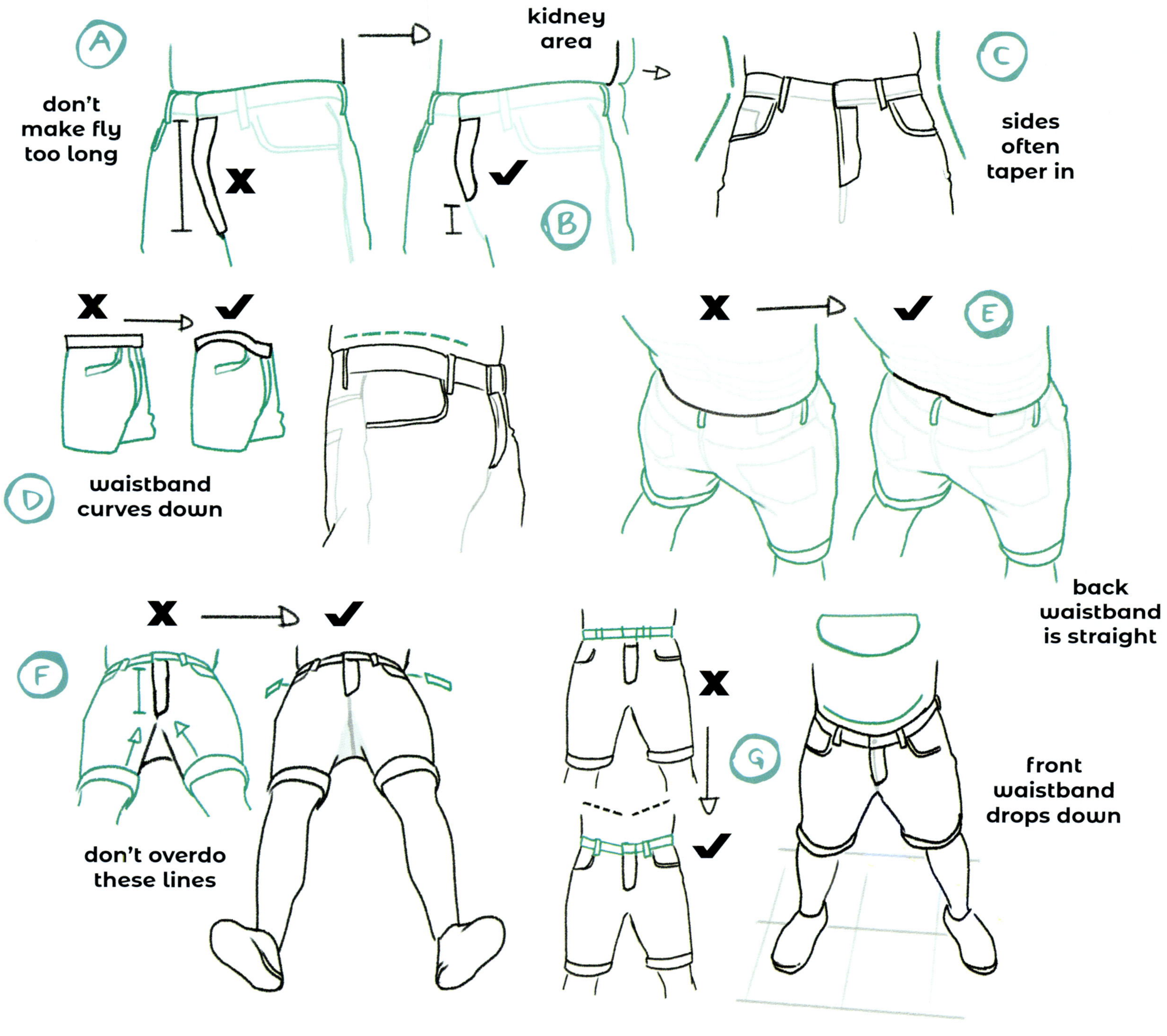

Let's look at this top-left example, where several simple-to-adjust errors have been made (H). The belt has been drawn horizontal, but it should have a slight angle **(1)**. The fly has been drawn straight, but it should bulge forwards slightly **(2)**. There are also too many belt loops **(3)**. The pockets are too flat – although jeans-style pockets are almost horizontal, most pockets are closer to vertical **(4)**. Garments usually have five belt loops, so we can remove some of those (I). On the back, jeans typically have some extra panels and patches (J), and the rear pockets should include a triangle on the bottom and have some additional stitching. Folds often appear below the glutes, particularly in standing poses where the legs are straight (K). When adding folds, you often see these forms drawn (L), but it's more appropriate to add compression below the waistband, and below the pockets on the sides (M). Usually there's no need to add folds to the front of the thigh.

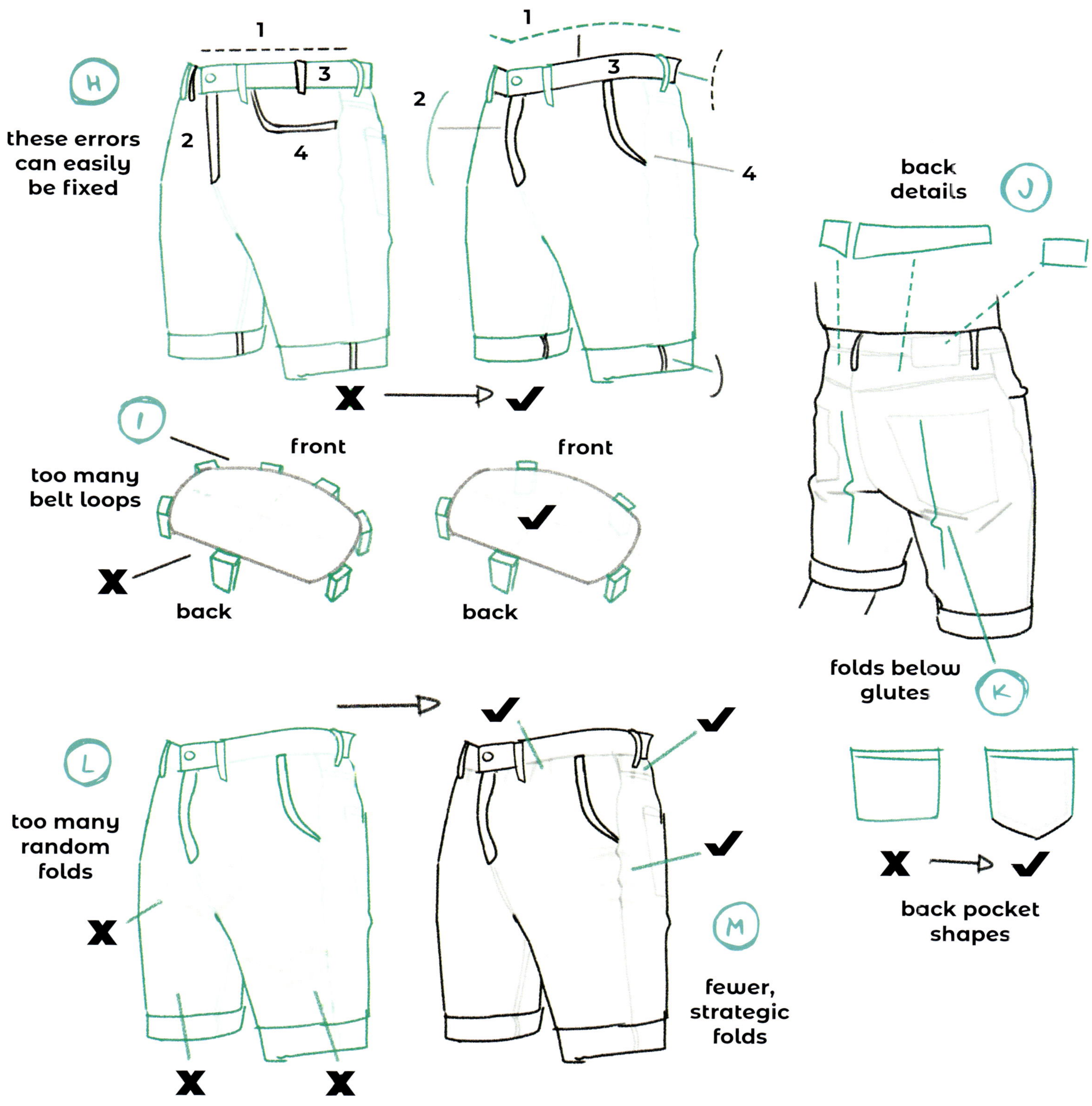

walking to running

As the front leg is brought forwards, compression occurs between the hips and top of the thigh, and just below the rear knee (A). Between strides, you'll see messy, random folding between the knees (B). This side region is often drawn too straight, without getting wider (C). When this happens, it looks like some of the outside of the legs and glutes has been removed. The neckline of a dress can be challenging, but it's also a great tool for indicating twist. Make sure it wraps up and over the trapezius muscles (on either side of the neck) and isn't a simple U-shape (D). When fully running, the forward knee may pull so strongly that the fabric above the back of the rear knee is raised and compressed on the back of the thigh (E).

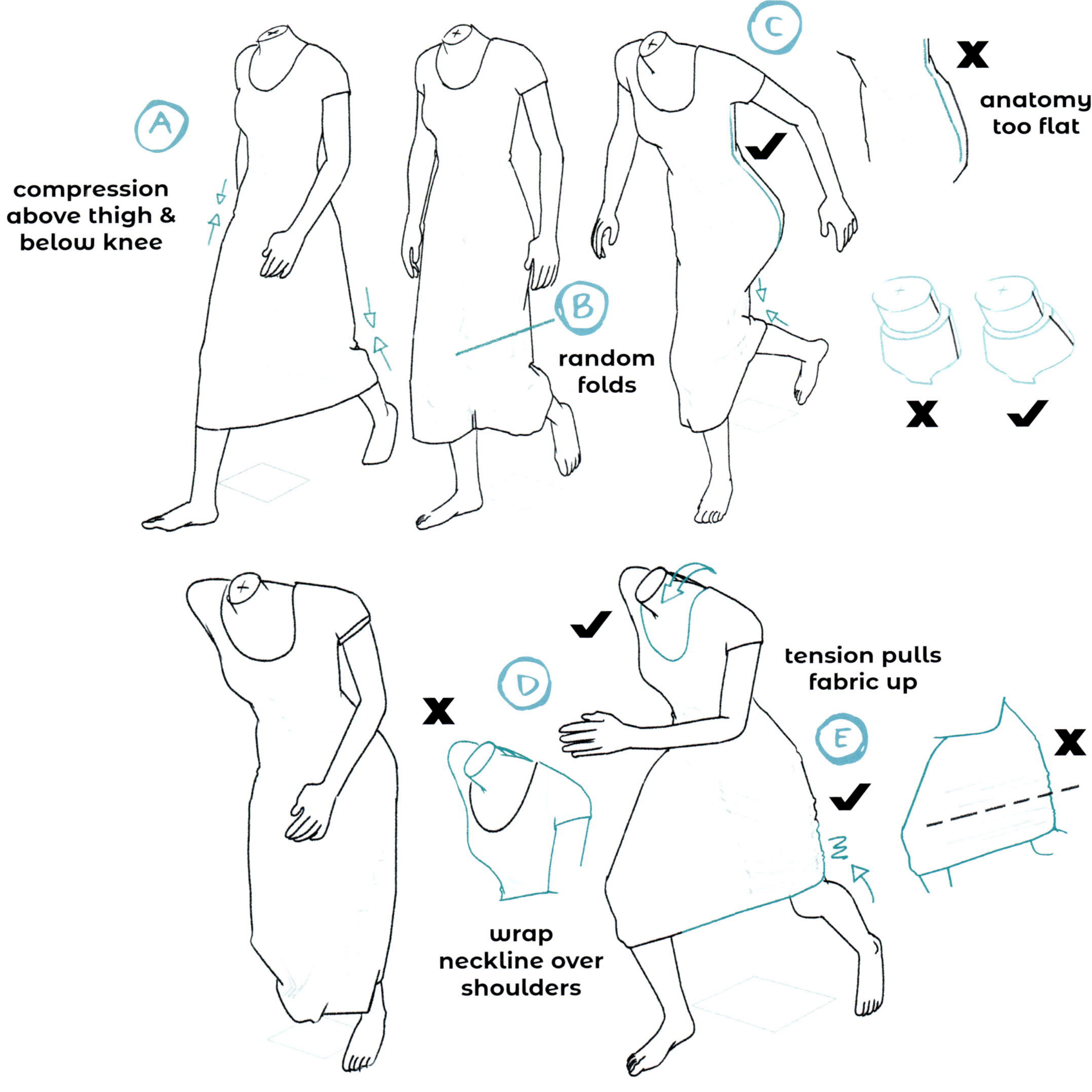

The first thing to pay attention to in these references is the indicated angles of the folds. For example, notice that the angle of the folds just above the thigh **(1)** is not the same as the angle lower down **(2)**. These angles change throughout the running process. The second thing to pay attention to is the areas where there are no folds. I've indicated one here **(3)**, but it's better to leave you to observe them, without making the drawings too noisy. Regions with no folds tell you just as much about the simulation as regions with folds.

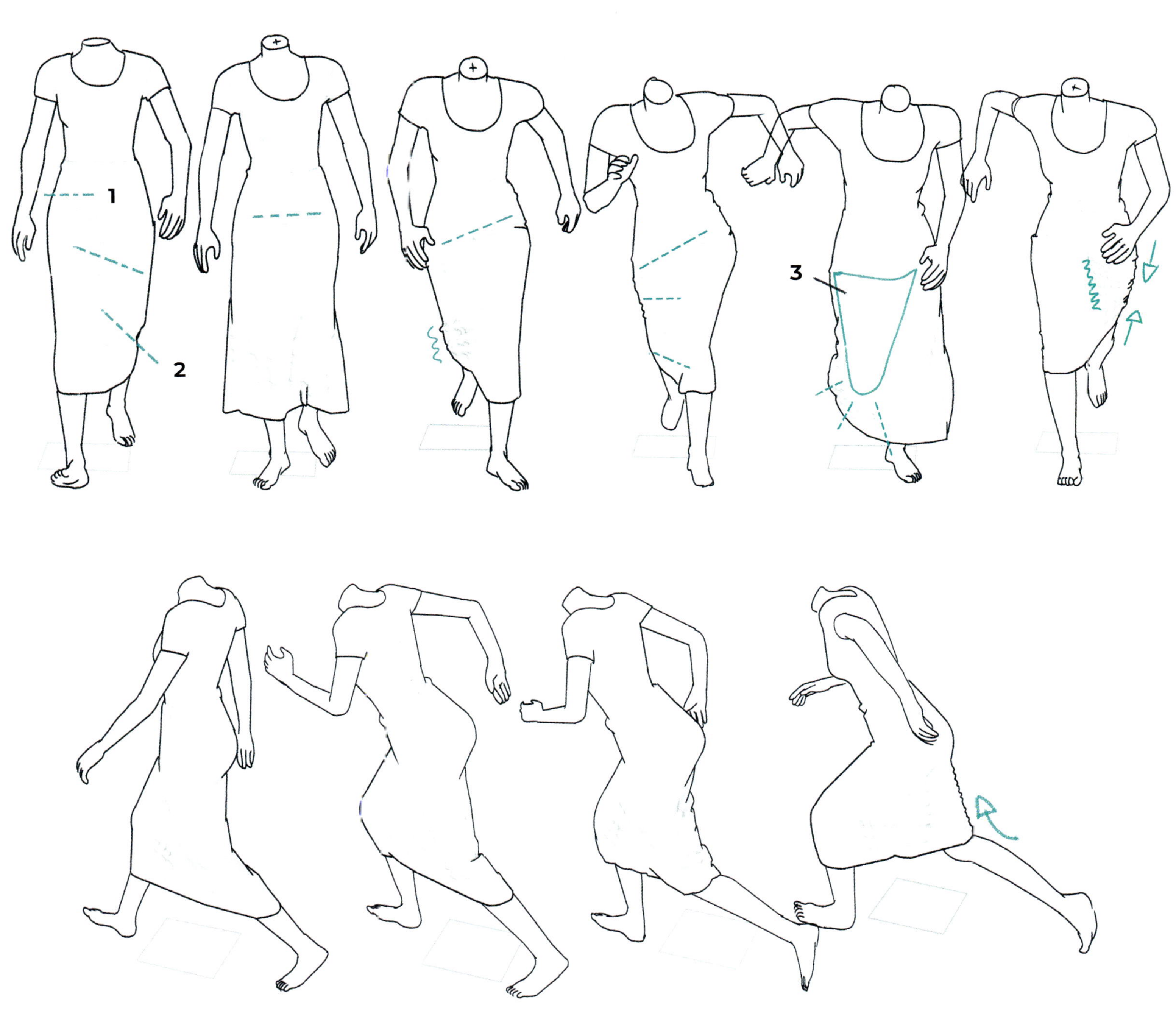

jogging

When jogging, the shoulders are held back to allow for easier breathing, which creates these folds on either side of the upper back (A). When one leg is extended and impacts the ground (B), the momentum creates shallow folds across the top of the torso **(1)**. At the same time, the opposite arm is brought back, which causes a series of diagonal folds starting here **(2)** and wrapping up and under the rear armpit **(3)**. The forward leg also causes compression here **(4)**. Between strides, the folding is more central (C). From behind (D), these diagonal folds are mirrored, wrapping from here **(5)** to here **(6)**. As the shoulder swings back, this form appears behind it (E).

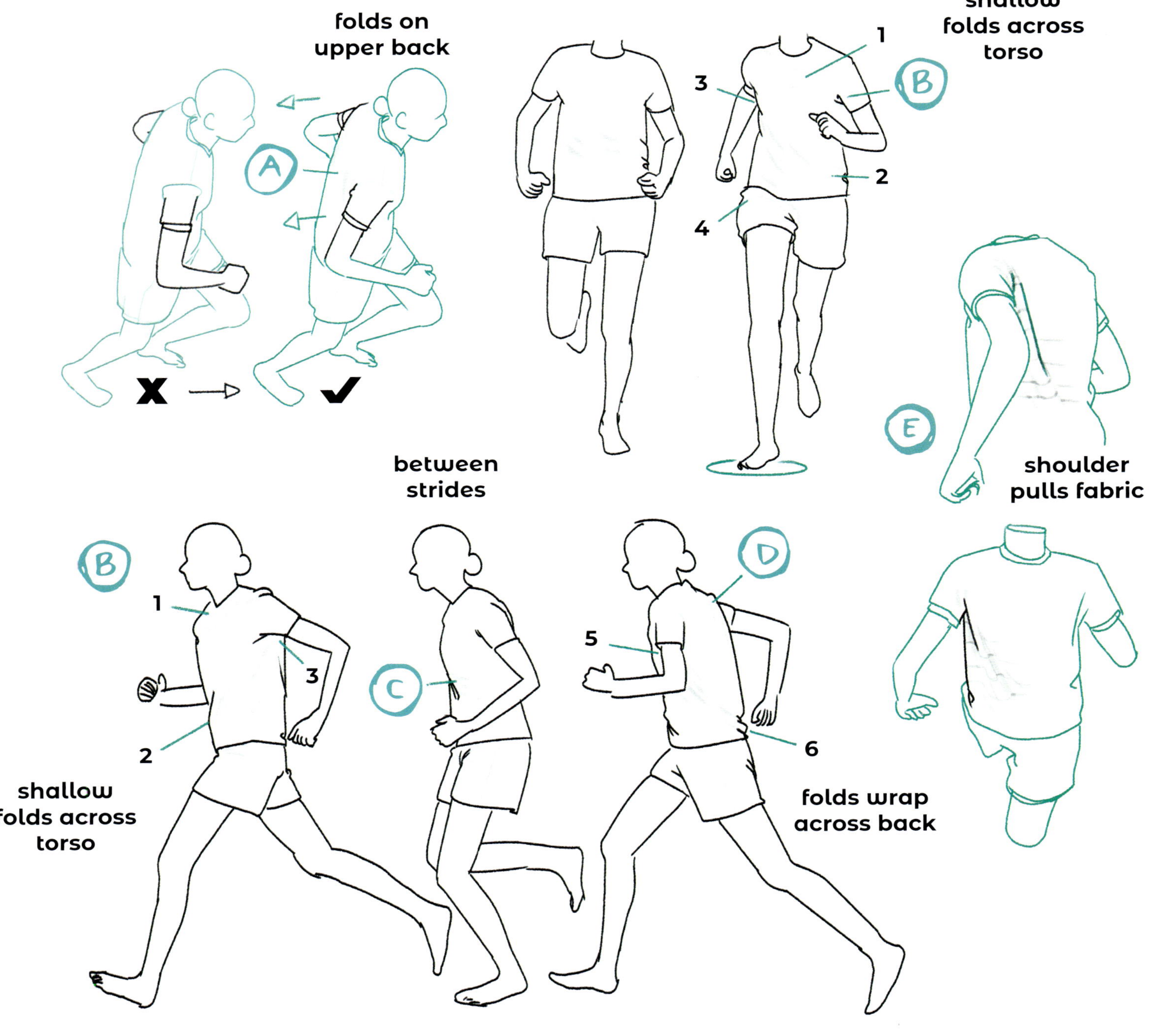

When drawing this seam (F), think of a circle in perspective. As the ellipse narrows, it changes our impression of which way the arm is facing. Try to get it as accurate as possible, so it doesn't confuse the viewer (G). The buttons below the collar are another powerful symbol you can use to influence the twist of the torso – a slight adjustment can make the whole torso look like it has rotated (H). These folds on the inside of the arm often have a lovely curving shape to them (I). Add this conical shape onto the side of a bent arm (J). These folds on a backward leg will flow out and back from the inside (K).

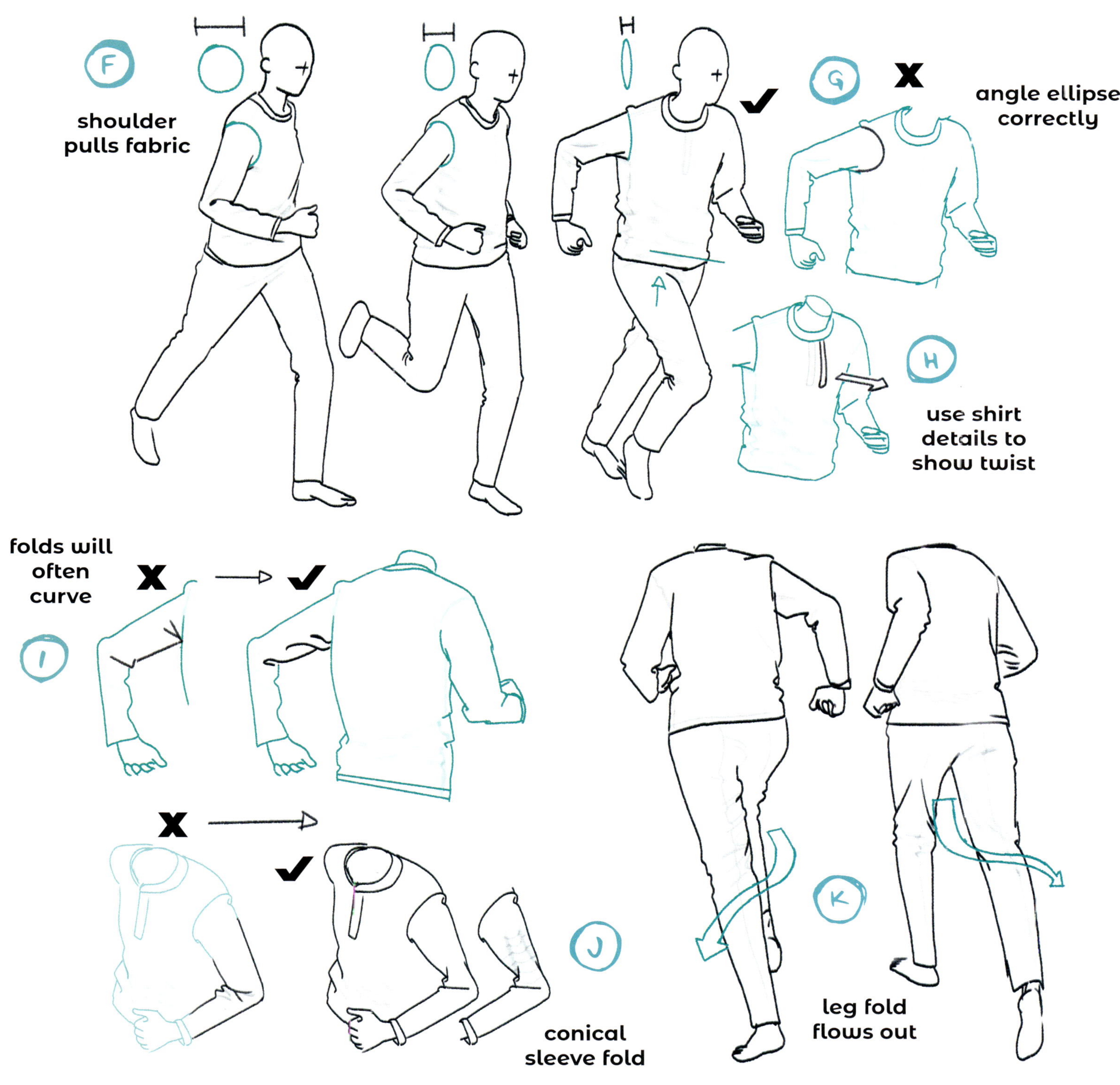

running

It's important to get these sleeve overlaps right – the arm should look like it's rotating inwards, rather than simply being straight (A). Tracksuit bottoms typically have quite low crotch areas. Because of this, you'll often see a sort of 'ledge' of material form when the legs are between strides (B). When one leg is extended, the folds around the fly sit at this angle (C). Use the pocket of the hoodie – or any graphics on the chest – to help demonstrate twist (D). The fold on the inside of this arm is sometimes difficult to imagine (E). Finally, we see the flow of folds up and over the calf, when the leg is extended back (F).

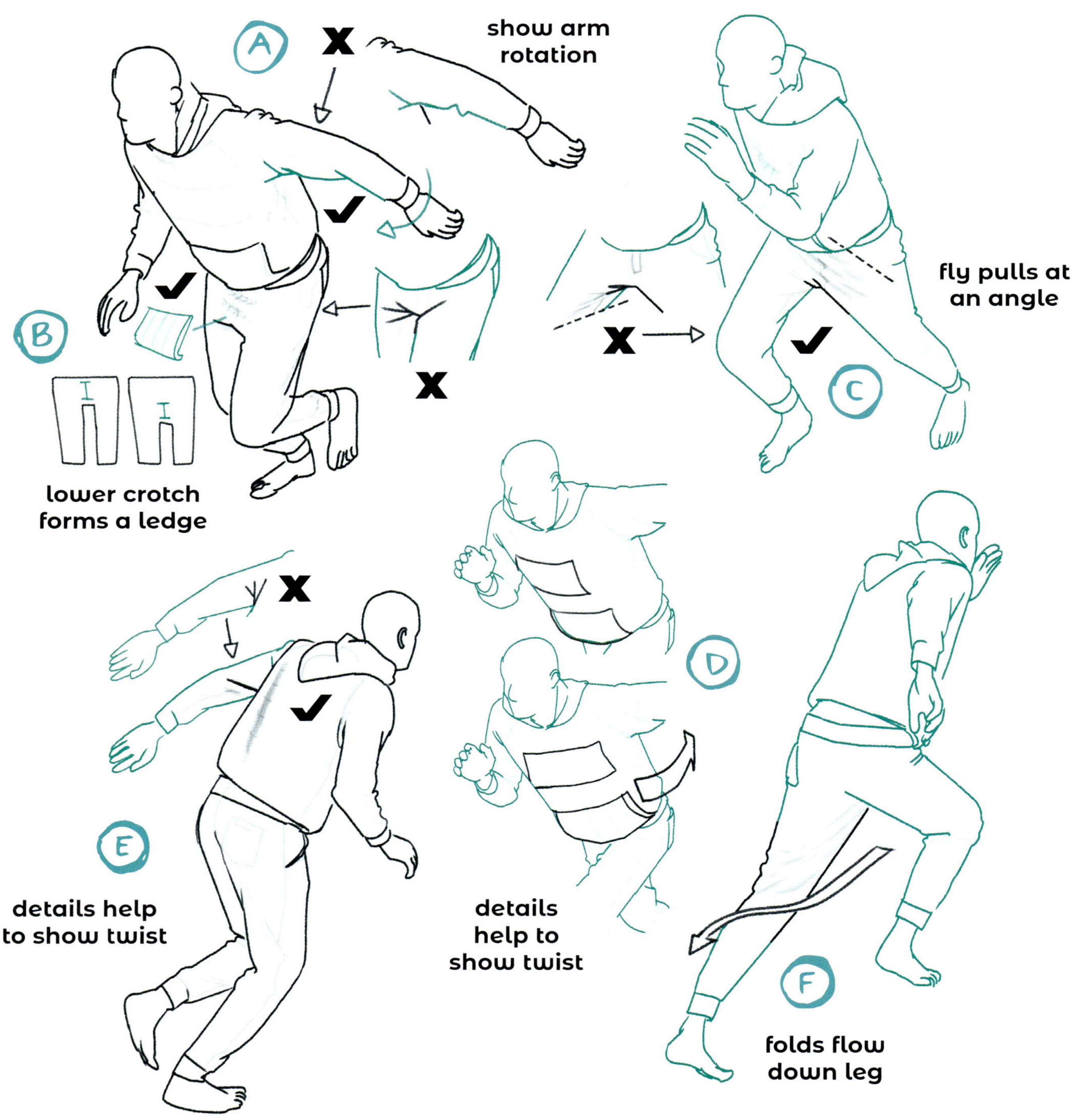

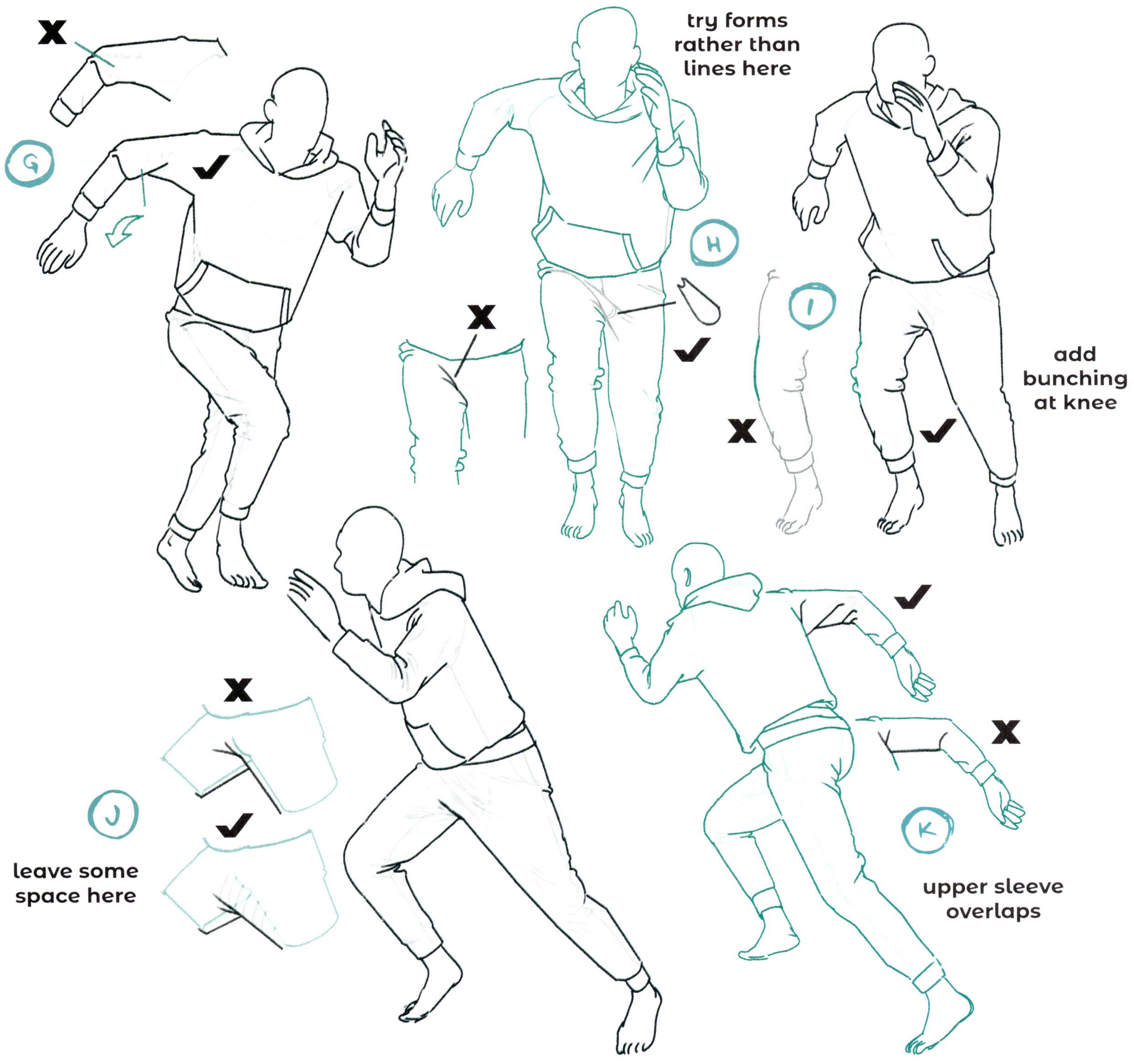

When the arm is raised back like this, the upper sleeve often falls down upon itself (G). When drawing the crotch region, don't think, 'What lines do I need to draw here?' Instead, ask, 'What new forms need to be added here?' In this case, you often see this additional form (H). It's tempting to draw the far side of the knee as a simple line (I), but there's often some visible folding from this angle. In this situation (J), include some space between the fabric and the mannequin – the raised thigh pulls the fabric further from the anatomy beneath. These overlaps are tricky to get right, so it's worth learning this pattern (K).

When one arm is brought forwards, you can use this useful shape to help describe the folding that occurs (L). The raised leg on the opposite side will cause bunching at the bottom of the T-shirt (M). The highest level of compression around the waist occurs when neither arm is fully forwards (N). Note this sleeve shape – rather than being rounded, it stays quite angular (O). Sometimes the momentum of the movement causes larger sleeves to flare outwards (P). If you squint at this page, you'll see that the contours and internals are really not important when it comes to drawing this motion. What matters are the major overlaps and the silhouette of the sleeves and mannequin.

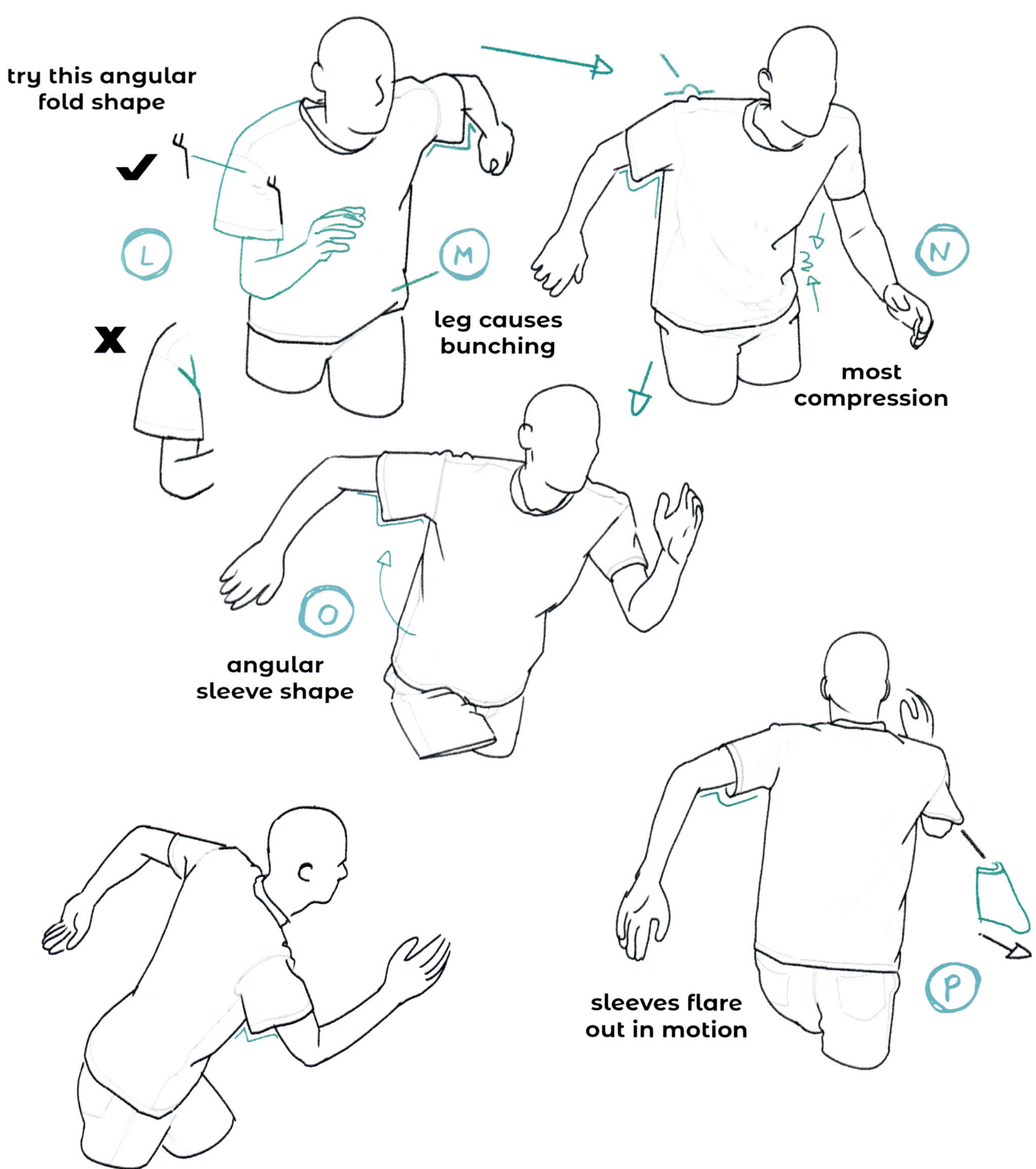

When the arms are swinging, these seams will rarely be flat (Q). Instead, you'll often see gentle folding across the top of the shoulders (1, 2). When one arm swings forwards, this broad, shallow fold may appear (R). As one arm swings back, compression occurs in the middle of the upper back (S). From this angle, you may see these folds, which help to suggest the twist (T). When drawing a raised leg from the front, people often leave the outer side smooth, when you'd most likely see some folding on both sides (U).

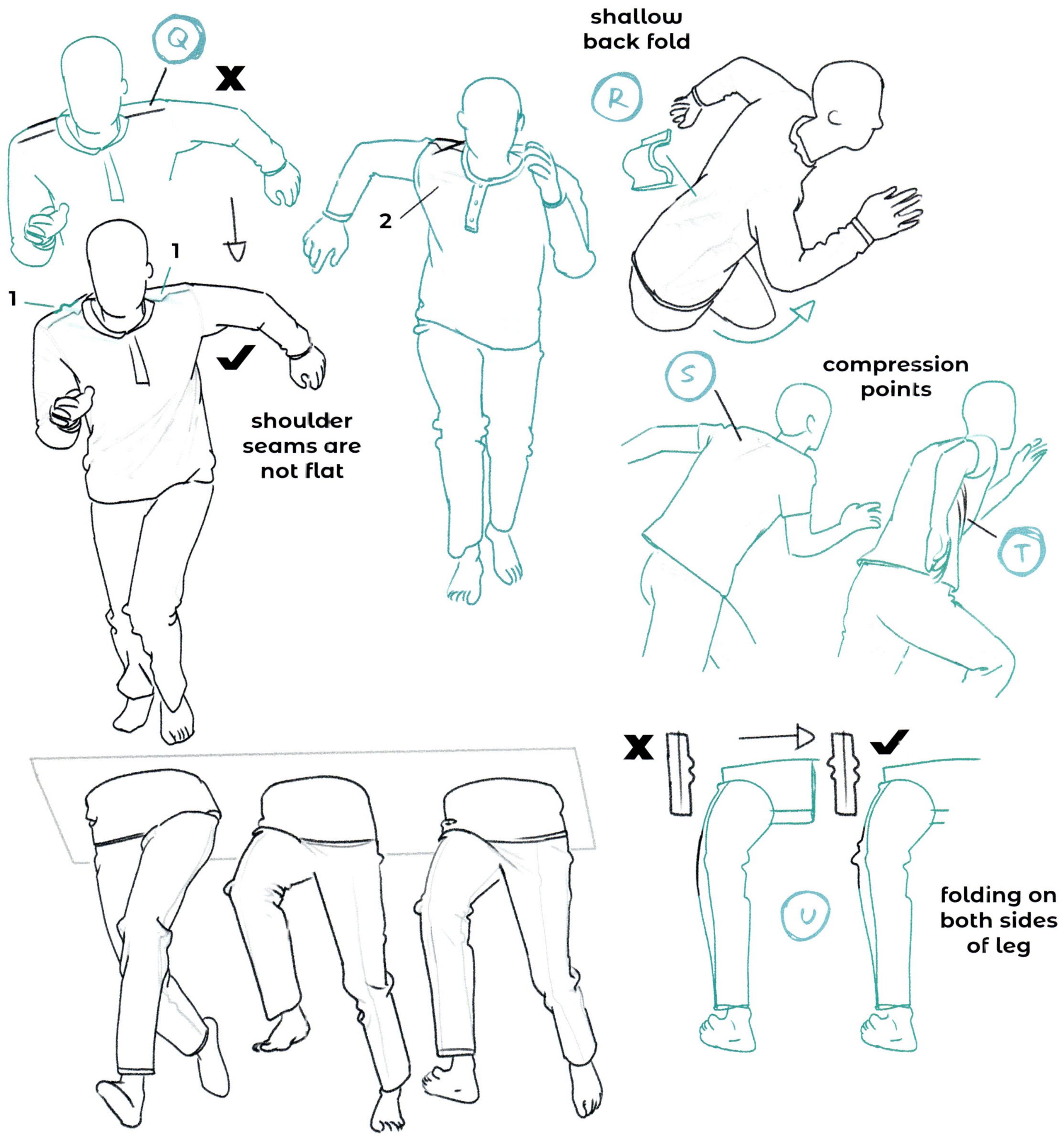

running jump

The back leg is bent to generate the power to leave the ground (A), and then the arms are thrown up to add momentum (B). Once in the air, the arms reverse position: the front arm swings back and the back arm swings forwards (C). As the arms move, the torso twists, too. Near the top of the jump, the fabric of the top of the T-shirt lifts up and folds gently (D). When this arm is back, make sure there are clear overlaps (E). When the arm is extended high, this part of the silhouette should be pulled taut (F). The forward arm also appears to drag material with it from the other side of the torso (G).

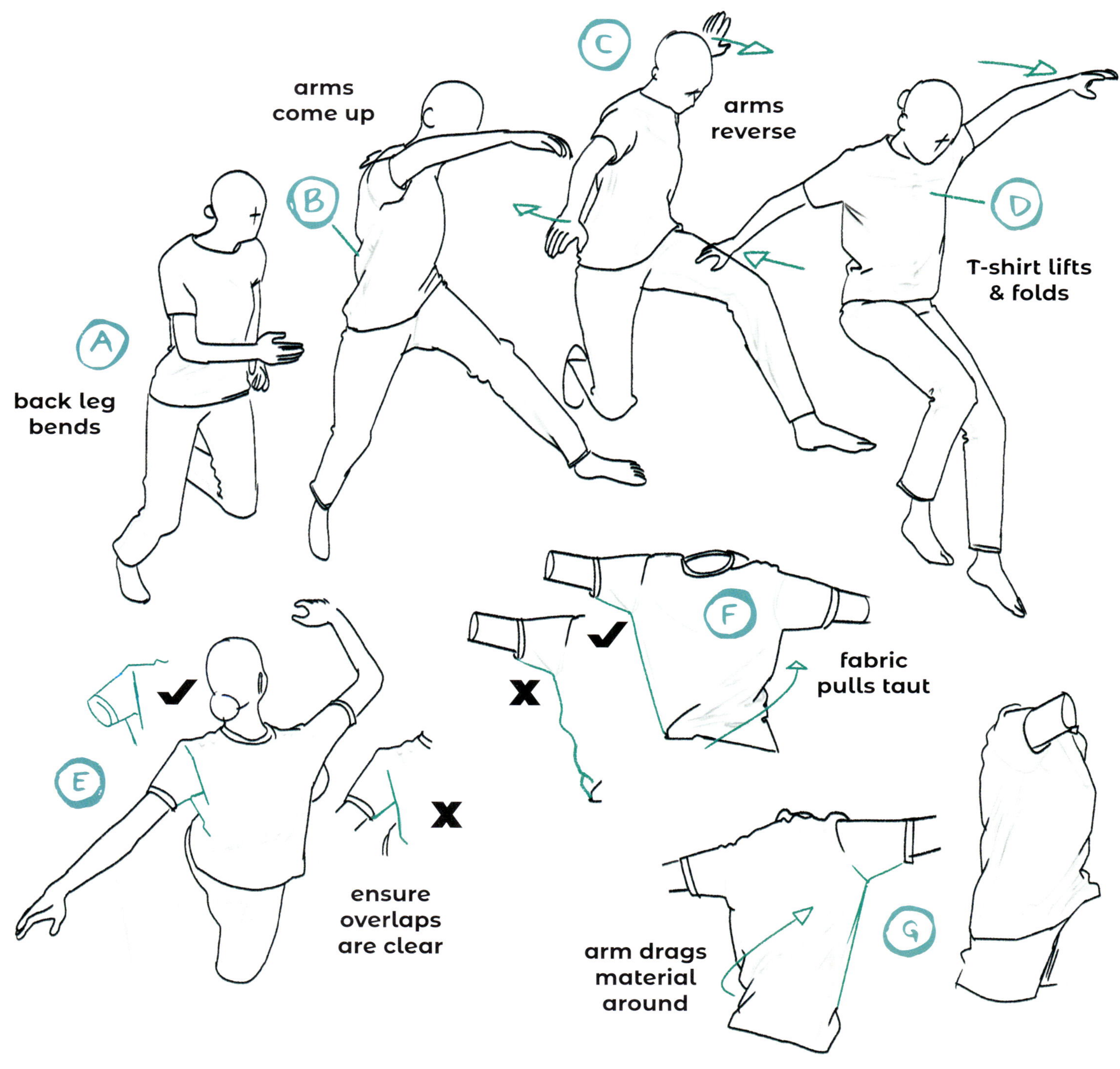

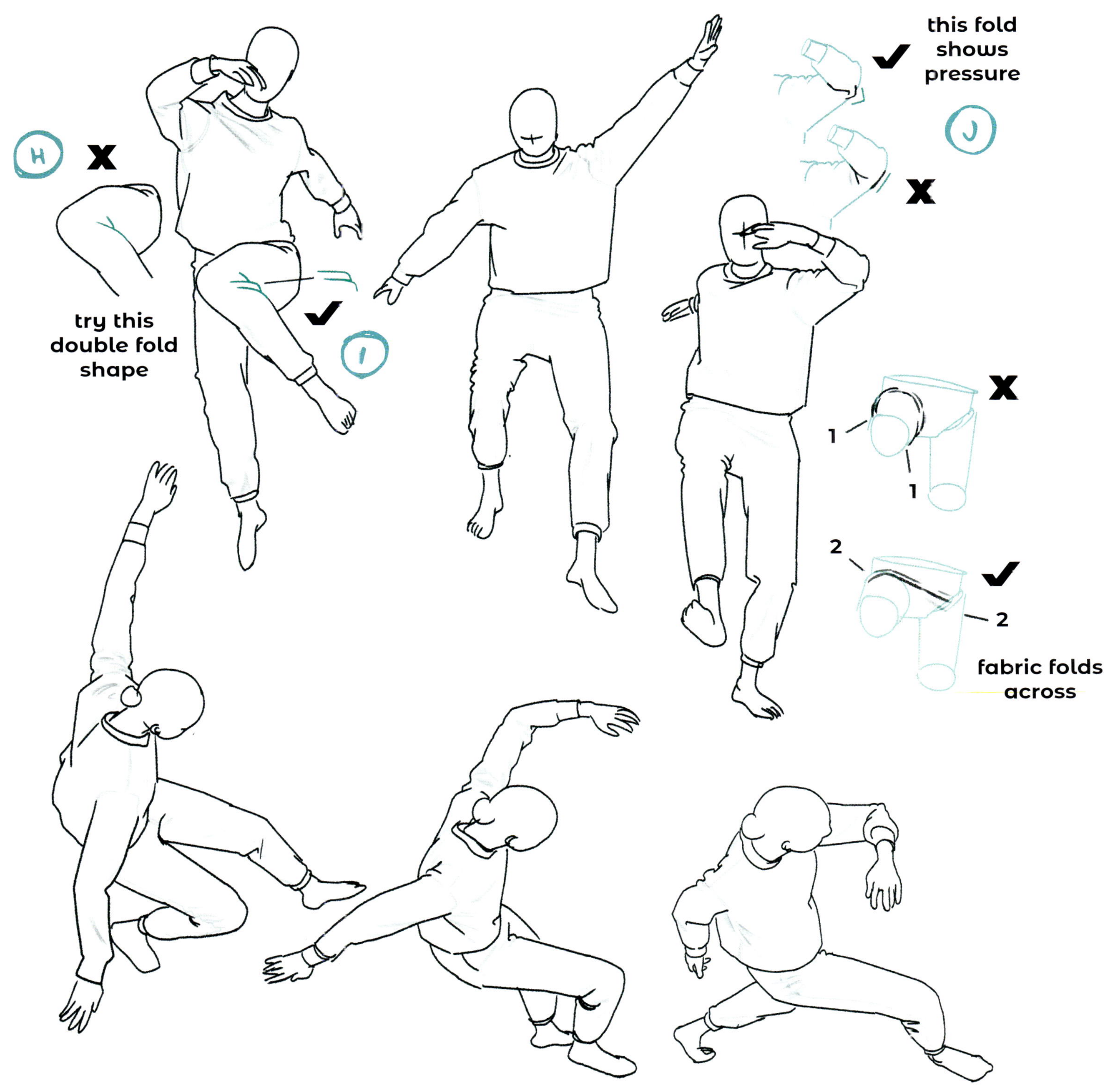

This is an interesting line pattern that describes folding: rather than a 'V' shape (H), we see a double line (I). This folded sleeve also shows a interesting fold pattern: we have a Z-line and a slight bulge that helps indicate the pressure (J). When drawing a raised leg, the folding shouldn't look like it's connecting these two points **(1)**. Instead, it usually connects these **(2)**.

vaulting

The bunching on the front of the torso won't be evenly distributed – the heaviest bunching will occur near the legs (A). As you move forwards, one arm is planted to support some weight. When both arms are raised, folds connect these two points rather than dropping down towards the waist (B). The crotch region tends to expand outwards further than you'd expect, rather than always folding higher up (C). That sort of folding does happen, but mostly on trousers with a tight fit. The same is true when viewed from behind (D). Note this fold around the knee – it will almost never be a simple radiating fold (E). In order to indicate that the figure is leaning over to one side slightly, these overlaps are important (F) – avoid drawing a straight line here.

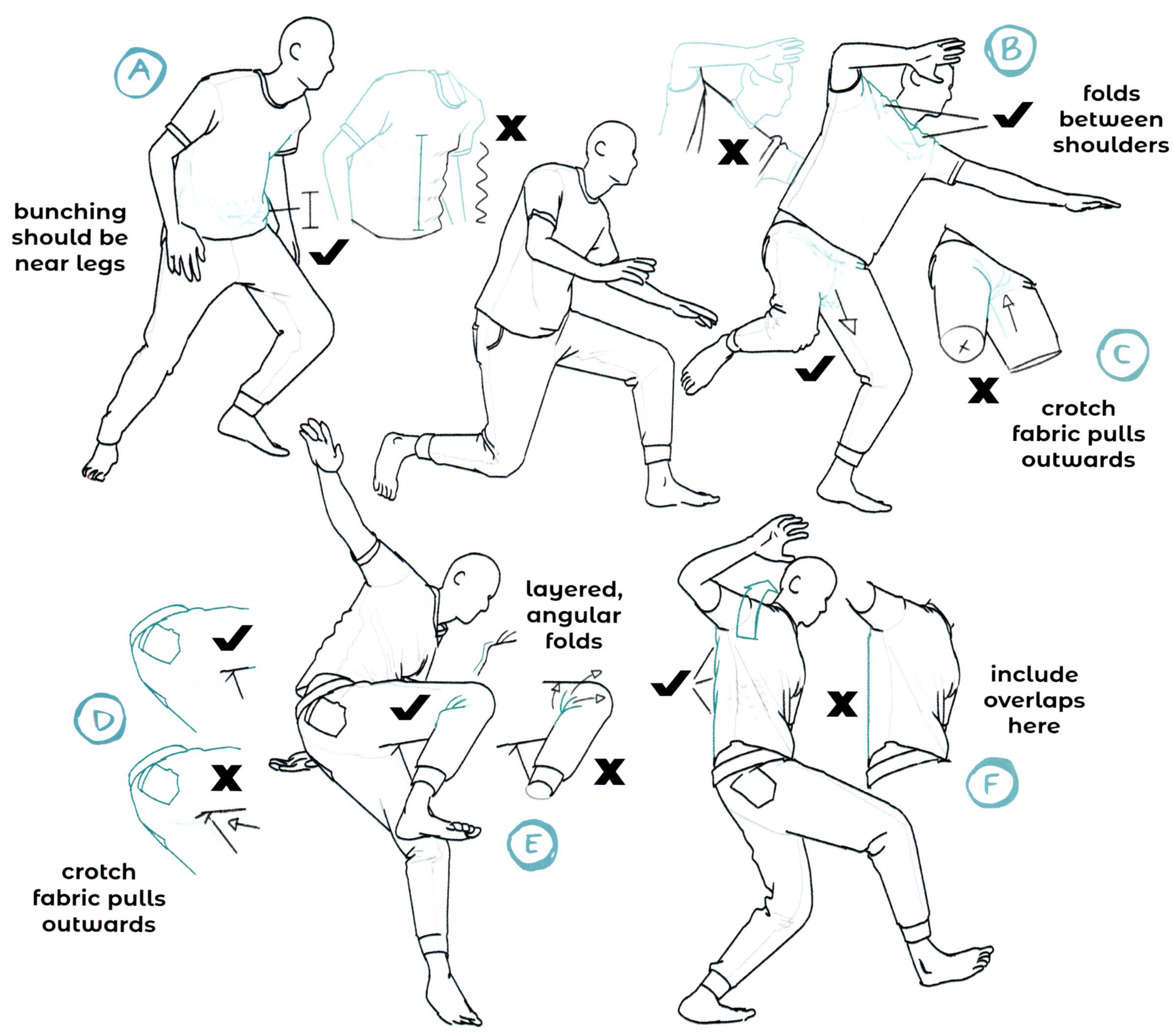

When running, the flaps on the shirt pockets may fall forwards, which helps suggest movement (G). The side of the shirt isn't level, but raised in the centre (H). When you start to drop, the shirt raises up, which may cause bunching on the back of the neck (I). The bottom edges of the shirt will lift too, but they'll only rarely turn upwards. Instead, they'll raise, but still curve downwards (J). When a shirt compresses forwards, this front section is usually the part furthest forwards (K). It forms a sort of 'wedge' shape.

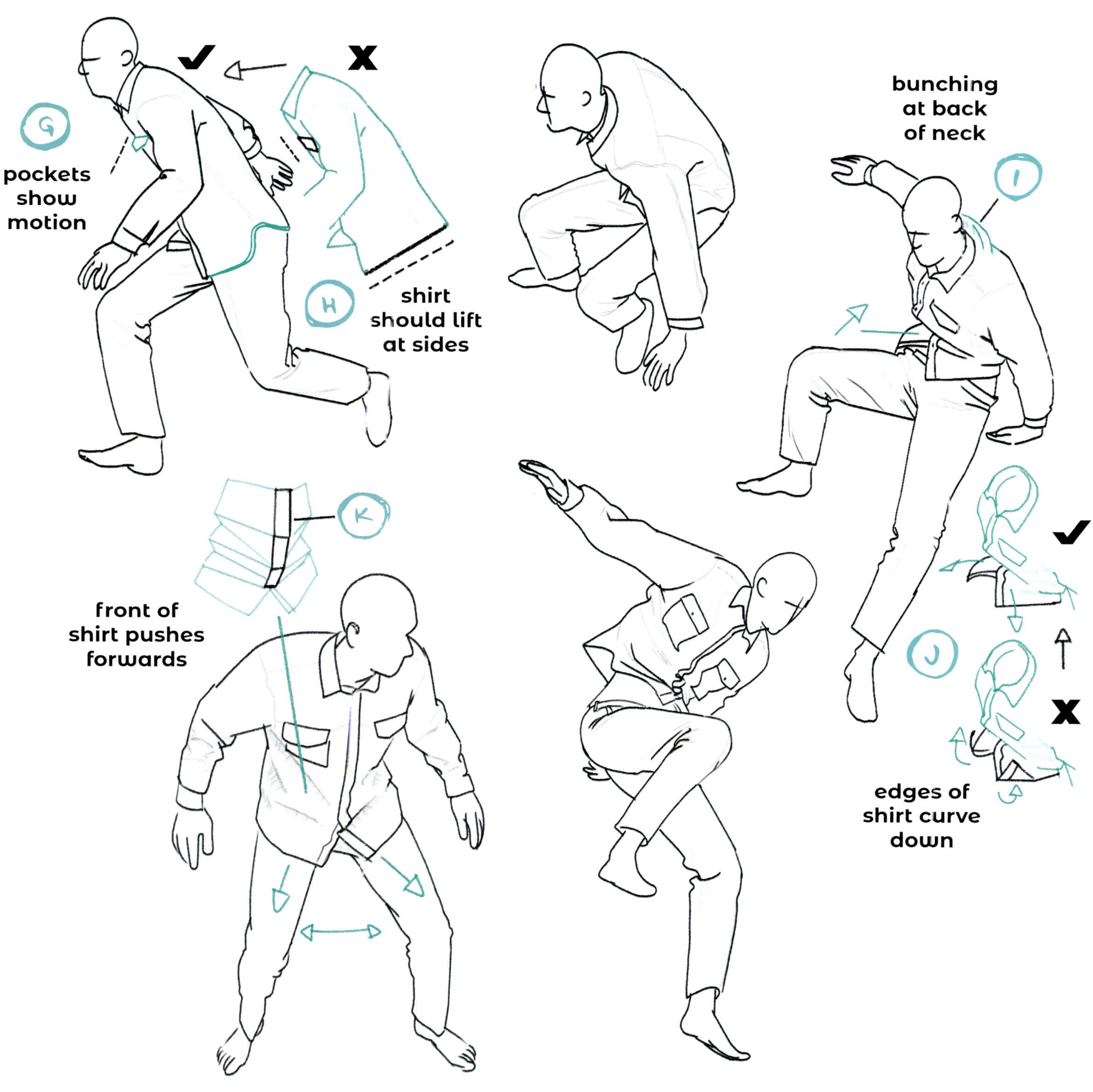

shoulder carry

When a character leans forwards this far, the T-shirt won't hang evenly down. Instead, the sides usually compress inwards (A). On baggier trousers, the bending of the knees causes this shape to stick out in front of the shin **(1)**. Folding happens on the top of the lower back **(2)**. This is a challenging fold to imagine – the sides are pushed out by the inside top of the thigh, causing this form to appear (B).

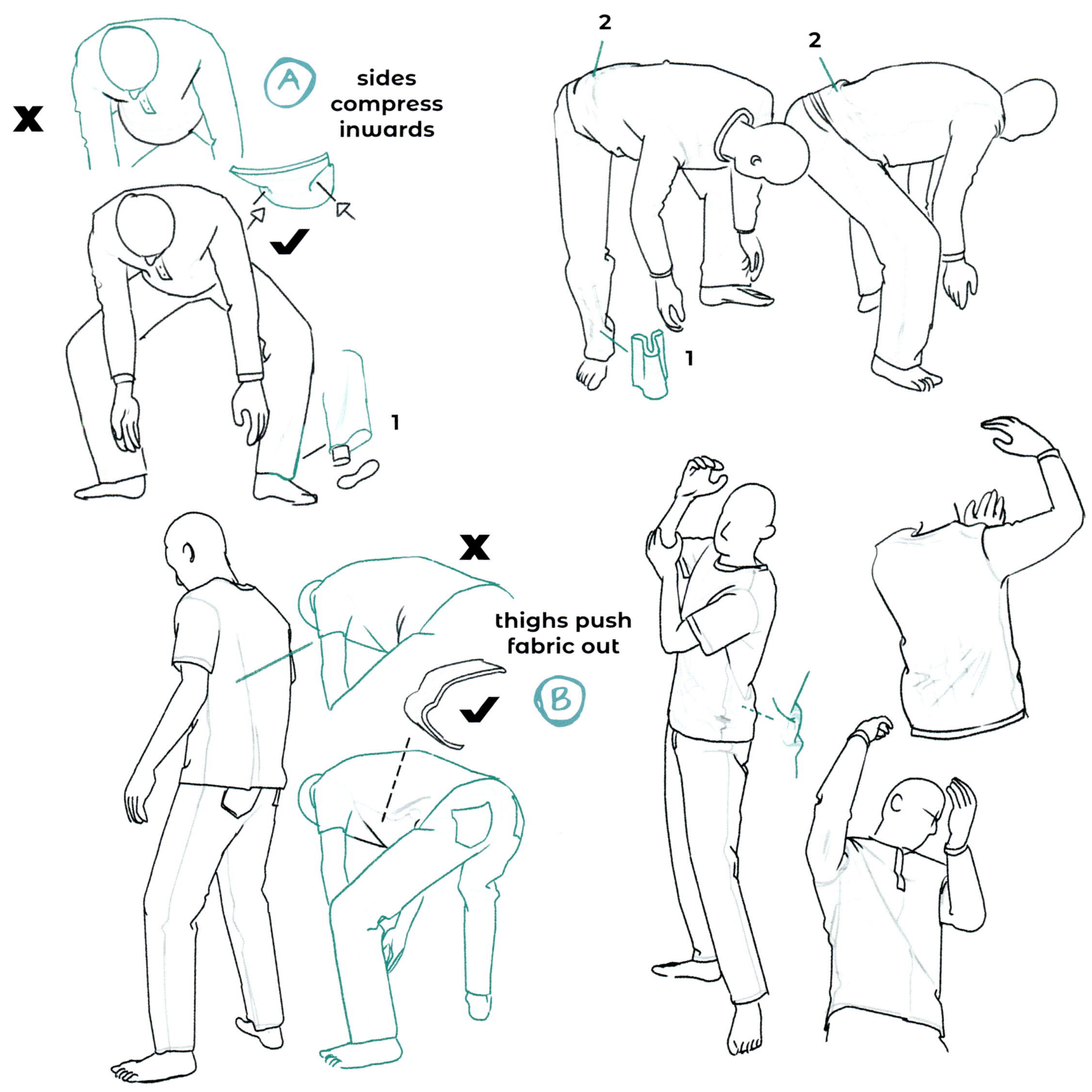

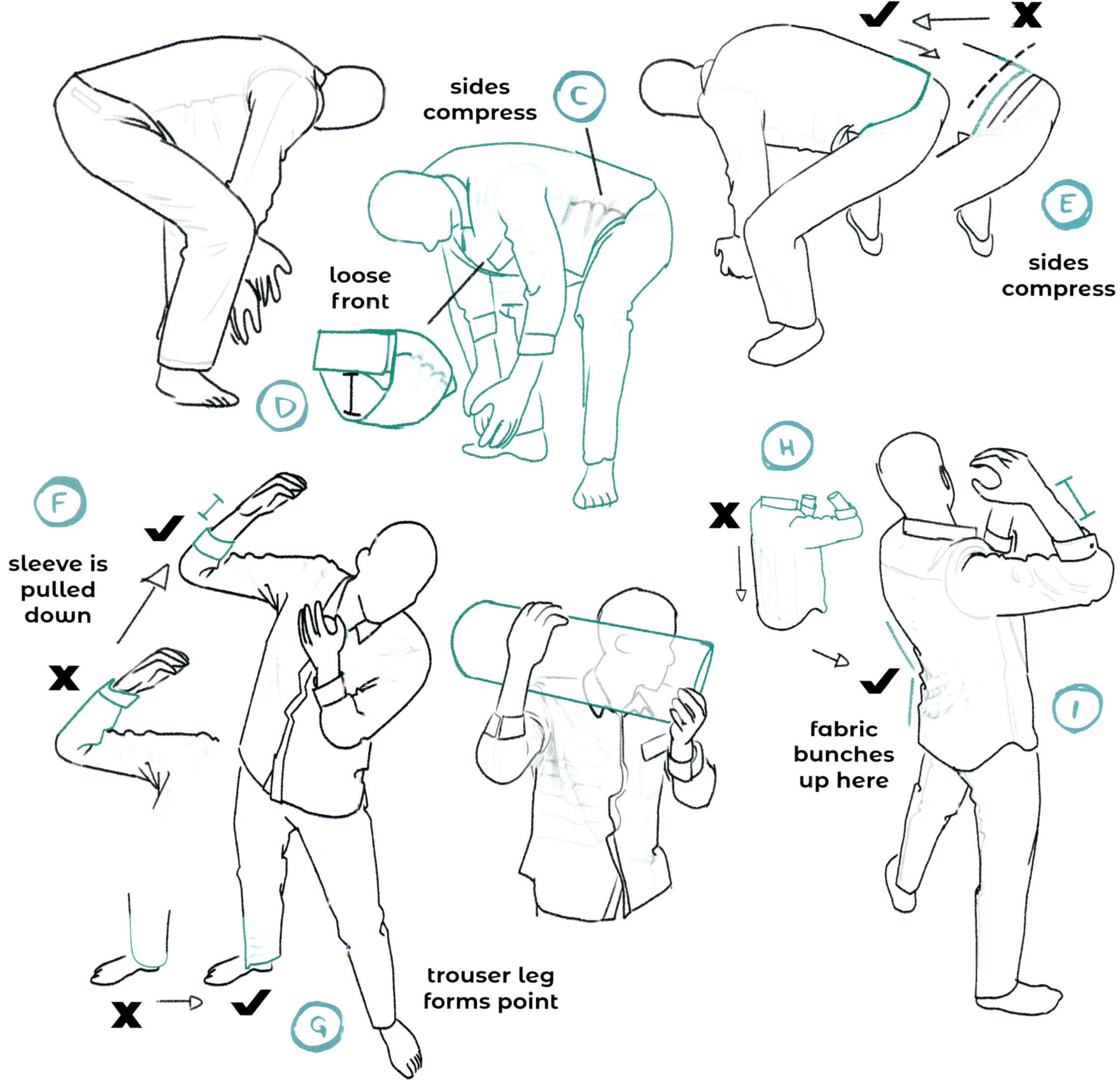

When bending like this, the torso and core are squeezed between the legs, compressing the sides of the shirt (C). Most shirts are loose enough to leave a gap between the mannequin and the front of the shirt (D). The back of the shirt is lower than the sides, so it continues down the torso when you bend (E). When the arm is bent like this, the sleeve is usually pulled down the arm (F).

When the leg is just slightly bent, the front of the trouser leg often forms a sharp point (G) – particularly if it has a strong crease on the front. When you carry something on your shoulder, you often lean back slightly. Rather than drawing a shirt hanging straight down (H), the fabric will usually be pulled inwards, and bunch around the lower back (I).

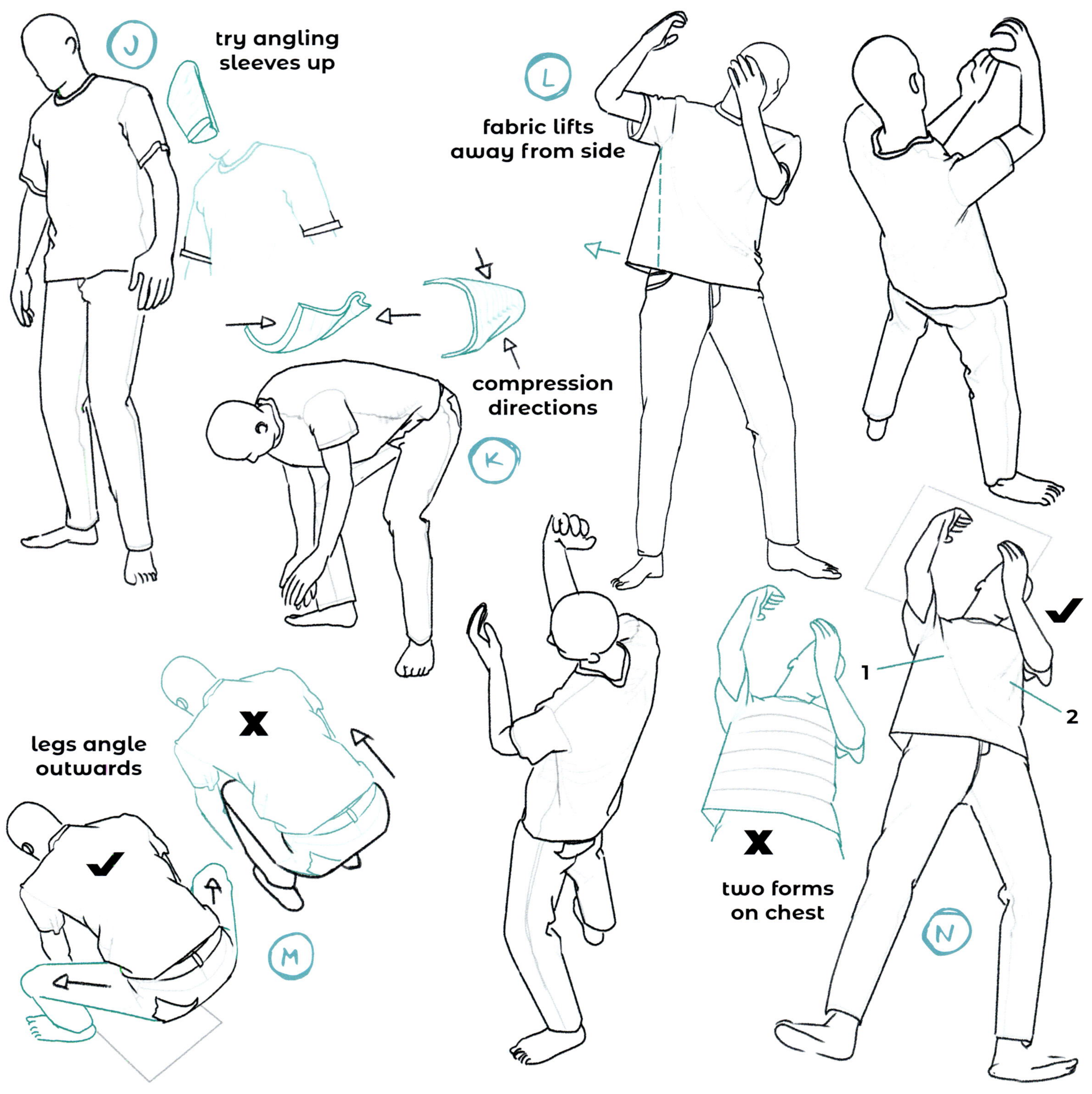

To add variety to your T-shirts, try angling the sleeves up for a different 'fit' (J). When bending forwards, compression occurs in two directions – from the bottom to top, and from the front to back (K). Raising this arm often causes the seam below the armpit to pull the fabric below it up and away from the body (L). When bending down, the legs usually angle outwards, rather than facing forwards (M). If they faced forwards, you wouldn't be able to pick up any large objects. Seen from below, when both arms are lifted high (N), these two forms are created on the sides of the chest **(1, 2)**.

heavy lifting

When the arms come together like this, you'll see some interesting forms on the front of the torso. Rather than being a smooth curve (A), you'll often find two bunches just on the inside of the arms (B), and a rounder form falling away from the core (C). The distance between the mannequin and garment will be larger at the core than near the chest. These seams are often drawn vertically, but should usually be angled outwards (D). From behind, the back often forms this wedge shape (E), widening towards the bottom.

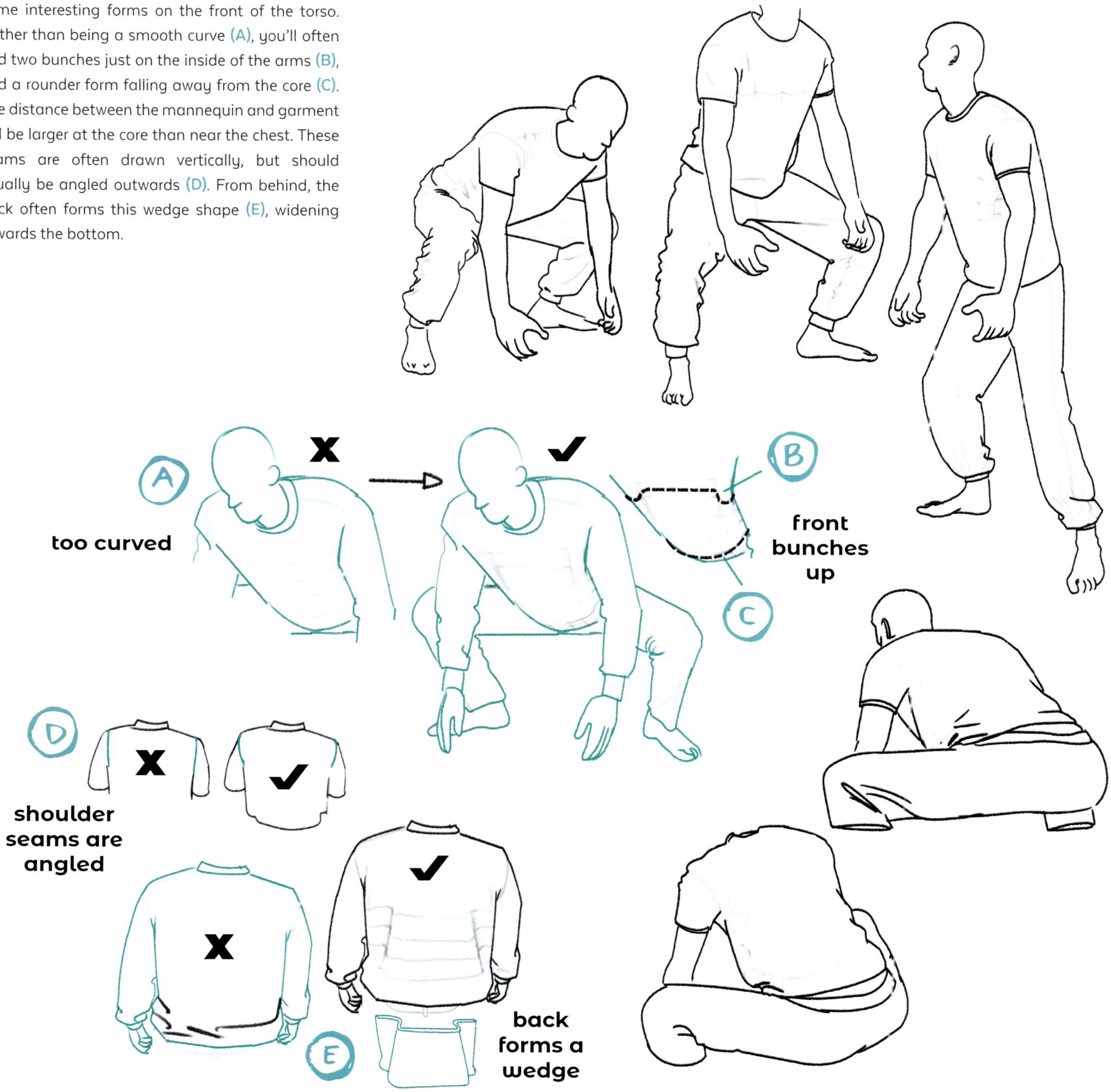

carrying a box

Many pairs of trousers have shallow folds along the back of the leg, even when a mannequin is standing with straight legs (A). When picking up a box like this (B), your left arm twists outwards slightly **(1)** and you lean back. As this arm is squeezed against the side of the torso, this fold appears **(2)**, which changes the silhouette (C). The more you lean back, the greater the compression around the backs of the knees **(3)**. The back of the sweatshirt also falls away from the core (C), which causes this form seen from above (D). Bunching still happens around the waist, so this ledge is created by leaning back (E). Note these diagonal folds, created by the leg swinging forwards (F).

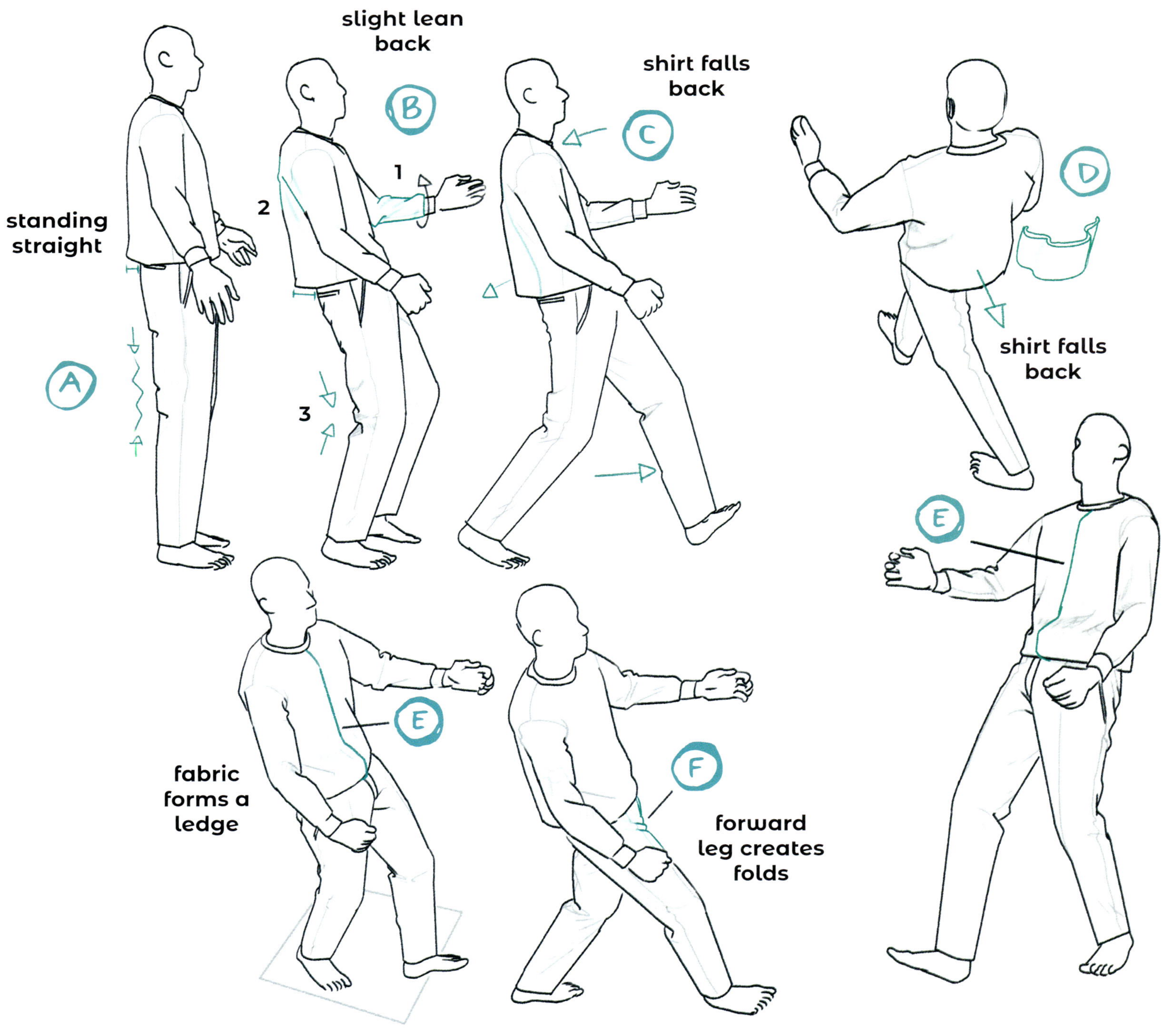

pushing

Drop one shoulder and move it forwards when suggesting a really strong push (A). Any contours on the top of the thigh should have this curving pattern (B), to reflect the underlying anatomy, rather than being a straight line. The fabric on the front of the core often bulges outwards rather than sitting flat (C). The raised arm should affect both the area immediately under the arm, and the lower back (D). As both arms are raised, a fold will wrap the lower back (E). When drawing a straight leg, make sure there's enough curvature on the back of the calf (F).

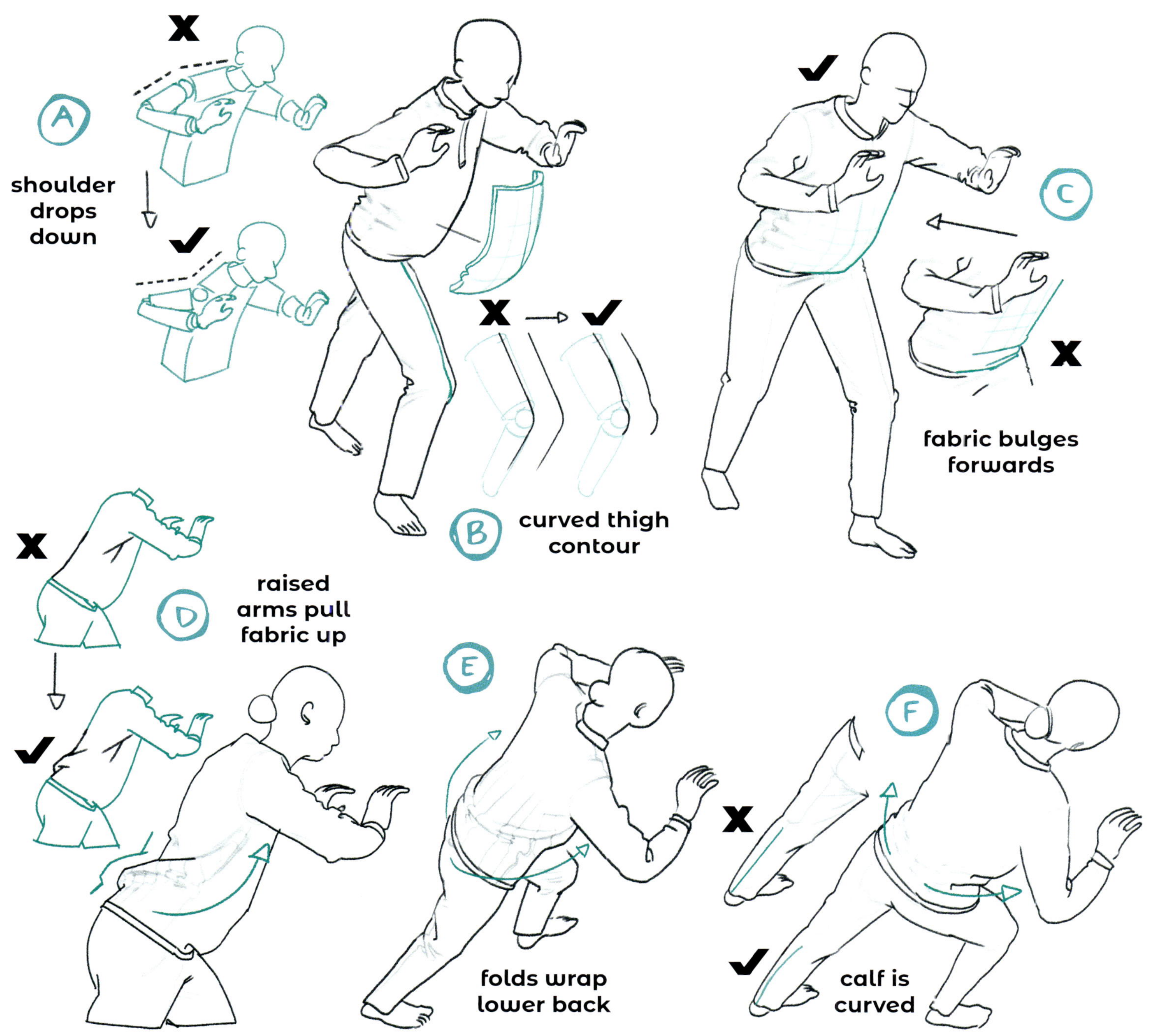

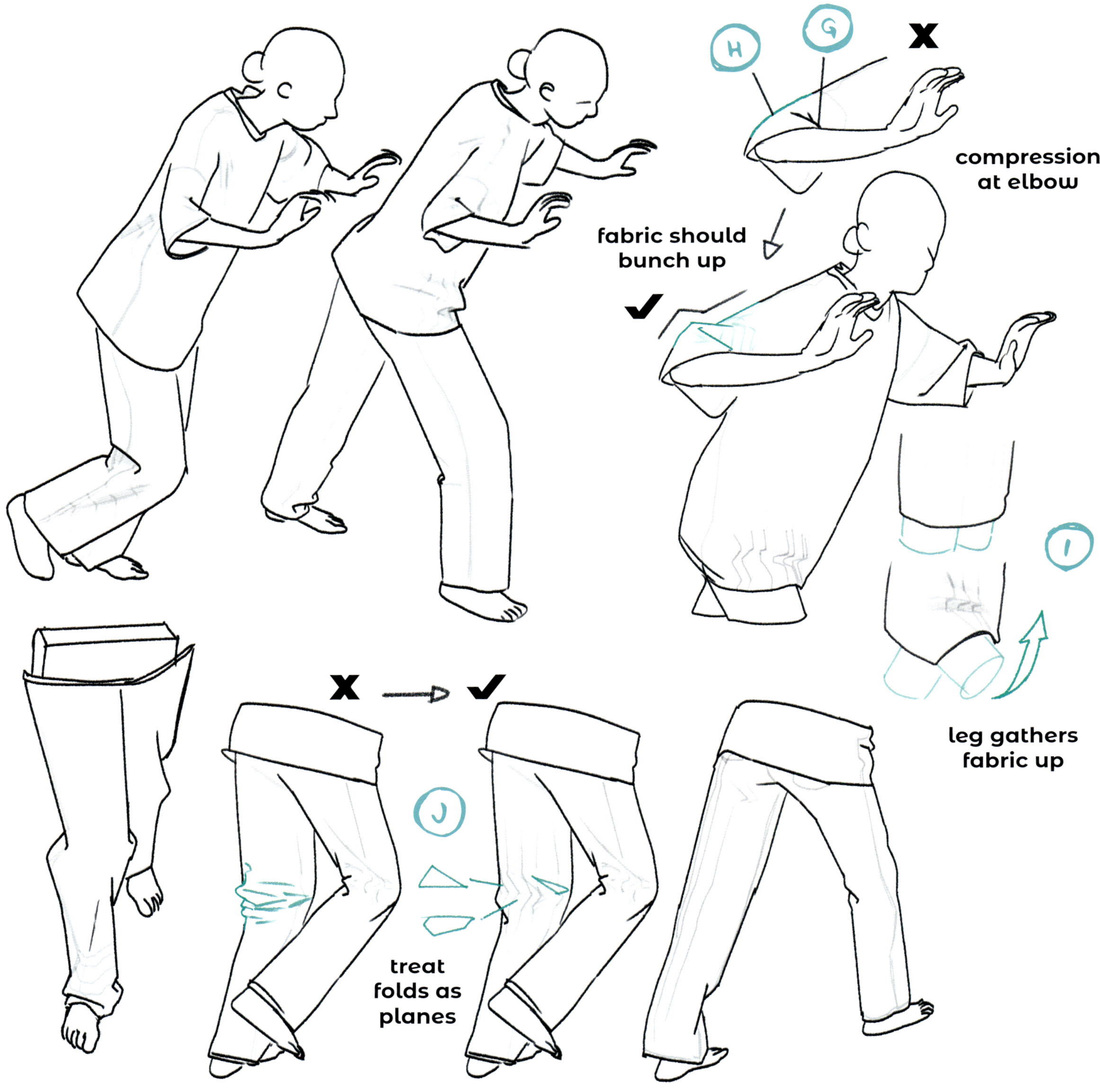

When a sleeve is this length, it often forms interesting drapery. Pay careful attention to when the arm bends. The compression here (G) should cause a deformation in the silhouette – it shouldn't be smooth, like this (H). When the leg swings up, the bottom of the garment will be gathered up and compressed (I). When you're adjusting your drawing, try to imagine the folding forming big planes, rather than a larger number of smaller, round, narrow tubes (J).

dragging

I always find this fold counter-intuitive (A) – it usually curves down, rather than up. We tend to bend down with a straighter back, which then 'rounds' as we begin dragging (B). The area between the upper thigh and side of the core is a region of compression (C). This is another unusual – but very common – fold, where the fabric on the shoulder partially conceals the upper arm (D). When dragging, there's often a strong lean to the side (E). This line extends further across the torso than you may expect, and needs to be included to make the drapery feel like its hanging over the core (F). Finally, the pockets must look like they sit on a curved surface, rather than a flat plane (G).

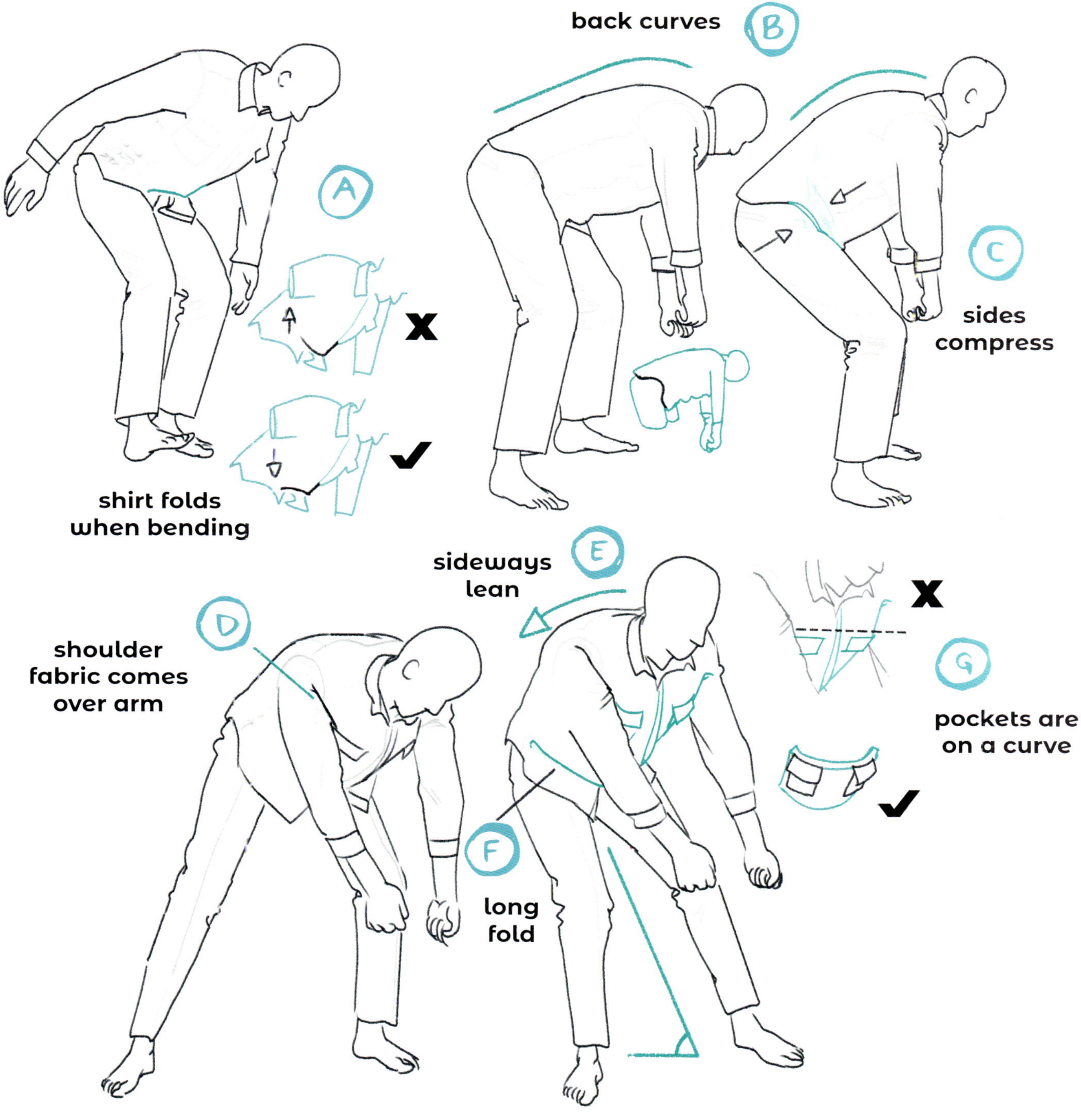

If cuffs are elasticated, it should be clear in the drawing. Avoid using a straight or single line, and instead give it a series of curves (H). When a character bends down quickly, the underside of the hood should fall away from the neck (I). Sometimes the momentum is enough to lift the hood up onto the back of the head (J) – this helps to suggest that the drawing is a snapshot of a quick movement.

Don't be afraid to have the pocket of a hoodie fall almost completely horizontal when a character is bending (K). It's easy not to foreshorten it enough, which makes the torso look like it's twisting (L). From behind, the folds should reflect the underlying anatomy (M). The waist is often noticeably slimmer than the shoulders. The backs of the legs show the same conical forms that we've seen before (N).

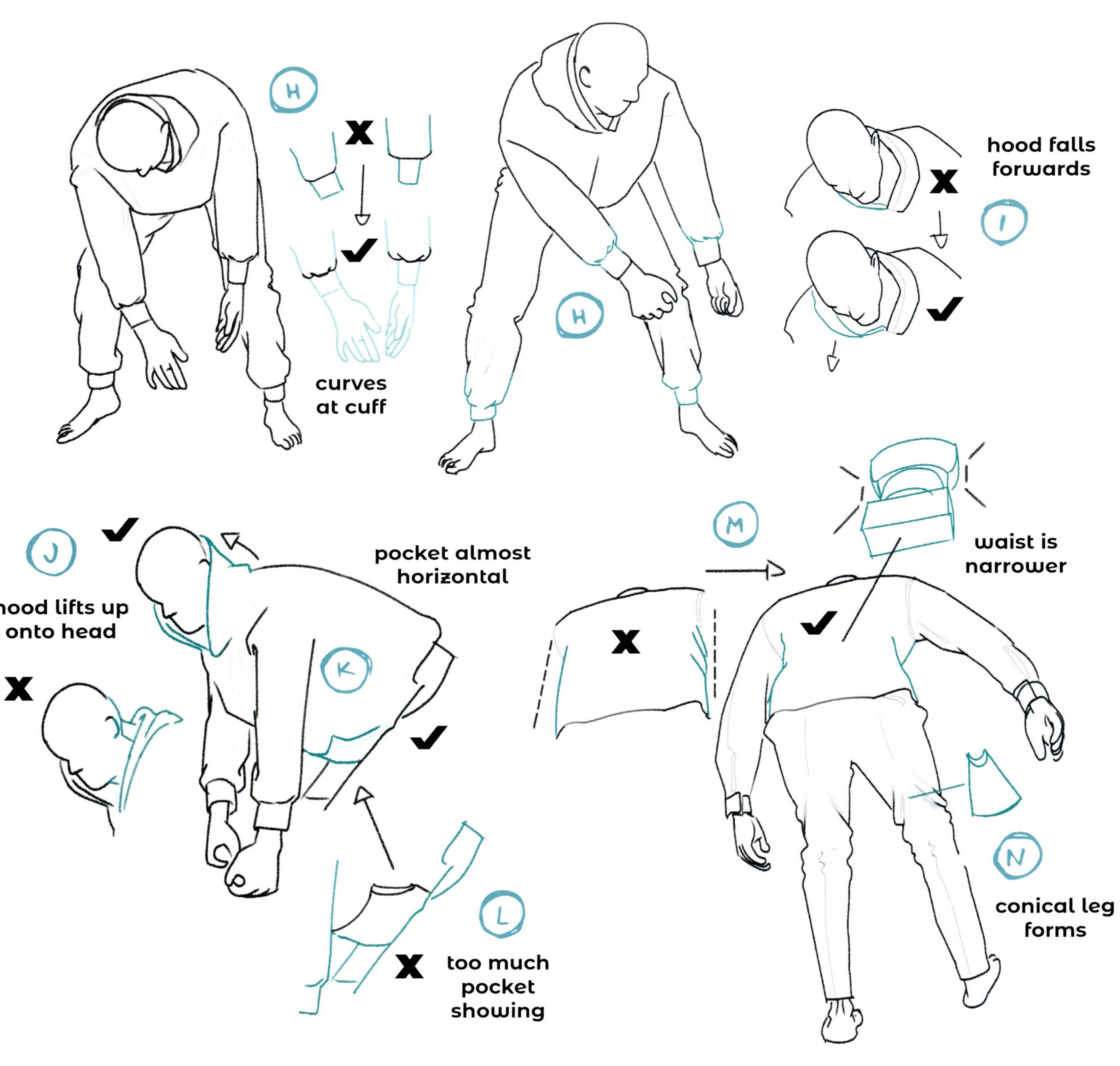

stealth

When you move in a stealthy crouched position, the torso leans forwards over the thighs – the front of a sweatshirt or hoodie will fall forwards and usually hide the waistband of the trousers (A). Don't be afraid to really foreshorten any front pockets. During this movement the rear leg continuously swings forwards and around the current front leg (B). When the legs are held apart (C), the folding is mostly horizontal and the inner seam is visible (D). However, when the leg is extended back, it rolls inwards, which hides the inseam (E). The folds around the fly will be angled towards the forward leg (F).

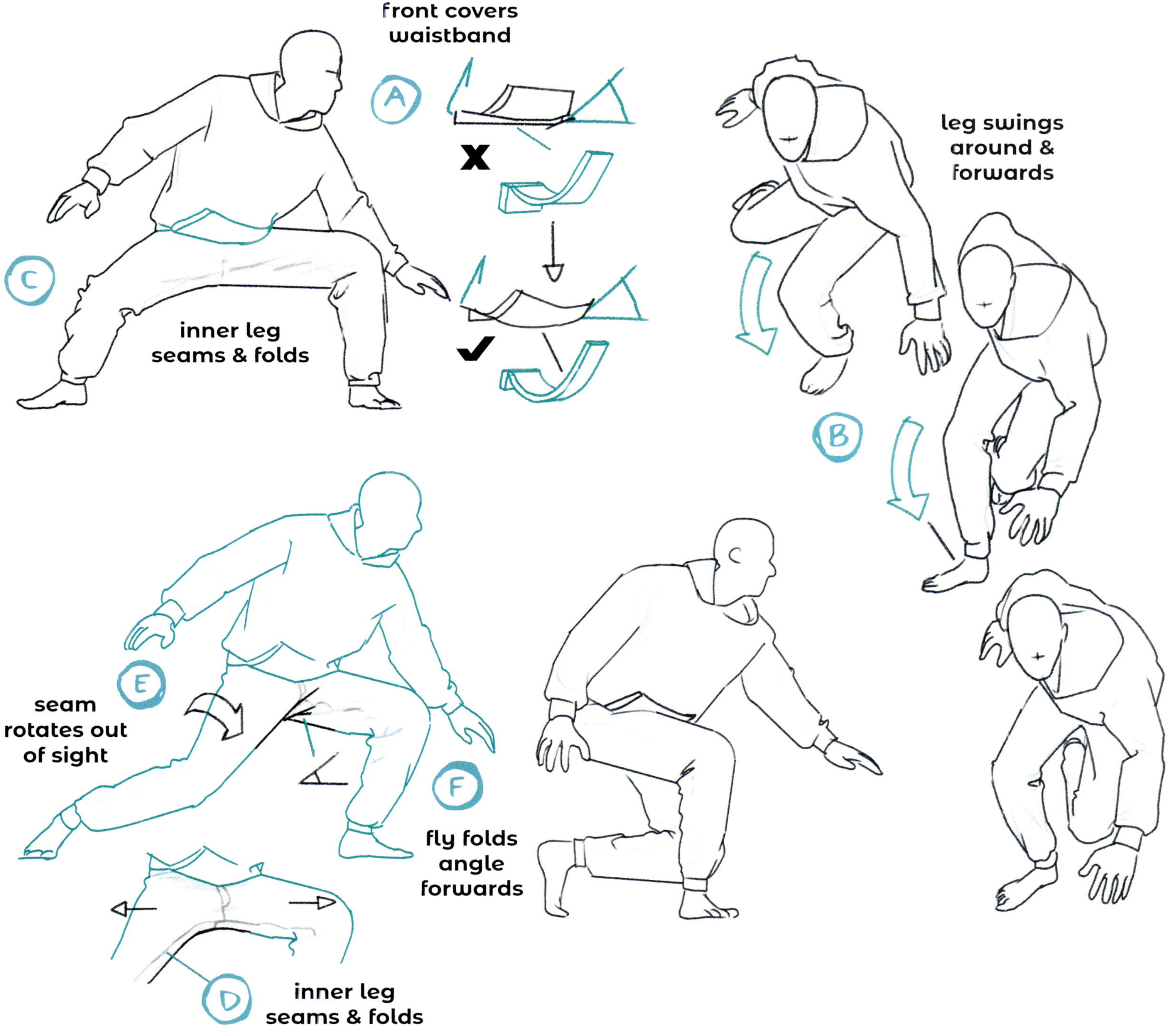

On the side with the higher shoulder, folds wrap up under the arm (G). On the other side, compression occurs between the thigh and torso (H). When the arm is raised even slightly, that compressed material becomes more taut (I). When drawing folds across the front of a T-shirt, avoid drawing simple horizontal ones (J). The central section should either come away from the torso in some variation of this wedge (K), or it should hug the body more closely and wrap up and around under the armpits (L). Finally, when the hand and forearm are rotated forwards (M), shallow folds occur across the top of the chest (N).

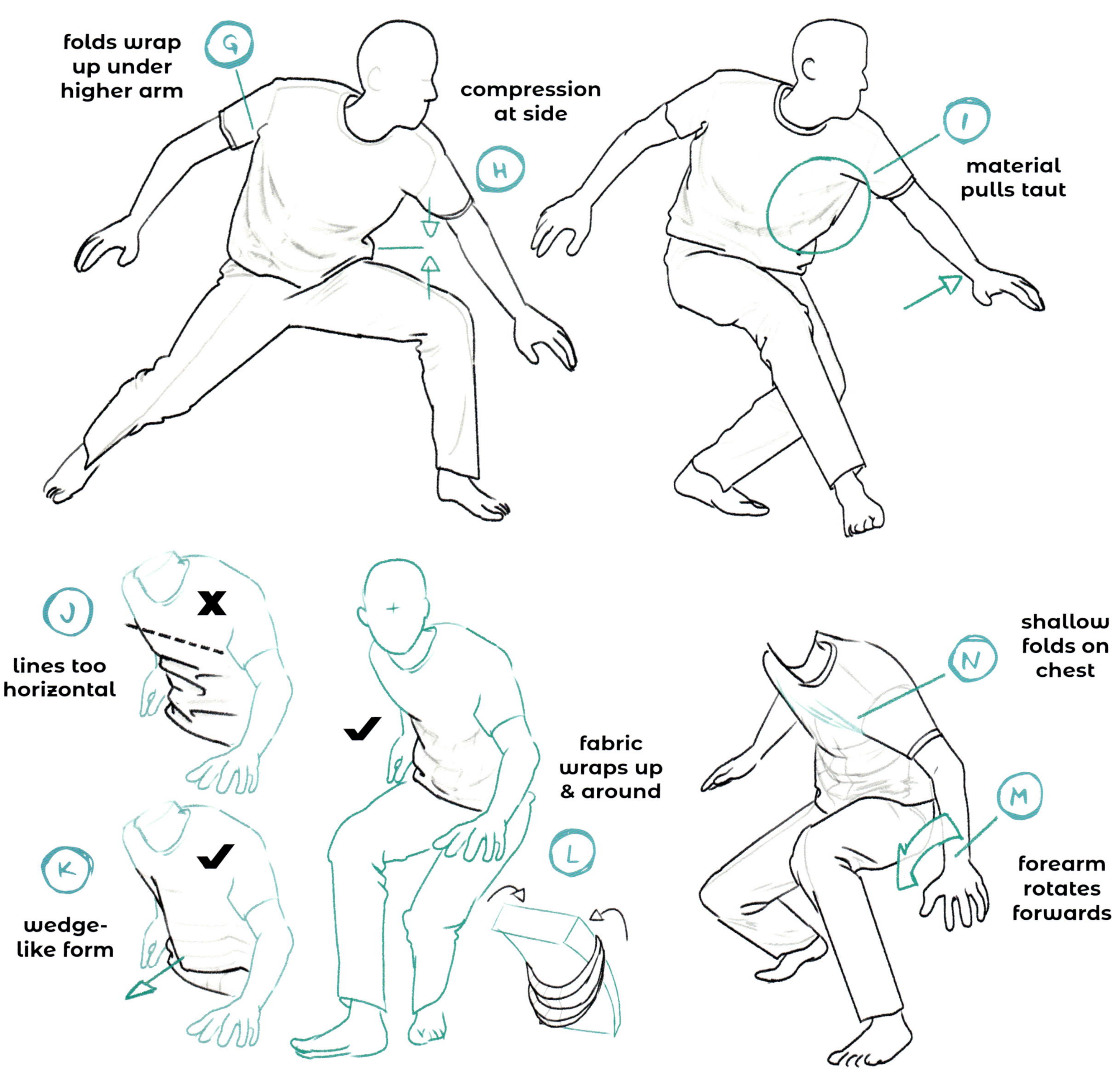

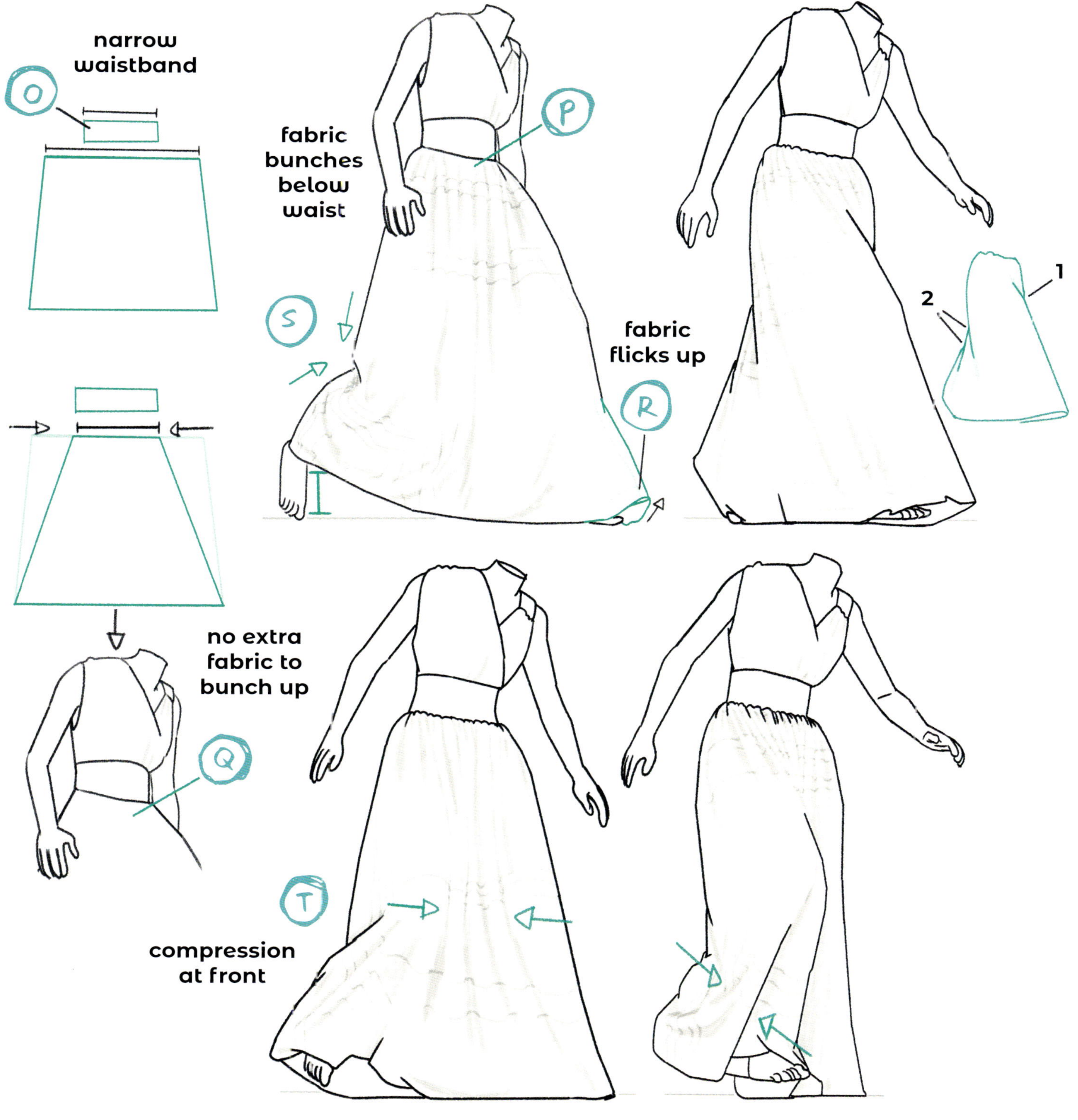

The waistband of this dress is not as wide as the bottom section (O). This is a design choice, which causes bunching below the waistband (P). If we adjusted the bottom part to be narrower, to match the waistband, the result would be no bunching below the waist (Q). When one foot is brought forwards, the fabric here (R) sometimes flicks up in front of the shin. When the rear foot leaves the ground, compression occurs here (S). When one leg is midway through moving forwards, there'll be compression between the knees (T). The success of drawing this dress hinges on getting these overlaps right **(1, 2)**.

When the legs are wide apart like this (U), visualize a connecting piece of fabric between these two points **(1, 2)**. The top of the thigh acts as an area of support (V). When the rear foot is lifted forwards, avoid the temptation to draw a straight line (W). When the rear leg is brought forwards, this bunching doesn't simply fall straight down (X), but is partially pulled round the outside of the thigh (Y). When the thigh isn't as raised as in example (U), note how the thigh is still an AoS, but there isn't as much bunching around the sides (Z).

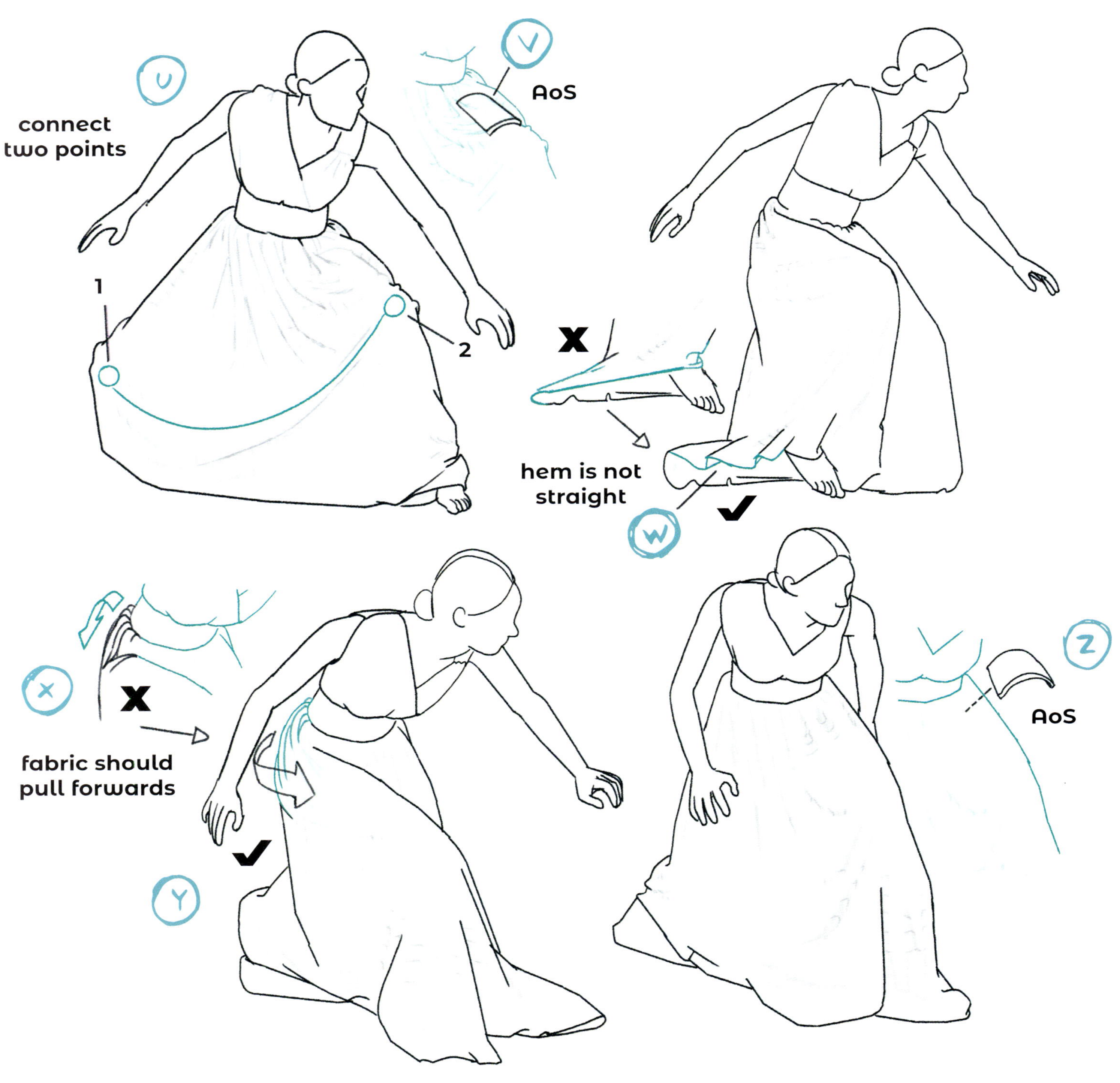

jumping onto a wall

When approaching something high, you'll usually lean back (A) and to the side (B), which makes it easier to raise your leg (B). When bending the knee, it's often more effective to draw a fold like this (C). This line helps to suggest that compression is happening, and the surface of the side of the knee is also deforming. When one arm is thrown up, you can help suggest momentum by showing a little of the belt/waistband (D). To generate enough momentum to jump up, an arm and a leg on the same side are thrown up simultaneously (E). In this position, both legs are brought slightly forwards, which causes concentrated folding around the fly (F). Make sure the seam is running from the side of the leg rather than simply near the middle (G).

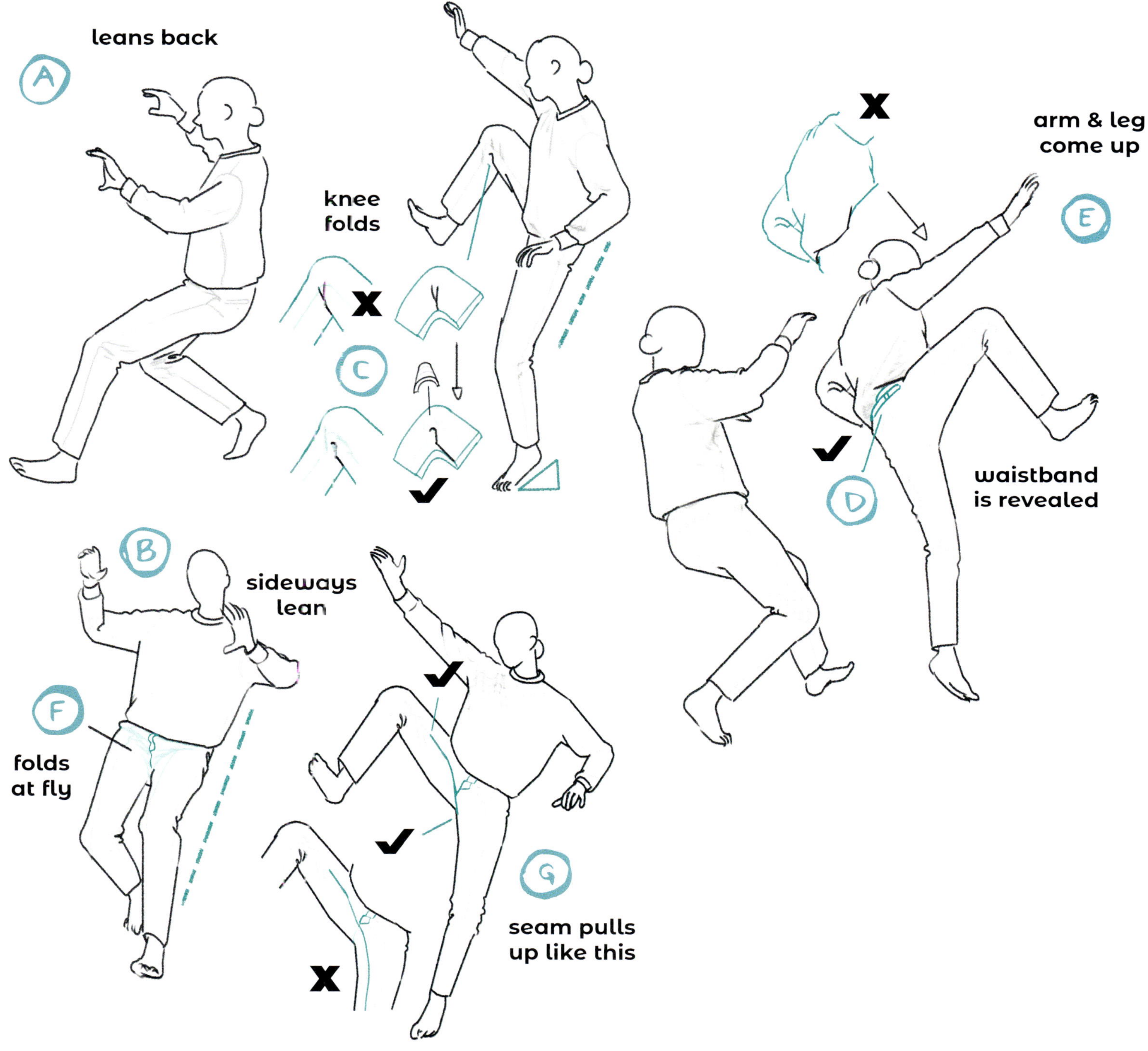

Most sweatshirts bunch around the bottom when worn (H). In this pose, there'll be compression here (I) caused by the arms being held back. When the leg is lifted up, the whole limb is tilted inwards, so the inside of the thigh faces almost straight down (J). Leave plenty of room for the fabric to hang off the back (K). When one arm is held back, the collar often deforms in response to the pressure (L). Don't draw too many lines on the glutes, as they are a pulling surface (M). These shallow folds on the back of the thigh are helpful (N), but they don't usually extend into this area (O).

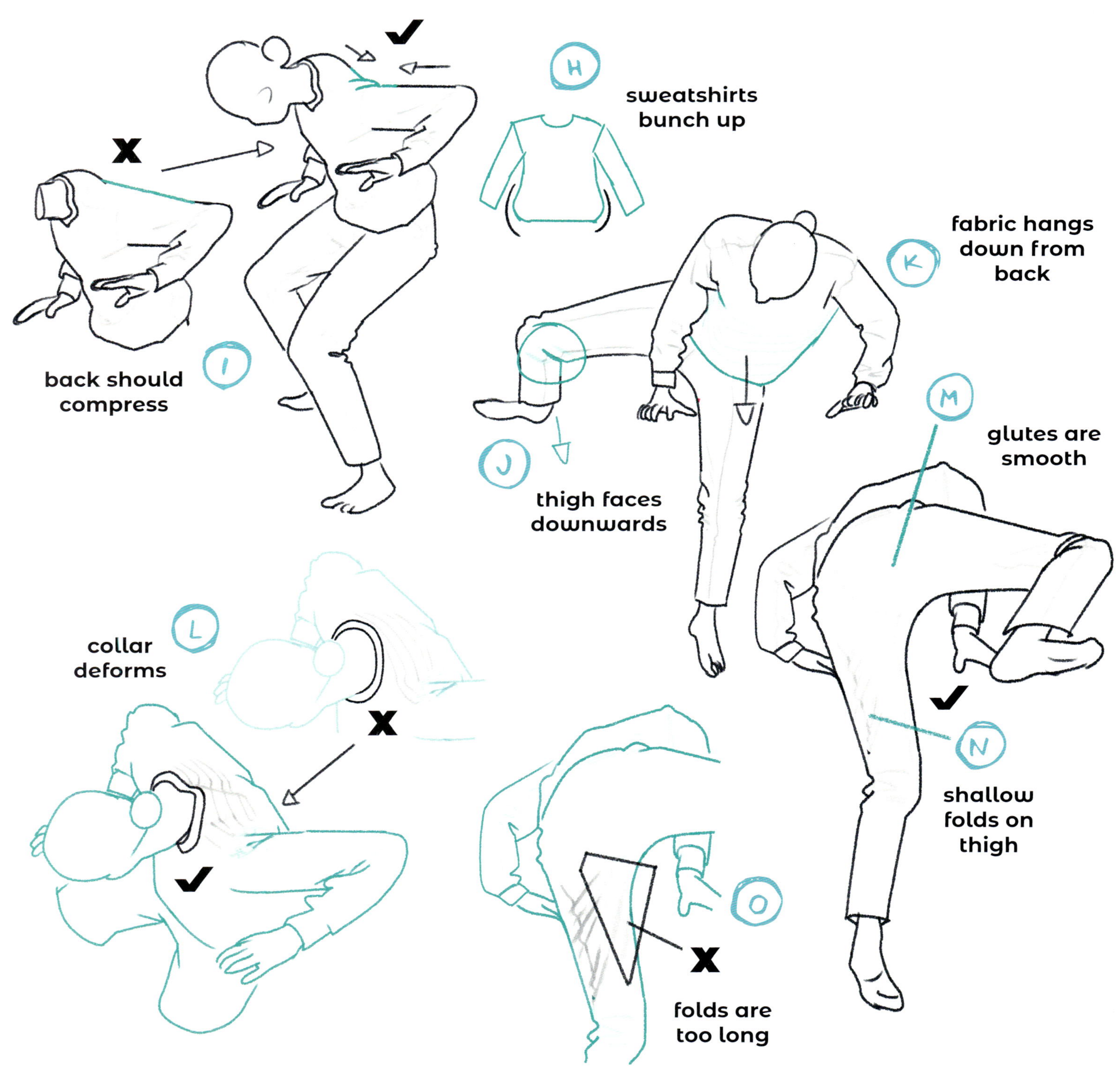

climbing

If one arm is extended straight, then the leg on the same side is probably nearly straight, too (A). A raised arm may lift the waistband (B) causing the front pocket to deform and fold upon itself (C). There's often a lot of side-to-side movement when climbing. To reflect this, have the hood swing to one side rather than hanging straight down the back (D). Most of the power comes from the legs, so make sure it looks like your character is 'lunging' up the wall rather than hanging from both arms. This is another example of a fold that runs in the opposite direction to what you'd expect (E). You may initially try drawing something like this instead (F), but it's rarely as effective.

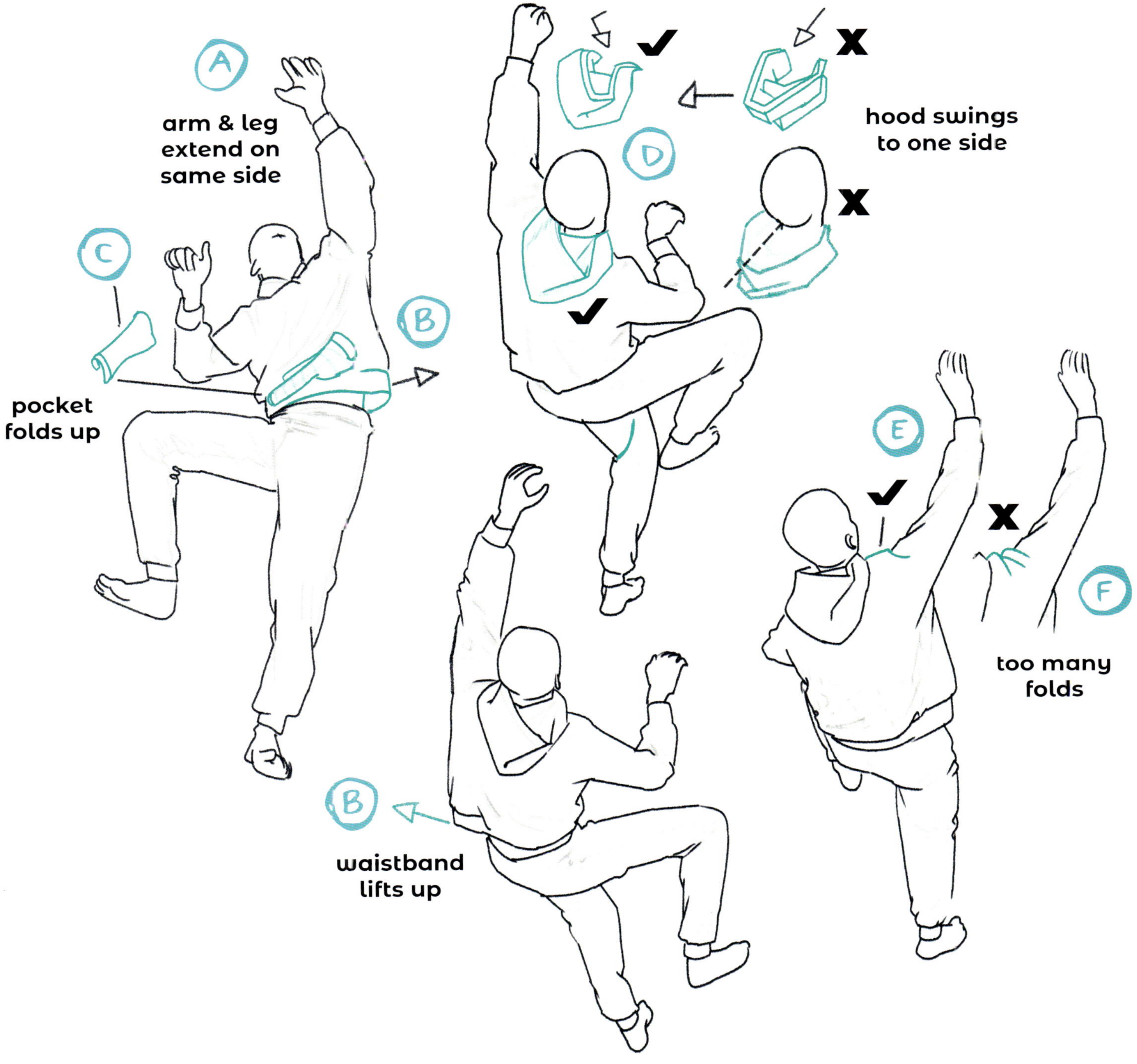

When climbing, the legs are usually held out at an angle rather than straight in front (G). This lets you position yourself closer to the wall. Be mindful of drawing the folds on either side of the knee too close to the kneecap itself. They should be set back a little (H). There's normally strong compression on the back of the neck when both arms are raised (I). Angle the seam to reflect the raising of the armpit (J).

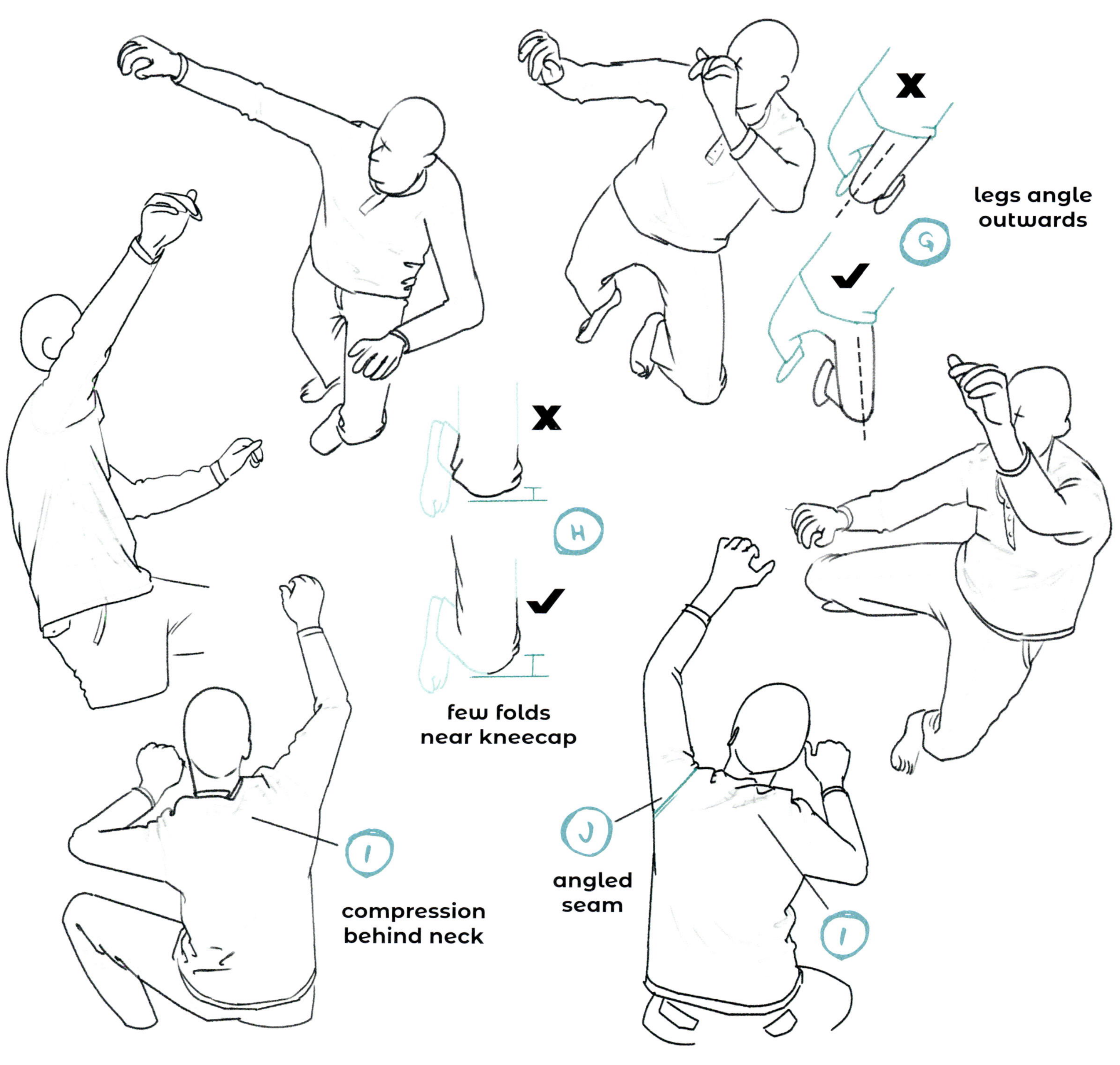

cycling

It's always tricky to draw a character cycling. From this sort of angle (A), try to make it clear that the arm **(1)** is in front of the torso **(2)**. Often, that'll involve using some variation of this shape (B). The folds around the waist shouldn't wrap up and around like this (C), but should change in angle (D). The upper back is often more arched than you'd expect (E), and this is partly because the shoulders drop lower down the sides of the torso than you'd imagine (F).

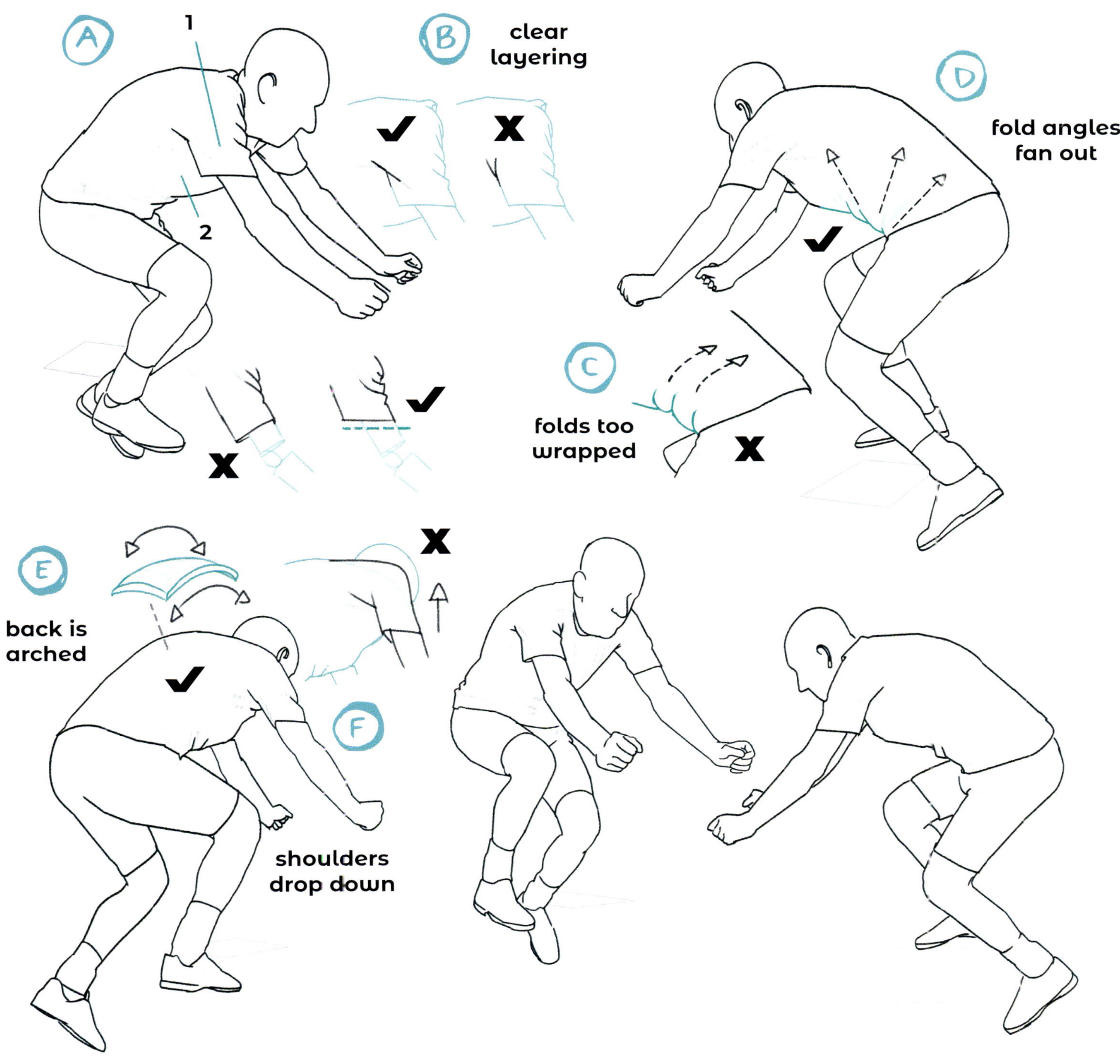

motions:
standing

slight lean

Identify the direction of the lean, then try to keep the lines on the outside edge simple (A). In this case, that's the back of the leg. When the legs are held this straight, folds may appear around the knees (B). The crotch area shouldn't normally have even folding, but should have lines that angle to one side (C). These shallow folds on the front of the leg are important to indicate that the foot on that side is slightly further forwards **(1, 2)**. The back of the hoodie will be fairly flat (D), whereas the sides will 'kick out' like this (E). The seams on the shoulders shouldn't meet the ends of the folds under the arms – they're usually lower than that (F). Finally, on a baggy garment, the arms will likely get wider towards the elbow (G).

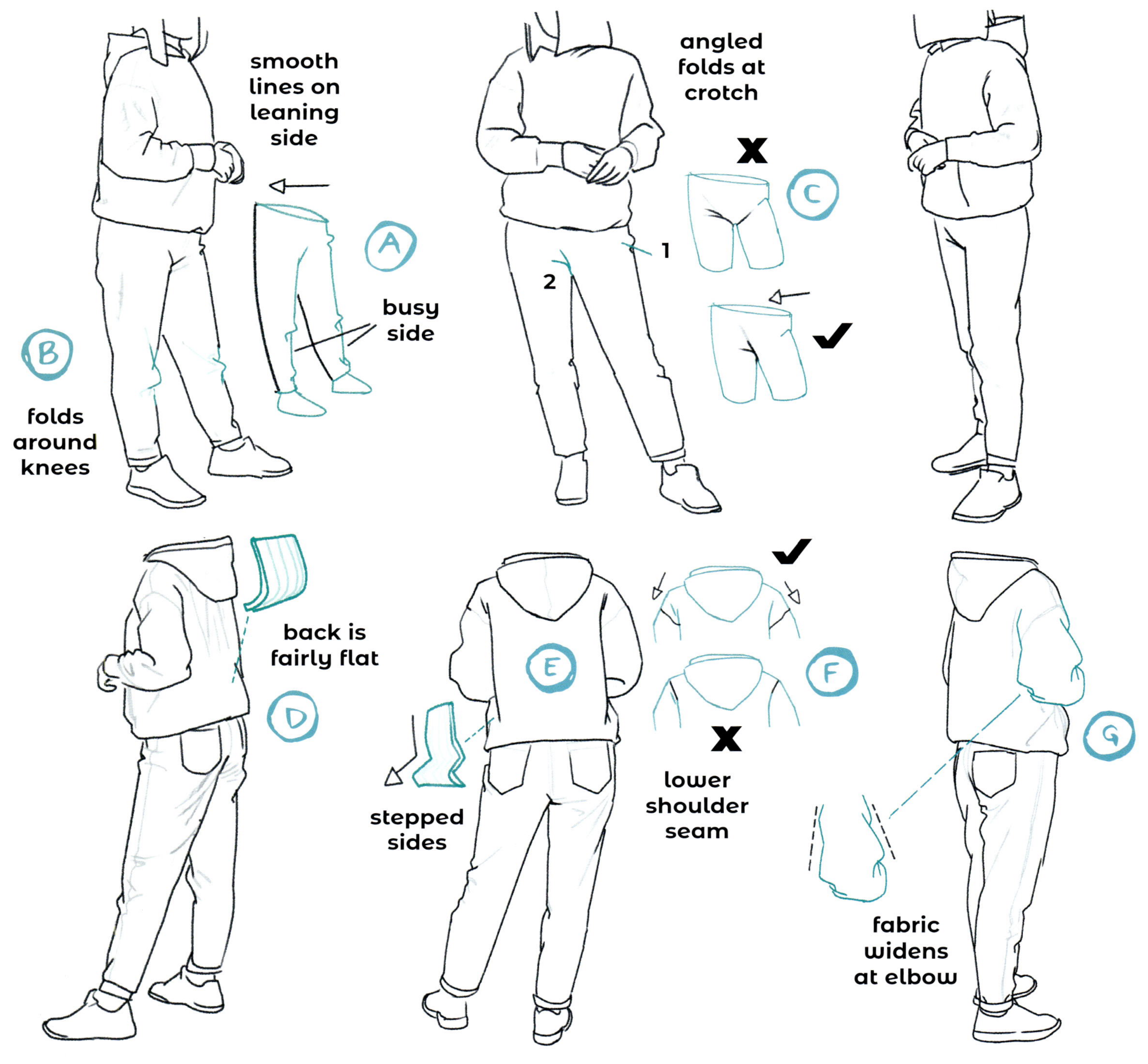

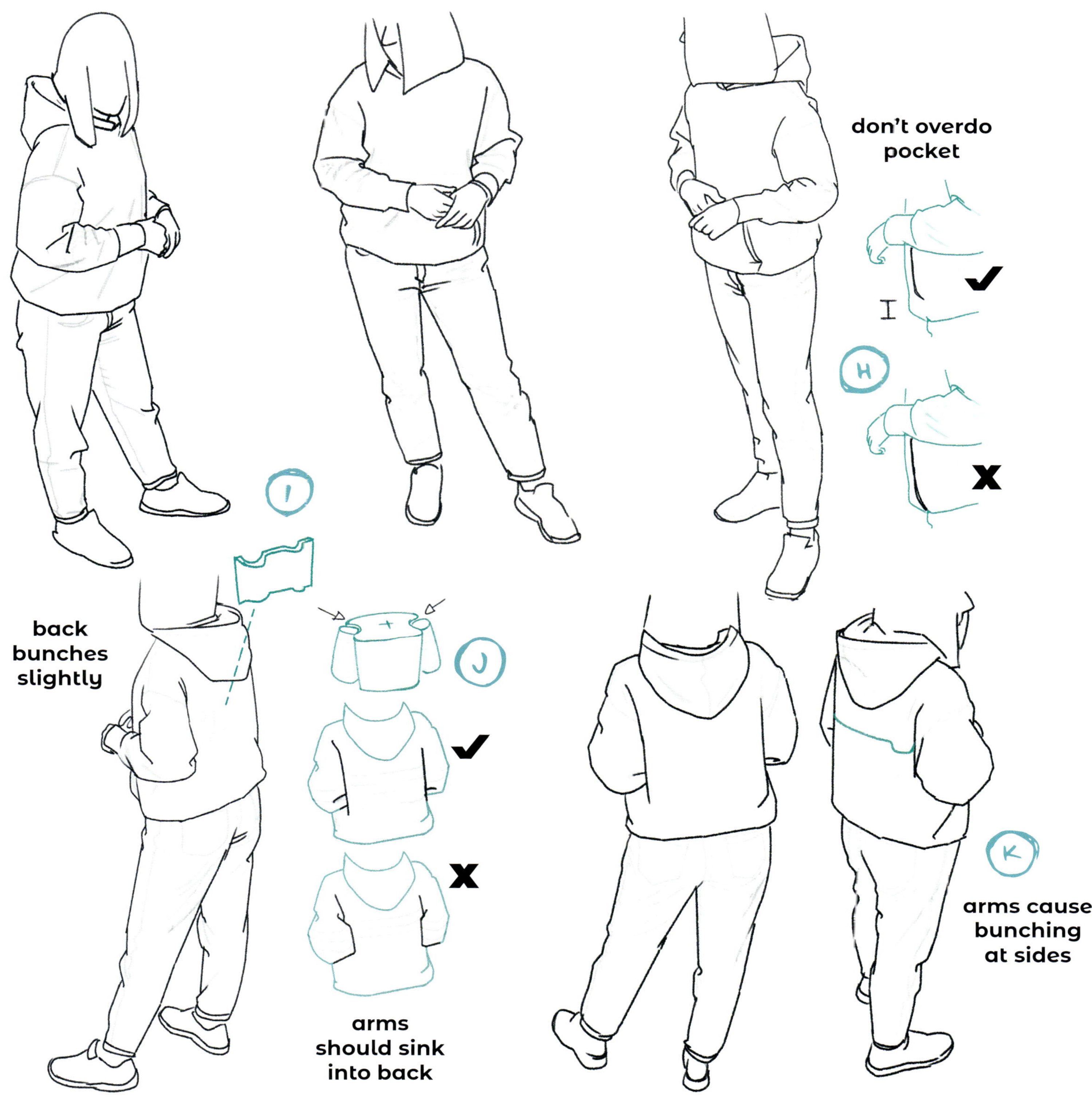

The sides of the kangaroo pocket should stop before reaching the bottom of the garment (H). When the arms are held back, gentle bunching occurs across the back (I). The arms should sink into the mass of fabric of the back rather than sitting above them (J). Where the arms wedge into the back, there will be a slight bunching at the sides (K).

tip: feet & shoes

The top of the foot is arched in both length and width (A). Draw the shoe with enough height to reflect this (B). The toe end usually lifts upwards, so make sure to include this detail (C). The tongue isn't flat, but curves to wrap the front of the shin (D). The ends of most shoes are slightly pointed, and rarely fully rounded (E).

The heel collar is a reinforced area around the top of the back of the shoe. Give it plenty of thickness (F). Give the toe box the appropriate level of volume for the style of shoe. Generally, smarter shoes have less volume in this area and are pointed. By contrast, skate shoes are very rounded and raised (G).

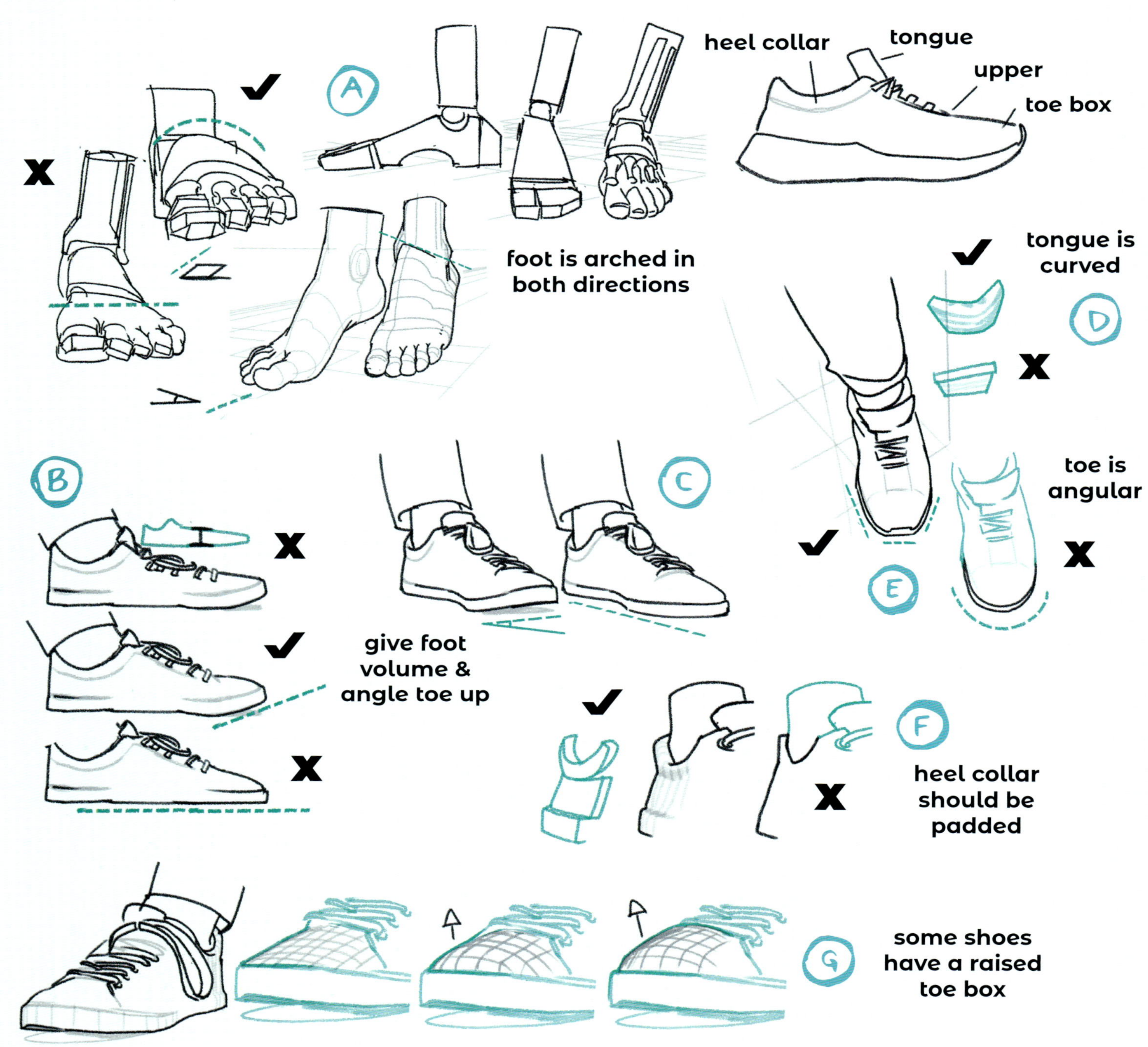

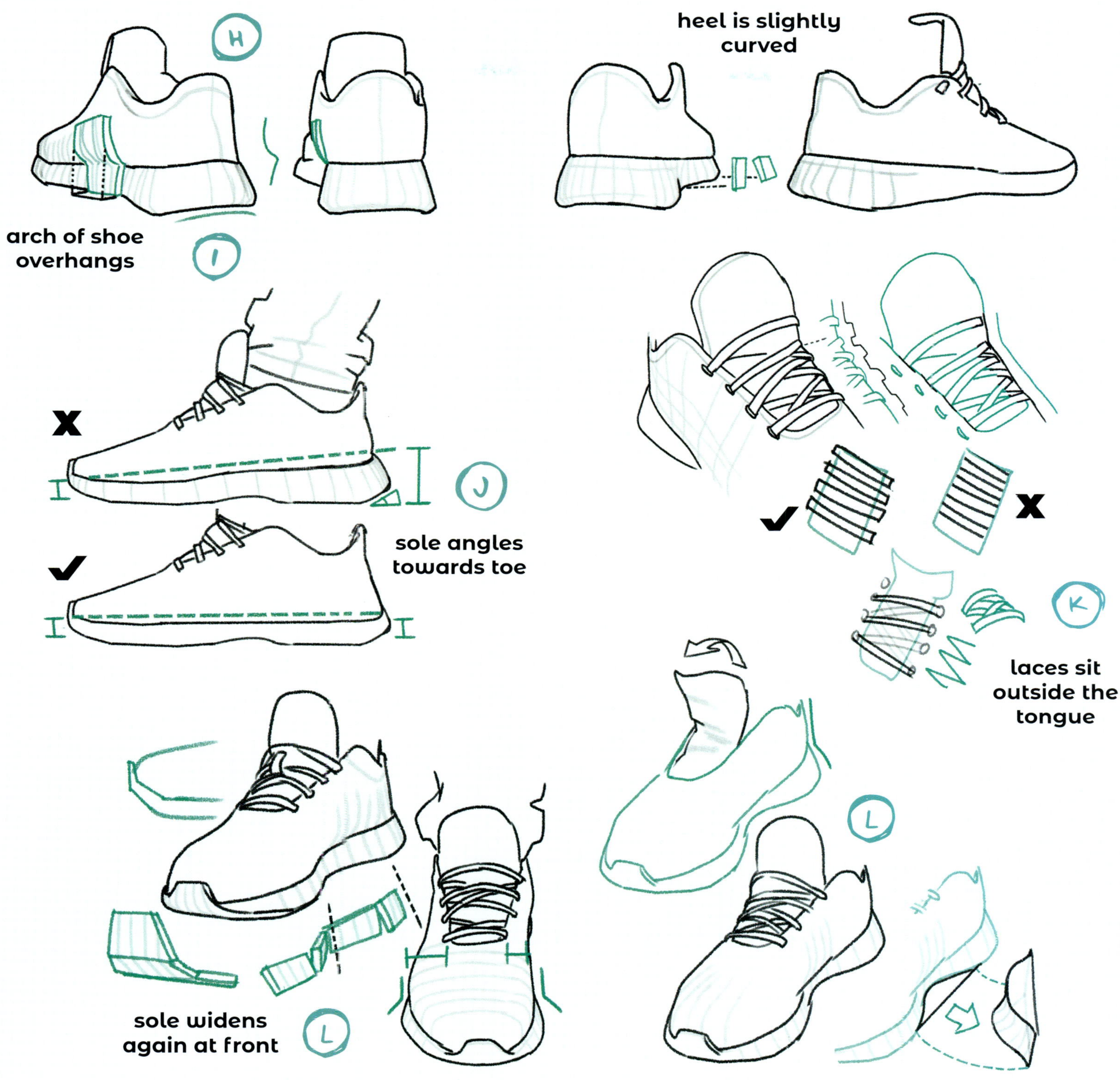

On the inside surface of the shoe, there's an overhang (H). On sport shoes there's often a gentle curve to the back of the 'crash pad', which is where your heel strikes the ground when running (I). It's also slightly raised. The whole sole is angled down towards the front of the shoe (J). The laces should sit on the outside of the tongue rather than under (K). The silhouette is angular, rather than smooth. The sole flares out at the front to give extra stability and help prevent you rolling your foot and twisting your ankle (L).

crossed legs

As mentioned before, when drawing a hoodie pocket, don't extend the pocket openings all the way to the bottom of the pocket. Instead, there's normally a gap between the bottom and the sides (A). The folds of the upper arm usually don't converge downwards like this (B). Instead, there is an obvious form that hangs just below the shoulder and forms a triangle of material (C). That's what you'll see most often when the arms are held down by the sides. When the arm is bent, the folds won't cross straight across the arm (D). Instead, they'll curve around the inside of the bend, which reflects the direction of the pressure shown by these arrows (E). This pressure often causes obvious bulging, which can be seen from multiple angles, even from behind (F).

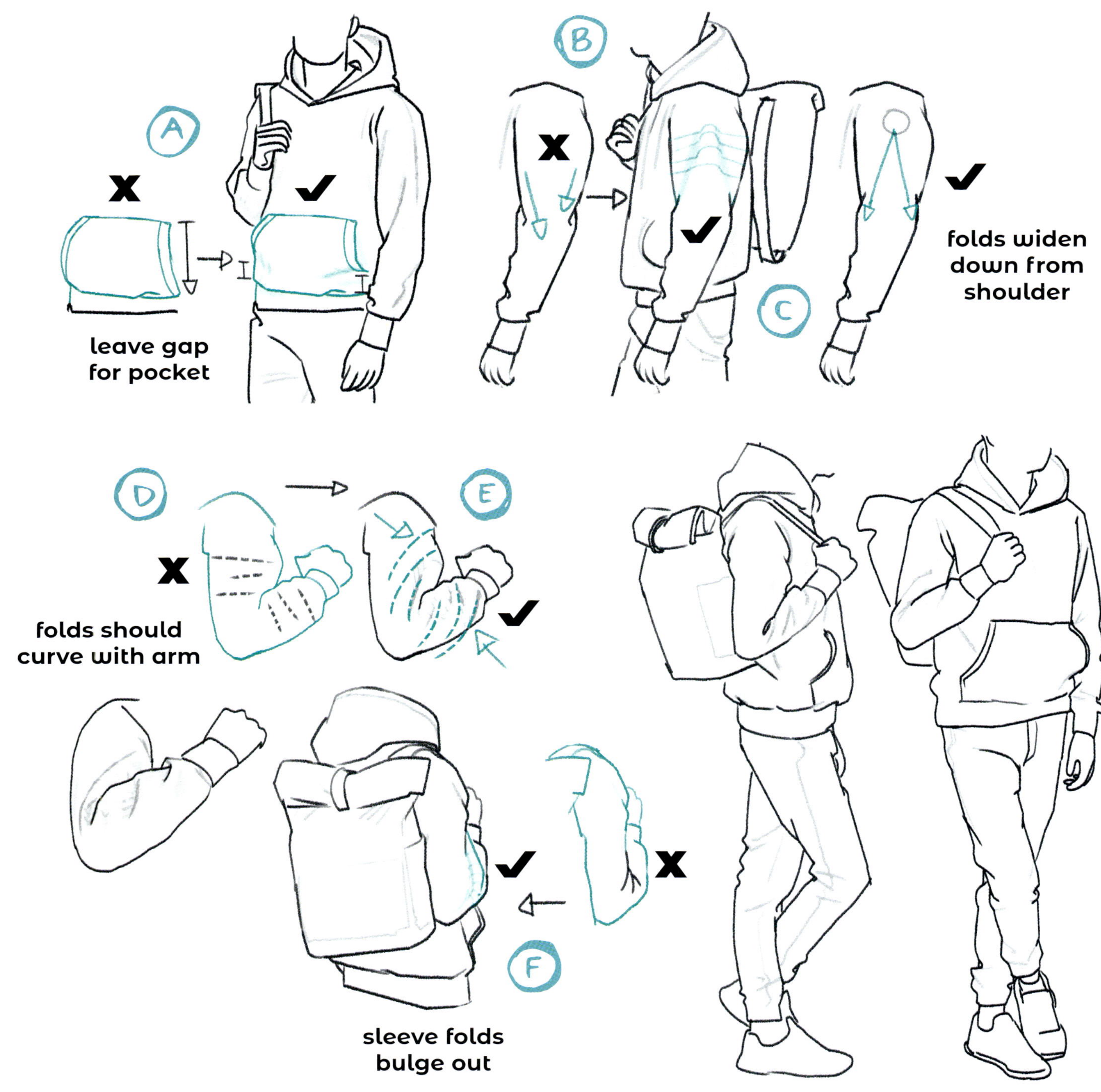

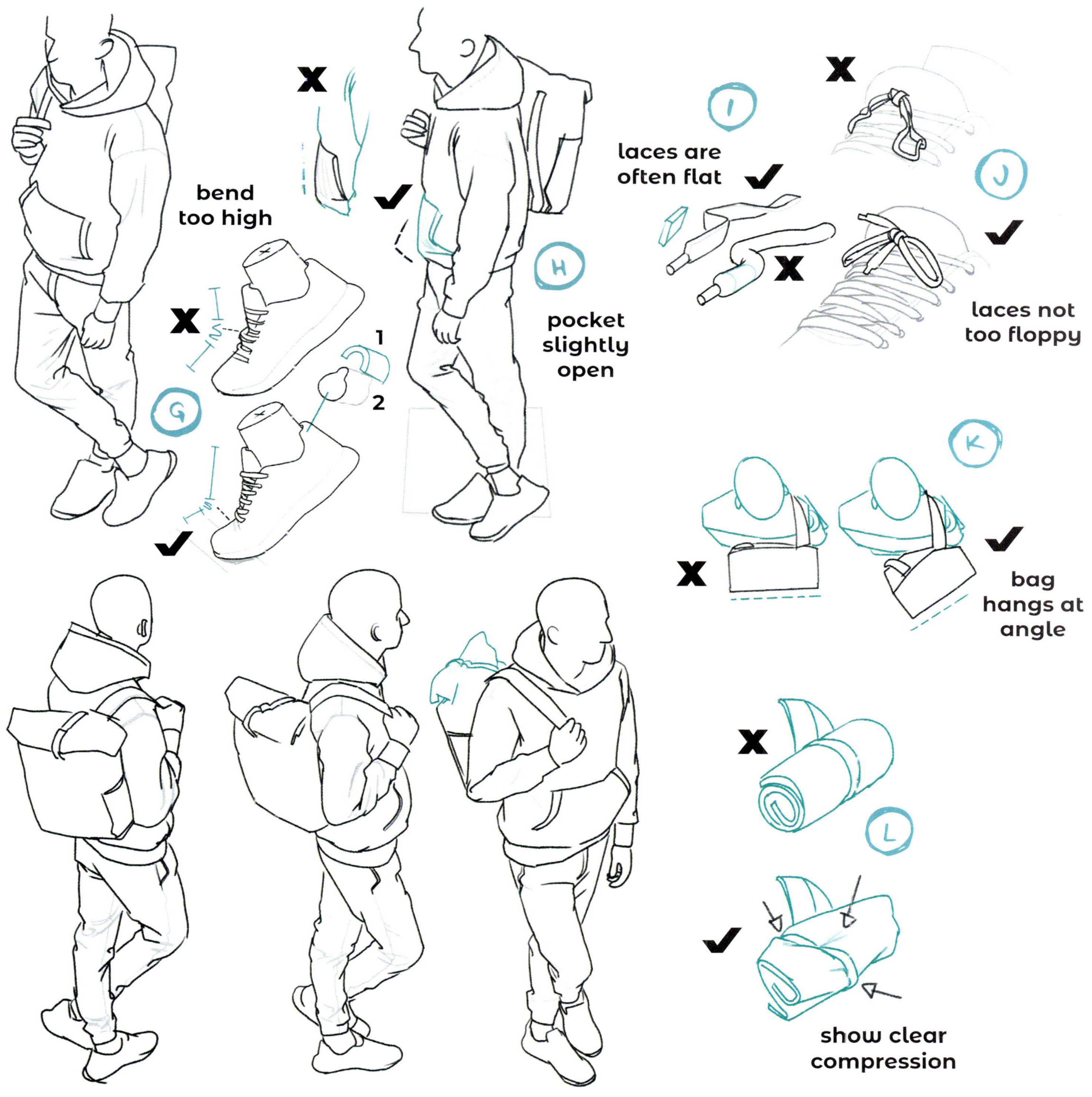

When lightly pressed against the ground, most shoes bend just below the laces, rather than across the arch and laces (G). The back of the heel collar **(1)** should wrap around the Achilles tendon **(2)**, rather than being flat. Even when standing relatively straight, the hoodie pocket will often be 'open' from the side (H). Shoelaces are often slightly flattened, rather than perfect tubes (I). You often see them drawn too floppy, but they should easily support their own weight (J). When you hold a bag with one hand, it usually falls away from the back at an angle (K). If you include a strap that could compress another part of the garment, then it's best to draw it compressed, for clarity (L).

hands together

When the sleeves are rolled up, they rarely form a smooth tube. More often, the form is twisted (A). It's natural to want to draw the pocket flaps bulging outwards when a shirt is open, but just as often they fold inwards (B). The area above the cuff should indicate compression and the squeeze caused by the rolled cuff itself, rather than being smooth (C). When the arms are brought inwards, the main compression happens from the sides, rather than being vertical from the top and bottom (D).

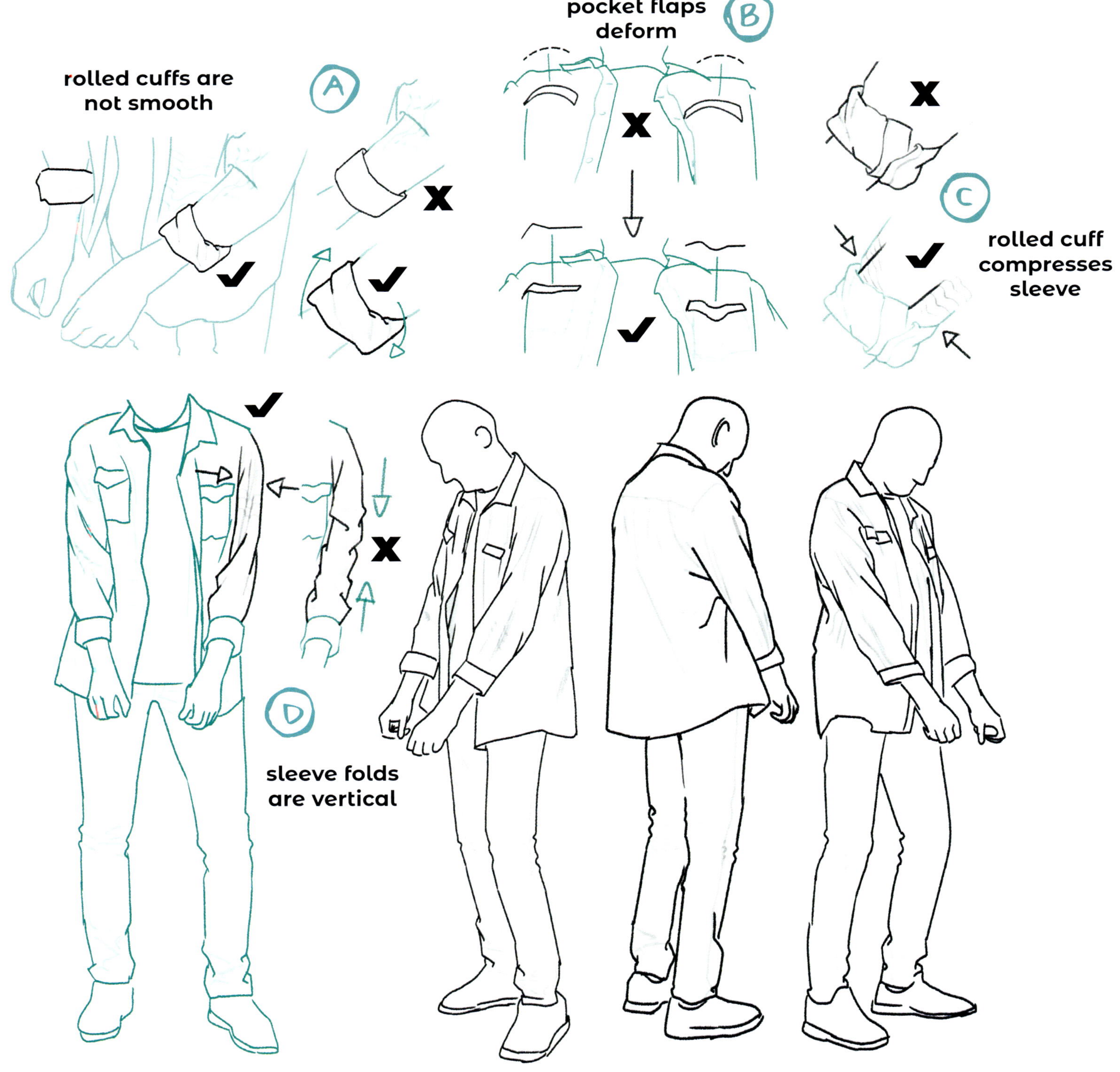

This is the cuff **(1)** and this is the placket **(2)**. It's easy to forget to draw the placket. It has a button hole which is often left loose. The placket rarely sits flat on top of itself – there's usually a small gap between the two pieces **(3)**. When the cuff is buttoned, add a small angle between them rather than making them perfectly parallel **(4)**. When the sleeve is rolled up, the placket opens up, and eventually a small 'V' is created in the rolled sleeve – don't draw the roll as a closed loop (E). Across the back of the shirt you'll usually see multiple small, shallow folds. Although they can appear on both sides of this seam, they usually first appear below it (F).

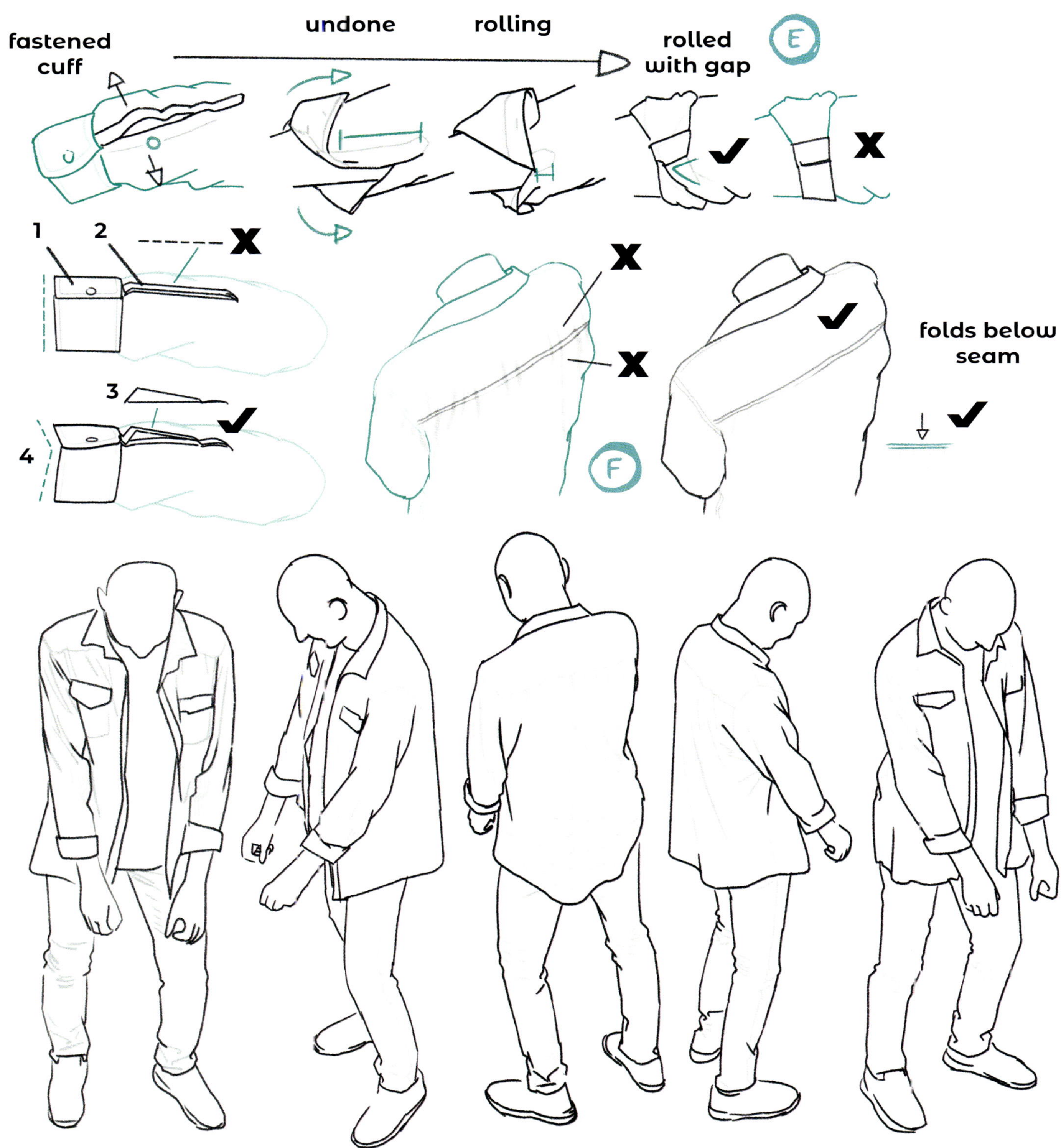

waiting

Backpacks should generally hang below the shoulders, not be level with them (A). To suggest the weight of the bag, give it a bottom-heavy shape, rather than making it boxy (B). When tucking hands into trouser pockets, make sure the pocket is angled enough, and that the fabric slopes down both in front and behind (C). The shirt will often compress here, and its front should fall in a 'U' shape (D).

This sort of raised jacket collar should be thick at the back and thin at the front where the zip is located, and the open collar will angle outwards at these points (E). When drawing this kind of padded jacket, don't try to draw in every separate panel – just indicate them (F).

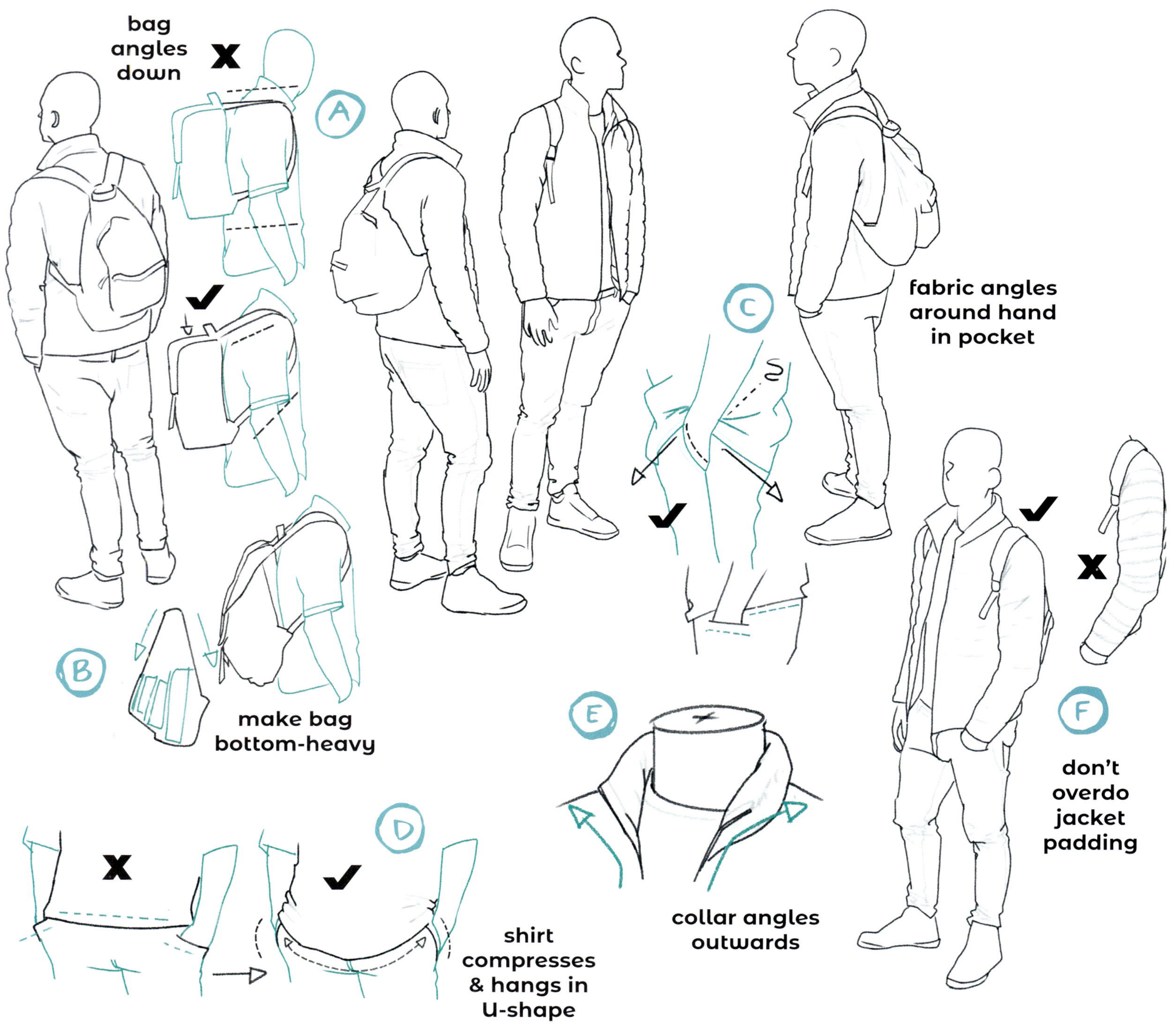

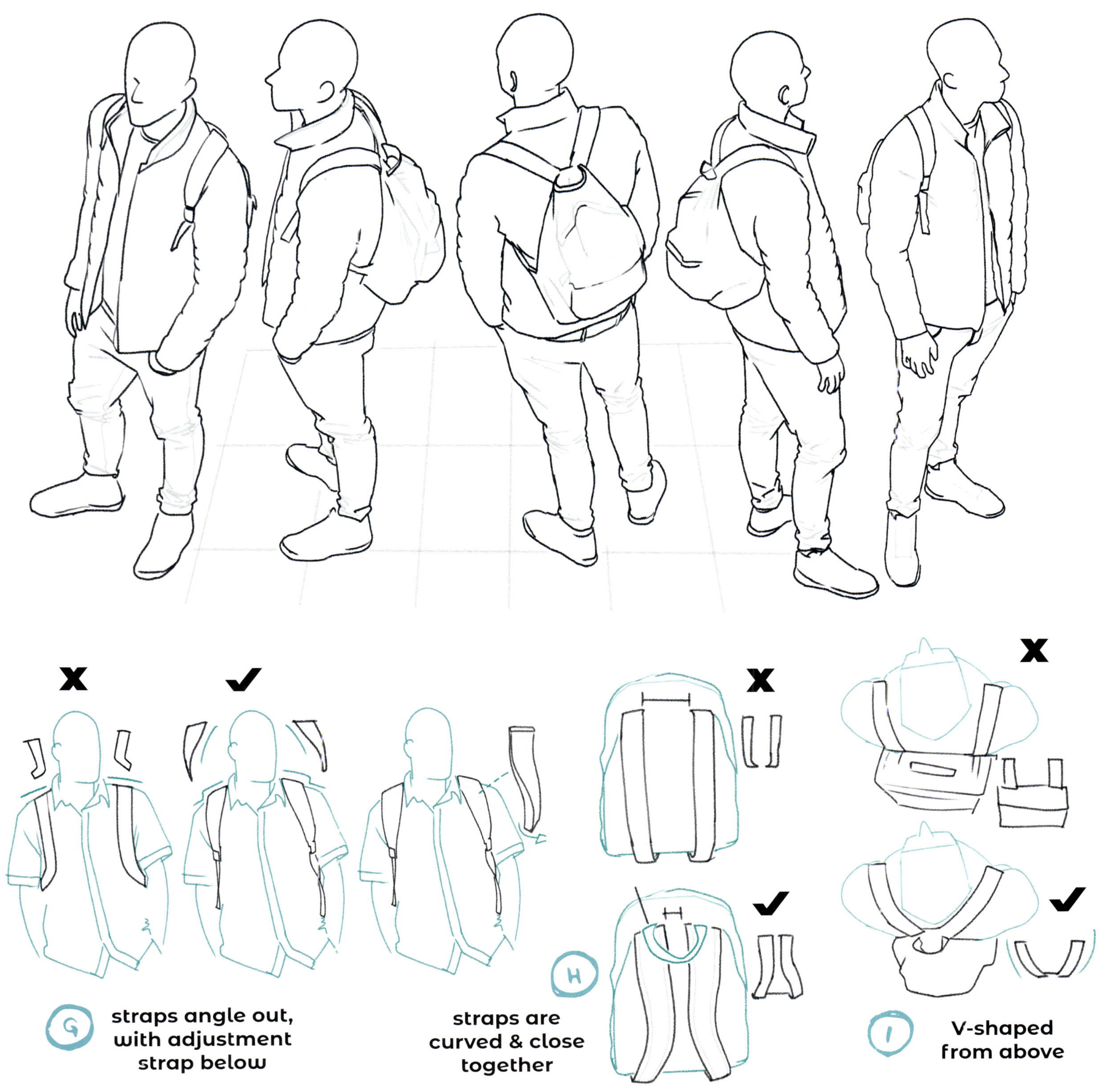

The straps of a backpack should turn outwards, rather than inwards. Don't forget to add the adjustment straps hanging near the armpit (G). Avoid drawing the backpack straps too straight and far apart from each other. Instead, they're usually close at the top, wider towards the bottom, and often partially covered by a carry handle (H). Viewed from above, they should flare outwards in a 'V' shape, rather than two parallel lines (I).

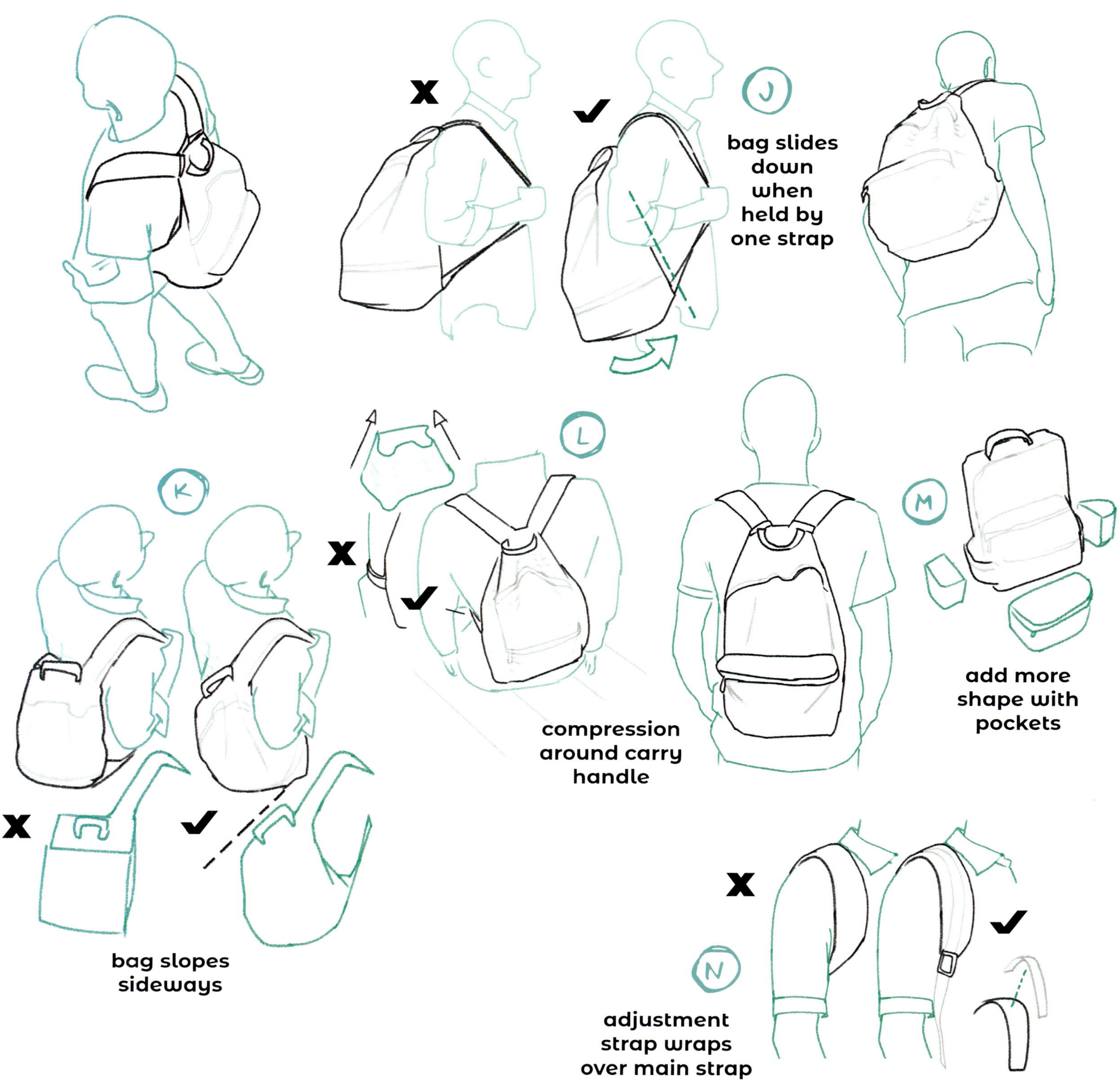

When held with one hand, bags often slide down and under the arm holding the strap (J). The whole bag will also slope down to one side (K). Don't forget to include folds that reflect the compression of fabric near the carry handle (L). If you want to draw a more solid backpack – for carrying a laptop, for example – it's helpful to add a lower rear section and side pockets to make the shape look more organic (M). Often the adjustment straps' material wraps the top of the main straps (N).

crossed arms

The kangaroo pocket of the hoodie usually bunches near the bottom in a U-shape (A) rather than folding straight across. The direction of this fold on the upper arm is very important to get the arms to look convincingly crossed (B). From this angle, the tip of the elbow is very obvious - avoid drawing it rounded (C). Avoid drawing wavy lines here (D). Instead, add a reversed line to help indicate the compression across the front of the arm. When the arms are crossed, a pulling surface is created across the upper back (E). Most of the folds on the lower back and sides angle up towards this area rather than running horizontally (F). Don't forget: the arms aren't just raised up, but twisted inwards, and this should be fairly obvious to the viewer (G). Again, from this angle, the tips of the elbow are clearly seen, because the fabric on the outer arm is under tension **(1, 2)**.

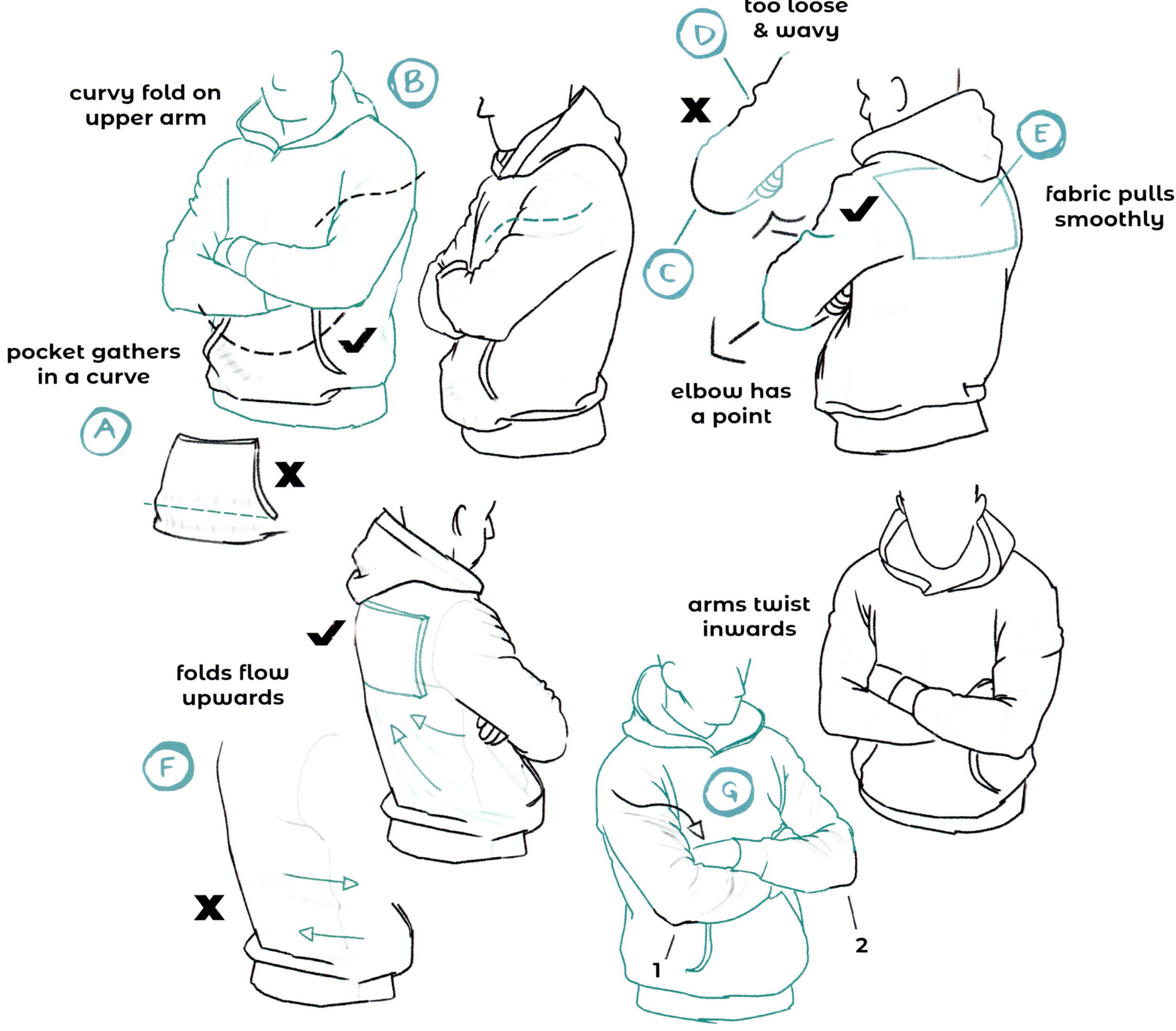

When drawing folded arms, you rarely see both hands on top of the arms (H). Usually, you'll see one hand above and one under the arms. When the character has a protruding core, they'll be able to tuck both hands in and rest them on top of their stomach (I). The stacked forearms put pressure on each other – ensure the drapery isn't rounded, but has some horizontal folding (J). On sleeves that aren't tight, you'll clearly see the compression of the two forearms sitting on top of each other. Again, avoid rounding the arms too much, or they will look like they aren't touching (K). When drawing a larger stomach, keep this area clear of lines (L). You'll rarely find lines crossing horizontally on this section.

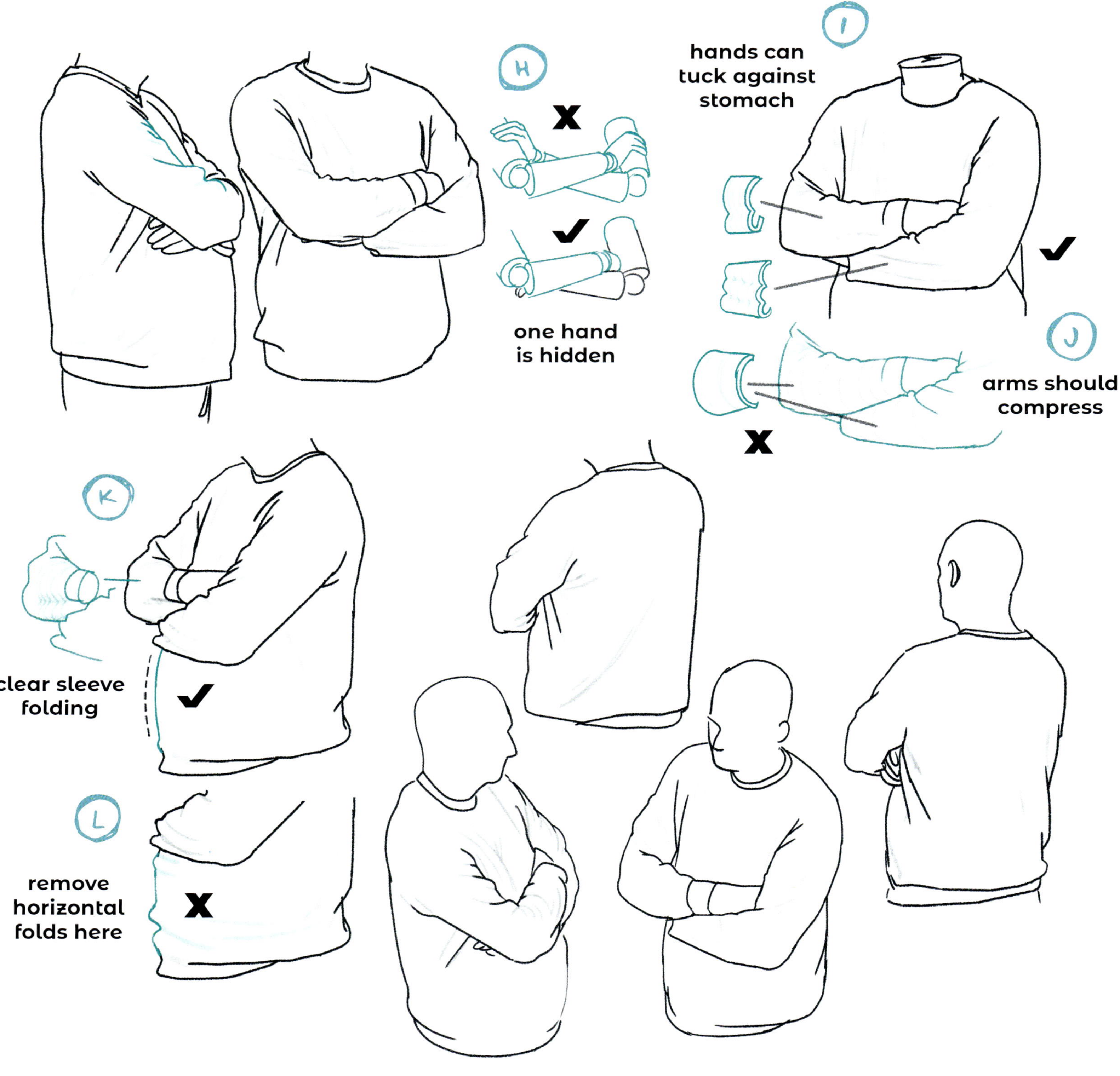

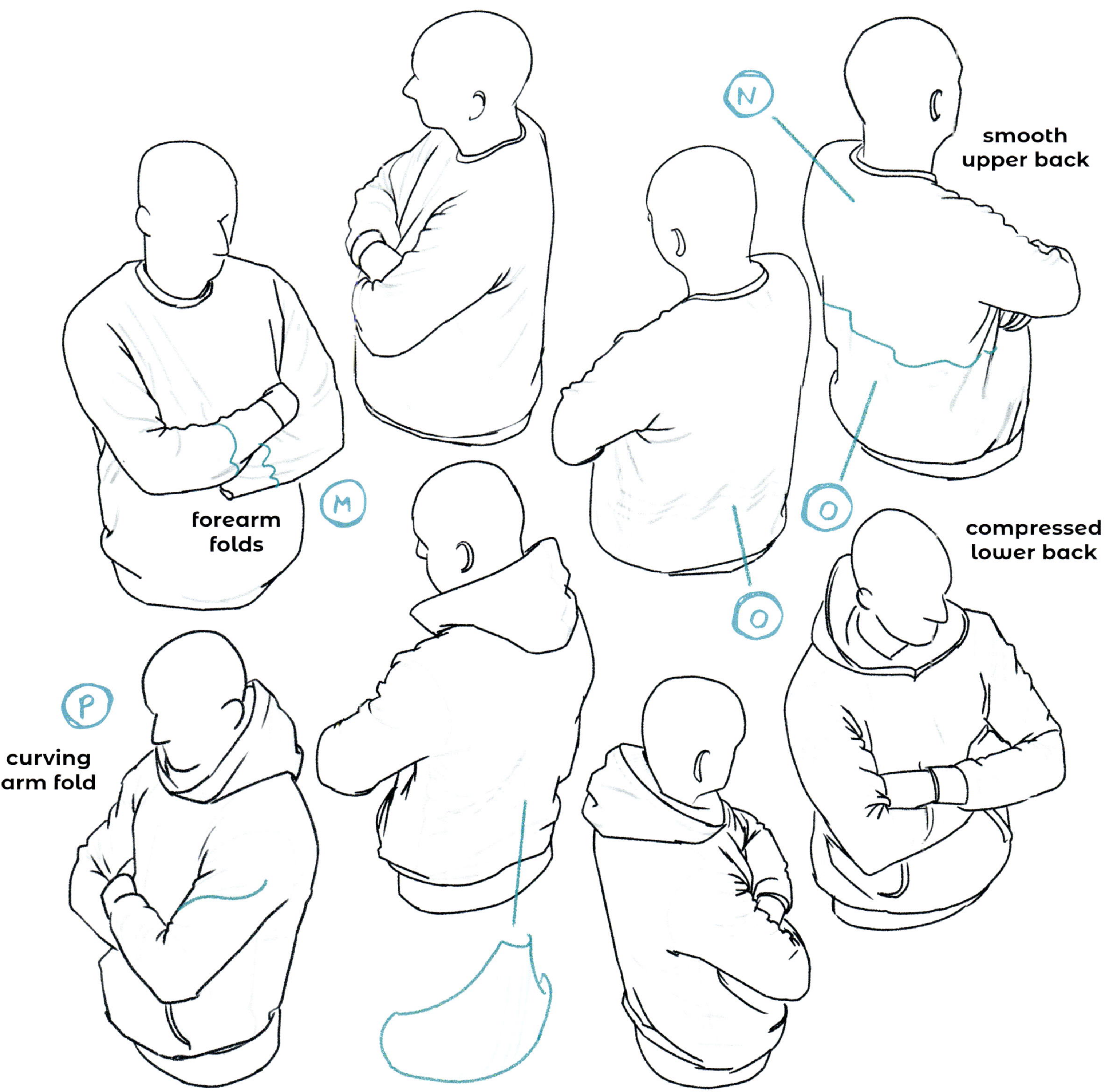

These references are the same poses as on the previous two pages, but seen from different angles. These poses are so frequently used that it's important to study them closely. Note the compression on the forearms (M), the upper back empty of lines (N), the compression across the lower back (O), and the flow of the curve on the inner forearm (P).

talking

When talking, the hands are often up in front of the torso, or gesturing out to the sides. This form is often visible (A). When drawing an arm bending from behind (B), many people forget to include these folds **(1)**. They're visible from most angles, so leaving them out is visually confusing. This line reverses on itself at the very end **(2)**. When you rotate you hand and arm inwards, there'll be very little twist in the drapery (C). When you turn them outwards, as if explaining something, the twist appears (D). The seam running across the back is rarely horizontal – it's normally angled up slightly (E). Note this common line, which indicates compression from both above and below (F). When the arms are brought up, the angle of these folds changes (G). This sleeve (H) will often appear to sit under the fabric of the back (I).

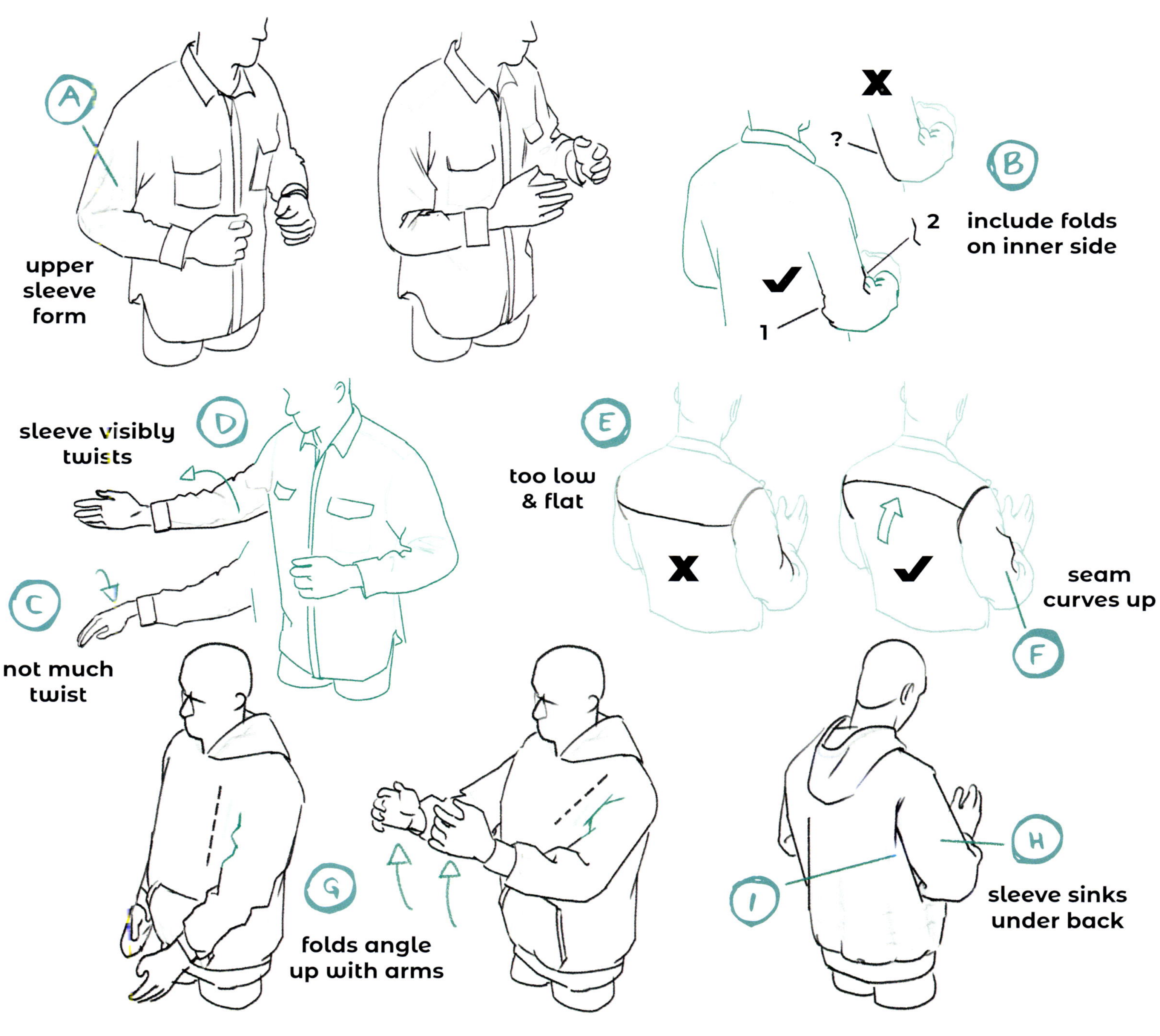

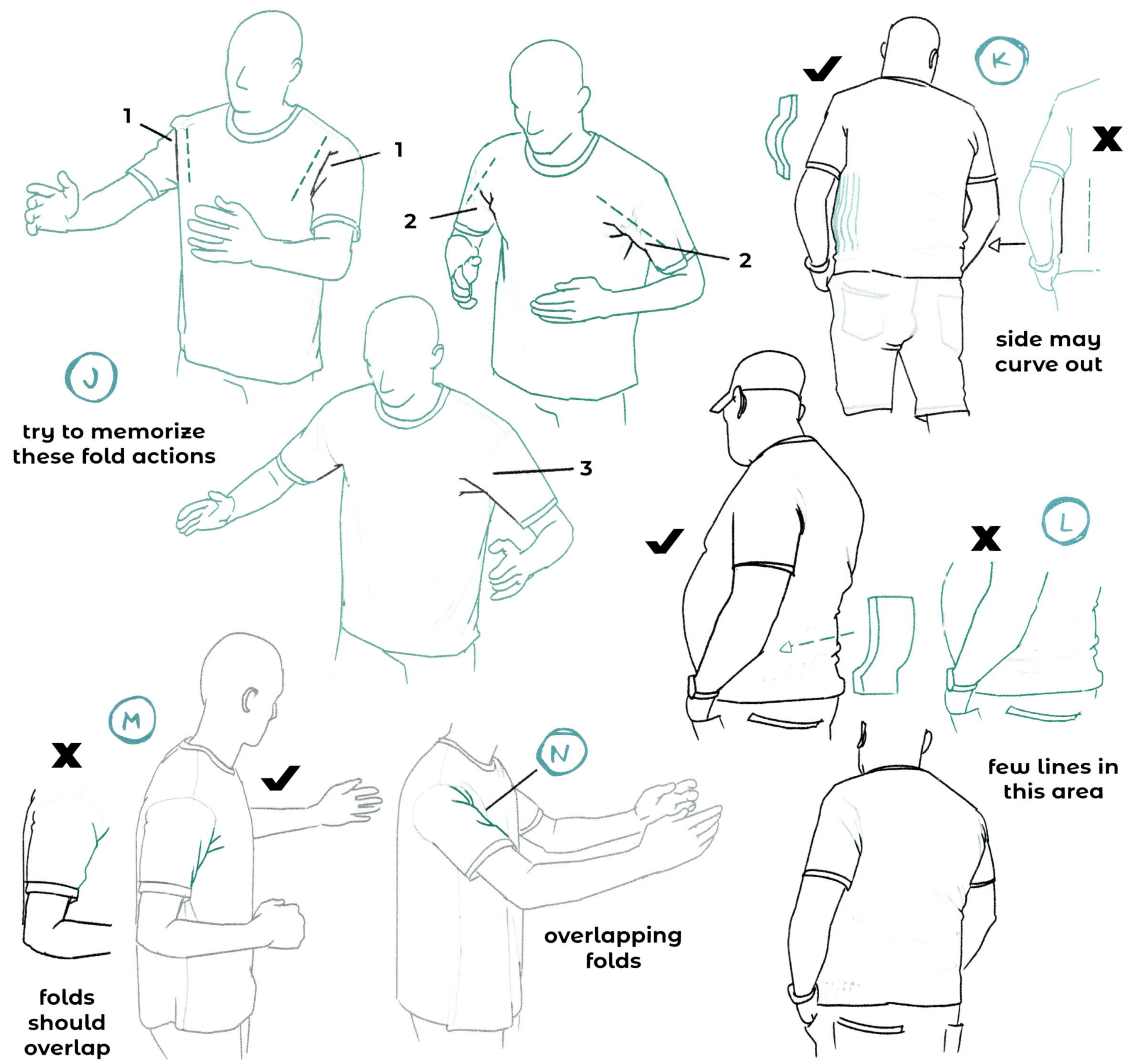

The folding around the armpits is not always intuitive, but it's worth taking the time to get it right (J). When the arms are held up and forwards, these folds angle back **(1)**. When the arms are down nearer the sides, and the elbows are pulled back, this angle is reversed **(2)**. Note the bunching just above the darker lines. When the elbows are back but the arms are raised, this often disappears **(3)**. On individuals with higher body fat, you may see some bulging here (K), where the T-shirt is pulled against the kidneys and lower back, which is a common area of fat accumulation. You'll rarely see many lines in this area (L). If you want to make the arm look like it's being held against the side of the chest, you'll need a series of overlaps (M). This series of folds indicates the compression between the shoulder and the upper arm (N).

Here are some great references for a character in different conversational poses. By raising and turning the hand outwards, you add a delicate twist to the sleeve (O). When the elbows are closer to the sides, there's more compression here (P).

When an elbow is raised up higher, you'll see gentle folding on the top and back of the shoulder (Q). Sometimes you'll see this bump appear in the silhouette (R), where the arm has pushed the fabric up.

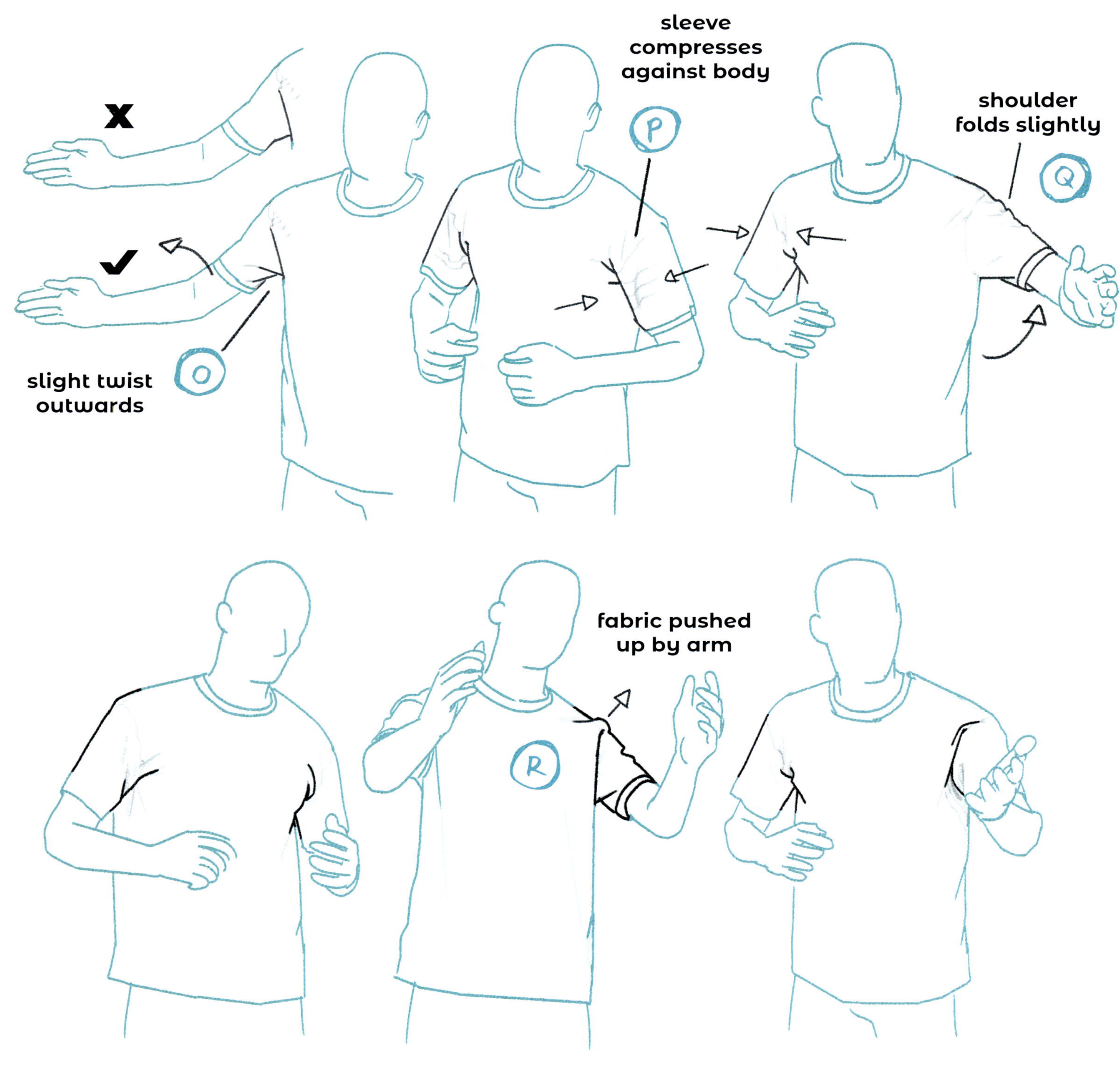

hands on hips

When the arms are on the hips, they're usually angled backwards slightly, rather than straight out to the sides (A). When this happens, the shoulders subtly roll forwards, which sometimes creates this delicate folding (B). The area above the rolled sleeves should have its own subtle folds, rather than being smooth (C). As we've said before, the roll should split into a 'V' shape (D). It's not easy to imagine how the fabric here flares out, so take note of that (E).

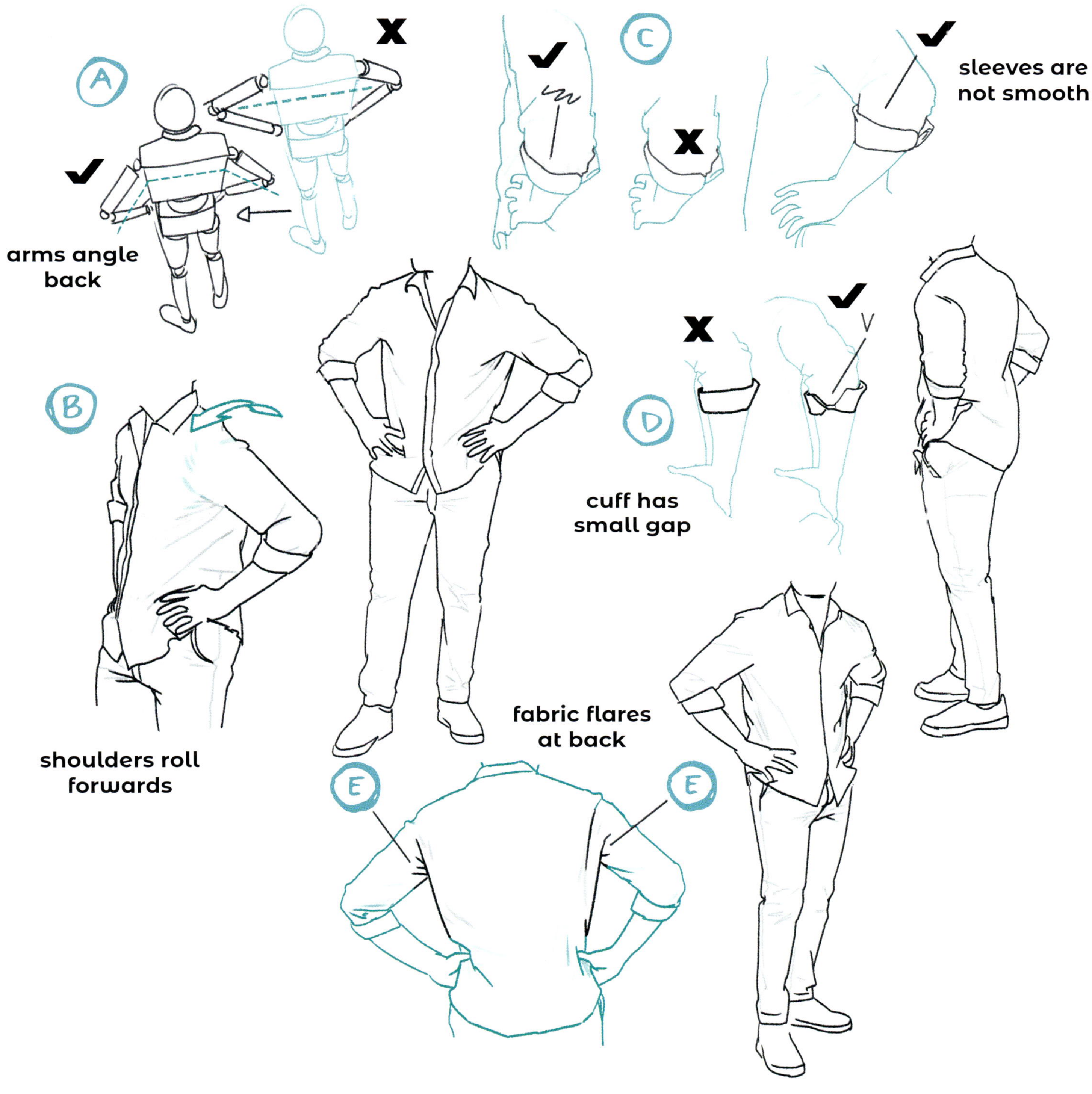

The forward rotation of the shoulders causes folding on either side of the neck (F). Viewed from above, the front of an open collar will lie almost straight across the top of the chest (G). As the shoulders rotate forwards, they push the fabric up and over here **(1)**, and cause this part to be pulled up and back **(2)**. This is why you get so much folding here **(3)**. Note again how the rolled sleeves sit at an angle when the arm is bent (H). When the hands are on the hips, avoid drawing the thumbs on the back. Most of the time, the hands are covered by the folding material above them (I). The back of the shirt shouldn't drop down vertically, but should instead fold in on itself (J) – the lumbar region of the spine curves inwards, which allows space for this to happen.

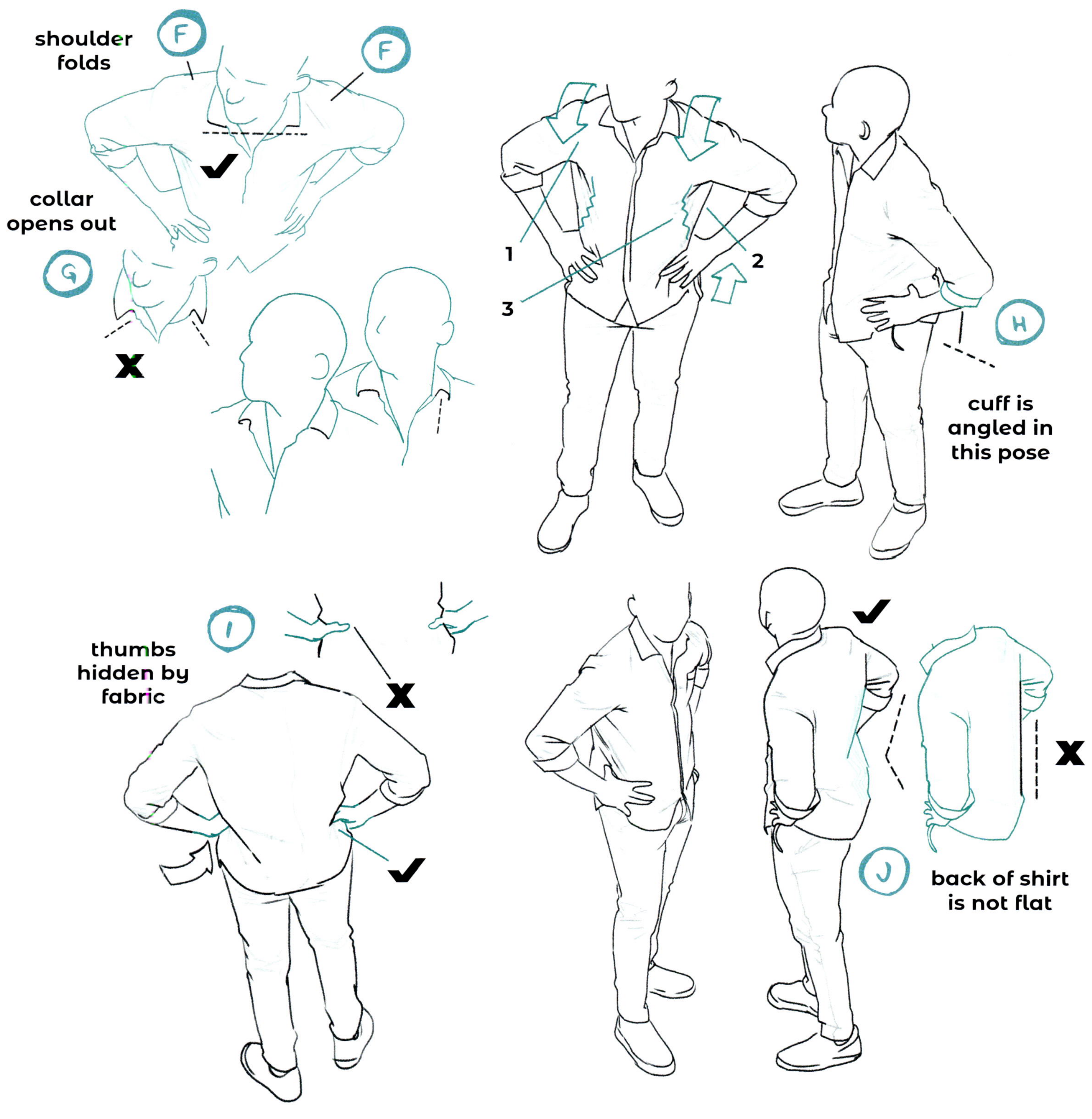

on the phone

Before the phone is lifted to the ear, there may be a gentle curve to the back of the sleeve (A). When the arm is raised, this line straightens, often causing this small hollow to appear (B) – a cross section of the upper arm won't be completely round (C). The shoulder of the arm holding the phone is normally lowered slightly, causing compression below it (D). The raised arm pulls material forwards and up (E). Seen from below, a cross-section of the arm won't be tubular (F). Finally, an arm that's raised up onto the hip often shows a fold on this angle (G).

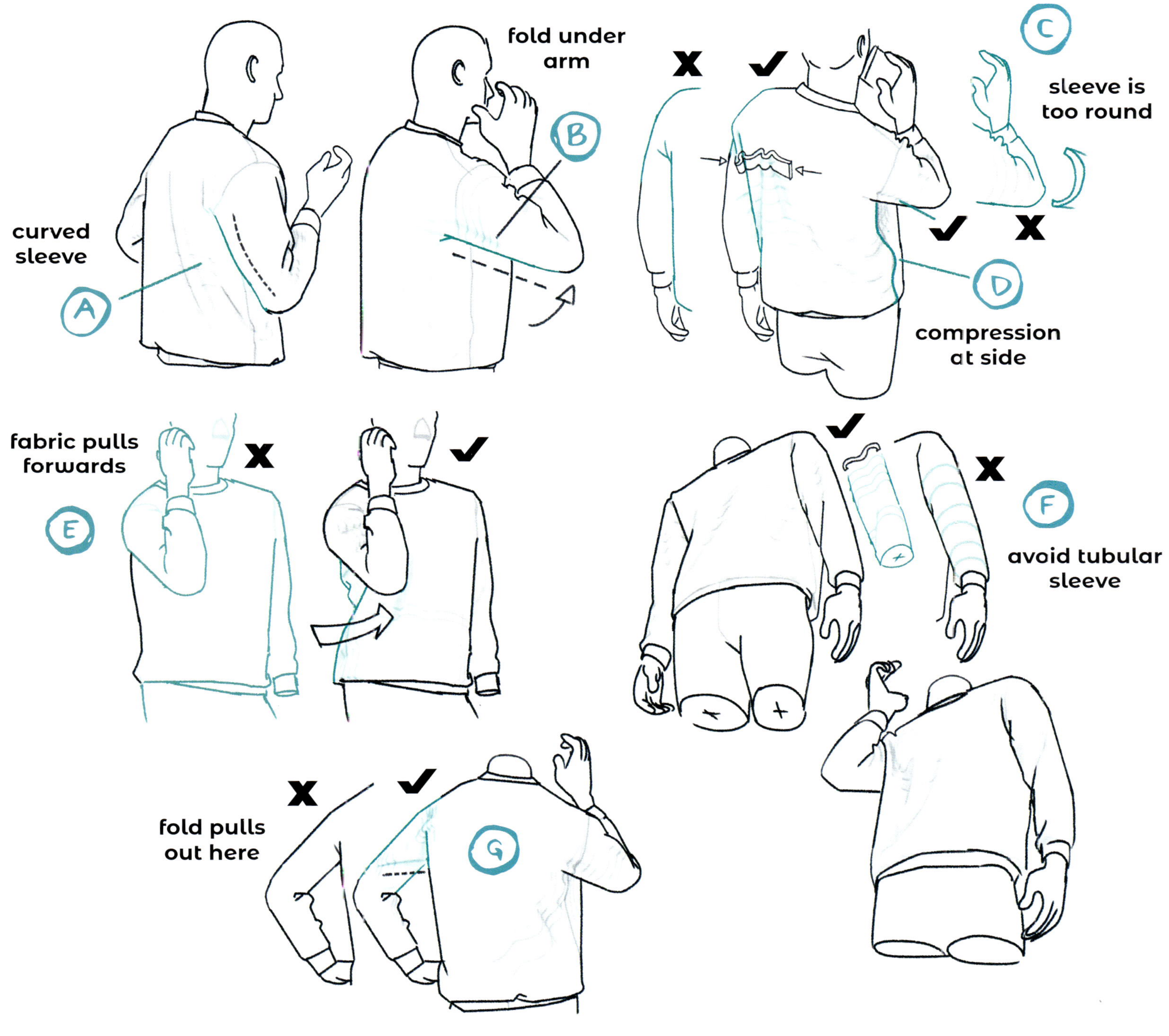

As we've covered, a hand on the hip may rotate the shoulder forwards, causing a small depression below the shoulder (H). In this situation, the back of the sleeve will lie close to the back of the arm **(1)**, and there'll usually be a slight gap at the front **(2)**. Oversized garments tend to have this triangle of fabric between the torso and the back of the arm (I). The bag strap should have some folding beneath it to indicate the compression it's causing (J). This helps to show that the two garments are physically affecting each other, as opposed to lying on top of each other lightly. Most of the folding on the front of the torso originates below the line connecting the breasts (K). The front of the hood often holds itself higher than you'd expect (L). To add variety to your character, try adding a low-resistance hood that collapses inwards, rather than supporting its own weight (M).

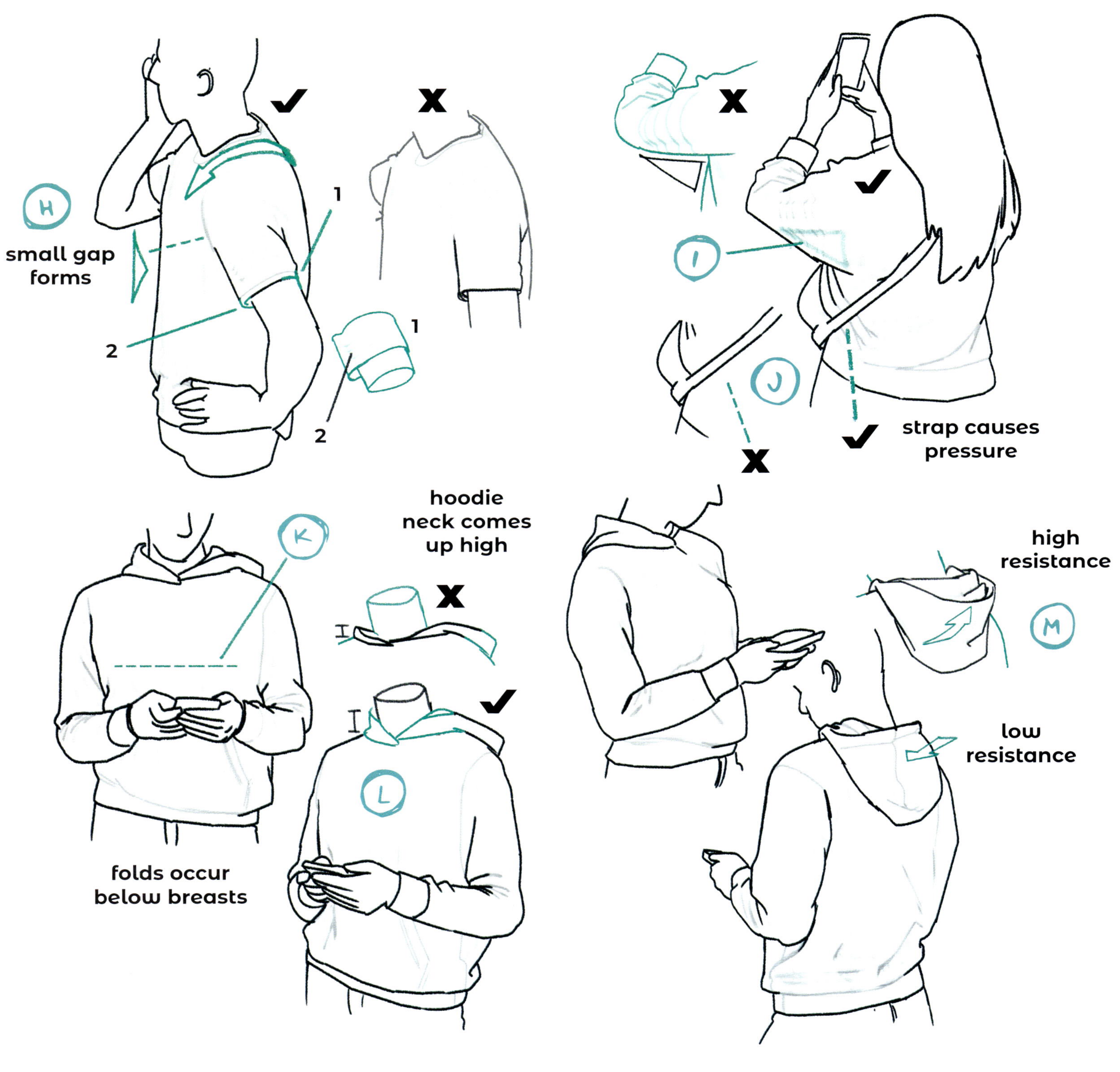

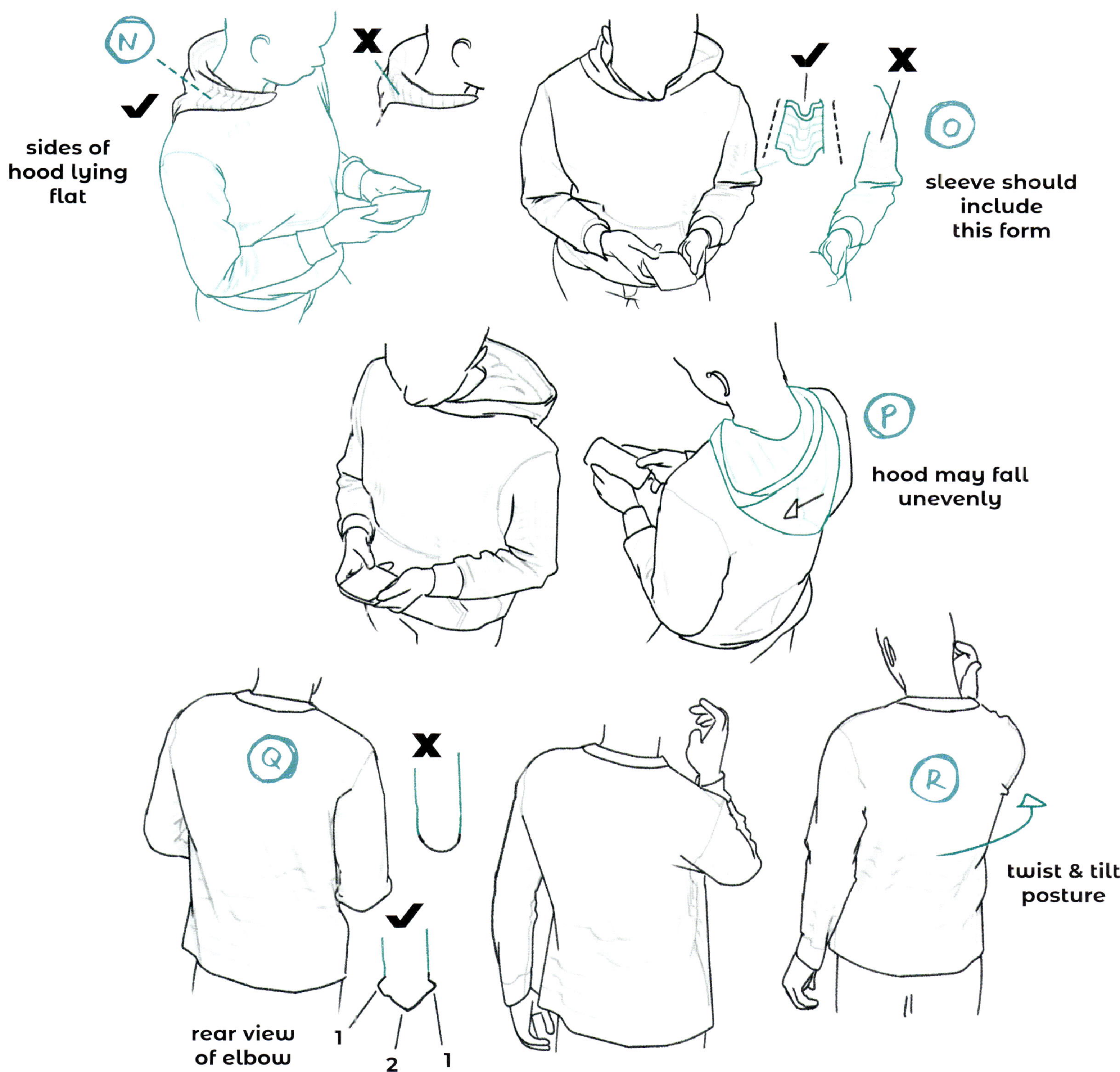

Often, the sides of the hood lie flatter than you'd expect (N). This form on the upper sleeve is also likely to occur (O), rather than the simple tube-like shape next to it. You can also add interest by drawing a hood that folds unevenly to one side (P). From this rear angle (Q), the bulging of fabric at the sides of the elbow should be clear **(1)**, and the elbow should be quite pointed, rather than round **(2)**. One of the best ways to make it look like your character is really on the phone, rather than standing stiffly, is to add some twist around the core, and to have them angle their head as if in thought (R).

reaching up

When one arm is raised, the underside of the sleeve shouldn't be drawn too baggy. Instead, draw it with relatively simple straight lines (A). Remember that the raised arm will pull the material of the torso out to the side and will cause compression on the opposite side. The arrows here indicate major regions of compression (B). When drawing a partially raised arm, it's tempting to curve the fold in towards the elbow, and while this does sometimes occur, it's often reversed (C). When the arm is raised high, the seam of the armpit should also be raised (D). When extended, the sleeve should smooth out rather than bulging at the elasticated cuff (E). Finally, when both shoulders are raised, you'll see extensive folding across the top of the back (F).

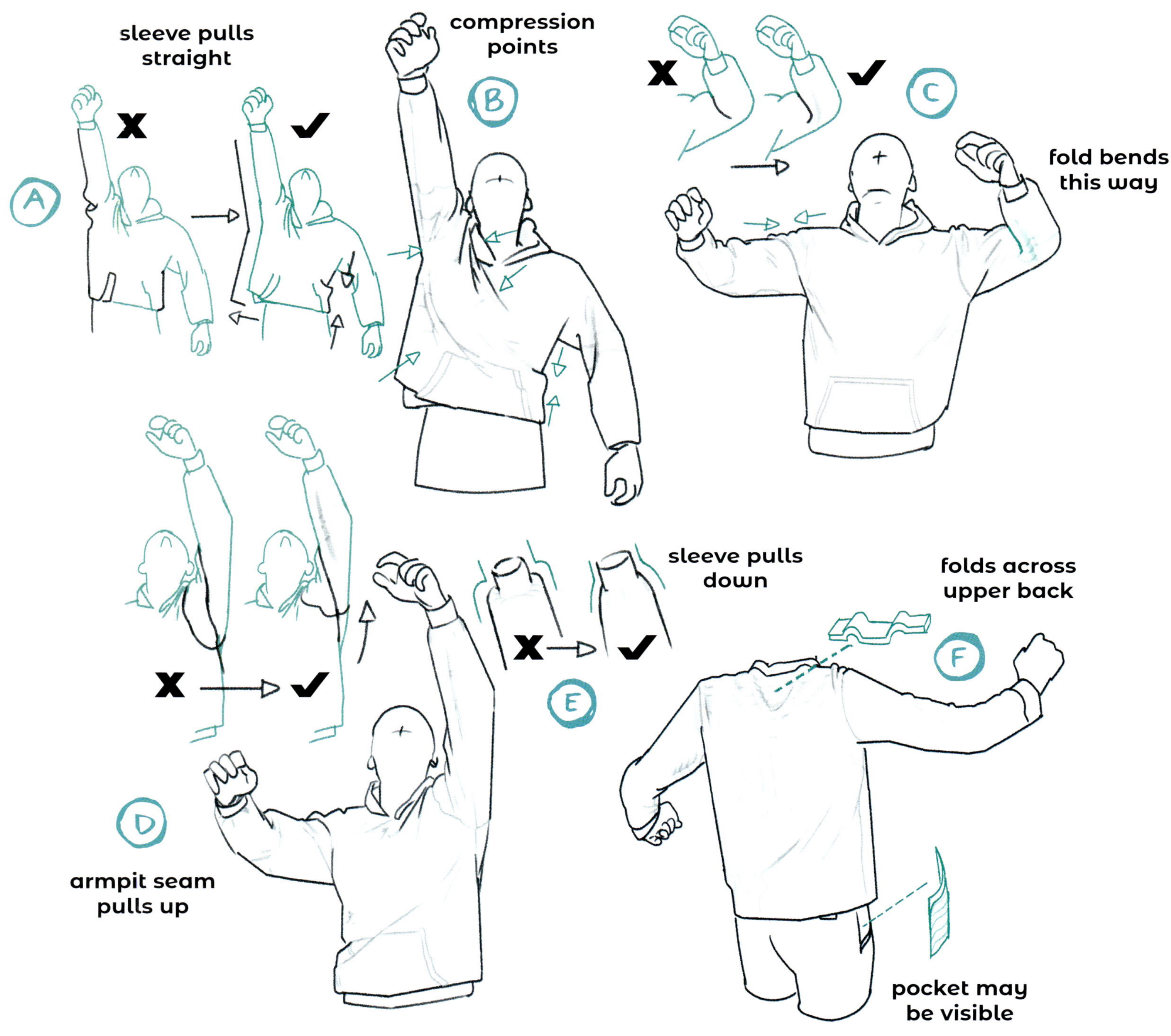

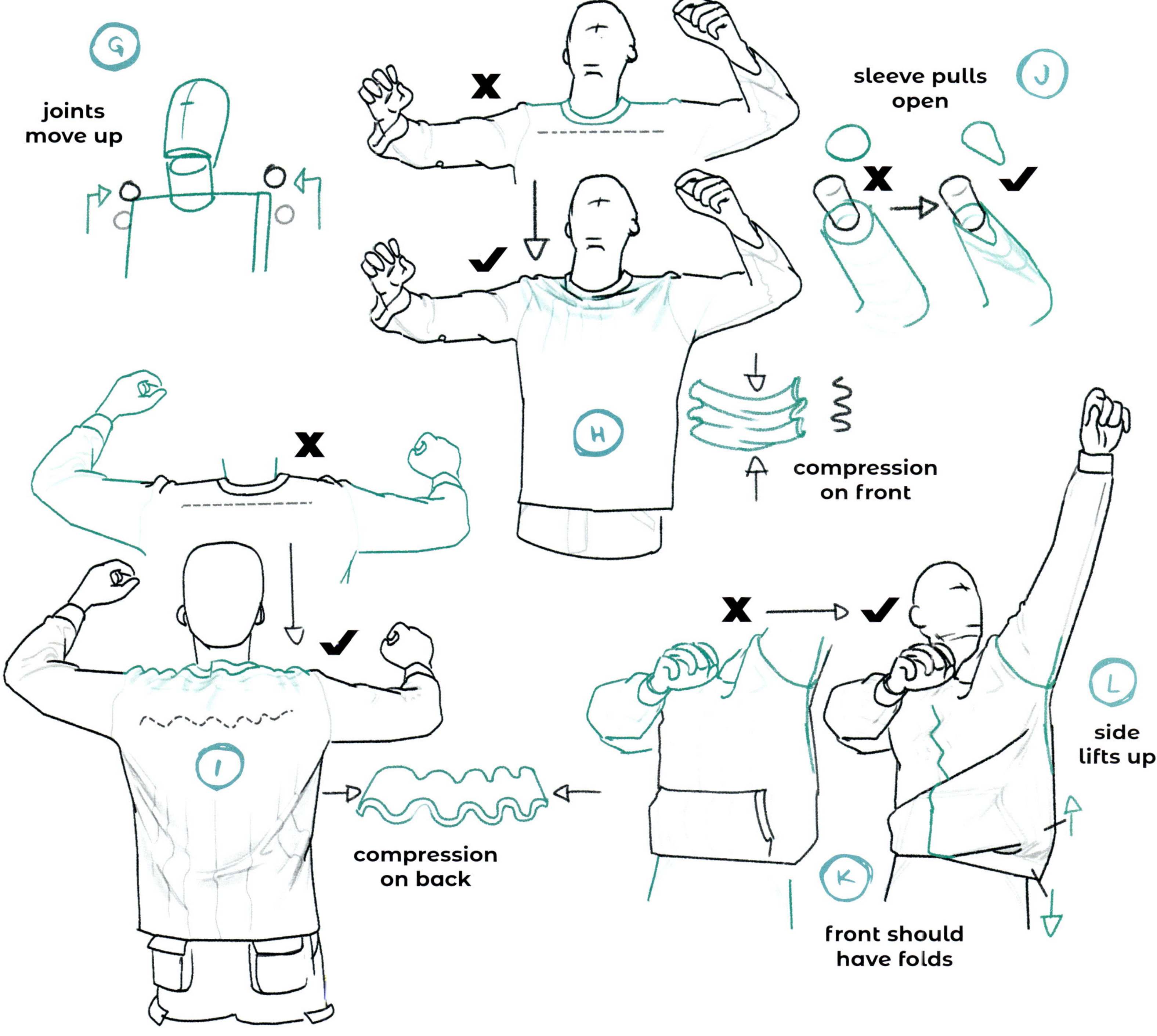

When the arms are raised, the shoulder joints move both upwards and inwards (G). On the front of the torso, this movement causes compression below the neck – mostly vertical compression (H). However, on the back of the torso, the compression is mostly horizontal (I). Rather than drawing the sleeve openings as circles or ellipses, draw a teardrop shape to reflect the pressure created by the arm raising up and inwards (J). When one arm is raised high, the seam under the armpit is also raised, which deforms the fabric across the front of the torso (K). This can sometimes cause the waistband to drop further down, rather than being pulled up (L). This will only happen if the fabric was initially hanging far over the waistband.

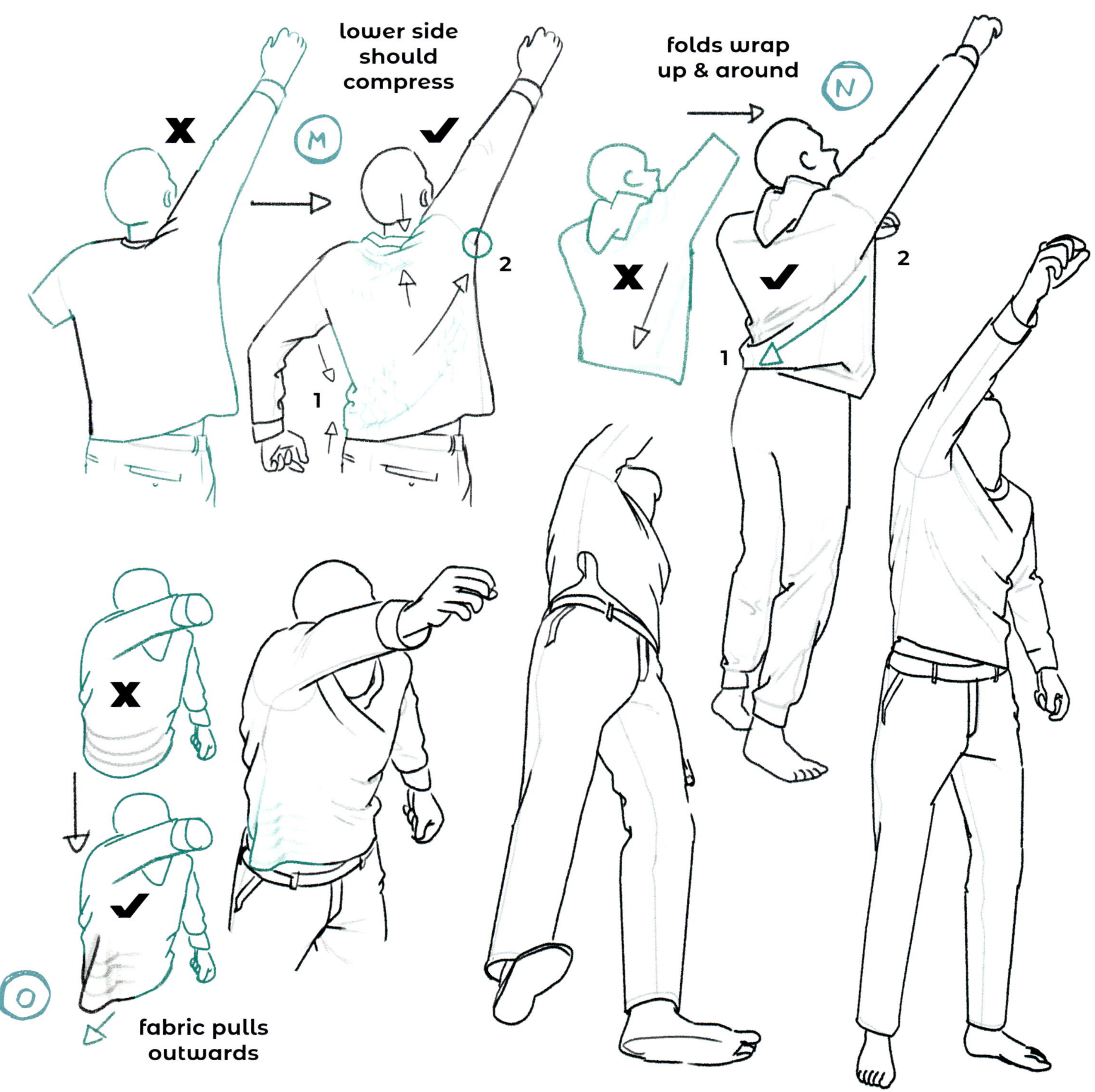

When one arm is raised there will usually be compression on the opposite side (M). You'll also see diagonal folds running up from this compression **(1)** towards the seam at the armpit on the other side **(2)**. Avoid drawing folds falling down from the armpit – they need to wrap around and across the lower back (N). On the side of the raised arm, don't draw the waist section too rounded – there should be a triangle of material that is pulled out (O).

holding neck

When holding your neck, both arms are angled outwards slightly, and the underside of the sleeve is curved, which reflects the anatomy beneath (A). Folds will gather up towards the armpit, and the placket of the cuff will usually be slightly opened by the forces on the forearm (B). This region across the back will have very few folds present (C). When the material of the back 'steps' out, it will usually step inwards first (D).

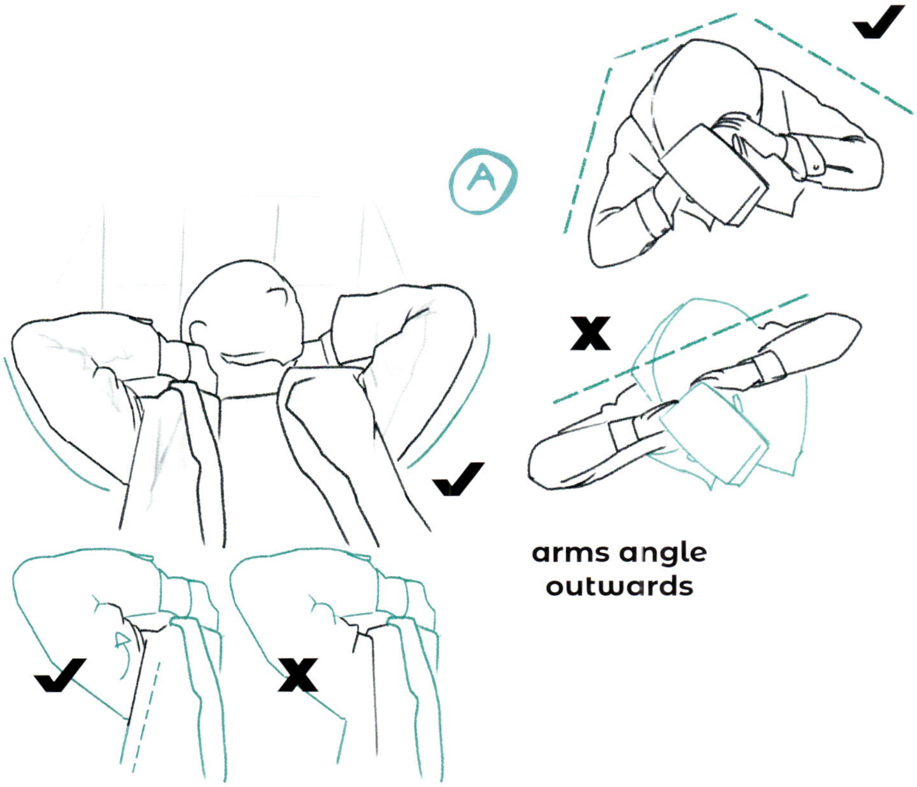

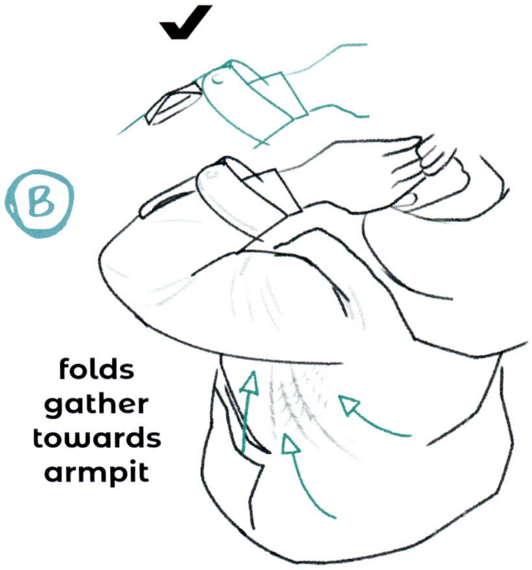

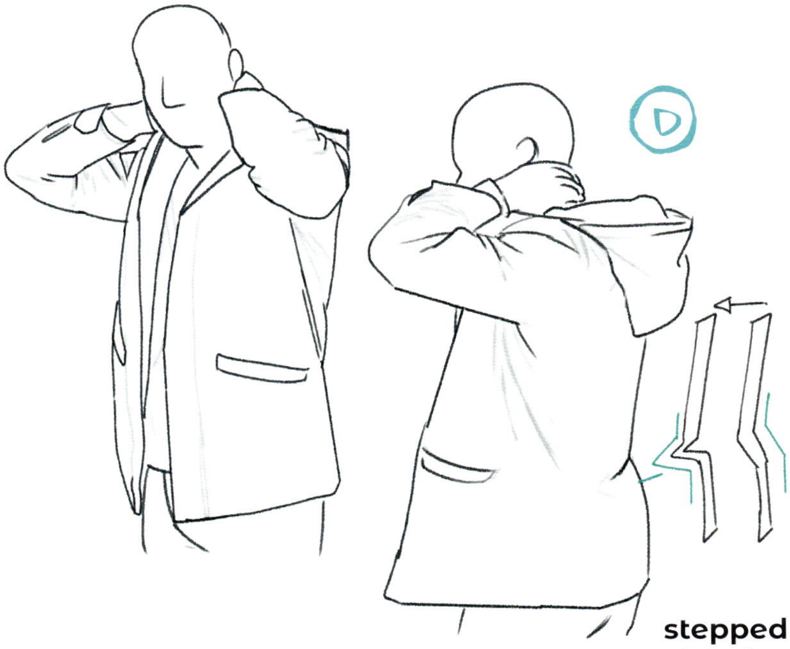

arms angle outwards

folds gather towards armpit

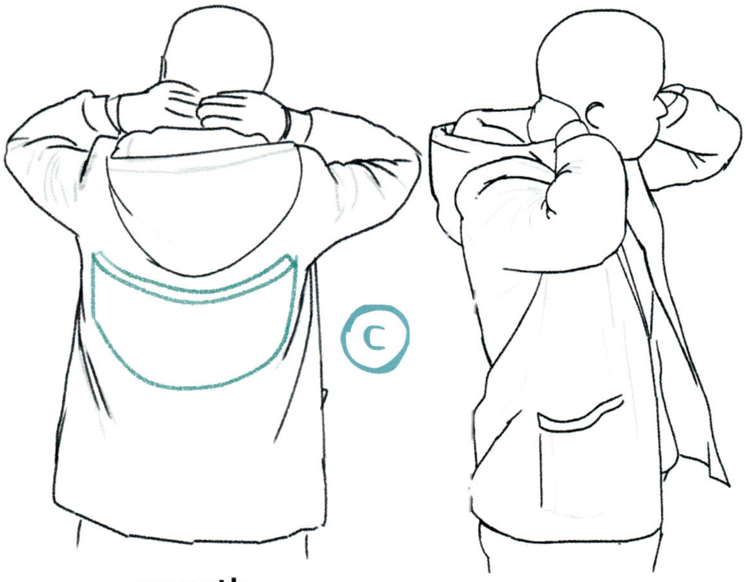

smooth upper back

stepped fold in lower back

When the arms are bent and raised like this, the cuff won't sit evenly across the wrist. Instead, it'll flare out and up (E). Sometimes the outer part of the hood falls down on itself, and sometimes it's able to support its own weight – you'll have to consider the level of resistance of the fabric you're trying to draw (F). When the cuffs are buttoned up, they won't form a neat loop, but will sit on an angle relative to each other (G). The actual edge of the lip of the hood often has some thickness (H), although it can also be drawn thinner (I).

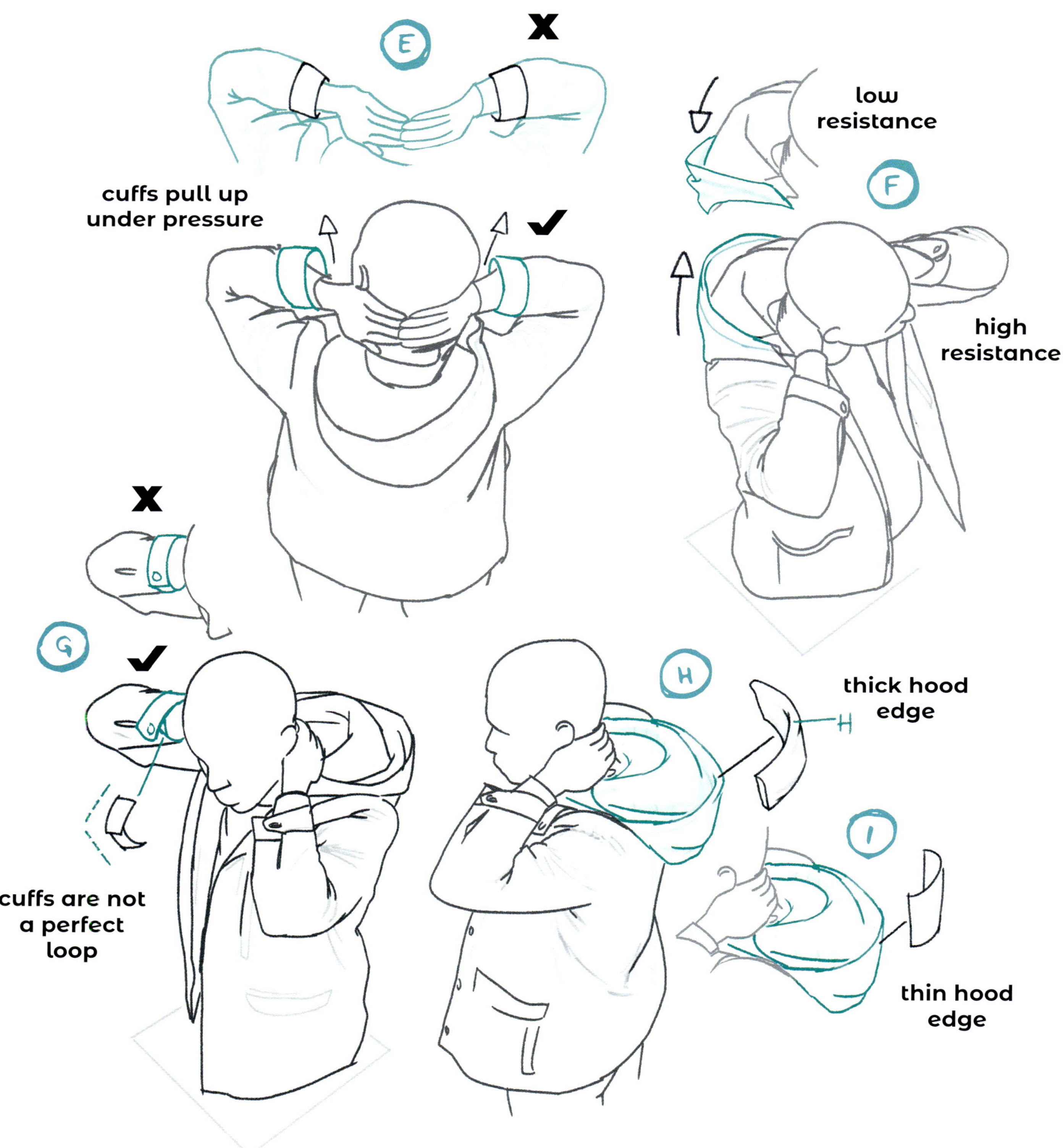

hands in pockets

In this pose, one leg is held forwards (A). Because of this, the folding across the glutes won't be even. The leg that's straighter will show more compression below the glutes **(1)**, and the one held out in front will have fewer folds **(2)**. There will be strong compression at the bottom of the sleeve, because the pocket itself is resisting being pushed down (B). Hands in these pockets will usually force the whole section forwards and slightly inwards. The bottom corners may hold themselves outwards on a high-resistance material, but usually they fold in on themselves (C). The weight of the arm forces the whole pocket down, causing these folds at the back and beneath the pocket (D). The top of the back is rarely a smooth curve. Instead, there will often be two raised areas which reflect the location of the scapulae, or 'shoulder blades' (E).

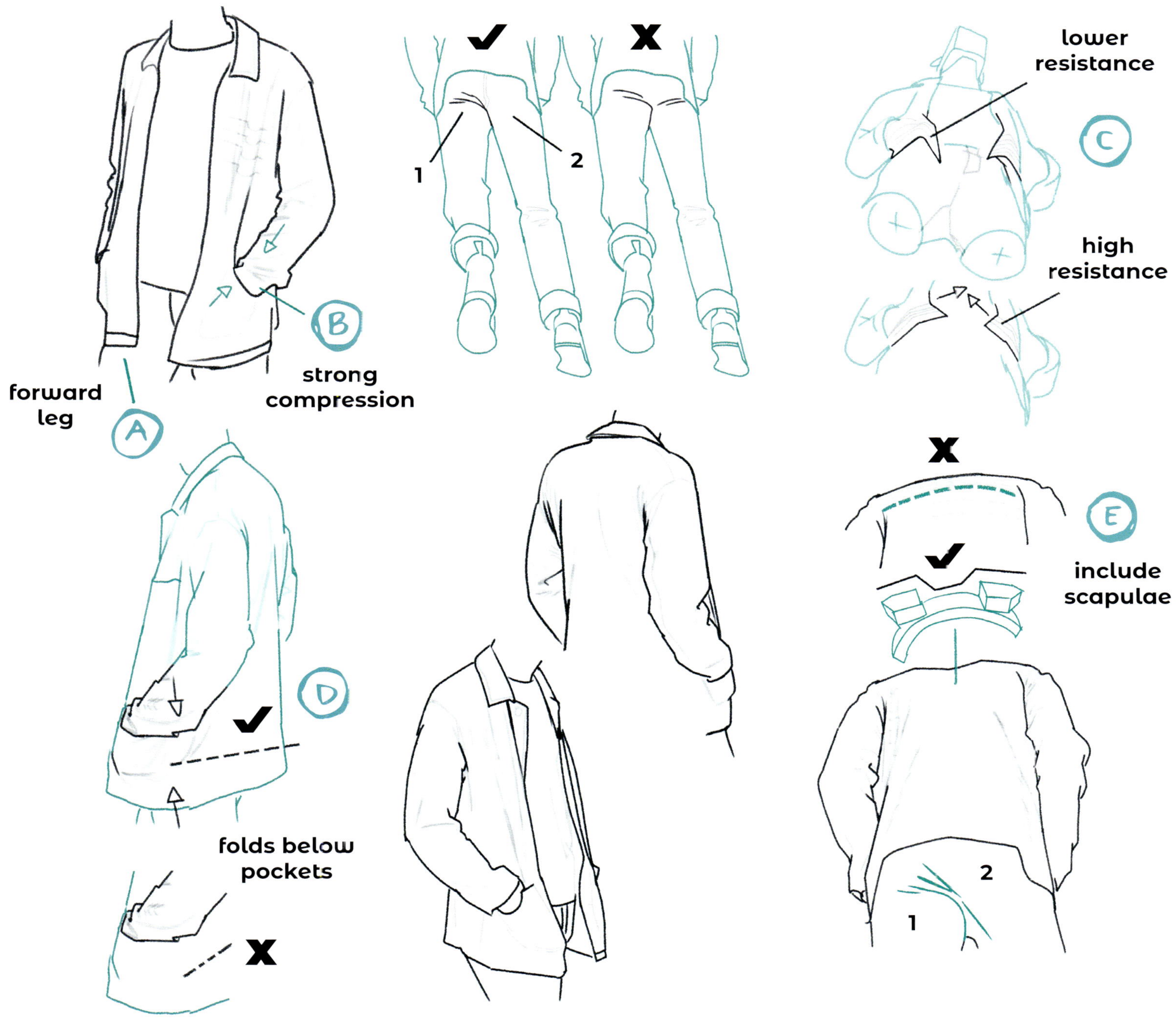

When the hands are in the pockets, the jacket will rarely hang straight down, and the breast pocket will rarely sit flat (F). Instead, the weight of the arm will force this section forwards and in, and the pocket will deform (G). The sleeve will likely bulge out and hang over the top of the pocket, and the bottom corner of the pocket will sometimes merge into the rest of the jacket (H). Because the underlying anatomy creates a 'shelf', there'll be very little folding in this region (I) – give it the appropriate depth, as you often see it drawn too narrow. From above, this form on the back appears to create a narrowing of the waist (J).

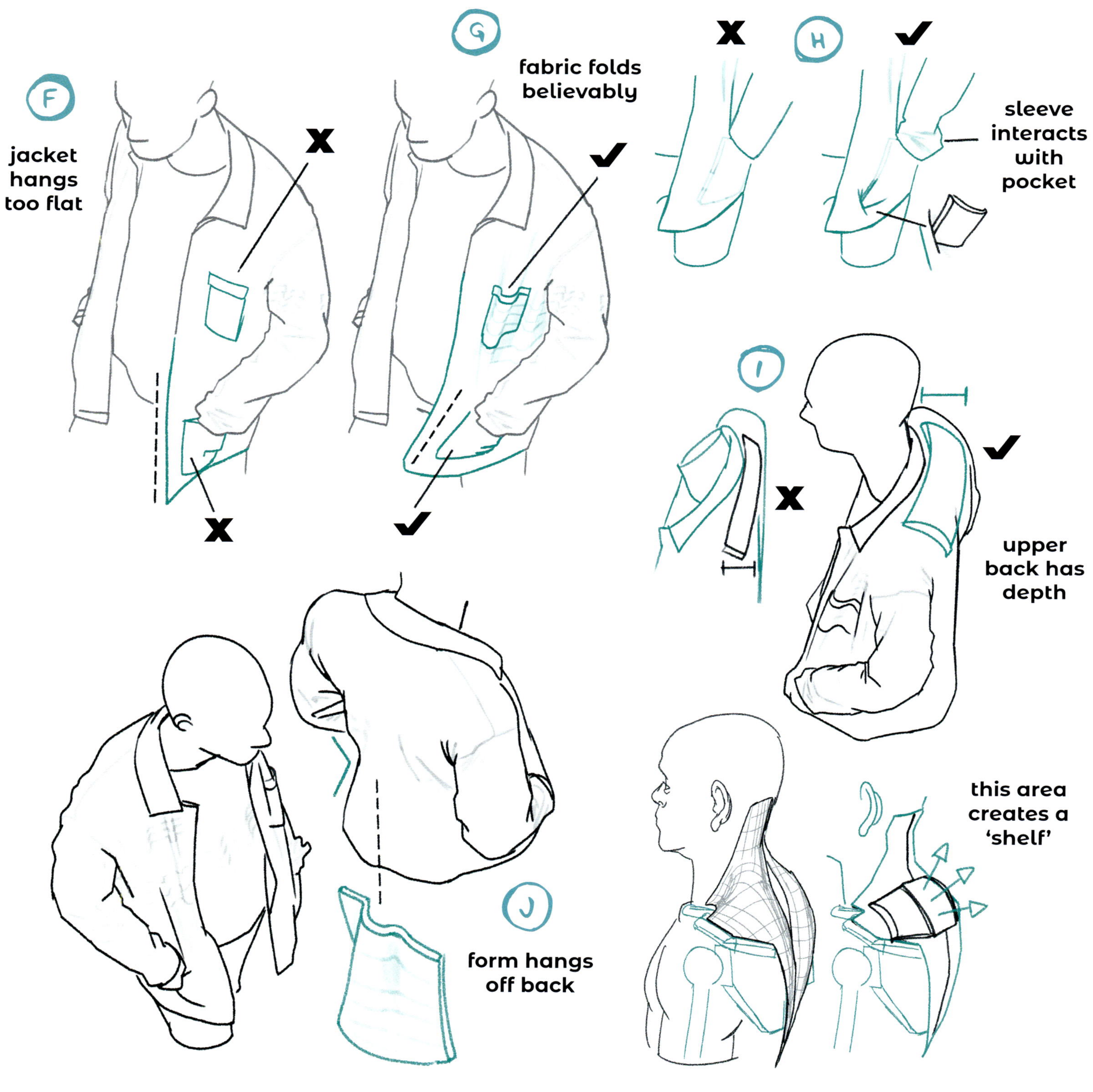

suit pockets

Don't forget to indicate some folding in the shirt below the suit (A). The hand in the pocket usually sweeps the side of the jacket backwards, rather than raising it (B). The bottom part of the jacket (C) gently curves outwards as it reaches the bottom of the lapel **(1)**, then curves slightly inwards again at the hem **(2)**. Remember the adjustment about surface orientation? There will be fewer drawn folds on this surface (D) because it's facing directly towards the viewer. However, this surface (E) will have more, because the whole back is angled further away from us. Finally, the bottom of the tie should almost touch the belt buckle (F). Be careful not to draw it too long or short.

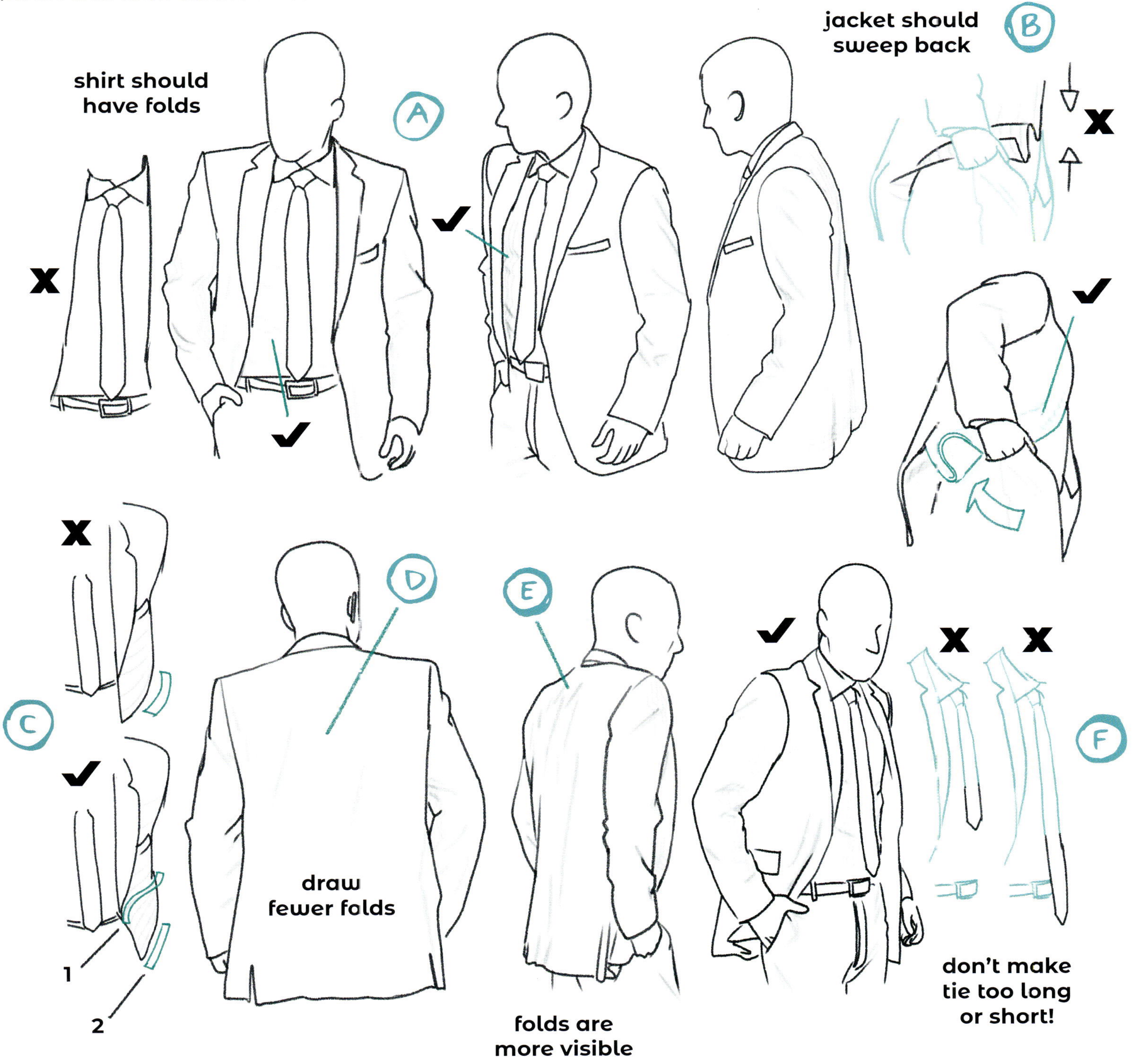

As you move down the lapel, it twists and faces forwards (G). There's often too much thickness at these ends (H), because this twist is forgotten. It's closest to vertical at the back of the neck. Just below this point, you tend to see a slight 'ledge' of material (I). On very slim individuals in standing poses, the belt buckle is nearly vertical (J). However, most people's belt buckles will be angled slightly outwards when standing (K), and angled much further forwards when sitting, due to the bulging of the core.

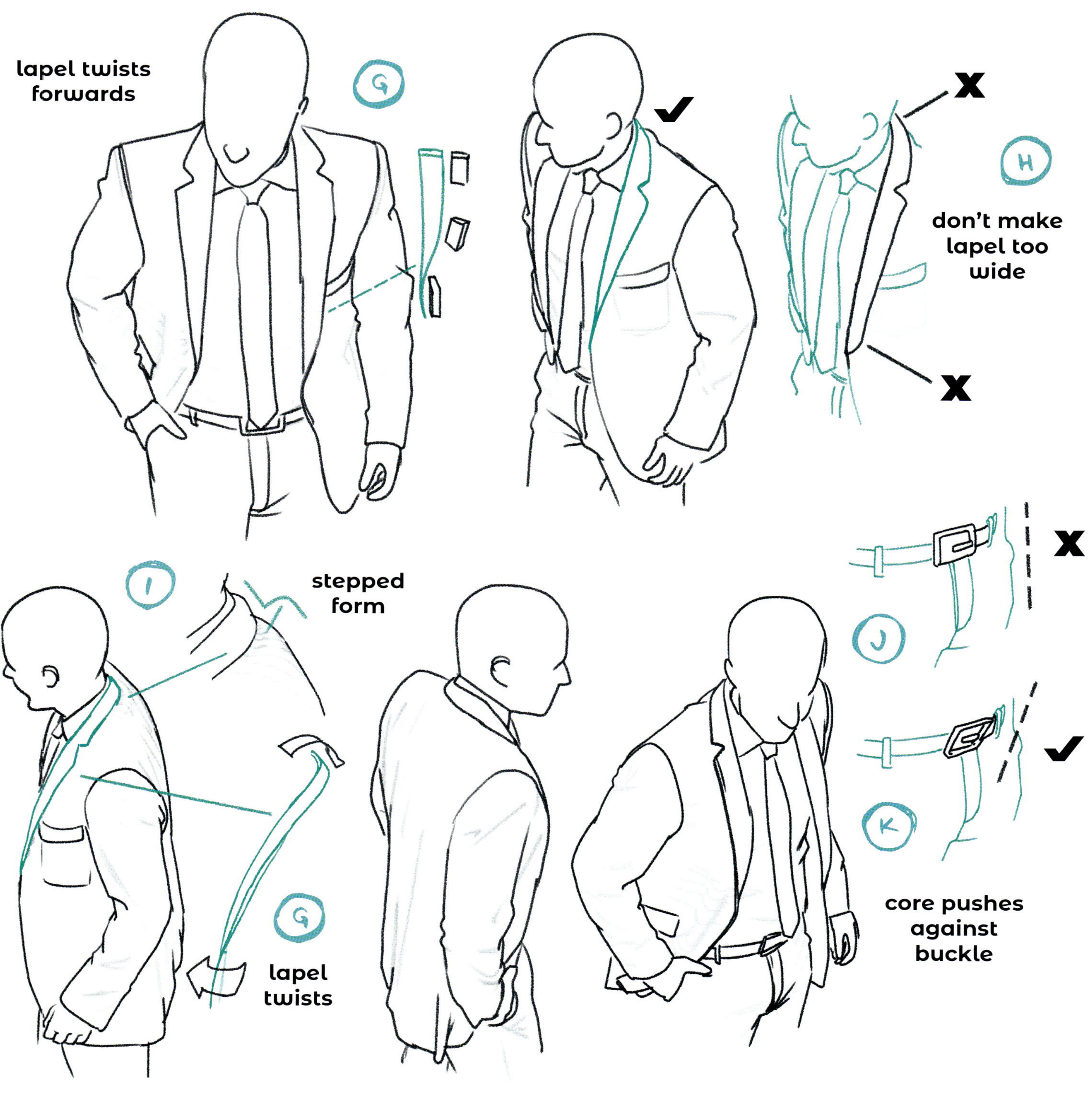

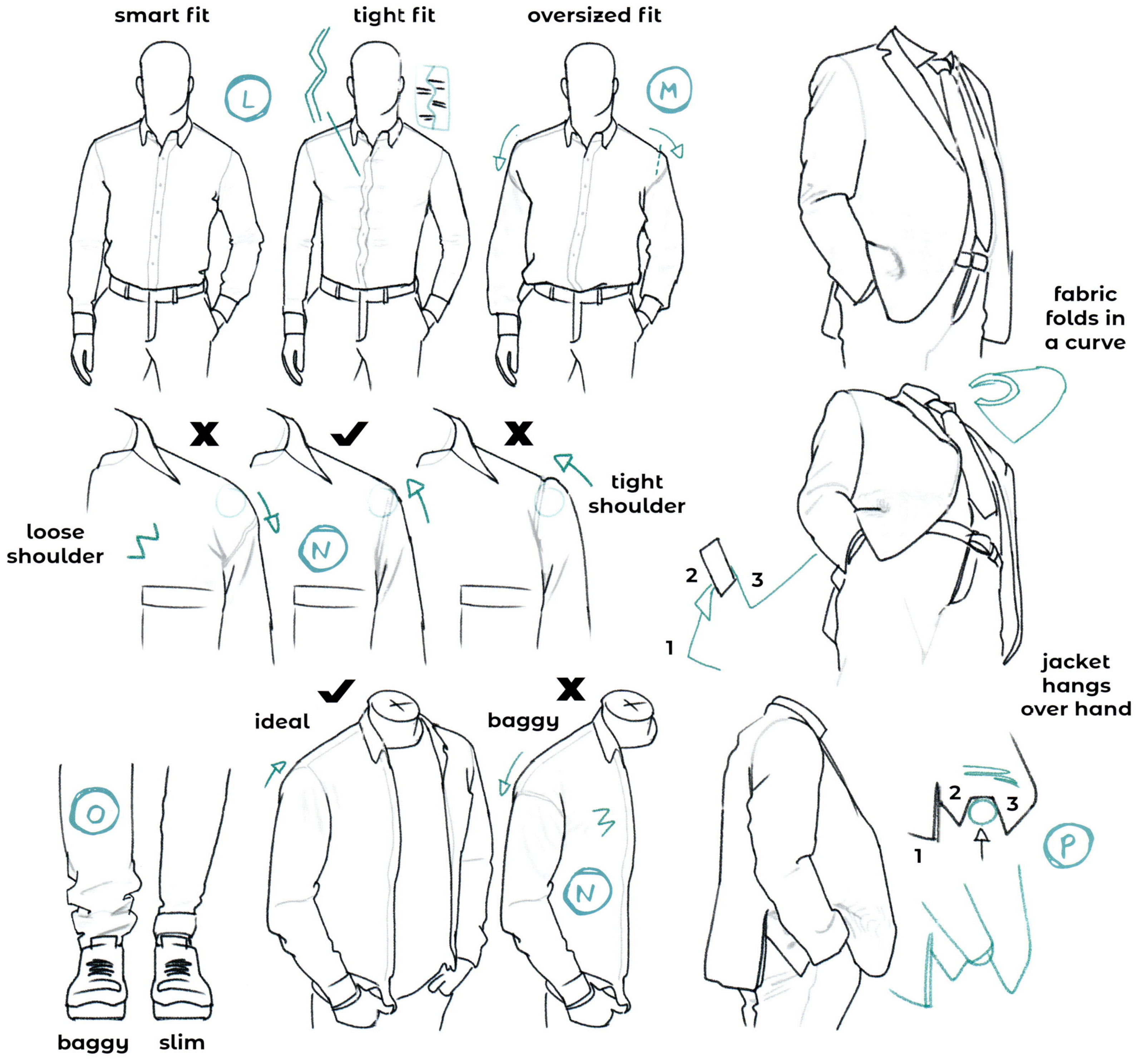

Shirts have a placket down the centre, to which the buttons are attached. When a shirt is tight, small folds will appear either side of this placket (L). The placket will also be more angular. On oversized shirts the shoulder seam drops down from the top corner of the shoulder (M). When this happens, you'll usually see multiple complex and shallow folds around the armpit (N). This is usually considered a poor fit. Jeans and trousers will also show folds or compression depending on whether they are loose or slim-fitting (O). Sometimes the jacket hangs both in front and behind the arm, bunching up the front panel. In this situation, don't forget to include the separation of the back panel (P). Visualizing this in segments **(1, 2, 3)** can help.

cheering

When both arms are raised (A), there's strong bunching both in front **(1)** and behind the neck **(2)**. These triangular volumes will hang from below the sides (B). When the arm is pulled back and bent, there's strong tension on the outside edge of the arm, and the cuff will be pulled up the forearm and will deform (C). As both arms raise up and come together, the back of the collar will deform, and bunching will occur at the very tops of both deltoids (D).

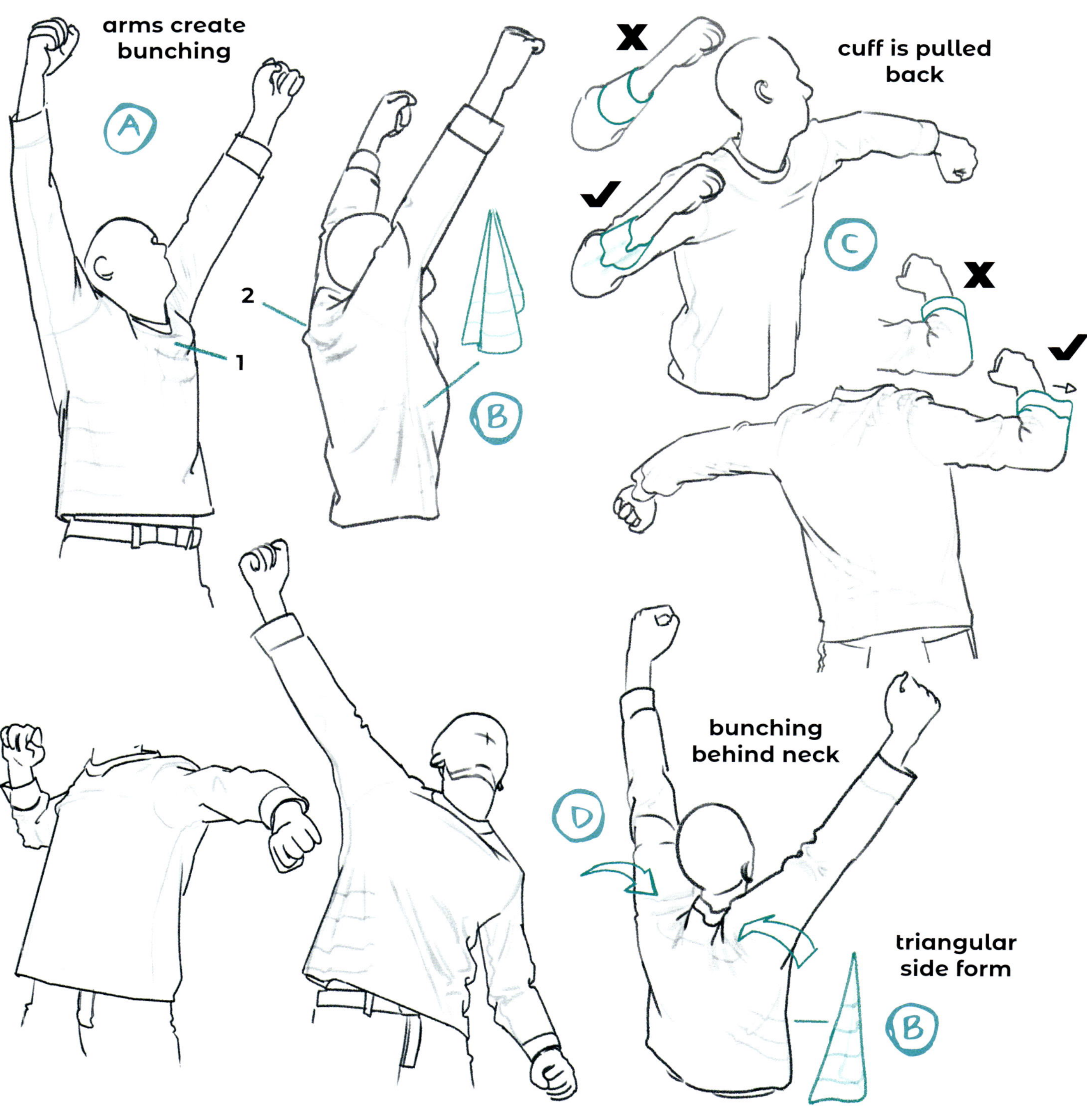

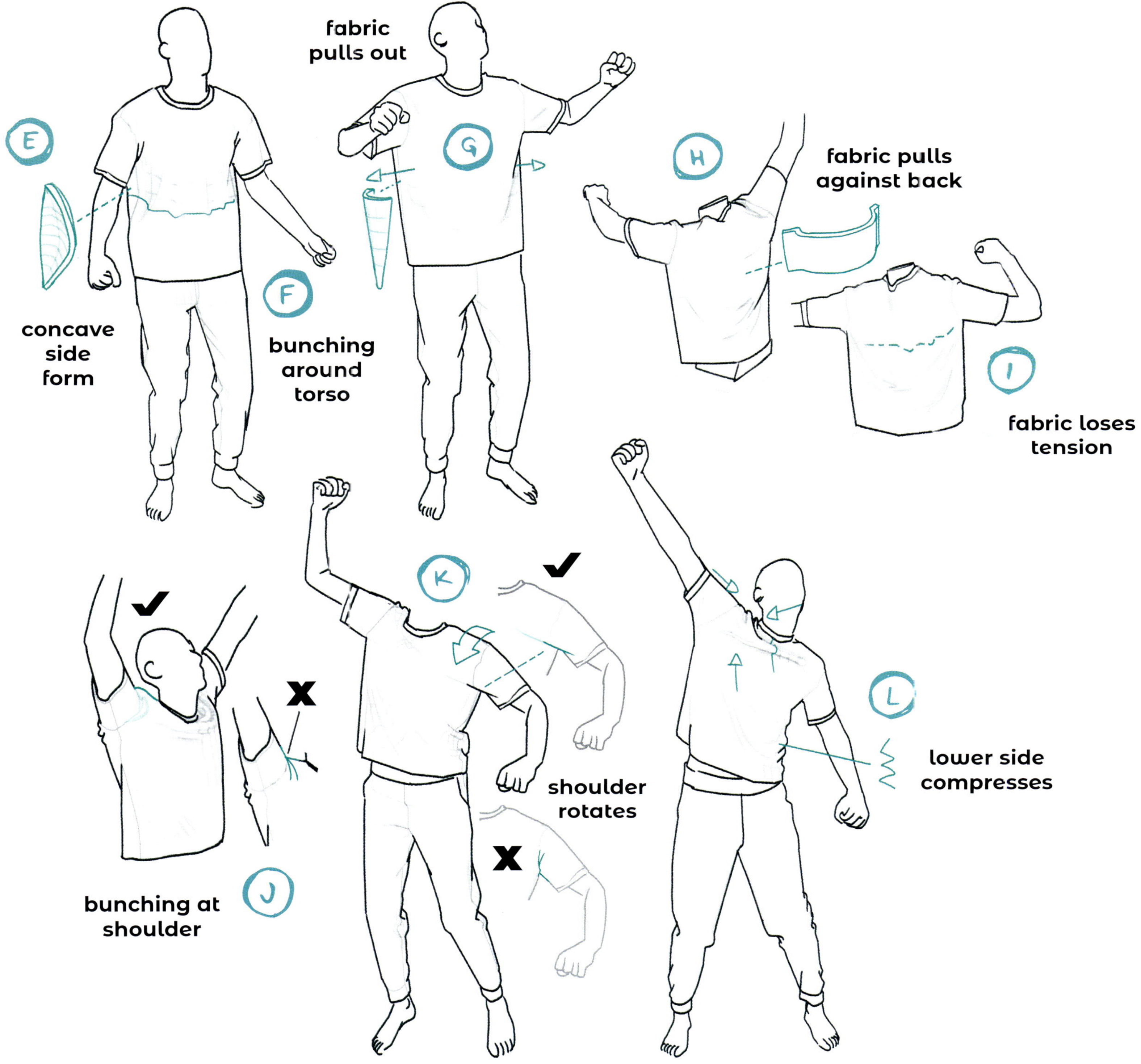

With the arms near the sides, a gentle concave form may appear under the arms (E). Shallow bunching may also occur around the circumference of the torso (F). As the arms are raised, this concave section 'inflates' and expands outwards, creating these upside-down triangle forms (G). When one arm is raised, the back of the T-shirt is often pulled against the back of the ribs (H). When the arm is brought down and back, the tension eases and gentle folding appears (I).

When drawing folds, don't think, 'What lines need to go here?' Instead, ask yourself, 'What new forms might appear?' For example, when the arm is raised, you don't just see folds appear – you see a whole new form appear above and inside the shoulder (J). This shoulder is slightly rotated forwards, so make sure your lines reflect this (K). When the shoulder is raised on one side, the other shoulder drops, which creates compression below (L).

lifting arms

These compression lines should curve and wrap the front of the chest, rather than being straight (A). The raised arm usually causes compression on the front of the torso, forming this pattern (B). Avoid drawing it in a V-shape. When the arms are lowered, the fabric across the back isn't flat, but stepped (C).

When the arms raise, the fabric compresses just below the back of the neck, which really sells the idea (D), and the steps of hanging fabric are flattened out (E). Compression originates at the hand on the hip, and wraps up and around to inside the armpit of the raised arm (F).

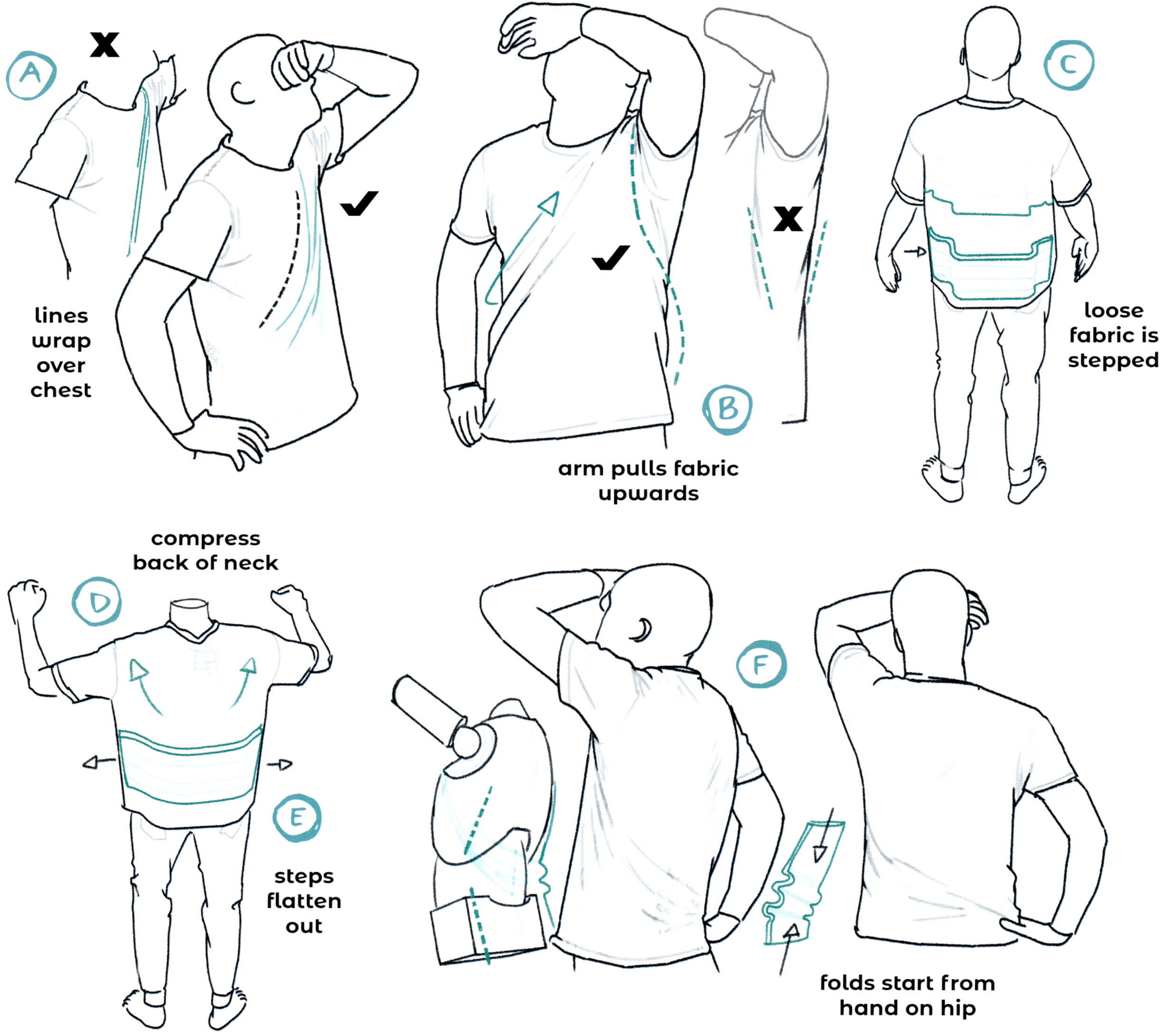

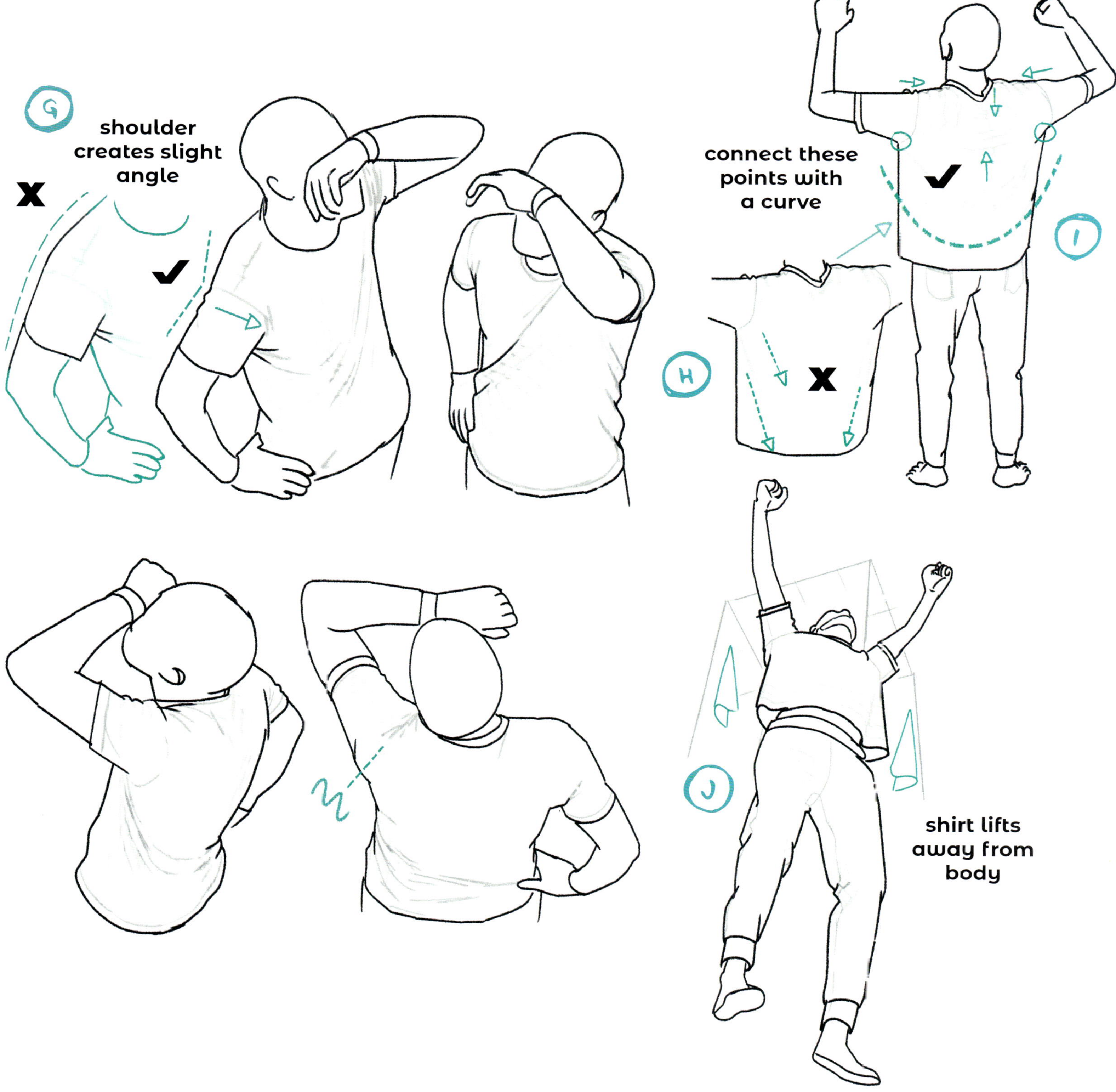

Again, when one hand is on a hip, the shoulder moves forwards. Avoid drawing the shoulder rounded – instead give it this concave angled shape (G). With raised arms, sometimes people draw folds in a V-shape (H). Instead, try to connect these two circles so that the folds 'hang' from them (I). As mentioned before, there'll also be inward compression and an area of folding below the back of the neck. There's a lot going on here! Finally, when the arms are raised, the shirt will lift away from the core (J).

swinging a bat

These folds should originate just above the breasts, not below them (A). The trailing elbow should be tightly tucked into the side, causing compression here (B). The leading shoulder should be tucked right into the torso, creating pressure here (C). The compression at the thigh may cause the pocket to open slightly (D). The trailing arm releases the bat, but the momentum carries it further round (E).

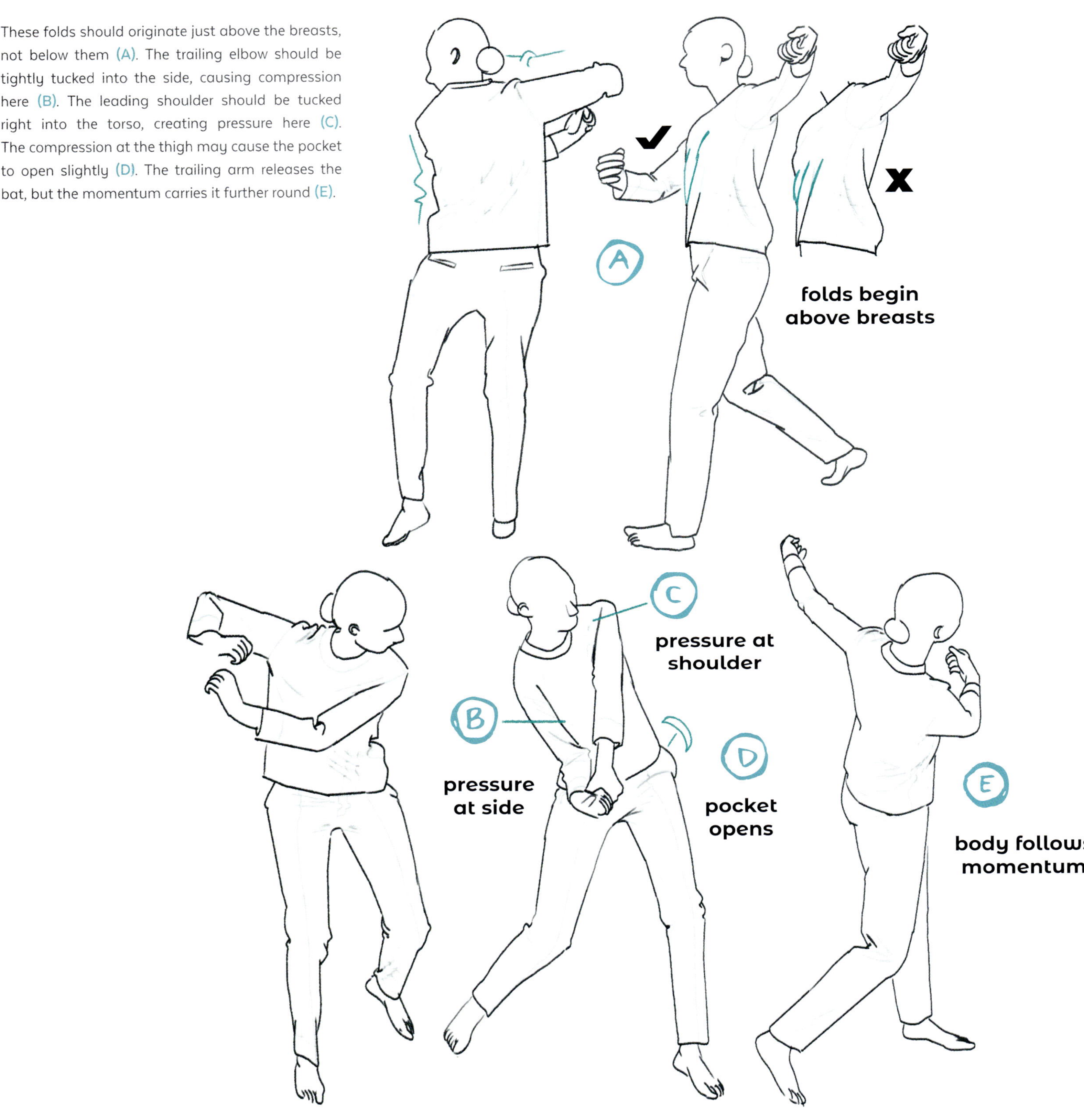

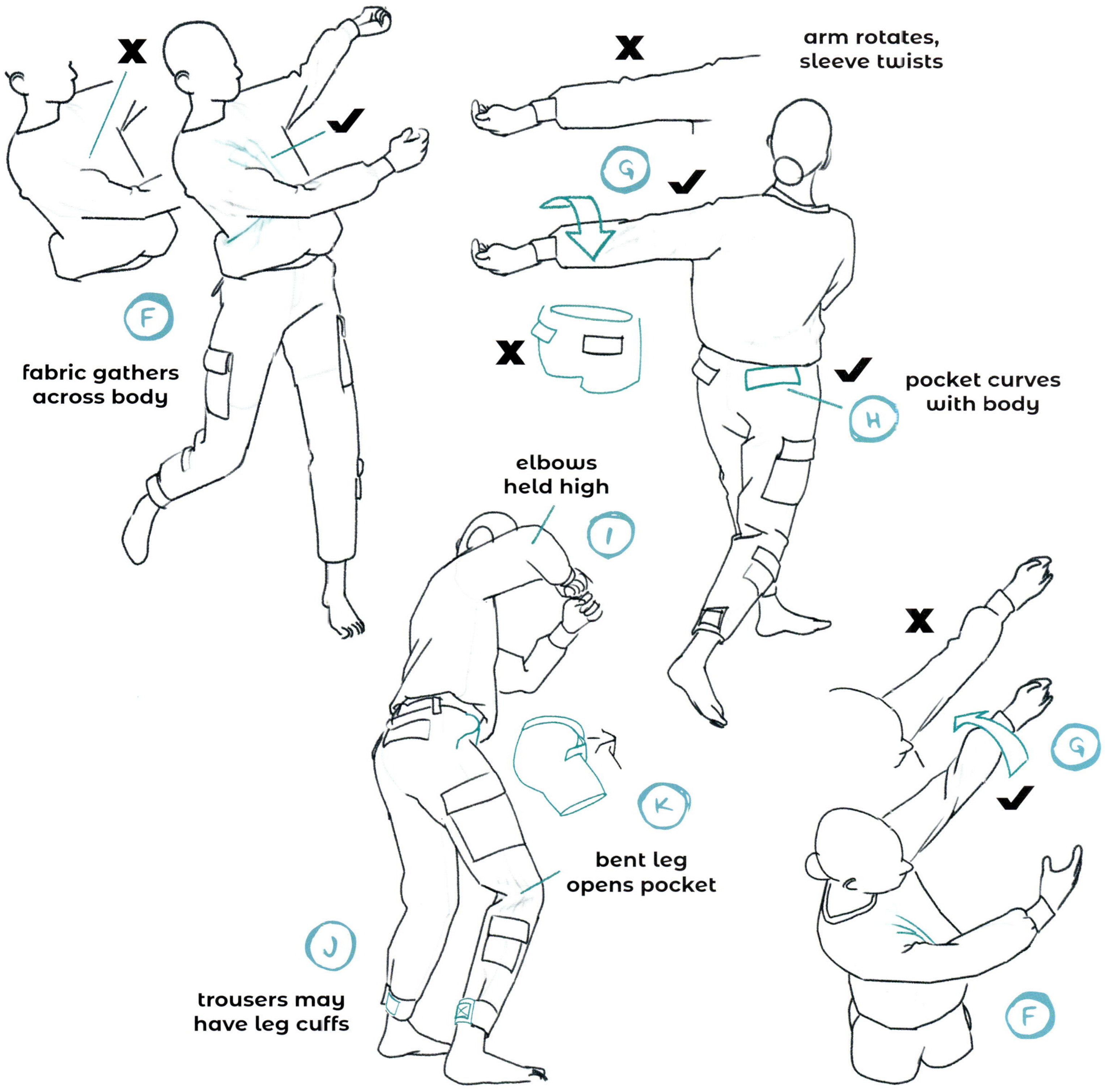

When the trailing arm moves across the body, it often gathers up fabric before it (F). The leading arm, once swung round this far, usually shows signs of rotation (G). This pocket may reflect the fact that the rear leg is held further back and face upwards (H). Before the hit, the elbows are held high and stick out to the sides (I). On cargo trousers, there's often a little patch that fastens the bottom cuff (J). Bending the leg may cause the pocket above to open forwards (K).

wheelbarrow

When both arms are brought back, the upper back is compressed (A). When the mannequin leans back, the bottom of the T-shirt usually falls backwards (B). When the arms are pushed forwards, the T-shirt can't simply fall forwards like this (C) because there isn't enough material along this length to allow it (D). Instead, you'll see bunching both behind **(1)** and in front **(2)**. When the arms are outstretched, the bunching on the back will only happen above and below this smooth area (E), which will have very little, if any, folding at all.

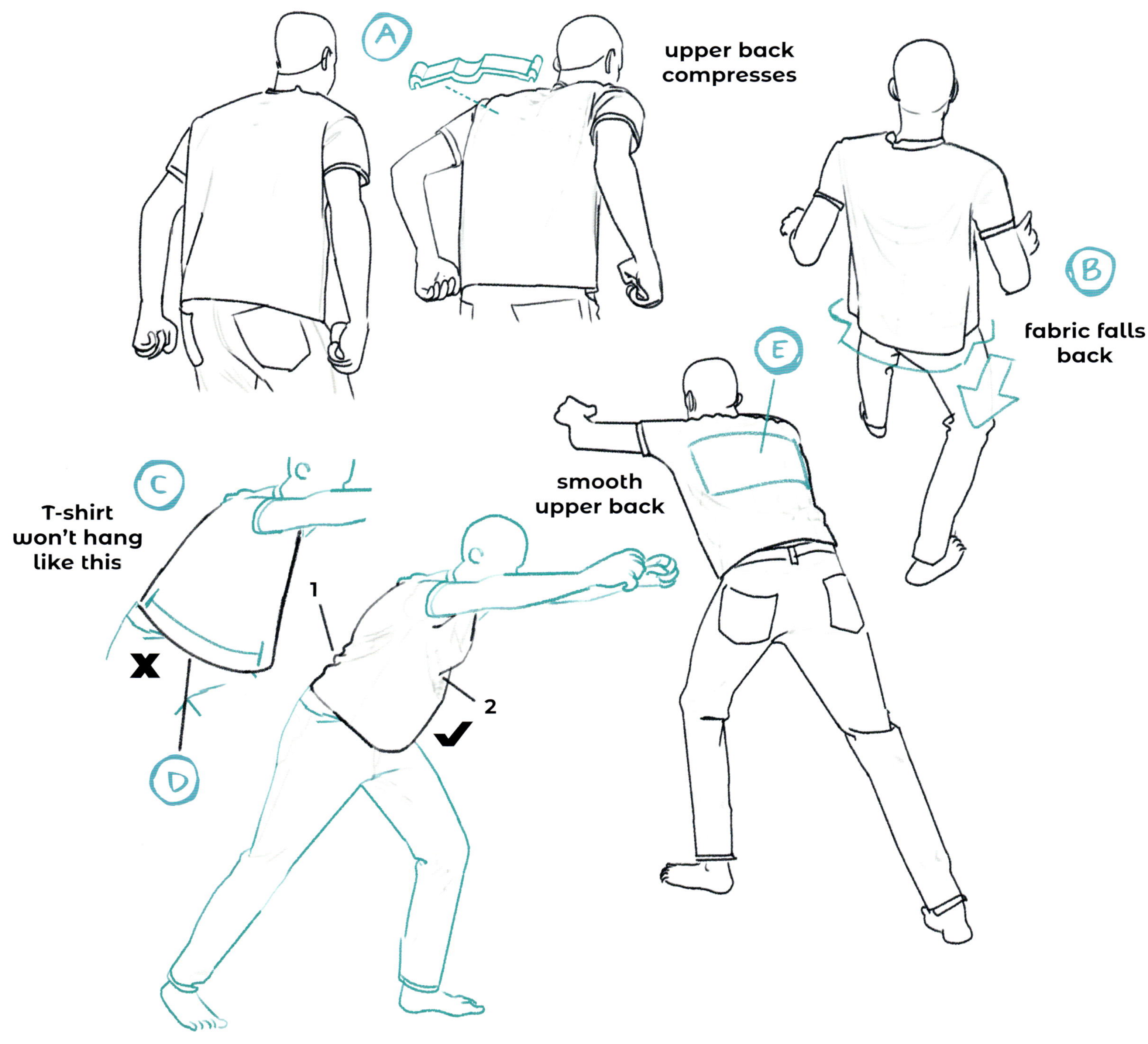

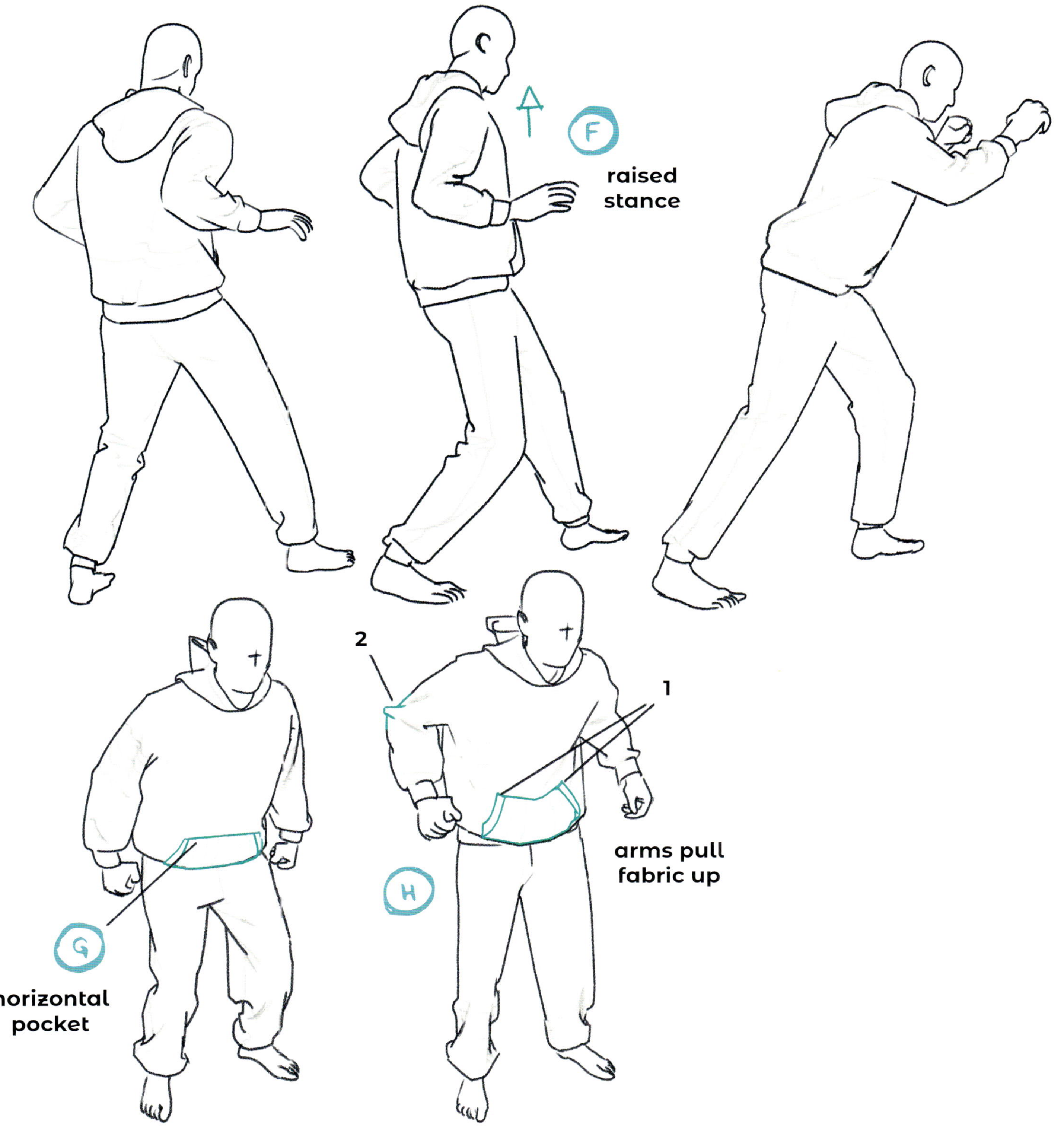

Here's the same action in looser clothing. Note that the character is raised up in the middle of the motion (F). When the arms are down, the top of the hoodie pocket is nearly horizontal (G). However, when the arms are raised up and back (H), the top corners of the pocket raise up (**1**). The material on the front will also be more vertical and less folded. The tight bending of the elbow causes this bunching to occur (**2**).

Remember: these poses aren't included to give you lots of reference for drawing characters with wheelbarrows! This movement is included because these references give you a range of useful component parts relating to lifting the arms. Rather than thinking, 'I'll never use that because I never really draw characters with wheelbarrows', think of it as parts for your collection. There are many situations when you'll want to draw a character using both arms like this. For example, this could be used for someone carrying two large pieces of luggage (I). Pay particular attention to the shape of the sleeves in these examples.

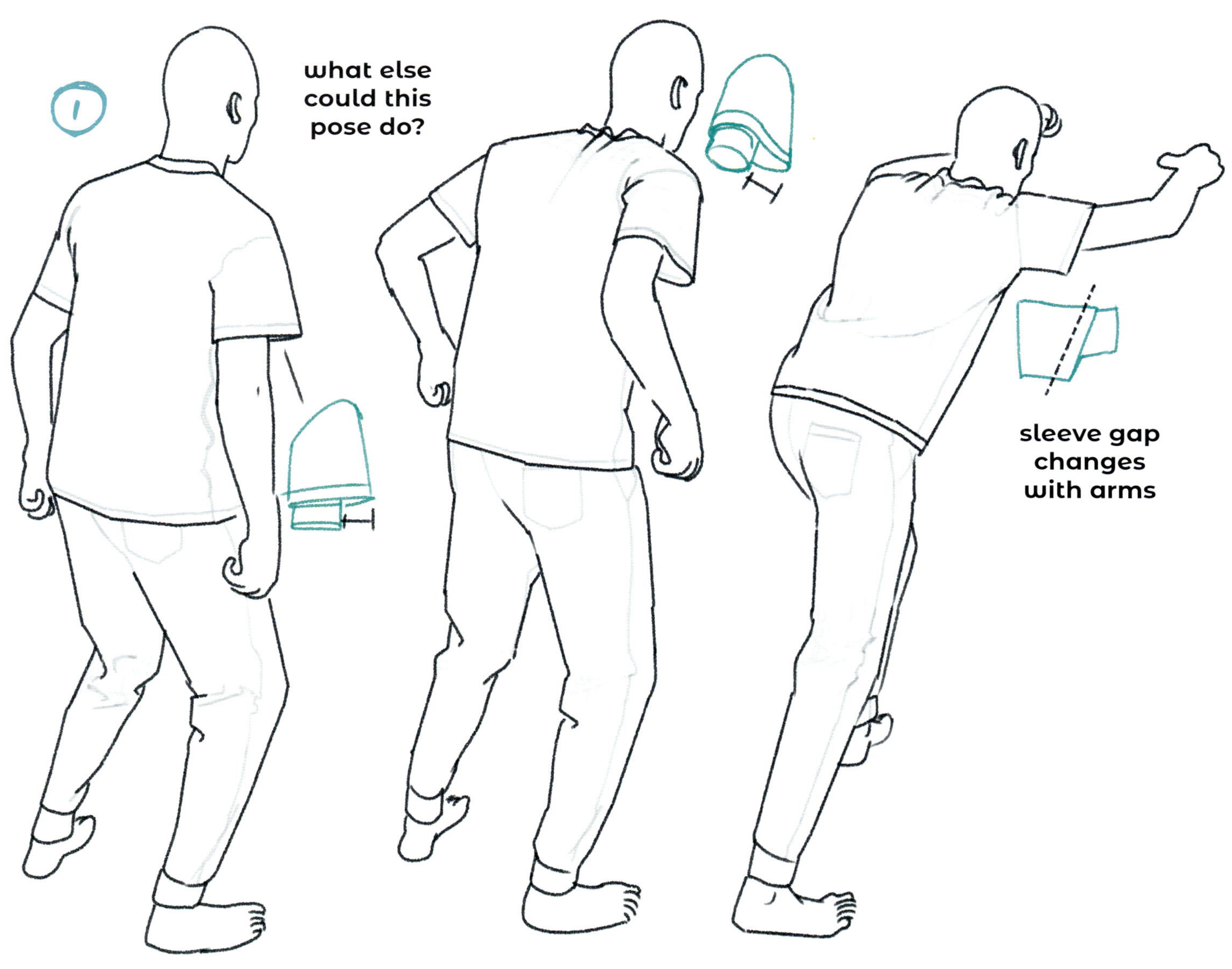

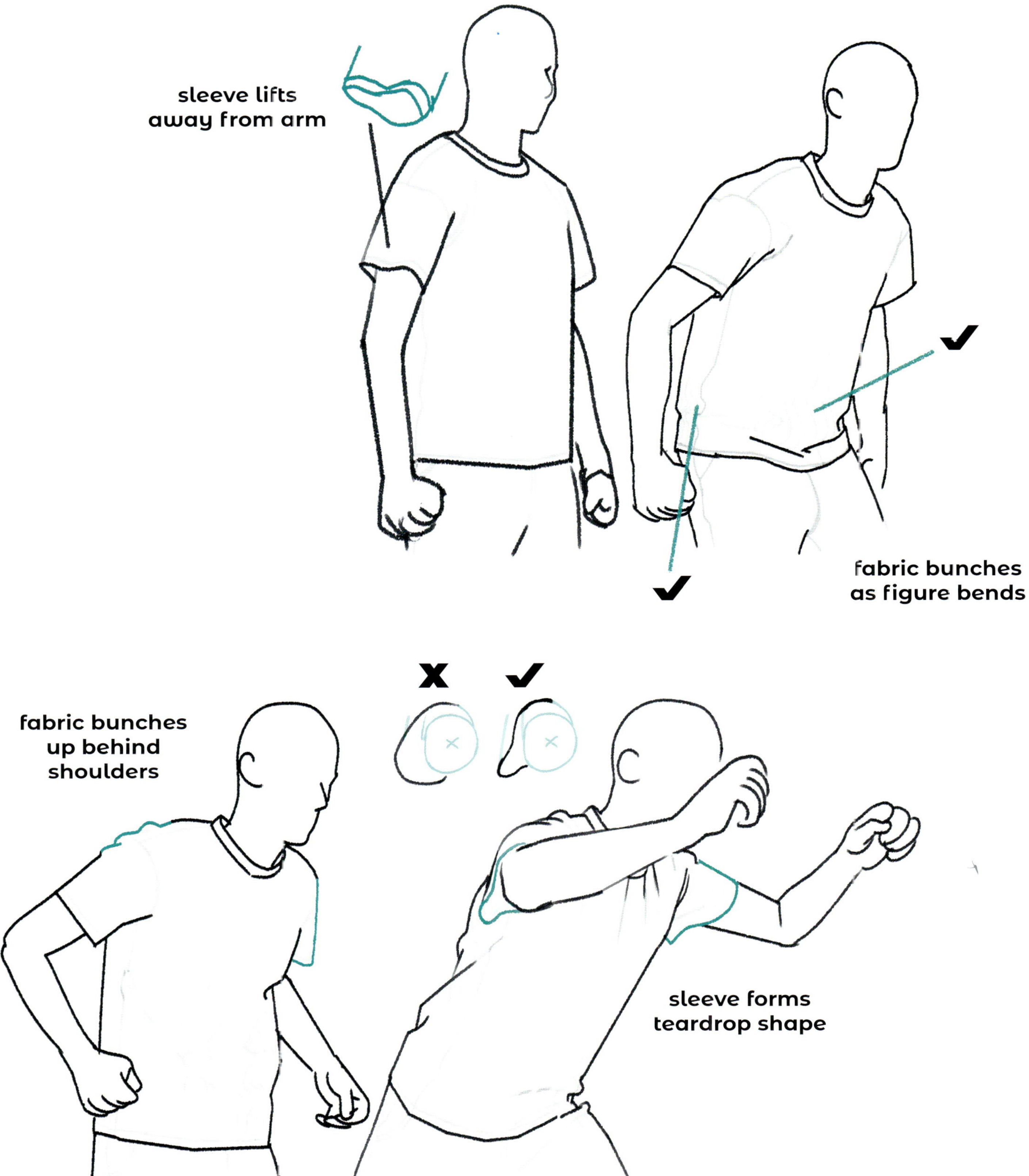
sleeve lifts
away from arm
fabric bunches
as figure bends
fabric bunches
up behind
shoulders
sleeve forms
teardrop shape

motions: bending

setting a table

The collar should taper from the widest point at the front to almost a point at the back of the neck (A). Avoid drawing it an even height the whole way around (B). Remember the angles we covered in the pages on collars (page 112). When the arms are brought together at the front, these folds appear (C). Without them, it won't look like the arms are being squeezed together and rotated inwards.

Remember one of our very first adjustment tips: use fewer lines. When the legs are straight, it's often more effective to keep them as a simple silhouette, perhaps with a seam or two as a hidden contour (D). Not only is this quicker to draw, but you are saving the detail and emphasis for the upper body, which is usually where you want the viewer to look.

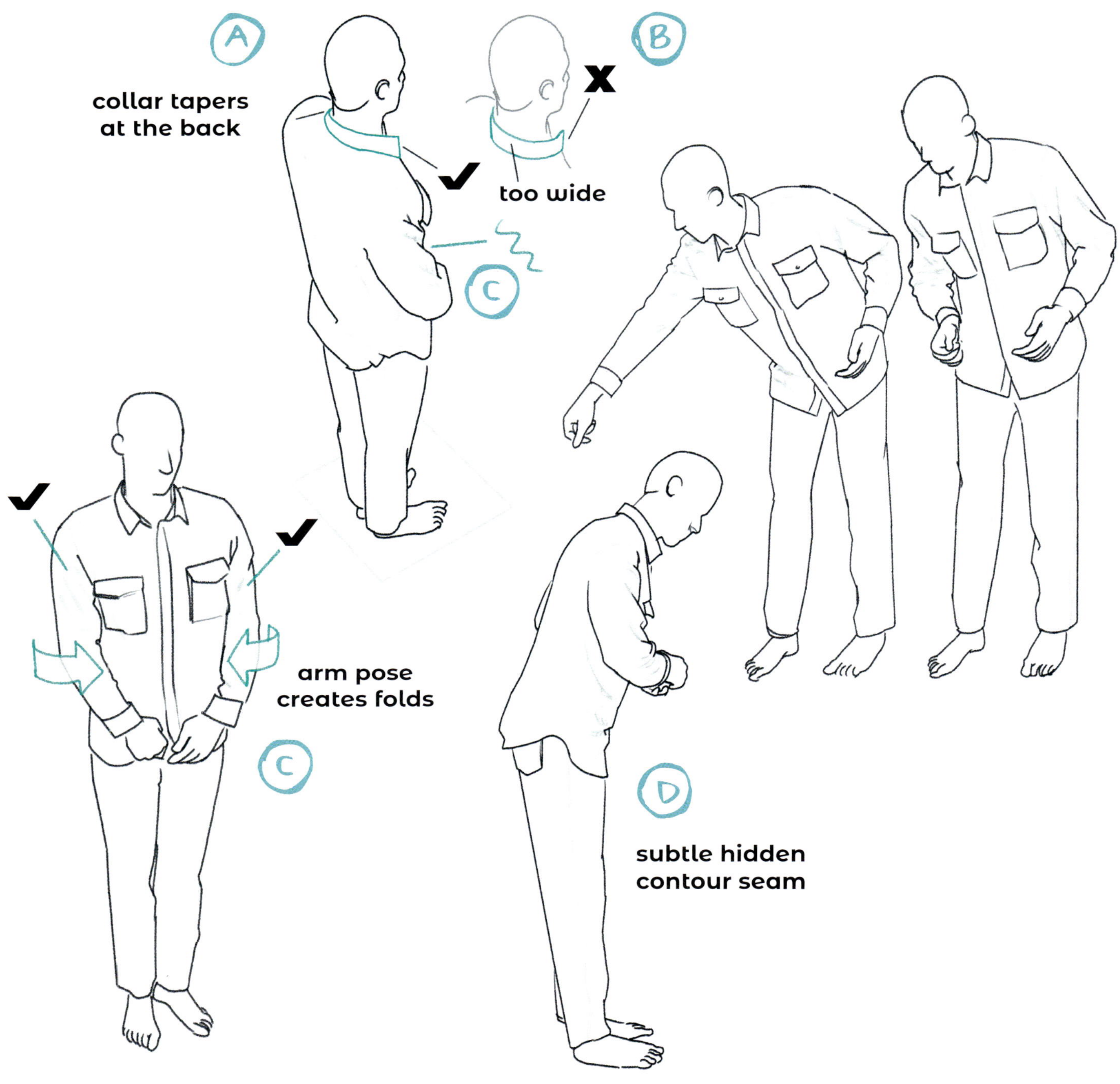

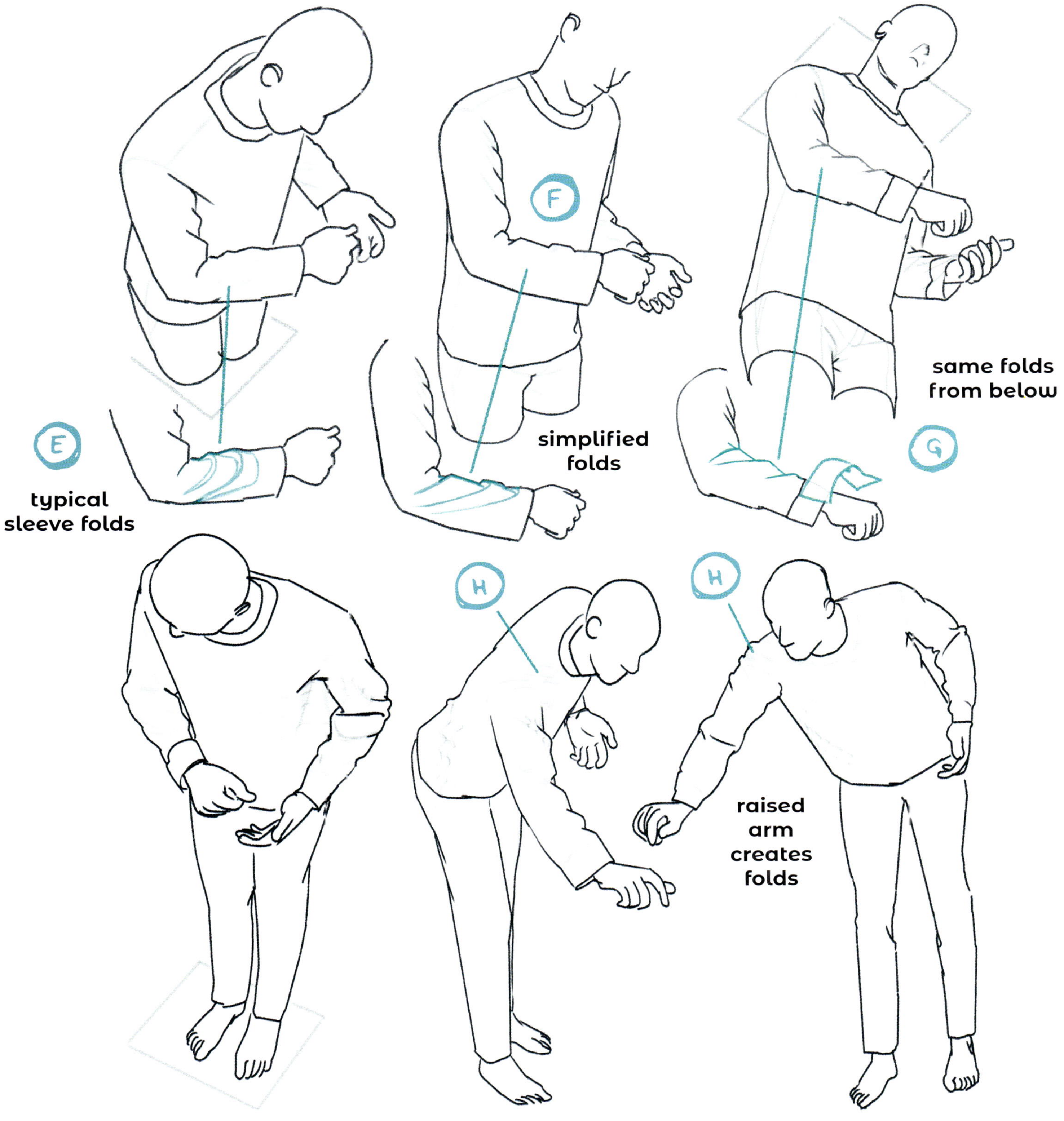

This pattern of folding is very, very common (E), so let's see it from a few different angles to better understand it. This simplified version can help clarify what you're looking at (F). These forms wrap the top of the arm, which is the most compressed side. As we rotate under it, the same form is almost unrecognizable (G). This is why you need to pause and consider the viewing angle at all times. When you lean forwards and extend an arm, you'll often find this folding here (H).

water cooler

Here the figure bends at the waist and holds a leaning pose, with the hands close together. In the case of the cargo trousers shown here, all the additional pockets and seams increase the garment's resistance. So, if you don't want to draw many folds, throw some pockets on there to help 'bulk out' the fabric! The sides of the collar are far more gently angled than the back, which is nearly vertical (A). Compression at the front pushes the bottom of the shirt out to the sides (B), even while the knees move inwards. We often see a box pleat here in the upper middle of the back (C).

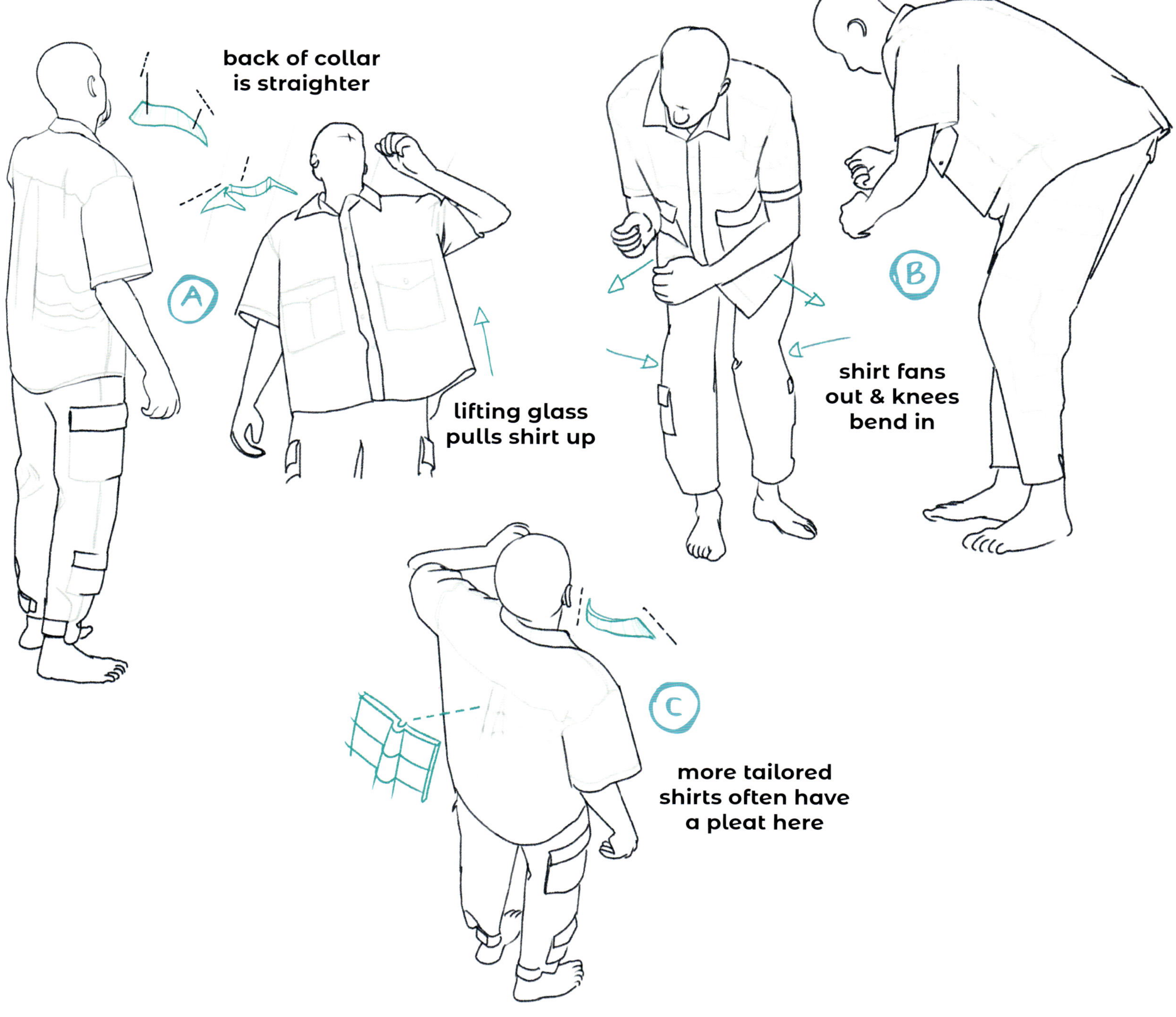

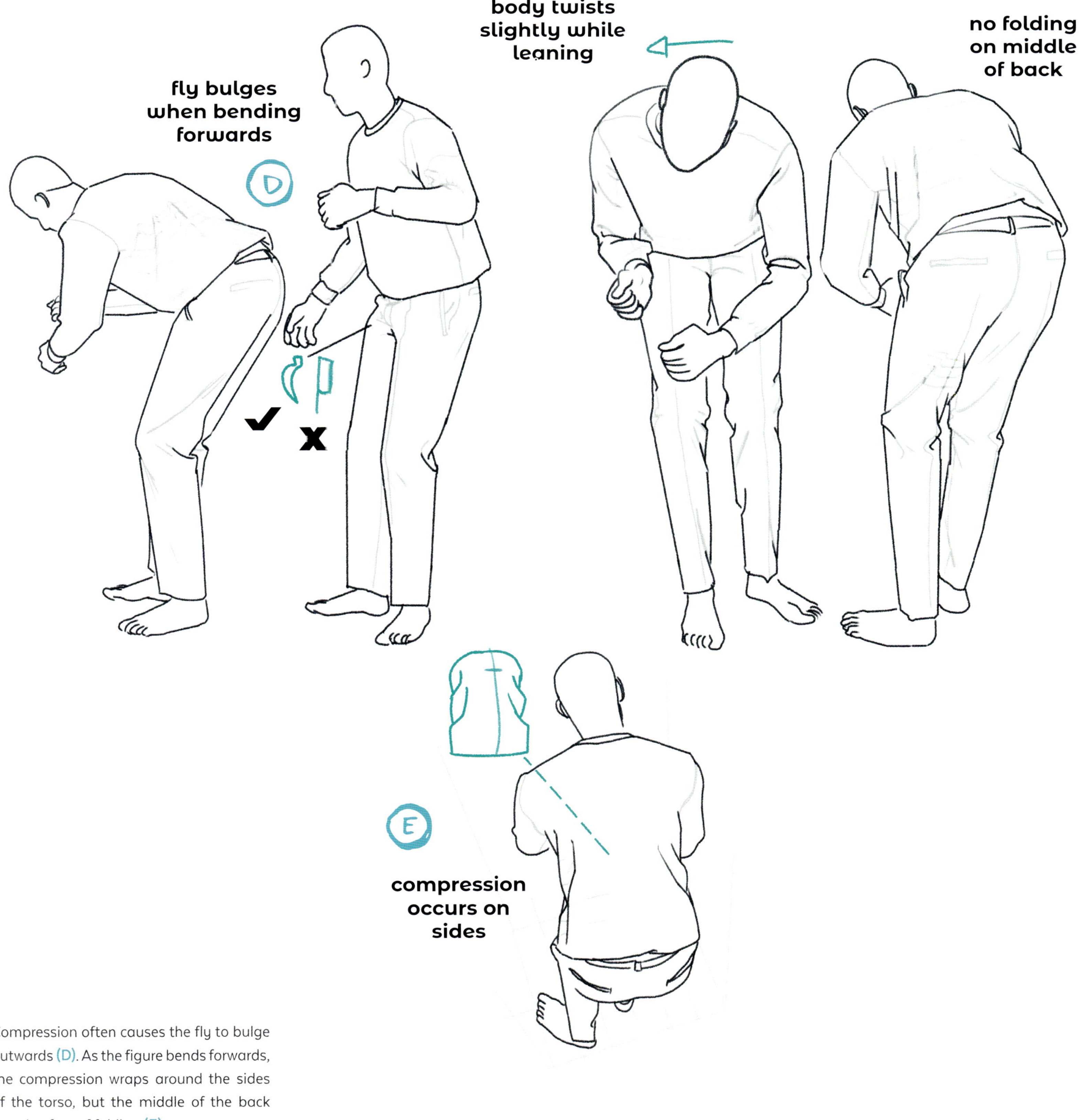

Compression often causes the fly to bulge outwards (D). As the figure bends forwards, the compression wraps around the sides of the torso, but the middle of the back remains free of folding (E).

checking a bag

The side pockets on cargo trousers don't sit flat against the leg, but wrap around (A). The centre of the back is usually flat between the shoulder blades, rather than rounded (B). The pockets are often made from four sections (C) – a flap above and three sections below – which allow it to expand outwards as it's filled. In this gentle bend forwards (D), the back of the T-shirt rises, and the knees bend slightly; the legs will almost never be straight in this position. The shoulder blades drop down lower than you'd expect, so avoid drawing the top of the back too flat (E).

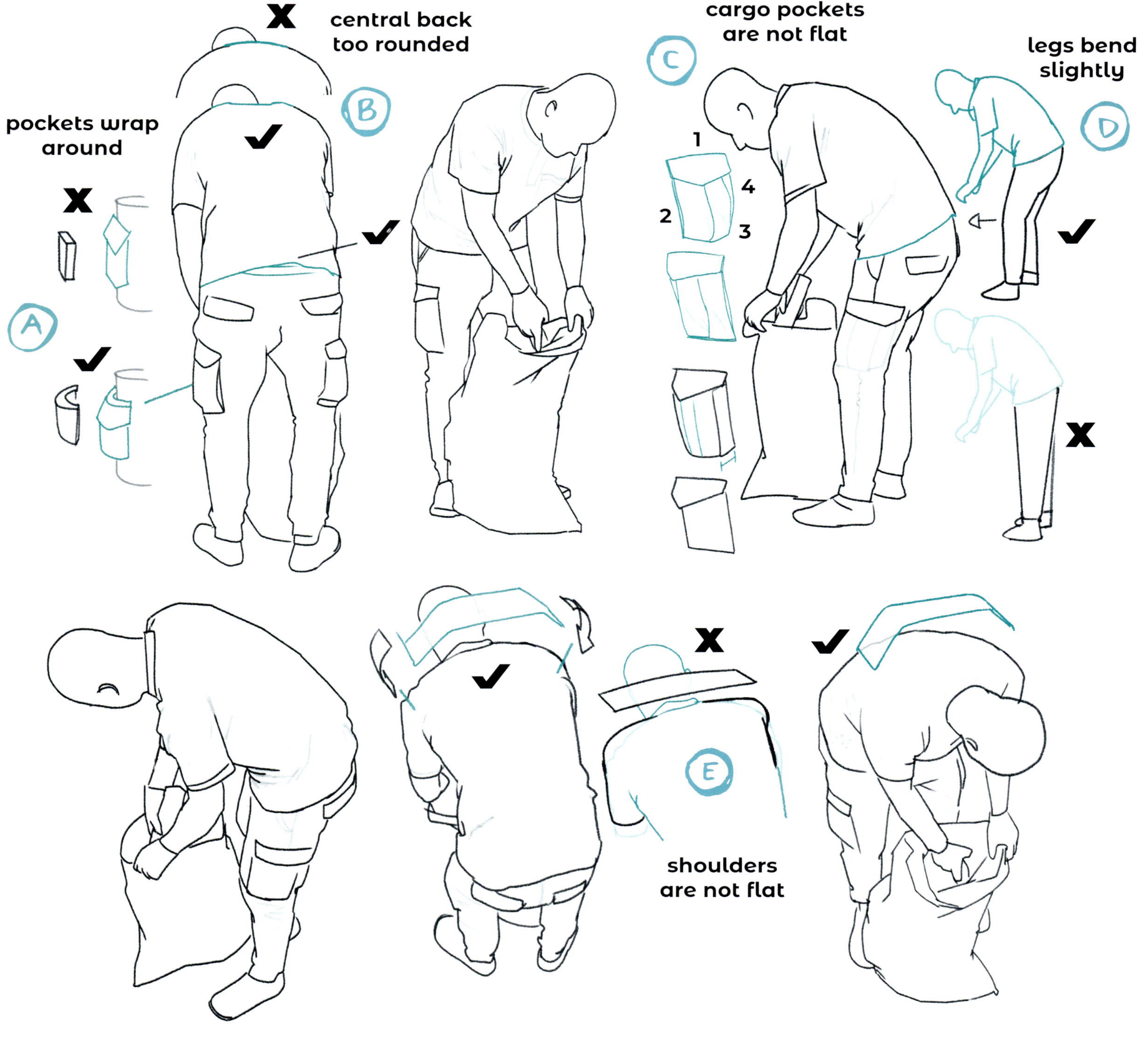

leaning

The back of the glutes and side of the leg should have a simple line here, to represent the tension caused by this position (A). The front of even fairly slim garments should hang from the torso rather than cling to it (B). As the upper arm is held forward, there should be compression on the front of the shoulder (C). You can use these jean pockets to emphasize the curvature of the glutes. Carefully consider whether the surface you're drawing them on is facing up or down. In this pocket's case, this curve should wrap up, rather than down (D). Because the straight leg is held slightly back, you'll likely see small folds here (E). Most of the folding on the back will be found on the lower section (F). It's rare that you'll see it occur higher up because the arms are creating a pulling surface across it.

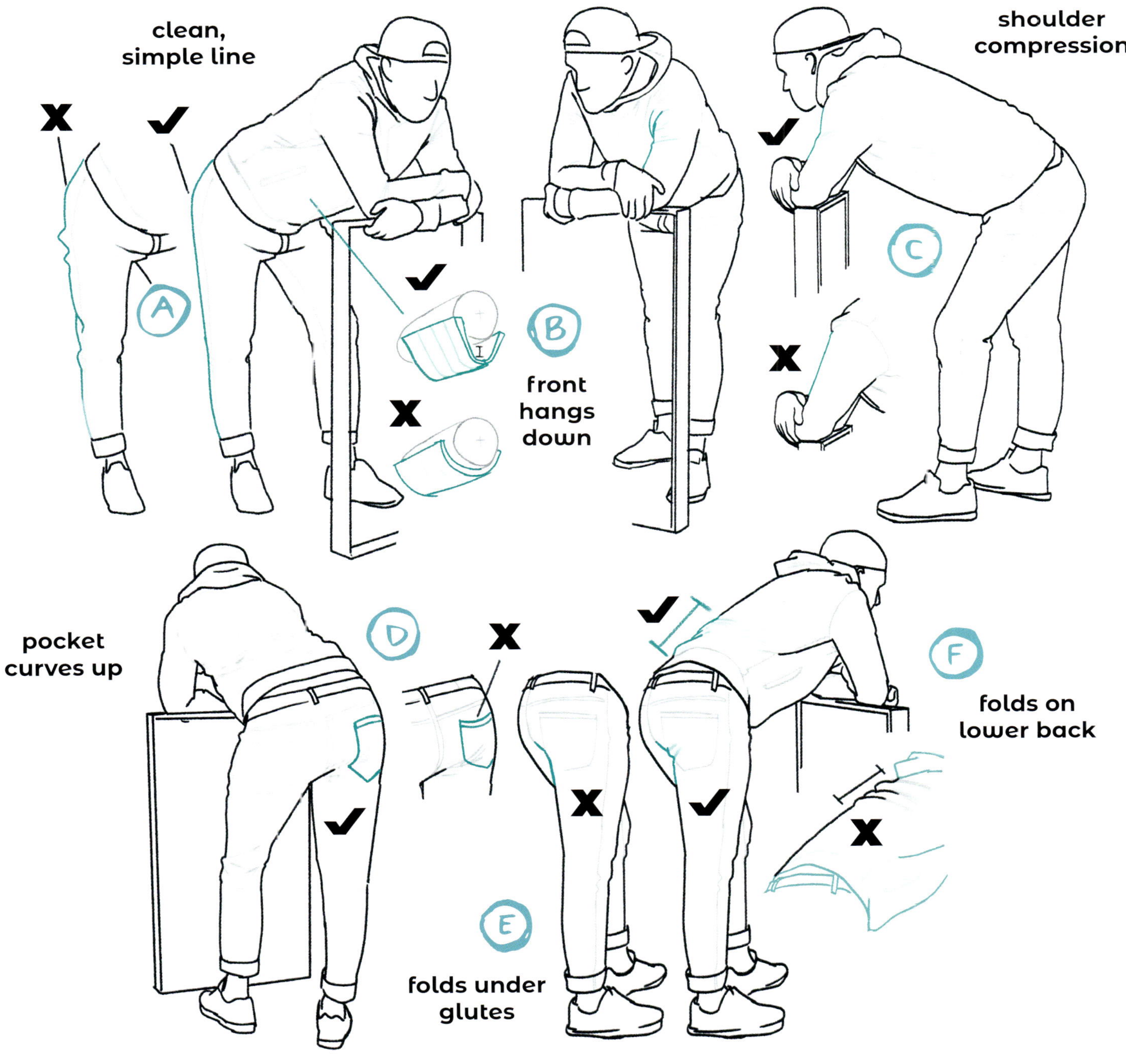

On the straightened leg, you'll see gentle folding occur below the kneecap (G). When the leg is partially bent like this, the kneecap sticks forward a little from the lower leg (H). If you're drawing relatively slim trousers, they'll follow that kneecap contour. It is possible for fabric to hang from the kneecap, but it's less common in this position.

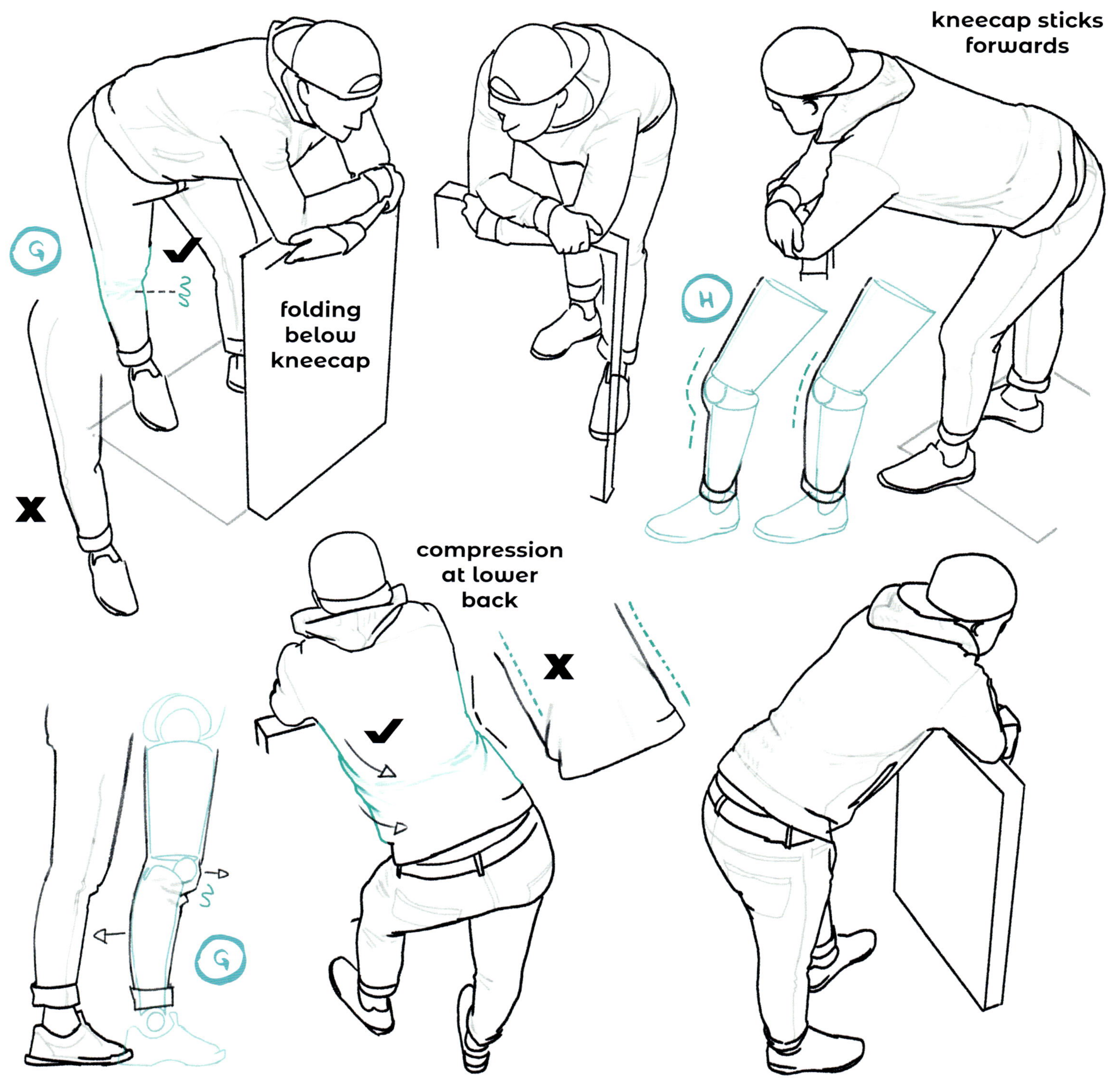

taking a photo

The end of a shirt sleeve isn't a simple tube. It should be smaller than the width of the sleeve (A). The 'cuff' actually consists of a cuff **(1)**, which is the single piece that folds over itself, and a placket **(2)**, which is the opening for ease of putting your hand through the sleeve. When the cuff is unbuttoned, the placket twists and moves with the end of the cuff (B). The placket is almost always found on the pinky side of the hand (C). When a photographer is keen to get a good picture, they rarely stand upright. Instead, they'll lean forwards, and put their head forwards (D).

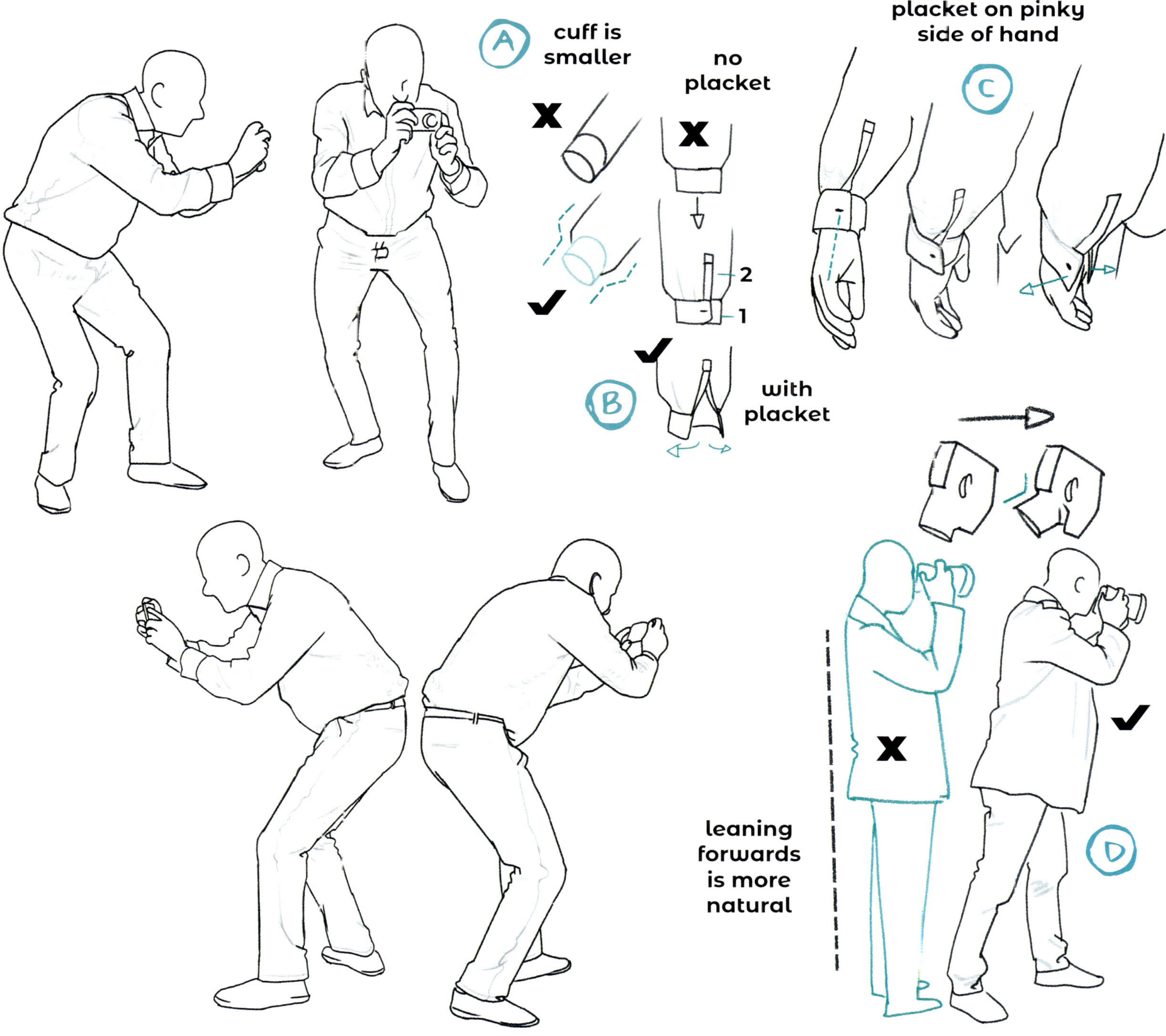

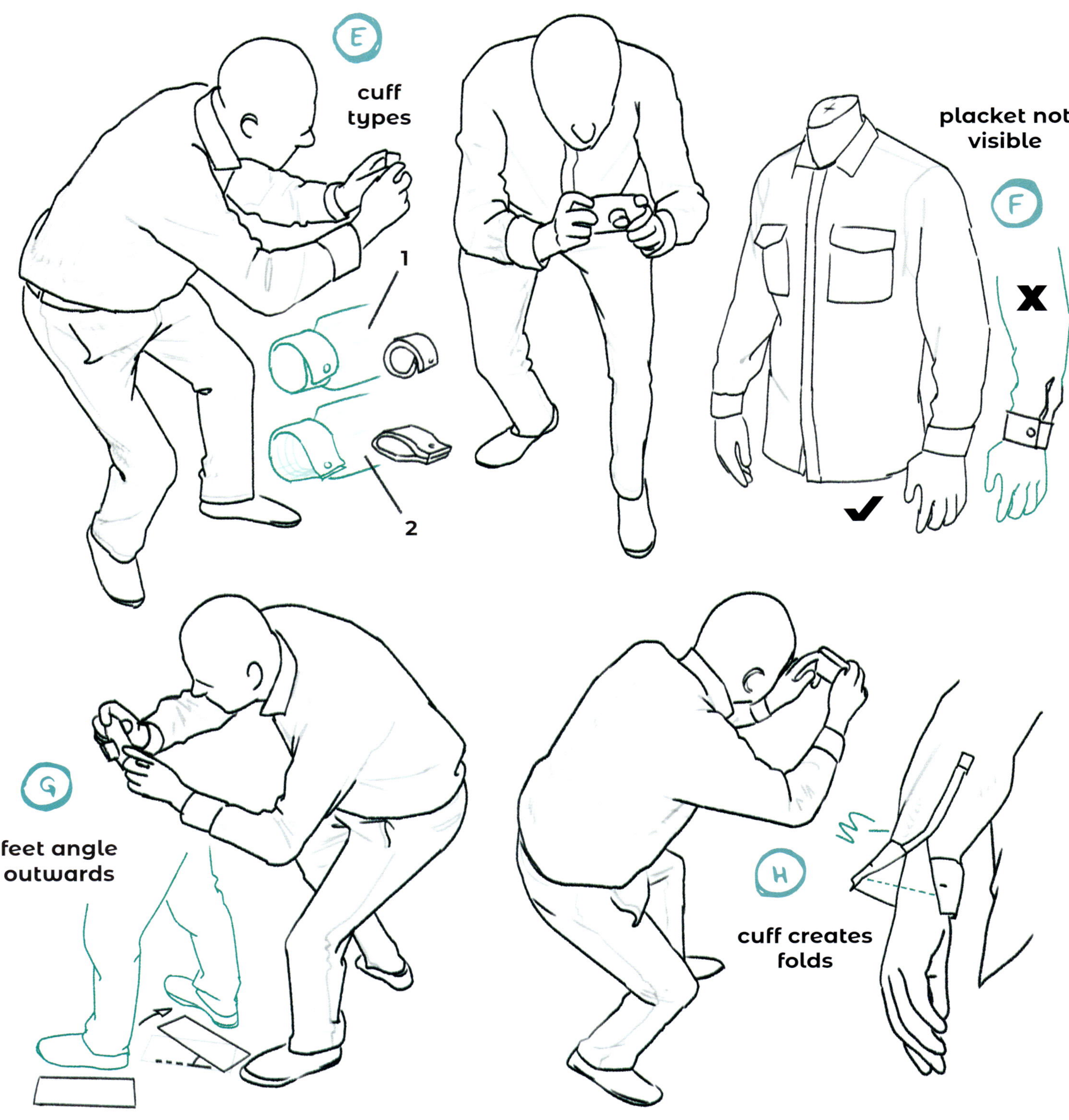

Here are two common types of cuff (E). In the first, one end overlaps the other end **(1)**. In the second, the two ends are pressed together; this is generally a more formal style **(2)**. When looking at a sleeve from the front, you won't usually see the placket (F). In this stance, the rear foot turns outwards to provide stability (G). Don't forget to include the folding created by the cuff itself acting on the sleeve (H).

picking up

One way of picking something up is to take a small step beforehand, place one foot forwards, and then lean over with almost all your weight on that leg (A). In order to get closer to the ground, you'll usually also drop the leading shoulder and keep the other raised for balance (B). This naturally causes the rear heel to lift (C). Seen from this angle, you'll have to include these lines (D) to indicate the twist.

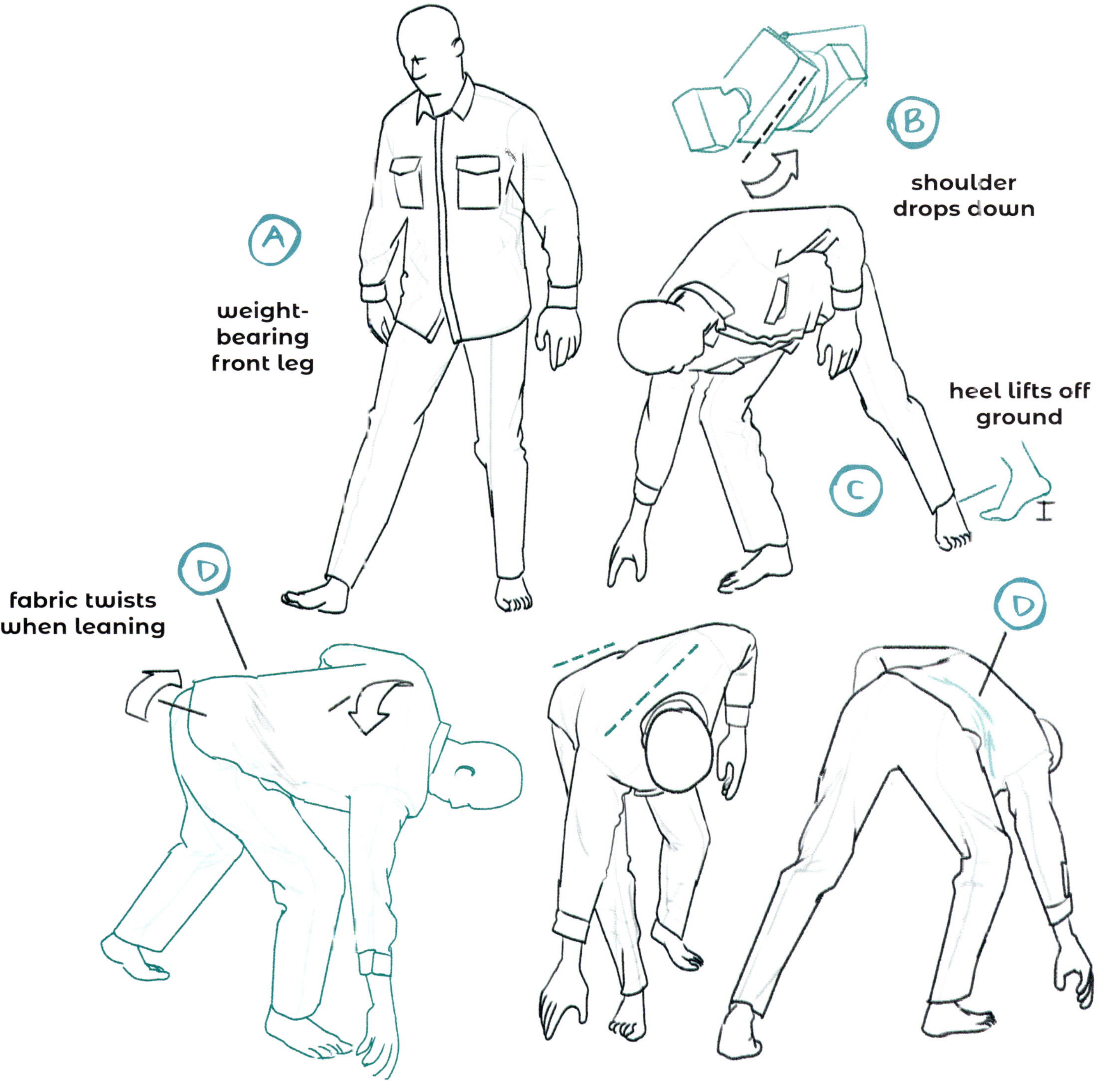

Rather than putting your weight over one leg, you can pick something up by bending more evenly and distributing your weight over both legs (E). When wearing an open shirt, the bottom corners will open out and wrap around the thighs (F). However, don't expect the shirt to drop a long distance down from the core (G). The corners of the shirt are prevented from doing this by the fact that the back of the shirt still rests on the lower back (H). When drawing this line, it will rarely flow straight into the edges of the legs, but usually wrap around and under (I). The main direction of the compression in this figure is between the thighs and the chest (J). The hem at the back of the shirt often folds gently, rather than forming a perfectly smooth curve (K).

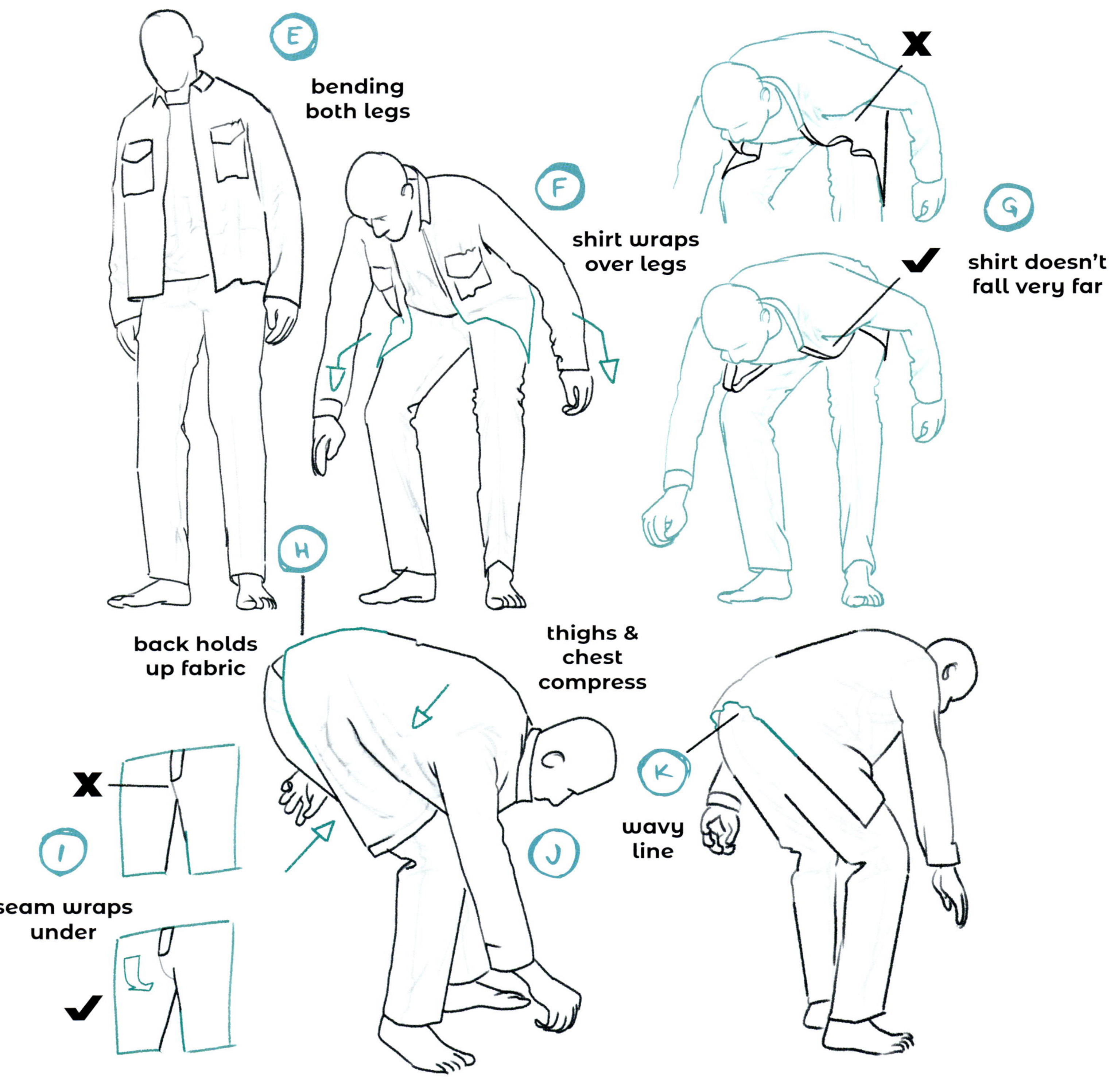

picking up a gun

When you bend down quickly to snatch something light off the floor, the knees often come together (A). This is one of the relatively rare views and occasions when you see these bunching lines between the legs **(1)**. The top garment usually deforms into this shape **(2)**, with concave sections on either side, rather than being rounded (B). The front centre of the top often drops into the valley between the legs (C).

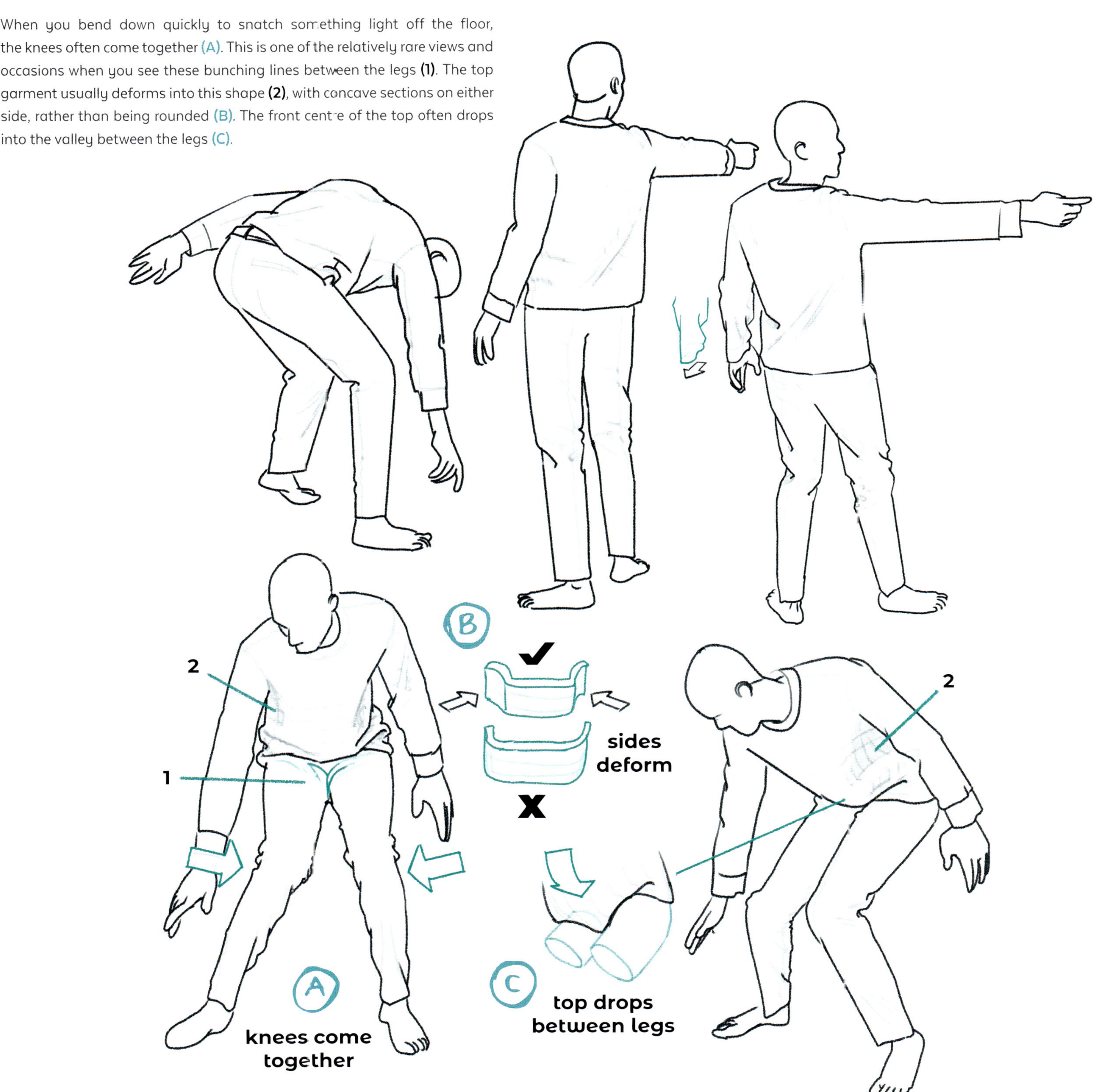

If this standing character rotates their arm inwards or outwards, the folds themselves will rotate around this point on the shoulder (D). That's the most important way to convey twist in the arm in a garment like this. When bending down, the hood usually falls to one side (E). If you forget to include this, the pose will look very static. A raised arm will often 'fill in' this triangle (F). Folds should converge towards this point (G). The drapery of the arm normally suggests rotation inwards, rather than outwards (H).

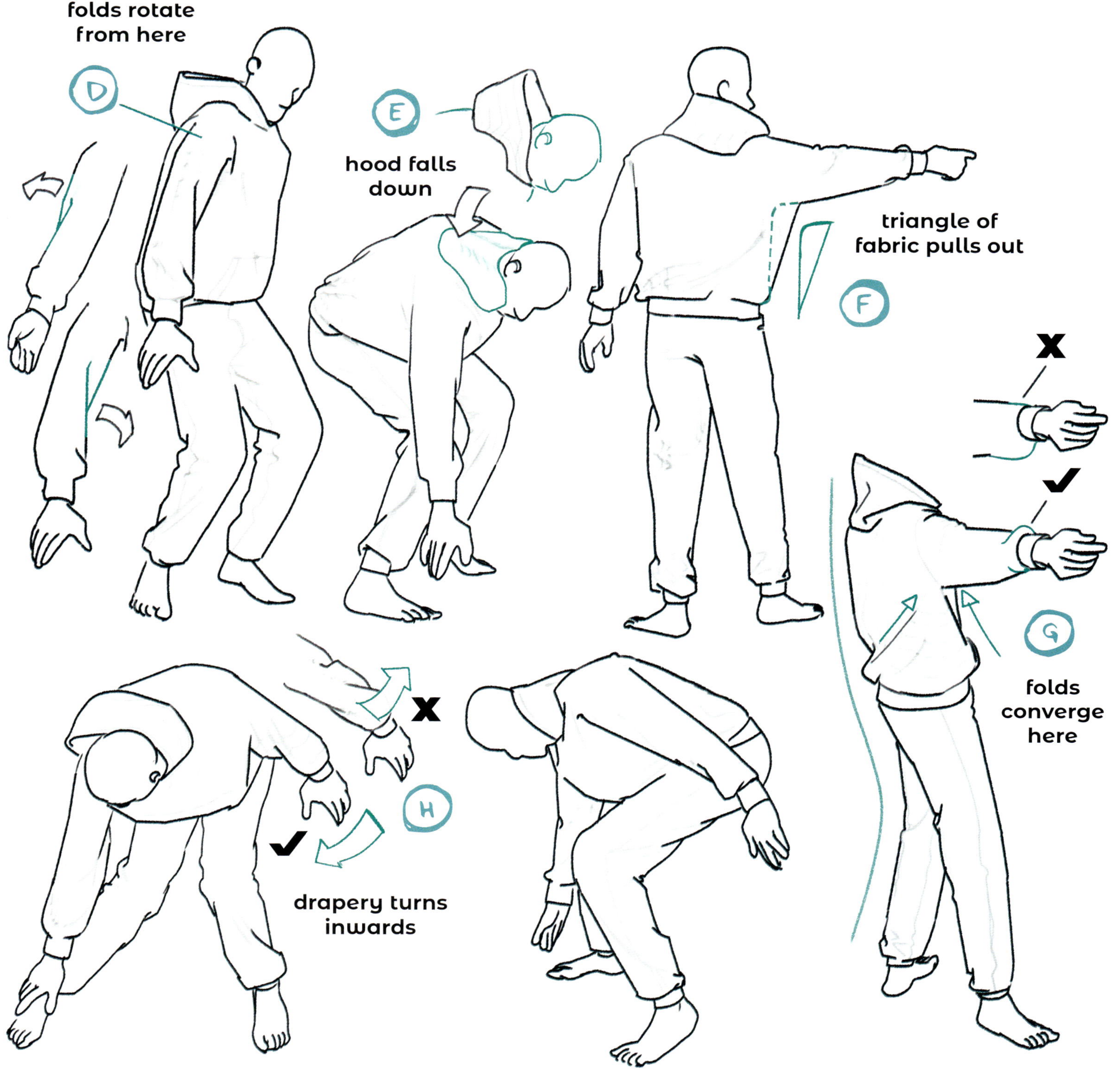

These folds converge on the underside of the raised arm (I). There is also folding on top of the shoulder. You can add interest to your garment by giving it wide sleeves, which will provide a lot of horizontal folding (J). Note the slight backwards lean of the torso when holding a pistol (K). When the leg is bent like this, the drapery bulges out to the side (L). As you lean forwards, the opposite arm is thrown back (M). Remember one of our first adjustments: 'fewer lines'. Less is often more – particularly when you want the viewer to be focusing on the gun itself, or the character's face, more than the legs – so keep the drapery on the trousers quite simple and avoid too many internals (N).

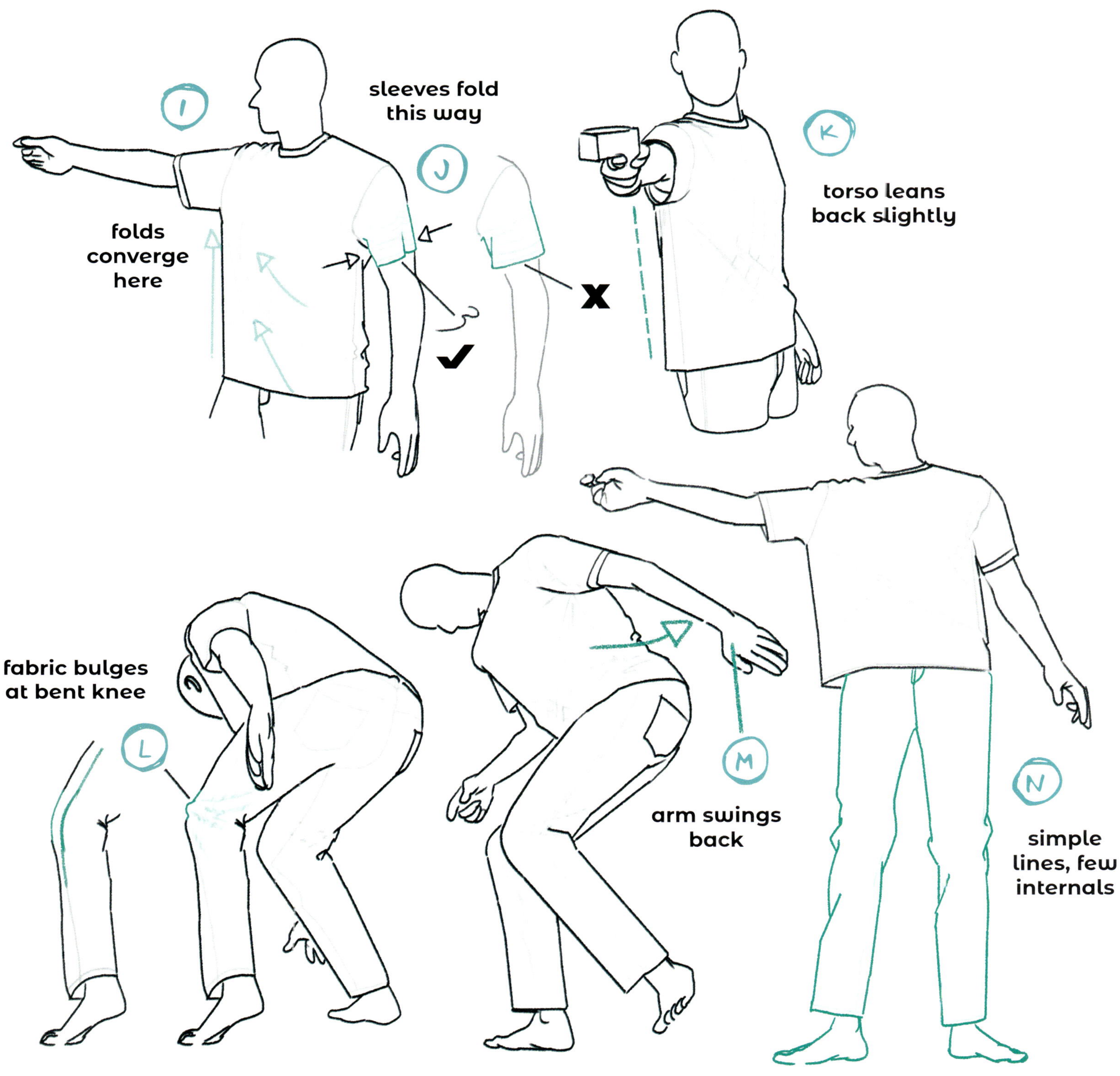

Folds converge upon the bottom of the sleeve from both sides (O). As we saw on the last page, the sleeve may gently fold upon itself, adding interest to a simple pose (P). Aiming a pistol often involves a slight bend in the legs – causing gentle folding on the back of the knees (Q). This is the same fold (R). You see it frequently when drawing trousers with quite high resistance. Indicating these lighter planes (S), with either tone or contours, is essential to create the illusion of compression.

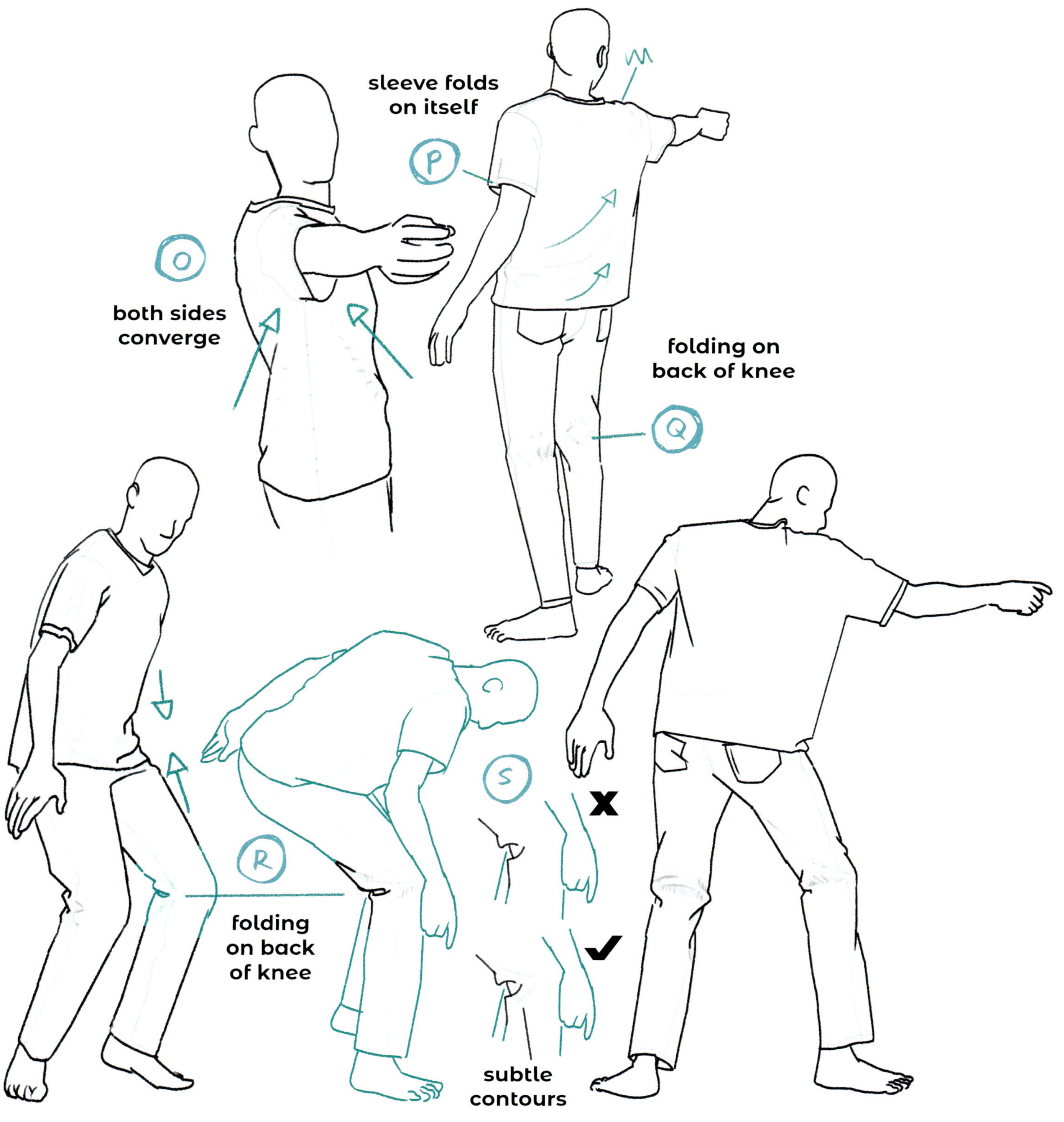

throwing

In this position the lower arm is often subtly rotated backwards, causing folding that wraps up and over the back of the arm (A). As the leading arm is raised up and slightly outwards, these folds appear (B). From behind, there'll be a twist between the upper torso and the core (C). In the wind-up to the throw, the shoulder on the rear side is dropped, which causes folding on the same side of the waist (D).

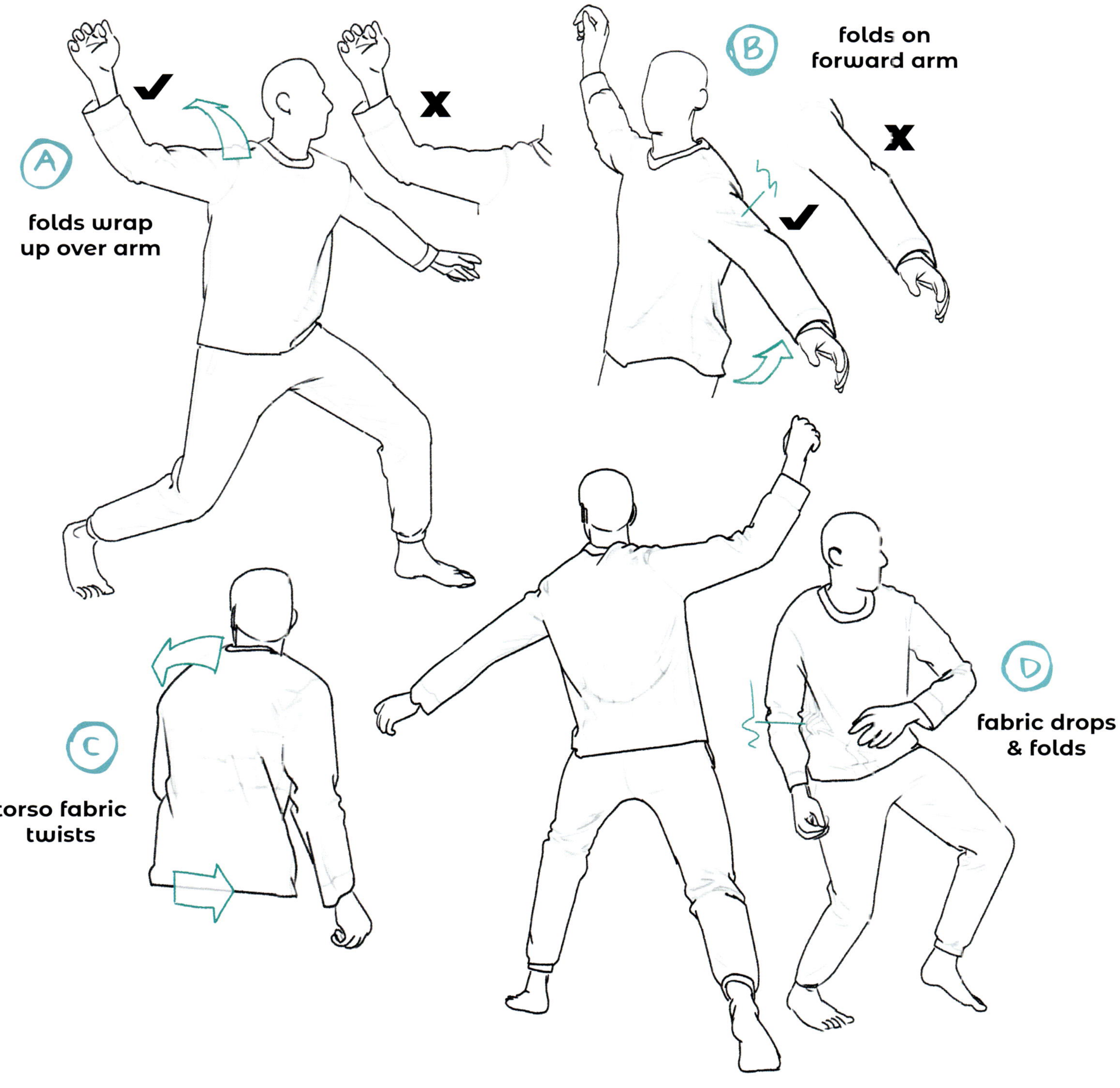

When bending down like this, it's tempting to draw a horizontal shirt fold, but most often multiple folds radiate out from the lower back (E). The front of the shirt should flare out with only a small amount of bunching, rather than stacking (F). The bottom of the shirt won't hang vertically down (G) – it will be pulled forwards by the front of the thigh (H). Remember our adjustment about 'snapshots' (page 29) – you could draw the shirt like this (I), but if you imagine (or act out) the whole movement, you'll find it makes more sense to have this side of the shirt show the forwards momentum (J).

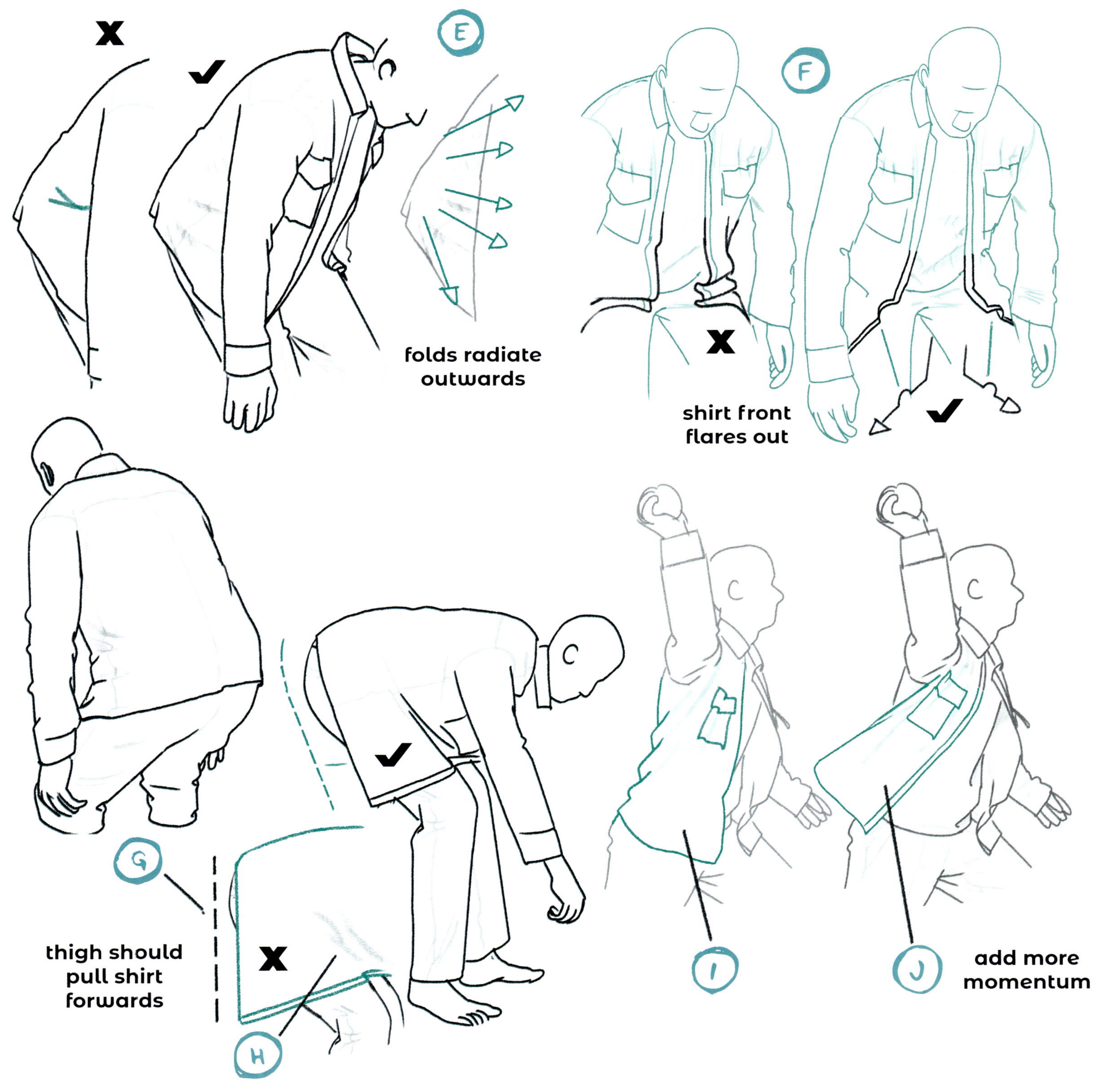

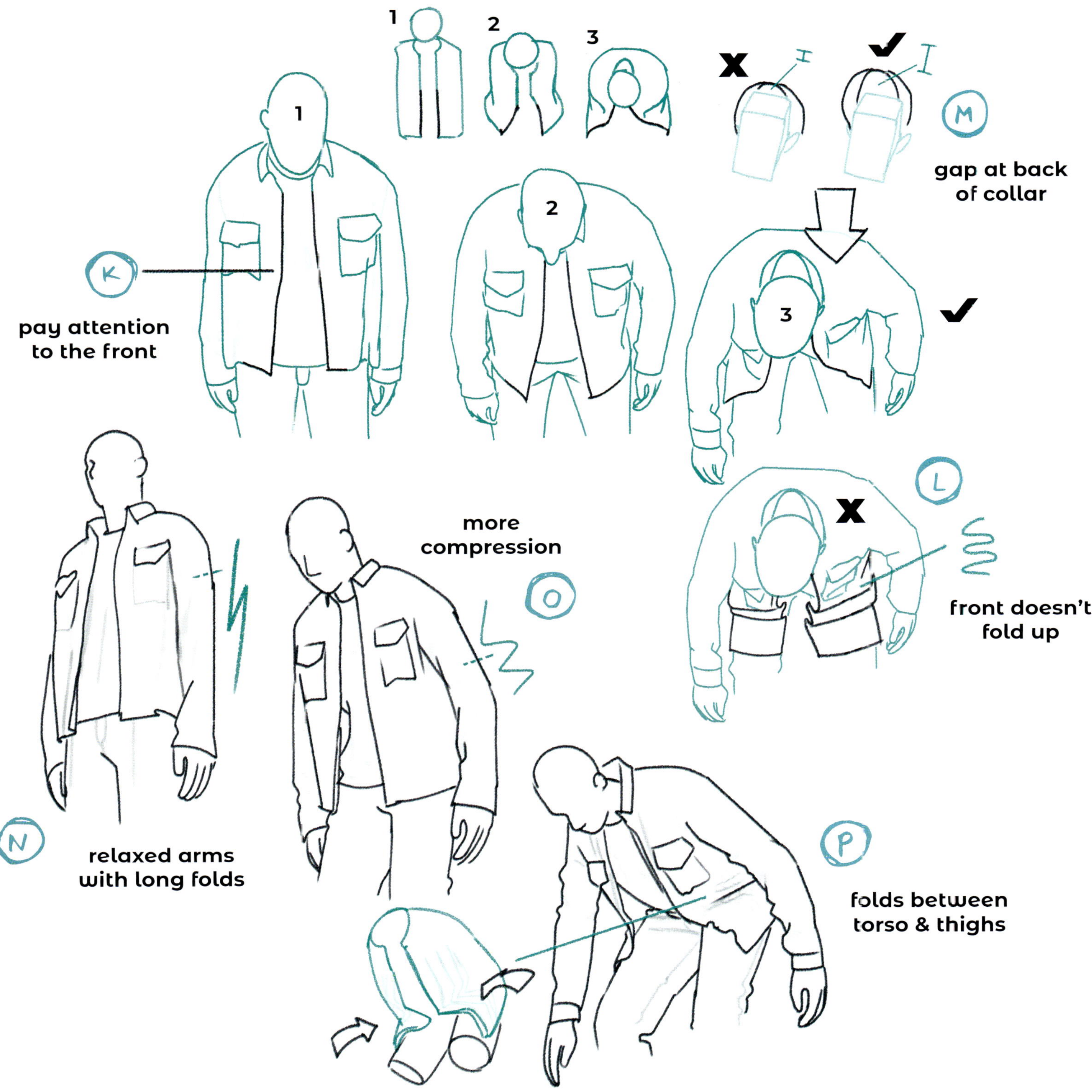

When a character bends forwards in an open shirt, pay attention to this line (K). It won't fold forwards upon itself (L), but will fall down and outwards (1, 2, 3). The head usually drops, exposing a gap between the collar and the back of the neck (M). When the arms are at the sides, the overall 'flow' of the folding on the arm is vertical (N). As you bend forwards, you tend to bend your arms to help balance, which causes a more compressed pattern on the inside of the arm (O). Here's the same forward fold from another angle, where it's easier to see that the shirt folds into the gap between the torso and the tops of the thighs (P).

digging

The numbered poses are a rotation around the same subject. Thinking about the whole movement, outside of the pose we've drawn here, you'll notice that the hood has fallen down to one side of the head, which shows there was a movement just before this one (A). Note the fold on this arm (B). In comparison, the arms below it are not as effective at communicating the drapery. Why? Because without that fold, the arm looks like compression is only happening within this narrow band (C). In reality, there'd be some compression in a much wider area, and that's what this fold shows (D). Notice that this pattern of lines represents the forms seen in rotations **1** and **2**, but from another angle (E). It's not an easy pattern to visualize, so it's worth taking some time to really try to understand it.

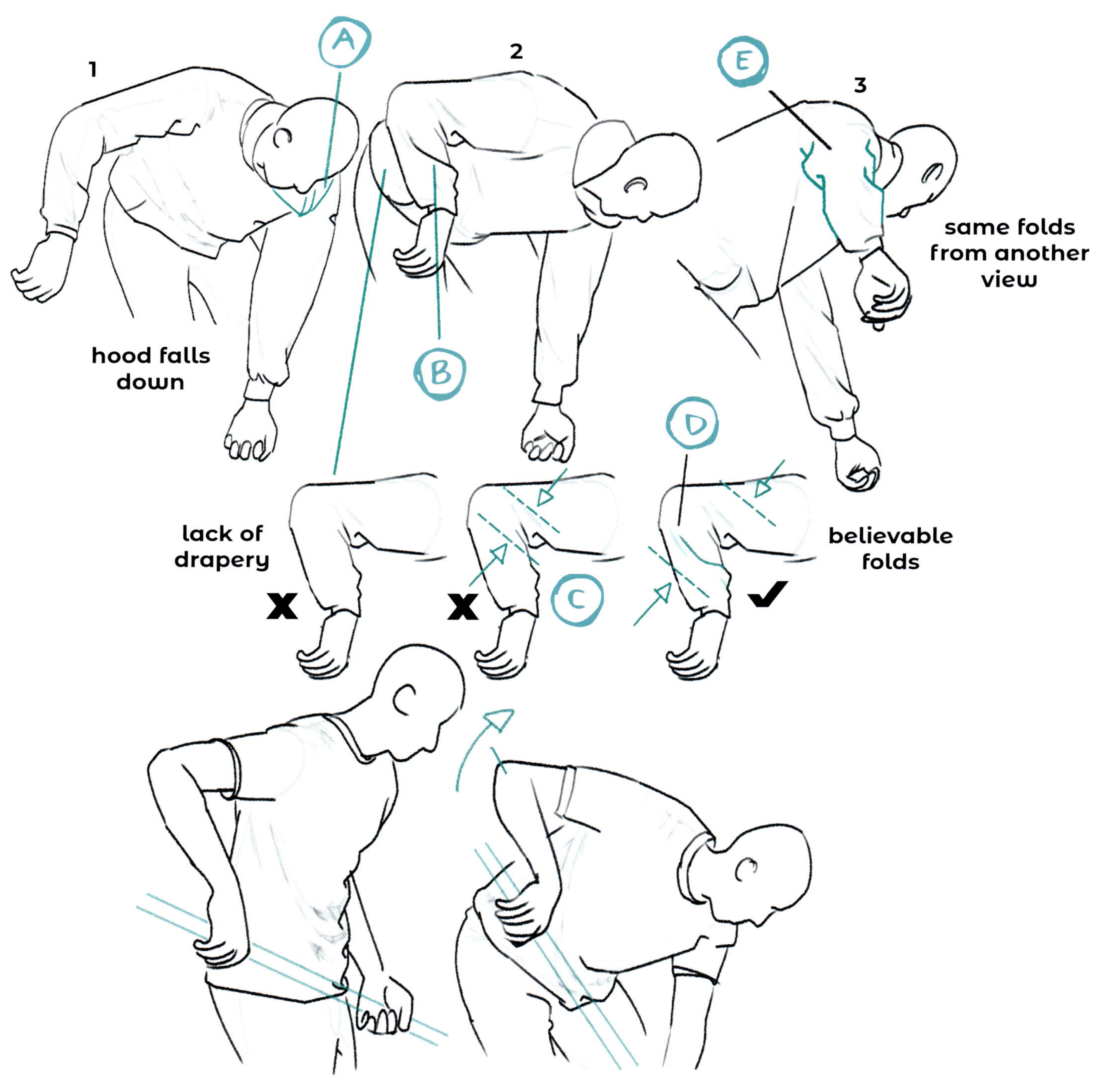

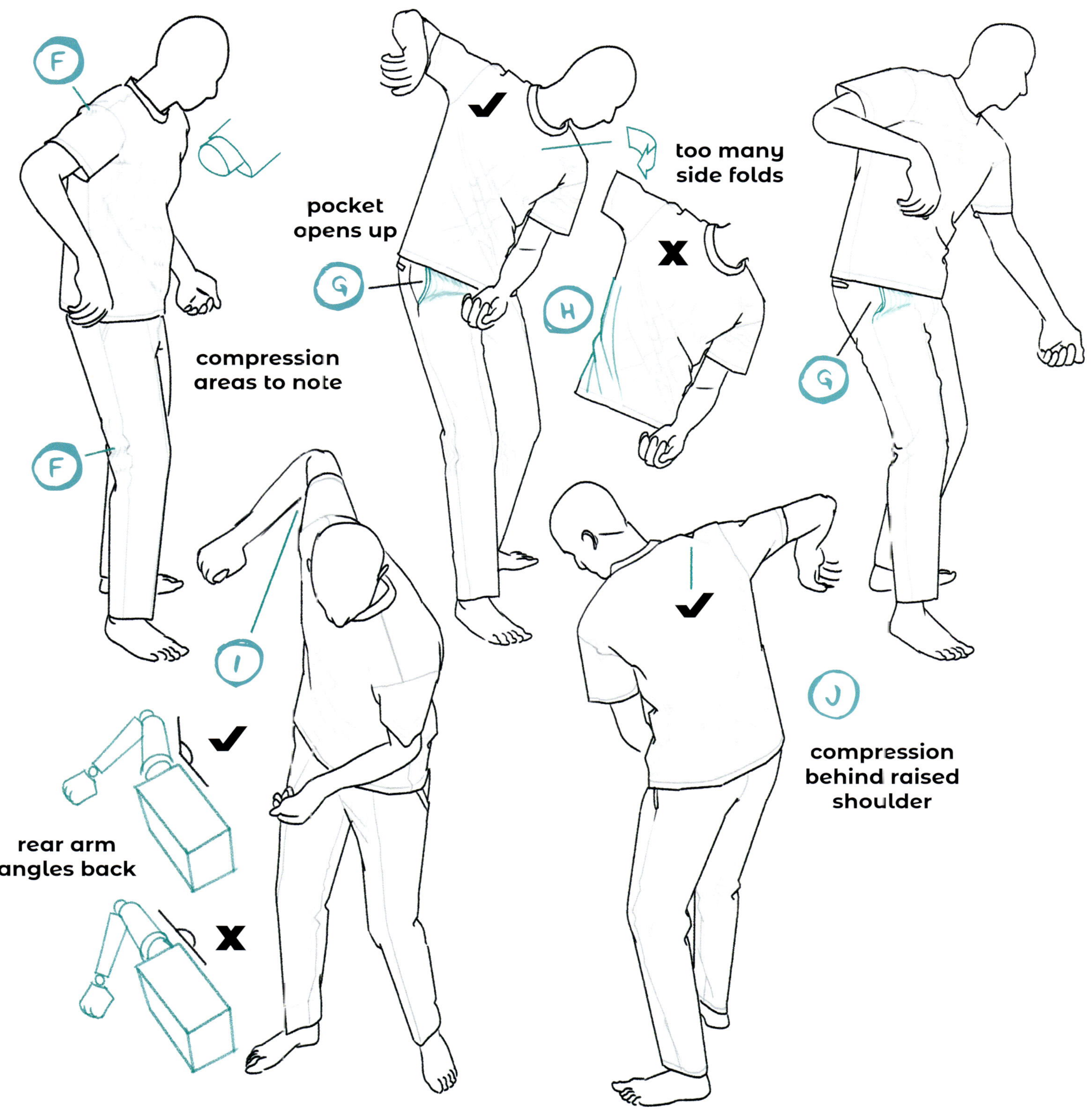

Here are some of the regions of compression when digging (F). As the right leg is slightly further forwards, the pocket may open slightly (G). The diagonal lines across the front of the torso help indicate a twist in the upper body. However, you generally shouldn't extend them into the hip area (H). The rear arm is raised up and back, further than you'd imagine (I), which is why you get such strong compression on the rear of that shoulder (J).

Some styles of trouser, including jeans, have a couple of extra pieces included in their pattern below the waist at the rear (K). If you don't include them, the jeans may look odd (L). As denim is usually quite high-resistance, it's often better to draw it angular rather than more softly curving (M). This shape is very useful when showing compression around the elbow (N). Add some interest to the hood by having it collapse in on itself (O).

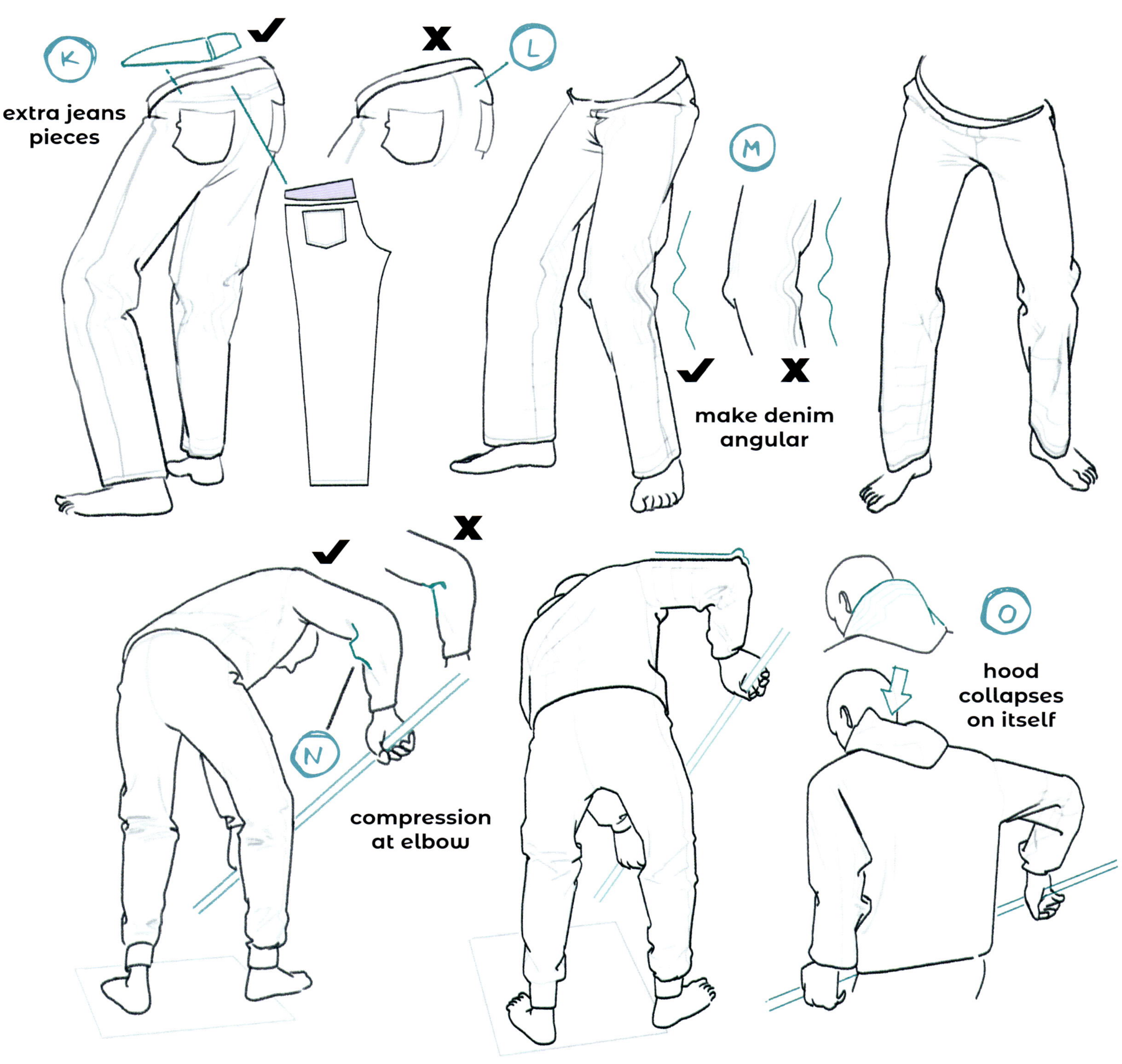

kneeling

When the arm is raised, as if to swing a hammer, folding occurs across the upper back (A). This line is important (B) – it shows that the shoulders are twisting round (C).

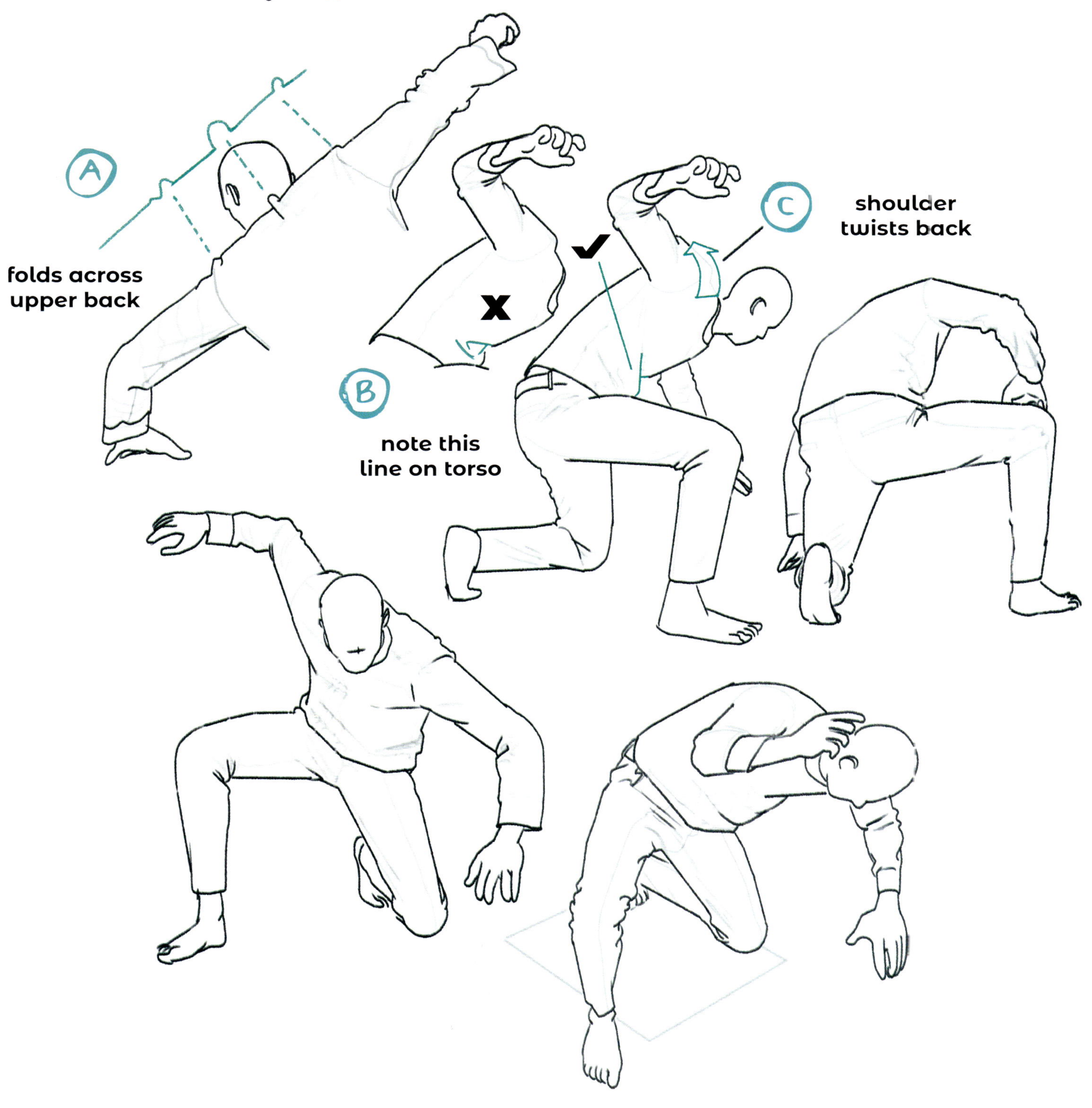

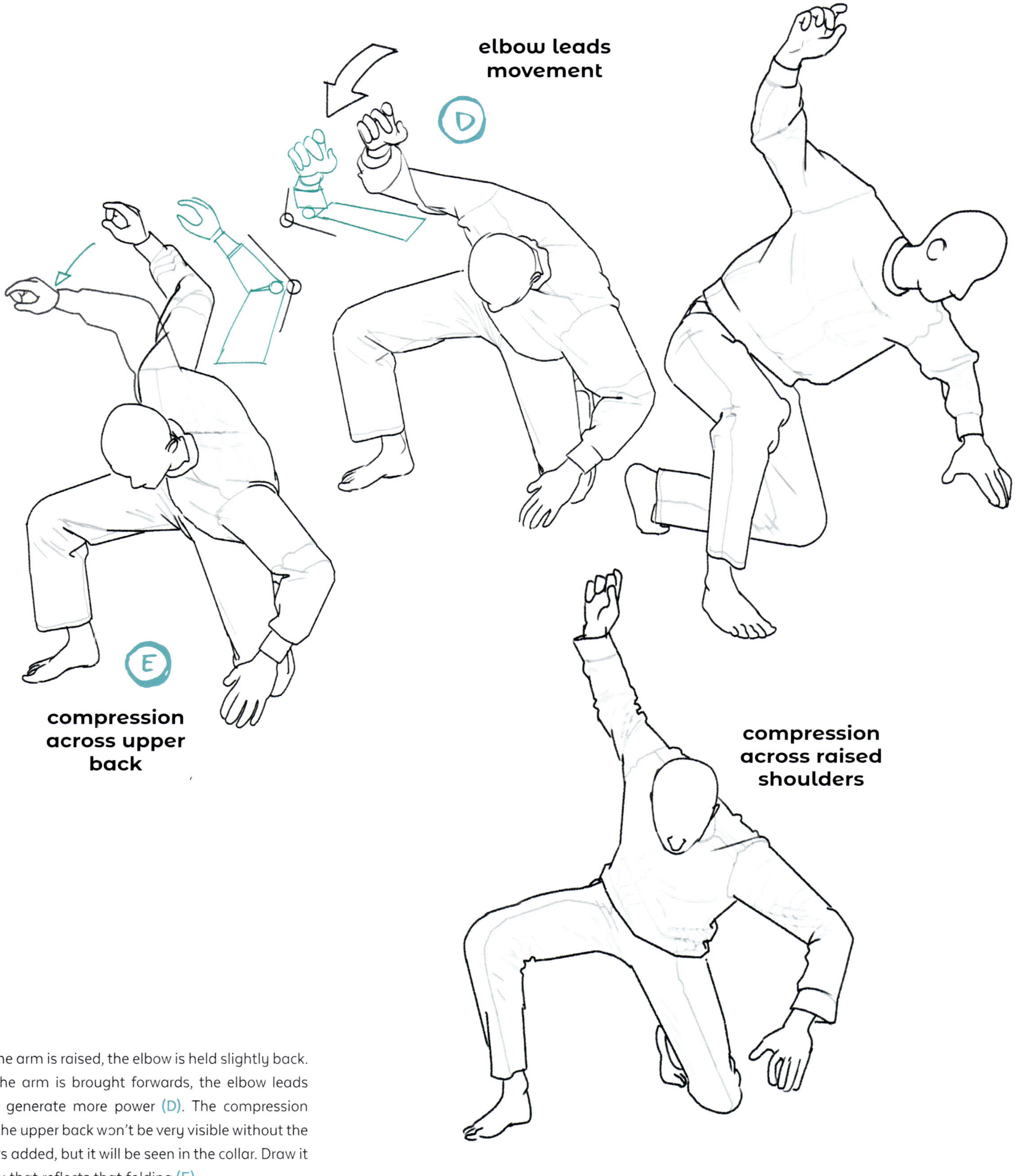

When the arm is raised, the elbow is held slightly back. When the arm is brought forwards, the elbow leads to help generate more power (D). The compression across the upper back won't be very visible without the contours added, but it will be seen in the collar. Draw it in a way that reflects that folding (E).

crouching

When drawing a character crouching with their legs together, you'll usually want to draw the fly area pulling up towards the higher leg (A). At the side of the core, a shirt is more likely to fold inwards in an angular way, rather than fold upon itself (B). From behind, many figures have this hourglass shape (C). If the head is tilted forwards, you'll see a gap between the collar and the back of the neck, rather than the neck touching the collar (D).

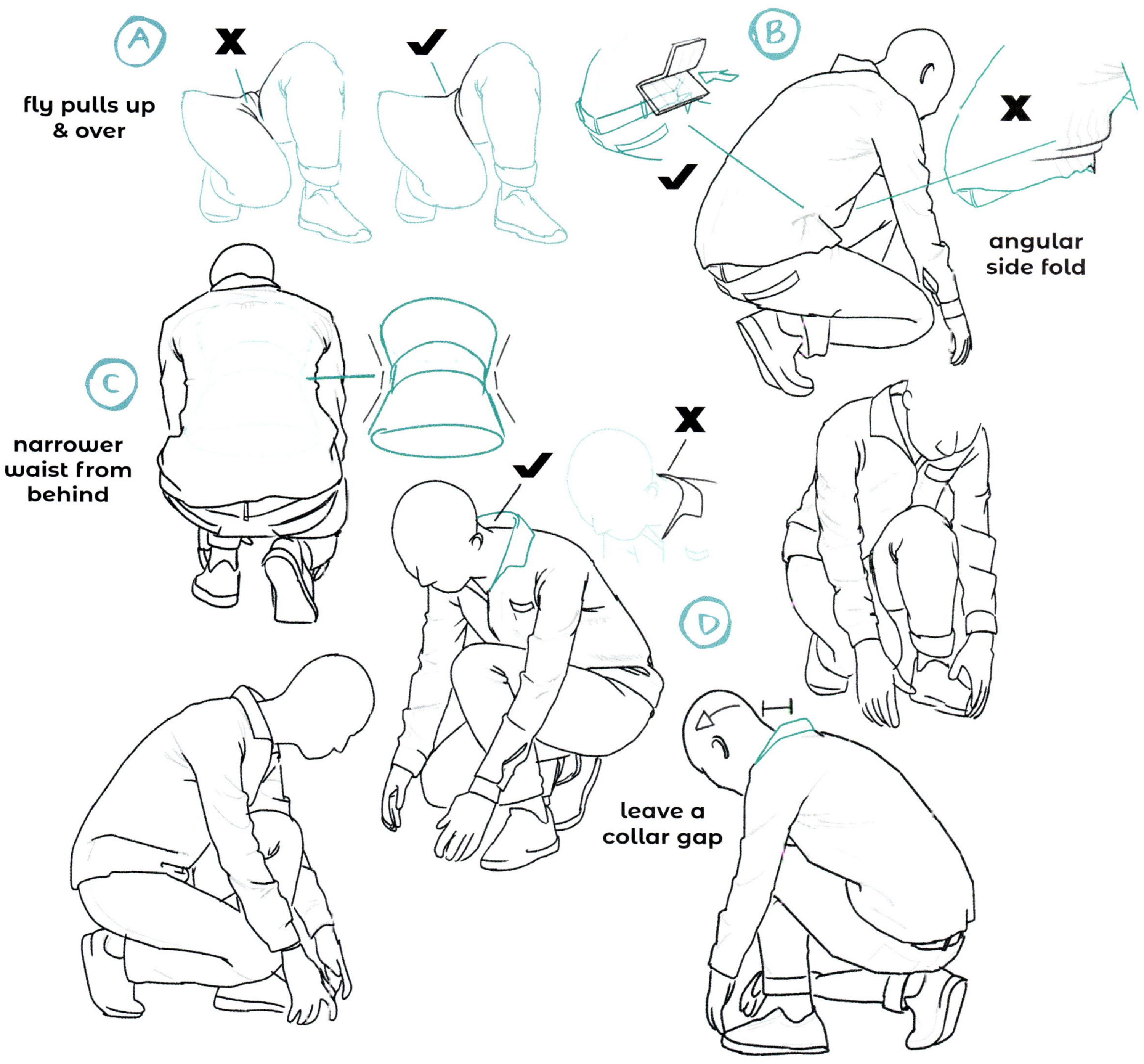

Here's the same crouching pose seen from above, with several rotations. This includes some excellent reference for collar shapes from various angles, so pay attention to those. Note how simple the folds around a bent knee can be from this angle (E). When the leg is bent like this, the fabric on the front of the shin will almost never be completely rounded, but will have a central section that protrudes forwards (E). It's tempting to draw this darker line meeting the folds under the arm (F). Instead, it's usually more accurate and believable to leave a slight gap between them (G).

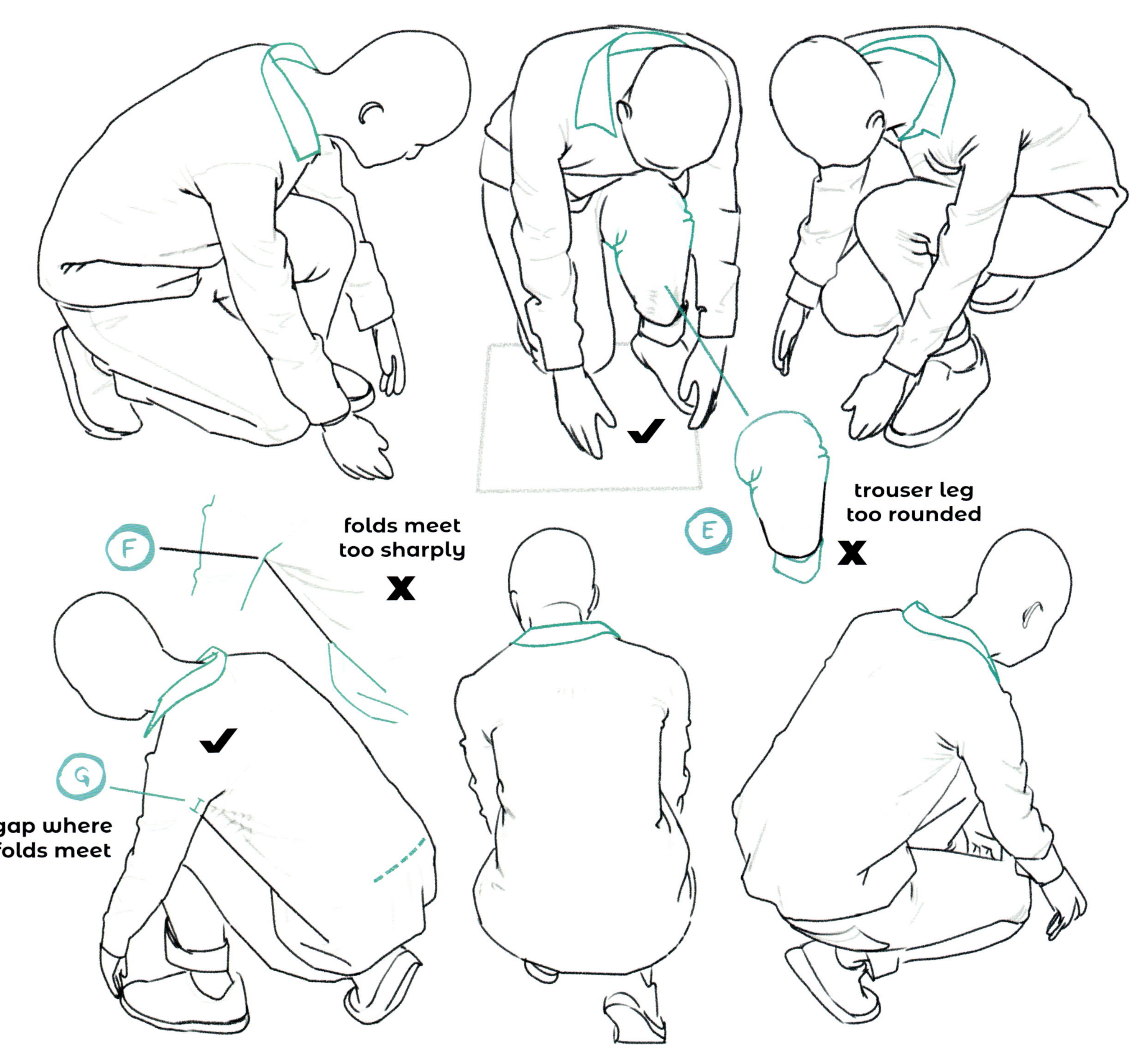

This sort of crouched pose is incredibly difficult to draw, so it's always worth using references. When the torso leans forwards, it's important to get these folds correct (H) – the ends of these lines usually reverse direction, rather than continuing to curve up. There's so much pressure between the upper and lower leg above the knee that folding occurs on either side of this line (I). More often than not, one foot is further forwards, and the other is angled out to the side (J) – it's rare that both feet face forwards. The fabric across the top of the chest and shoulder usually sits on top of the fabric of the arm, not the other way around (K). It's not easy to get the direction of these folds correct, but they should both sweep up and around the torso (L). They shouldn't meet in the middle, as the central back is an area of support.

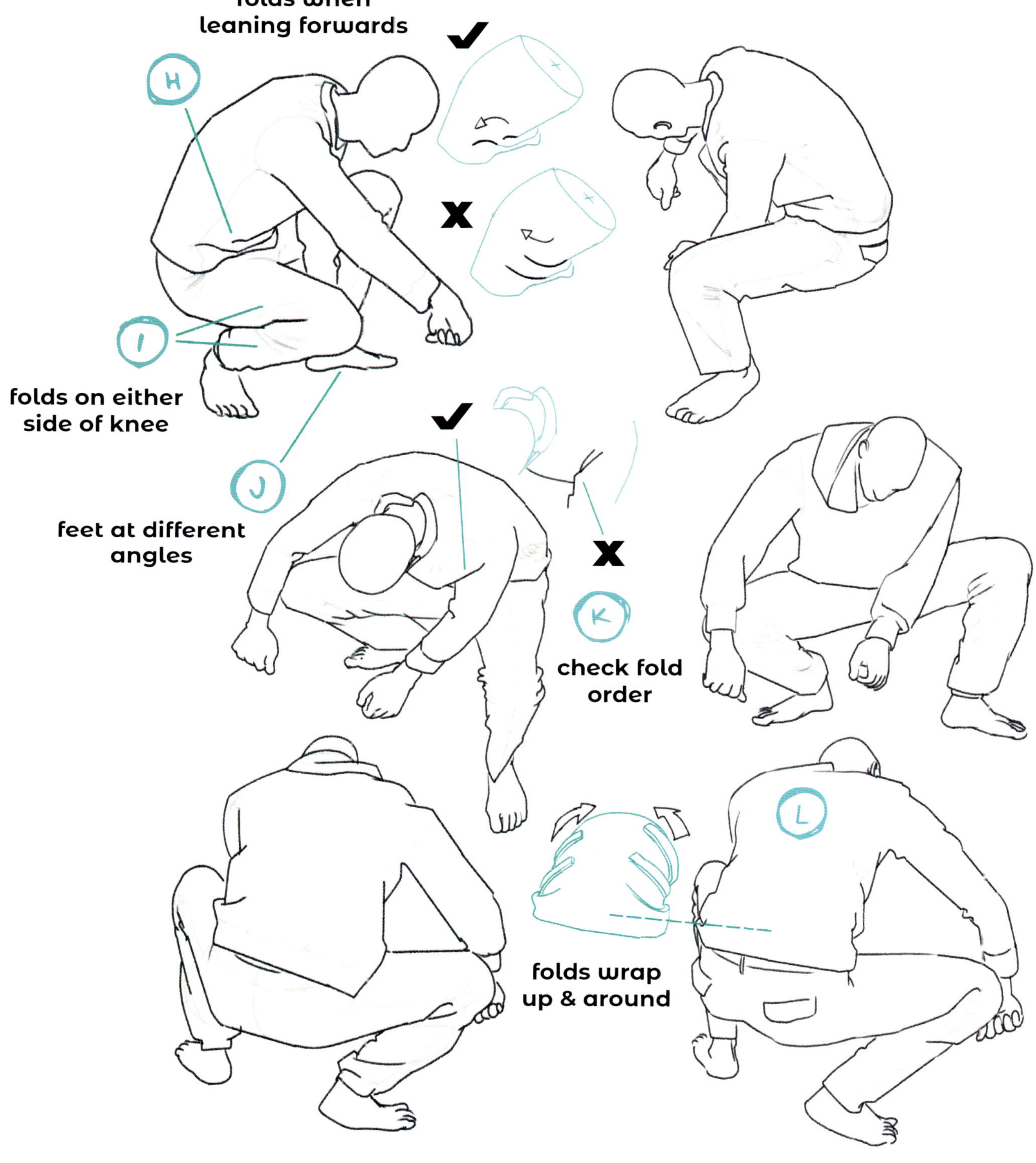

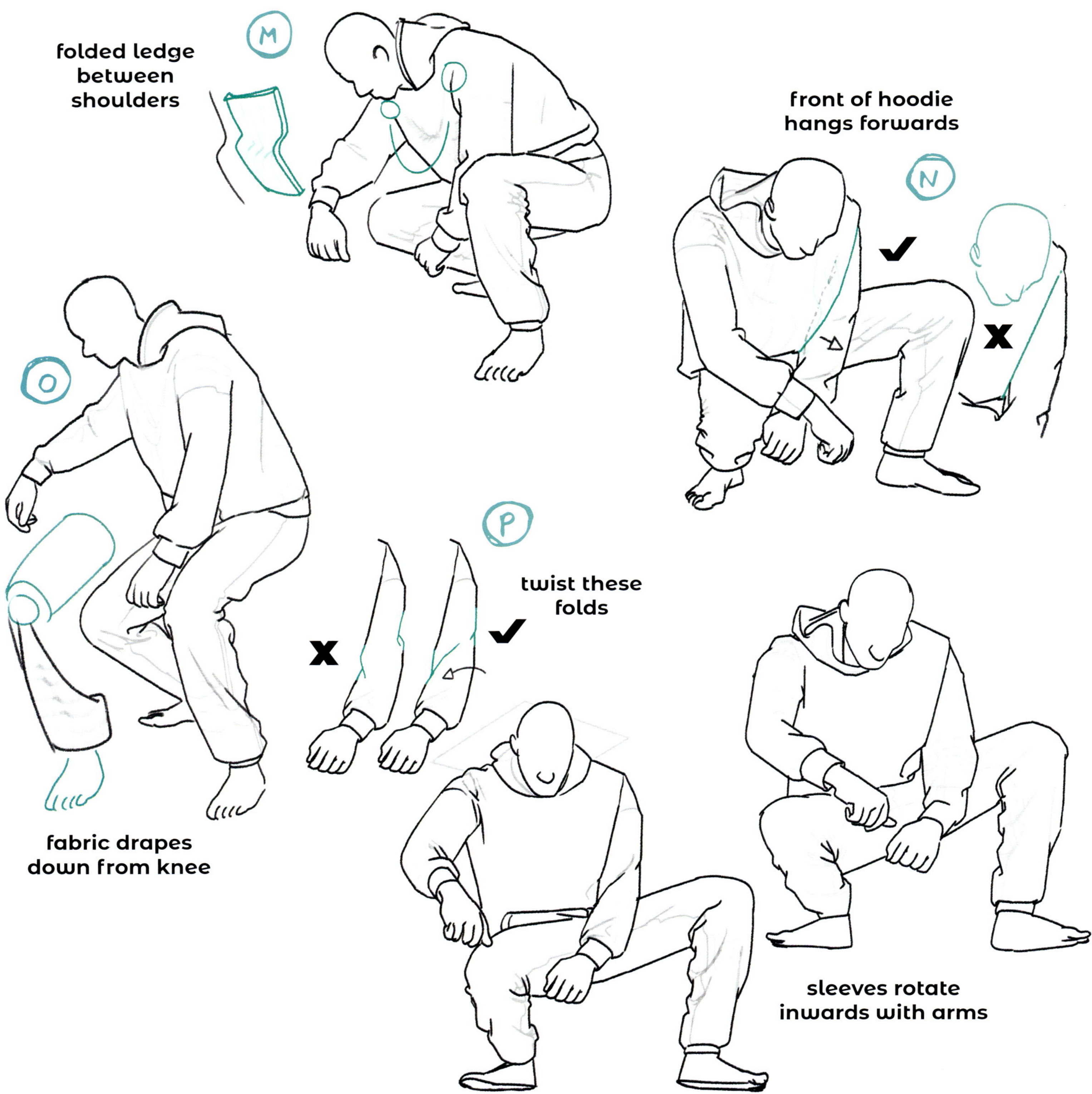

With oversized tops, when a character leans forwards you'll often see this ledge connecting the raised shoulders (M). Ensure that the fabric of the front of the hoodie hangs in front of the rear arm rather than creating a straight line (N). The arm should wedge into this material. Fabric will often drop away from the knee, and seamlessly join with the bunched form above the ankle cuff (O). When the arms are rotated inwards, there will often be two critical overlaps that really communicate the twist. Make sure that they're the right way around (P).

squatting

The front of the hood should clearly converge to a point below the chin (A), rather than forming a loop. This usually causes folding here (B). The cuff itself is often smaller than the sleeve, so you'll see some folding around the cuff (C). The back of the hood should fold upon itself, rather than dropping straight down (D), and the folding is usually angled up from the chin rather than from the back of the neck. The top of the knee often causes the outside edge of the arm to be pushed upwards (E). The backs of the thighs put pressure on the fabric around the shins, which may cause these folds to appear (F). The overall pattern of the folding on the arms is an outward spiral (G).

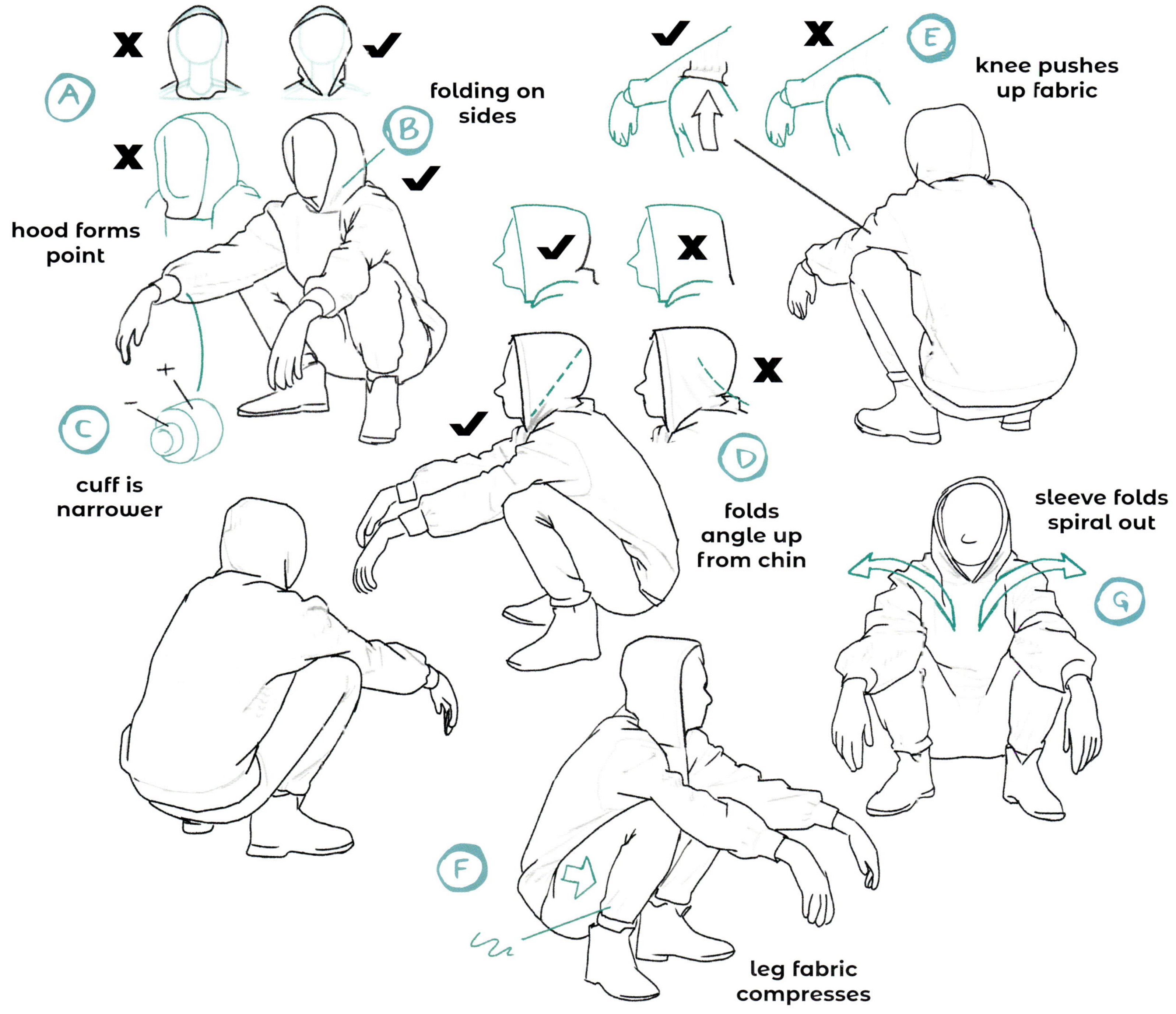

These folds at the sides of the hips require more than one line, and need to bunch out of the silhouette here (H). When squatting, the arms are very often held out like this to help balance the character and stop them falling backwards (I). The major direction of compression is between the tops of the thighs and the front of the hoodie (J). To show that, this form should sit on top of the thighs (K). Notice how few folds occur on the back (L) – this is one large pulling surface, and should be kept clear.

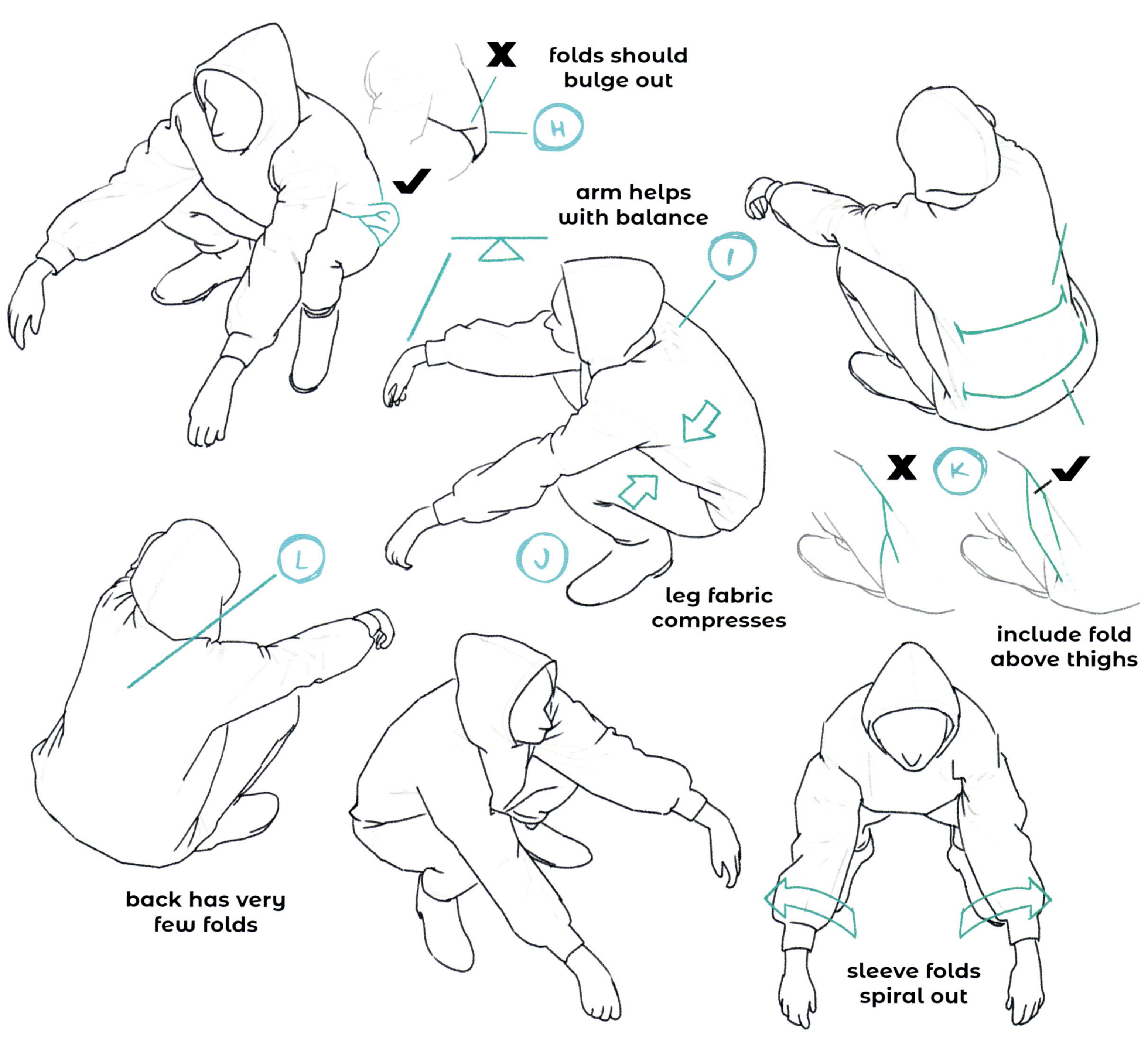

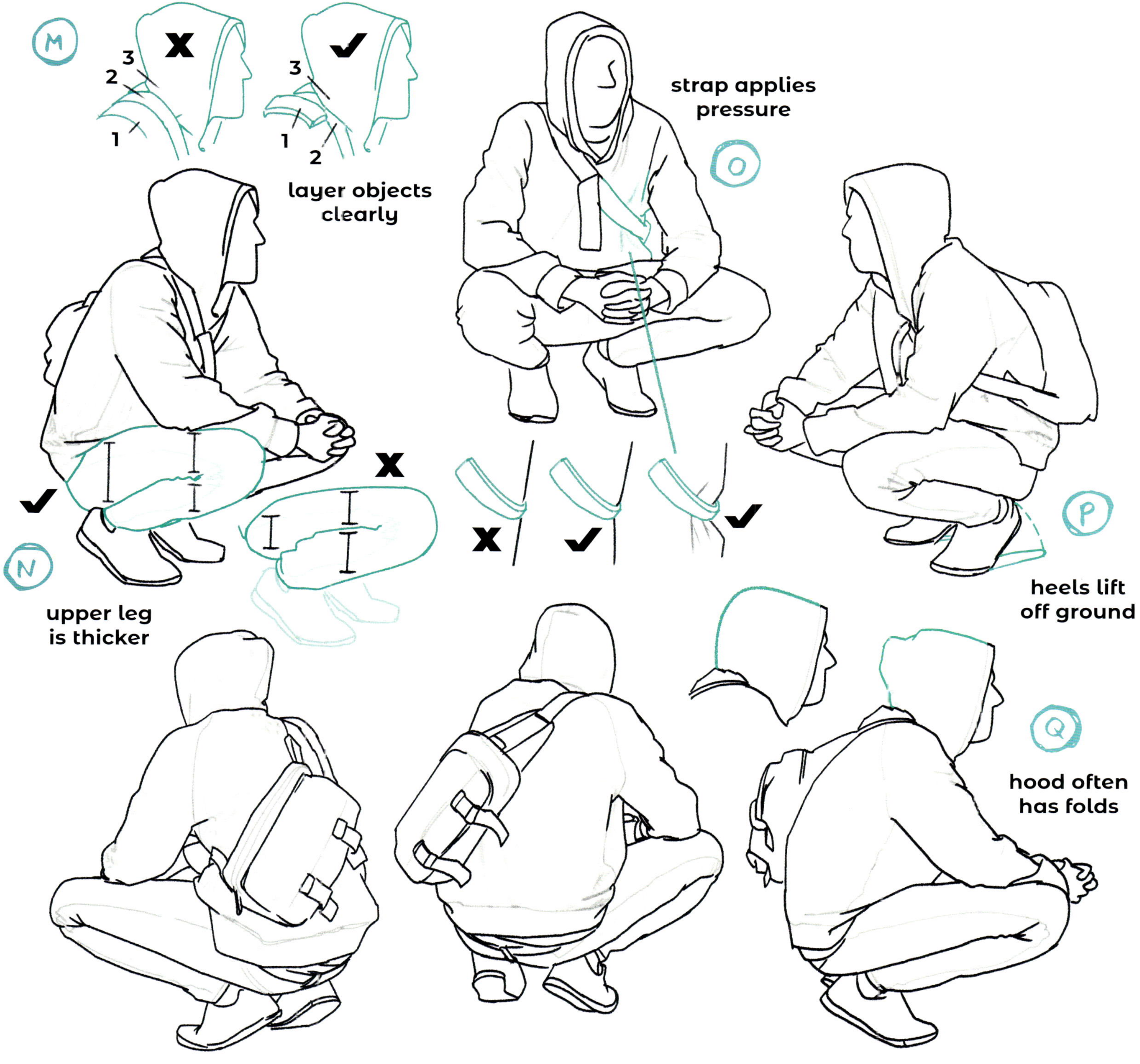

The more interacting forms you have, the more important it is to make the overlaps clear. In this situation, we have the bag strap, the hood, and some fabric between the two (M), and it's unclear what is in front of what if they are not overlapped well **(1, 2, 3)**. When the upper leg is stacked on top of the lower leg, the two have very different heights – they won't have an even spacing (N). There should be a clear taper in thickness from the glutes towards the knee. Bag straps are a common source of problems for artists. The bare minimum effect a bag strap should have is to change the silhouette (O). If you can add some compression on the fabric within the silhouette, that's even better! When most people squat, their heels are raised off the ground, and their feet subtly turn outwards (P). The back of the hood is sometimes a soft curve, but more often it tapers to a slight point and contains some angular folds (Q).

When drawing a bag strap from above, be bold with these overlaps (R). The hood or the shoulder on the outside of the strap will often fully cover a strap like this. The same strap, seen from this angle, pulls the fabric on the chest inwards (S), rather than wrapping a rounded form (T). This form is seen all the time - whenever the forearm is bent and placed on top of a surface (U). Note the indentation here in the top of the hood (V). Finally, a hood will rarely be rounded at the back like this - more often, it'll form a point (W).

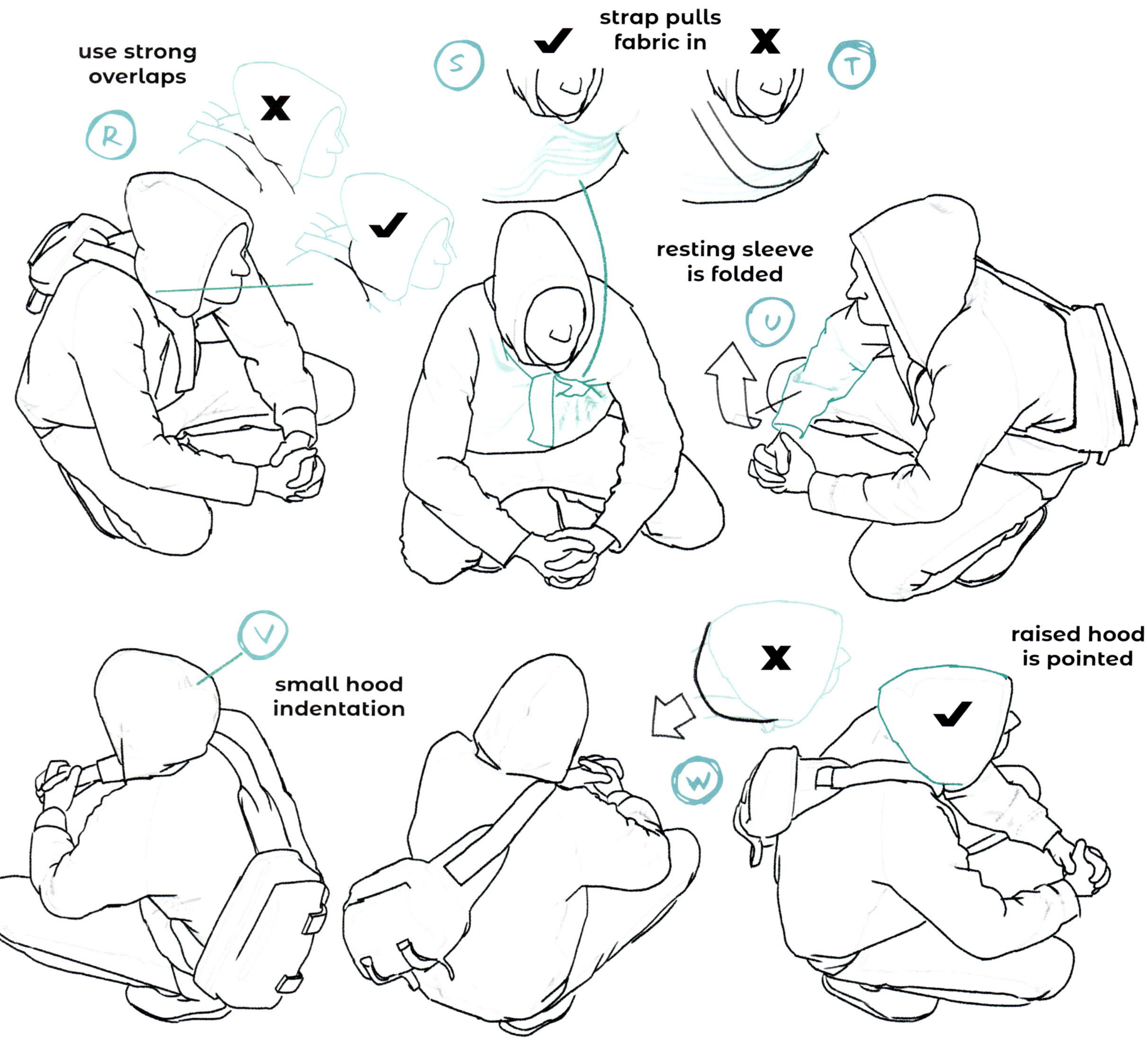

squatting in a dress

When squatting in a dress, these folds should be orientated upwards, rather than downwards (A). Ideally, the muscle of the calf will bulge out to the side, as it's compressed against the thigh, rather than sitting directly beneath it (B). Fabric doesn't follow the legs exactly, but usually hangs down from the forward knee (C). The thighs will rarely be even heights, and as a result one knee will usually be lower or further back (D). Finally, from in front, the folds around the lower legs will usually be concave (curving in), rather than convex (bulging outwards) (E).

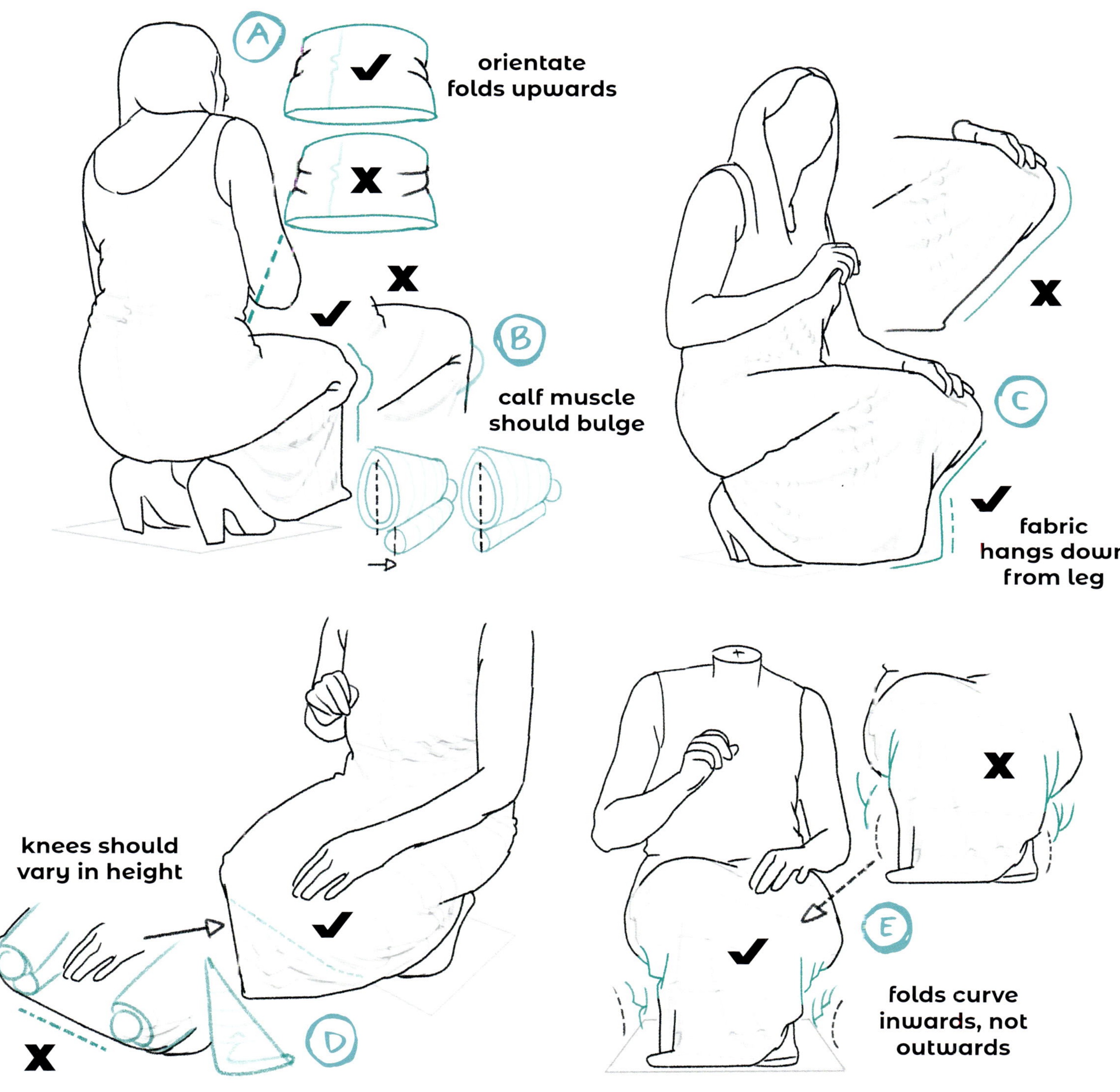

motions:

sitting & lying

sitting in a skirt

When one leg is on top of the other, you won't see a long line of overlap (A). Instead, you'll see fabric bulge outwards. Some fabric will be pinched between the legs, but only the part near the knee; as you move up the leg, the overlap disappears (B). You may find two bulges on either side of the top leg, too (C).

The back of the skirt won't hang down in curtain-like folds, but will compress vertically instead (D). Unless the skirt is very tight around the thighs (which is completely possible), these lines will sag in the gap between the thighs (E).

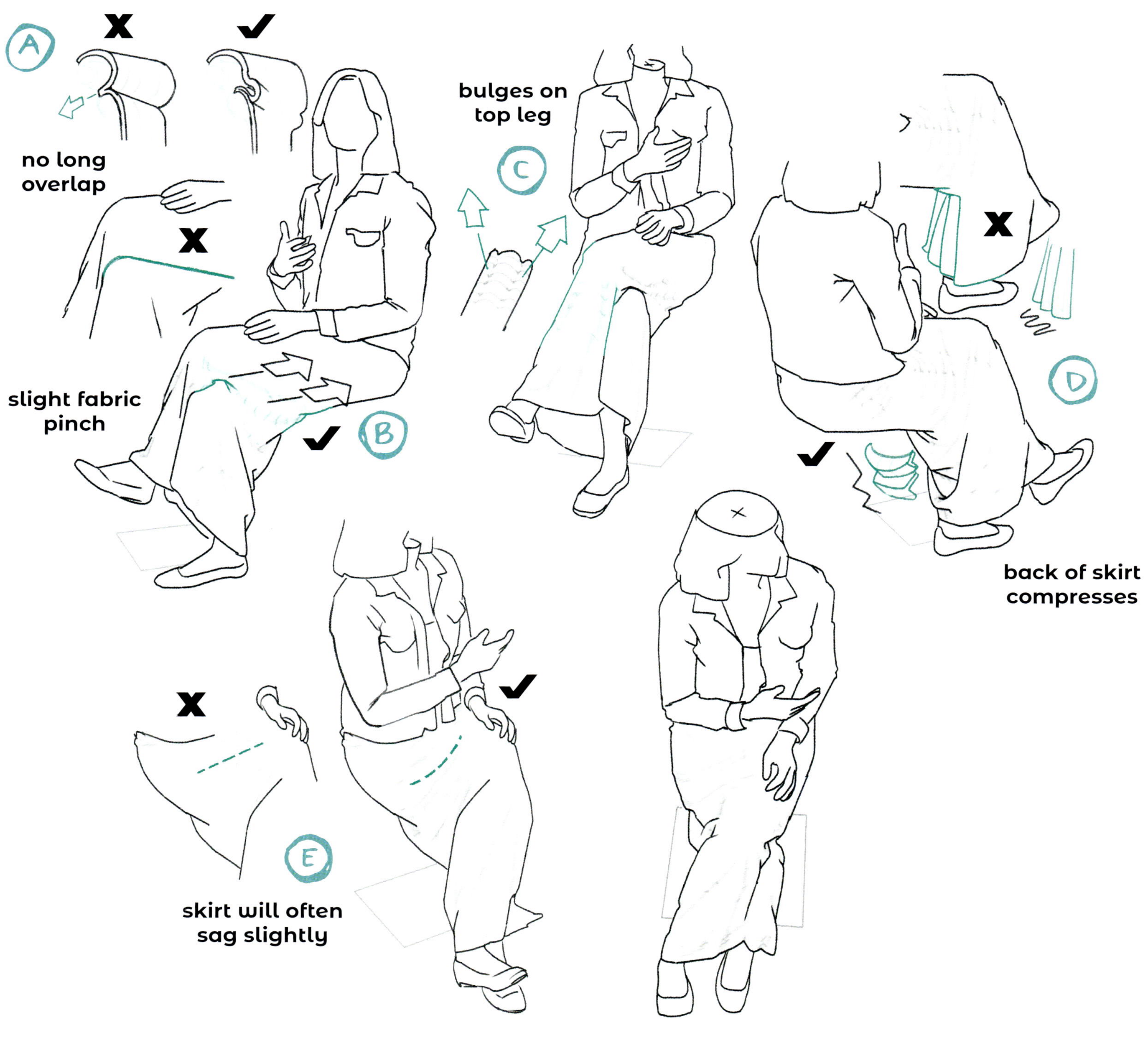

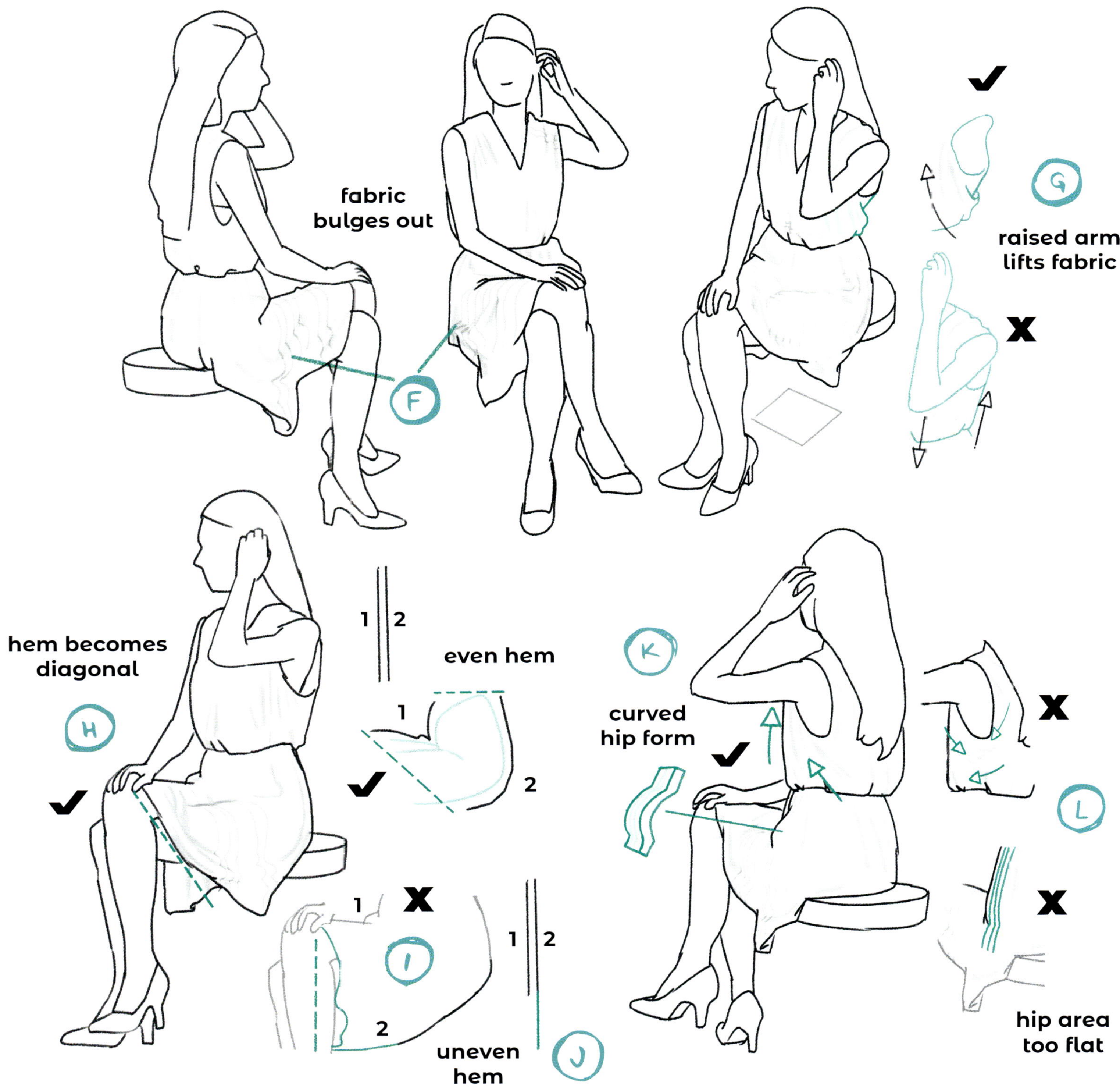

With one leg on top of the other, a fold often forms on the outside of the thigh (F). The raised arm pulls the fabric forwards and up, creating diagonal folds rather than the vertical ones (G). Imagine a line down the front of the dress **(1)** and a line down the back **(2)**. If these lines are the same length, when the thighs are raised, the end of line 1 will reach further forwards than the end of line 2 (H). Therefore, the fabric on top will reach further forwards than the fabric at the back, making the hem fall at a diagonal when sitting. For the bottom of the dress to do this (I), the back of the dress would have to be extended down (J), which would look odd when standing. On the outside edge of the hip, you'll likely see this form (K) – be careful not to draw the surface too flat (L).

When there's plenty of width in the fabric around the thighs, you may notice that the fabric connects the upper thigh to the front of the hips, almost like two triangles (M). If the waistband is narrower than the fabric below it, the dress will bunch around the circumference of the waist (N). When the knees are held together, the fabric in front of the knees may bunch **(1–3)** (O). This area on the side will usually be quite flat and won't contain folds (P). The area in front of the knees forms an arch, rather than hanging flat, and the arch subtly angles outwards (Q). At the back, the hem also lifts up (R), and there'll almost always be an overhang over the waistband (S). Resist drawing these folds like this (T) – in reality they would be reversed, partly to reflect the triangles of material mentioned before (M).

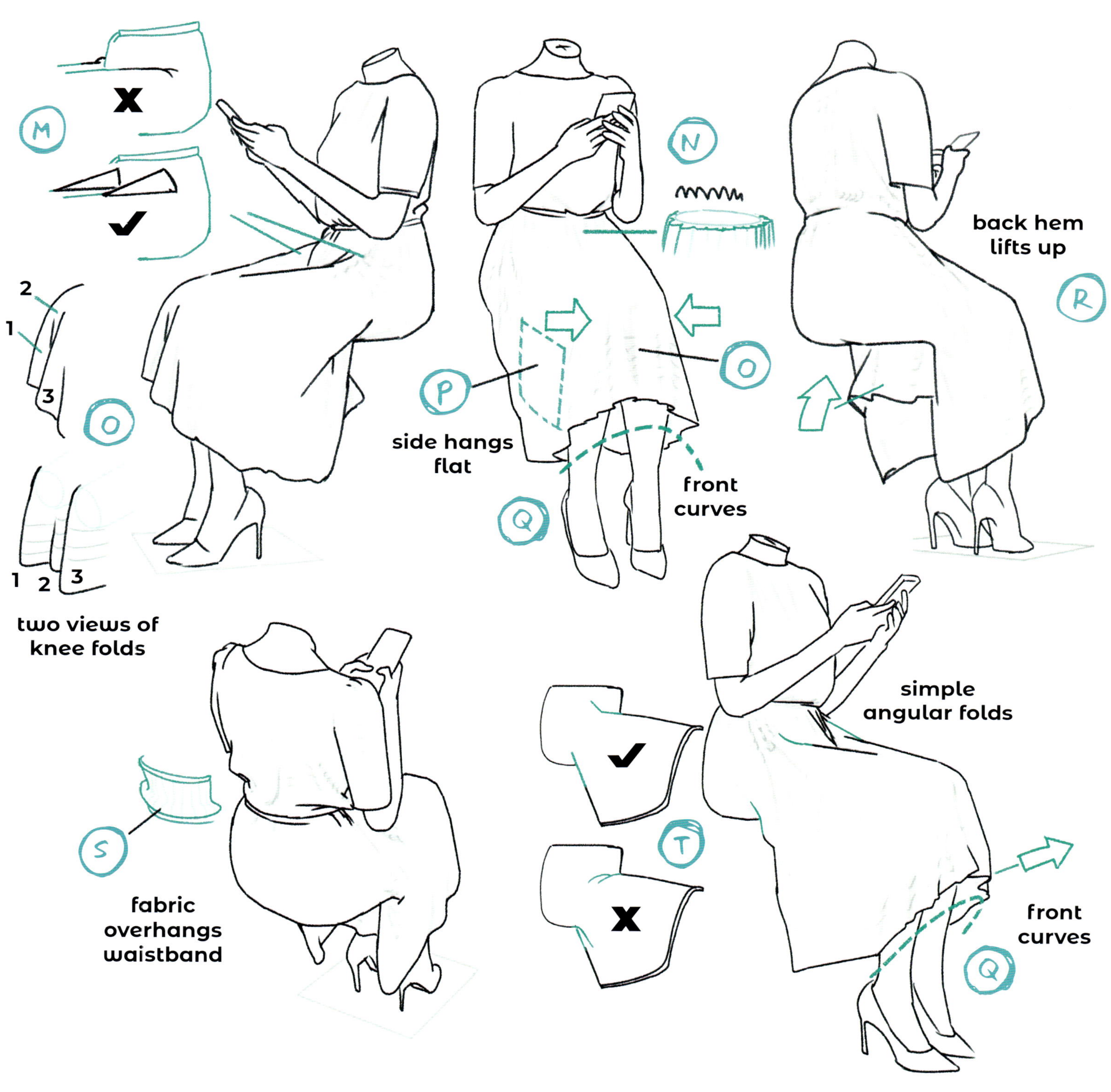

listening

Tilting the head is almost essential to show that a character is listening. When leaning forwards with the hands clasped together, the back should be rounded, particularly across the shoulders (A). When the front leg is resting on the back leg, the fabric should be pushed up to reflect the pressure (B). The shoulders should be well forward of the back rather than lined up (C)

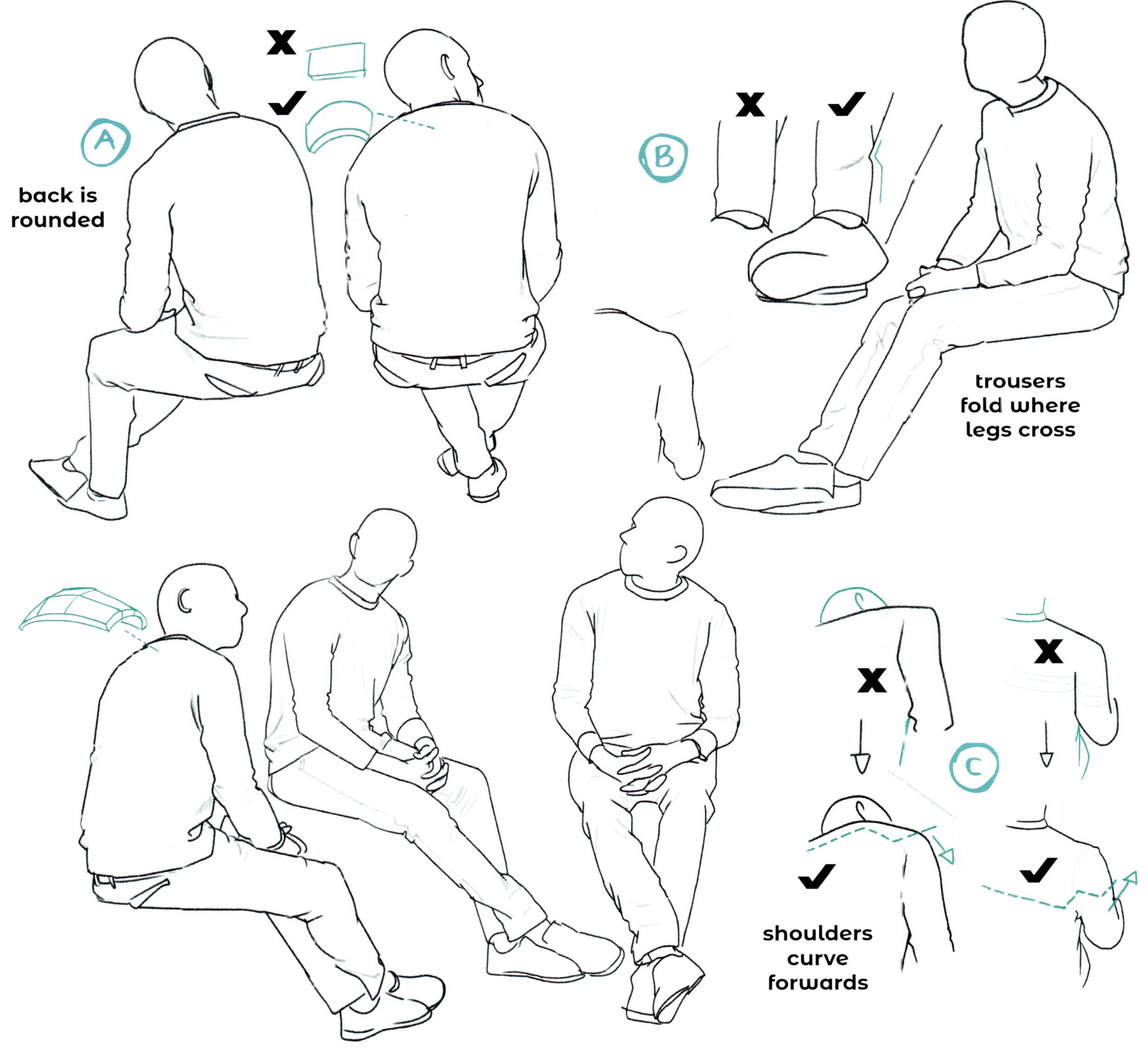

This pose and character are full of examples of forms pressing against each other in subtle ways. These details can make or break your drawing, so they're worth paying attention to. In this first example (D), the arm is resting on the leg, and the cuff is pushed up by the pressure from below. Here, the upper arms are pressing against the lats and upper torso – shown by these small folds here (E). Without them, that pressure wouldn't be apparent. Here (F), the rear leg is pushing the fabric forwards, in a way that adds a lot of believability to the drawing. These three lines (G) clearly indicate – without much detail – that the fabric of the chest is above the upper arm, and that the upper arm is swinging forwards and in. Again, these may seem like small details, but they add a lot of believability to the character.

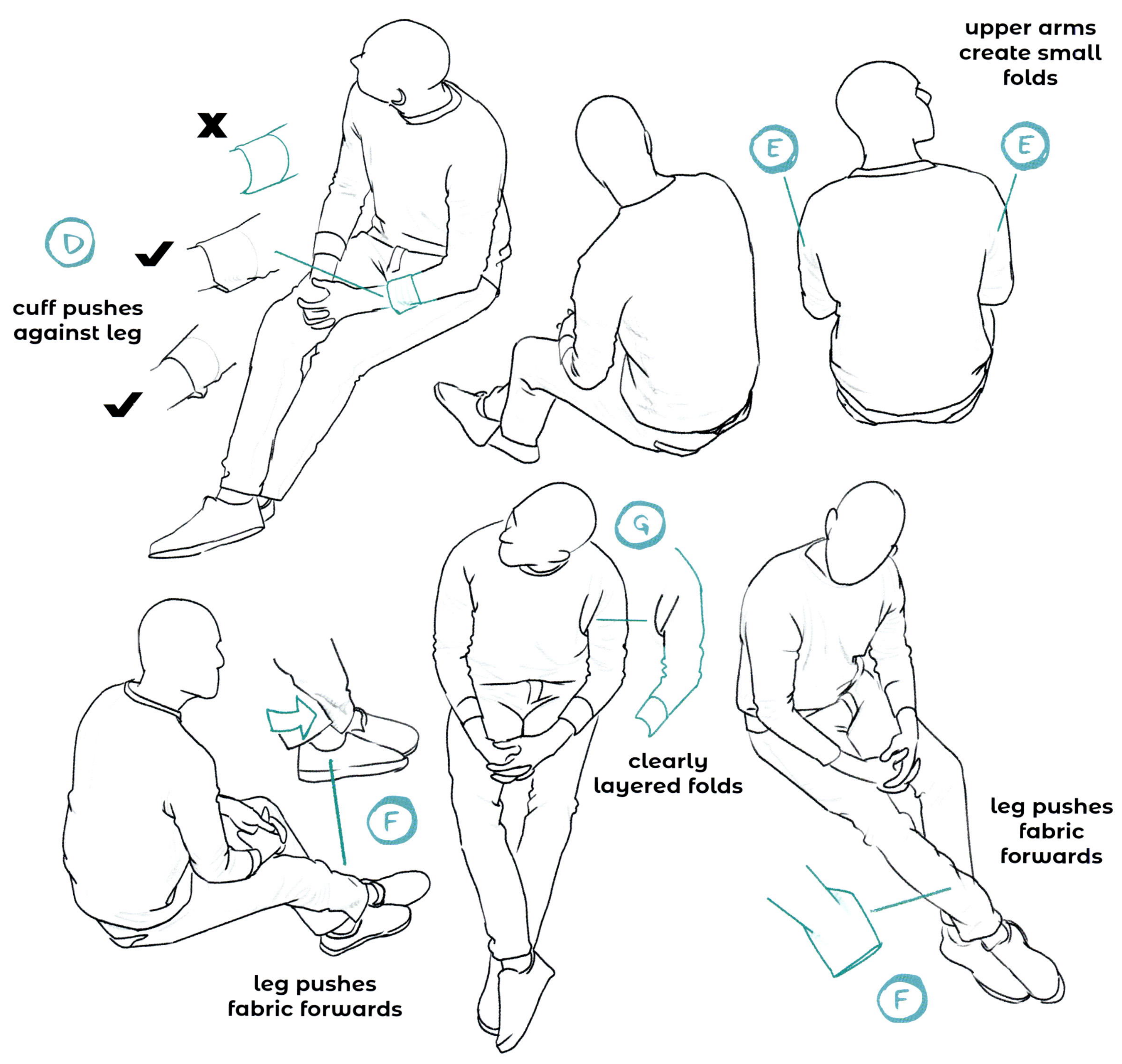

eating

When sitting with an open jacket (A), sometimes the side of the jacket partially bunches up on the top of the thigh **(1)**, and other times it falls straight down the side of the leg **(2)**. It's tempting to draw the top garment falling down over the fly area (B), but very often it tucks behind it, and the fly sticks upwards (C). From behind, the elbows are partially raised out to the sides, which causes gentle folding (D). This page and the next are full of great examples of ways to simplify the complex folds at the bottoms of the legs into minimal lines (D). I've highlighted a few recurring patterns that are worth remembering or examining more closely (E).

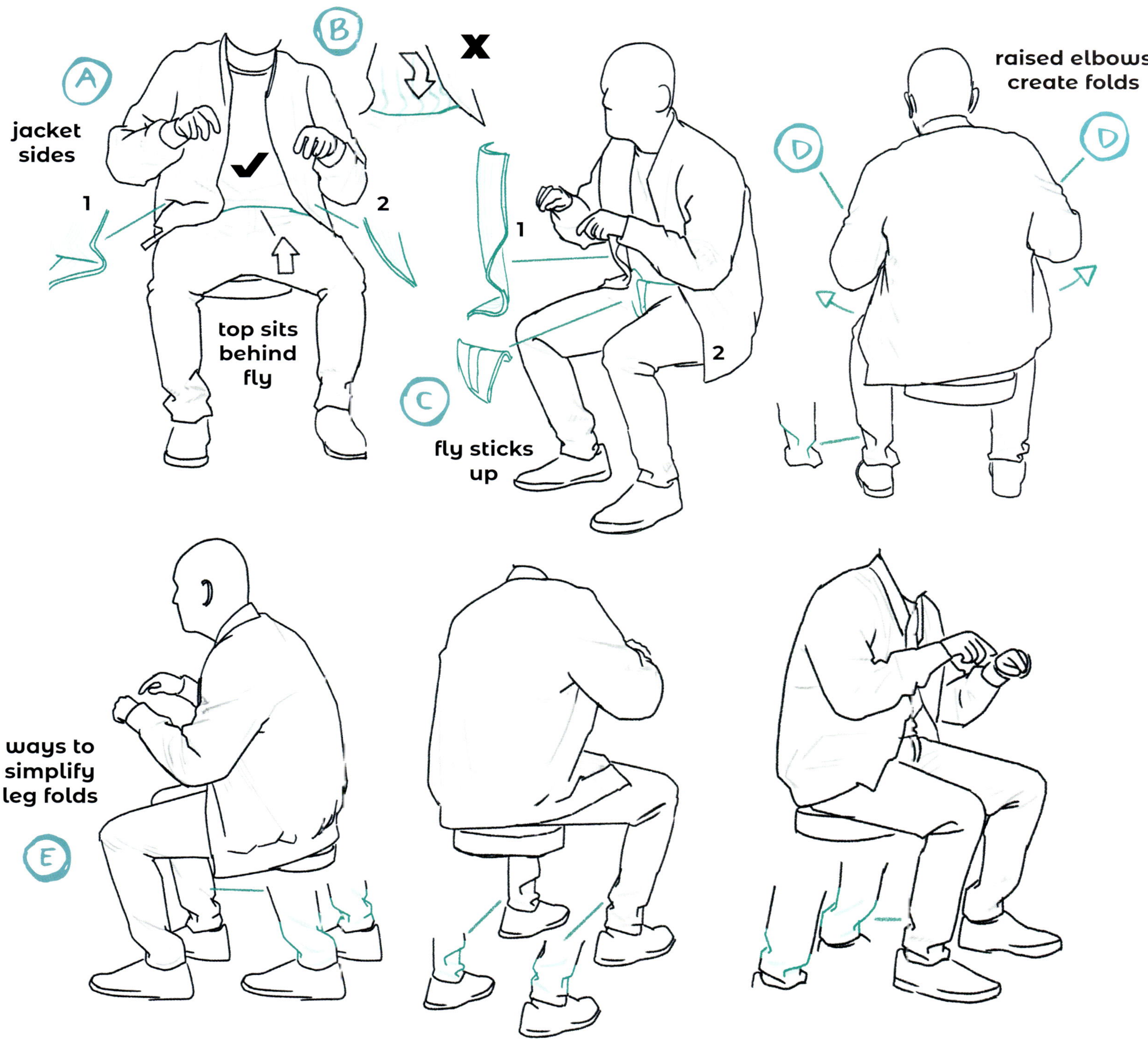

As mentioned on the previous page, here are a few patterns that are frequently used. Legs bending like this are seen so often that it's worth trying to memorize some of these patterns. Then you'll have a sort of helpful 'shorthand' for when they're needed.

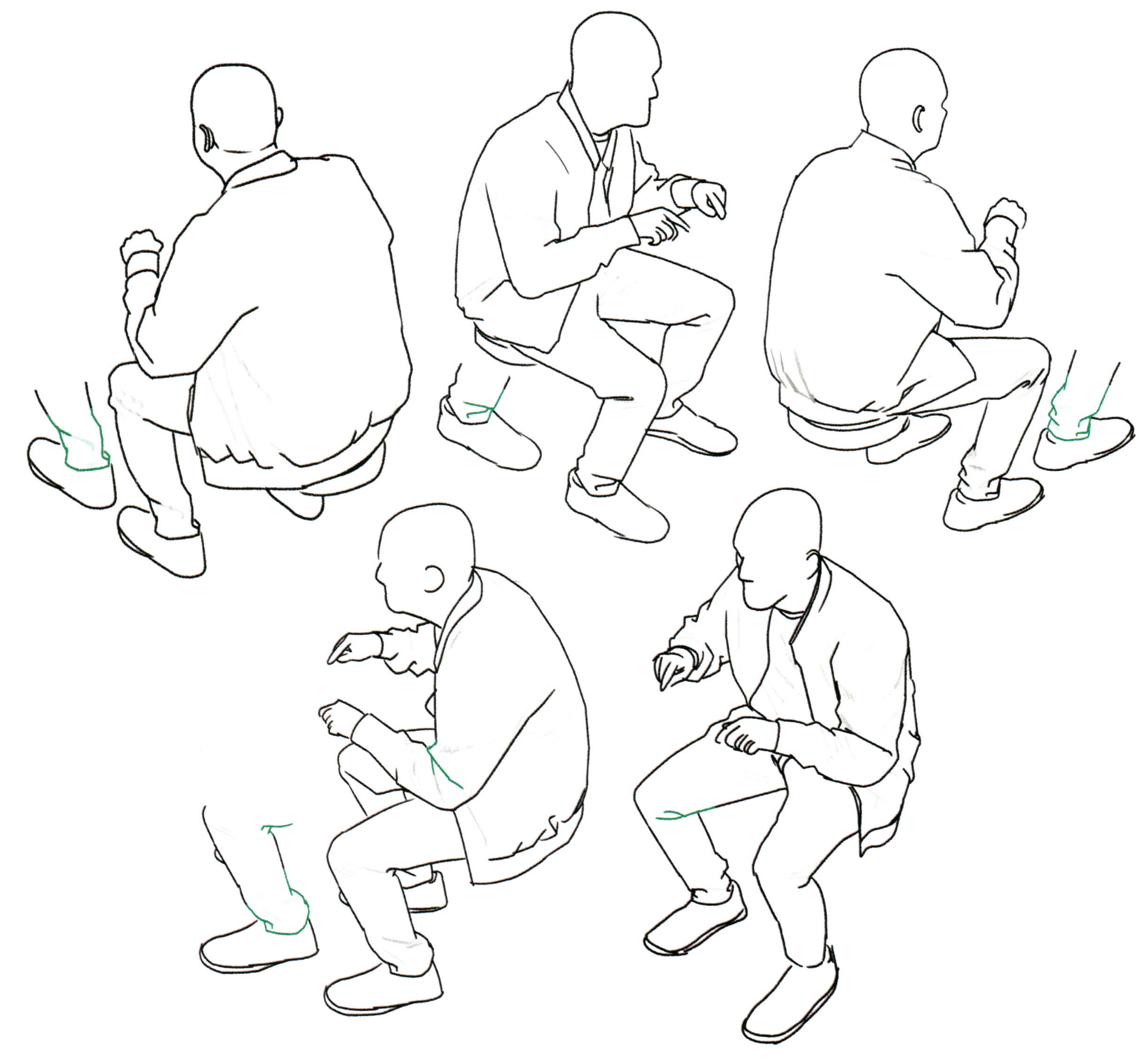

laptop

In this pose, the foot rarely holds itself parallel to the leg. Instead, angle the foot downwards (A). Fabric usually hangs from the end of the vertical leg in a cone (B). You'll often see strong compression behind and below the shoulders, because the elbows are usually held close to the body when typing (C). The front of the trouser leg may fall in front of the tongue of the shoe, but it will often be caught, causing an overhang (D). This is a nice detail to add. Pay attention to the way the sleeves fall. In oversized T-shirts, their outer edge will often lift off the arm (E).

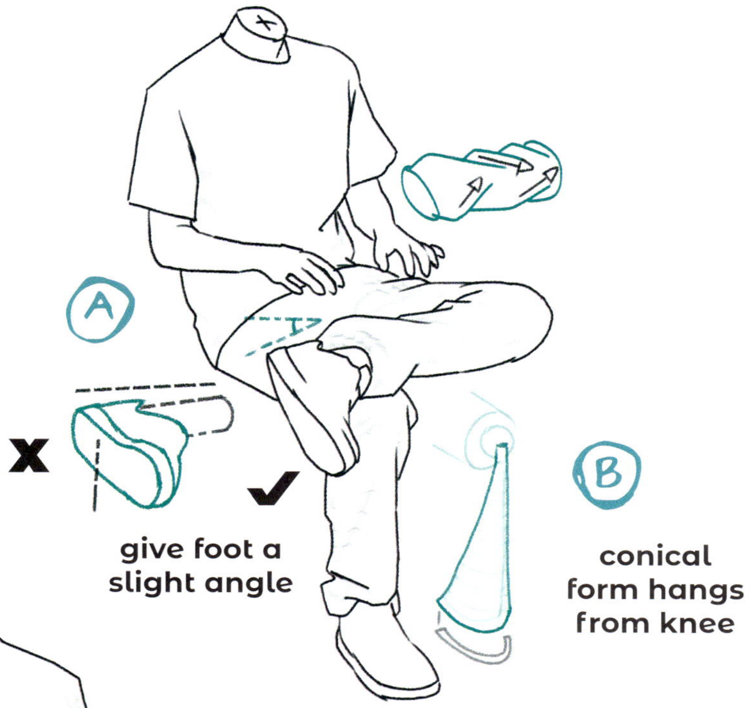

A

give foot a slight angle

B

conical form hangs from knee

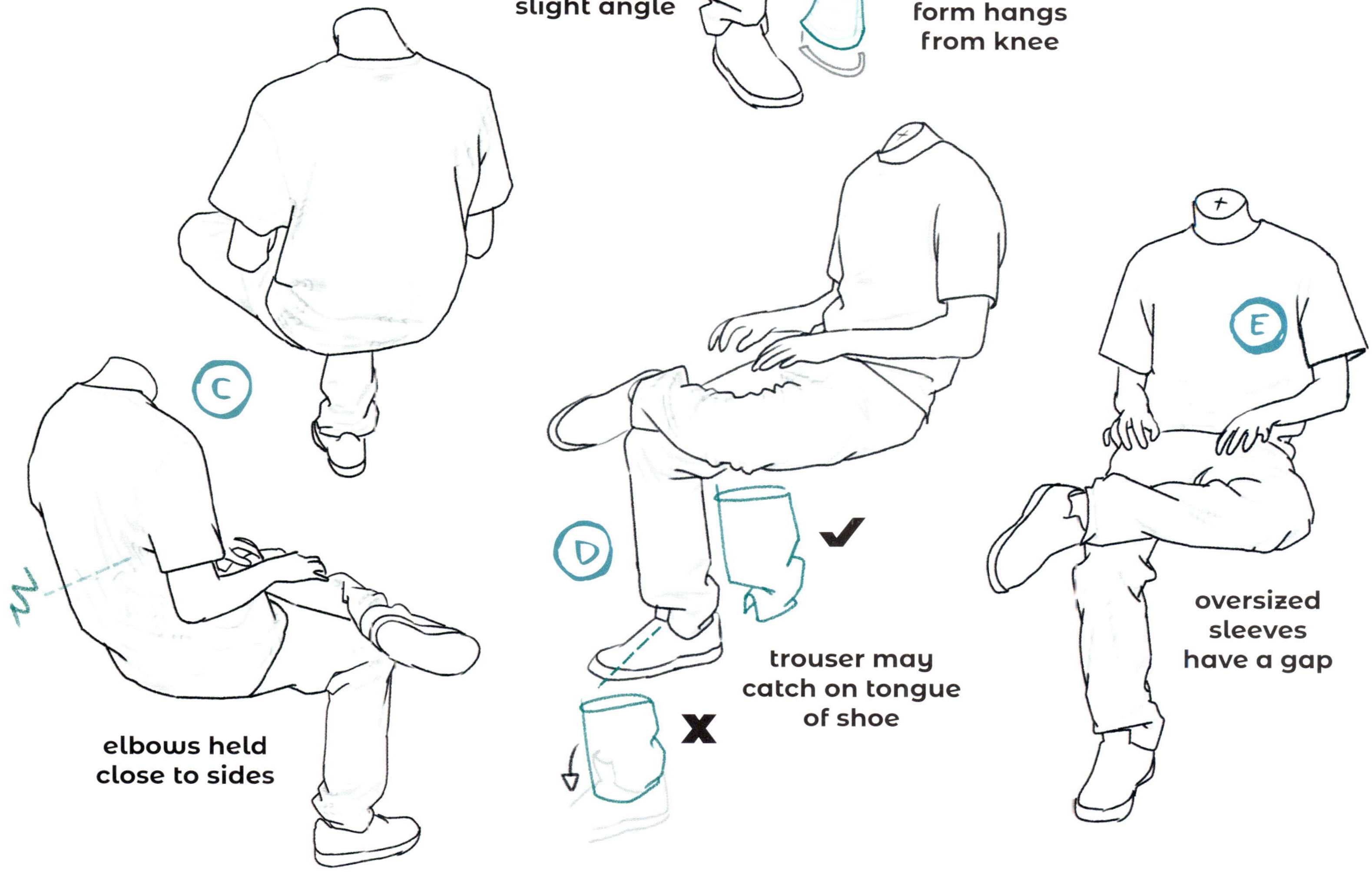

C

elbows held close to sides

D

trouser may catch on tongue of shoe

E

oversized sleeves have a gap

stretching

When the arms are raised in a stretch, the shoulder-blade area becomes a pulling surface (A). At the same time, the bottom of the shirt forms a curve (B), to reflect that the sides of the shirt are higher than the front and back. One arm often twists back, causing folds to appear under the arm (C). Be careful not to draw the underarm in a way that suggests the arm is simply lifting up (D). The forearm is pulled so tightly against the upper arm that the cuff may be forced upwards (E). This is a particularly tricky part to draw: the folds should show the compression, but also the twist, while joining the underarm to the top side of the forearm (F). When the arms are raised, they pull the fabric at the bottom of the shirt up and also out (G).

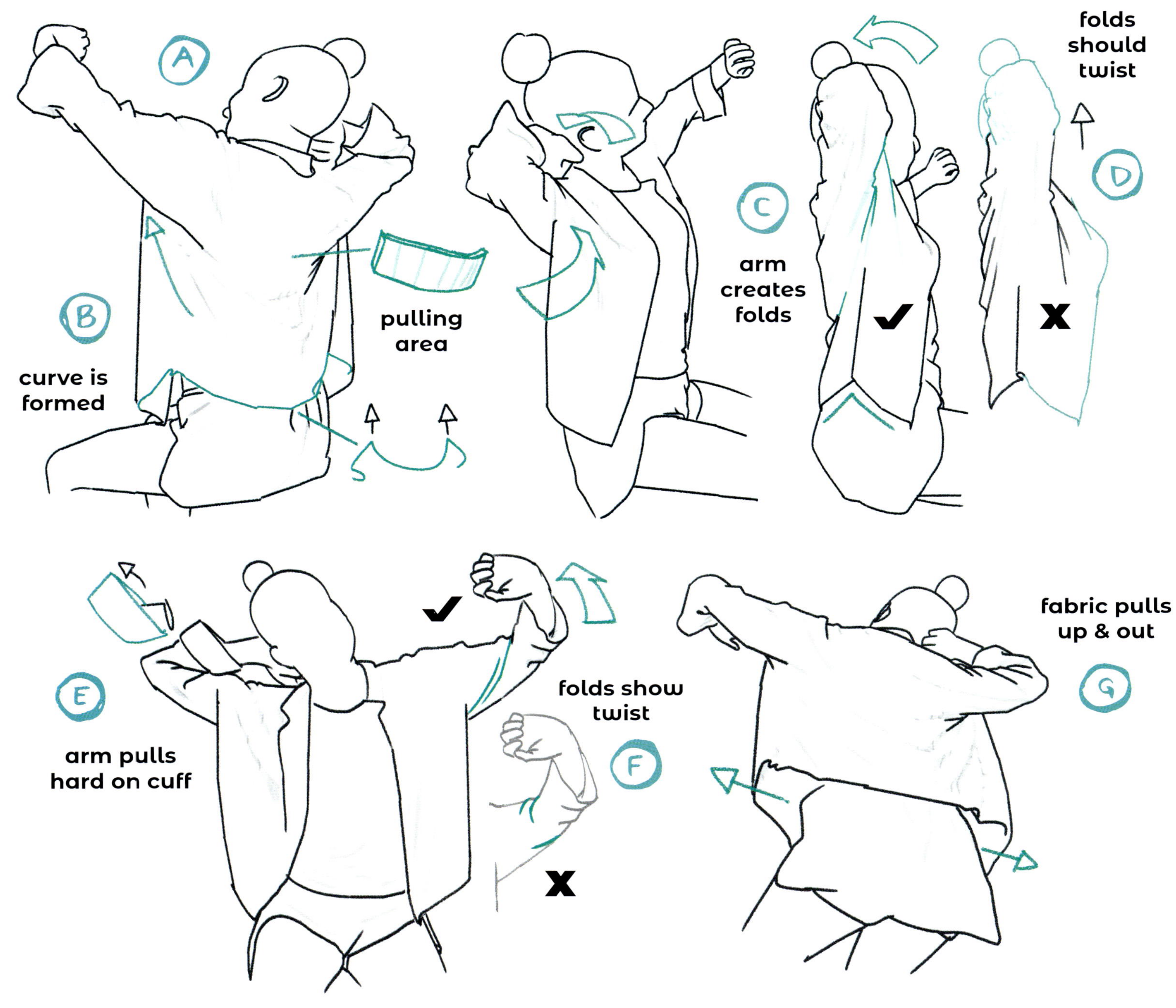

leaning forwards

When a figure really bends forwards like this, it's tempting to add in a lot of lines to try to make it clear that there's strong compression. Resist this urge. You can show just as much with one or two simple lines (A). With a large hoodie like this, the line extending from the back of the arm should 'wrap' around the ribcage rather than being straight (B). The folds below the waist will be flatter (C), and those around the waist will wrap around more (D). From below, don't forget to keep the gap between the legs and the glutes quite large. This line is often drawn extending too far (E).

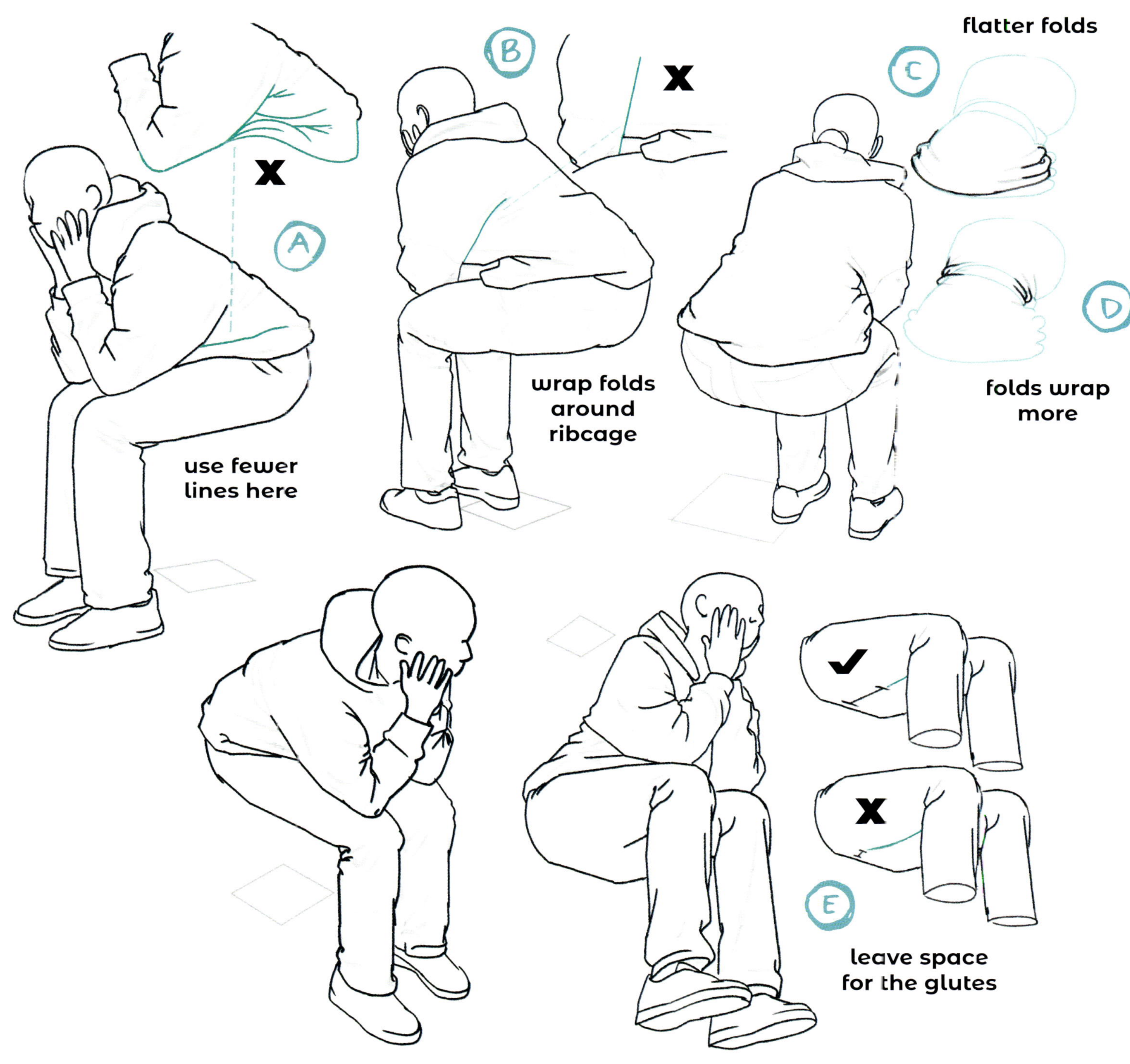

It's helpful to show an obvious 'inner' **(1)** and 'outer' to the hood **(2)**, rather than drawing forms that are difficult to interpret. When the zip is fully undone, the fabric near the zip often opens outwards (F). Sometimes hoods support their own weight, but often they collapse down (G). As the zip is raised, the edge of the hood curls in on itself (H).

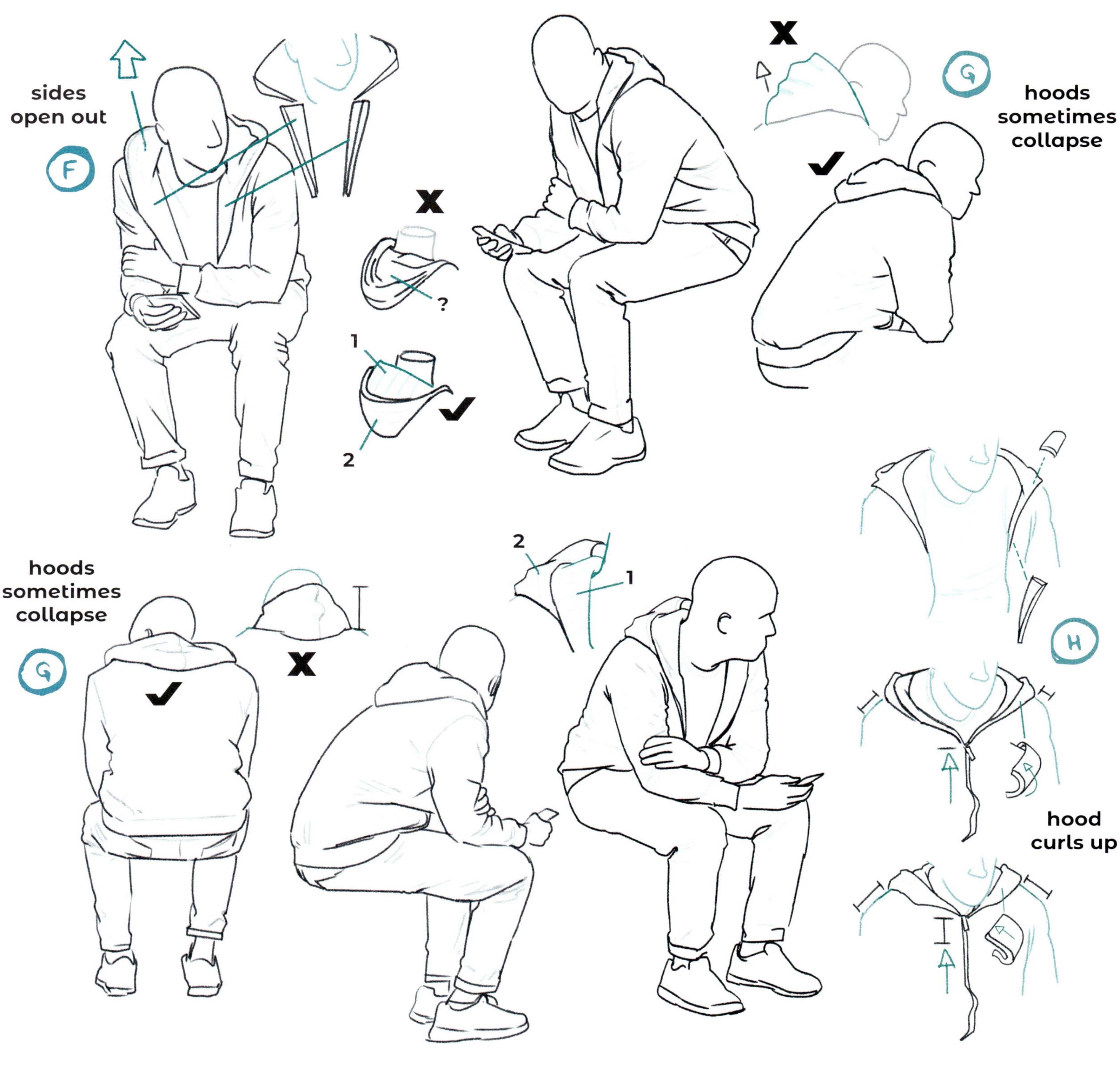

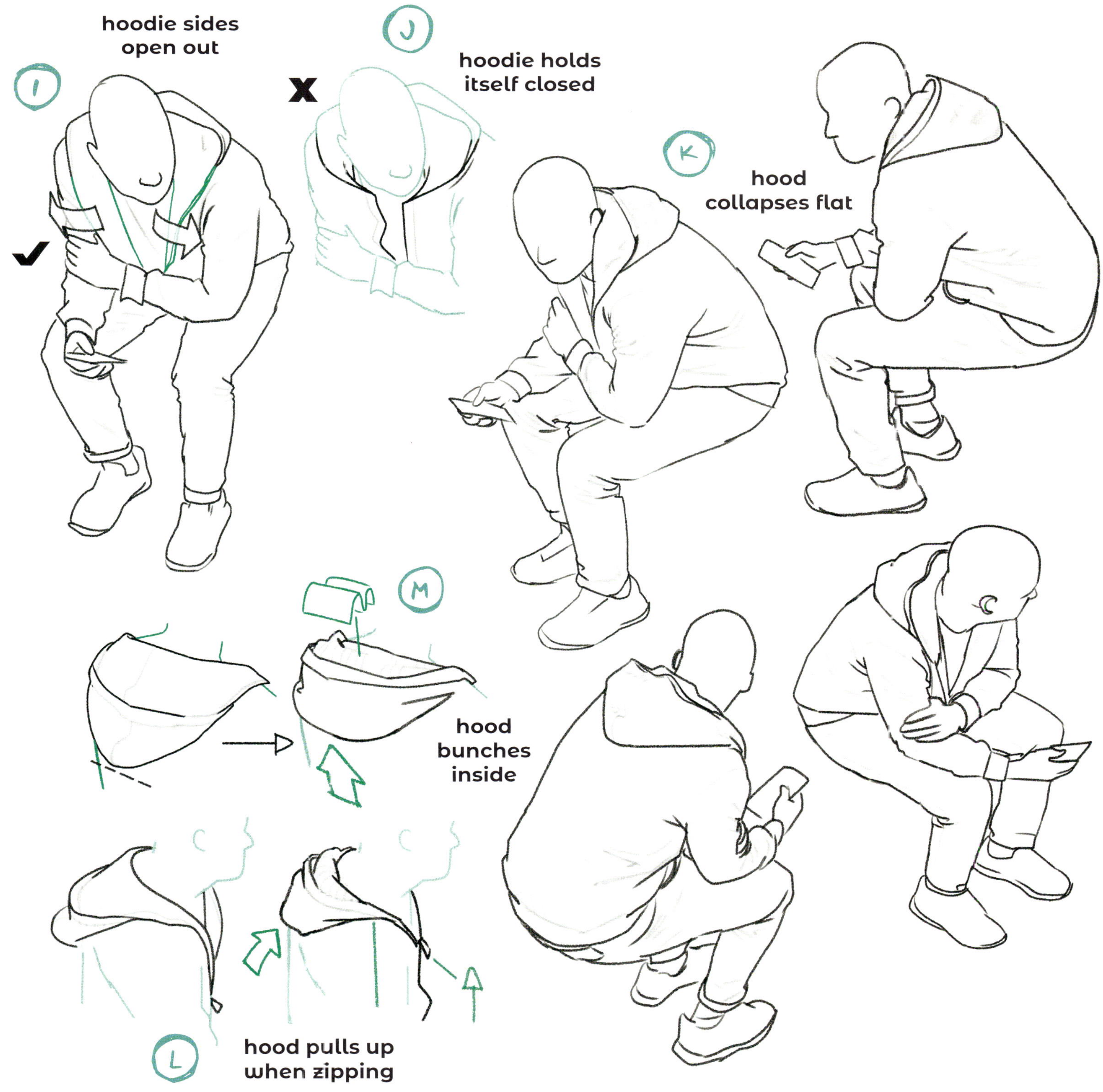

As seen on the previous page, when the zip is fully undone, the fabric on either side folds out (I), rather than forming this shape (J). From this angle, it's obvious how flattened the hood is across the top of the back, and how it struggles to support its own weight (K). When the zip is done up, the back of the hood rises up (L), and hood's inner section bunches in response (M).

reading

The tie knot usually bulges outwards slightly, rather than lying flat (A). The bottom of the jacket has three sections (**1–3**). The cuff of the jacket should have button holes as well as the buttons themselves (B). The lapel and collar of the jacket will follow these angles (C). This is an interesting example where the front of the fold (**4**) obscures the back (**5**) – difficult drapery to imagine without a reference. Often, the shallow folds on the inner thigh are only found above the inseam (D). The jacket lapel usually curves inwards (E). At rest, the legs often angle inwards, rather than being vertical (F).

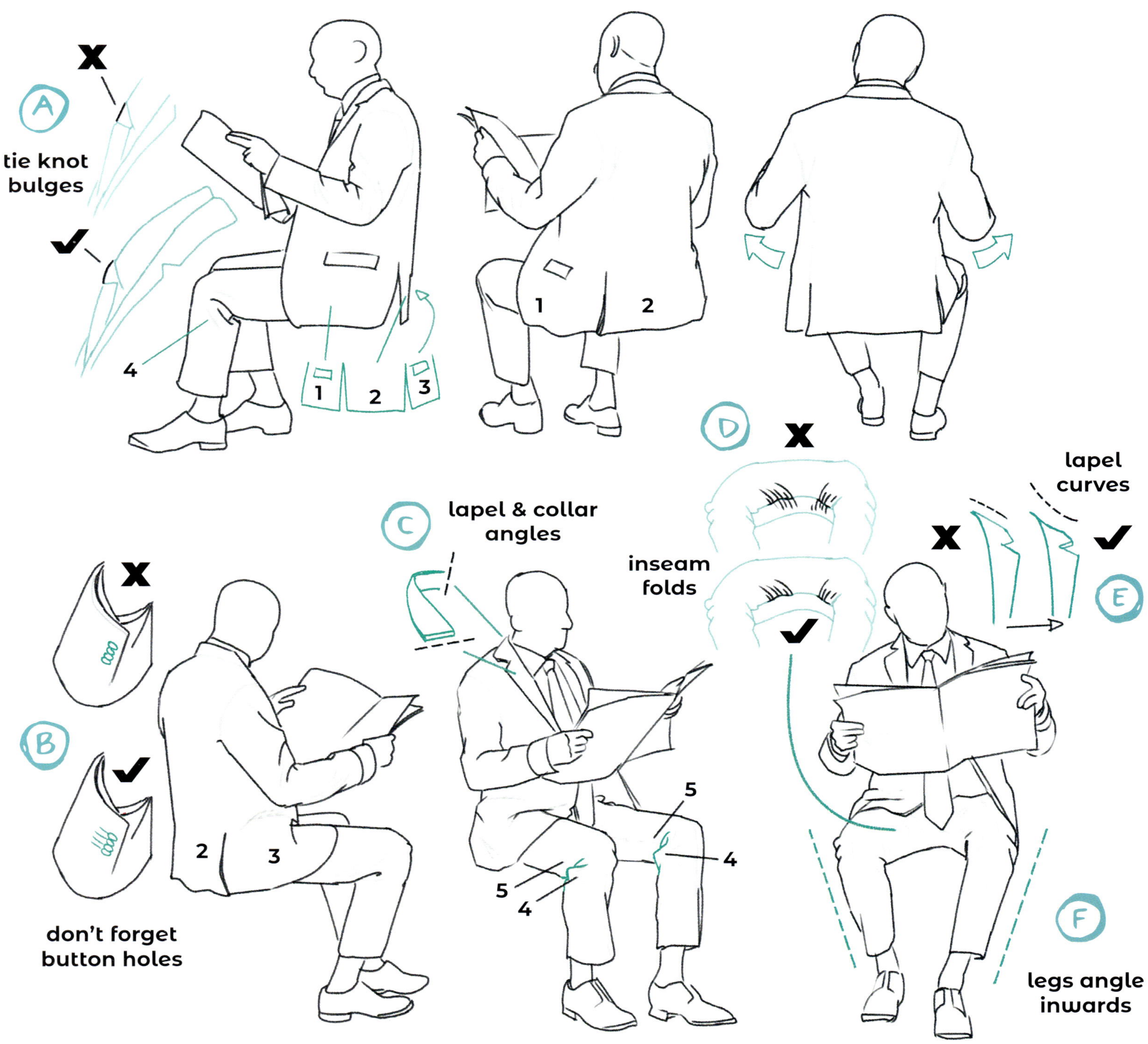

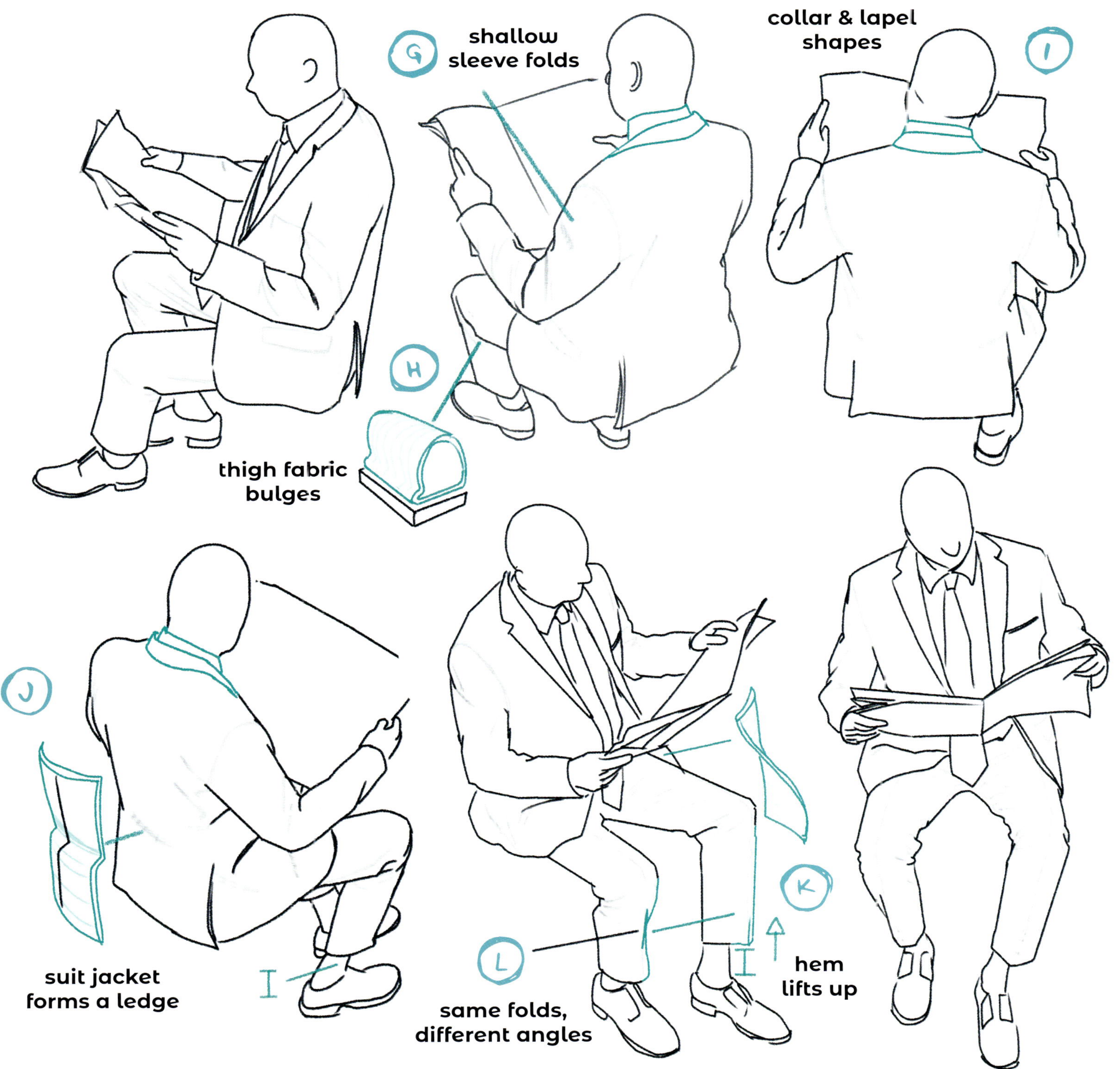

When the arms are raised out to the sides, we expect to see some shallow folding on the outer arms (G). When the thigh rests on a chair, there is often a bulging of material out to the side, near the contact point (H). This page contains some great references for collars and lapels from different angles, which aren't always easy to imagine or remember (I). A 'ledge' often forms here (J), just above the rear section of the jacket. When suit trousers 'fit' properly, the bottoms rise when sitting, revealing the socks (K). These two legs show the same form, but the closer one shows it from an interesting angle (L). With only three lines, you are able to communicate this form.

tip: ties & dress shoes

The thickness of the lapels should be evident when they sit on top of the shirt collar at the back of the neck (A). The knot of the tie shouldn't be flat and even, or sit above the collar (B). Instead, it should sit under the collar, and be irregular in shape, reflecting the pressure of the knot wrapping around the inner fabric (C). The knot should compress the part of the tie that hangs down. Add a notch into the lapels on either side, and try to show the thickness of the fabric (D). Smart shoes have a more obvious heel platform, and the back of the shoe is curved (E). When viewed from directly below, the overhang of the inner arch is clear (F). On smart shoes the laces are normally very slim, rather than chunky, and the toe is pointed rather than rounded (G).

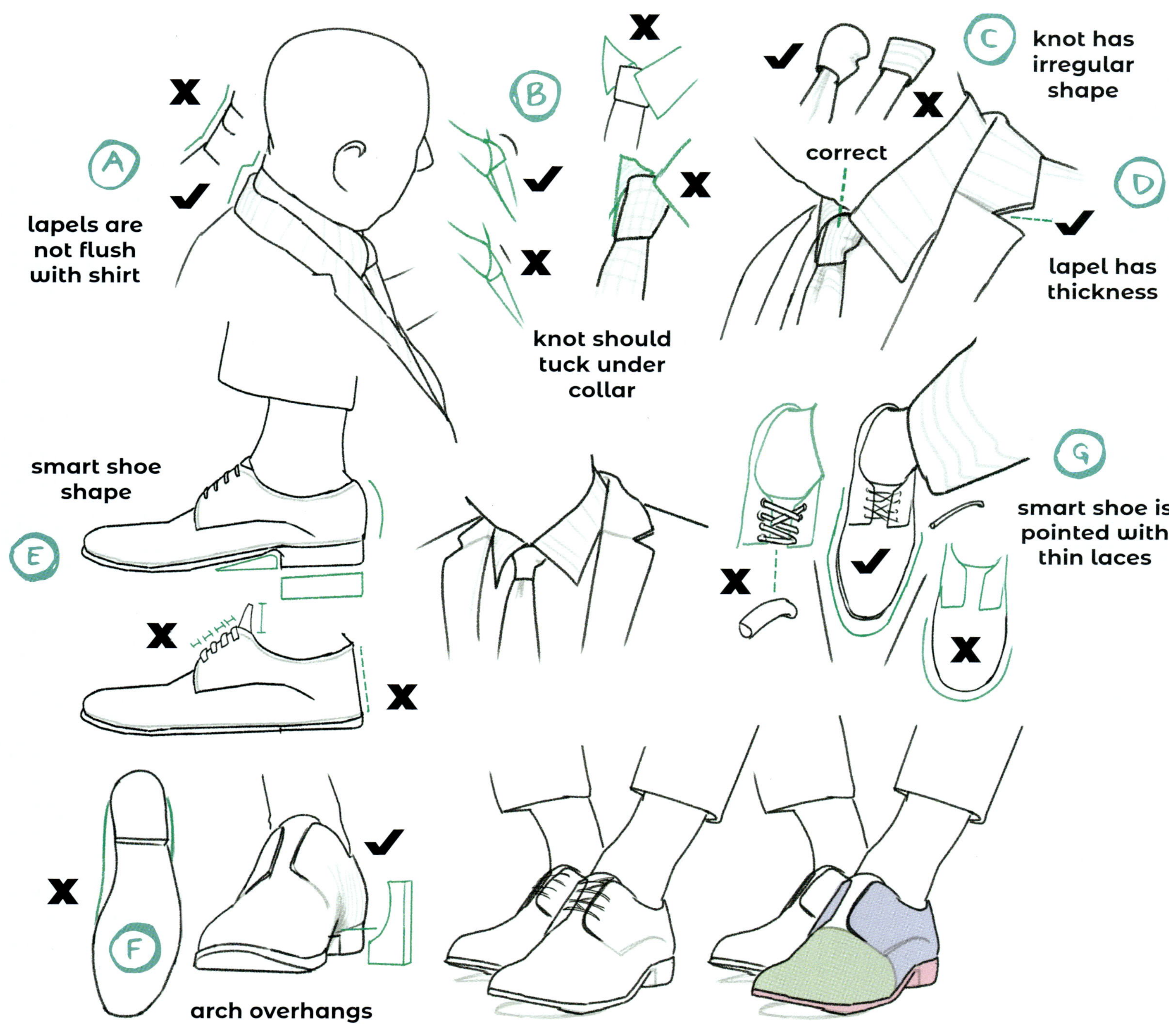

writing

When the belt is too long, the end may stick out all the way back here (A). Don't be afraid to extend this fold all the way to the knee, from the side, it shouldn't stop short (B). As we've already seen, the belt is lower at the back (C). The glutes usually form a delicate curve rather than a straight line (D). The lining of the pocket is usually reinforced to make it last longer and give it a neater edge. Because of this, it's usually more resistant than the rest of the trouser fabric. To show this, draw it more angular when it's compressed (E) rather than leaving it rounded. This shirt is fairly tight. To show this, most branches of the secondary silhouette won't travel very far internally (F). It's often more challenging to draw tighter-fitting clothing because you really need to understand the anatomy well. So, if you want to make things easier for yourself, it's generally better to rely on baggier clothing for things like background characters.

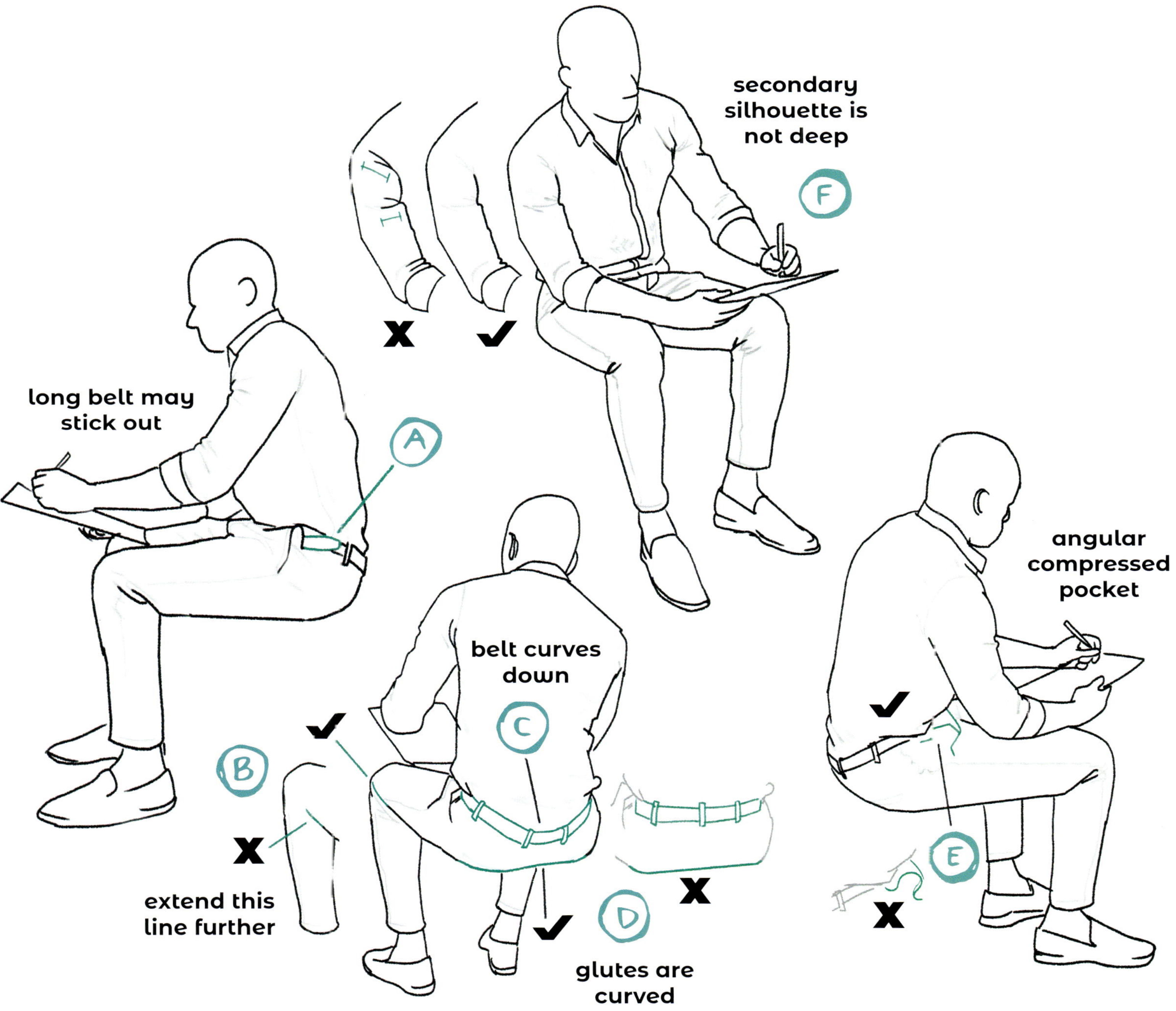

Because this shirt is a slim fit, and it's a fairly smart shirt, the material is likely quite low-resistance. It's probably quite a thin material, too. For this reason, we should pay careful attention to the fold width – folds should be narrow and close together, rather than broad and spaced out (G), which suggests a higher level of resistance. In this position (H), shirts usually hang over the belt at the front, but won't conceal the rear section of the belt. If the fabric hangs over the belt at the back (I), it will either appear loosely tucked or not be believable. When the arms are held forwards, we'll usually see strong compression on the front of the deltoids, and at the front of the arm around the elbow (J). Don't draw many folds in the gap between these areas where the biceps fills the volume.

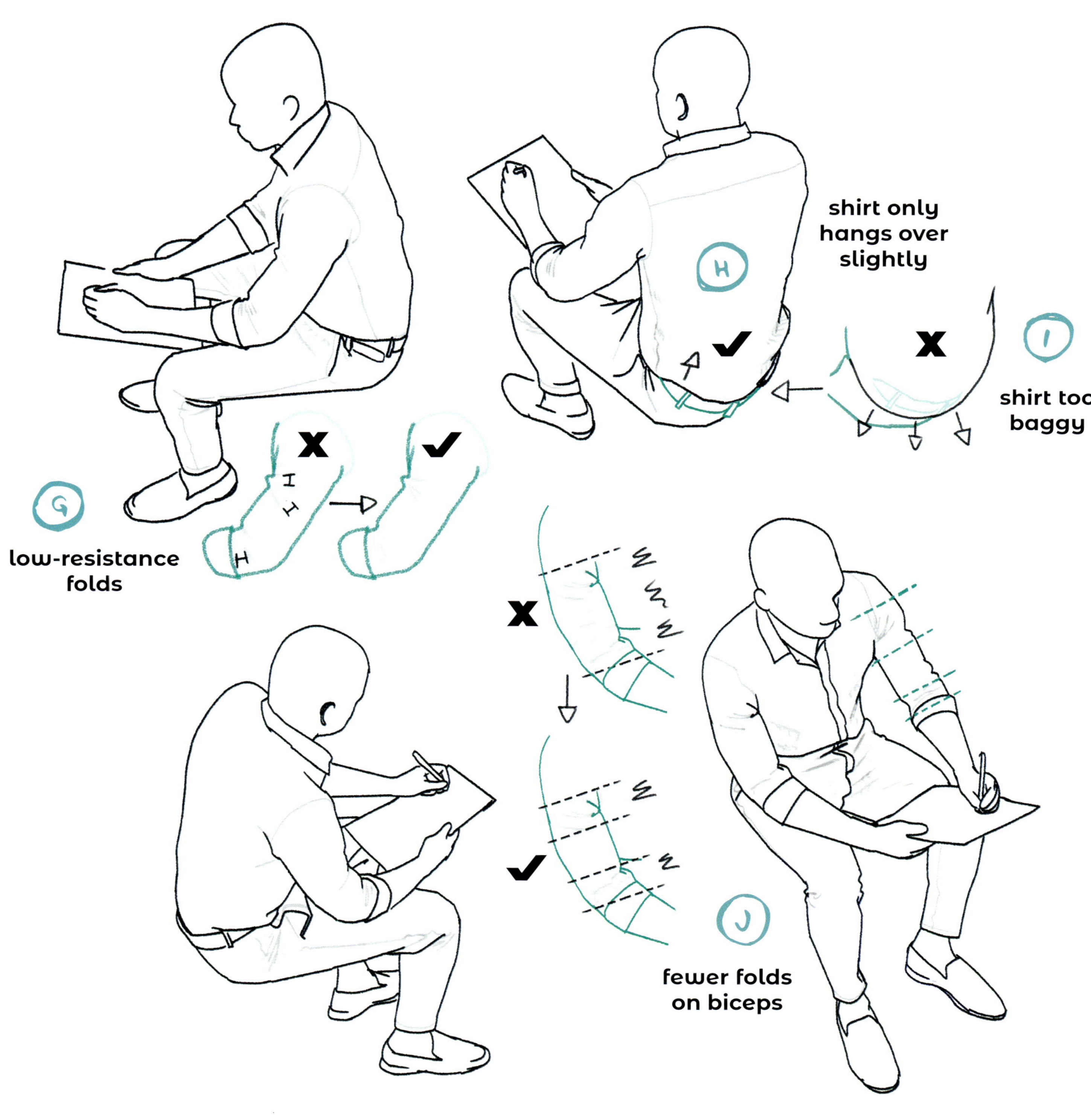

drinking coffee

In a large shirt like this, you'll often see these two lines running up and inwards towards the front of the breasts (A). In fairly fitted trousers, it's often best to leave the internal areas clear of lines (B) – unless absolutely necessary – because any folding that occurs here will be mostly small and shallow. As this shirt is so large, it has a bit more mass to it than a more fitted shirt. As a result, when the front is undone, the collar will be dragged backwards more than you'd expect (C). Also note this fold on the underside of the arm (D). This bulging fabric on the back, near the arms, is clear from multiple angles (E) This form is small, but it conveys a lot of information, so don't forget it.

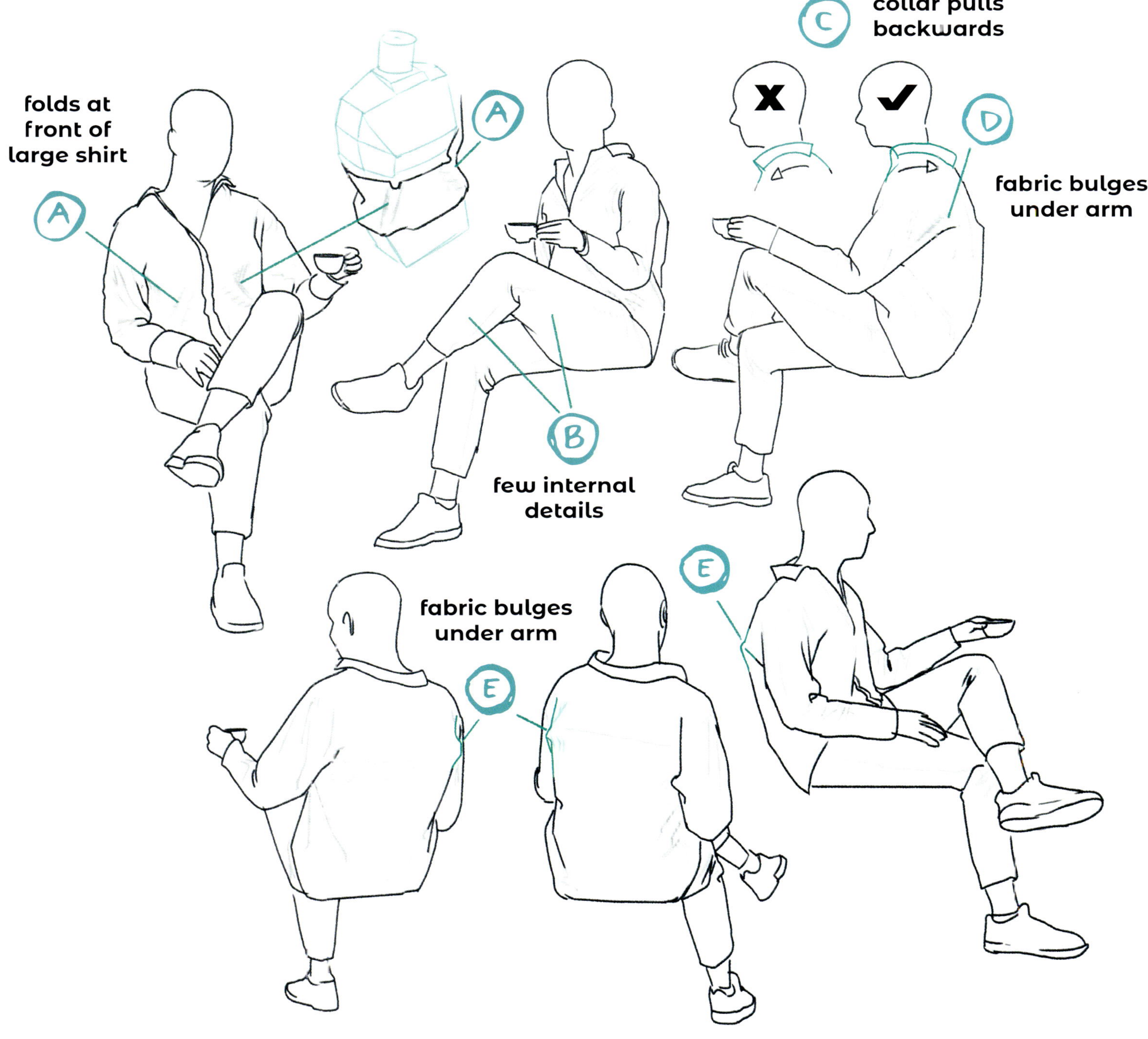

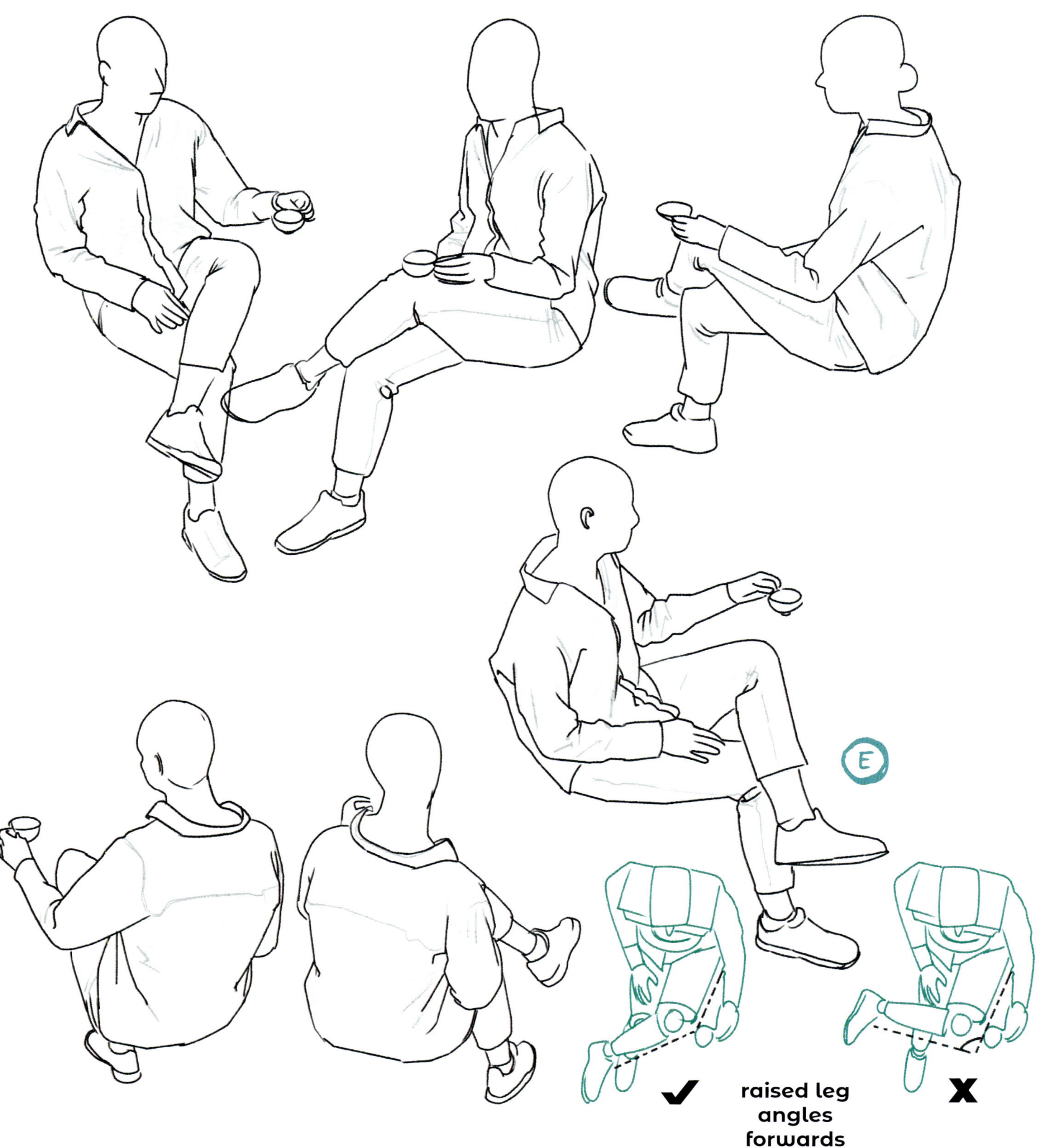

The top leg rarely sits at 90 degrees. Instead, it's more angled forwards (E).

When the arm is held forwards like this (F), there's often more of an angle to the bottom of the sleeve than you'd expect. From this angle, sometimes the shoulder is drawn 'bulging out' from the side of the torso (G). Try to avoid that, and keep them in line (H). When crossed, most people won't hold their leg perfectly horizontal. Instead, it'll be at a slight angle (I). This small fold helps indicate the slight inwards twist of the upper arm (J). In this position, the lower back is tilted backwards more than you'd expect (K).

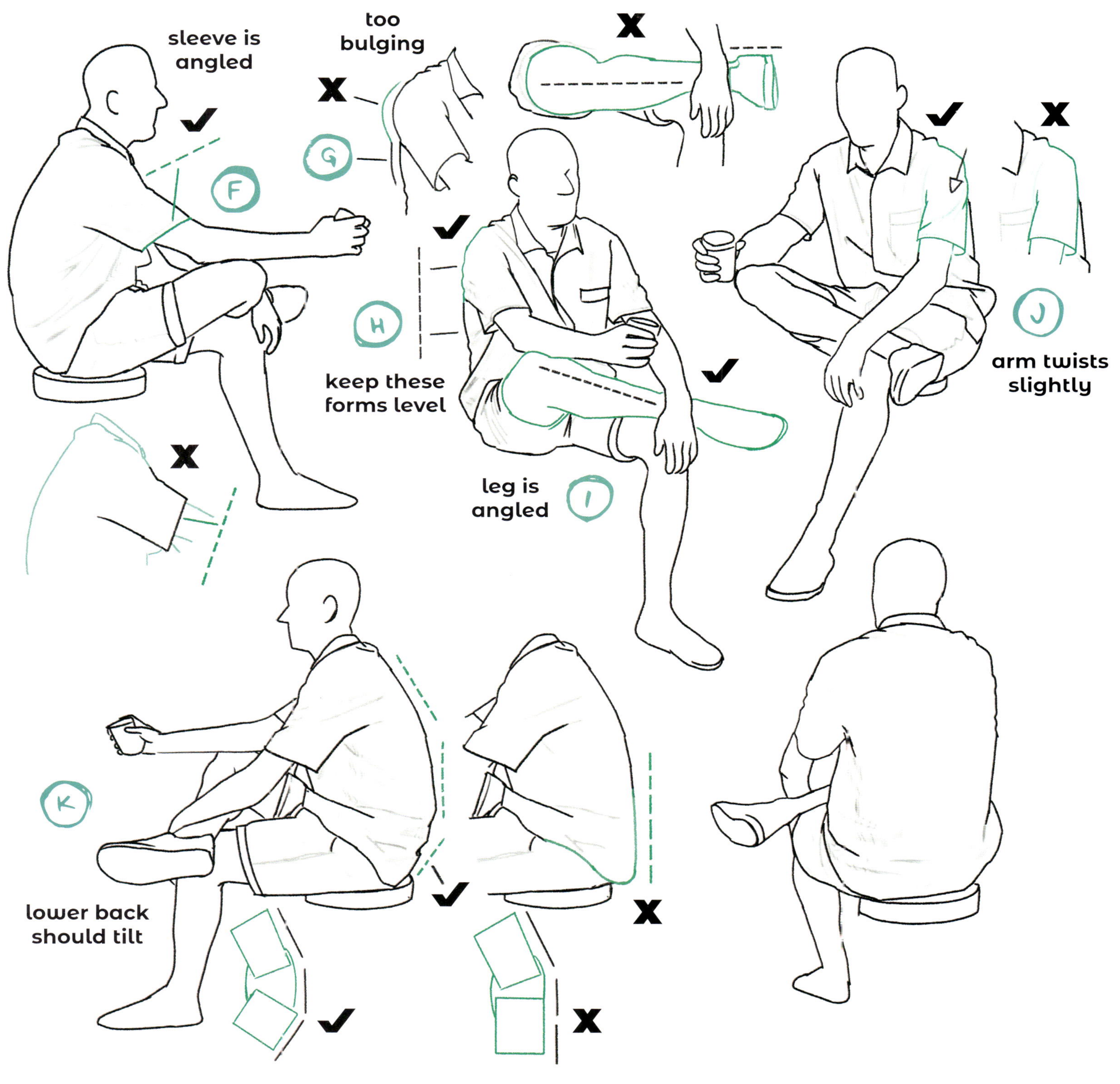

Because the arms are held forwards, the fabric just inside the arms may bulge (L). When so much material folds over itself around the front of the core, we usually see bulging at the sides of the waist (M). The fabric will bulge out furthest at the sides of the waist (N), and cling most closely to the spine at the back (O). When one leg is raised like this, a fold will appear, crossing from one thigh to the other side (P).

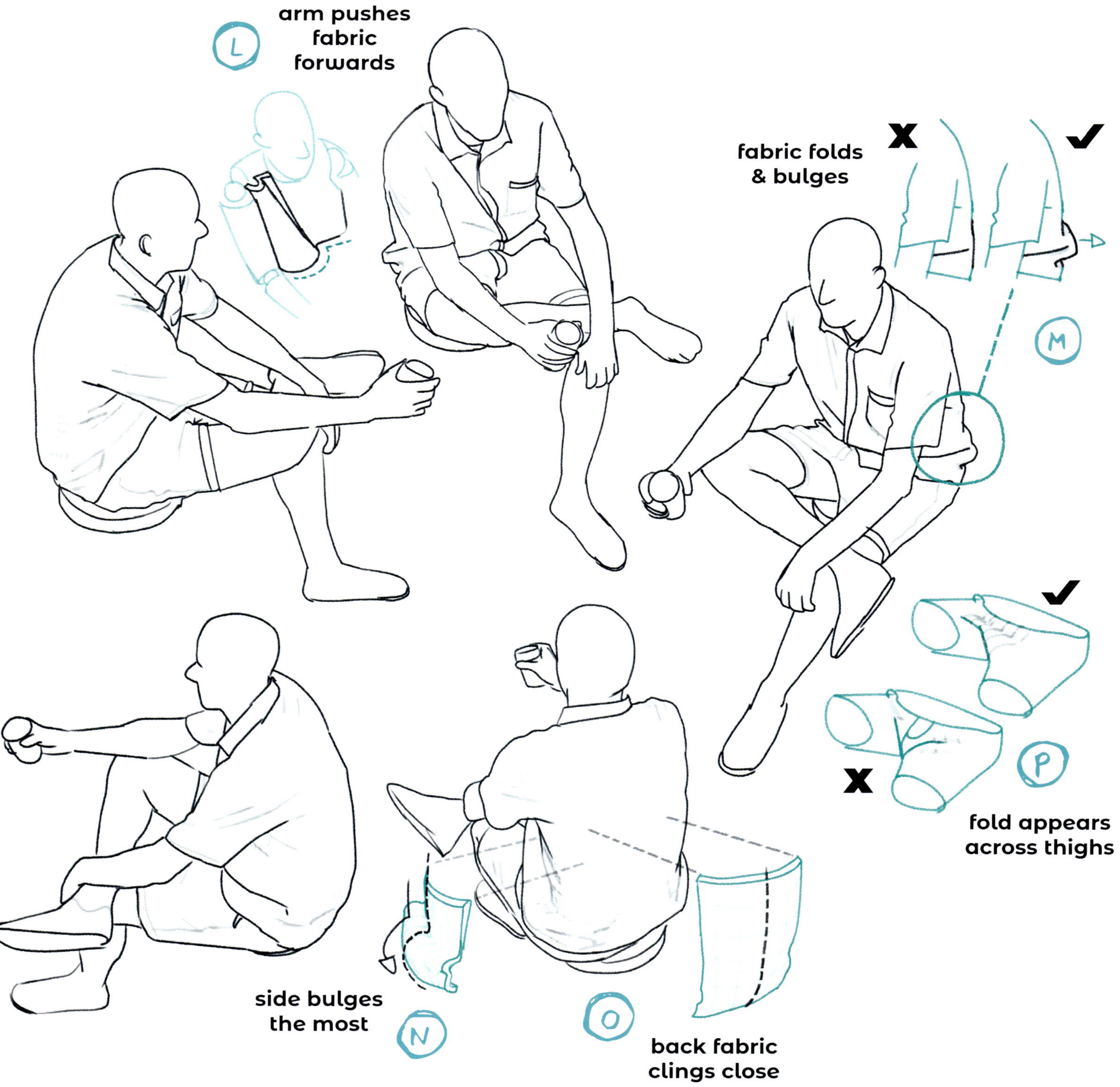

driving

When driving, the trousers often bunch up around the crotch, which causes the pockets and the fly to raise upwards (A). It's very rare that they'll sit flat (B). This line along the underside of the raised arm should almost connect to the silhouette of the back, and causes a small fold (C). The belt rarely sits vertically (D) – partly because the hips are tilted backwards – and the raised pockets are obvious from this angle (E). Finally, the collar doesn't sit on a straight line across the back, but appears to sit on the raised platform of the traps (F).

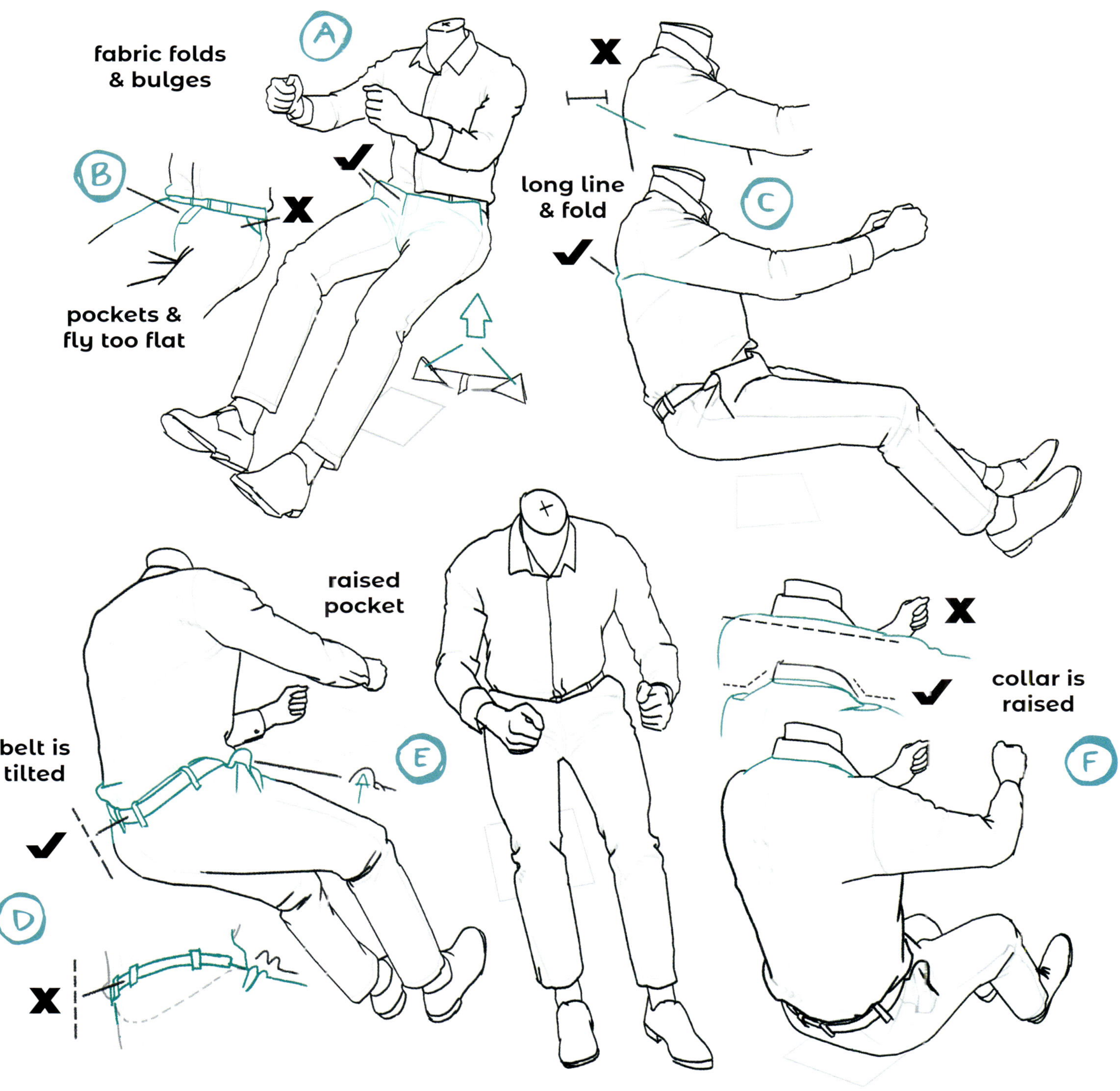

holding one leg

The belt and pockets shouldn't be drawn flat across the glutes (A). Instead, they should both curve and wrap the surface (B). The pocket covers should flare outwards, too, rather than sitting perfectly flat. When the leg is raised, avoid drawing the pocket too flat, as it often bulges upwards (C). When the shin of one leg rests on the knee of the other, don't draw the material like this (D). It should deform, to reflect the pressure applied to it, and fold into itself once or twice (E). You can draw this as a single fold or have it fold over itself twice – whichever you prefer (F).

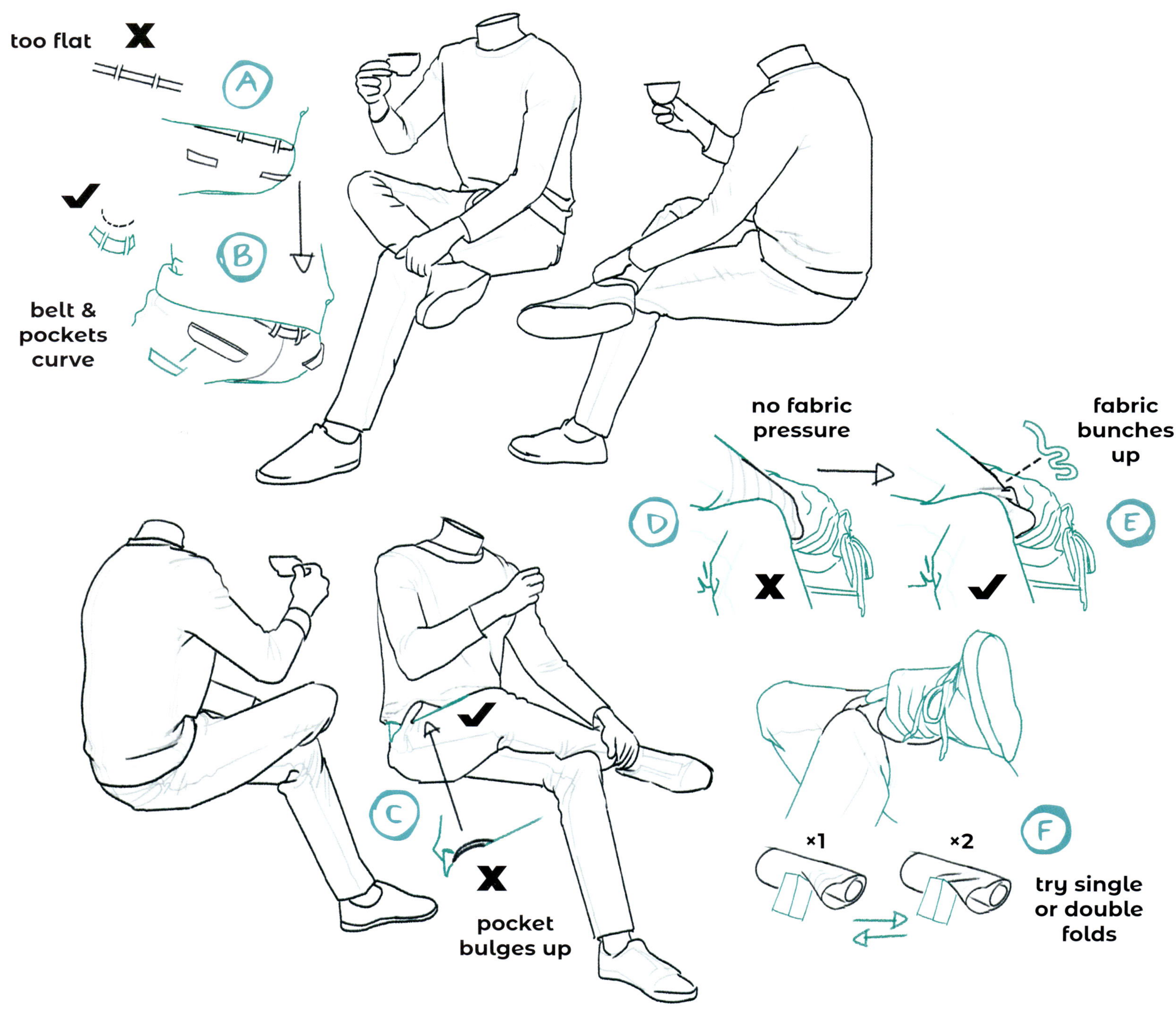

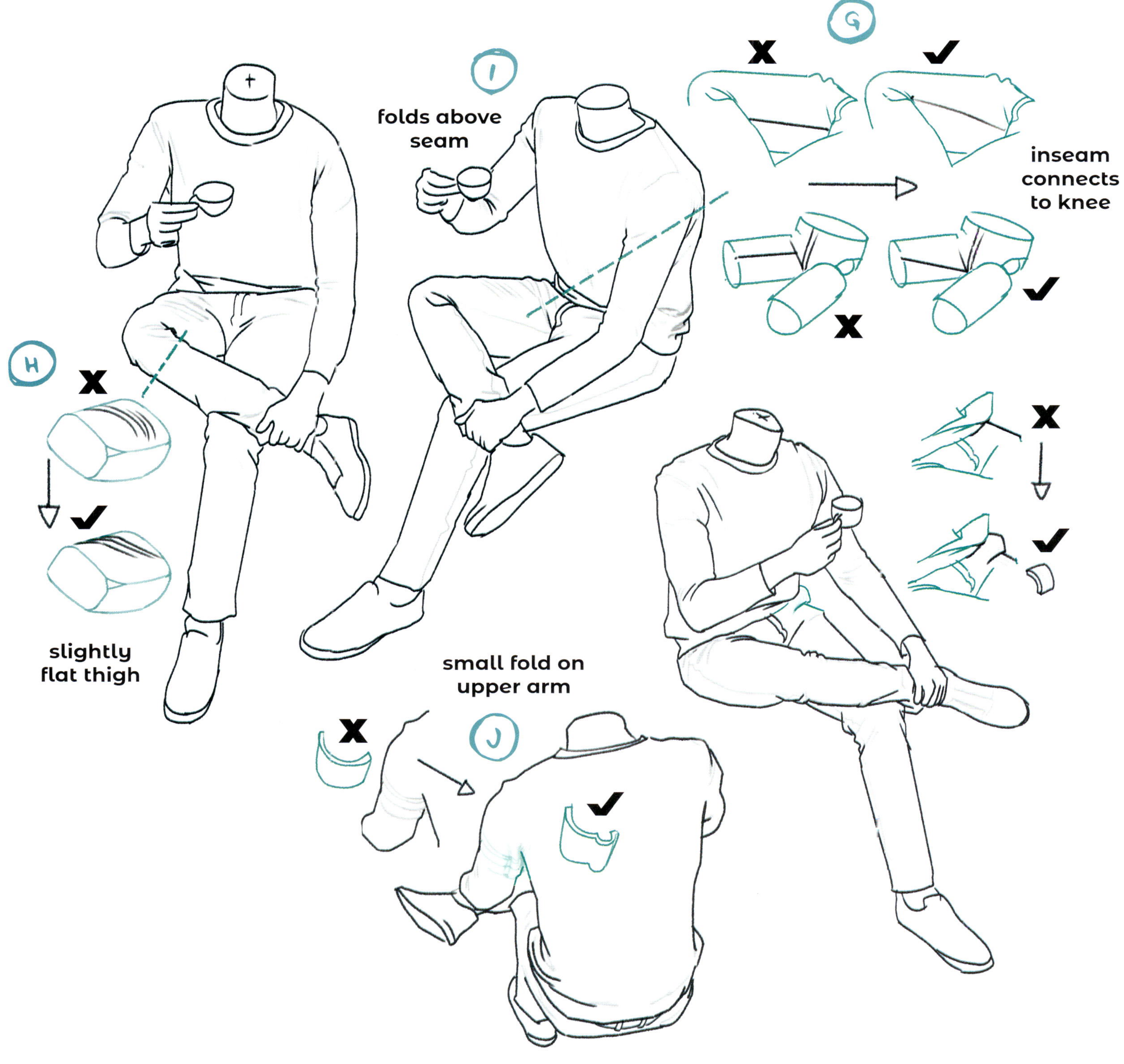

The seam on the inside of the thigh shouldn't run straight across the leg, but instead connect under the fly to the side of the knee (G). When the thigh is raised, the inside surface isn't cylindrical, but has a slightly flattened shape (H). In this pose, you'll often see shallow folds on the inside of the thigh. Keep them above the seam, rather than below it (I). The lowered arm often shows the pressure between the back of the arm and the torso. Don't draw the drapery fully rounded on the upper arm. Instead, add this small pressure fold (J).

phone call

When the shirt is heavily compressed around the core, the two plackets of the shirt often twist and separate rather than remaining on top of each other (A). You'll usually need some sort of buckle here to allow for adjustment – easily forgotten (B). The strap itself usually runs through a sort of 'tube' of thicker material (C), which is designed to sit over the top, or just behind the shoulder (D).

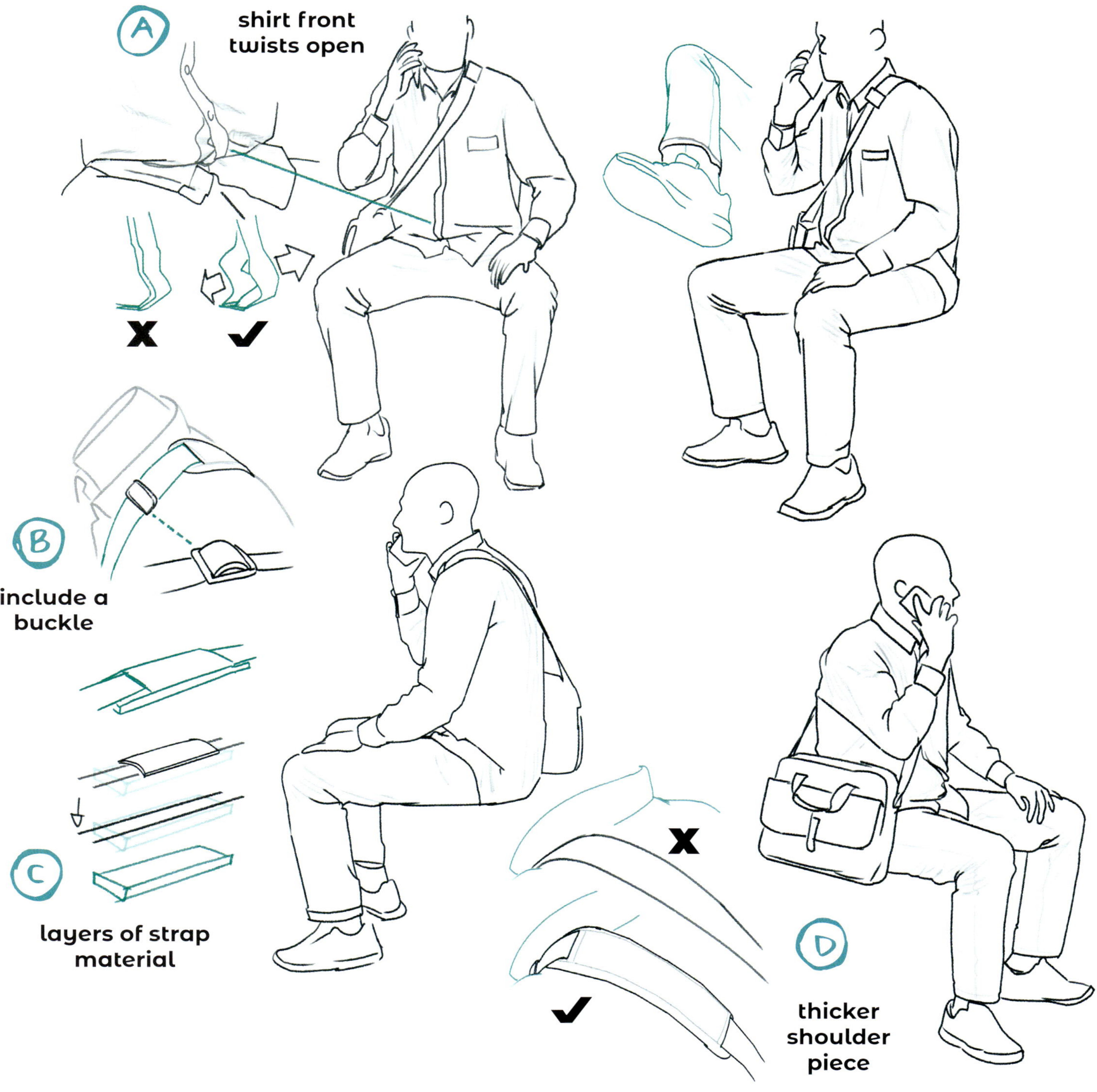

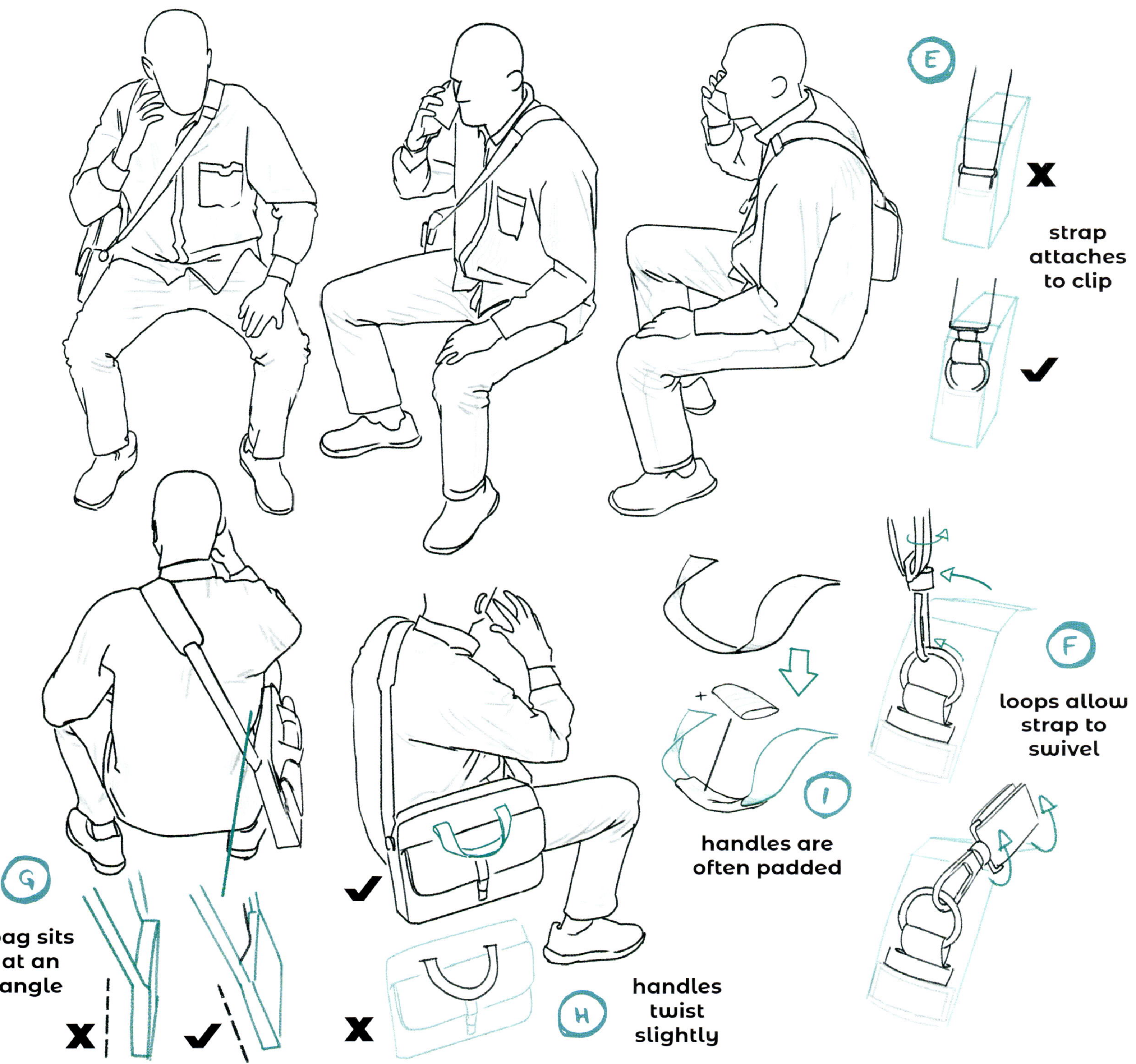

Bag straps like this don't attach straight into the sides of a bag (E). Instead, they usually end in a loop that connects to a clip with a swivel on it. This allows the whole connection to move in multiple directions, and the strap to twist (F). Seen from the side, this bag will rarely be vertical (G), and the shirt above it will overlap slightly. The carry handles shouldn't be drawn as simple loops (H), but will twist as they fall down, and usually have a loop of padded material to make the handle more comfortable (I).

sitting cross-legged

With baggier trousers, the crotch often extends out to form a 'shelf' (A), rather than sitting flat (B). This shelf extends further at the top/front, and then curves inwards. When one arm is brought forwards, the sleeve forms this teardrop shape rather than a simple curve (C). Some oversized T-shirts have thick collars, which makes them more resistant. When one arm is brought back, the collar may deform and bend out (D).

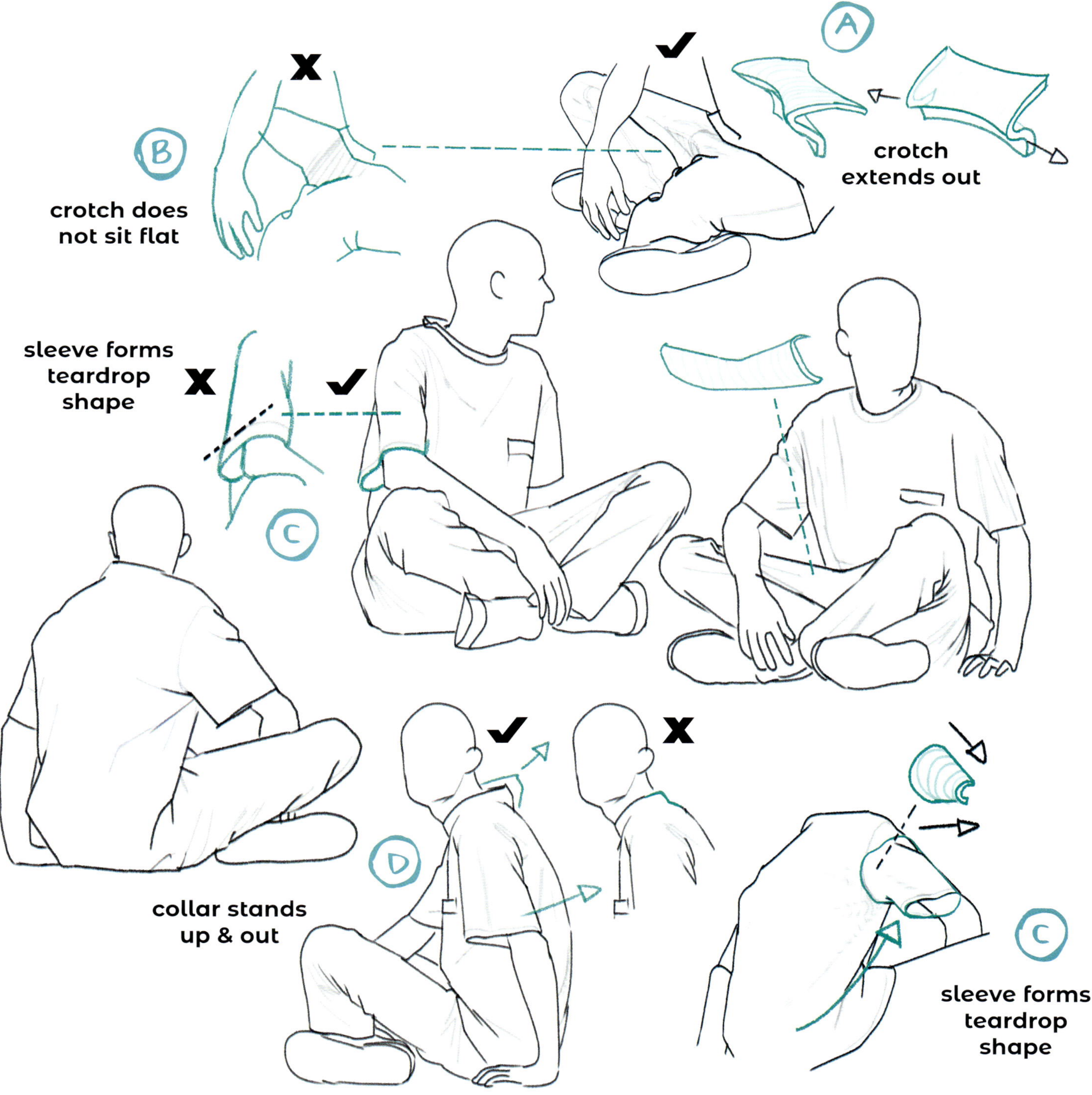

On a T-shirt with an 'oversized' fit, the bottom of the sleeve is rarely straight. When the arm is brought forwards, like this, you'll usually see a curve here (E). When sitting on the floor, the forward fold of the torso is strong. Keep the folding on the front of the torso angular, rather than using a series of curved folds (F). This line behind the arm will usually sit lower than you'd expect (G). When one arm is held back, suggest some pressure between the back of the upper arm (triceps), and the shoulder blades (scapulae) (H).

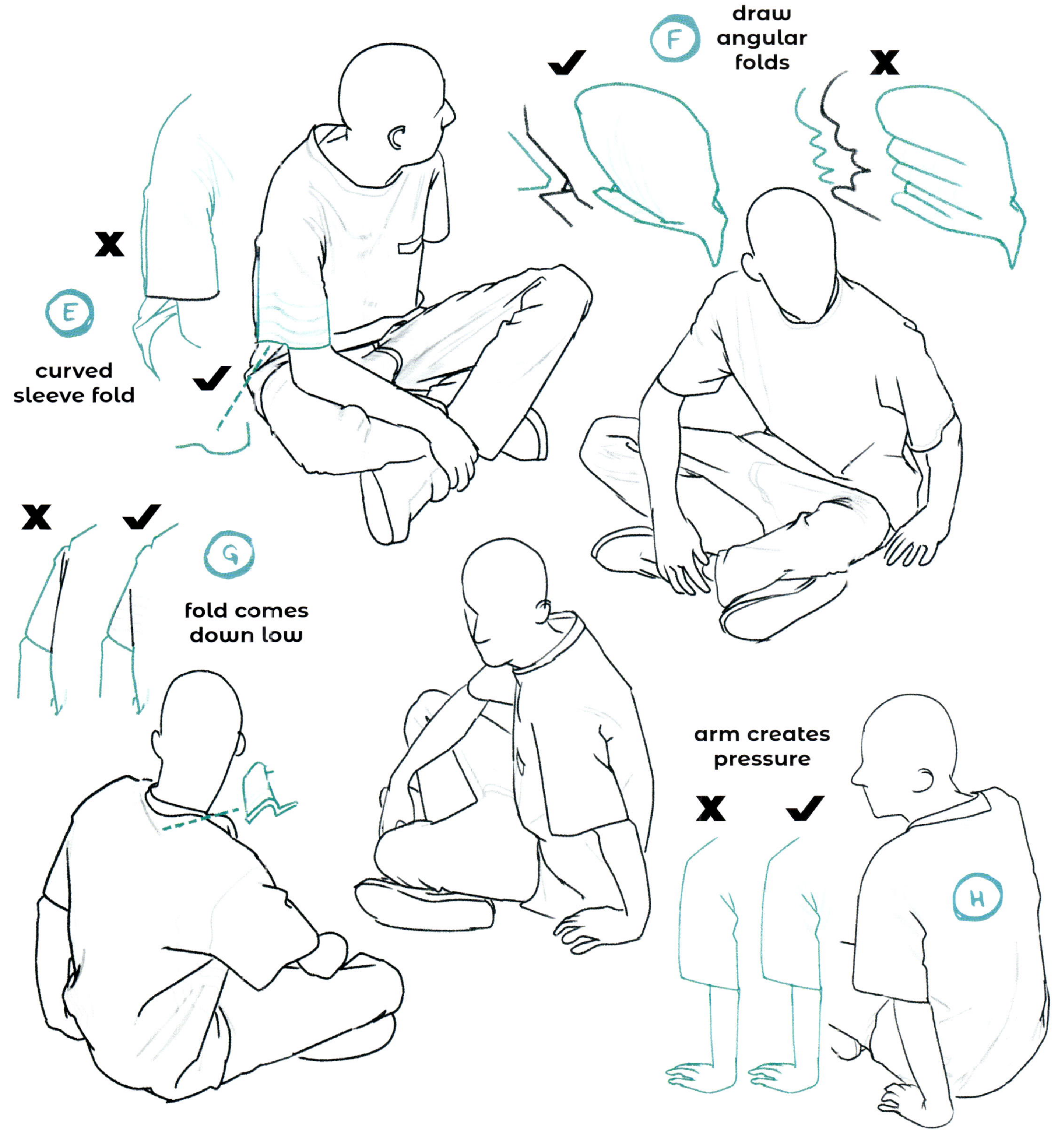

leaning back

When the legs are crossed, the feet aren't an even distance from the hips. Both legs rest on top of the feet, but one is necessarily in front of the other (A). The elbows will usually be close to the sides, with the hands a little further apart. This gives the impression of the arms splaying out (B). As usual, the most intense folding occurs below the chest, and the upper area is quite free from folds (C).

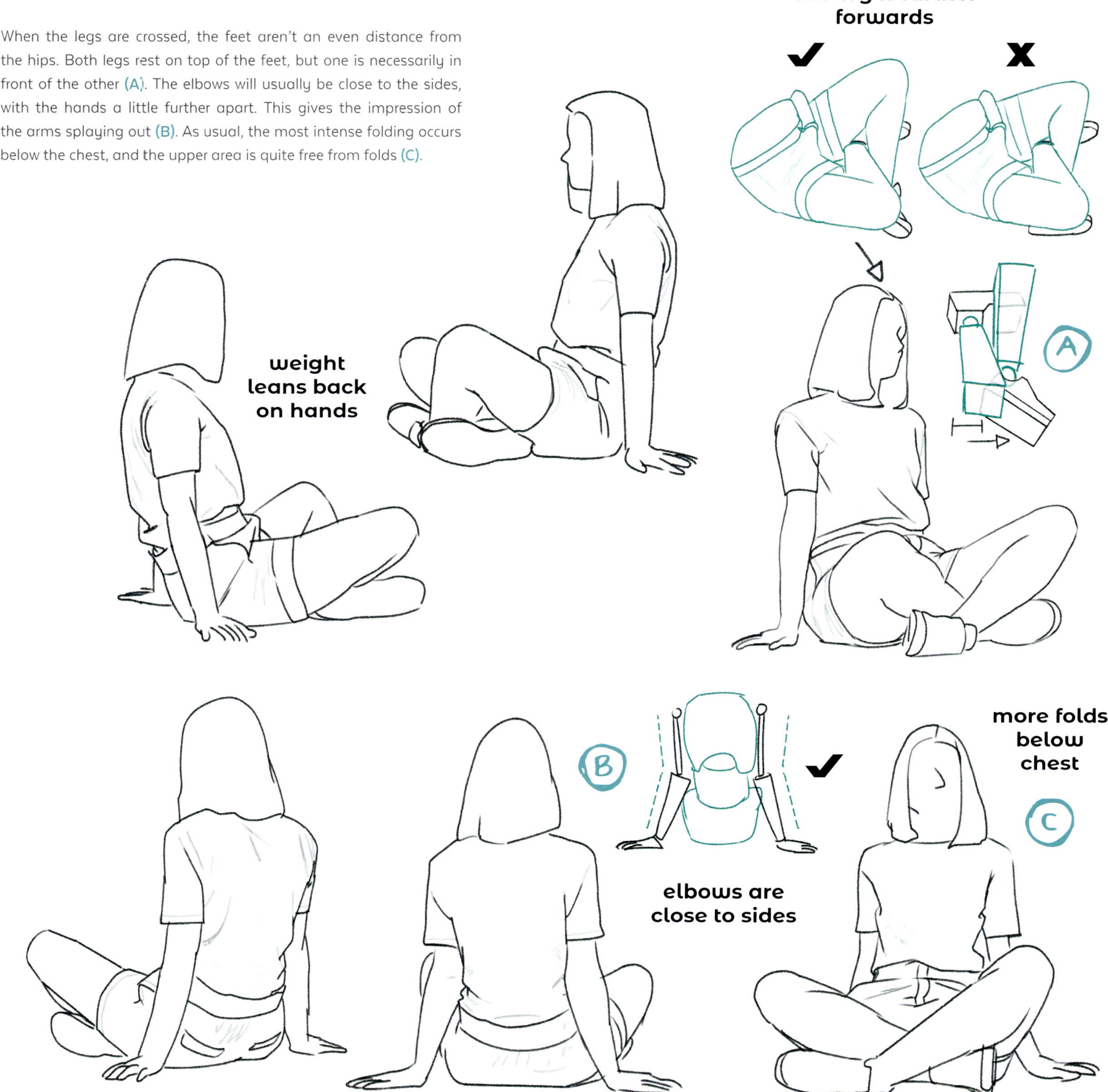

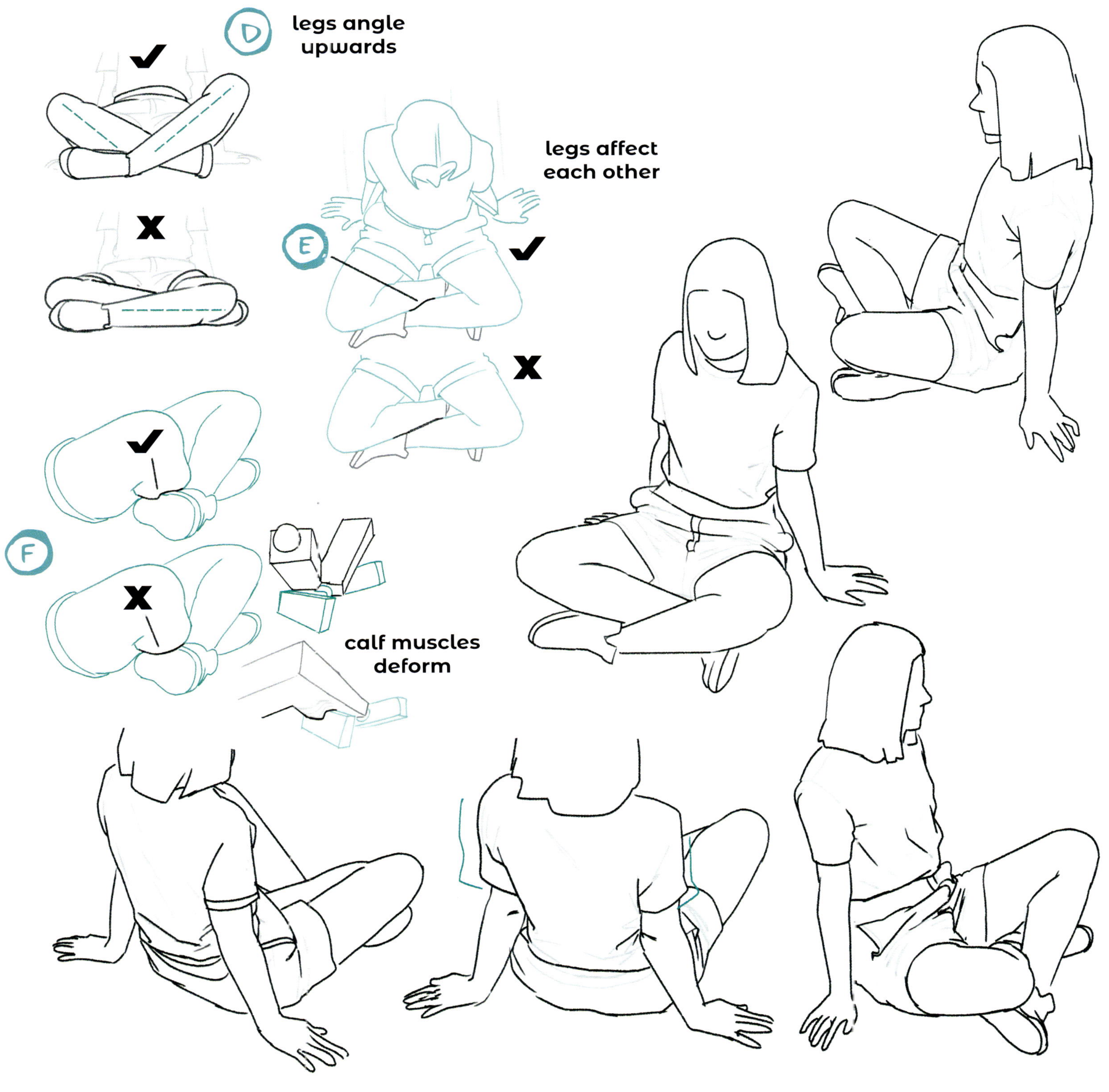

When sitting on the ground like this, the legs are usually angled rather than flat (D). Try to convey the weight of the top leg resting on the bottom. Often this is done through very small adjustments to the silhouette of the legs (E). Ideally, the weight of the leg resting on the foot is also obvious, as the calf muscles might deform slightly (F).

When the legs are bent, you rarely see folds radiating out evenly (G). Instead, there are usually fewer on the thigh, and more on the calf side of the knee (H). Viewed from in front, these folds don't always wrap inwards, but often turn in the other direction (I). When one leg is raised, there's usually a fairly large 'wedge' of material connecting the two thighs. You'll rarely see a form like this (J), as more often the crotch will fold like this (K). The top's fabric is often pushed into the centre by any raised pockets (L).

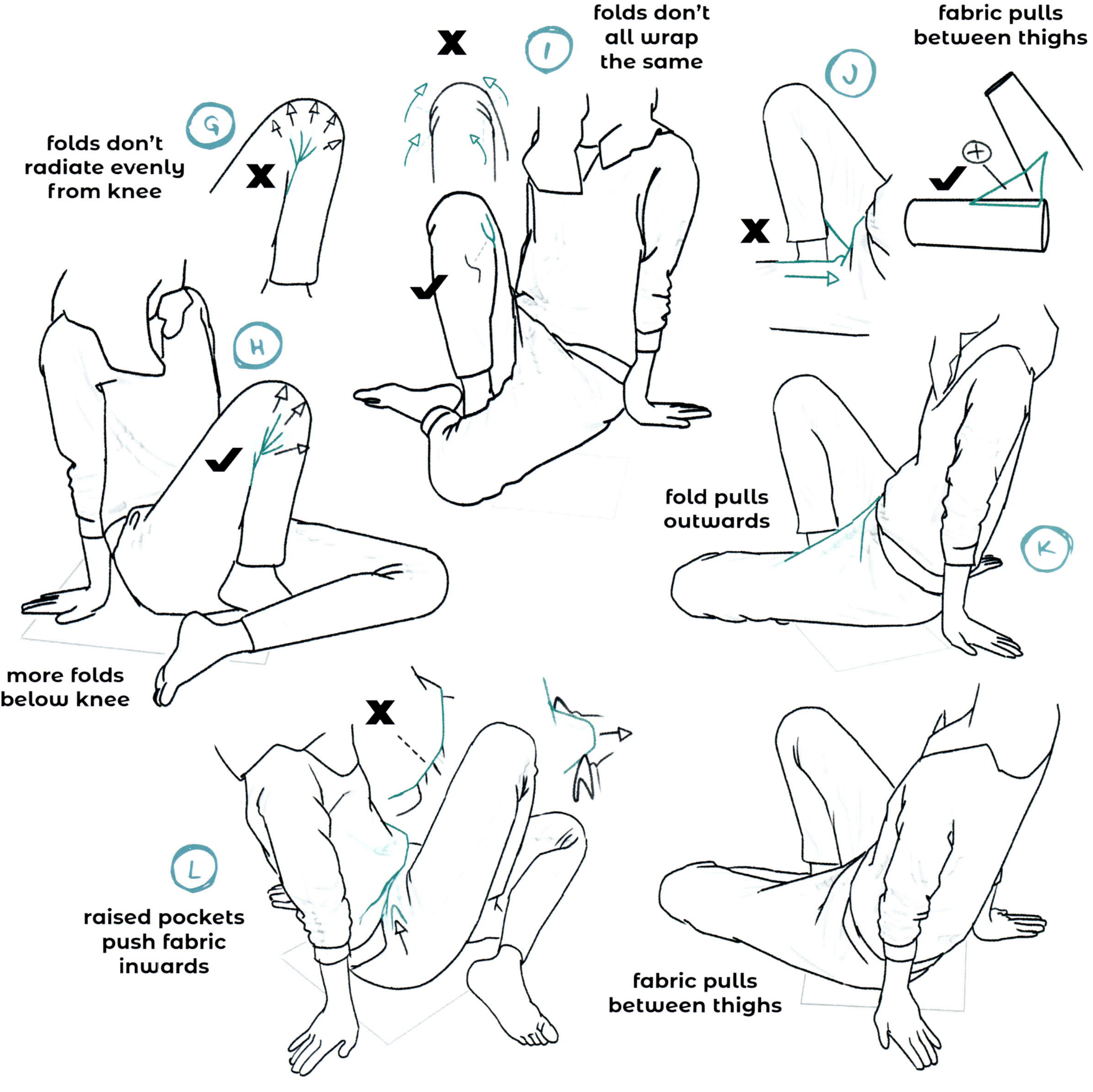

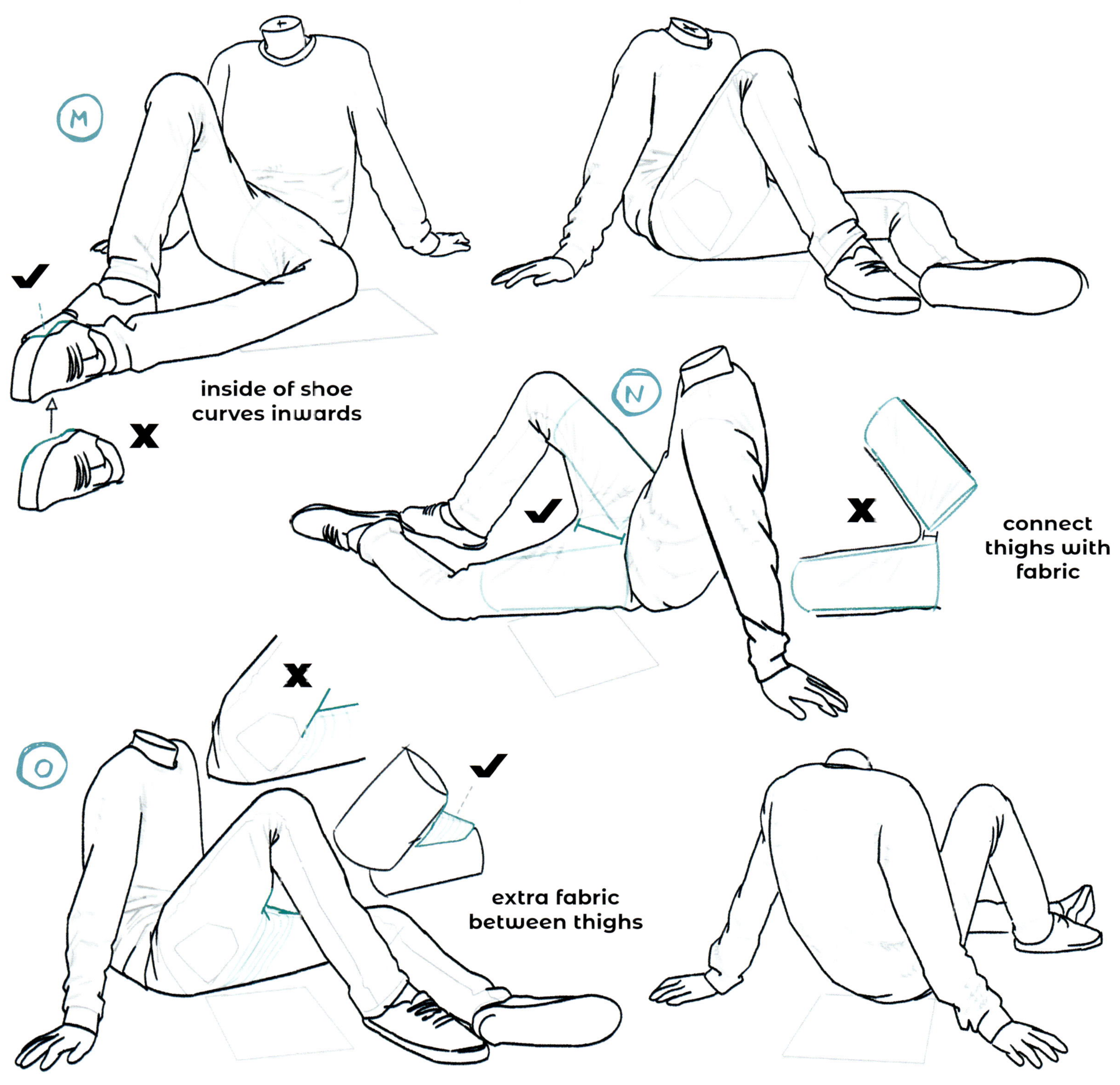

From the side, part of the inside sole of a shoe often seems to disappear (M). Again, allow for excess fabric around the crotch to connect the thighs when held apart (N). When viewed from below, this fabric is more clearly seen (O).

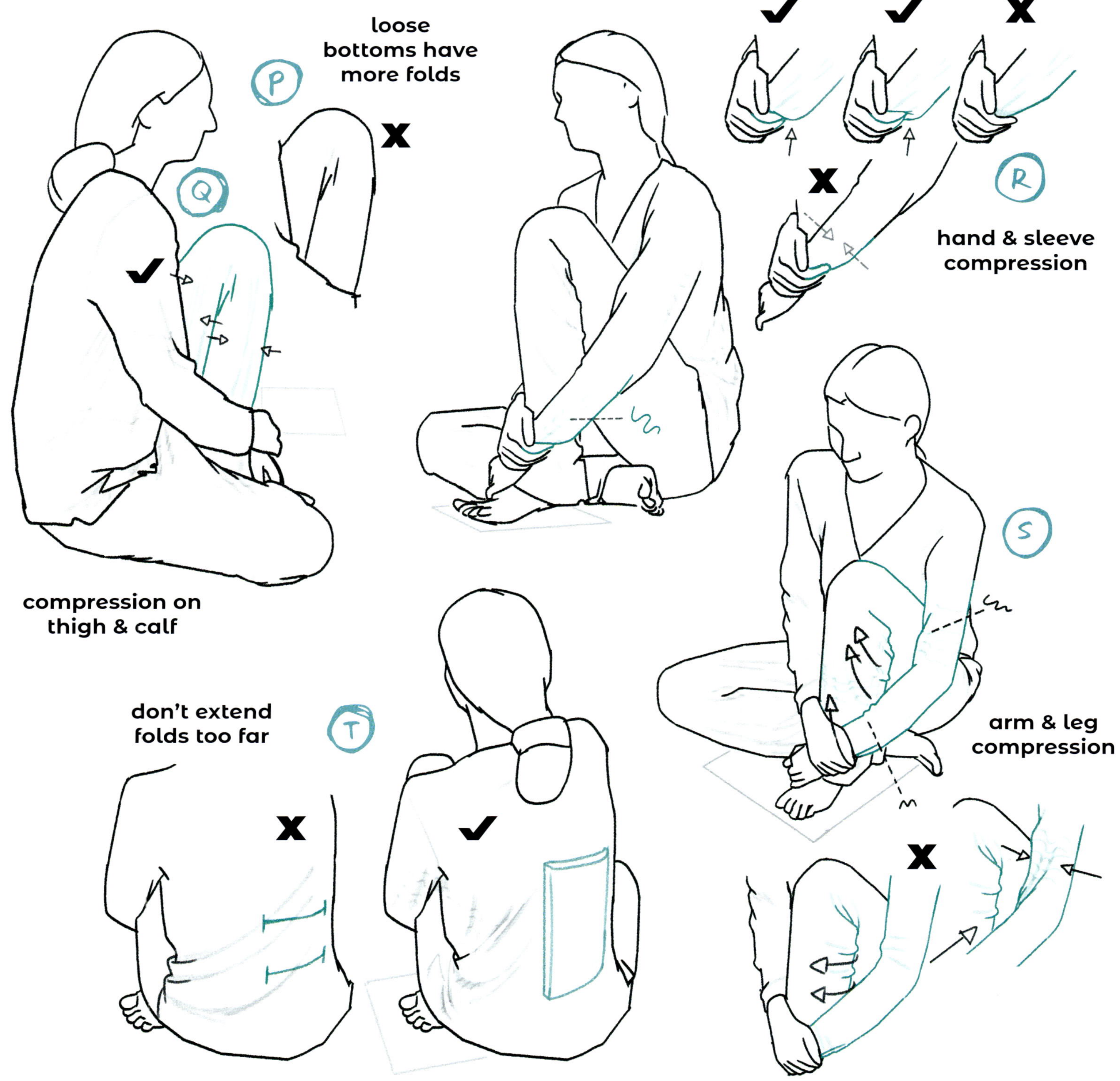

In looser garments, like pyjama bottoms, the compression of a bent leg spreads out to affect the whole limb, rather than just one point (P). In this context, you'll often find shallow folding across the thigh and calf (Q). The challenging thing about drawing a character like this is that all the limbs are interacting and compressing each other in different directions. For example, the hand is gripping the sleeve (R). Make sure that there some clear overlaps and shallow folding to show that the hand is holding on to the wrist rather than just sitting on top. The folded leg is also pressing hard against the inside of this arm (S). When drawing a slight lean to one side, avoid drawing diagonals the whole way across the figure. Keep them mostly on one side (T).

sitting on a sofa

When the arms are held back, tension is created across the top of the chest, which causes shirts to pull open slightly (A). This tension isn't present further down. When the legs are raised, the pockets open far enough that you can often see slightly inside them (B). The main folds across the top of the thighs occur near the fly (C). Don't draw them extending too far down. The region around the fly folds upwards, and the pockets are usually raised slightly behind the fly region (1, 2, 3) (D). Because the hips are still tilted backwards, the belt will be angled back, too.

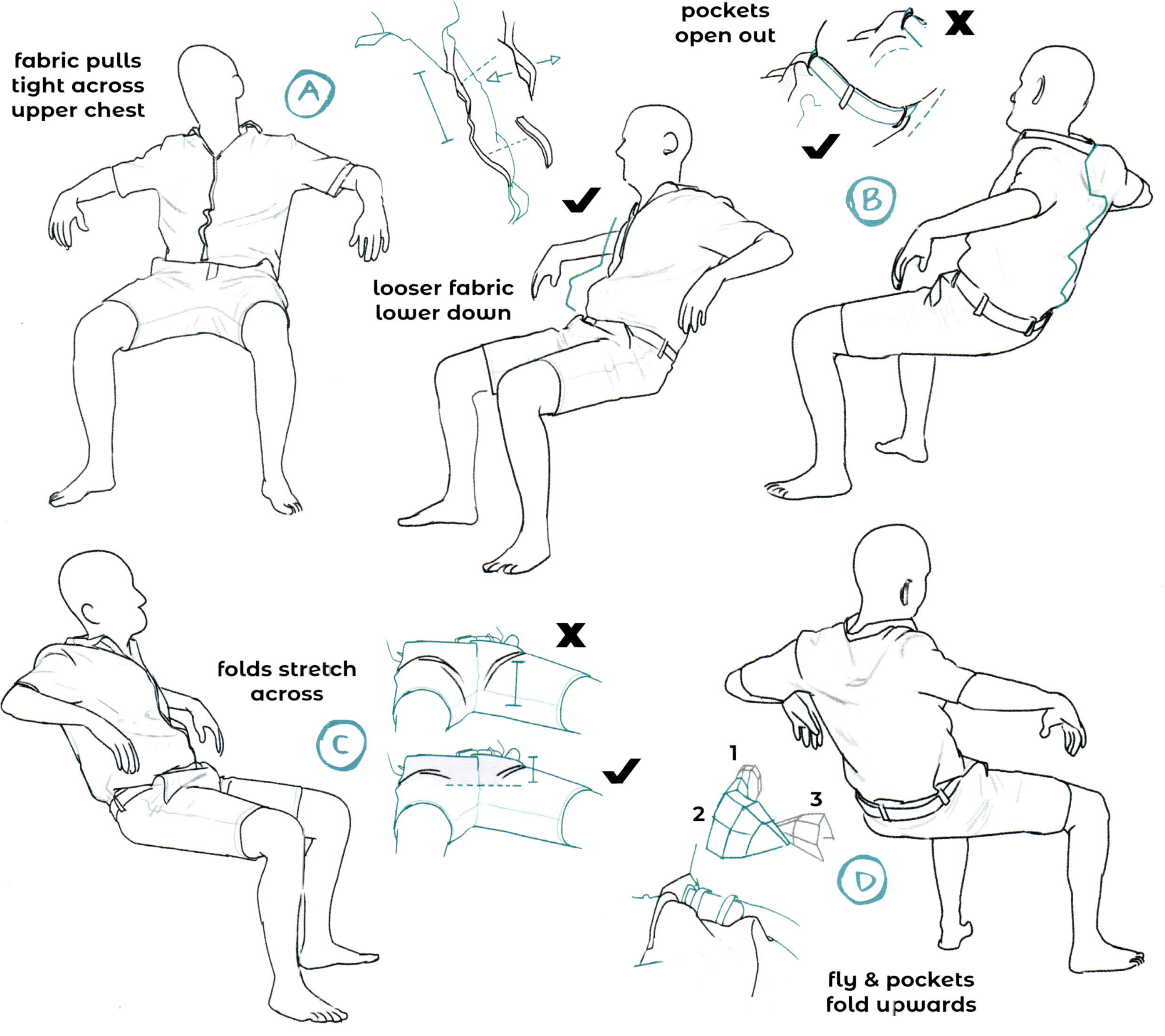

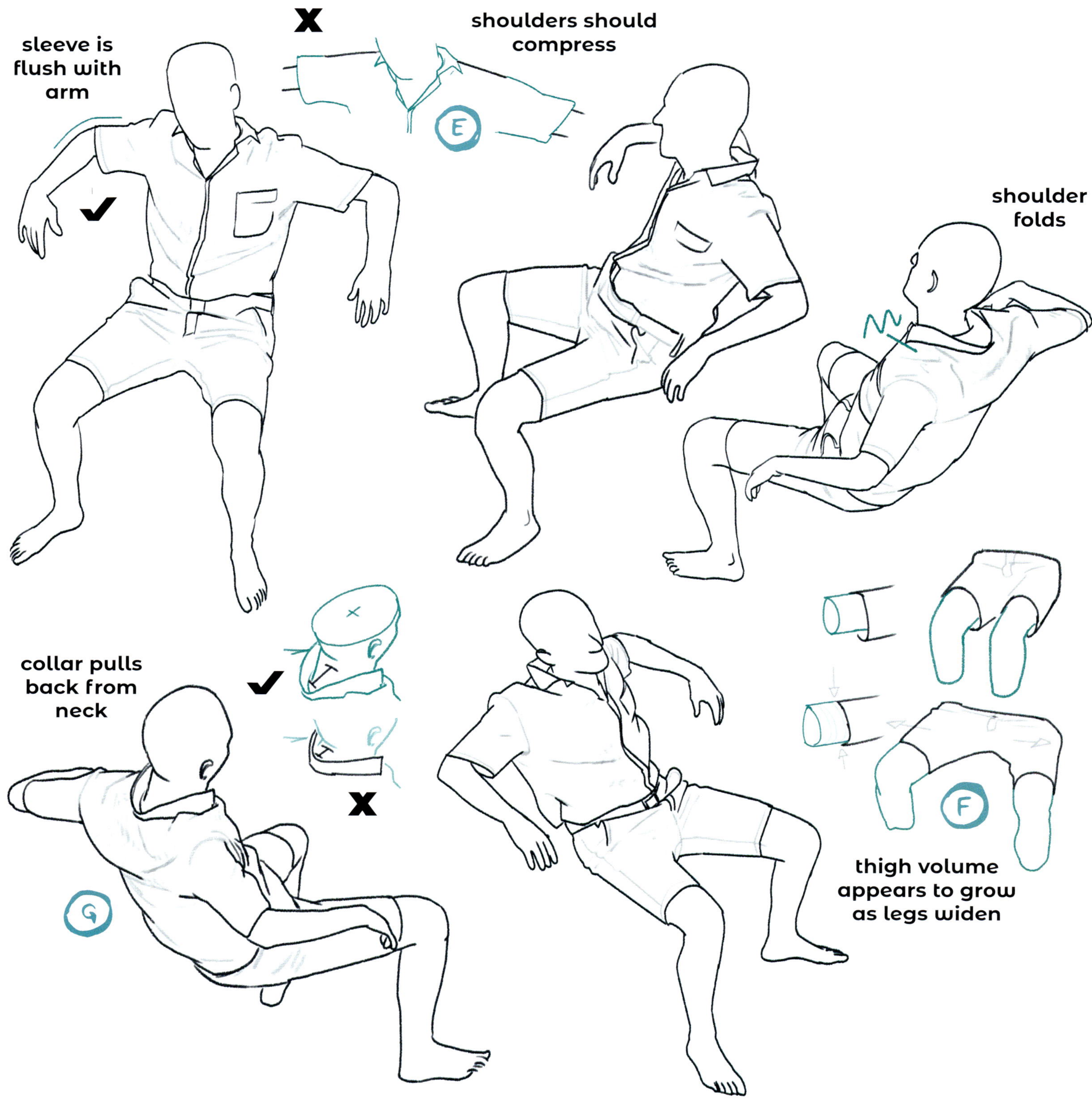

With the arms raised, compression must be shown across the top of the shoulders, and the sleeves should join into the arm almost seamlessly (E). When the legs are held apart like this, shorts and trousers often appear to tighten (F). Because the arms are also moving back, the collar will be compressed into more of a V-shape, and will move away from the neck (G).

hands behind head

When the arms are held behind the head, the roundness of the chest is clear (A). Viewed from above (B), most of the folding should occur at the top and bottom, with the central section left relatively clear. Viewed from the side, the folds along the underside should sweep up from the lower back to the front of the shoulder (C). With the legs held slightly apart, shallow folding will fan out rather than stretch directly across (D).

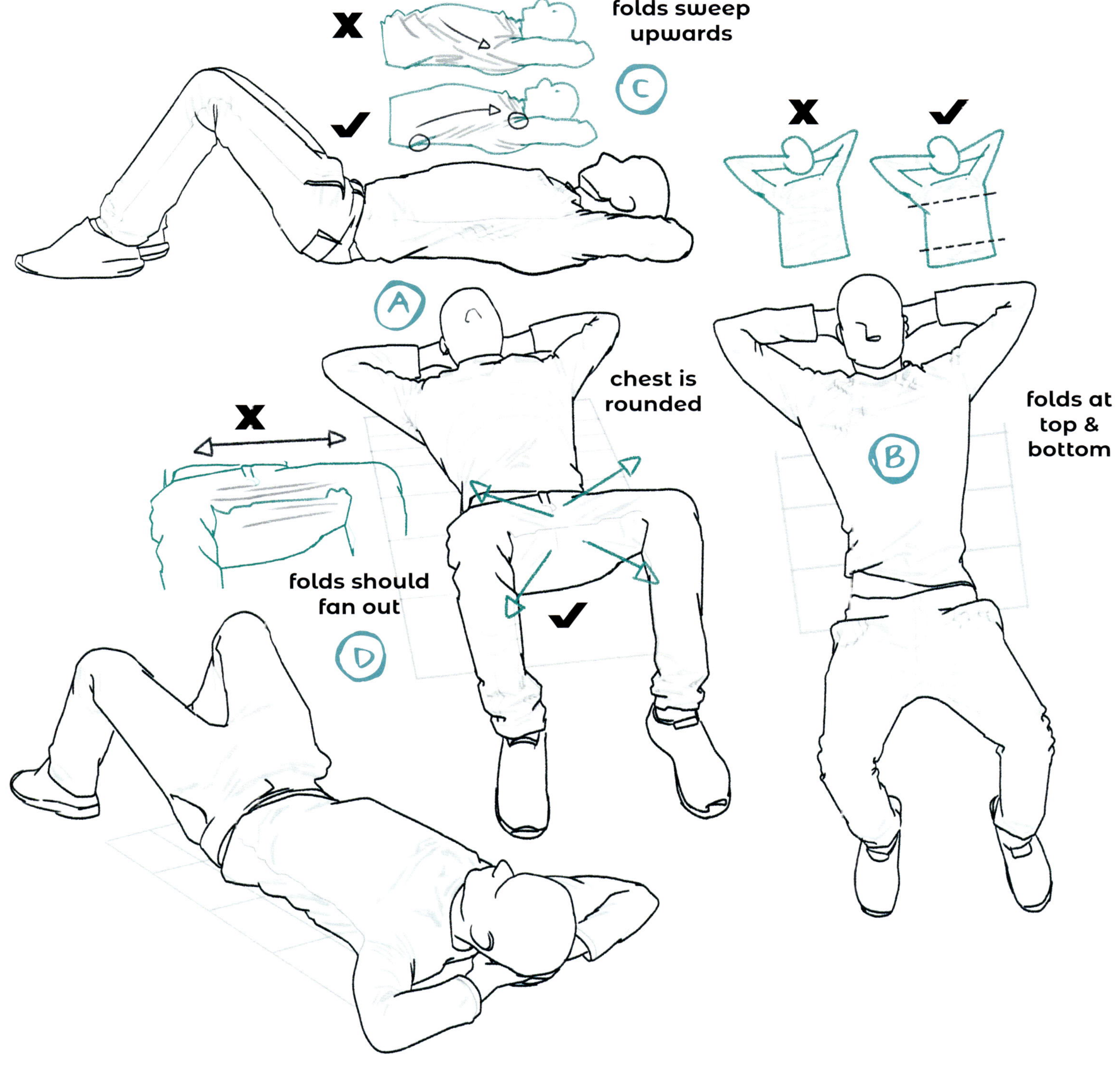

sleeping on your side

When the legs are stacked on top of each other, they lose some of their roundness and bulge out to the sides (A). When the arm drops down, the roundness of the ribcage should force it to narrow near the top (B). The material below it often bulges out rather than dropping straight down. The bottom of a longer jacket or coat shouldn't sit smoothly on the curve of the glutes, but often becomes wavy and supports its own weight (C). The upper back usually sits on an angle rather than vertically (D). The bottom arm often falls down on an angle rather than sitting under the bent arm (E). The folds across the side of the core sweep up to the underarm rather than wrapping evenly (F).

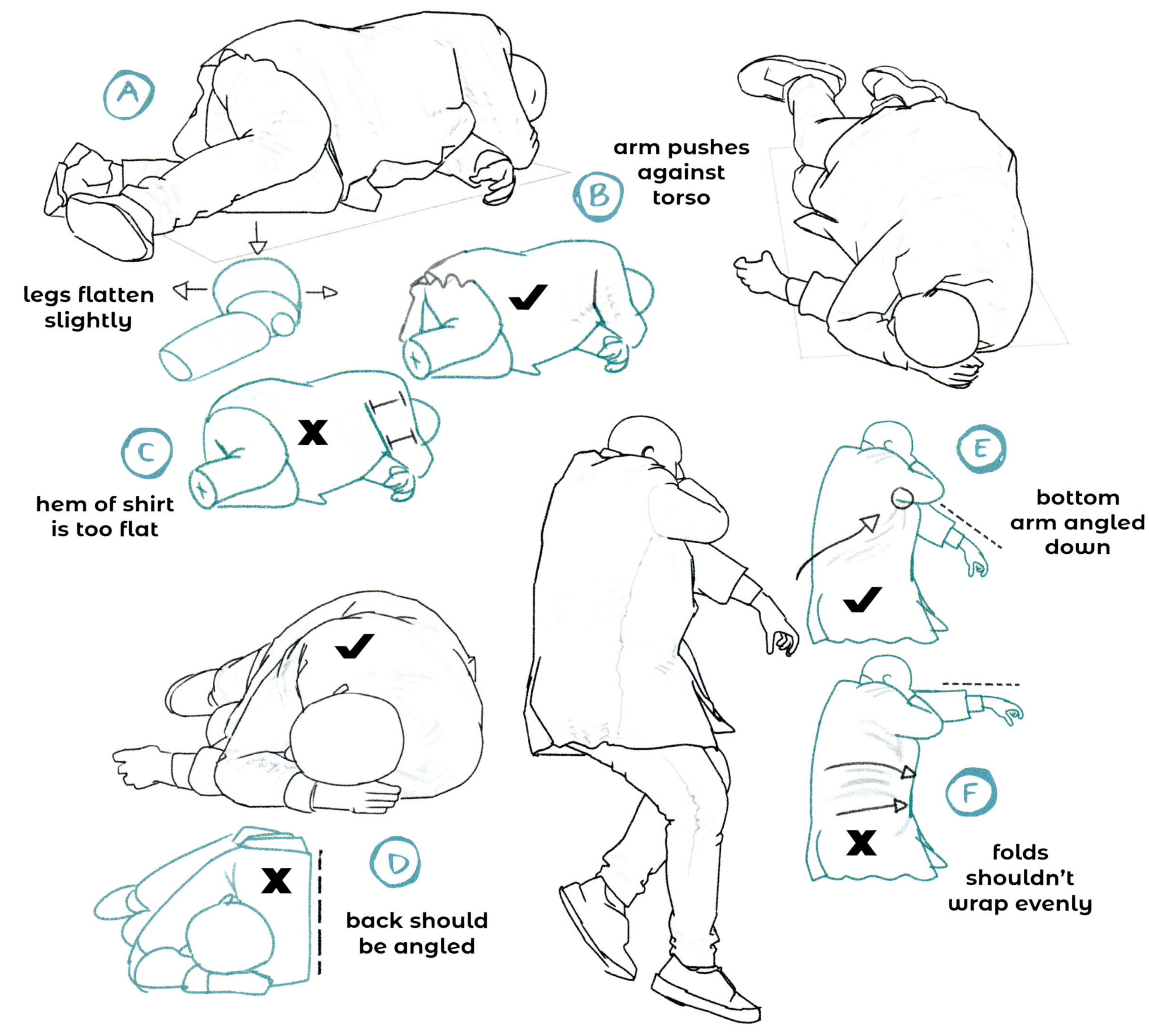

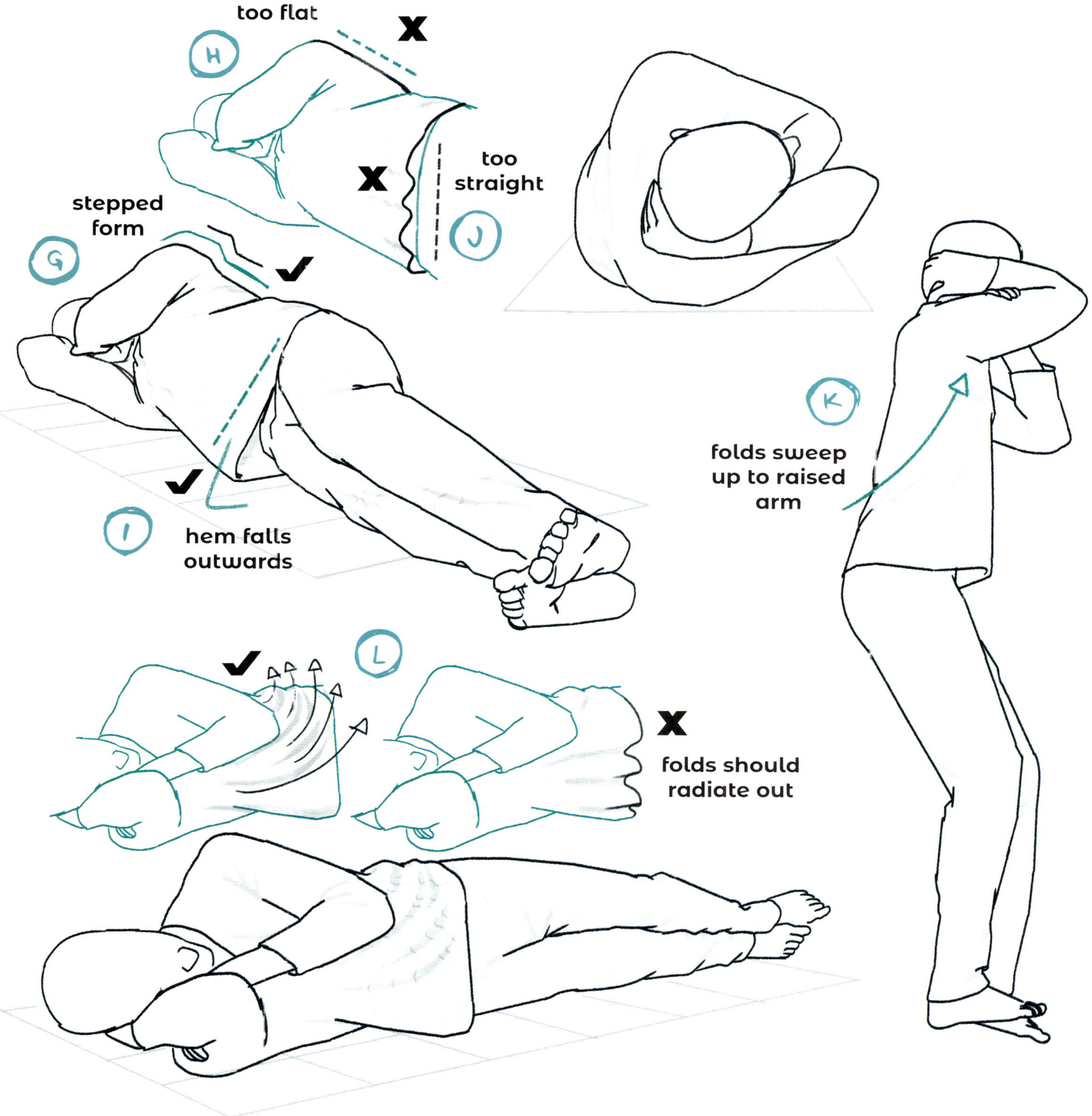

The line connecting the back of the arm to the torso will often 'step down' (G), rather than running smoothly into the back (H). The bottom of the top should fall down and out, to create a sort of triangle (I), rather than a simple series of shallow folds (J). As we saw on the previous page, the sweep of the folds flows up from the lower back to under the raised arm (K). Here's another angle showing that (L). Folds should radiate up and out rather than down the body.

lying with a phone

The folds across the torso should fan out and down rather than crossing evenly (A). The raised shoulders often also show compression here **(1)**. The pressure between the front of the torso and the top arm should be clear (B). When drawing the folds at the knee, don't be afraid to have the inner lines cause a bulge in the silhouette (C). When drawing the crotch, you'll only see strong, deep folding on the far leg, while the side that's closest to the viewer has a simple silhouette (D).

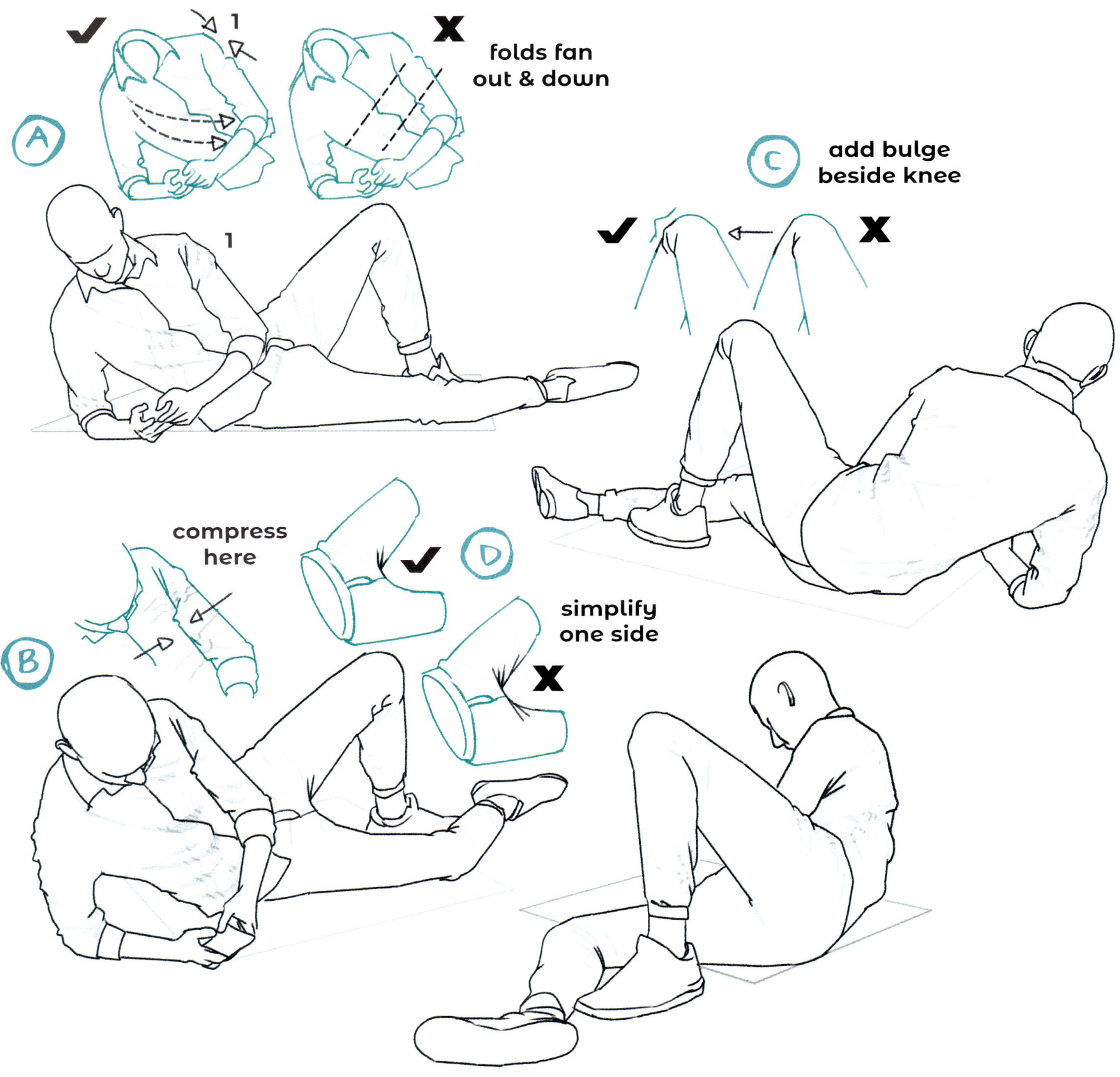

lying while talking

It's not easy to draw someone leaning on their elbow, because the pose often doesn't look like it's balanced. For starters, the elbow is often tucked in rather than extending vertically (A). It's also usually tucked backwards (B). Because the elbow is brought so far back, folds often wrap across the front of the torso, heading towards the armpit (C). When the thighs are brought this close together, the crotch area often bulges outwards and you see V-shaped folds at the top of the front of the thighs (D).

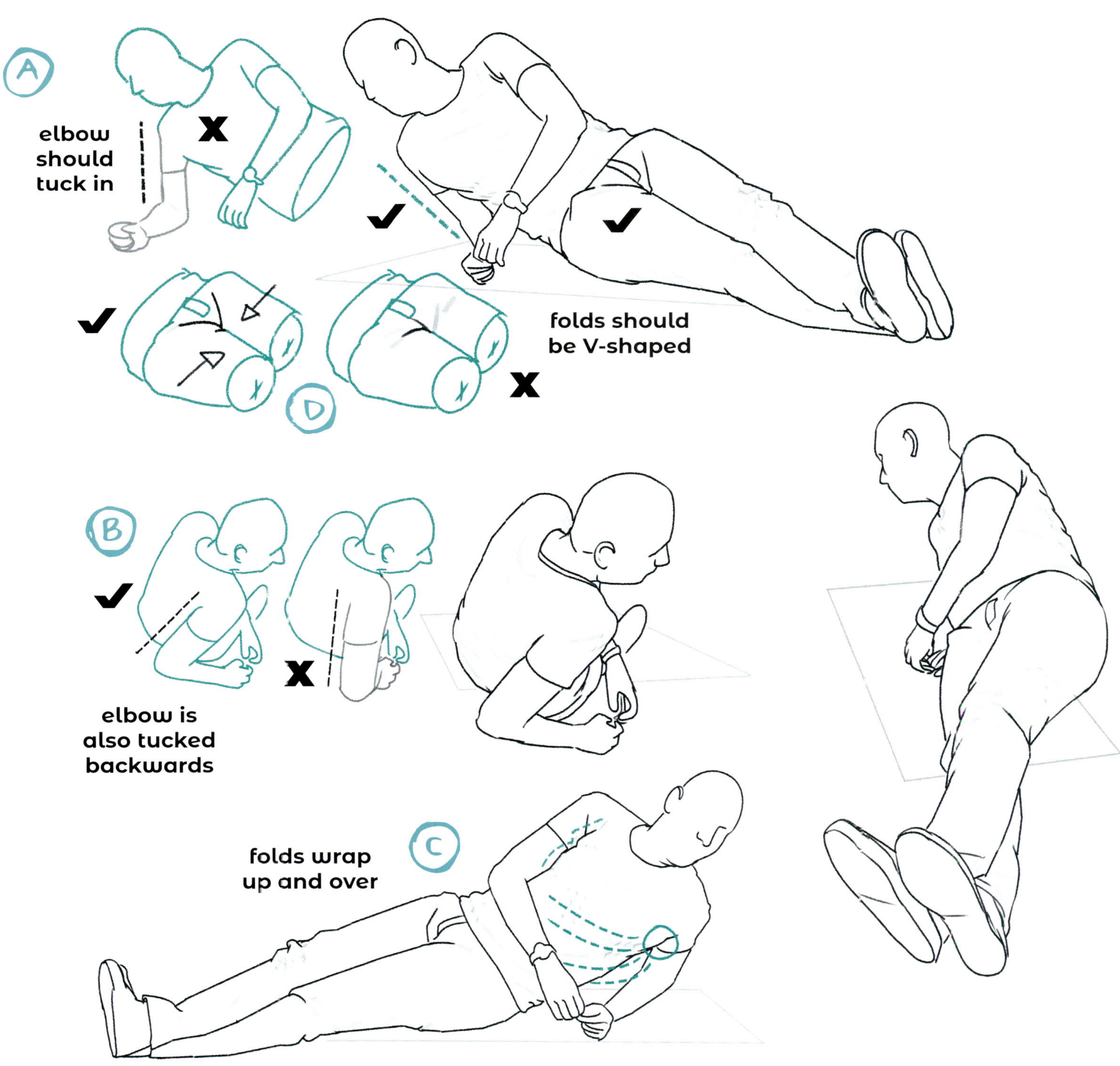

watching tv

We often lie at an angle on the sofa. Viewed from below, you can see that just a few overlaps are crucial to making this leg look believably foreshortened (A). If the overlaps are the wrong way around, we feel like we're looking up at the upper leg and down at the lower leg, which is very confusing. From behind, the crotch often extends further down away from the glutes than you'd expect (B).

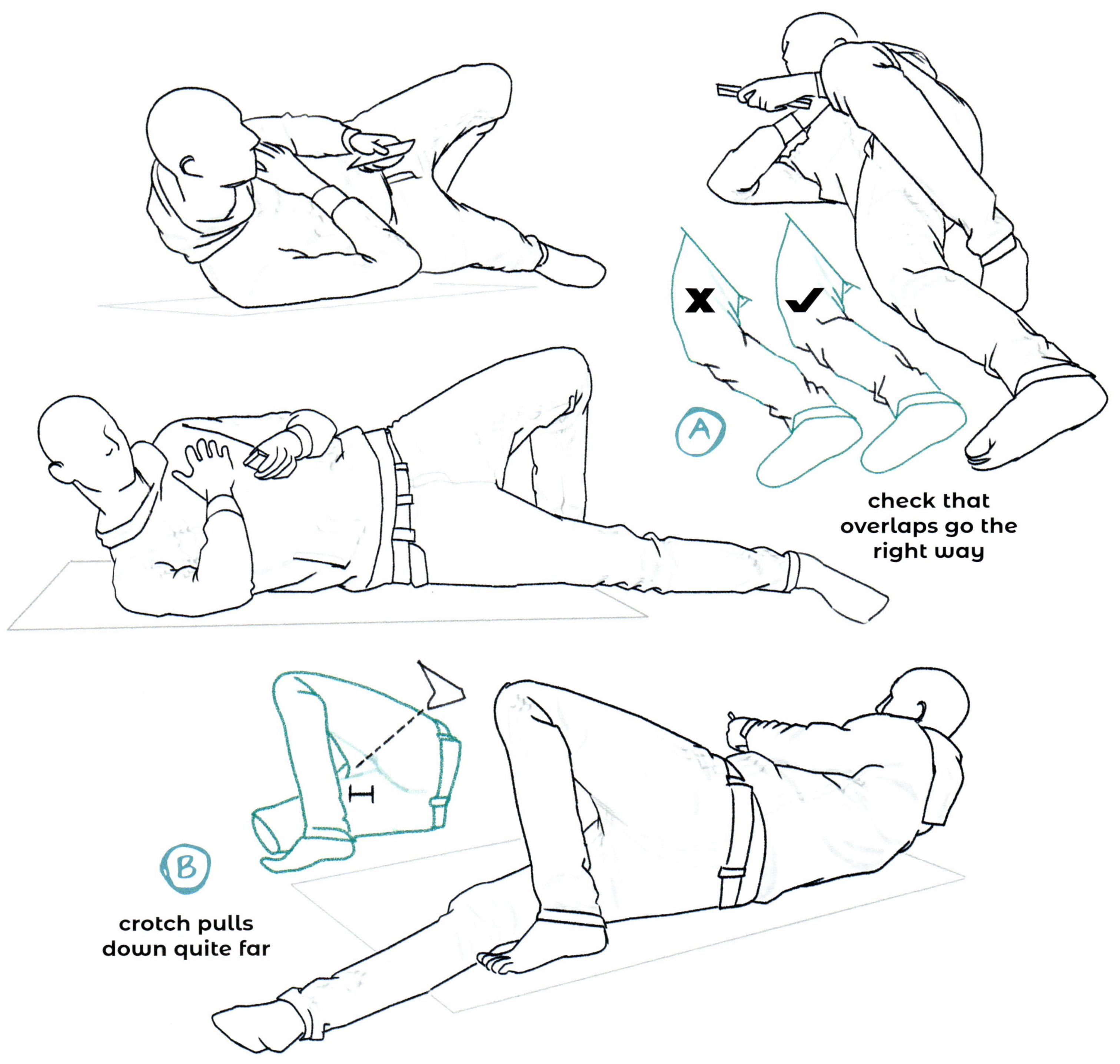

lying on your back

When the arms are folded across the chest, the fabric across the stomach often bulges out and partially covers the arms (A). This is particularly true when a pocket is present on a hoodie. The inside of the crotch should be given enough depth to be believable (B). When the arms are folded, the upper arm often forms a 'triangle' of material (C), as opposed to a tube. Don't forget to include a small fold where the sleeve makes contact with the torso (D).

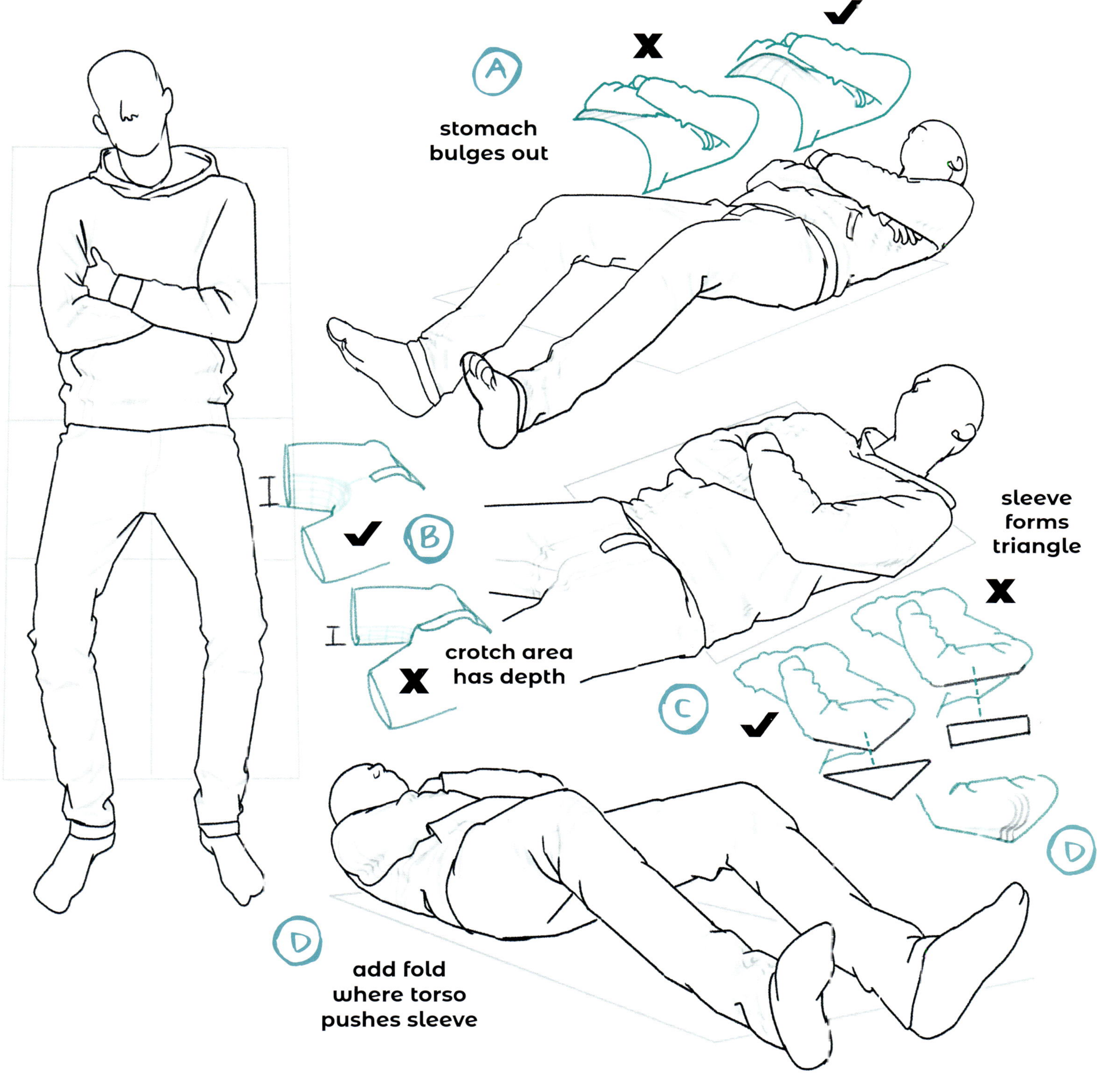

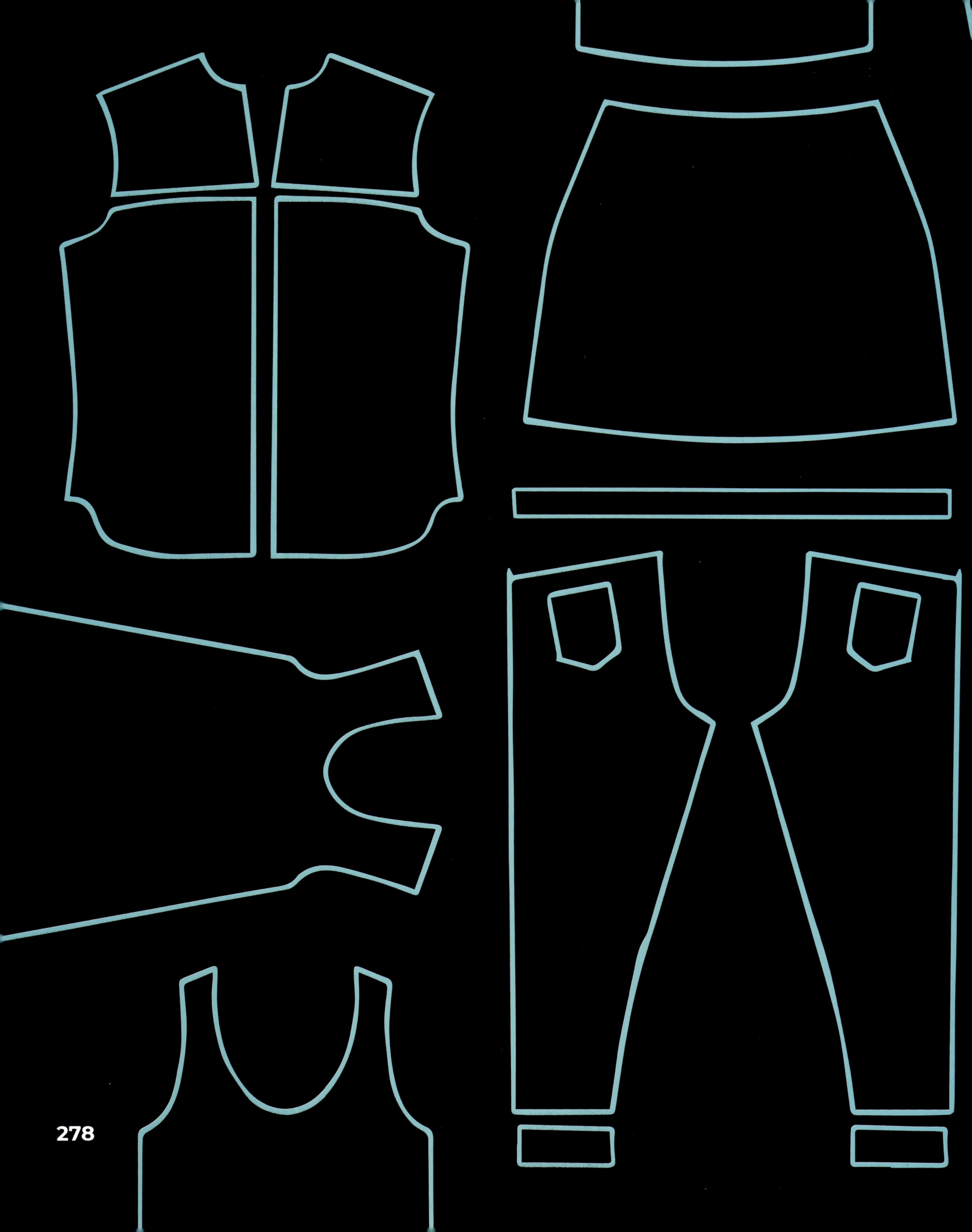

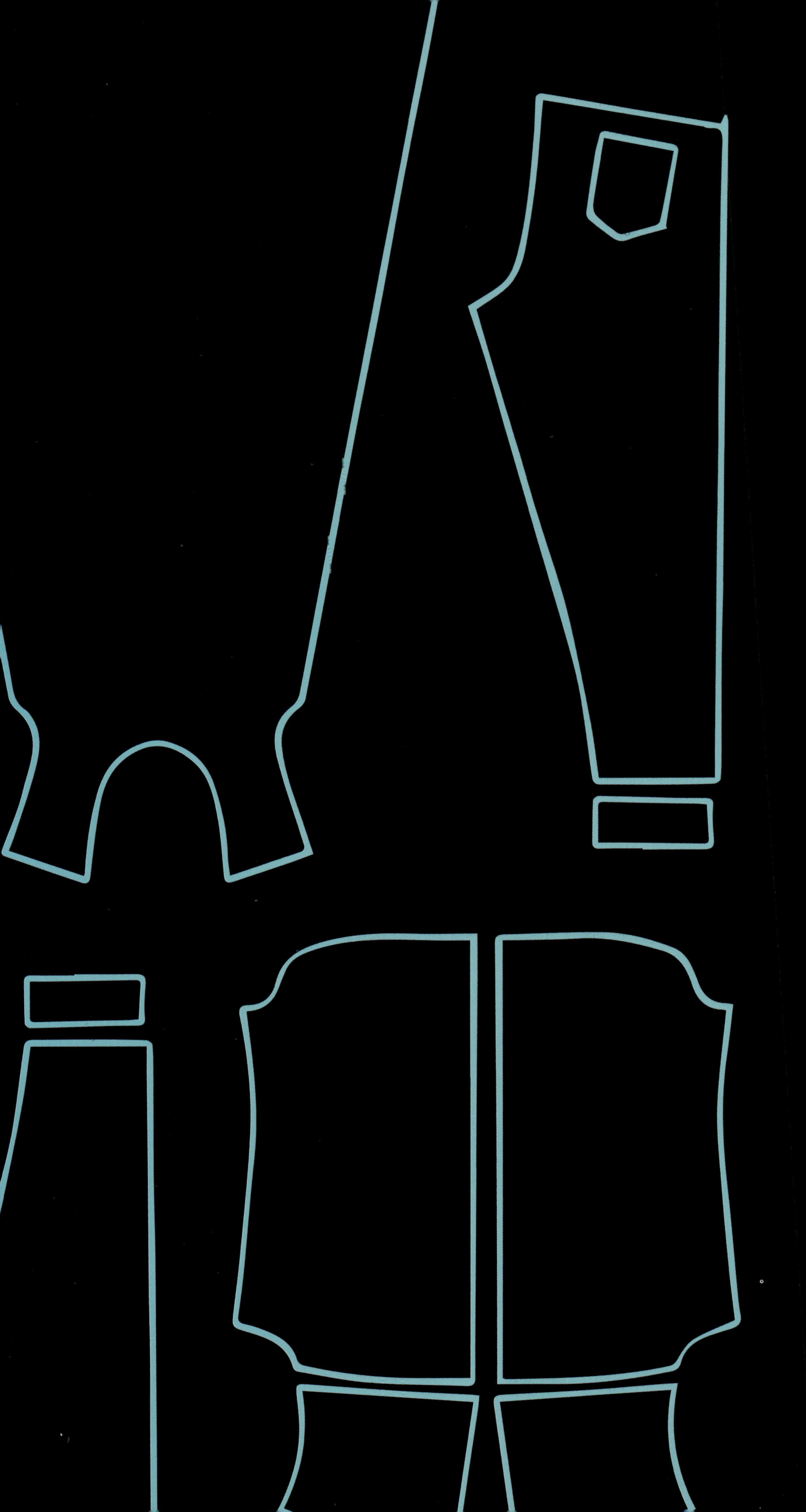

common patterns

trousers

A standard pair of trousers has a pattern something like this. The waistband is usually slightly curved, rather than straight, and has five belt loops (A). On jeans, you'll often see two additional pieces shown here in purple (B). The fly is sewn directly into the side of the front of the leg, shown in yellow (C). The widest point of the leg and trousers is circled here (D). For trouser legs that fit more closely around the calf and ankle (E), bring in the bottoms of the trousers here (F).

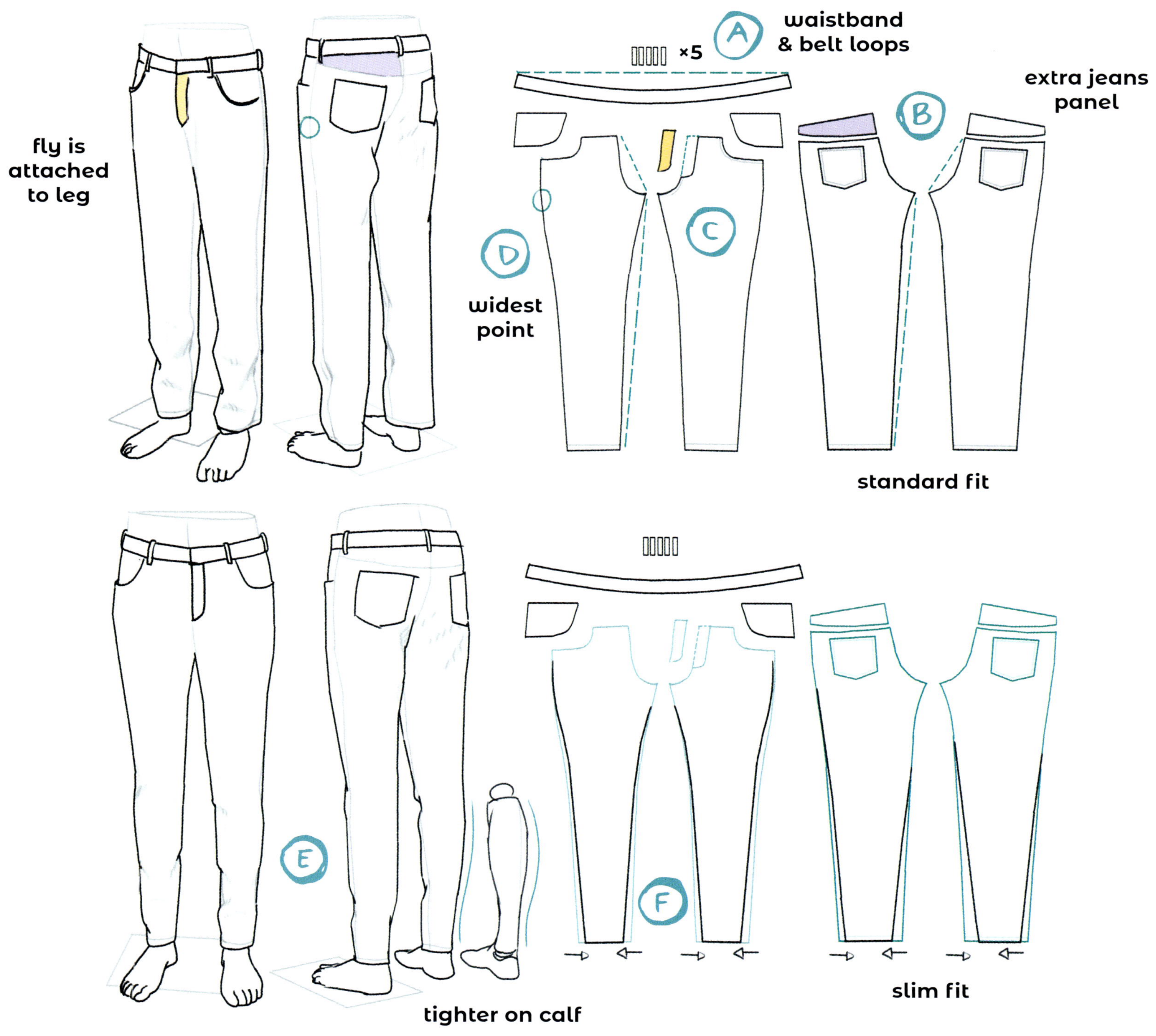

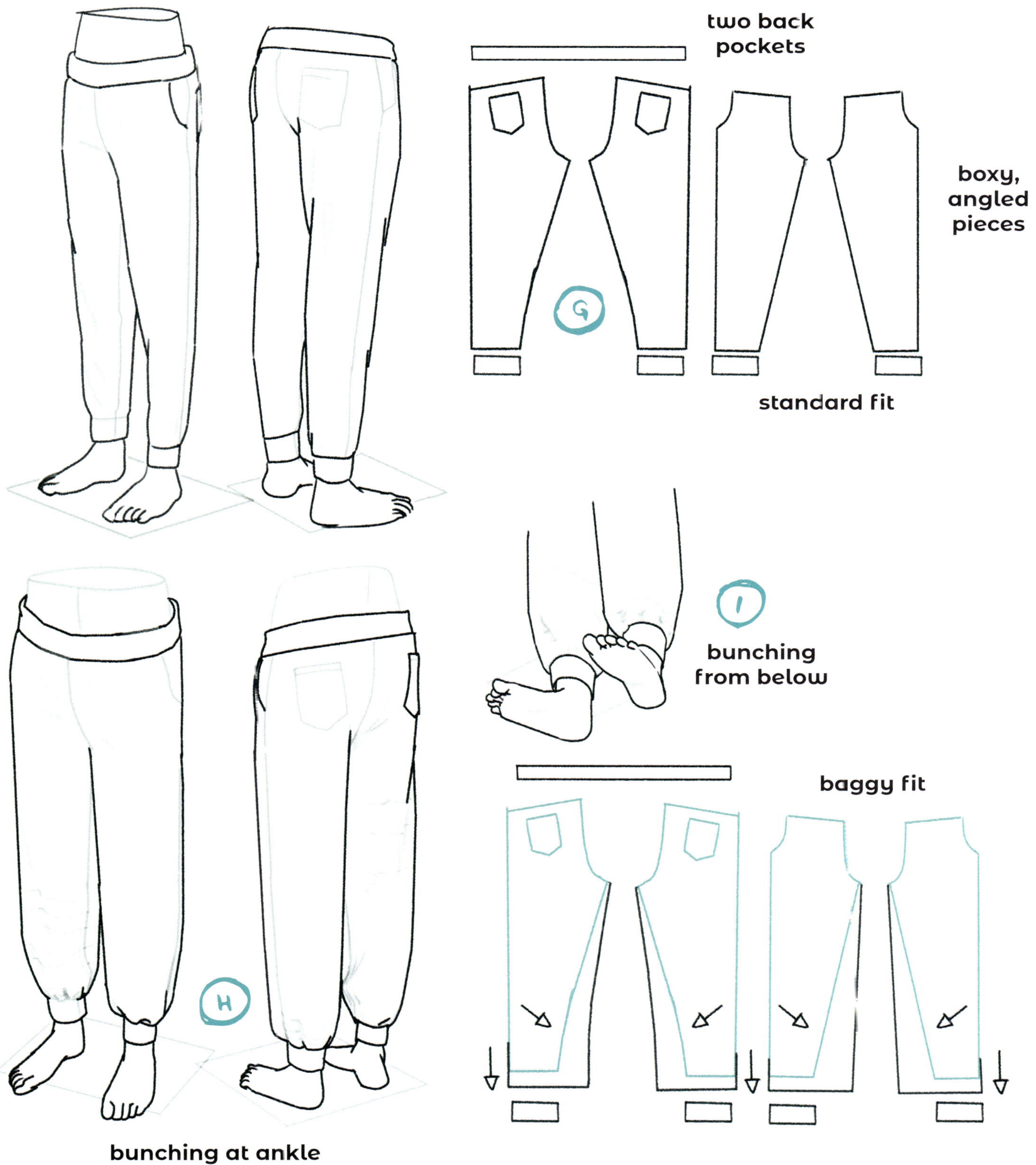

With tracksuit bottoms, the pattern is more 'boxy' There's less curvature to the pieces. You'll often see two pockets on the back pieces, which are angled rather than sitting vertically (G). If you lengthen the trousers and widen the bottoms, you'll see this bunching occur at the bottom (H). In this situation, the elasticated cuffs can't drop lower, so the material will bunch both vertically and horizontally. Here's the same thing from below (I).

T-shirt

The neck of a T-shirt is lower at the front than at the back (A). The sleeves wrap around the top of the arm, with the seam joining the two ends under the arm. If you bring in the ends of the sleeve, it will grip the arm more tightly (B). If you widen them out, the sleeve will land more loosely (C).

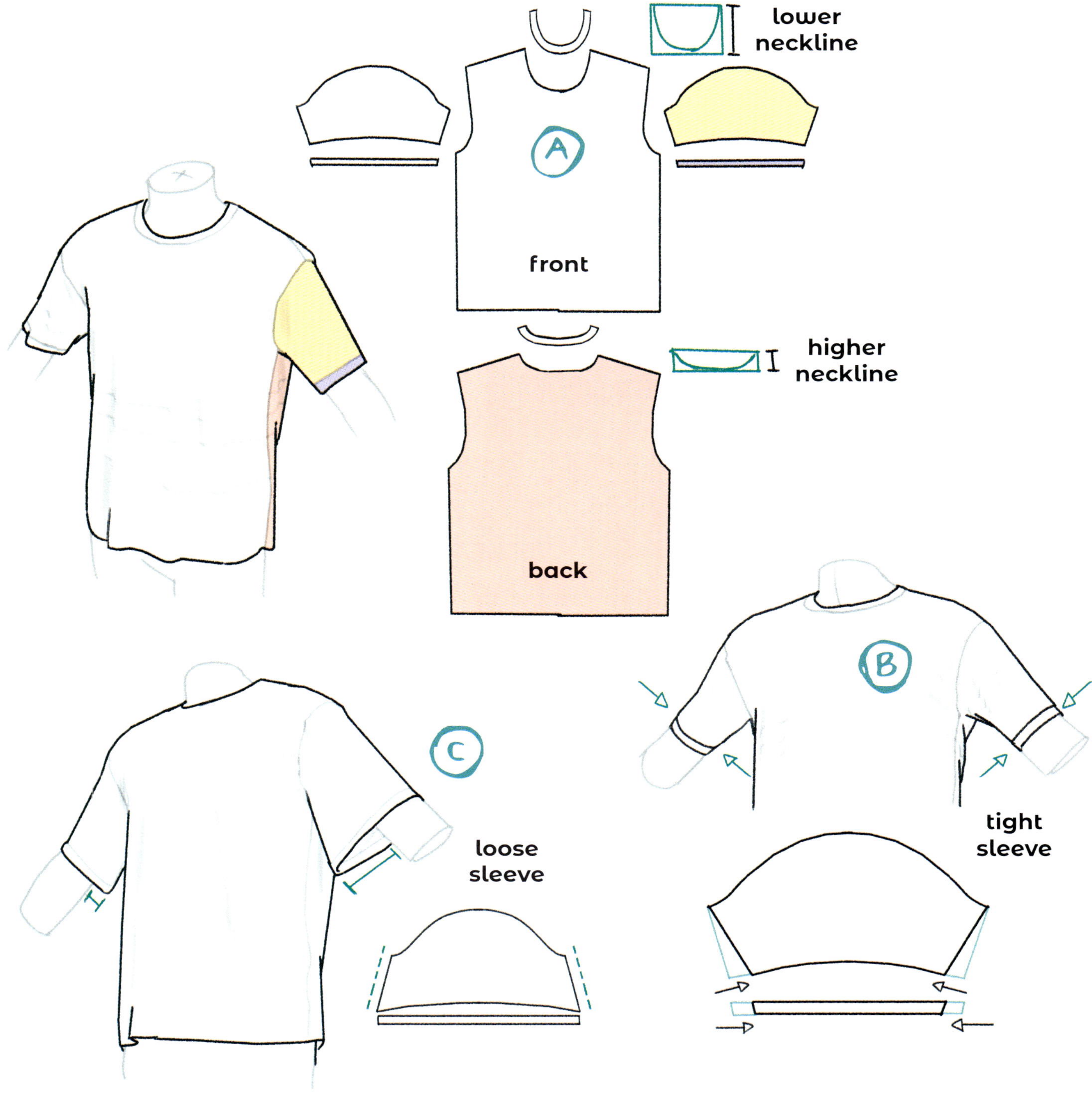

long-sleeved T-shirt

You'll notice that the pattern is almost exactly the same as the one used for a short-sleeved T-shirt. The main difference is simply that the bottom of the sleeve has been extended, creating more length (A). The sides of the sleeves aren't straight, but curve inwards slightly to account for the tapering of the arms (B). If you reverse this curve, so it bulges outwards, you see sleeves like this (C).

If you instead widen the sleeve and make it more boxy, you see drapery like this form (D). This is very similar to the result of doing the same to our tracksuit bottoms on page 281. Finally, if you widen the sleeve but remove the bottom cuff, the sleeve will hang loosely (E).

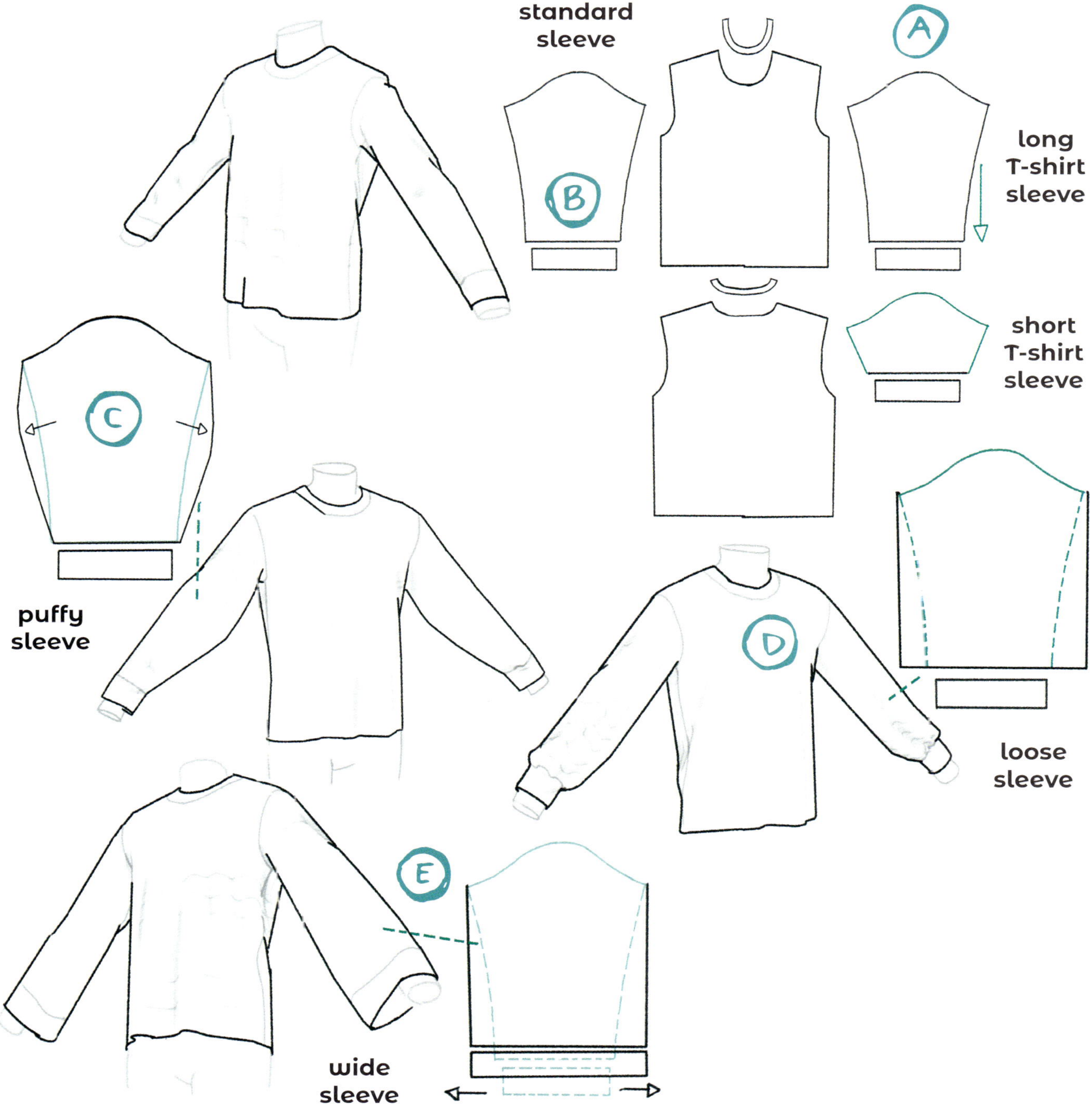

shirt

Shirts have a similar shape, but the pattern usually has more pieces. The front piece is split vertically (A), and sometimes horizontally, too (B). There is often a pocket on the left side, and sometimes the right as well. As seen on page 112, the collar consists of two pieces: an outer and an inner (C). Some shirt sleeves are made from several pieces (D), and some are made from a single piece (E). Either way, the final shape is similar. The end of the sleeve is composed of a placket running up the shirt, which fits into this gap (F), and a cuff. The placket usually runs up the arm on the 'back' of the arm, in line with the pinky (G). The placket isn't located exactly in the middle of the sleeve, but just to one side.

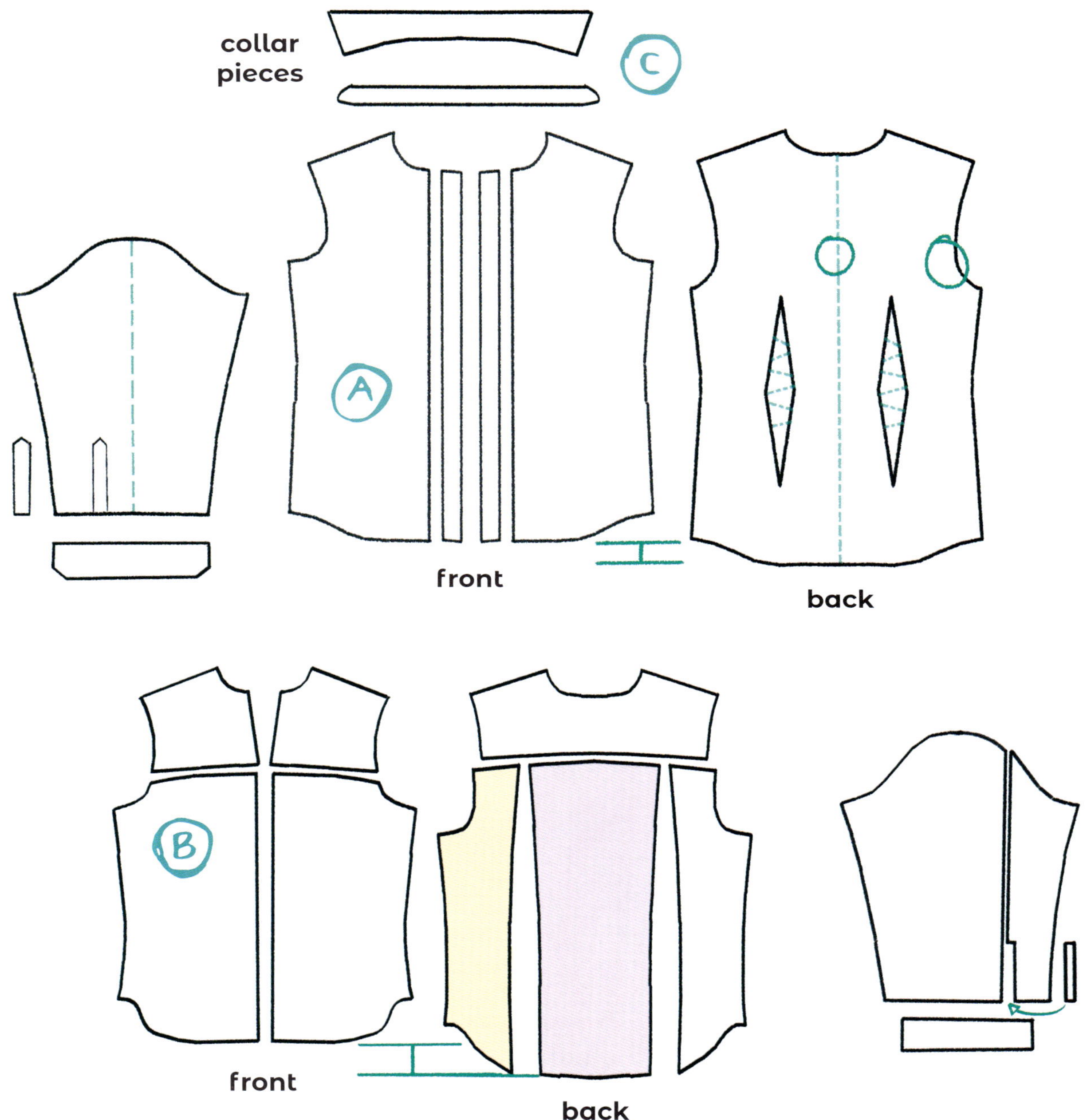

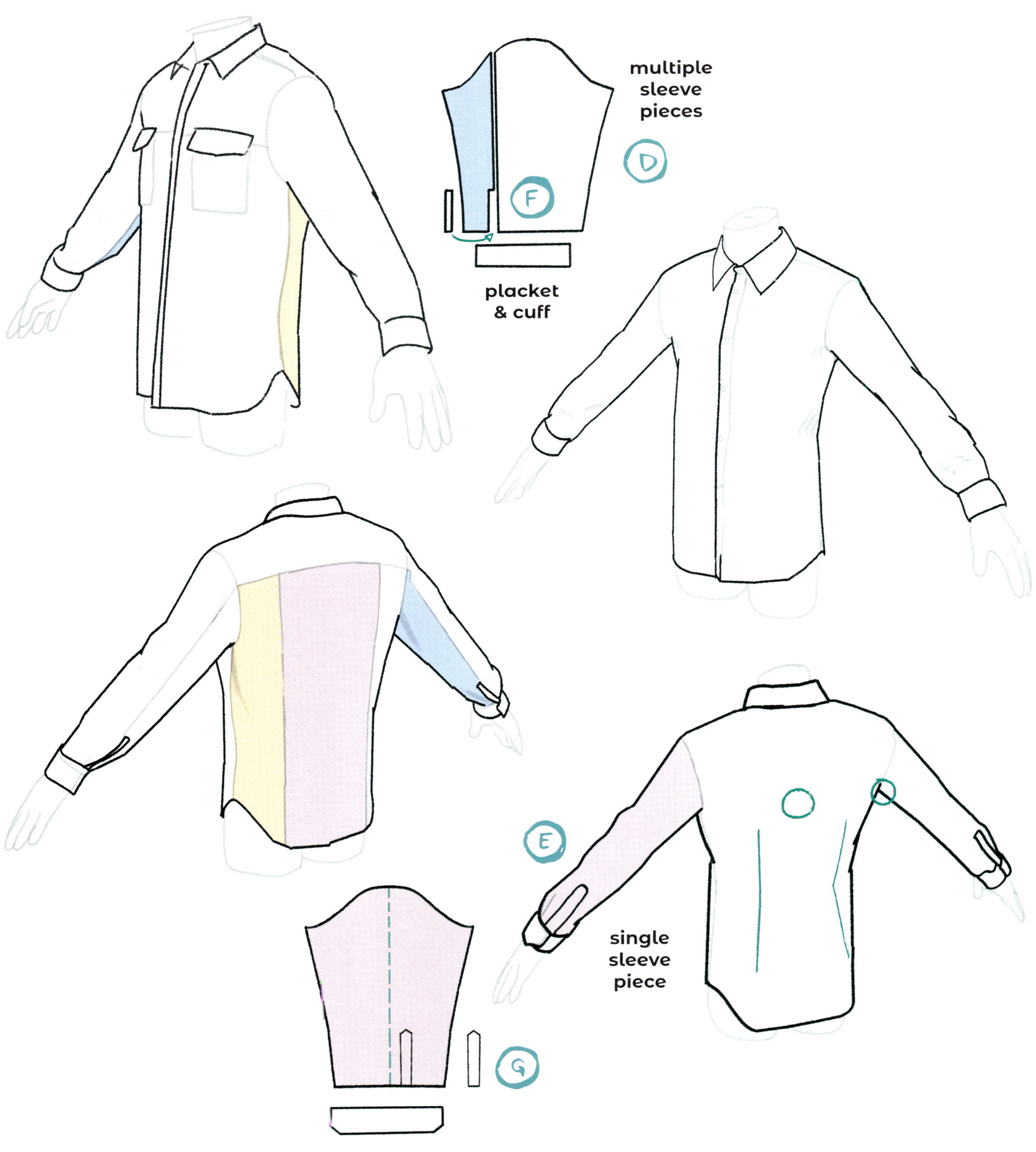
multiple
sleeve
pieces
D
F
placket
& cuff
E
single
sleeve
piece
G

hoodie

The basic pattern of a hoodie is something like this. Note that the hood isn't flat on the bottom, but slopes down at the front, just as your neck and chest do (A). The hand holes for the front pocket also don't extend the whole way down (B). For a baggier sleeve, just take the sleeves and extend them downwards (C). When this happens, we see this drapery form (D). Don't forget: we may have lengthened the sleeve, but the elasticated cuffs probably won't fall over the hands, so the sleeves must compress along their length. Folding on the sleeves is often confused for additional width in the pattern, when it's really just extra length.

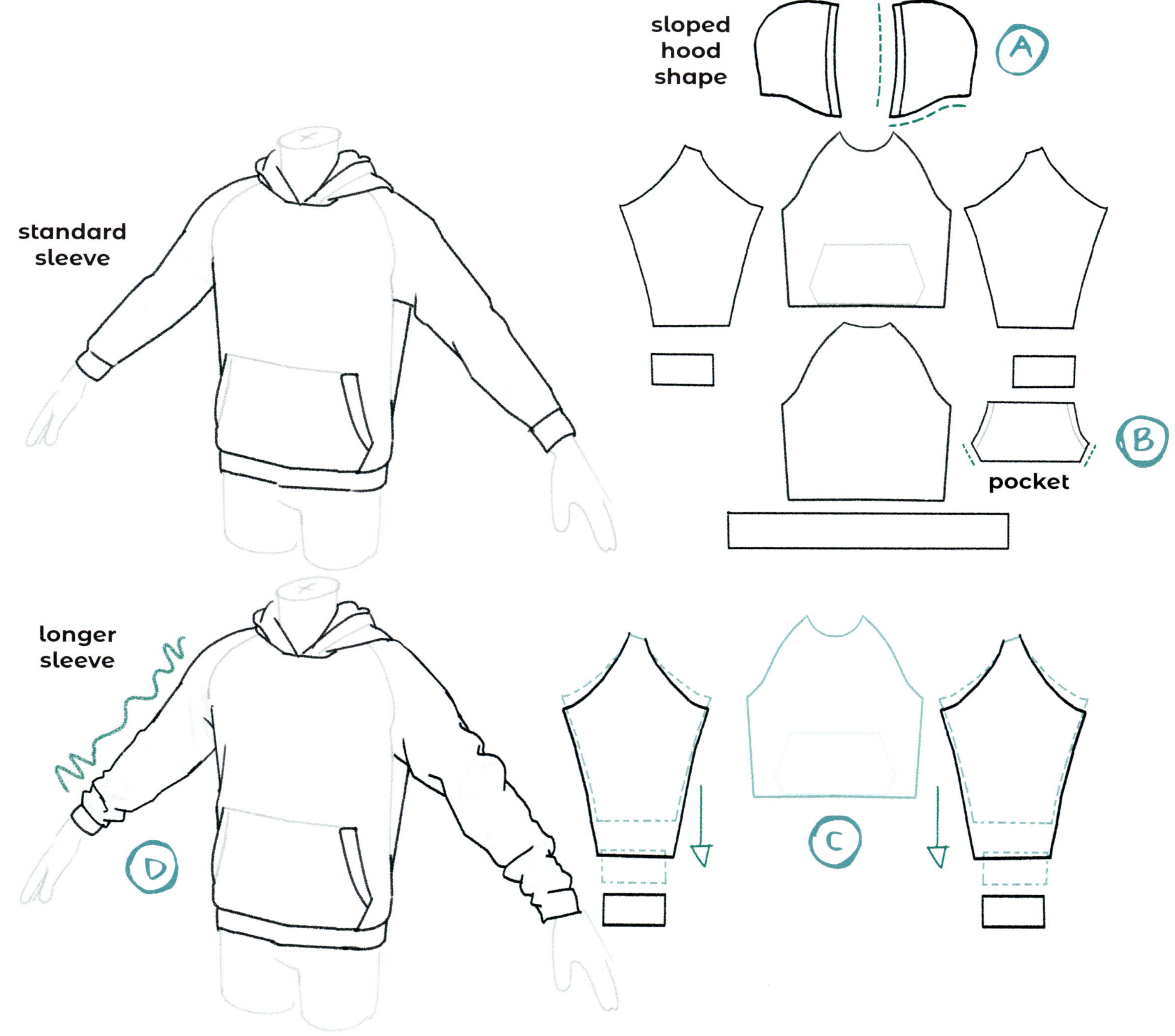

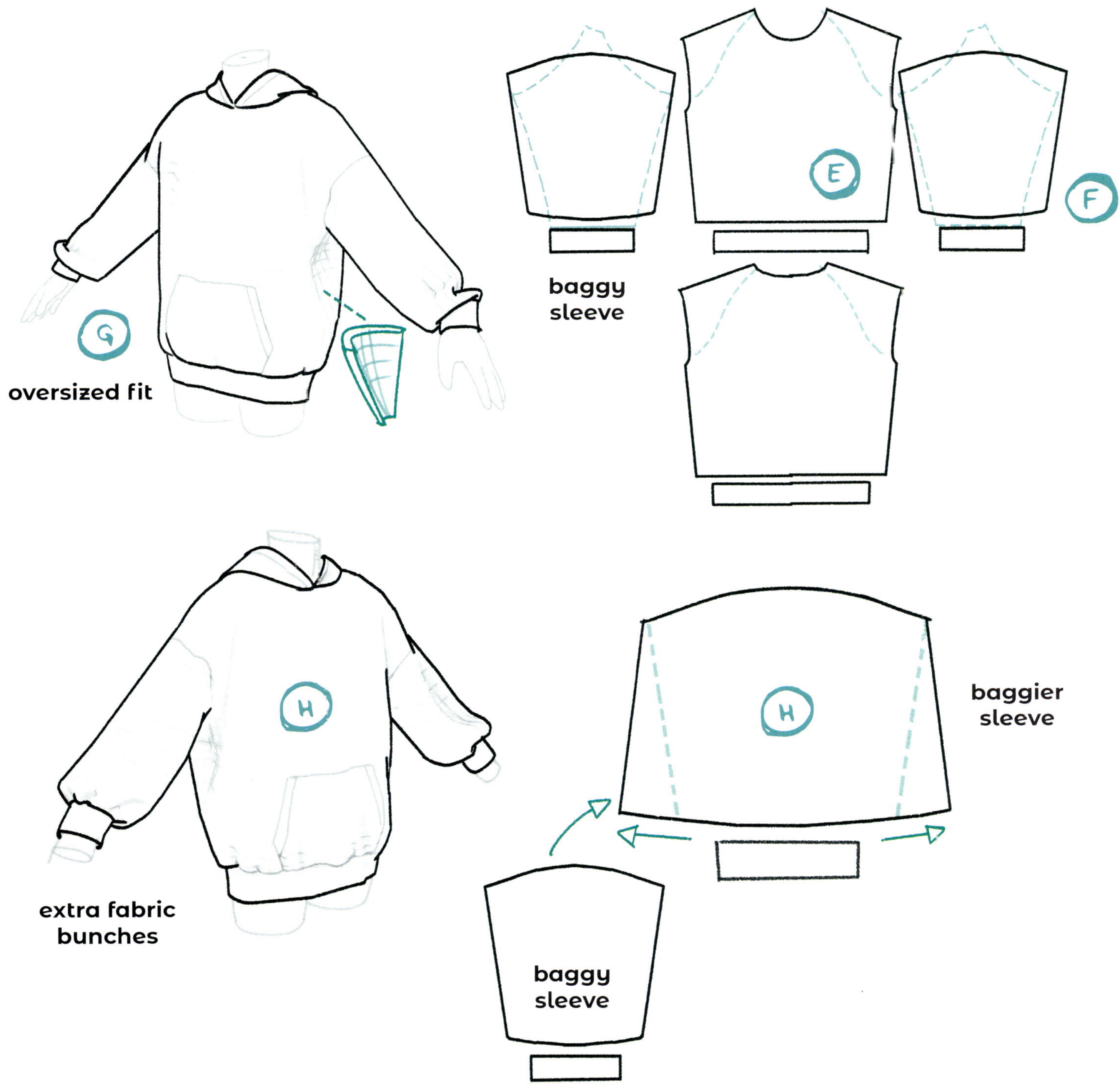

Here's an example of an 'oversized' hoodie pattern (E). The original pattern is below, in a lighter colour. Notice that the new pattern is more 'boxy': more straights and strong angles, and fewer delicate curves. The sleeves are also much wider (F). Because of this, the whole garment is less 'fitted'. In hoodies like this, you often see this concave form (G). If we take the sleeves and widen the bottom, we see this drapery form (H). The width is limited by the elasticated cuff, so the fabric must bunch over itself.

skirt

This is a simple skirt and vest pattern (A). Note how the vest bunches up slightly at the back, and in this position there's a general flow of folding from the lower back forwards and around to the breasts (B). The shoulders of the vest usually angle further backwards at the front, while at the rear, they're nearly vertical (C).

Most skirts keep tapering out right to the bottom, but some then taper inwards again (D). This is restrictive in terms of movement, so it's not as common. In a high-waisted skirt (E), you may see this plane around the lower back and top-rear of the glutes **(1)**. This will then reverse a little on the underside of the glutes **(2)**.

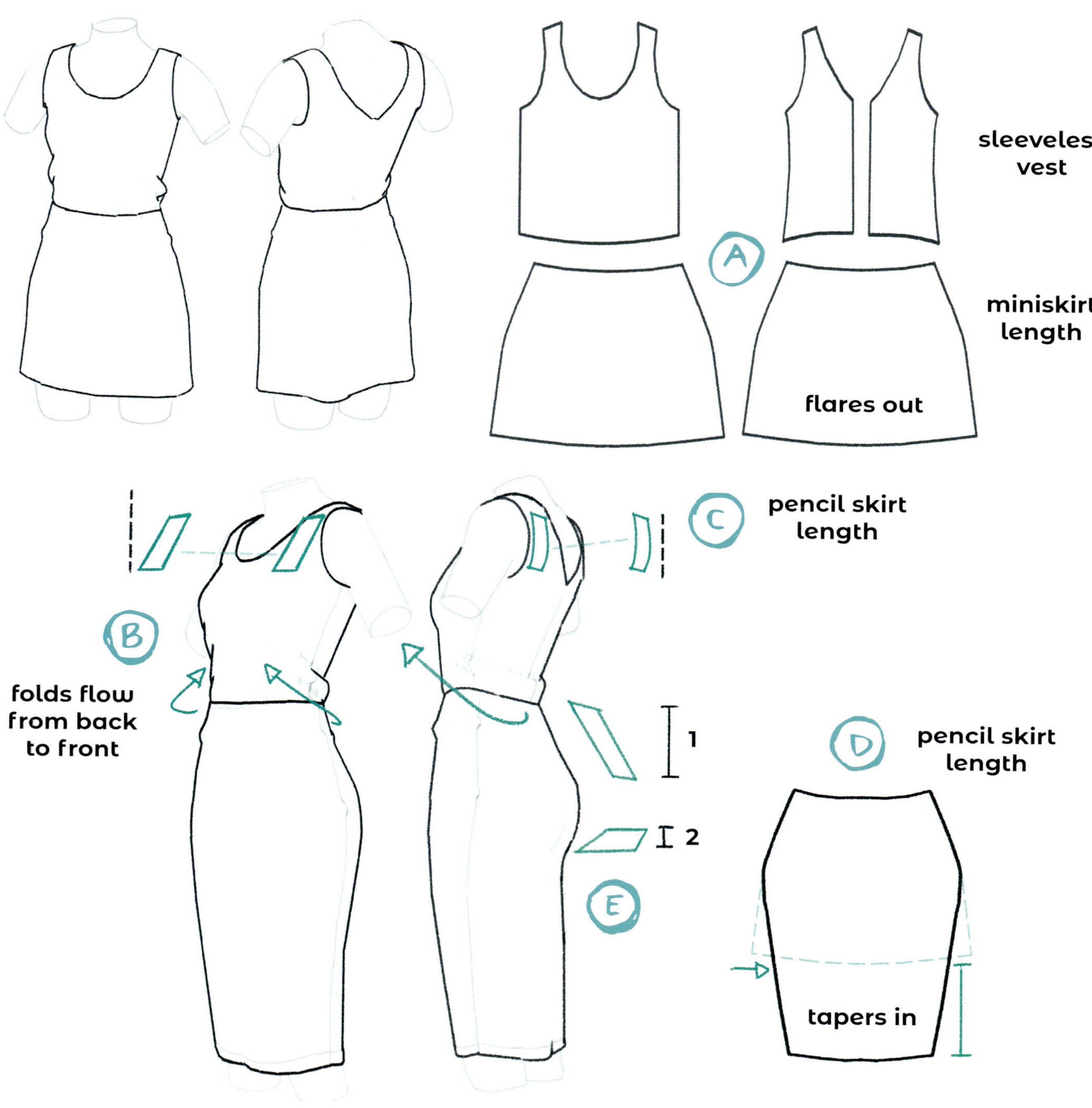

dress

This dress (A) corresponds with this pattern (B). As with most garments, the neckline at the front is lower than at the back (C). The sleeves are very short (D). The pattern widens towards the bottom of the dress, which is why you see this horizontal compression near the feet. For the dress on the right (E), the pattern has an extremely large piece below the waist (the front and back patterns are identical, and only one is shown here). The top of this piece is sewn directly onto the waistband (F). This causes horizontal compression immediately below the waistband, which continues all the way down (G).

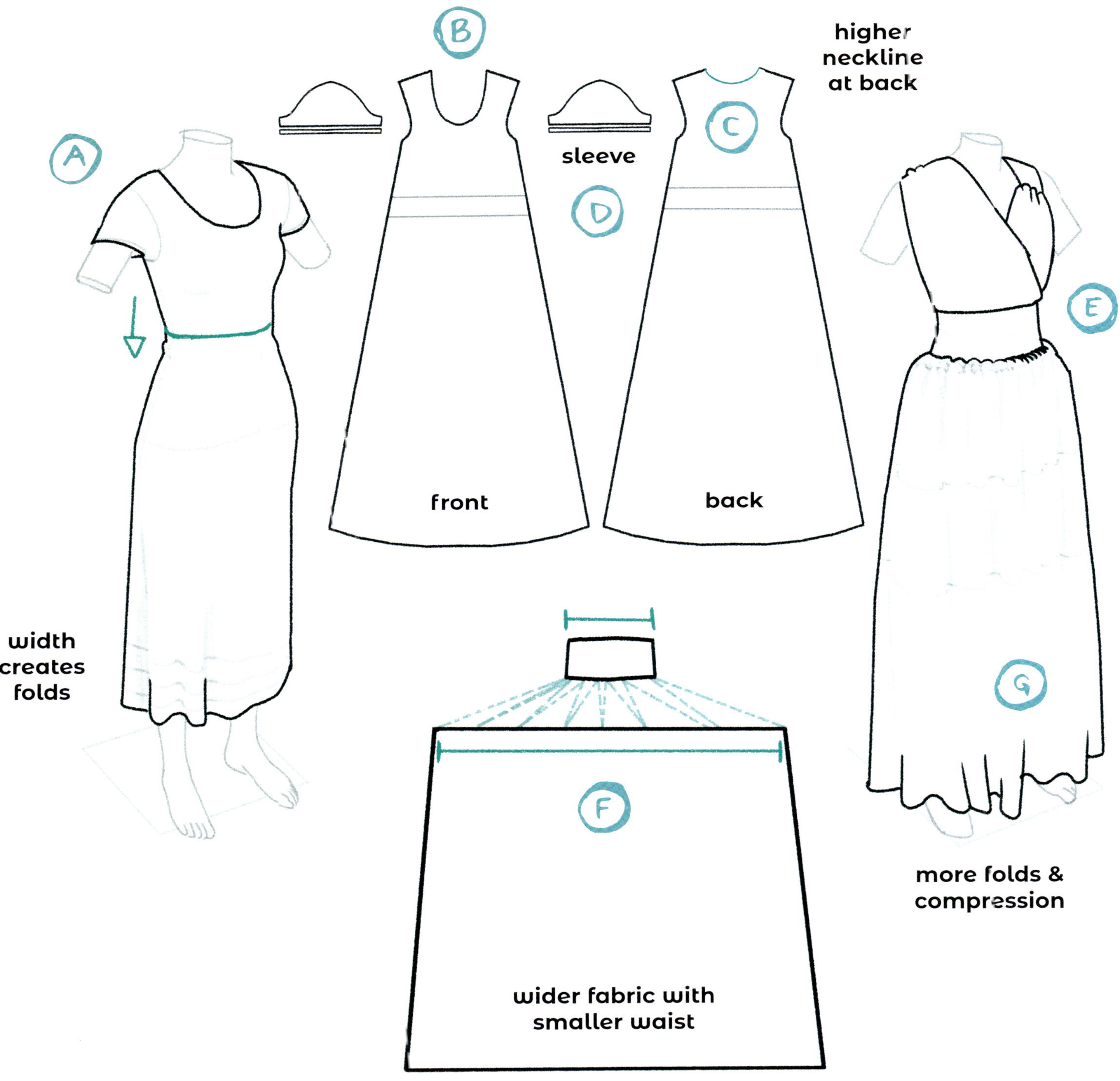

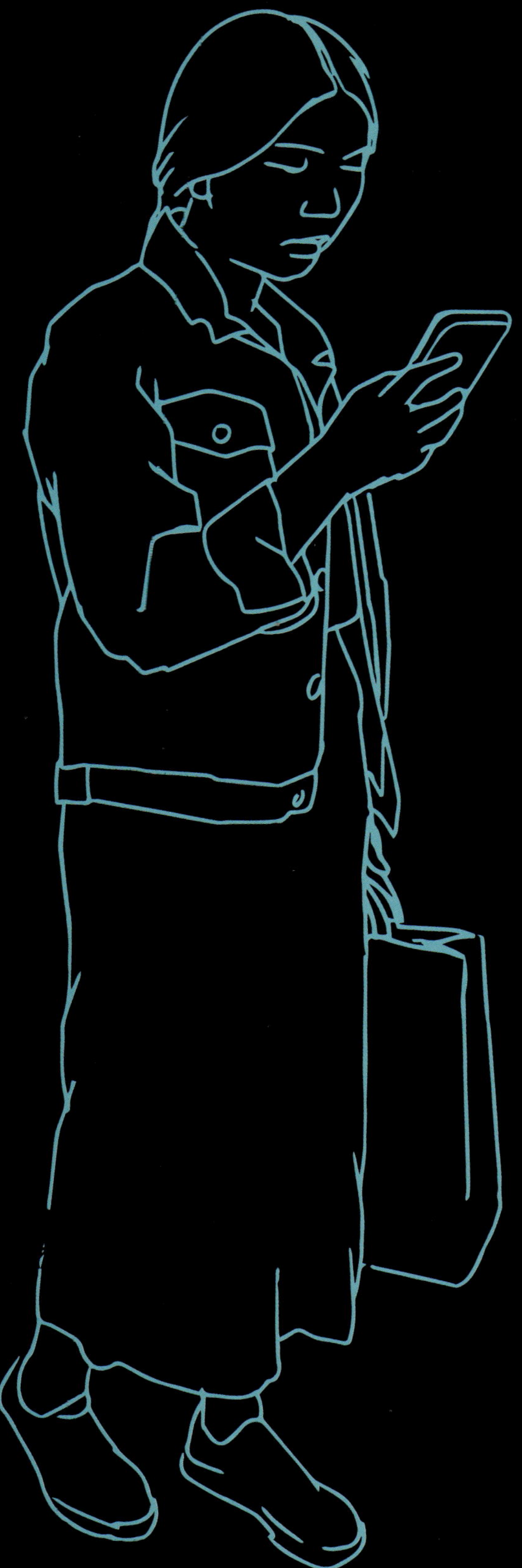

over to you...

You've covered a lot. Some adjustments were simple, others more challenging – but all of them were designed to help you see your drawings with more clarity. Now is a good time to take a step back and give yourself space to practise.

These ideas won't settle in all at once. They need to be tested, revisited, adjusted, and tested again. Real progress often feels slow from the inside, but that's how deep learning usually works – quietly, in layers, over time. There's no need to rush it.

You won't need all 42 adjustments for every drawing. A few will stick with you and become part of how you naturally work. Some might only click later. Others you might leave behind – and that's fine. This kind of knowledge develops through use.

This book is the first part of the learning process – the part where you observe, notice, and start to see your drawings more clearly. If you'd like to take things further, the companion workbook gives you a space to apply what you've learned, solve drawing problems directly, and build that clarity through repetition.

For now, just keep going. Keep drawing. Keep adjusting.

Really, the only important thing is that you're enjoying it.

tom fox

Tom Fox

---

follow tom...

instagram.com/tomfoxdraws

tiktok.com/@tomfoxdraws

twitter.com/tomfoxdraws

youtube.com/tomfoxdraws

glossary

area of support
In this book, this refers to a prominent point of the figure or object, from which the fabric hangs downwards.

compression
In this book, this is the 'bunching up' of fabric caused by the figure's movement or the pattern of the garment.

cuff
The end of a sleeve – often a band-shaped piece that surrounds the wrist.

drapery
The way a garment or cloth sits in response to all the forces affecting it.

fold
A line or ridge created by bending something (in this case, compressing fabric).

fly
In clothing, this refers to the front opening on a pair of trousers, which is usually fastened with a zip or buttons.

glutes
Short for the *gluteus* or buttock muscles.

hem
The folded and sewn edge on a garment, such as at the bottom of a trouser leg or end of a T-shirt sleeve.

inseam
The length of the seam on the inside of the wearer's leg, also called the 'inner leg'.

patella
The kneecap – the small bone at the front of the knee joint.

pattern
In clothing design, this is the template of flat pieces from which a garment is constructed.

placket
An opening in a garment, such as on a sleeve or front of a shirt, which is reinforced with extra fabric and usually has fastenings (such as buttons).

pleat
A type of fabric fold, intentionally built into the design of a garment.

scapula
The shoulder blade – the flat, triangular bone on the upper back.

seam
A line indicating where two pieces of fabric meet and are sewn together.

tension
The state of being pulled.

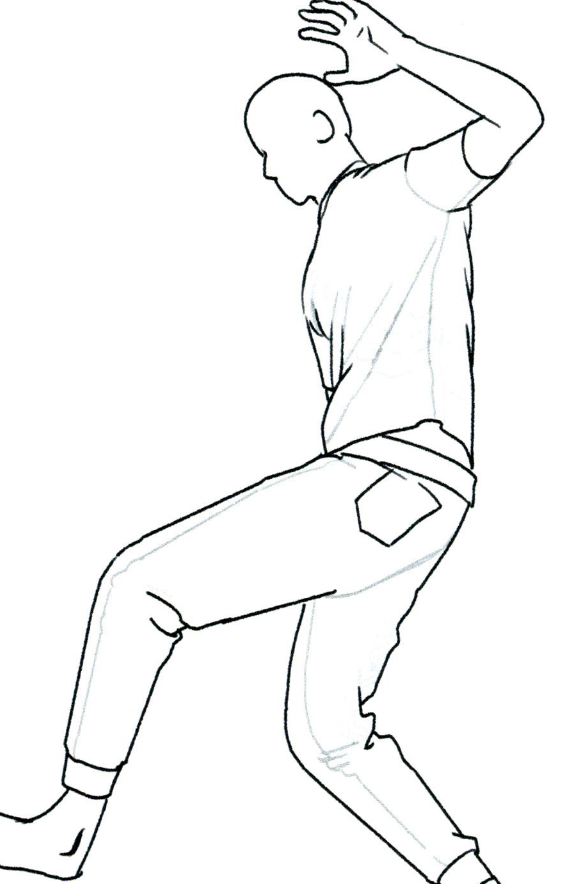

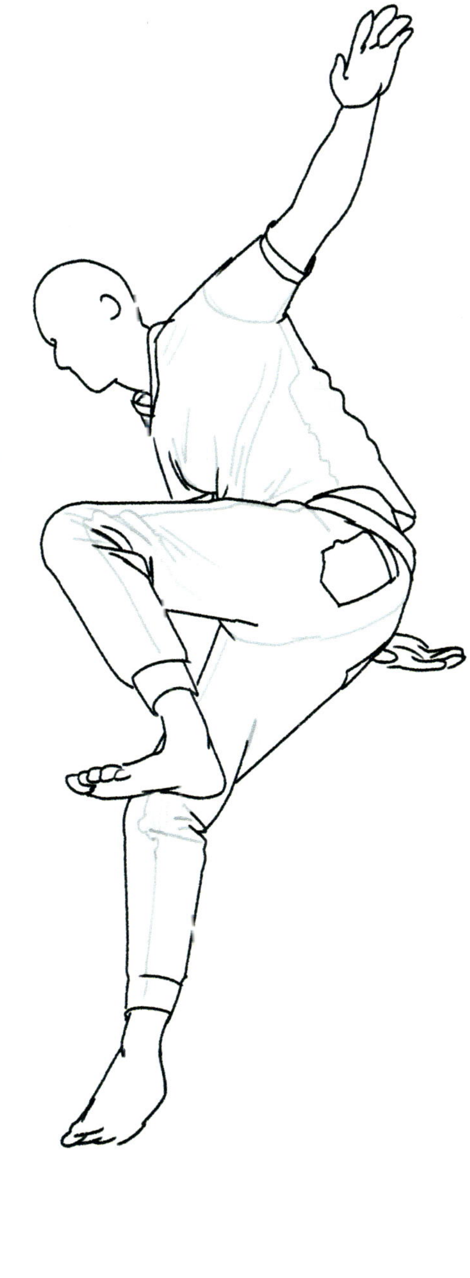

index

R

S

T

U

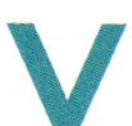

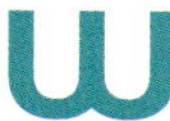

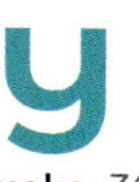

Z

also by tom fox...

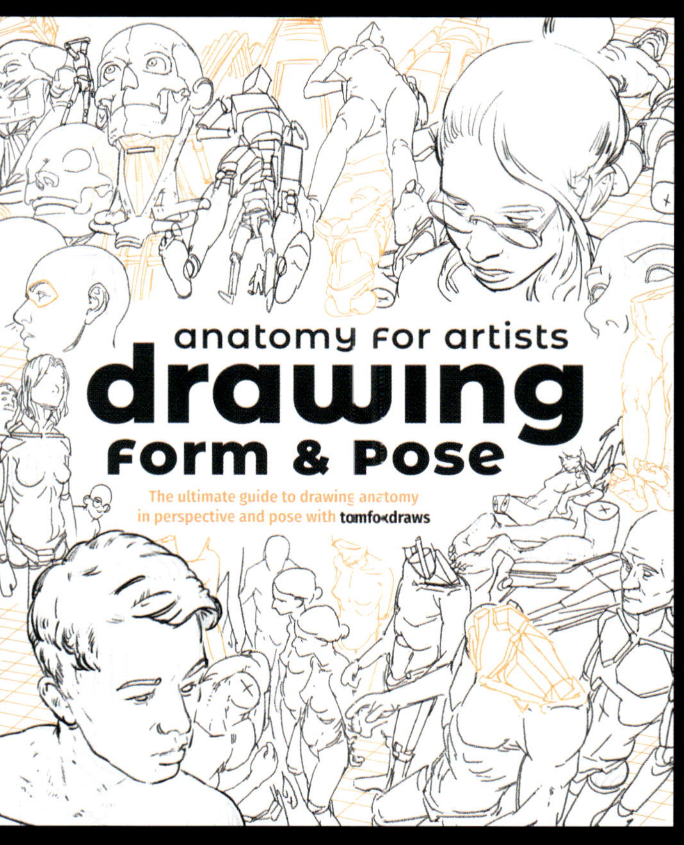

Discover a brand-new approach to drawing the human form with this unique guide by expert Tom Fox, aka tomfoxdraws.

The instructor's trademark teaching style uses innovative box mannequins made from simplified shapes. Tom's less-is-more approach to drawing the body ensures believable results even when tackling traditionally tricky subjects such as perspective, proportion, and three-dimensional form.

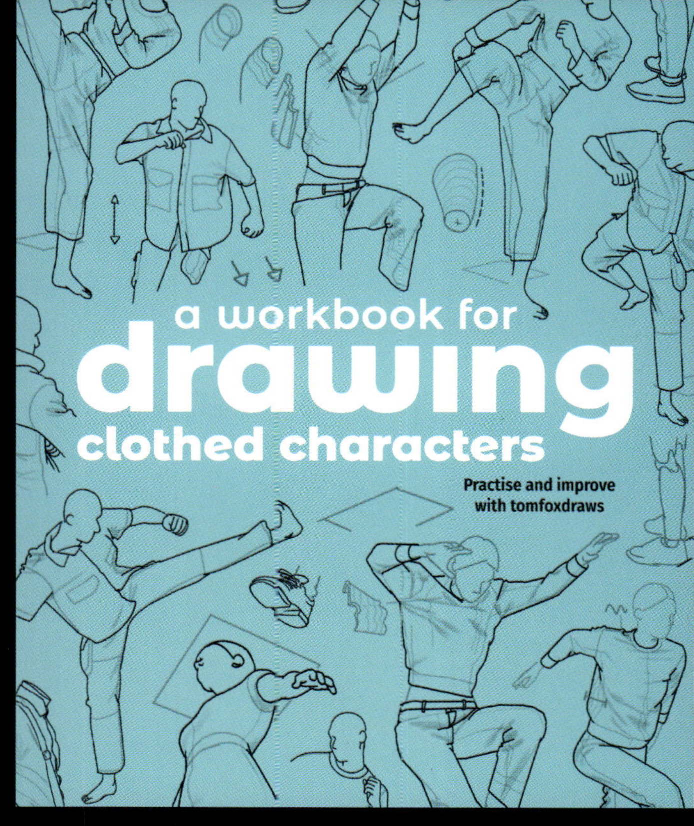

Practise drawing clothing and drapery directly on the page with expert guidance from artist Tom Fox, aka tomfoxdraws.

Specially crafted as a companion to Tom's book *An Artist's Guide to Drawing Clothed Characters*, this collection of interactive challenges and exercises provides a valuable space to test your knowledge of garments and drapery.

Available now at
store.3dtotal.com